UNIVERSITY OF LAUSANNE
CENTRE OF COMPARATIVE, EUROPEAN, AND INTERNATIONAL LAW

NATIONAL ACADEMY OF SCIENCES OF UKRAINE
VOLODYMYR KORETSKY INSTITUTE OF STATE AND LAW
CENTER OF COMPARATIVE JURISPRUDENCE

UNIVERSITY OF PALERMO
FACULTY OF POLITICAL SCIENCE AND INTERNATIONAL RELATIONS
CENTRE OF ADVANCED STUDIES "A. S. CENT"

PENNSYLVANIA STATE UNIVERSITY
DICKINSON LAW

The World Picture *of* Comparative Law

JCL Studies in Comparative Law: Second Series

Series Editors

Professor William E. Butler

Professor Michael Palmer

1. W. E. Butler and O. V. Kresin (eds.), *Discovering the Unexpected: Comparative Legal Studies in Eastern and Central Europe* (Clark, New Jersey, Talbot Publishing, 2021). ISBN 9781616196554

2. Simon Palmer and Zhai Xiaobo (eds.), *Bentham Around the World* (Clark, New Jersey, Talbot Publishing, 2021). ISBN 9781616196561

3. O. V. Kresin, *Comparative Law in Warsaw: 1800-1835*, transl. W. E. Butler (Clark, New Jersey, Talbot Publishing, 2022) ISBN 9781616196585

4. W. E. Butler and O. V. Kresin (eds.) *The Comparative Method in the Science of Law* by Lev Rebet (Clark, New Jersey, Talbot Publishing, 2022) ISBN 9781616196653

5. Horst Dippel, *Modern Constitutionalism*, 2 vols. (Clark, New Jersey, Talbot Publishing, 2022) ISBN 9781616196769

6. Stephan Meder, *Legal Machines* (Clark, New Jersey, Talbot Publishing, 2023) ISBN 9781616196813

7. Ama F. Hammond, Folashade Rose Adegbite, Maame Yaa A. Mensa-Bonsu, Prosper Batariwah (eds.), *Family Law in Africa: Perspectives on Selected Systems of Marriage* (Clark, New Jersey, Talbot Publishing, 2023) ISBN 9781616196844

8. William E. Butler and Oleksiy V. Kresin (eds.), *The World Picture of Comparative Law* (Clark, New Jersey, Talbot Publishing, 2024) ISBN 9781616196905

STUDIES IN COMPARATIVE LAW
JCL
SECOND SERIES

The World Picture *of* Comparative Law

EDITED BY
William E. Butler
JOHN EDWARD FOWLER DISTINGUISHED PROFESSOR OF LAW,
PENN STATE DICKINSON LAW
EMERITUS PROFESSOR OF COMPARATIVE LAW,
UNIVERSITY COLLEGE LONDON
FOREIGN MEMBER RUSSIAN ACADEMY OF NATURAL SCIENCES,
NATIONAL ACADEMY OF SCIENCES OF UKRAINE;
NATIONAL ACADEMY OF LEGAL SCIENCES OF UKRAINE

AND
O. V. Kresin
PROFESSOR, DOCTOR OF LEGAL SCIENCES (DR. HAB.),
ASSOCIATE, IACL,
HEAD OF COMPARATIVE JURISPRUDENCE CENTRE, VOLODYMYR KORETSKYI
INSTITUTE OF STATE AND LAW, NATIONAL ACADEMY OF SCIENCES OF UKRAINE,
GENERAL SECRETARY OF UKRAINIAN ASSOCIATION OF COMPARATIVE JURISPRUDENCE,
PRESIDENT, UKRAINIAN NATIONAL COMMITTEE OF IALS

TALBOT
PUBLISHING
Clark, New Jersey

ISBN: 978-1-61619-690-5

TALBOT PUBLISHING

AN IMPRINT OF
The Lawbook Exchange, Ltd.
33 Terminal Avenue
Clark, New Jersey 07066-1321

Please see our website for a selection of our other publications and fine facsimile reprints of classic works of legal history www.lawbookexchange.com

Library of Congress Cataloging-in-Publication Data

Names: Butler, William Elliott, 1939- editor. | Kresin, Oleksiĭ, 1976- editor.
Title: The world picture of comparative law / edited by William E. Butler, John Edward Fowler Distinguished Professor of Law, Penn State Dickinson Law Emeritus Professor of Comparative Law, University College London Foreign Member Russian Academy of Natural Sciences, National Academy of Sciences of Ukraine; National Academy of Legal Sciences of Ukraine; Oleksiy V. Kresin, Professor, Doctor of Legal Sciences (Dr. Hab.), Associate, IACL, Head of Comparative Jurisprudence Centre, Volodymyr Koretskyi Institute of State and Law, National Academy of Sciences of Ukraine, General Secretary of Ukrainian Association of Comparative Jurisprudence, President, Ukrainian National Committee of IALS.
Description: First edition. | Clark, New Jersey : Talbot Publishing, an Imprint of The Lawbook Exchange, Ltd., 2024. | Includes bibliographical references and index. | Summary: "An anthology of essays on comparative law by an international team of scholars"-- Provided by publisher.
Identifiers: LCCN 2024023776 | ISBN 9781616196905 (hardcover)
Subjects: LCSH: Comparative law.
Classification: LCC K559 .W67 2024 | DDC 340/.2--dc23/eng/20240528
LC record available at https://lccn.loc.gov/2024023776

Printed in the United States of America on acid-free paper

Table of Contents

SECTION 2.

Law: Spaces of Order and Interaction

SECTION 3.

At the Margin or in the Centre? Teaching and Doing Comparative Law

The Authors

Butler, William E., John Edward Fowler Distinguished Professor of Law, Penn State Dickinson Law; Emeritus Professor of Comparative Law, University College London; Foreign Member, Russian Academy of Natural Sciences; National Academy of Sciences of Ukraine; National Academy of Legal Sciences of Ukraine; Associate, International Academy of Comparative Law; co-editor, The Journal of Comparative Law; editor, Jus Gentium: Journal of International Legal History.

Kresin, Oleksiy Veniaminovych, Professor, Doctor of Legal Sciences (Dr. Hab.); Associate, International Academy of Comparative Law; Head, Center of Comparative Jurisprudence, Volodymyr Koretsky Institute of State and Law, National Academy of Sciences of Ukraine; Research Fellow, Faculty of Political Science and International Relations, University of Palermo; Visiting Professor, Centre for Comparative, European and International Law, University of Lausanne (2022-2023).

***

Behruz, Hashmatulla, доктор юридичних наук; professor; Head, Chair of International and European Law, National University "Odessa Law Academy".

Cordero, Jorge A. Sánchez, Ph.D. (Law), University Pantheon-Assas, Paris II; Dean, Governing Council. International Institute for the Unification of Private Law (UNIDROIT); Director, Mexican Center of Uniform Law.

Damirli, Mehman A., Doctor of Legal Sciences; Associate, International Academy of Comparative Law; Faculty of Law, Near East University (Cyprus).

Egorov, Aleksei V., Rector, Belarus State University of Economics; доктор юридических наук; professor.

Giraudo, Marco, Ph.D. (Law); Researcher, Law Department, University of Torino.

Gordley, James, W. R. Irby Distinguished University Professor, Tulane Law School.

Graziadei, Michele, Professor of Comparative Law, Law Department, University of Torino; Titular Member, International Academy of Comparative Law; Member, Academia delle scienze, Torino, Collegio Carlo Alberto Fellow.

Gutan, Manuel, Ph.D. (Law); Professor of Legal History and Comparative Law, Lucian Blaga University of Sibiu (Romania), Faculty of Law; Editor in Chief, Romanian Journal of Comparative Law.

Halabudenko, Oleg A., Ph.D. (Law); Associate Professor, Department of Political Science and Law, Kyiv National University of Construction and Architecture.

Iuliis, Carmelo Massimo de, Professor of Corporate Law, Department of Public and Private Economy Law, Catholic University (Milan); lawyer, Supreme Court of Italy.

Kharytonov, Evhen O., доктор юридичних наук; professor; Head, Chair of Civil Law, National University "Odesa Legal Academy"; Honored Scientist and Educator of Ukraine; Associate, National Academy of Legal Sciences of Ukraine.

Kharytonova, Olena I., доктор юридичних наук; professor; Head, Chair of Intellectual Property Law and Patent Justice, National University "Odesa Legal Academy"; Honored Scientist and Educator of Ukraine; Associate, National Academy of Legal Sciences of Ukraine.

Mercescu, Alexandra, Ph.D. (Law); Lecturer, Faculty of Law, West University of Timisoara; Research Affiliate, Nomos Center for International Research on Law, Culture and Power (Jagiellonian University, Krakow, Poland); Research Affiliate, Centre for Legal Education and Social Theory (Wrocław, Poland).

Nicolini, Matteo, Ph.D. (European and Constitutional Law); Associate Professor of Comparative Law, University of Verona; Visiting Lecturer, Newcastle University Law School; external partner, Centre for the Study of Law in Theory and Practice, Liverpool John Moores University.

Ostroukh, Asya, Ph.D. (Law); Senior Lecturer, Faculty of Law, Cave Hill Campus, University of the West Indies.

Rabinovych, Serhiy P., доктор юридичних наук; professor, Chair of Constitutional Law, Lviv Ivan Franko National University.

Saidov, Akmal Kh., Academician, Academy of Sciences of the Republic Uzbekistan; доктор юридических наук; Professor of Comparative and International Law; Director, National Human Rights Center of the Republic Uzbekistan.

Samuel, Geoffrey, Ph.D. (Cambridge); Dr. (Maastricht); Dr. (honoris causa) Université Nancy II; Professor Emeritus, Kent Law School, United Kingdom, and formerly Professor affilié, École de droit, Sciences Po (Paris).

Tkachenko, Oleksandr V., Кандидат юридичних наук; professor, Institute of International Relations and Law, Kyiv International University.

Tykhomyrov, Denys O., Доктор юридичних наук; docent, Chair of Theory of State and Law, National Academy of Internal Affairs of Ukraine.

Tykhomyrov, Oleksandr D., Доктор юридичних наук; professor; Associate, International Academy of Comparative Law.

Valcke, Catherine, J.S.D. (Columbia University); Professor, Faculty of Law, University of Toronto; Associate, International Academy of Comparative Law.

Varga, Csaba, Professor Emeritus, Institute of Legal Philosophy, Péter Pázmány Catholic University of Hungary; Research Professor Emeritus, Institute for Legal Studies, Hungarian Academy of Sciences.

Chapter 1
Introduction

The chapters herein are partly based on reports made during a series of comparative law events – the International Symposium Drawing Legal Pictures: The Worldview and its Implication for the Purpose and Method of Comparative Law and International PhD Workshops Series Strategies in Comparative Legal Research, both held in May 2023 at Lausanne, Switzerland. They were organized and supported by: Swiss Institute of Comparative Law (ISDC); Centre of Comparative, European and International Law at the University of Lausanne (CDCEI UNIL); Koretsky Institute of State and Law, National Academy of Sciences of Ukraine; Association of Universities in Western Switzerland (CUSO); *The Journal of Comparative Law*; and the Swiss Society of International Law. [1]

The Symposium pursued the idea that every discipline perceives and constructs the world in its own way: it conceptualizes and structures an aspect or a fragment of (perceived) reality and develops a research program and method(s) that are apt to develop this construction process, having in mind a specific vision or mission. One can call such disciplinary perception and construction a special world picture of a discipline.

In various ways the appropriate concept had been considered by Sir Isaac Newton, Immanuel Kant, the Humboldt brothers, Dilthey, Martin Heidegger, and others. Depending on different modes of scientific rationality, the world picture can be seen as the object, subject, or aim of a scientific discipline. In any case, even if not explicitly stated, this construction is a core issue of any discipline.

In law, various (sub)disciplines such as legal philosophy, legal theory, and comparative law have developed sundry (albeit often mutually influenced) interpretations of the world. One could

[1] A detailed account of these comparative law events was published in *The Journal of Comparative Law*, XVIII (2023), pp. 592-601. We express here our deep appreciation for the efforts of Lausanne colleagues involved in the organization of these activities: Dr. Lukas Heckendorn Urscheler (vice-director of the ISDC), Prof. Andrea Bonomi (ex-director of the CDCEI UNIL), Prof. Andreas Ziegler (director of the CDCEI UNIL, President of the Swiss Society of International Law), and others, including the members of research, library, and technical staff of the ISDC.

argue that there has been competition between the (sub)disciplines for the right or the possibility to define a world picture generally valid for discourse about law.

The Lausanne symposium was intended to create an awareness of the fundamental experience and potential that comparative law possesses when conceptualizing the "legal". Relying on its rich experience, comparative law is well positioned to take into account current developments in the field when (re-)defining its world picture, in order to conceptualize perceptions of law in a truly global perspective. The symposium invited participants to discuss the dialectics of the Individual/unit (national and/or other legal systems), the Particular/common and the (non)existence of the General/global in the legal world as the material basis of a comparative law world picture.

Some core issues of the Symposium were reflected in the report of Dr. Lukas Heckendorn Urscheler. He pointed out that comparative law generally starts with the assumption that national law is the (main) "object" or "unit" of comparison. He expressed doubts as to whether the assumption still holds: there is great variety in comparative legal studies of "what" is compared, and the debates on classification of legal traditions/systems reflect a more open approach. In terms of origin and evolution, the notion of national states in the West contributed to the nationalization of law in nineteenth century; law previously had taken different (non-national) forms. In twentieth-century Europe, national law became a reality, and law finally became a "national" discipline, often considered as a system. This view, considered to be universal, disregarded the law of nations and non-Western realities, as well as the omnipresent interaction of State legal systems with other normative orders (religious and transnational norms, customary law, and others). These orders imposed limits on the concept of State law. Today, State law remains an important unit in legal development, but it is not necessarily fundamental for comparative law. In comparative law, there is growing awareness of this element, but profound paradigmatic shift has yet to occur.

The chapters herein, for the first time presenting the complex philosophical and historical vision of the world picture of law developed in comparative law (comparative jurisprudence), is considered by American, Cypriot, Italian, Moldovan, and Ukrainian scholars – Oleksiy Kresin, Mehman A. Damirli, Matteo Nicolini, Oleg Halabudenko, James Gordley, Michele Graziadei,

Marco Giraudo, Oleksandr and Denys Tykhomyrov, Oleksandr Tkachenko.

The second group of articles presents a vision of the spaces of legal ordering and legal interactions as addressed by American, Belarus, Italian, Mexican, Romanian, Ukrainian, and Uzbek researchers – Akmal Saidov, Aleksei Egorov, Hashmatulla Behruz, Serhiy Rabinovych, William E. Butler, Evhen Kharytonov, Olena Kharytonova, Manuel Gutan, Carmelo Massimo De Iuliis, and Jorge A. Sánchez Cordero.

Finally, the third block is dedicated to the issue of implementation of the elaborated comparative legal world picture in academia and legal practice: articles by scholars from Canada, Hungary, Romania, United Kingdom, and the West Indies – Geoffrey Samuel, Alexandra Mercescu, Csaba Varga, Catherine Valcke, and Asya Ostroukh.

A number of these chapters appeared in *The Journal of Comparative Law*, XIX, no. 1 (2024). Some have been subsequently revised, and others appear here for the first time. Seven chapters were translated by Professor Butler.

William E. Butler

Oleksiy V. Kresin

SECTION I.

The World Picture and Alternative Concepts

Chapter 2

World Picture of Comparative Law: "The Courage of Your Convictions"

O. V. KRESIN

If we assume that comparative law is an autonomous discipline and not something else, it has to be called *comparative jurisprudence* as first happened in English as early as 1827 in England[1] and by 1829 in United States,[2] following the original German concept of

[1] "Abolition of the Code Napoleon in the Rhenish Provinces", *The Jurist, or Quarterly Journal of Jurisprudence and Legislation,* I (1827), pp. 252-253: "It is well known that the art of surgery has, of late years, been indebted, for great improvement, to the advances which have been made in the science of *comparative* anatomy. The principle of improving our knowledge, by extending our researches into subjects analogous and collateral to the immediate object of our inquiries, may be successfully applied to the science of jurisprudence. We have arrived at an epoch when we should no longer hesitate to break down the absurd barriers opposed to the progress of knowledge, by prejudices erroneously called national. The people of different nations should mutually study and compare existing institutions: and when the public opinion of each nation, enlightened by the efforts of philanthropic jurists, the founders of *comparative* jurisprudence, shall have obtained institutions adapted to the national manners, and the national wants, we may begin to hope that justice will be established upon firm and permanent foundations".

[2] "The Civil Law", *The American Jurist, and Law Magazine,* II, no. 3 (1829), pp. 59-60: "Our statesmen at home, therefore, our diplomatic agents abroad, and our practicing lawyers of eminence, who are daily called to the examination of important questions more or less intimately connected with the rights and duties of foreign nations, must make themselves in some degree acquainted with foreign laws; and for this purpose a knowledge of the civil law is indispensable. We might add to these considerations, that in a liberal course of professional studies, general or *comparative jurisprudence* must be a constituent part; and in this point of view the Roman law is of far greater importance than that of any other nation". Ibid, p. 416 (Index): "... importance of the study of *comparative jurisprudence*". Also published as a separate brochure: *Remarks on the Study of the Civil Law* (Boston: Freeman & Bolles, 1829), pp. 23-24. The author was John Pickering (1777-1846), a noted jurist and philologist, and close friend of Stephen du Ponceau (1760-1844), the Philadelphia international and comparative lawyer. Pickering was "... one of the few Americans deeply interested in Roman Law". Quoted from Morris L. Cohen, *Bibliography of Early American Law* (1998), I, 1650.

vergleichende Jurisprudenz / vergleichende Rechtswissenschaft (1800). But let us leave this issue aside. Assuming that comparative law is a separate discipline means it has not only practical functions (if at all) and descriptive capabilities, but also the aim of deeper cognitive significance. This aim of comparative law is the construction of an own special comparative-legal picture of the world. To be sure, legal philosophy, legal history, legal theory, and legal sociology each offer their own pictures of the world and to some extent using comparative methodology. But who is to decide that their pictures are more adequate or precise than those fashioned by comparative jurisprudence?

If we assess the analogies and differences between various legal orders with a predominantly cognitive aim, and do this repeatedly or constantly – do we acquire a body of knowledge that could lead us to a system of knowledge with own theory and philosophy? Or should comparatists pass the knowledge obtained to someone else, regarding themselves as field agents for wiser theoreticians and philosophers? If we are to critically and intellectually elevate ourselves collectively, does this engage the autonomous formation of the foundations of comparative legal studies?

Does the "official" mantle of "philosopher" make a person wiser than others? If we return to a philosophical approach to comparative jurisprudence as a predominantly inductive discipline dealing with positive law and other social phenomena cognized with empirical research, is it possible to also imply the traditional metaphysical (with a concealed natural law base) and speculative/deductive philosophy merely with an improved conception of law? Or should we venture to speak about another type of philosophy?

Even if we do not assume the task to construct our own special picture of the world for comparative jurisprudence, it has done this successfully for more than two centuries. This special picture of the world, as the major and most generalized aim of the discipline, is the clearest sign that the last exists in its own right.

PHILOSOPHY OF COMPARATIVE JURISPRUDENCE

The possibility and necessity for comparative law to construct an own special world picture flows from the philosophical level of cognition. Questions arise: has comparative law ever achieved and, if not, can it now achieve this level? Are the philosophical grounds of comparative law somehow special, or are they identical with those of the metaphysical philosophy of law?

Inductive philosophy?

Might, according to epistemology, a predominantly empirical and inductive discipline form its own philosophy by generalizing and questioning the knowledge it obtains, and immerse itself in metaphysical reasoning? There are different views. Robert Audi notes that empirical, sensory experience becomes knowledge only when in combination with analytic propositions, including purely logical truths. Rationalists believe these truths have an *a priori* character; empiricists believe the logic of these truths is grounded in experience. Moreover, rationalists maintain that, in addition to logical truths, synthetic *a priori* truths exist, so all knowledge is deductive and grounded in reason.[3]

Alexander Bird advances the idea of inductive knowledge primacy. Results of inductions become the premises for the next inductive inferences, mediating the reasoning from the observed to the unobserved. Contrary to deduction, inductive inferences are ampliative, "where the conclusion 'goes beyond' the premises". Bird believes that in reality premises are not fully inductive; they appeal to some sort of externalist epistemology, so the inferences are not fully detached and contingent, but to some extent could be subject to apriorism.[4]

William Alston emphasizes the autonomy of perceptual knowledge which has an own *prima facie* justification, albeit defeasible, not absolute.[5] This means that perception can be just empirical and the results of perceptual knowledge may form the primary premises for the inductive generalizations.

The truth lies in between: some initial externalist epistemology elements in the inductive comparative legal research are unavoidable, but major premises are themselves the results of previous inductions. The logic of research is ampliative, which

[3] Robert Audi, *Epistemology: A Contemporary Introduction to the Theory of Knowledge* (3d ed.; 2011), pp. 116-117.

[4] Alexander Bird, "Inductive Knowledge", in Sven Bernecker and Duncan Pritchard (eds.), *The Routledge Companion to Epistemology* (2011), pp. 271-272, 282.

[5] Willliam Alston, "Perceptual Knowledge", in John Greco and Ernest Sosa (eds.), *The Blackwell Guide to Epistemology* (1999), pp. 223-225.

presupposes the possibility of critical assessment of any involved externalist epistemology to avoid deductive inferences. In this way comparative law may form an own philosophical discourse independently from the metaphysical philosophy of law.

Early philosophy of comparative jurisprudence: Feuerbach

From the very beginning comparative jurisprudence as a mode of scientific reasoning and disciplinary project included the philosophical level of comprehension of the plurality of legal orders and presupposed a type of philosophizing other than that of a newborn brother and *alter ego* – metaphysical legal philosophy. Disregarding numerous grandfathers for the moment, we concentrate on the ideas of the father of comparative jurisprudence (who did not predict the future strange creation of comparative law), Paul Johann Anselm von Feuerbach.

Feuerbach wrote about the inadequacy of legal theorizing built, explicitly or implicitly, on the generalization of Roman law. The substance and wisdom of the latter should be the impetus for the scientific legal thought of "enlightened peoples" and not a body of predictable and ultimately ossified results that deny contemporary realities and make progress impossible. The conflict between the right unreal Ought and the wrong real Is was not amenable to solutions; theory and practice in law became isolated and despised one another. Theorizing is dominant in its separate seemingly scientific imagined world, elevating the ideal of isolation from real life. And the legal practitioner became indifferent to the imagined theoretical world as empty and unfruitful.[6]

> From other side, the practice too often presented the means as the only and final end, hoarded whole treasures and left them unused, or lifted up whole layers and left the pearls

[6] Paul Johann Anselm von Feuerbach, "Vorrede. Blick auf die teutsche Rechtswissenschaft", in Carl August Dominik Unterholzner. *Juristische Abhandlungen* (1810). Herein we use the Ukrainian translation. Feuerbach, «Погляд на німецьке правознавство», transl. Olena Shabliy; ed. Oleksiy V. Kresin, in Порівняльне правознавство [Comparative Jurisprudence], no. 1-2 (2012), pp. 283-284; Kresin, «Формування теоретико-методологічних засад порівняльного правознавства у працях Пауля Йоганна Анзельма фон Фейєрбаха» [Formation of Theoretical and Philosophical Bases of Comparative Jurisprudence in the works of Paul Johann Anselm von Feuerbach], in Yuriy Shemshuchenko, Ivan Hrytsenko, and Oleksandr Marin (eds.), Порівн1яльне правознавство: сучасний стан і перспективи розвитку: Збірник наукових праць [Comparative Jurisprudence: Contemporary State and Prospects for Development] (2011), pp. 30-52.

> found in place, magnified the letter but killed the spirit, brought stones to the pile and constantly polished them without a thought as to what should come out of it[7].

Feuerbach wrote that philosophy first "tried to gain a foothold on the ground of jurisprudence" only during the time of Christian Wolf, in the first half of the eighteenth century. Even the attempts of philosophy to evaluate and conceptually organize jurisprudence according to mathematical logic, leaving aside experience and historical peculiarities "had very bad consequences": "What it displayed was nothing more than a flimsy web of concepts that neither shed light on new truths, nor cemented old ones", translated living truths "in a distorted and restricted form". This metaphysical and speculative philosophy failed, but returned in a "Kantian revolution" with more ill-founded pretensions.[8]

One embodiment of metaphysical philosophy is natural law teaching, modified by the philosophy of pure reason. It clearly distinguished between morals and law, so decisive for legal order, and certain key legal concepts (albeit not all adequate). But such a philosophy is ungrounded, empty, pure speculative, formalistic, and geometric; its main concepts are erroneous and harmful for the development of positive law. The only contribution of such a philosophy is the negative definition of law:

> The pure form of law, no matter how understood, is always negative. Nothing positive can be created from it, and therefore it is devoid of any content and serves as a criterion for determining the extent to which current and future laws are acceptable from a legal point of view. However, it is not the element from which the content of any legislation could develop.[9]

According to Feuerbach, philosophy in the sphere of law (just as in the sphere of any positive science) cannot be a creator or principal, but merely a teacher and companion; it cannot change the existing *materia* and legislate, but merely propose forms and ideas. There is no source, not even "eternal reason", for the

[7] Feuerbach, note 6 above, p. 284.

[8] Ibid, p. 285.

[9] Ibid, pp. 288-289.

authority of legal philosophy. It has no power over real positive law and no basis for despising it; philosophy can merely analyze and comment on existing law.[10]

Feuerbach mercilessly criticized the metaphysical, substantial, *a priori,* subjective philosophy as the irreconcilable enemy of science. But he was convinced that the philosophical level of comprehension has to be an integral part of jurisprudence in indissoluble connection with the "historical" (inductive study of positive law) level. Following Gustav Hugo (1764-1844), he proposed the other non-metaphysical inductive philosophy – the philosophy of positive law. In 1810 he wrote about a general jurisprudence in which the base has to be comparative jurisprudence and the top has to be the positive philosophy of law or "philosophy of the laws". The last "derives the General from the Individual and reduces everything to a large and meaningful Whole".[11]

In his later work Feuerbach defined both general jurisprudence and comparative jurisprudence as the "science about the State and history of law in human society as such", noting that: "Science as such consists in knowing the General and regular in their relation to the Individual and accidental. And only a comparison of different research subjects can bring us closer to this level of knowledge".[12]

In this work Feuerbach declared that this general or comparative jurisprudence has to provide legal disciplines or areas of legal research with scientific grounds. Whereas Kant presupposed the possible autonomic from the metaphysical philosophy existence of positive legal science, but suggested this would be a headless body, Feuerbach viewed comparative jurisprudence as this head.

Feuerbach believed that metaphysical philosophy is false and empty, and virtually unnecessary, just as any idea of law's substantiality is discredited. Moreover, the philosophy of

[10] Ibid, pp. 285, 290.

[11] Ibid., pp. 285-287, 289.

[12] Feuerbach, "Idee und Notwendigkeit einer Universal-jurisprudenz", in Paul Johann Anselm von Feuerbach, *Biographisher Nachlass* (1853), pp. 378-401. Herein is used the Ukrainian translation. Feuerbach, "Ідея та необхідність універсальної юридичної науки. Природне право, філософія права, загальне правознавство", transl. Olena Shabliy; ed. Oleksiy Kresin, in Порівняльне правознавство [Comparative Jurisprudence], nos. 3-4 (2012), p. 329. See a similar thought on p. 338, with a substitution of "regular" with "necessary".

natural law, seemingly built on consistent speculative "pure reason", conceals its true nature as merely the generalization of European legal orders (foremost Roman law). A true philosophy of law (or philosophy of legislation) and legal theory should be based on comparative legal studies attentive to both similarities and differences, presuming the equality of different peoples' experiences and able to comprehend their values. Universal human elements should be comprehended with the comparative study of nations as individuals; homogenous universal similarity being impossible, the General is the "movement to achieve maximum unity with the existence of the greatest possible diversity". The philosophical study of the values, spirit, and senses of positive law is seen here as a part of general or comparative jurisprudence: "General positive legal science (universal legal science) ... if, thanks to the comparative analysis of various laws and legal systems, it will be able to rise to the level of science, then it will be called comparative jurisprudence".[13]

Generally speaking and taking the Kantian terminology (the key consistency here, paradoxically at first sight, is Feuerbach taking some Kantian terms while rejecting his metaphysics), it can be said that Feuerbach doubts the reality and the need for the philosophy of pure reason as metaphysics continuing to predominate the sciences, including jurisprudence. Pure reason cannot determine the philosophical discourse in law. On the contrary, philosophical senses, or "universal wisdom", should be formed from below; not from the generalization and idealization of one nation's experience, but on the base of the comparative study of positive national legal orders. Comparative jurisprudence here stands as a dominant among general legal disciplines and as a multi-tiered project presupposing its own philosophical discourse.

These ideas of the philosophy of positive law of Gustav Hugo and of the own philosophical discourse or dimension of comparative jurisprudence of Feuerbach had extensive dissemination and influence and were reproduced by others, sometimes almost literally and without references. As a brief example: in his lectures at London University (now University College London) as the Professor of Jurisprudence and the Law of Nations from 1827 to 1832, John Austin (1790-1859) distinguished within the "province of jurisprudence" general jurisprudence or the philosophy of

[13] Feuerbach, note 12 above, p. 328-334, 337-339.

positive law (their identical content was repeatedly stressed) from the particular jurisprudence or the complexes of knowledge of individual national legal orders. Expressly basing himself on Hugo and implicitly reproducing key theses of Feuerbach, Austin viewed general jurisprudence / philosophy of positive law as

> concerned directly with principles and distinctions which are common to various systems of particular and [sic!] positive law; and which each of those various systems inevitably involves, let it be worthy of praise or blame, or let it accord or not with an assumed measure or test. ...is concerned with law as it necessarily *is*, rather than with law as it *ought* to be: with law as it must be, *be it good or bad,* rather than with law as it must be, *if it be good.*[14]

In the second, posthumous edition of Austin's work it was noted:

> the ampler and maturer systems of refined communities are allied by the numerous analogies which obtain between all systems, and also by numerous analogies which obtain exclusively between themselves. Accordingly, the various principles common to maturer systems (or the various analogies obtaining between them), are the subject of an extensive science: which science (as contradistinguished to national or particular jurisprudence on one side, and, on another, to the science of legislation) has been named General (or comparative) Jurisprudence, or the philosophy (or general principles) of positive law.[15]

Thus, John Austin proclaimed the identity of the spheres of general jurisprudence, comparative jurisprudence, and the philosophy of positive law, being opposed simultaneously to the metaphysical philosophy of law (including natural law teaching), science of legislation (embracing legal encyclopedia, legal deontology and ethics, legal technics etc.) and "particular jurisprudences".

We do not integrate here the rich material about the development of the philosophy of comparative law and present Feuerbach's views merely as an example, albeit a fundamental one.

[14] John Austin, *The Province of Jurisprudence Determined* (1832), p. iii.

[15] Austin, *The Province of Jurisprudence Determined* (2d ed.; 1861), II, p. 1107.

Contemporary philosophy of comparative law and the issue of its world picture

And what of the contemporary vision of the philosophical discourse of comparative law? This is addressed by many distinguished scholars writing about the theoretical and philosophical aims/goals of comparative law, something deeper than description and taxonomies, and rising to an own world picture conceptualization.

Max Rheinstein in his various works stated that comparative law has not just to describe legal systems and present the analytical legal geography as the result of such activities, but also is "concerned with law as a supra-national phenomenon", can in the future construct the general morphology of law, and form the general teaching on law. Legal concepts should be formed not from intellectual speculations, but be a result of comparative induction and generalization of the real law.[16]

Stephen Hicks suggested the shift in the perspectives of comparative law from the instrumental and evaluative to the interpretative one, being the only one legal discipline offering a "total overview" of legal phenomena and processes on the base of the experience of law. The widening of the scope of the discipline should include inductive forming of "the notion of the whole legal world and its intellectual development", in which every real form and mode acquires its meaningfulness.[17]

Petro Martynenko in 1990 stated that comparative-typological cognition is based on the spatial dimension of law, "spatial feasibility of law as the implemented state of the totality of its systems", being on an equal footing with historical and theoretical dimensions. It presupposes generalization and "produces new comparative knowledge about law on the base of typical models thereof and comparative study of legal systems and their elements", their interactions, applying the comparative-typological approach.[18]

[16] Max Rheinstein, "Comparative Law – Its Functions, Methods and Usages", *Arkansas Law Review and Bar Association Journal*, XXII, no 3 (1968), p. 415; Макс Рейнстайн, "Предмет и задачи сравнительного правоведения" [The Subject and Tasks of Comparative Jurisprudence], in Vladimir Tumanov (ed.), Очерки сравнительного права [Essays on Comparative Law], (1981), pp. 93-94, 97.

[17] Stephen C. Hicks, "The Jurisprudence of Comparative Legal Systems", *Loyola of Los Angeles International and Comparative Law Review*, VI (1983), p. 92.

[18] Petro F. Martynenko, «Целостность мира и сравнительное правоведение»

Martynenko proposed a precise conceptualization of a special picture of the world in comparative-legal studies. Although the subject-matter of comparative jurisprudence is legal geography (legal map of the world), the highest aim is the construction of a picture of the world. The essence of this picture is the dialectics of the General, Special, and Individual elements (institutionalized as legal orders or not) in legal development, where the interrelation of the General and the Individual is mediated by the Special.[19]

Tikhomirov relegated to a "picture of the general legal development in the world community": the nature of legal diversity and differences in law, the character and peculiarities of "legal formations" or legal complexes (national legal systems, legal families, branches of law, legal corpuses of inter-State associations, international law), the interaction thereof, and general and regional trends in the development of law.[20] Vladimir Ilich Lafitsky (1957-2023) stated without further details that the main aim of comparative law is the "creation of the universal picture of law in the all diversity of its manifestations".[21]

Samuel declared that the object of scientific thought, including in comparative law, is not "the facts of the social world", but the model in which and in relation to which every concrete fact obtains a sense.[22] Later he argued this thesis in detail. In search of an aim of comparative law as a scientific discipline he points on the need to clearly distinguish between ontological and epistemological dimensions of legal disciplines, the same as between science and the object of science. Researchers are studying empirical phenomena,

[Integrity of the World and Comparative Jurisprudence], in O. V. Kresin (ed.), Порівняльне правознавство: Антологія української компаративистики XIX-XX століть [Comparative Jurisprudence: Anthology of Ukrainian Comparativistics XIX-XX Centuries] (Kyiv, 2008), pp. 295, 297.

19 Ibid., pp. 282-283, 288, 298, 301, 303, 306.

20 Iu. A. Tikhomirov, Курс сравнительного правоведения [Course of Comparative Jurisprudence] (1996), pp. 2, 6-14, 16, 19-20, 247-248.

21 Vladimir I. Lafitsky, "О предмете сравнительного правоведения и методологии его исследования" [On the Subject-Matter of Comparative Jurisprudence and Methodology of Its Study], in Iu. A. Tikhomirov (ed.), Методология сравнительного правоведения: материалы конференции [Methodology of Comparative Jurisprudence: Materials of the Conference] (2012), p. 44.

22 Geoffrey Samuel, Comparative Law, in C.B. Gray (ed.), *The Philosophy of Law. An Encyclopedia* (1999), p. 207.

but they reacting to existing facts by construing abstracted conceptual models of the reality, and the last become the object of science. The model, and not empirical facts themselves, "produce explanations and predictions", and scientific theories.[23]

The model is valid/credible when it has no visible contradictions with reality, is formally coherent internally, is consensual/ conventional (accepted/agreed by "members of a specified community"), and these three requirements are at the same time the ways of verifying a model. The first two factors seem to be most important, but the decisive factor in discarding and replacing the model with another is the loss of conventionality.[24] Therefore models, Samuel stated, are "more or less *indirectly* connected to empirical phenomena": "Science is about the construction of schemes and models and empirical reality is understood not so much by imposing the model onto this reality but by schematizing an empirical phenomenon and inserting it into a system of concepts where it gains its scientific and referential sense".[25]

Models in legal science mediate between law and reality.[26]. Samuel repeatedly noted the significance of developing theory and methodology of comparative law, the inadequacy of works on legal philosophy for comparatists, the potential and even naturalness of the deductive and axiomatic stages of development for every science that begins with description and induction. But for him there is only one conceptual model of reality interpretation for legal science. He prefers comparative law to play a central role in the development of this single model which could become "post-axiomatic".[27]

Rodolfo Sacco (1923-2022) believed that "science does not need to borrow its justification from practical needs" and saw the

[23] Geoffrey Samuel, Epistemology and Comparative Law: Contributions from the Sciences and Social Sciences, in Mark Van Hoecke (ed.), *Epistemology and Methodology of Comparative Law* (2004), pp. 36-38, 43.

[24] Ibid., p. 44.

[25] Ibid.

[26] Ibid., p. 46.

[27] Ibid., pp. 35-36, 54-56; Geoffrey Samuel, Law of Obligations & Legal Remedies (London, 2001). See also: Horatia Muir Watt, "New Challenges in Public and Private International Legal Theory: Can Comparative Scholarship Help?", in Mark Van Hoecke (ed.), *Epistemology and Methodology of Comparative Law* (2004), p. 273.

principal/essential/chief goal of comparative law as "to access and understand the differences that exist between divergent laws and to discover the attendant benefits of these differences", "weigh the analogies and differences existing between the legal systems that they study".[28] William Ewald wrote about the "jettisoning of philosophy" from comparative law, leaving "the dry skeleton of the law", and proposed to return to a philosophical approach "based on a richer and more defensible conception of law" which presuppose a new deeper subject-matter for the discipline transformed into comparative jurisprudence.[29]

Pierre Legrand called for the "lucid theoretical undergirding of comparative legal studies and for methodological humility"; that presupposes moving upwards from description and compiling to the previously repressed "more vital roles such as critic and intellectual".[30] He defines the whole enterprise of the comparatist and comparativistic reasoning as a philosophy:

> The task of the comparatist is to lift himself out of his mundane existence and to attempt an 'appropriation of the foreign', to confront the enigmatical as he discerns it in other legal cultures in the full knowledge that the study of different lifewords will tax his empathic powers. Beyond the challenge to the foundational assumptions by which he leads his legal life within his local community, the comparatist must engage in the hermeneutical act that will allow him, through his intrusion into alien forms of discourse, to decipher and explicate a range of phenomena that appear inhospitable to interpretation... The comparatist aims to demonstrate that the discursive practices and the mental representations operating within a legal culture, often at a level beneath consciousness, are able to serve as a focus for speculative inquiry into significance in that they can communicate the specific legal and cultural sensibility of a given interpretative community.[31]

[28] Rodolfo Sacco, "One Hundred Years of Comparative Law", *Tulane Law Review*, LXXV (2000-2001), pp. 1162, 1170.

[29] William Ewald, "Comparative Jurisprudence (I): What Was It Like to Try a Rat?", *University of Pennsylvania Law Review*, CXLIII (1995), pp. 1953, 2114, 2145.

[30] Pierre Legrand, "The Return of the Repressed: Moving Comparative Legal Studies Beyond Pleasure", *Tulane Law Review*, LXXV (2000-2001), pp. 1034-1035.

[31] Legrand, "Alterity: About Rules, For Example", in P. Birks and A. Preto (eds.),

Perhaps paradoxically, Legrand at the same time argued that no methods, including the said "hermeneutical act", could cross the boundaries of an own legal tradition for the comparatist, and calls this situation "epistemological incommensurability". But he uses the available comparative methodological instrument for other purposes including the understanding of own legal tradition, the impossibility of interchanging "here" and "elsewhere", and of the imposition and distorting of foreign law, which "deserves to be elucidated, as much as possible, *on its own terms*".[32]

Jaakko Husa distinguishes dogmatic and non-dogmatic disciplines in general legal studies. Legal theory is maximally close to national legal dogmatics. Comparative law is also close to legal dogmatics methodologically, but is different in ontological and epistemological issues, for it has not a national, but a supranational character. At the same time, comparative law is close to legal philosophy from the view of its issues and objects of study, epistemological supra-national prospects, but differs in its ways of argumentation and research tradition.[33]

Husa considered that the ontology of law lay in the research sphere of comparative law just as in the philosophy of law, and that a division of labor exists. Husa supports the idea that the highest existential aim of comparative law is mostly the same as those of legal theory and legal philosophy – the production of a theory of law independent from the differences of legal systems. Legal philosophy transcends legal science, whereas the philosophical discourse of comparative law operates inside it. But within legal science, legal theory and legal philosophy have no monopoly on the philosophical comprehension of law, and "comparative law is at least for the same degree philosophical as legal theory" dealing with the ontology and epistemology of law.[34]

Husa observed that all branches of jurisprudence with an object transcending national boundaries, and especially comparative

Themes in Comparative Law. In Honour of Bernard Rudden (2002), p. 21.

[32] Ibid., pp. 22, 32.

[33] Jaakko Husa, "Nicht nur juristische Auslandsforschung: Rechtsvergleichung als Rechtsphilosophie", *Rechtstheorie*, XL (2009), pp. 3-5, 8; Jaakko Husa, *Interdisciplinary Comparative Law. Rubbing Shoulders with the Neighbors or Standing Alone in a Crowd*, (2022), pp. 3, 6.

[34] Husa, note 33 above (2009), pp. 7-8, 17-18.

law, raise theoretical and philosophical questions. And underlying these questions are "fundamental theoretical assumptions laying under the surface" of comparative law that could be cognized without own ontological and epistemological discourse.[35]

Esin Örücü noted that comparative law has its own philosophy – "the understanding of another". That is why comparison as comprehension, mode of thought, and lifestyle to be genuine cannot confine itself to empirical comparison, but "must end in explanations, answering the question: why?" These inductive explanations lead to "three essential gems of comparative law": "theories of methodology; theories of legal families; and theories of transfrontier mobility of laws".[36] In earlier work, however, Örücü saw comparative law as a branch of social science based on positive observation that anyway "must exist with symbiosis" with the philosophy of law, for the latter is not merely speculative and really acquires a "true knowledge of law".[37]

Mehman Damirli and Iryna Kryvtsova suggested to consider the legal map of the world as a special scientific picture of the world of comparative jurisprudence.[38] In their view, the forming of the legal map of the world should be perceived as a scientific research program of comparative jurisprudence. This view would appear to confuse interconnected, but essentially different, phenomena: the objective forming of the legal map of the world, the doctrine on the legal map of the world, and the doctrine on fundamental objects and processes in the sphere of law as the foundation of the legal picture of the world.

[35] Ibid., pp. 18-20.

[36] Esin Örücü, "Comparative Motley: Offerings from a Comparative Lawyer", *Critical Analysis of Law*, VIII, no. 2 (2021), pp. 9-10, 13.

[37] Örücü, *The Enigma of Comparative Law. Variations on a Theme for the Twenty-first Century* (2004), p. 14.

[38] Mehman Damirli, "Предметне поле порівняльного правознавства: комплексне бачення" [Subject-Matter Field of Comparative Jurisprudence: The Complex Vision], Порівняльне правознавство [Comparative Jurisprudence], no. 1-2 (2012), pp. 79-80, 86; Iryna S. Kryvtsova, "Научная картина мира, картина мира правовых наук, правовая карта мира (юридическая география мира): от общего к частному (некоторые размышления)" [Scientific Picture of the World, Picture of the World of Legal Sciences, Legal Map of the World (Legal Geography of the World): From the General to the Special (Some Reflections)], Правова держава [Rule-of-Law State], no. 27 (2016), pp. 439, 442-443.

Aleksei Egorov said that comparison becomes scientific only when it rises to the theoretical and philosophical levels, creating a theory of its objects with the model of their comparative relations – a special comparative world picture of law.[39]

Oleksandr Tykhomyrov distinguished three main components of the bases of comparative jurisprudence: ideals and norms; special scientific picture of the world; philosophical bases. They are mutually dependent, but each has its own sense and performs certain functions.[40] He noted that the philosophical bases of comparative jurisprudence are similar to, but not identical with, those of legal philosophy, just as philosophy and science are close but not the same. Comparative jurisprudence is "choosing and adapting the philosophical-legal knowledge to its nature and necessities through their concretization, clarification, adaptation, filling with new senses".[41] These philosophical bases of comparative jurisprudence

> reflecting it as a form of culture, on the worldview level determining its ideals and norms, scientific picture of the world, providing for a mutual relation of science and worldview, culture, social practices in temporal and spatial contexts, i.e. in certain historical epoch and in certain space … The comparative mode of thinking to some extend is specifying itself in the philosophy of post-postmodern – transmodernism, transversal philosophy, including the philosophy of comparativism, and as not a substantive philosophy, but a mode of philosophizing.[42]

[39] Aleksei Egorov, «Философия правового сравнения» [Philosophy of Legal Comparison], in Oleksiy V. Kresin (ed.) Філософія порівняльного правознавства: Збірник наукових праць [Philosophy of Comparative Jurisprudence: Collected Articles] (2015), pp. 189-191.

[40] Oleksandr Tykhomyrov, «Філософські засади порівняльного правознавства» [Philosophic Bases of Comparative Jurisprudence], in Oleksiy V. Kresin (ed.) Філософія порівняльного правознавства: Збірник наукових праць [Philosophy of Comparative Jurisprudence: Collected Articles] (2015), pp. 129.

[41] Tykhomyrov, «Філософсько-наукознавчі засади юридичної компаративістики» [Philosophic and Science of Science Bases of Juridical Comparativistics], Порівняльне правознавство [Comparative Jurisprudence], no. 1-2 (2012), p. 28.

[42] Tykhomyrov, note 40 above, pp. 129-130, 138.

According to Tykhomyrov, the philosophy of comparativism by rational means eliminates universality and uniqueness, determinacy and spontaneity, chaos and order, is "based on their relativity, supplementarity, on the cyclicity and accidentality of mutual transformations, and through them it is optimizes, harmonizes modernism and postmodernism, comprehends the world as pluralistic, multidimensional, multipolar".[43]

Fundamental for the philosophy of comparativism is the dialectics of One, Another, and the Other and its comprehension is based on the categories of common and different, proportionality, necessity and accidentality, constancy and changeability, on the philosophies of identicality, difference, and existence.[44]

Tykhomyrov views the special scientific picture of the world of comparative jurisprudence as a fragment of juridical (legal) and comparative (glocal, civilizational, cultural) scientific pictures of the world. Its role is the systematization of scientific knowledge of legal and regulative reality and to determine the tasks of comparative legal studies and the choice of the means of their realization. Whereas scientific facts reflect the images of the common and different in the fragments of reality, the picture of the world is the ordered image of reality in the specifical for comparative jurisprudence mode – through General, Special and Unique.[45]

Oleksandr Tkachenko based his philosophy of comparative jurisprudence on the delocalization of philosophy – "the impossibility of its existence as systemic, *a priori*, transcendental, unitary, timeless, and single horizon of philosophical senses".[46] Comparative jurisprudence, Tkachenko noted, had been not freed from metaphysics. The metaphysics symmetry in legal philosophy is the opposition between the jusnaturalist tradition, as its legitimation, and positivism. The autonomic metaphysical symmetry in comparative jurisprudence, which "is not a simple

[43] Ibid., pp. 138-139.

[44] Ibid., p. 139.

[45] Tykhomyrov, note 41 above, pp. 27.

[46] Tkachenko, "Постметафізична інтерпретація tertium comparationis — конституант права-як-філософії" [Postmetaphysical Interpretation of Tertium Comparationis – Constituent of Law-as-Philosophy], Порівняльне правознавство [Comparative Jurisprudence], nos. 3-4 (2012), pp. 423-424.

translation of philosophical problematics onto new subject-matter, and, in addition, deforms and dismantles legal philosophy", is the opposition between universalization and singularization of legal traditions.[47]

A new perception of intellectual space is underway through the overcoming of metaphysics, a change in the construction of thinking from the vertical to horizontal: "philosophy is possible only as the way of processualization of thinking within concrete disciplinary discourses, and not in some supradisciplinary, metadygmal space". The philosophical comprehension of law does not transcend the confines of legal science, is immanent, and constitutes as autonomous philosophical discourse. Comparative jurisprudence no longer has the aim of abstracting conclusions from cultural historicity to be used on an imagined higher level of legal philosophy, and no longer applies the ontological and epistemological axiomatic truths of legal philosophy; it becomes post-metaphysical. Existence could not be deprived of languages, and the mathematical principle of thinking is inadequate. Comparative jurisprudence in the context of post-nonclassical scientific rationality is constructing an own gnoseological framework and becomes an autonomous sphere of philosophical and methodological reflection: "philosophical senses could not be brought into comparative jurisprudence, but could be only produced by the latter, in particular by autonomous rebuilding of phenomenological or hermeneutical approaches to the world".[48]

Post-metaphysical comparative legal thinking perceives the place and the language not as the surface that hides a deeper sense, but as parts of the latter, so any singular unity and substantiality of law are abandoned. But the content of these local senses, embodied especially in national legal orders, is not self-sufficient; it is hetero-*materia*, applicable to other legal orders, and the comprehension of these processes has the speculative effect of producing "disciplinary philosophical senses". The comparison of law becomes philosophical and a "special procedure of

[47] Tkachenko, "Негативний простір юридичних конструкцій – територія правового порівняння як правової філософії" [Negative Space of Legal Constructions – Territory of Legal Comparison as Legal Philosophy], in Kresin (ed.) Філософія порівняльного правознавства: Збірник наукових праць [Philosophy of Comparative Jurisprudence: Collected Articles] (Kyiv, Lviv, 2015), pp. 233-234.

[48] Tkachenko, note 46 above, pp. 423-424.

processualization of legal thinking embodied in the discursive form with the legal deconstruction of own law".[49]

Tkachenko argues that – in the situation of inability of universality-singularity opposition to be an orientator for the philosophical identity of legal science – post-metaphysical construction of comparison becomes "the conceptual space of law-as-philosophy": "Positive space of legal constructions is the only sphere of legal senses existence. Its ontologization means that legal sense cannot be metajuridical, it is always immanent for materia of law".[50]

The specifics of legal reality and the special style of legal thinking, according to Tkachenko, are embodied exclusively in legal dogmatic constructions. They are not and cannot be the sphere of philosophical discourse, for the truth cannot be deduced from the existent – it is a stepping out of sense. That is why philosophy is localized in the negative space of legal constructions – the appeal to another law being the "nothing" of own law providing the sense of the last in the motion. "Foreign law is not an ontological phenomenon, but the gnoseological construction of own law comprehension", and awareness of own law's non-self-sufficiency leads to the procedure of comparison being a philosophy.[51]

Anastasia Saparova clarified such theses by noting that "law is itself a culture, and not just something existing in its confines, is simultaneously a process and a result of constant movement of senses, their mixing and combination". The comprehension of the constant legal transplantation processes should be a central subject of philosophical and methodological discourse providing the denial of both universalization and singularization of law.[52]

Of relevance are the present writer's thoughts expressed in earlier publications.[53] Legal philosophy studies ideal primary bases

[49] Ibid., pp. 425-427.

[50] Tkachenko, note 47 above, p. 236.

[51] Ibid., pp. 236-238.

[52] Anastasia Saparova, "Переосмислення правових трансплантантів як механізм оновлення філософії правознавства" [Rethinking Legal Transplants as the Mechanism of Legal Philosophy Renewal], in Kresin (ed.) Філософія порівняльного правознавства: Збірник наукових праць [Philosophy of Comparative Jurisprudence: Collected Articles] (2015), pp. 386-393.

[53] Kresin, "Філософія права і філософія порівняльного правознавства:

of law, objective and universal regularities of the origin, structure, functioning and development of law, and the specific features of the manifestation in law of regularities inherent in nature and social phenomena. Legal philosophy forms the doctrine on extra-legal grounds of law and its ideal primary bases, that is, natural (or reasonable, philosophical) law. Positive law as such is not within the subject-matter of the legal philosophy, and is of interest only in correlation with the ideal natural law (even if it is not called such). Such a legal philosophy: has a regional character, is not universal; does not directly correlate with the development of positive law and legal culture in concrete societies and States at certain stages of their development. This is not a shortcoming of legal philosophy, but a limitation thereof, an assumption of the existence of its limits. It cannot claim to a disciplinary monopoly in the sphere of a connection between philosophy and jurisprudence and in the sphere of the philosophical contemplation of law – especially if we refer to a contemplation of law in force.

At the same time, the philosophy of positive law formed during the second half of the eighteenth to the early nineteenth century is necessarily empirical and social. It provides for the non-incidentalness and rationality of the existence of the diversity of legal systems. And irrespective of whether the General in law is drawn from them inductively or is ascribed externally and deductively by the philosophy of natural law in the form of final reasonableness, the philosophy of natural law does not absorb temporary rationality, just as philosophy does not absorb jurisprudence.

A comparativistic legal worldview (or comparativistic elements of a worldview) became a generalization of the philosophy of positive law, in essence being non-monist, non-metaphysical, non-deductive, but pluralist, social, and inductive. Thanks to it and the comparative-legal approach and the complex of comparative-legal disciplines generated by it, the unity of the system of legal knowledge was established – from practically-

деякі міркування" [Philosophy of Law and Philosophy of Comparative Jurisprudence: Some Considerations], in Iu. S. Shemshuchenko and Ia. V. Lazur (eds.), Сучасні проблеми порівняльного правознавства: Збірник наукових праць [Contemporary Problems of Comparative Jurisprudence: Collection of Scientific Works] (2015); Kresin, "Зрозуміти Патрика Гленна" [Understanding Patrick Glenn], Порівняльно-правові дослідження [Comparative-Legal Studies], no. 2 (2014); Kresin, *Comparative Legal Studies: 1750 to 1835. Approaches to Conceptualization*, ed. and transl. William Elliott Butler (2019).

oriented studies of national law to a determination of the universal in legal development. The philosophy of positive law in the works of Anselm von Feuerbach and his followers in essence became comparative, and the comparative jurisprudence designed and identified by him finally absorbed such a philosophy and should have produced knowledge about law at the highest possible level of generalization. The entire system of legal knowledge and disciplines, according to Feuerbach, was permeated with comparativism. This comprised the first system of the philosophy of comparativism.

The philosophy of comparativism is in constant development, is pluralist, and is difficult to systematize. The very identity thereof is plural. Martynenko, for example, considered this problem more within comparative jurisprudence, and Glenn and Tykhomyrov – within legal science as a whole.[54]

An opposition exists between traditional legal philosophy as one reflecting an *a priori* and metaphysical, universalist, and monist worldview and the philosophy of comparativism and comparative jurisprudence as reflecting an empirically oriented, historical, social, pluralist, spatial worldview. The philosophy of comparativism is a philosophy of the Individual, Particular (Special), and General being sited horizontally relative to one another, in mutual linkage, and mediated by time, space, and social development. Therefore, on one hand, comparative jurisprudence needs an own philosophy and creates this, using own experience and the achievements of various sciences, and, on the other – comparativism and its philosophy never can be embodied in a single discipline.

The philosophy of comparativism, just as legal philosophy, has to do with ideas concerning law, including various law-comprehensions. But it considers and evaluates them not in individual or group personalized, but in social existence, as elements of a legal worldview of concrete societies, dominating law-comprehension. It considers these law-comprehensions not as absolute, not as emanations of pure reason, but as pluralist and relative, localized in time and space.

[54] For Patrick Glenn's views, see his entry in: Elisabeth Zoller, George A. Bermann, Patrick Glenn, Kim Lane Scheppele, Amr Shalakany, and David V. Snyder, "Comparative Law: Problems and Prospects", *American University International Law Review*, XXVI, no. 4 (2011); Kresin, "Зрозуміти Патрика Гленна", note 53 above, pp. 59-68.

Categorical propositions of a legal philosophy *a priori* in essence and abstract in orientation act for the philosophy of comparativism merely as hypotheses and ways of thinking, and also one of many variants which may be topical or not topical with regard to a concrete time and place. But comparativism does not coincide also with materialist philosophy; it provides an indirect link between material conditions and sphere of law (positive law, legal culture, legal consciousness) because the autonomy is recognized of the last and the possibility of various variants of the development of law in similar material conditions. Legal philosophy, claiming the perpetuity of truth in law, is in its essence, materialized. The philosophy of comparativism is always uncompleted, for the objects of comparative jurisprudence are dynamic, and therefore it is to a greater degree processual.

WHAT IS THE SCIENTIFIC PICTURE OF THE WORLD?

The scientific picture of the world as a concept can be analyzed from different vantage points, among them: philosophy of science, science of science, and history of sciences.

Philosophy of science

We begin with Immanuel Kant (1724-1804), whose ideas were key for the transformation and institutionalization of the social sciences two centuries ago. In his concise article "What is Enlightenment" in 1784[55] he insisted the humans rise from "self-imposed nonage", blaming the inability to form own understanding without the guidance of an imposed metaphysics of theology and philosophy. A new model of thought, stepping away from indecision, "the courage of your convictions", "dare to know!", is the essence of Enlightenment. This could not be achieved at once; it is a slow process of freeing from prejudices, a process of conscious and consistent use of practical reason.

In the Kantian vision this use has to be scholarly and public (sharing and discussing the obtained knowledge), and be realized in practice (for example, in the civil service). This scholarly quest

55 Immanuel Kant, *What Is Enlightenment?*, transl. Mary C. Smith (available online).

leads to the formation of an order, both an intellectual scheme and its realization, that is not absolute and eternal, but relative and temporary, to be changed subsequently with a new order in the never-ending process of intellectual progress ("progress in enlightenment"). Moreover, this order is to some extent conventional because it rests on the convention of the majority of scholars, but does not eliminate the dissenting views of a scientific and non-scientific character.[56]

The essence of the conventional intellectual order was subjectivized in the ideas of scientific worldview and world picture of a number of philosophers of science, among them Wilhelm Dilthey (1833-1911) and Karl Jaspers (1883-1969). Dilthey in 1911 claimed that every worldview "is historically conditioned and therefore limited, relative", separated from other worldviews by its "inner law". And at the same time, every worldview is "grounded in the nature of the universe and the relation of the finite knowing mind to it" and so "each of them expresses one side of the universe within the limits of our thought", being one-sided true while "it is not granted to us to see these sides all at once". So, "the pure light of truth can be seen by us only in variously broken rays".[57]

The key conclusion of Dilthey is that the cognition of the world is only one among important moments in worldview formation. These moments result from reasoning, pre-position, pre-experience, all our psychological integrity, and so could be destroyed by mere factual or logical argument.[58]

Dilthey wrote that the worldview could be not only personal, but also characteristic for some climate, race, nation, and conditioned by particular history, influence of State order, life conditions, interactions between peoples, being at the same time typical in essence for an epoch of general history. Just as living beings are struggling for territories, different worldviews are

[56] A contemporary scholar has observed that the concept "worldview" (Weltanschauung), important in principle for understanding the world picture as a sub-concept, appeared first in Kant's *Critique of Judgement* (1790). See David Naugle, *Worldview: The History of a Concept* (2002).

[57] Dilthey's fragments are presented in David Naugle, *The Age of the "World Picture": Hermeneutics and Weltanschauung Theory*, pp. 29-30 (available online).

[58] Wilhelm Dilthey. Типы мировоззрений и обнаружение их в метафизических системах [Types of Worldviews and their Appearance in Metaphysical Systems], in Культурология. XX век. Антология [Culturology. 20th Century. Anthology] (1995), pp. 216-229.

struggling for souls. Worldviews better able to explain themselves win out and become long-living and stable, developing themselves organically and becoming more systematic.[59]

The substantial changes in life conditions, state of science, interaction of peoples, and major political events create new combinations of living experience and orientations, which together influence the power of certain ideas and evaluation of the importance of problems. These new integral intellective complexes contradict the settled and conventional worldview, and this may lead to the transformation or creation of a new worldview.[60]

Three grand types of worldview are distinguished by Dilthey, historically consecutive but co-existing: naturalistic (nature influencing humans), subjective idealism (human spirit influencing nature), objective idealism (harmony between humans and nature).[61]

Dilthey used the notion of world picture / *Weltbildes* (connected with, but separate from worldview / *Weltanschauung*) as being the system and the result of the consistent cognition which summarizes and interprets perceived objects and their relations with other objects and with us, moving from the known and from our values to the as yet unknown. Then in turn the world picture becomes the base for the evaluation of particular objects and filling them with sense.[62]

An insightful analysis of Dilthey's views on the subject is presented by Eric Nelson. First, the worldview in the theory of Dilthey is not a passive meditation, but the "interpretive perception or picturing [anschauen] of a world": "A historically situated and self-reflexive life interpretively pictures and forms a world for itself and expresses and communicates this world in myriad ways throughout its life".[63] So the *Weltanschauung* means the active appropriation, conceptualization, modelling, construction; the world picture is a necessary and inalienable

59 Ibid., pp. 216-229.

60 Ibid., pp. 216-229.

61 Ibid.

62 Ibid.

63 Eric S. Nelson, "The World Picture and its Conflict in Dilthey and Heidegger", *Humana.Mente Journal of Philosophical Studies*, XVIII (2011), p. 19.

function of a worldview. Second, the individual forms his/her world picture not "through the self-intuition or self-assertion", but in relation to other individuals in a certain surrounding, and so this world picture is always necessarily concrete social-cultural, belonging to some "social-historical worlds".[64] Third, social sciences produce their own world pictures based on the aspects of social reality they study. These world pictures are empirically-based within their subject-matter and at the same time may be metaphysical in conceptualizing matters that are involved, but external.[65] Fourth, the only world picture for all times, "social-historical worlds", and sciences is impossible, and so the idea of the unity of the world, speculation, metaphysics, and ontology give way to "non-reductive or pluralistic empiricism in relation to knowledge", relativism, and "comparative coordinating strategy".[66] Fifth, philosophical reduction of the multiplicity of world pictures is futile, "leads to aporias and downfall", because every world picture is not fully rational, but self-interpretive and connected with concrete social experience; and reduction is dangerous because it "leaves us with an impoverished thinking that is only calculation and an instrument of domination ... The resolution of the antinomy in a projected systematic totality is to suppress the differences constitutive of life". Every world picture is based on the consciousness of real external world and not losing the link with Is while constructing its model. It follows, and this is important, that "the historicity of worldviews entails that there is no master worldview from which to neutrally rank others, even one that appeals to an ontological principle of difference".[67] Sixth, instead of previous statements, it is possible to speak of world picture of generation or age, but as "dominant yet no single unified tendency of an age, as anarchic possibilities of the creative, new, and otherwise — which contest the hegemony of the dominant worldview — emerge and defy control".[68]

Jaspers in his work of 1919 used the notion of world picture and provided its psychologically-oriented vision. But he also wrote

[64] Ibid., pp. 19-20.

[65] Ibid, pp. 20-21.

[66] Ibid., pp. 21-24.

[67] Ibid., pp. 24-28, 31, 33-34.

[68] Ibid, p. 28.

that individual world pictures are essentially close in some socio-historical context and could be seen as a point of view, variant or a fragment of the regional, historical, national world pictures, and assumed also the existence of the absolute universal world picture. Worldviews and world pictures are subjective, but they become also objective when they penetrate the world and are the part of the process of appropriation of thus understood/interpreted world.[69]

A more comprehensive philosophical vision of world pictures was elaborated by Martin Heidegger. In 1938 Heidegger delivered a lecture "Die Zeit des Weltbildes", that was published in 1950 in German. The lecture was translated into English at least four times with the titles "The Age of the World View" (1951) and "The Age of the World Picture" (1977, 2002, 2009).[70] Both the meaning of the title in translation and the time of the finalization of the author's ideas[71] have significance, but we analyze here the 1977 translation.

In Heidegger's view, research in the social and humanitarian sciences consists in principle in the criticism of sources and in the "comparing of everything with everything", making facts comparable and in this way intelligible, tracing them to laws and rules in order to reconstruct (and in fact to construct) "the ground plan of history".[72] This process, if it is "ongoing activity" with own methodology, is related and mutually reinforced with specialization and institutionalization, thus developing scholarly disciplines. The representing of the being by these disciplines means its objectification ("truth has been transformed into the certainty of representation") rising from the particular fact to the world (including the world of thought) in its entirety, not copying,

[69] Karl Jaspers, "Психология мировоззрений" [Psychology of Worldviews], transl. Cyril Golikov, in Философская антропология [Philosophical Anthropology], VII, no. 1 (2021), p. 120.

[70] Miles Groth, *A Bibliography of English Translations of the Writings of Martin Heidegger (1949-2011)*, p. 17 (available online).

[71] As Sidonie Kellerer suggests, the original content of the lecture had been modified for publication, at least for reputational purposes (to show Heidegger's "inner resistance" to the Nazi regime in 1930s). Sidonie Kellerer, "Rewording the Past: The Postwar Publication of a 1938 Lecture by Martin Heidegger", *Modern Intellectual History*, XI, no. 3 (2014), pp. 575-602. So, one may suppose other changes could have been made as well.

[72] Martin Heidegger, "The Age of the World Picture", transl. and ed. William Lovitt, in: Martin Heidegger, *The Question Concerning Technology and Other Essays* (1977), pp. 121-122.

but constructing the world picture as a system for each such discipline. These pictures of the world are temporal, for they are the pictures we are ready to see and understand now.[73]

Heidegger wrote that in the Middle Ages the world had been perceived as God's creation and so "to know is not to search out; rather it is to understand rightly the authoritative Word and the authorities proclaiming it". The world had been understood as objective, thought and being are the same (Heidegger used the citation from Parmenides), there is no place for the subjective perception and representation of reality.[74]

The time of the first scholarly world picture construction became the Modern Age. The representation in the Modern Age (Heidegger pointed more precisely to the end of the eighteenth century) means the relation of the something with oneself as "something standing over against" and creation of the conceptual model of this something while putting oneself in this model. Man intentionally stands in the center of the model of the new world he constructed and thus becomes a *subjectum* as "I am" and "We are", being a part of the concrete society and humanity, and the model becomes anthropological. "The word "picture" now means the structured image that is the creature of man's producing which represents and sets before".[75]

Science as research, and not a philosophy, becomes necessary for the construction of this world picture. Ordering knowledge and building an uncontroversial system of representation are essential for this picture. Research is a continuous and open process; if "the original power of the projecting is lacking" at a certain stage of picture development, it could degenerate into "the superficiality of a system that has merely been fabricated and pieced together".[76] "Original power" here may be understood as a reflection of a certain value and scholarly paradigm capable of adequately representing legal reality. It is always possible for a new world picture construction to exist, gaining conventionality and domination.

[73] Ibid., pp. 122-128.

[74] Ibid., pp. 121, 129-130, 140.

[75] Ibid., pp. 130-133, 151.

[76] Ibid., pp. 134, 139-141.

Some general grounds explaining Heidegger's notion of world picture could be found in his hermeneutic phenomenological ontology, namely in the concept of the fore-understanding. The last consists of fore-having, a fore-sight, and a fore-conception. The interpretation is conditioned not only by objective reality, but also by pre-assumptions and point of view on reality by the interpreter. Fore-having means that the interpreter presupposes to put the new interpreted object in a context of her/his previous experience of understood / interpreted objects. Fore-sight means the description of the new object with categories taken from previous interpretations. Fore-conception means the readiness of the interpreter to conceptualize the object with all he/she fore-has and fore-sees.[77]

Science of science

The concept "scientific picture of the world" has long since been recognized, extensively used, and researched in the science of science.[78] Viacheslav Stepin defined the scientific picture of the world as an "integral image of the subject-matter of a scientific study in its chief systemic-structural characteristics formed by means of fundamental concepts, representations, and principles of science at each stage of its historical development".[79]

[77] This is the present writer's interpretation of Heidegger's fragments in Naugle, note 57 above, pp. 16-17.

[78] See, for example: Oksana Basalaeva, "Функция понимания в частнонаучной картине мира" [Function of Understanding in Special Scientific Picture of World], Вестник Кемеровского государственного университета культуры и искусств [Herald of Kemerovo State University of Culture and Arts], no. 18 (2012), p. 215; Raphail Nurullin, "Метафизические основания научной картины мира" [Metaphysical Grounds of Scientific Picture of World], Вестник Оренбургского государственного университета [Herald of Orenburg State University], no. 7 (2011), pp. 186, 191.

[79] Viacheslav Stepin, "Научная картина мира" [Scientific Picture of the World], in Ilia Kasavin (ed.), Энциклопедия эпистемологии и философии науки [Encyclopedia of Epistemology and Philosophy of Science] (2009), p. 581. Also see Tatiana Kubanova, "Картина мира как философское понятие и мировоззренческая система взглядов: история и перспективы изучения" [Picture of the World as Philosophical Concept and Worldview System of Views: History and Prospects of Study], Общество. Среда. Развитие [Society. Environment. Development], no. 1 (2011), p. 190; Svetlana Chernova, "Научная картина мира как форма развития знания о реальности" [Scientific Picture of the World as Form of Development of Knowledge about Reality], Вестник Вятского государственного гуманитарного университета [Herald of Viatka State Humanities University], IV, no. 4 (2010), p. 27; Mikhail Soroka and Igor

Oleksandr Petryshyn relegated the scientific picture of the world to types of perception of the environment which are formed at each stage of the development of society and science. It determines the development of methodology as "progress of cognitive possibilities of man and society".[80]

General scientific, socio-historical, natural science, and special (disciplinary, individual scientific) pictures of the world could be singled out.[81] The existence of such a special picture is the evidence of the generalized vision of the subject-matter of research, constituting a certain domain of scientific knowledge in the form of a separate science.[82] Some authors, however, doubt the possibility of a general-scientific picture of the world, it being impossible to observe the world as a whole, and here there is place for a philosophical (worldview) picture of the world.[83]

Bulychev, "Проблема структуры научной картины мира" [Problem of Structure of Scientific Picture of World], Вестник Пермского университета. Философия. Психология. Социология [Herald of Perm University. Philosophy. Psychology. Sociology], no. 3 (2015), p. 33.

[80] Oleksandr Petryshyn, "Проблеми соціалізації права та соціологізації правової науки" [Problems of the Socialization of Law and Sociologization of Legal Science], Право України [Law of Ukraine], no. 8 (2011), p. 135.

[81] Stepin, note 79 above, p. 581; Sergei Khizhniak, "Национальная культура как фактор формирования языковой и концептуальной картин мира (на примере научной картины мира юриспруденции)" [National Culture as Factor of Forming Linguistic and Conceptual Pictures of World (Example of Scientific Picture of World of Jurisprudence)], Известия Саратовского университета. Новая серия. Серия: Филология. Журналистика [News of Saratov University. New Series. Series: Philology. Journalistics], XVI, no. 2 (2016), p. 130.

[82] Stepin, note 79 above, p. 581; Tykhomyrov, note 41 above, pp. 27; Nikolai Sharov, "Природа научной конвенциональности: когнитивно-языковой аспект" [Nature of Scientific Conventionality: Cognitive-Linguistic Aspect], Вектор науки [Vector of Science], no. 1 (2013), p. 270; Chernova, note 79 above, p. 27.

[83] Pavel Kopnin, Гносеологические и логические основы науки [Gnoseological and Logical Foundations of Science] (1974), pp. 384-388, quoted from P. S. Dyshlevyi and L. V. Iatsenko, "Научная картина мира и мир культуры" [Scientific Picture of the World and the World of Culture], in Dyshlevyi and Luk'ianets (eds.), Научная картина мира: логико-гносеологический аспект [Scientific Picture of the World: Logical-Gnoseological Aspect] (1983), p. 8; Soroka and Bulychev, note 79 above, p. 33; V. V. Kyzyma, "Научная картина мира в культурно-историческом контексте" [Scientific Picture of the World in the Cultural-Historical Context], in Dyshlevyi and Luk'ianets (eds.), Научная картина мира: логико-гносеологический аспект [Scientific Picture of the World: Logical-Gnoseological Aspect] (1983), p. 78.

Notions of "fundamental objects from which presumably all other objects are structured which are studied by respective science", typologies of objects, peculiarities of their interaction, and spatial-temporal structure of reality are involved in the scientific picture of the world.[84] The scientific picture of the world may be integral or be reflected in the form of competing notions which, nonetheless, have unified theoretical grounds conventional in character.[85]

Each scientific picture of the world is concrete-historical and over time is replaced by another. Moreover, the possibility of universal pictures of the world, especially in the socio-historical sphere, is doubtful because of the influence of culture on them.[86] Some scholars point to the obligatory presence of value socio-cultural orientations, a certain attitude towards the phenomena and processes of reality in the scientific picture of the world.[87] Thus, the scientific picture of the world has localization in space and time, and also transcends purely scientific limits.

The scientific picture of the world is a type of theoretical knowledge, is the most general theoretical model of reality, functionally acts as a research program, and is the basis of a certain strategy for the investigation and structuring of theories within a scientific discipline, "advancing hypotheses concerning the nature of phenomena discovered in experience" (link with culture and worldview).[88] With regard to knowledge already received, the

[84] Stepin, note 79 above, p. 581; Tykhomyrov, note 41 above, p. 27; S. K. Buldakov, "Научные, философские и методологические основания классической науки" [Scientific, Philosophical, and Methodological Grounds of Classical Science], Вестник Костромского государственного университета им. Н. А. Некрасова [Herald of Kostroma N. A. Nekrasov State University], no. 2 (2013), p. 69.

[85] L. A. Mykeshyna, "Научная картина мира как мировоззренческая форма знания" [Scientific Picture of the World as Worldview Form of Knowledge], in Dyshlevyi and Luk'ianets, note 83 above, p. 63.

[86] Sergei Khizhniak, "Национальная культура как фактор формирования языковой и концептуальной картин мира (на примере научной картины мира юриспруденции)" [National Culture as Factor of Forming Linguistic and Conceptual Pictures of World (Example of Scientific Picture of World of Jurisprudence)], Известия Саратовского университета. Новая серия. Серия: Филология. Журналистика [News of Saratov University. New Series. Series: Philology. Journalistics], XVI, no. 2 (2016), pp. 130-132; Chernova, note 79 above, pp. 27-28.

[87] Kubanova, note 79 above, p. 190; Soroka and Bulychev, note 79 above, p. 33.

[88] Viacheslav Stepin, note 79 above, pp. 581-583; I. A. Gorkovenko and

scientific picture of the world acts as a theory thereof, and with regard to receiving new knowledge performs a methodological function.[89]

At the same time, the scientific picture of the world itself represents a system of theories, and therefore changes when a significant part of the last ceased to correspond to accumulated empirical knowledge, or when changes in worldview, or in reality being researched occur.[90] As Chernova noted, the history of science as a result appears as a continuously-interrupted process, and the transition from one picture of the world to another acts as a qualitative transformation of theoretical principles of science, that is, as a scientific revolution. A new picture of the world from the outset is advanced as a hypothesis which passing through stage of substantiation and may for a long time coexist side by side with the previous picture. Most often it is confirmed as a result of verification by experience of the principles and use of these principles for new theories.[91]

History of sciences

The emergence of scientific pictures of the world was preceded by mythological, religious, and philosophical ones. In the sixteenth and seventeenth centuries a natural-philosophical picture of the

V. I. Strel'chenko, "Идея научной картины мира: постклассическая рациональность" [Idea of Scientific Picture of the World: Post-Classical Rationality], Вестник Ленинградского государственного университета им. А. С. Пушкина [Herald of Leningrad A. S. Pushkin State University], no. 2 (2010), p. 133; Kubanova, note 79 above, p. 189; Chernova, note 79 above, p. 29; G. M. Purynycheva and Iu. P. Kul'kov, "Научная картина мира как мировоззренчески-информационный концепт" [Scientific Picture of the World as Worldview Information Concept], Вестник Чувашского университета [Herald of Chuvash University], no. 1 (2006), p. 10.

89 A. F. Kudriashev and O. I. Elkhova, "Общенаучная картина мира: старое в новом одеянии" [General Scientific Picture of the World: The Old in New Dress], Вестник Башкирского университета [Herald of Bashkir University], XVIII, no. 4 (2013), pp. 1255-1256; Iu. V. Dzhulai, "Научная картина мира и условия познания" [Scientific Picture of the World and Conditions of Cognition], in Dyshlevyi and Luk'ianets (eds.), note 83 above, pp. 59-61.

90 Sharov, note 82 above, pp. 270-271; E. E. Sokolova and R. V. Gurina, "О соотношении языковой и научной картин мира" [On the Correlation of Linguistic and Scientific Pictures of the World], Знание. Понимание. Умение [Knowledge, Understanding. Skill], no. 3 (2010), pp. 83-84.

91 Chernova, note 79 above, p. 29.

world was formed. It was connected with the development of religious doctrines and philosophy and with the progress of the natural and technical sciences and development of a new cultural-historical picture of the world. Researchers asserted the presence in scientific works of the concept of a picture of the world from the early eighteenth century,[92] but in its essence it was created for the first time in the natural sciences in the seventeenth century by René Descartes and other scholars and completed and named by Sir Isaac Newton (1642-1727) the "synthesis of the system of the world" in the second half of seventeenth century, which often is pointed to as the date of the ultimate completion of the natural sciences and the emergence of science as an autonomous social system.[93]

Isaac Newton in 1685 wrote *De mundi Systemate* (*System of the World*), that two years later in revised form became a part (Book III) of his fundamental treatise *Philosophiæ Naturalis Principia Mathematica*. He argued that the system of the world could be comprehended as something purely objective, with mechanical/mathematical principles of reasoning (of philosophy) free from metaphysics.[94] At the same time, he was conscious of limiting his subject, speaking on behalf not of all sciences, but of "the science of Mechanics". He implicitly presupposed the possibility of another (biological, social, humanitarian) world picture: "Our design not respecting arts but philosophy, and our subject, not manual but natural powers".[95]

92 Kubanova, note 79 above, p. 189.

93 Buldakov, note 84 above, pp. 69-70; A. V. Shutaleva, "Классическая естественнонаучная картина мира: особенности формирования новоевропейской науки и трансформация принципов античной рациональности" [Classical Natural-Science Picture of World: Peculiarities of Forming New European Science and Transformation of Principles of Antique Rationality], Вестник Ленинградского государственного университета им. А. С. Пушкина [Herald of Leningrad A. S. Pushkin State University], II, no. 2 (2011), p. 128; Stepin, note 79 above, p. 583; Dyshlevyi and Iatsenko, note 83 above, p. 36; A. M. Rubanets, О категориальной структуре научной картины мира [On the Categorial Structure of the Scientific Picture of the World], in Dyshlevyi and Luk'ianets (eds.), note 83 above, p. 57; Kyzyma, note 83 above, pp. 75-76.

94 Isaac Newton, *A Treatise of the System of the World*, transl. into English (2d corr. ed.; London, 1731), pp. v, vi; Newton, *The Mathematical Principles of Natural Philosophy*, transl. A. Motte (London, 1729), I, p. 3.

95 Newton, note 94 above (1729), I, p. 3, 5.

The sharpest criticism of Newton, albeit latent, was the theology grounded on metaphysics, but his formal negative accent is on metaphysical philosophy. What is not sensible or technically observed and cannot be verified, cannot be the subject-matter of science: "which forces being unknown, Philosophers have hitherto attempted the search of Nature in vain".[96]

Newton did not believe in fate (in fact – in the non-comprehendible God's plan for the world) as blind necessity, "which is certainly the same always and everywhere, could produce no variety of things".[97] And he did not believe in God Who was independent from people and not a living being:

> For God is a relative word and refers to the living: and Deity is the dominion of God not in his own body, but in his servants. God is the supreme Being, eternal, infinite, absolutely perfect; but a Being, however perfect, without dominion, is not the Lord God... The word God occasionally means Lord, but every Lord is not God. The dominion of a spiritual Being establishes God, truths truth, the highest supreme, fictions fiction. And from the dominion of truths it follows, that the true God is living, intelligent, and powerful; to be the highest or the most perfect of the rest of the perfections.[98]

For Newton, God has to be understood as living most perfect being and part of nature. All we know about God comes from the "appearance of things" and from "the ways of mankind". So, God should be cognized as natural phenomena; this knowledge "belongs to Natural Philosophy".[99]

Newton's way of reasoning (experimental or natural philosophy) and comprehension of the system of the world, his methodological principles ("General Scholium" and the "Rules of Reasoning") are observation and inductive generalization from particular to universal (rule III), using reliable and sufficient

[96] Ibid., I, p. 6; II, p. 203.

[97] Ibid., II, p. 391; Newton, *Philosophiae naturalis principia mathematica* (2d ed.; 1713), p. 483.

[98] Ibid., p. 482.

[99] Newton, note 94 above (1729), II, p. 388-389, 391-392; Newton, note 97 above, p. 483.

empirical data collection (rule IV), experimental verification (rule I), and analogy (rule II):

> ... whatever is not deduced from the phenomena, is to be called a hypothesis; and hypotheses, whether metaphysical or physical, whether of occult qualities or mechanical, have no place in experimental philosophy. In this philosophy particular propositions are inferred from the phenomena, and afterwards rendered general by induction ... But these are things that cannot be explained in few words, nor are we furnished with that sufficiency of experiments which is required to an accurate determination and demonstration of the laws by which this electric and elastic spirit operates.[100]

Specialists define such a scientific picture of the world as classical (and correlative to the classical type of rationality) and single out such principles and provisions thereof: (1) determinism (unequivocal causal links of natural phenomena); (2) pure objectivity and absolute truth of scientific knowledge; (3) universality of the scientific method; (4) unity of truth and existence of one conception about one subject-matter; (5) progressive, continuous, gradual development of science.[101] Such a universalist, ahistorical, objectivist (identity of thought and existence), mechanical-mathematical, and out-of-value picture of the world might be and was solely natural-technical, not taking into account the peculiarities of the socio-humanitarian world.

As Shutaleva noted, "nature was regarded as a material *universum,* as the sole true reality from which the spiritual component was eliminated".[102] The last was logical, for this picture of the world reflected the aspiration of the natural sciences to get out from under the dominance of theology and philosophy, but in this way it became one-sided, although it claimed a general scientific character.[103]

The emergence of special scientific pictures of the world specialists link with the development of the discipline-organized

[100] Newton, note 94 above (1729), II, pp. 392-393, 387, 202-205; Newton, note 97 above, p. 484.

[101] Shutaleva, note 93 above, pp. 122-123, 128; Buldakov, note 84 above, p. 70.

[102] Shutaleva, note 93 above, p. 125.

[103] Buldakov, note 84 above, p. 69.

science at the end of the eighteenth and early nineteenth centuries.[104] Theoretically this was thought out with respect to biology and comparative linguistics by the brothers Friedrich Wilhelm Heinrich Alexander von Humboldt (1769-1859) and Wilhelm von Humboldt (1767-1835), and Kant emancipated and separated out the non-mechanical sphere of the sciences on the spirit (humanities and social sciences) from the natural sciences.[105]

Alexander von Humboldt in his influential *Essai sur la géographie des plantes* (1805), on the basis of a geographical approach to botany successively studied the dissemination of plants in the world (science of the geography of plants) and proposed the concept of the empirical scientific picture of the world and concrete picture of nature. The methods of the structure thereof he named as fixation, verification, identification, quantitative measurement, localization, correlation, and juxtaposition of all observed phenomena within the framework of the subject-matter of research, determining their mutual links, typology – purely empirical and without "delving into the nature of things" (all categorization outside the citation is added – ОК). Moreover, he asserted the possibility of forming on this basis a nature-philosophical picture of the world of a "much higher order", especially on the basis of the philosophy of Friedrich Wilhelm Joseph von Schelling (1775-1854), but noted that both pictures of the world were self-sufficient and had a different character.[106]

As Vul'f noted, "the thought of the linkage of all physical-geographical phenomena with live nature in one unbreakable chain" runs like a red thread through Humboldt's works. Humboldt attempted to "comprehend the world of flora on earth not from the standpoint of descriptive botany, which aspires only to identify species, but in all the diversity of its manifestation", and on the basis thereof the "linkage of the geography of plants not only with space, but with time" is identified.[107]

[104] Stepin, note 79 above, p. 583; Buldakov, note 84 above, p 70.

[105] Sokolova and Gurina, note 90 above, p. 83; E. K. Pogorskii, «Картина мира» [Picture of the World], Знание. Понимание. Умение [Knowledge. Understanding. Skill], no. 4 (2012), p. 322; Buldakov, note 84 above, p. 71.

[106] A. Humboldt, *География растений* [Geography of Plants] (Moscow-Leningrad, 1936), pp. 51-52, 55-56. For the English-language edition, see A. von Humboldt, *Essay on the Geography of Plants*, transl. Sylvie Romanowski (2009).

[107] Evgenii V. Vul'f, "Значение работ Гумбольдта для географии растений"

In his first important work on the comparative study of languages with regard to different eras of their development (1820) Wilhelm von Humboldt proposed not ultimately differentiated doctrine concerning a linguistic picture of the world and a scientific picture of the world of linguistics.[108] In this theoretical complex one may single out ideas relating to: the nationality of languages (and the impossibility of a universal world language), the historicity and conditionality of their development by spiritual-social factors, the processes of the interaction of languages (differentiation, mixing, and others), classification of languages (idea of linguistic families – by analogy with families of plants – as the Particular (Special) in linguistic development, between the Individual and the General), universal linguistic development as the sum of evolution and interaction of all languages, comparison as the method of building not only comparative but also historical linguistics.[109]

With regard to the language family, Wilhelm von Humboldt noted:

> The form of individual genetically related languages should be found to be in accordance with the form of the entire family. There cannot be that which would be not consistent with the general form; moreover, each of their peculiarities, as a rule, is conditioned by this general form in one or another way. In each family languages exist which more purely and completely than others have preserved the initial form.[110]

These ideas were developed in a later work.[111]

[Significance of Humboldt's Works for the Geography of Plants], in A. Humboldt, География растений [Geography of Plants] (1936), p. 8.

[108] W. von Humboldt, "О сравнительном изучении языков применительно к различным эпохам их развития" [On the Comparative Study of Languages Applied to Different Epochs of their Development", in V. A. Zvegintsev, История языкознания XIX – XX веков в очерках и извлечениях [History of Linguistics of 19th – 20th Centuries in Sketches and Fragments] (3d ed., 1964), I, pp. 91, 101.

[109] Ibid., pp. 75-79, 81, 83, 87, 91, 94-95.

[110] Ibid., p. 95.

[111] W. von Humboldt, Über die Verschiedenheit des menschlichen Sprachbaus und ihren Einfluss auf die geistige Entwicklung des Menschengeschlechts (1836), available in English as: W. von Humboldt, *On Language. On the Diversity of Human Language Construction and its Influence on the Mental Development of the Human Species* (2d rev. ed; 1999).

The doctrine on a scientific picture of the world as an integral notion concerning subject-matter was activated in the mid-twentieth century by physicists Max Planck, Albert Einstein, and others, and later also developed, with specific meaning, by philosophers, representatives of the humanities and social sciences.[112]

SPECIAL WORLD PICTURES OF GENERAL LEGAL DISCIPLINES

Even branch legal disciplines form their own special pictures of the world. They are to some extent compatible, to some extent conflicting, as between civil and labor law. The pictures of the world of the so-called general legal sciences differ even more, mutually complementary and competing in the explanation of the processes and their results, the whole reality of the world of law. Comparative law (comparative jurisprudence) has real advantages in this competition, working with real phenomena using the inductive methodology and not so deeply infected with deductive speculations. Konstantinos Kerameus meant essentially this when wrote: "In a world which is slowly but undoubtedly converging, comparative law is best structured and better adapted than any other legal discipline to respond to the challenges and make a legal contribution to resolving the problems of society and life as a whole."[113]

Is it possible that one disciplinary picture of the world may dominate, may win in the competition? Yes, of course. Metaphysical and speculative visions are dominant in the science of law. Above the practical comparative legal enterprise and description, the building of comparative jurisprudence (or comparative law) in

[112] Soroka and Bulychev, note 79 above, p. 33; Kubanova, note 79 above, p. 189. Also see B. G. Kuznetsov, Эволюция картины мира [Evolution of the Picture of the World] (1958); Serhiy Kryms'kyi, «Зміст та функції природничо-наукової картини світу» [Content and Functions of Natural Science Picture of the World], Філософська думка [Philosophical Thought], no. 2 (1976); Dyshlevyi and Iatsenko, note 83 above, p. 7; Basalaeva, note 78 above, p. 215; Pogorskii, note 105 above, p. 322.

[113] K. D. Kerameus, "Message from the President of the International Academy of Comparative Law", in Ежегодник сравнительного правоведения [Yearbook of Comparative Law], (2001), p. 268. Let us leave aside the issue about the reality, scope, and fate of convergence.

the views of the larger part of comparatists is not finished. Some scholars doubt that it needs to be finished.

A "nature of law", "legitimate reserved territory", and the ambition of legal theory

Here we turn to discussions in the theory of law about its character, its encounters with metaphysics, and the pretense of the theory of law to present an only world picture suitable for use by all other legal disciplines and legal practice.

Joseph Raz (1939-2022) has stated that the sense of the theory of law is "an explanation of the nature of law", and this is "central to philosophical reflection about the law throughout its history". To be successful, a theory of law should consist simultaneously of the Ought ("propositions about the law which are *necessarily* true" ... "wherever and whenever it is to be found") and the Is (but only in the explanation by the Ought). The first element and its comprehension are primary, the second is secondary and supplementary to the first. But when stating that "a theory consists of necessary truths, for only necessary truths about the law reveal the nature of the law" Raz meant that the theory of law never reaches the Is.[114]

The objective nature of law is part of the nature of things, it contains "essential properties" of law ("which make law into what it is"), is universal, eternal, and always the same, not depending on human understanding. The different and mutable positive law is mediated by its nature through concepts – various "local" social understandings of the nature of law. Only "nonessential properties" of law are subject to change, which is reflected in a concept of law there and now.[115]

> More specifically, what counts is not the common understanding of expressions like "the nature of law," nor even the fact that the concept of law changes over time. What counts is the nature of the institution which the concept of law (i.e., the one we currently have and use) designates. To make its case the objection has to show that

[114] Joseph Raz, "Can There Be a Theory of Law?", in Martin Golding and William Edmundson (eds.), *Blackwell Guide to Philosophy of Law and Legal Theory* (2004), pp. 324, 328.

[115] Ibid., pp. 325, 327-331, 334, 340.

> our concept of law (as it is at the moment) does not allow for the application of the (philosophical) notion of essential properties to the law, that is, that the law has no essential properties.[116]

When we are studying the nature of law, we are improving our concept of law. Law in different concepts is law because it is referential to the one nature of law. Although law is a social phenomenon, the views of humans and their societies on the nature of law are not important; law and legal system can exist and function even in a society without any concept of law. And the theory of law is so universal, unnational, and unlocated that it can be a disinterested and objective denominator for what law is in every society even if this society does not recognize this something to be law.[117]

The theory of law is concerned with the universal nature of law and, subsidiarily, with the relation of concepts of law to its nature, but not with positive law. Moreover, the study of the latter has little academic value. Raz considered the comprehension of alien legal systems in principle possible only in relation to our culture (so, it is subjective) and in practice imprecise because of the incommensurability of concepts of law: "So our understanding of their cultures differs from their own understanding of their own cultures, and cannot be altogether objective, or perfect, or something like that". The only possible objective, albeit "blinkered", understanding of law outside own country is theoretical, provided by theory of law, for "understanding consists in knowing important relations among the essential properties of the things the concepts apply to, and among them and some other properties".[118]

A critic of Raz, Paula Gaido, claimed from the position of non-individualistic conceptual relativism that "the properties associated with law are contingent in the sense that the necessary character of these properties is restricted to the conceptual

[116] Ibid., p. 329.

[117] Ibid., pp. 331-332, 334-335, 337-338.

[118] Ibid., pp. 338-340.

scheme at stake. Thus the concept of law cannot have a pattern of correctness extrinsic to the practice that constitutes it".[119]

The nature of law, eternal (or semi-eternal) and independent from the culture and the will of society as well as from particular social conceptualizations is a fantasy ("non-realistic ontological conception"), a concept of law is concrete and belonging to a concrete society in a certain time, and every theory of law studies one of these concepts. "Natural" and "essential" are what they are in the view of the community. No theorized "nature" could be "the pattern of correctness of the concept of law" and "no ontological space for the nature of law" exist. And law cannot function in a society and have any "defining properties" without a concept of law:[120]

> Concepts understood as cultural products establish the necessary properties of an object for the concept to apply to it. Concepts are what establish the defining properties that outline the world, and given that concepts depend on the thoughts of a group of people, they are subject to the variations these thoughts impose. Therefore, conceptual correctness or incorrectness cannot be asserted in absolute terms.[121]

Gaido concluded that the only theoretical task of the legal theory is "to articulate the essential properties that our concepts highlight".[122]

William Twining (and he is not alone) proposed that the "theoretical part of law as a discipline" (claiming to embrace any "activity of theorizing" and all "general questions relating to the subject-matters of law as a discipline"), with the inclusion of legal philosophy (as "the most abstract part" of legal theory and not a co-extensive discipline) and all "heritage" in legal science, be called general jurisprudence. In Twining's opinion, the latter should be viewed, *inter alia,* as an ideology presenting the world picture ("links one's beliefs about law to one's more general beliefs about

119 Paula Gaido, "The Purpose of Legal Theory: Some Problems with Joseph Raz's View", *Law and Philosophy,* XXX, no. 6 (2011), p. 688.

120 Ibid., pp. 686-688, 691, 693, 697.

121 Ibid., p. 688.

122 Ibid., pp. 689, 691, 697.

the world —whether or not they are systematic", "whole views or total pictures", "picture of law in the world", "obvious trilogy of global, regional, and nation-state").[123] Twining believes that one research objective of legal science should be the "aspiration to build up an accurate and sophisticated total picture (or series of pictures) of law in the world", geographical and temporal, mentioning also the different levels of law (local, sub-global and global).[124]

Twining sees general jurisprudence as cosmopolitan and relativistic, overcoming Western centrism, statism, and unempirical character. He stresses that traditionally legal theory was and is mostly the theory of national / municipal law, and predominantly of the theorist's own legal system:[125]

> In the present context, an important implication of this is that nearly all of our stock of concepts and theories has similarly been relatively local, or at least geared to a single legal tradition. Indeed, nearly all legal concepts, including many "fundamental legal conceptions", that have been the focus of attention of analytical jurists are "folk concepts".[126]

Twining (and not only him, of course) proposes a quite contradictory view. He understands that a theory of law is either "folk" knowledge unjustly applied to any law and so, if self-critical, necessarily becomes more reductionist when encountering reality; or pure abstraction and ignorant of reality. He states that the present theory of law is the theory of national law: "none of our stock of theories of municipal law can provide an adequate theoretical basis for a cosmopolitan and reasonably inclusive discipline of law". He sees the way out in empirical comparative legal studies – "particular inquiries" and generalizing projects like "Glenn's account of legal traditions", but paradoxically calls them "examples of the synthesizing function of legal theory".[127] So the theory of law to be "cosmopolitan", "adopt a global perspective",

[123] William Twining, "General Jurisprudence", *Anales de la Cátedra Francisco Suárez*, XXXIX (2005), pp. 646-648, 651, 653, 656-657, 664, 675.

[124] Twining, "Globalisation and Comparative Law", in Esin Örücü and David Nelken (eds.) *Comparative Law: A Handbook* (2007), pp. 70, 72, 79.

[125] Twining, note 123 above, pp. 647, 650, 652-653.

[126] Ibid., p. 652.

[127] Ibid., pp. 653-654, 658.

"thinking in terms of total pictures", cease its "collective ignorance" of reality and living "by abstractions alone", should become comparative law, or the theory of comparative law, or even comparative theory of law, and abandon the essence and heritage of the theory of law. Even John Austin's idea of "general jurisprudence" is understood by Twining (and, maybe, taken just for this reason) as the general theory of law[128] and not just as a synonym of comparative jurisprudence – as it was in original.

It is likely that Twining understood the shortcomings of such logic when he proposed a vision of general jurisprudence as the "theoretical study of two or more legal traditions, cultures, or orders", which has to encompass "all levels of legal ordering, not just municipal and public international law", "broaden its geographical reach to take more account of non-Western legal traditions, a broader range of legal phenomena, and different levels of normative and legal relations and ordering".[129] But this is the fragment of the definition of comparative law – without the word "theoretical". Because for comparative law the generalizing, including theorizing, is the result of the empirical inquiry and induction. So is general jurisprudence in the Twining view theoretical comparative law? But he consistently ignored comparative law as a discipline in his article. Why? Perhaps because Twining believes that only now "the discipline of law becomes more cosmopolitan".[130]

Twining proposed to "de-centre the state" in the world picture of law ("without denying that it is for most purposes the most, powerful, complex, and sophisticated form of law around"), giving a place to public international law, religious legal traditions, and customary legal orders; this would help the reduce the marginalization of non-Western legal traditions. In this context he speaks about "comparison and generalization across legal traditions, cultures and other boundaries", but within the framework of theoretical jurisprudence.[131] Twining in fact rejected comparative law as a discipline or research subject,[132], so too its

128 Ibid., pp. 654-656, 664.

129 Ibid., pp. 655-656, 660.

130 Ibid., pp. 660.

131 Ibid., pp. 664-666, 669.

132 But he once mentioned comparative law as being among the "specialized

experience of generalizing the empirical studies of all the said legal phenomena. He further denied the theoretical essence of the theory of law, seemingly suggesting that the latter become empirical, inductive, and comparative to conceptualize an adequate world picture of law. He rejected the ability of legal theory to perform this task on its own, only "on the back of specialized areas of legal scholarship" producing middle order theories to serve as subject-matter for critical scrutiny and appraisal by legal theory as the "heading" discipline.[133]

The insufficiency of comparative law was addressed by Horatia Muir Watt. Even the title makes it clear that comparative scholarship is helping legal theory, and not working for itself. Watt states that legal theory (including international private and public law theory, quite contradictory simplification) and legal philosophy (named here casually and more as the metaphysical bases of legal theory) are patently inadequate in explaining changes in contemporary legal phenomena and cannot "accept diversity and acknowledge commensurability"; Watt points to the need for "new forms of knowledge capable of embracing complexity". Within this framework, "pieces of comparative legal scholarship" provide the inspiration for a renewal of legal theory, giving new insights when involved in interdisciplinary dialogue, and help to "develop more sophisticated models with which to understand the interdependencies and multiple identities which undermine traditional categories". It seems that Watt may consider comparative law to be a discipline (albeit not so named), but existing at a lower level of data processing than legal theory, and thus supplies the latter with semi-finished products. Apparently another model is provided by Watt – the "trans-disciplinary crossfertilisation of ideas" that could help construct a "post-axiomatic" model of knowledge about law (after Geoffrey Samuel) single model for all legal disciplines to replace the existing "flat schemes issuing from present legal theory". But this would also lead, in Watt's vision, merely to "structural changes in present legal theory".[134]

areas" or "transnational fields" that obtained "greater prominence" thanks to globalization processes, and produced some "assumptions and discoveries" for the critical scrutiny and appraisal by legal theoretician. See: Ibid., p. 680.

133 Ibid., pp. 680-681.

134 Watt, note 27 above, pp. 271-274.

Having mentioned "comparative theory", Watt points to the "comparative scholarship reflection on commensurability and the acknowledgement of the Other", but observes that the level of formulating paradigms and conceptual models belongs to the discipline of legal theory.[135] In the present writer's view, the proposed changes mean that the essence of legal theory would be crushed and replaced by comparative law: "International legal theory therefore should turn its back on the metaphysics of conformity, on the ethics of a center and a periphery and aim to build a relational, pluralistic model, open to dialogue and mediation and allowing for constant readjustment". But Watt does not acknowledge this and believes it is merely a "rewriting of the metaphysical narrative".[136]

There always were seemingly more realist views. Mark Van Hoecke and Francois Ost were not the first to observe that the theory of law truly originated no earlier than the mid-nineteenth century in response to the needs of European societies. They noted the deep identity crisis of legal doctrine and all legal science in the first half of nineteenth century caused by codification in comparison with successes of "positive science" (authors meant the so-called exact sciences). Van Hoecke and Ost note that "It is readily understandable that in this climate several jurists should from the middle of the century start to question the scientific nature of their discipline", which led to the creation of the legal theory as the "empirical natural law", so based on empirical methods, "in a comparative legal perspective".[137]

These assertions by Van Hoecke and Ost are ambiguous. It is important that they, unlike many, understand that legal theory has a proper disciplinary beginning and has not existed from times immemorial. But they, like most legal theoreticians, seem to believe this discipline has a unique given place in the system of knowledge about law that was intentionally left free. They are not ready to see that the said ways to overcome the crisis in legal science (positivization, empiricization, comparativization) were proposed a half of century earlier by the philosophy of positive

[135] Ibid., pp. 282-283.

[136] Ibid., p. 283.

[137] Mark Van Hoecke and Francois Ost, "Epistemological Perspectives in Legal Theory", *Ratio Juris*, VI, no. 1 (1993), pp. 30-32.

law and comparative jurisprudence. They were extensively popularized and integrated into legal education in some countries.

This means that the approaches proposed by scholars in the mid-nineteenth century were not new, not "the ambition", but just adapted from other well-grounded legal disciplines to create a new one – "general theory of law". But were these approaches introduced with the intention to create a discipline "running counter to any speculative approach of a metaphysical type", an "ideological alternative" to a metaphysical philosophy of law",[138] or just its succession? The question remains open.

In the view of Van Hoecke and Ost the theory of law should prioritize global approaches (leading to a world picture drawing), which gives the discipline a special place in a triad with "traditional jurisprudence" and the philosophy of law. The key here is the comparative approach, helping the theory of law to overcome "limiting itself to some intellectual construction and/or criticism based on a kind of self-created reality". But Van Hoecke and Ost conclude that reaching "more general valid results" than a theory of law within the limits of some legal culture, at most a "Western" one, is not possible "at this moment".[139] Thus, the theory of law is pretending to an integrative and higher position among legal disciplines (giving primacy only to the philosophy of law), ignoring comparative law as a discipline and separate way of reasoning and theorizing, reducing the latter to an approach within its own framework. And it seeks to draw an own and the only world legal picture, but is unable to do so.

Paradoxical it may seem, but preferable is the position of Watt which mercilessly criticizes the real abilities of legal theory to develop a world picture. Using human rights ideology as an example, "presented as having universal, objective validity", she shows its "flattening effect of abstraction" and fundamentalism, leading to the negation of peoples' history and reduction of diversity, "refusal of otherness", "reducing the Other to one's own image", cultural imperialism. The prescribed *tertium comparationis* here is "a projection of a purely European axiological model". The metaphysical ideas about the "essence of the human being" provide here the false universal legitimacy for abasement and erasing the

[138] Ibid., p. 32.

[139] Ibid., pp. 44-45.

vast plurality of experiences.[140] But, while understanding the depth of the problems raised by the example, Watt nonetheless calls not for the rejection of metaphysical narrative, but for rewriting it.

Forever infantile comparative law with "walk-on role"?

The widely-shared ignorance of the true historical path of comparative jurisprudence has far-reaching implications for understanding its character and potential for presenting an own picture of the world. What creates the illusion that the theory of law heading all legal studies, concentrating the entire heritage of general legal studies, has the right to speak in the name of all jurisprudence, being "an integrative discipline able to coordinate and systematize the approaches and the results of these disciplines on an interdisciplinary base"[141] and to propose the only possible world legal picture suitable for all peoples, all legal disciplines, and even for all social sciences?[142] One reason is the long-imposed pretense that legal theory as a discipline has ancient origins and non-existence or relatively late origin of comparative jurisprudence (comparative law).

Many believe, consciously or unconsciously, that legal philosophy and legal theory have existed from the time immemorial. And comparative law is believed to have emerged for primarily practical reasons in recent times as a weak movement. Comparative law in this scenario appears late, relies on the philosophical and theoretical foundations of other well-established legal disciplines, and performs a function for those disciplines, supplying crude or partially processed materials?

To some extent the notion of the recent or late development of comparative law was supported by iconic comparativists. David in his treatise written in 1950s claimed that the importance of comparative law as "an independent science" came to be recognized, and its method and aims were systematically studied no earlier than in the second half of the nineteenth century with positivization and nationalization in the science of law.[143] To be

140 Watt, note 27 above, pp. 282-283.

141 Van Hoecke and Ost, note 137 above, p. 33.

142 Ibid., p. 44.

143 René David and John E. C. Brierley, *Major Legal Systems in the World Today:*

clear, David is not stating that comparative law is an offspring of other legal discipline, but the words "late" and "recent" mean that some other legal disciplines have an earlier origin. He views legal history, philosophy of law, and general legal theory as given parts of legal science or cluster of legal sciences with "reserved territory", and comparative law gets its justification and recognition from them as their subsidiary discipline, supplying field materials for their consideration, and being thus useful or even very useful. Words like "utility", "benefit", "profitable", "help", "promote", "assistance", "draw attention" are used here. In this perception, the discipline has merely a service role, is not self-sufficient, and no existence in its own right. Comparative law is rather a way of gathering legal information without a "reserved territory", although it could be seen as "an autonomous branch of legal knowledge". Legal comparatists are needed just for preparing the ground for other legal scholars and practitioners. Other proclamations in David's book like "comparative law has a primary role to play in the science of law" and in the progress of law[144] look purely rhetorical in comparison with the service role; or the word "primary" has to be understood as the "lowest level". What one can expect from other authors?

But in the introductory chapter for the *International Encyclopedia of Comparative Law,* written in 1972 and published in 1976, David focused not on legal systems, but on conceptions of law and, more widely, on conceptions of normative regulation of relations in society. He avoided entering into a discussion of a single nature of law, but in fact showed the inadequacy of the discussion and dedicated most of his attention to the historical-cultural conditionality of every conception of law. He proclaimed the "overcoming any scruples about excessive widening of the field of comparison" and advocated the individual empirical search for norms, principles, and doctrines that are working and are legal in every particular society and become subjects for comparison between societies. David named this work both comparative and theoretical and made not a single reference to the theory of law. He did refer to the philosophy of law, stating that comparative law should pass results of own research to it, for "this is legitimate". But at the same time he claimed that the comparative lawyer can,

Introduction to the Comparative Study of Law, (3d ed.; 1985), pp. 2-3.

[144] Ibid., pp. 4-17.

if he wishes, become a philosopher of law or sociologist of law and modify attitudes of these disciplines by declaring there could be no universally accepted conception of law, merely conceptions historically predominant in a particular country. He himself proposed "philosophical considerations" of certain important issues, such as equity or subjective rights, from the pluralist and relativist positions of the comparative lawyer and not the legal philosopher.[145]

Based on sociological concepts, David stated that law should be treated not as an ideal, but as a "makeshift" – something that is man-made, suitable for particular time and place, and subject to further change, as well as only a part (and in some instances not the most just or effective one) of a concept of social order created by particular society, with its tradition, popular feelings, beliefs, and intellectual doctrines. Finally, all the latter elements that cannot be transferred from the subject of comparative law to legal philosophy even though they are not "the rules which are in fact enforced". Global comparison necessarily transcends "a strictly legal level" and engages the sociological level.[146]

In a later text, written in 1981 and published in 1984, David harshly criticized the theory of law for "divorce from reality" (and even "complete distortion of reality"), "based on an outdated ideology" whose formulas could be satisfied only with fictions. This is historically rooted in European and Islamic university legal education, which taught ideal theoretical-philosophical law instead of the real one. Nothing changed in principle with modern scientific approaches because of the impossibility to come theoretically and philosophically to any "agreement on what the law is" and of the strong wish "to force the hand of fate by stating principles which did not correspond to the truth of things at the time". General legal philosophy abstract concepts have nothing in common with what really happens in a particular society at a particular time. In this situation, coupling the approaches of comparative law and sociology of law have the merit of considering whether dormant rules are law and whether rules never recognized but obeyed by the members of community may be called legal norms. And

[145] David, "Introduction", in *International Encyclopedia of Comparative Law. Vol. II. The Legal Systems of the World. Their Comparison and Unification. Chapter 1. The Different Conceptions of the Law* (1976), pp. 3-5, 7, 12.

[146] Ibid., pp. 4-13.

generally, what concept is working in the particular society?[147] After publication of his treatise, the concepts of David substantially evolved to an understanding of comparative law as a self-sufficient legal discipline with own theoretical and philosophical inferences different from the disciplines of legal theory and legal philosophy because of different scholarly premises and different methods of acquiring knowledge.

Konrad Zweigert and Hein Kötz in their iconic treatise reiterated as something obviously known that comparative law as a science, field or "at any rate" comparative method "started in Paris in 1900" and was unequivocally oriented towards the universal unification of law. It was always practically useful in spite of changing approaches, but has no "immediate aim", just "the ultimate goal of discovering the truth". But Zweigert and Kötz did not provide for comparative law any sufficient and final cognitive goal, reducing it to enriching legal knowledge, and to the auxiliary role of method and approach ("the gradual approximation of viewpoints, the abandonment of deadly complacency, and the relaxation of fixed dogma", "to afford a glimpse", "permit us to catch sight", "deepen our belief", "refresh and enrich", "let one see", "it can help"). They assumed, following Edouard Lambert (1866-1947), that any legal study to become "truly scientific" should "rise above the actual rules of any national system". Finally, comparative lawyers, in the view of Zweigert and Kötz, just "compare the legal systems of different nations" and provide their reflections for "the proper policy for the law to adopt", because the real accent of the authors is not on "discovering the truth", but on social engineering as an aim of legal science and comparative law in particular. To be precise, Zweigert and Kötz believe that this "may involve a reinterpretation of his [comparatist] own system", enhance critical thinking skills, and cultivate attitudes of tolerance.[148]

Zweigert and Kötz believe in the objective system of "branches of legal sciences" whose subject-matter is clearly distinguishable. Some deal with foreign law, in particular, pure sciences: legal history, legal ethnology, sociology of law, and comparative law.

[147] David, "Sources of Law", in *International Encyclopedia of Comparative Law. Vol. II. The Legal Systems of the World. Their Comparison and Unification. Chapter 3* (1984), pp. 201-202, 204.

[148] Konrad Zweigert, Hein Kötz, *Introduction to Comparative Law*, transl. by Tony Weir, (3rd rev. ed.; 2011), pp. 2-4, 6, 15-16, 21, 34, 45.

They are distinct, but interact. For example, Zweigert and Kötz point to two versions or forms of comparative law, "applied" and "theoretical-descriptive". The principal aim of the latter is "to say how and why certain legal systems are different or alike", rising above proper comparison. But to do this comparative law uses both "theoretical models and empirical data produced by the sociology of law". Zweigert and Kötz borrowed functionalistic dogmas from sociology of the 1970s without doubts or discussion. Paradoxically, after laying down strict imperatives to some extent predicting a result of any comparative inquiry (presumption of similarity, and others), Zweigert and Kötz alleged comparative law to be inductive and an experimental "basis for a universal legal science". But the upper limit for comparative law in their view is a "critical evaluation" of which law among those compared is "most suitable and just". "Scientific or theoretical comparative law" is also possible, but just "to improve our legal knowledge"; comparative law pursues utilitarian aims, and anything beyond is a discrete and ambiguous movement with "no recognized place in legal science".[149]

Let us consider some examples of less classical recent literature. For Jaakko Husa, as for many others, comparative law was born in 1900 at the Paris congress. Its history since that day is quite discrete. It was "fashionable" once, looking "again promising", "second coming", "splintering ... into different branches and schools of thought", "passing ... into a phase of scholarly disintegration". At a certain stage during the twentieth century it achieved an idealistic "understanding of its goals, approaches and theories", then "shattered into pieces and fragments", now exists "in a state of scholarly crisis", and never had a "truly uniform self-image of what it was itself". For Husa, only now we can begin to consciously construct the "sharp theoretical" disciplinary view of comparative law, but even this "bears the birthmark of a serious paranoia".[150]

The doctrinal study of law, which Husa considers to be a separate scientific discipline, but mostly identifies with legal theory, has "a strong footing in the legal academia" and is "the

149 Ibid., pp. 6-12, 32-47, 51-53.

150 Jaakko Husa, "The Tip of the Iceberg or What Lies Beneath the Surface of Comparative Law (Review Essay of: Mark Van Hoecke (ed.), Epistemology and Methodology of Comparative Law)", *Maastricht Journal of European and Comparative Law*, XVI (2005), pp. 73-94.

mother discipline of all legal disciplines", whereas comparative law has no stable footing and possesses "a kind of a walk-on role", lacking any outside intellectual support (as philosophy is for legal philosophy), appeared late, lacks sufficient recognition, its status in the family of legal disciplines is unclear, marginal, and doomed to eternally "searching for itself", "repeatedly questioning its own role, approaches, and legitimacy".[151]

It seems that for Husa comparative law is not and never has been a clearly established project of research and discipline like legal philosophy or legal theory; it is just a more or less (of course, less) successful movement. If we see no initial paradigm embodied in a world picture, and believe in the superficiality and semi-marginal character of comparative jurisprudence / comparative law that never rises above creating some theoretical observations (never been uniform, always fragmentary and conflicting), then any new trend or school appears to be the discipline's new birth, or principal transformation, or death.

In another article Husa addressed the hidden epistemic model ("primary epistemic foundation for legal understanding", "implicit mono-epistemology", "mono-epistemic platform", "one-system-centered provincialism", "mono-system thinking") stimulated by traditional legal education focused (at least at the initial stage) on a domestic legal system. The last began to be viewed as the standard reference point for evaluating law, and this makes difficult the impartial, distanced appreciation of different models and approaches, especially of "transnational pluralism". This type of teaching / learning seeks to form an axiomatic ("certain invisible theoretical commitments") base of thinking about law. While doing so, the hidden epistemic curriculum "offers a representation of the inner order of the world of law" ("world-of-law representation", "the picture", "shared comprehensive mental image of world of law in general", "shared legal world view"), being both conceptualization and cognitive pattern, that is, national law and domestic legal system centered and in which "foreign and comparative material ... does not appear legally relevant".[152]

151 Husa, note 33 above (2022), pp. 3-6.

152 Husa, "Turning the Curriculum Upside Down: Comparative Law as an Educational Tool for Constructing Pluralistic Legal Mind", *German Law Journal*, X, no. 7 (2009), pp. 914-919.

Husa contends that legal education should start with "general legal questions", implying (here one might add "*inter alia*", but nothing else was found) the addition of international law and comparative law as "subject areas", because law students "learn law well when they construct their own legal understanding from multiple sources". Excellent, and what, and what it for? For knowing "different foreign approaches to similar types of questions" as a "valuable tool for the construction of a primary pluralistic legal mind", to enable "the cultivation of a kind of legal Anschauung that would make it cognitively easier for future lawyers to adapt in pluralistic global and transnational law". Apparently far-reaching, but the final aim is to have "competing legal discourses alongside one's own national law", "to build a legal mind that starts from many possible solutions, instead of one legal base", and "to try to make students to actually attempt to use the laws of systems that differ from their own". Comparative law and foreign law courses have to be taught in the second or third year of legal studies because the first "should be reserved for such basic skills as ... general legal studies and/or legal theory".[153]

Husa leaves the construction of the legal picture of the world to general legal studies and/or legal theory. Comparative law is not "general"; it does not provide general knowledge; it is merely a practically oriented subject intended to find solutions for domestic problems in foreign experience and to provide an understanding of foreign and international law interacting with own national law.

Another example. Helge Dedek sees the origin of comparative law in the general trend of the nineteenth century to form disciplines on the base of the comparative method. The latter was permeated with imperialism and engaged with colonial differences and the unification movement. Any other contexts of the origin of comparative law are "ahistorical" and invented later; if original comparative law is deprived of its colonial context, it appears to be a "strange outlier" in European legal thought.[154]

In the view of Dedek, the first world picture of comparative law was imperial, based on "perfidious dialectics of Western universalism and exclusion by comparison", to some extent

[153] Ibid., pp. 914-918, 923-925.

[154] Helge Dedek, "The Tradition of Comparative Law: Comparison and its Colonial Legacies", in Mathias Siems and Po Jen Yap (eds.), *The Cambridge Handbook of Comparative Law* (2d ed., 2023), pp. 13, 15-16, 18, 22-23.

inherited from the universalism of the Enlightenment and filled with racial and evolutional or developmental theories, where law itself was an instrument of domination:[155]

> The scope of European empires and their power allowed Europeans to view the world as a totality and an object of study. It was not a mere coincidence that such a comparative epistemology rose to prominence in the exact same period as the most extreme expressions of empire and colonial expansion. On the contrary: the very project of colonialism necessitates, inescapably, a world view structured by the 'colonial difference' (Mignolo) between the coloniser and the colonised, which must and can only be established through comparison. Comparison, in this sense, is not meant to 'bring together peers', to reconcile, or to point out commonalities; rather, it establishes a ranking, a hierarchy.[156]

The only truth here is that the original "label" and historical context of origin with the original epistemology matter in principle for understanding a discipline trajectory of development, but Dedek's view of comparative jurisprudence is incorrect precisely because of this argument – the discipline appeared earlier, in other contexts, and drew quite a different world legal picture. The evaluation of comparative law as an "undertheorised field of study" that only recently formed its "intellectual ambition" of transforming comparison from method to subject[157] – is, of course, also not correct.

Not all believe in the close-to-marginal or subsidiary status of comparative law, but the tendency is strong. However, first, every discipline has its proper disciplinary beginning, even legal philosophy and legal theory, although they pretend to be the only legitimate heirs of all teachings about law from ancient times to the present. Legal philosophy as the discipline with its scope, name, and "scientific research program" (the term of Imre Lakatos)[158] appeared at the turn of the eighteenth and nineteenth

155 Ibid., pp. 19-22.

156 Ibid., p. 19.

157 Ibid., pp. 6, 23.

158 Imre Lakatos, *The Methodology of Scientific Research Programs. Philosophical*

centuries. Legal theory as a discipline appeared later.[159] To be sure, they are based on a massive corpus of earlier legal teachings, just as any other contemporary legal discipline. But their structured, systematized, relatively uncontroversial visions of the legal world, or world pictures, were formed two hundred years ago. Second, comparative jurisprudence (but not comparative law) was formed in the same period as legal philosophy. This is not the place to exhibit all the sources of this statement. But many share this view.[160]

FIRST SPECIAL PICTURE OF THE WORLD OF COMPARATIVE JURISPRUDENCE[161]

Comparative legal thinking and origin of comparative legal disciplines

A result of the three centuries of the development of social thought in Europe (sixteenth through eighteenth centuries) was the destruction of the idea of a theo-centric hierarchical world and confirmation of a new social worldview – secular, horizontal, pluralist, and comparativist in essence, the principal subjects of which became the social associations formed on the basis of a rational or irrational will of people – societies, nations, States. The monist and total world gradually dissolved into petty volitional monads – individuals, and a new world was constructed on its ruins – world of social political and legal totalities, equal and sovereign by virtue of being endowed with equal and sovereign will through a positive social contract (society, State) and social consciousness (nation).

Papers, ed. John Worral and Gregory Currie (1978), I.

[159] See for example: Ewald, note 29 above, pp. 2118-2119.

[160] For example: E. Amari, *Critica di una scienza delle legislazioni comparate* (1857); G. Rolin-Jaequemyns, "De l'etude de la legislation comparée et du droit international", *Revue de droit international et de législation comparé*, I, no. 1 (1869); G. Hamza, *Comparative Law and Antiquity* (1991); Ewald, note 29 above; Ch. Donahue, "Comparative Law Before the Code Napoleon", in M. Reimann and R. Zimmermann (eds.), *The Oxford Handbook of Comparative Law*, (2006); H. Mohnhaupt, "Vergleichung in Zeiten des Naturrechts der Aufklarung als Erkenntnismethode", in O. V. Kresin and I. M. Sytar (eds.), Історія порівняльного правознавства як сфера наукових досліджень: Зб. наук. праць [History of Comparative Jurisprudence as the Sphere of Scholarly Studies: Collected Scientific Articles] (2015); Kresin, note 53 above.

[161] This paragraph is based on Kresin, note 53 above.

A world was born of peculiarities and differences which could not be cognized by metaphysical philosophy, natural law, or dogmatic legal thought. The methodologies based on the approaches of theosophy, philosophy, and natural and technical sciences proved to be inadequate to cognize this new social (including socio-legal) positive reality, which finally materialized after the French Revolution and Napoleonic wars). This cognitive crisis led to the forming (or fundamental transformation) of positivist social sciences as a whole and confirmation of the transformed jurisprudence as a positivist social science in particular.[162] One constitutive element which might have ensured its unity given the bankruptcy of philosophical monism should have been comparative-legal knowledge.

Comparative jurisprudence was defined for the first time as a theoretical-methodological approach in 1800, and as a scientific discipline – in 1810, and consciously elaborated during the early nineteenth century, primarily by Germans, but also by other European legal scholars – Italian, French, Polish, Ukrainian, English, and others. Comparative jurisprudence was regarded as one of the basic general legal disciplines (together with history, encyclopedia, and philosophy of law), subject-matter of which are national legal orders and the processes of their interaction, and the object – the trends of the development thereof, and the determination of the Individual, Particular (Special), and General in the elements thereof. This is the basis for forming a general doctrine on law, concepts, and the creation of theoretical-methodological grounds for branch legal sciences and country-based legal disciplines.

The rise of the comparative (universal) history of law is linked with the claim of legal scholars of the early nineteenth century to universalize the subject-matter of the history of law, actively being formed at that time, and with the gradual separation of the politico-legal field within the framework of universal (worldwide) history. Contemporary levels of processing the sources enables the emergence of this discipline to be dated no later than 1818. The comparative history of law in its conceptualizations of that

[162] We do not analyze here various definitions of the term "positivistic jurisprudence". The first positivism in legal science was properly created and firmly established between the late 1780-s to 1830, starting with post-critical Kant, Gaetano Filangieri, and Gustav Hugo, was sociological in its essence, and not as legalistic or normativist as some better known later teachings.

time was defined as a separate legal (and also comparative and historical) science formed at the juncture of the history of law and comparative jurisprudence, which should accumulate and generalize, particularly on the basis of comparative and chronological analysis, knowledge about history and the contemporary state of law and legal thought of various peoples. This material would serve as the basis for clarifying concepts and cognition of the essence of legal phenomena.

An analysis of a significantly broader range of sources than those used previously by legal scholars gives ground to assert the existence in the first third of nineteenth century, despite lengthy discussions of clarification, of uniform theoretical foundations of comparative-legal thinking which rested on a significant corpus of comparative-legal studies, logic, and motivations of legal scholars relating to the organization of comparative-legal knowledge in both comparative-legal disciplines. The most important manifestation of comparative-legal thinking of legal scholars, irrespective of its being embedded as a particular scientific discipline, was the formation against the background of the bankruptcy of universalist legal ideologies of that time of a non-metaphysical scientific picture of the world – the Individual, Particular (Special), and General in legal development.

National legal orders and their distinctiveness

The basis of this scientific picture became the conceptualization of a legal map of the world formed solely from national-State legal orders as individual units, territorial and total in their scope. During the period here considered, two theories of national-State law were elaborated – the socio-volitional and the organic, which in material moments coincided as the formal and substantive aspects of a single doctrine and simultaneously correlated with the theory on the distinctiveness of the Individual in law.

The socio-volitional theory of national-State law was based on the requirement that the territorial-subject legal order conform to a civil society, nation, and State, and their identity relative to the contemporary development of law, despite their historical and functional differences. Thanks to the State, national law acquires a final and expressive institutional form and territoriality. The territoriality of national-State legal orders enables the legal map of the world to be constructed solely from them. The sociality of will and statehood enables the legal order to be objectified and the individual to be removed as a subject of law and the subjective right thereof, and transforms national law into the individual unit of legal development. The socio-volitional nature of law also enabled the identity to be proclaimed of the Is with the Ought, which meant the self-sufficiency and exclusiveness of a positivist legal order. The requirement of statehood for the national legal order finally separated law from other social regulators. The consideration of national-State legal orders as based on social will enabled them to be viewed as of equal value.

The organic theory of national law also considered the State to be a unit of legal development, a totality removing the individual and the subjective right thereof. It was based on a consideration of the nation/people as a natural population, simultaneously endowed with a number of social and ethno-cultural characteristics and socio-psychological unity. Within the framework of such a vision, lawmaking is part of the life of a nation and constantly accompanies its development irrespective of State-building, although the last is considered as an indicator of its maturity. This does not deny the idea of social will, but makes the last derivative and determined, one of the manifestations and a consequence of the life activity of a nation, and not its constituent, refuses the social will and State to be a value in themselves, and subordinates the State to the nation. The organic theory more consistently created the grounds for consideration of national legal experiences as equal in character and individuality, and respective national legal orders – as non-incidental and phenomena of considerable duration. At the same time, the organic theory to a greater degree provided not only for formal autonomy, but also for substantive non-repetitiveness of national legal experience, considered such experience in inextricable unity with the spiritual and cultural calling and development of the nation.

The formal separateness of a national legal order, determined, on one hand, by the will of the national society and, on the other, by international law, did not explain the substantive non-identicalness of legal orders – because they might be regarded as purely utilitarian, functional branches of law general to all people (irrespective of the origin and character thereof – divine, natural, reason). The question arose as to the substantive distinctiveness of each national legal order – its unique elements and the specifics of its common elements (found in more than one legal order).

The notion of the distinctiveness of national law rested especially on the organic theory of national law and was derivative therefrom, emphasizing the material role of self-development in the evolution of a people. During the first third of the nineteenth century, legal scholars advanced the thesis of the non-self-sufficiency of the influence of immutable climatic conditions and, to significant degree, of the requirements and economies of peoples derivative from them. They acted as the frameworks of the possible in the process of the development of a people whose culture and self-awareness cognize these limitations and juxtapose them. Social life was considered as free and self-determined, and law as an integral element thereof within the framework of a cultural tradition and manifestation of its awareness and contemplation.

The grounds in principle of understanding distinctiveness in law by legal scholars of that period were: historicity of peculiar elements in national law which are determined by social development in concrete conditions while completely or basically rejecting these distinctive elements in substantiality; impossibility, at least with respect to their societies and States, of the existence of absolute autochthonic law in the contemporary world; non-self-sufficiency of the distinctive elements, and also in principle the openness of legal orders to interaction; dependence of the expansion or narrowing of the sphere of distinctive elements in national law on the will of society and other factors, possibility of alternative variants of the development of this sphere; impossibility of the complete deprivation of national law of its distinctive elements without the termination of its existence, the necessity of these elements.

General in law, Special in law, and interaction of legal orders

The determination by legal scholars of the second half of the eighteenth and first third of the nineteenth centuries of the exclusiveness of the Individuals (national legal orders) on the legal picture of the world was accompanied by the rethinking in principle of the essence and role of the General in law.

The bankruptcy of ideas concerning the possibility of the formalization of any General in law in the form of a single legal order was realized by many legal scholars of that period, who pointed to the absence of normative space for this given the recognition of the territoriality and sovereignty of States, and also to its unsuitability – for each concrete nation this speculatively constructed legal order would prove to be nil and alien simultaneously. This had been reflected in the evaluations of the possibility of an extra-national legal order which emerged in views on the nature of international law and dominance of some peoples over others. Legal scholars concluded that the formalization of the General in law was impossible outside the framework of national legal orders: the dominance was always in essence territorially and socially limited, leading to limited substantive changes, but could not overcome the Individual without the complete destruction thereof; and international law acts as an external confirmation of the national-State legal order and has only a concrete-national material expression. The General in law, in the view of legal scholars of the period, should have been embedded inside the national-State legal orders, and outside them could exist only as a characteristic of a process.

Given the general understanding of legal scholars of that time relating to the insuperability and totality of the form of the Individual (national legal order), quests for the General in law were manifested in attempts to determine the substantive similarities in the development of legal orders through ideas of their substantive identity or relative substantive similarity. During the period here considered, legal scholars concluded that the substantive identity of legal orders was impossible, as was single invariable progress in the legal sphere, which always is affected primarily by a number of peculiarities and factors of concrete societies at a concrete time. Accordingly, there was not and could not be a universally suitable positive law which might be accepted by all legal orders.

Less radical than uniformity and more acceptable for legal scholars at the time was the idea of the relative substantive similarity of legal orders. Given the multiplicity and non-coordination of the content of national legal orders, is the material unity and stadiality of world development of the principles of positive law possible? Legal scholars have acknowledged the limited suitability and relativity of the idea of such development – as one of the immanent trends towards doctrinal convergence (together with the trend towards the preservation and deepening of individuality), and critiqued its possible teleological implications. The grounds for such a vision were the notions that the General in law, which has no own form, correlated only with the distinctive within the framework of the Individual (national law), and the transmission of social legal experience is historical and concrete – from one Individual to another.

Another approach to the study of the General in law during the period here considered was the doctrine of the dialogue of legal systems. Legal scholars singled out two inter-connected, but distinct, spheres of this dialogue: within and between national legal systems. The internal dialogue, relying on the idea of the non-self-sufficiency of distinctive elements of national law in the world of that time, consists of singling out, identifying, and being aware of certain elements as in essence General (and their form always is national-distinctive). Moreover, the aggregate of the general and distinctive elements of national law is not the simple sum thereof, but represents a struggle and a balance, and the result and the components thereof may, consequently, be determined only *a posteriori*. The dialogue became an internal interaction of singled out and aware distinctive and general elements, and legal scholars or lawmakers, depending on their position, might make a choice in favor of the priority development of the first, second, or both – understanding the inevitability of internal pluralism of any national legal order.

The conception of an external dialogue of legal orders provided for the generalization of the processes of similarities arising in law as a result of borrowing, correlation, and competition of legal orders. Although the general element may emanate from the unity of biological, physical, and anthropological nature of man, it, unlike this nature, is transformed in the process of human interaction in society and between societies. Legal scholars agreed that during the interaction of Individuals between themselves they act as wholes (unities of the general and distinctive elements), and the result of such interaction will be an increased role and volume of the common elements (disseminated in more than one Individual), which nonetheless do not lose their immanent character in national legal orders. The Common in the concept of external dialogue ceases to be perceived as General and unavertable, but is perceived as concrete-social (disseminated within a certain limited group of legal orders) and mutable, as a variable aggregate of interactions which primarily is not material, but a procedural reality, and may be materialized outside national legal orders only in a scientific text – as an analytical unity. At the same time, the idea had been developed of the procedural character of national distinctiveness in law as peculiarities of the dialogue with others and of participation in the creation of an era.

Acknowledgement by legal scholars of the inevitability of national diversity and non-total, non-transcendental, non-material, procedural, and immanent character of the social General in law placed their own national law in dialogue with others. This dialogue might have primarily a positive (exchange of experience) or negative (the other is a negative identificatory of one's own) character. But the emphases and stresses did not change acknowledgement of the fact that there are not two dialogues, but merely two aspects of one dialogue, the result of which is the perception by the parties (lawmakers and legal scholars) of some elements or principles of law – the General is conventional.

During the period here considered, a general theory of the interaction of legal systems was formulated. The grounds of the conceptions in this sphere were compatible, and the most principled of them coincided: an understanding of contemporary legal orders as open, recognition of the inevitability of their interaction and greater or lesser use from this; acknowledgement of the existence of similar problems in different legal orders and, respectively, an assumption of the existence of more perfected models for resolving them which may be borrowed; allowing the possibility of carrying over elements of law from one legal order to another without the loss of the content thereof; the idea of voluntary and limited reception emanating from realized requirements of the recipient society and compatibility of the legal orders; requirement of adaptation of the form of borrowed elements and correlation of their content for ensuring conformity to the conditions of the recipient society; presumption of the formation of the immanent General in law as a result of historical, concrete, and constant interaction of legal orders. Moreover, the coordinated complex of stable basic concepts in this sphere was elaborated.

During the second half of the eighteenth and first third of the nineteenth centuries, the idea was elaborated for the first time of the social Special (Particular) in law as an element of the comparativistic picture of the world. It arose from the contradiction between the *a priori* proclamation of the universality of legal development and studies of concrete mechanisms of the interaction of legal orders, and also from the contradictoriness of determination of the limits of ethno-cultural traditions of peoples not coincident with the boundaries of States and the identification of links not of equal value between different national legal orders.

The theory was developed of the families of legal systems as a middle and, simultaneously, maximum possible objective entity between a national legal order and universal legal development, an internally-linked phenomenon whose existence is materialized in the form of special immanent elements within national law. This Special in law, according to legal scholars of the first third of nineteenth century, may be defined as the sum of material elements and interactions formed historically and being common to certain groups of legal orders. The problem field of the Special in law and the classification of legal orders by a number of scholars already had been singled out as a sphere of scientific knowledge.

The most elaborate approach to the definition and classification of the Special in law was linguistic-cultural, the grounds of which were: the presumption of the conformity of linguistic-communicative, spiritual-cultural, and legal development, on the basis of which the theory of linguistic families was carried over to legal science as the theory of legal families; the consideration of the legal family as a unit of legal development, according to characteristics approximating a national legal order; confirmation of the forming of a legal family as a result of the division of a single people with its single law at a certain stage of historical development, preservation of its basic characteristics and a vector of development by peoples derivative from it and their legal orders; the notion of a legal family as a relatively cultural solitary space of constant internal legal interaction (mutual borrowing, convergence, coordination) not growing into an integral national legal order.

In addition to the linguistic-cultural approach, other criteria underlay the identification of the Special in law, but the respective ideas discovered their own inconsistency, and also subsidiarity with regard to the theory of legal families – each was supported only by some legal scholars, they did not have sufficiently developed and relatively uncontradictory theoretical foundations, and always were put forward in the works of legal scholars together with the division into legal families. These ideas are united by a quest for a unit of legal development broader than the legal family, which during the first third of the nineteenth century was not successful.

CONTEMPORARY MOSAIC OF WORLD PICTURE RECONSIDERED IN COMPARATIVE LAW

5.1. Attempts to find and not to lose

The first world picture of comparative law did not remain unchanged. For example, serious influential factors were a social crisis and the suppression of European revolutions in the 1830s that cast doubt on a nation's ability to contain within itself most interests of society, as well as to be a key actor of State-building. Another serious factor became the transformation of international law from the 1940s. But mostly the original world picture remained the same, with some changes of emphasis and non-conceptualized additions. We continue to face to a major extent an obsolete and inadequate model that require reconsideration.

There is a serious difference between the uncommon suggestion to reconsider the world picture in comparative law and massive efforts to rethink its different elements because of the substantial changes in the composition, importance, functions and interactions of different legal orders that occurred during last two centuries. Examples are given below to understand the scope and directions of such searches.

The idea of reconsidering the world picture of comparative law without losing the discipline as a historically continuous project is timely. For example, Dedek believes that generally comparative law is "an arguably undertheorized field of study" and sees a place for a "new intellectual ambition" in the theoretical contemplation of the subject. Comparison should become rather the subject-matter, than the method of the discipline. One problem is that a newly conceptualized (albeit known from times immemorial) phenomena such as transnational law are seen by many as subject-matter of its own, outside of comparative law, "calling the very future of Comparative Law as a discipline into question". Dedek considers that this and other examples demonstrate that every discipline has its historical and continuous "ideological matrix"; that is why it is regarded as not adequate for contemplating new subject-matter. Dedek thinks that the initial matrix of comparative law, including the comparative method mode, is colonialism, but presupposes decolonialization as a change of the matrix is possible.[163] Dedek,

[163] Dedek, note 154 above, pp. 6, 10, 16, 19, 22-23.

following Patrick Glenn (1940-2014), has stressed the "necessity to challenge the methodological nationalism in law that is such a strange anachronism in our global age".[164]

An attempt to theorize the whole issue of world picture change in comparative scholarship is connected with the juxtaposition of premodern, modern, and postmodern legal worldviews, in which postmodern is resolving inherent and developed inadequacies of modern based on to some extent reconsidered and refined potential of the premodern worldview. Anne Peters and Heiner Schwenke observe that postmodernist thought "considers as basic the experience of plurality and difference", "welcomes these heterogenous positions and find their discordance absolute", "protests against the totalizing monopolization of certain types of rationality and against universalist concepts that raise false allegations of absoluteness". In comparative law postmodernism points to different contexts, especially "cultural frameworks", of law and legal thought developments. These contexts are to some extent incommensurable and the frameworks are non-transcendable, which casts doubt on the very comparison.[165]

Nico Krisch noted two competing "imaginations of law": "modern" (orderly and systematic) and "postmodern" (complex and multivalent, "an order of multiplicity"), and said with respect to modern national law: "This image – the systemic, hierarchical and exclusive one – may well constitute the exception rather than the rule ... The legal order as such can then no longer be understood without an account of the ways in which its different parts are entangled".[166]

Some interconnected areas or grounds where ideas of the postmodern world legal picture were unwittingly or consciously formulated are: deconstruction of legal systems, legal pluralism, interactions of legal orders, and the cultural turn in theory and methods of comparative law. All these areas or grounds are connected with the denial of the possibility of aprioristic theoretical

164 Dedek, Mindful of the World: "A Cosmopolitan Jurisprudence", in *ASCL Blog* (available online).

165 Anne Peters and Heiner Schwenke, "Comparative Law beyond Post-Modernism", *The International and Comparative Law Quarterly*, LI (2000), pp. 801-802.

166 Nico Krisch, "Framing Entangled Legalities beyond the State", in Nico Krisch (ed.) *Entangled Legalities Beyond the State* (2021), p. 31.

construction of what is law's nature and what should be the legal order. The issue of the special nature of law is artificial; it is always a concrete concept, created and accepted by certain individuals or stable groups as society. As Niklas Luhmann put it, "even the most detailed legal propositions happen to emerge in society and society alone".[167]

Mireille Delmas-Marty observes that the world legal landscape is characterized by disorder and fragmentation from the structural point of view and rash unification (and even "totalization") by means of hegemonic integration. Potential legal unity is utopian, complete autonomy of national legal orders no longer exists, and the actual task for jurists should be bringing order to pluralism, building a globally "ordered legal area". Delmas-Marty proposes that jurists not insert facts into pre-established and inadequate categories of legal systems, but instead "adapt categories to shifting realities" – a non-Euclidean or postmodern situation. The national legal system is challenged from within and without; "new legal ensembles" have difficult natures, and the concept of legal order may be replaced with interconnected and interdependent "normative areas" structuring "normative masses".[168]

Deconstruction of national and international law

An influential deconstruction of the national legal system was presented by Rodolfo Sacco (1923-2022) in his legal formants theory. He characterized the systems approach as inadequate, noting that the hierarchy principle does not explain the real existence of interacting and conflicting legal formants instead of a single norm for each issue. The real comparative study of legal orders (not only national ones) has to be the fundamental cognitive goal of comparative law. The vision of legal theory for "proper law" contemplates reduction and interpretative engineering rather than the interpretative reconstruction of real law.[169] Some development of these ideas can be seen, for example, in the idea of

[167] Niklas Luhmann, *Law as a Social System*, transl. Klaus A. Ziegert (2004), p. vii.

[168] Mireille Delmas-Marty, *Ordering Pluralism: A Conceptual Framework for Understanding the Transnational Legal World* (2009), pp. 1-2, 5, 8-9, 12-16, 149-151.

[169] Rodolfo Sacco, "Legal Formants: A Dynamic Approach to Comparative Law (Installment I of II)", *The American Journal of Comparative Law*, XXXIX, no. 1 (1991).

molecular federalism of legal norms advanced by David Snyder.[170]

Several legal scholars considered the effects of legal transplants, a concept of Alan Watson (1933-2018),[171] within the receiving national legal system. That exercise was far-removed from the original intent of Watson and from the traditional systems approach to national law, deconstructing the latter and presenting its anatomy to be more complex and unpredictable and determined more by cultural processes than by normative algorithms. Gunther Teubner formed a new theory of legal irritants as imposed legal norms: these irritate law's binding arrangements with other social sectors and provoke fundamental change in the internal context of national law.[172] William Ewald proposed the mutual influences of legal systems to be a new subject-matter of comparative law.[173] Esin Örücü proclaimed the migration (transposition) of norms and their acculturation to be a major factor in legal development.[174] Valentine Vernon Palmer and others generalized both conceptually and geographically the concept of mixed legal system and proposed that every legal system is complex and plural because of the constant mixing.[175] Pierre Legrand wrote about the impossibility of legal transplants as meaningful constructions because of their embeddedness in socio-cultural and other contexts in home jurisdictions.[176]

No less important a deconstruction was proposed for international law by William Butler. He categorically confirms that the search for universals in international law is a useless undertaking. International law merely pretends to universality,

170 David V. Snyder, *Molecular Federalism and the Structures of Private Lawmaking* (2007) (Comparative Law and Political Economy Research Papers No. 1/2007).

171 Alan Watson, *Legal Transplants: An Approach to Comparative Law* (1974).

172 Gunther Teubner, "Legal Irritants: Good Faith in British Law or How Unifying Law Ends Up in New Divergencies", *Modern Law Review*, LXI, no. 1 (1998).

173 William Ewald, "Comparative Jurisprudence (II): The Logic of Legal Transplants", *American Journal of Comparative Law*, XLIII, 1995.

174 Esin Örücü, "Law as Transposition", *International and Comparative Law Quarterly*, LI, no. 2 (2002).

175 Vernon Valentine Palmer, "Two Rival Theories of Mixed Legal Systems", *Journal of Comparative Law*, III, no. 1 (2008).

176 Pierre Legrand, "The Impossibility of «Legal Transplants»", *Maastricht Journal of European and Comparative Law*, IV (1997).

but is not. The assumption of the universality of international law he considers to be dangerous and "originated in the absence of positive empirical evidence". Dangerous because the advisability of a universal legal system is doubtful. The reason for international lawyers proclaiming international law to be unique and universal Butler believes to be their aspiration that international law should be deemed to be a real legal system, and also the dream of a worldwide ordering of society and inter-society relations, the creation of a global community. Historically, international law has never been universal "except in the aspirations of its proponents (scientific works)". A multiplicity of "international systems" had coexisted (regional treaty, customary-law, doctrinal-ideological legal regimes and spheres), and there has never been an agreed concept of a universal international law and, the more so, such a law has never existed, at least down to the present. Moreover, historically, international-legal regimes had not recognized a hierarchy among themselves; they considered themselves to be superior in respect to other such regimes, if indeed they had any knowledge of others.[177]

And even at present, one may speak only of a "fictitious unity and wholeness of international law" and the real adversarial competition of centrifugal and centripetal forces in this domain, despite the fact that a hierarchy between international-legal regimes is supposedly established in part. The reason multiple international-legal regimes have arisen is the need to order and regulate concrete interactions between specific societies. And such interactions are growing. This does not threaten the development and operation of international law, but merely rejects its universal character. The perception of such a real state of affairs by international lawyers, Butler notes, is rather complex. Therefore, it is important to distinguish the real from the desired, an analysis of the state of affairs based on State practice and the doctrine of international law. One should speak not of the fragmentation of international law, but of its fragmentary nature or alternativity, which historically and now is a normal phenomenon and assumes the existence of "sub-systems or legal regimes of various types at various levels ... with a changeable degree of autonomy". Such

[177] William E. Butler (ed.), *International Law in Comparative Perspective* (1980); Oleksiy Kresin, Iryna Kresina, and Yuriy Shemshuchenko, "The Wisdom of Comparative Law: On the Contributions of William Butler", *Revue internationale de droit comparé*, no. 3 (2020).

regimes simultaneously may conflict, partially coincide and overlap, reinforce one another, or simply operate in parallel. Under this approach, Butler demonstrates, the opposition between international and national legal systems disappears; they become links of a universal, mutually-connected and partially structured aggregate of legal regimes of different types.[178]

A web of global legal pluralism

A cornucopia of scholarly works for some decades have been dedicated to the contemplation of global legal pluralism. Boaventura De Sousa Santos writes about three different legal spaces – local, national, and world – and three corresponding forms of law. Socio-legal life is constituted and simultaneously operating on different levels, so legal spaces constantly interact, and this creates interlaw and interlegality. This way of thinking Santos considers to be "a sociological attempt towards a postmodern conception of law".[179]

Santos considers legal pluralism to be the key concept of a postmodern view of law, albeit not a pluralism of separate entities in coexistence, but a pluralism of their interaction and of an awareness of such interaction, of "porous legality or of legal porosity, of multiple networks of legal orders forcing us to constant transitions and trespassings", and thus of interlegality with mixtures of legal semiotic codes, and with polycentrism, fragmentation, particularisms. In this postmodern living and interacting network of legal orders "the centrality of the state law, though increasingly shaken, is still a decisive factor".[180]

Mauro Bussani suggests a general justification for departure from absolute State-centrism in law ("legal monotheism") and for more pluralist approaches, including unofficial laws. The matrix of absolute clear State law was for some centuries justified by historically construed notions, but finally has to be acknowledged. For this, the abstract "battle of definitions" of law should be avoided

[178] Kresin, et al., note 177 above.

[179] Boaventura De Sousa Santos, "Law: A Map of Misreading. Toward a Postmodern Conception of Law", *Journal of Law and Society*, XIV, no. 3 (1987), pp. 287-288, 297.

[180] Ibid., pp. 297-299.

in favor of concrete empirical studies of the real frameworks in which law is embedded.[181]

Ralf Michaels, developing earlier ideas of Gunther Teubner, has directed attention to global legal pluralism that challenges "a perceived monopoly of the state in making and administering law", as well as law's "social embeddedness", and focuses on autopoiesis of law on the base of discourses, "autonomous global functional subsystems of world society" which coupled with different legal orders form internally differentiated global law. With this ignorance of supranational, international, and non-State law, as well as the focus on national legal systems and their classification, comparative law looks obsolete and inadequate.[182]

Michaels, to be sure, sees some slow changes in this sphere: new classification attempts are more anthropological and not centered on state law, and "internal heteronomy of legal systems" is acknowledged. The latter is realized, *inter alia,* in the mixed legal systems theory version stating that every legal system is mixed, and this version is closely linked to the theory of global legal pluralism. Some issues remain open in connection with these changes, especially a distinction between law and other normative orders. Michaels proposes that "The definition of law becomes a task neither for autonomous communities nor for neutral observers but instead for interpersonal and intercommunal negotiation and recognition", albeit with special recognition of the role of the State. The most adequate way of ordering the plurality of legal orders, in the vision of Michaels, is a new "general theory of interlegality" understood as global mutual recognition and conflict of laws teaching.[183]

Tamanaha's understanding of global legal pluralism is formulated as a sphere of considering a new world legal picture:

> Global legal pluralism apparently purports to encompass all legal orders in the world – local, state, transnational, customary, religious, non-state, etc. – considered together in a vast bottomless bucket. If the assertion is that all legal

[181] Mauro Bussani, "Legal Monotheism and Its Discontents", *AJCL Blog*. 25 January 2023 (available online)

[182] Ralf Michaels, "Global Legal Pluralism", *Annual Review of Law & Social Science*, V, 2009, pp. 3, 7-8.

[183] Ibid., pp. 8-9, 13-16, 21-23.

> orders in the world in the aggregate constitutes legal pluralism, it is a true but empty claim; if the claim is that their framework applies to all legal orders in the world considered together or whenever legal multiplicities of any kind arise, it is an audacious claim.[184]

Tamanaha is conscious that transnational legal pluralism is "constructing a wholly new paradigm" to address not only traditional, but also new forms of law. His generally seemingly theoretical view in fact presupposes pure empirical approach: law is something that is recognized by a certain community to be law:[185] "To know what law is for the purposes of legal pluralism does not require an abstract concept or definition of law stating essential or defining features – instead one must inquire into what people in a given social arena collectively (conventionally) identify as law".[186]

He proclaimed the denial of pure legal theory:

> ... transnational legal pluralists should not attempt to build on an abstract concept or definition of law (implicitly or explicitly). Not only is a concept of law unnecessary and superfluous..., but engaging in this theoretical project is a roadblock to progress. Theorists who attempt to base transnational legal pluralism on a definition of law will go in circles with other similarly engaged theorists and no prospect of resolution.[187]

Instead of "unnecessarily grand theories" trying to encompass everything and leading astray, it should be "modest, tailored theorizing that fits the matters at hand".[188] The abstract issue of law's nature is removed, and the task of researcher is to describe, compare, classify, generalize, and so on.

Tamanaha's article is a good example of the discussion and juxtaposition of "transnational and regulatory pluralist" against the principle that the legitimation of a particular legal order necessarily

184 Brian Tamanaha, "A Reconstruction of Transnational Legal Pluralism and Law's Foundations", in Krisch, note 166 above, p. 456.

185 Ibid., pp. 456, 469, 475-476.

186 Ibid., p. 471.

187 Ibid., p. 475.

188 Ibid., p. 477.

requires recognition from State(s), thereby presupposing the basic character of national legal orders. Tamanaha proposed three types of legal orders – community law, regime law, and cross-polity law (all three somewhere contained within national legal systems, somewhere not, somewhere even clashing) – and stresses that "these categories are inductively derived generalizations, not analytically derived":[189]

> Community law encompasses basic laws and institutions of social intercourse within communities addressing property, personal injuries, marriage, divorce, sexual restrictions, inheritance, debts and obligations and others; the body of rules through which people arrange their daily affairs. Every society has rules addressing these matters, which vary greatly across societies and change over time. Many existing systems of customary and religious law involve the lengthy continuation of fundamental rules of social intercourse going back many centuries, predating the establishment of state legal systems and evolving to adjust to the presence of the state (and the state to them). Regime laws are laws tied to ruling polities. They constitute, support and enforce the power of the governing regime, including taxation and customs fees, forced labour and military service, laws against sedition, border controls and much more, with governing regimes frequently nested within or encompassing in whole or part other subregimes. Cross-polity laws deal with matters between and across organized polities, consisting of national law (including conflicts of law), international law, transnational law and non-state forms of law that extend across states (like fatwa).[190]

Anne Peters developed a theory of the competition of legal orders within the framework of the legal pluralism paradigm and considers law to be the product of merchandise: "Just like a raw material, law seems to be a pre-product for the actual production of goods. This raw material is offered on the law-market". Under conditions of globalization, the State loses its monopoly for providing law because of choice of law options, the increasing role of international and supranational organizations, regional and

[189] Ibid., pp. 462-464, 469, 472-476.

[190] Ibid., pp. 472-473.

local authorities, and non-governmental actors, and competition with other national legal systems. A vertical and horizontal territorial and de-territorialized competition has its place between national law and other legal orders. Rules for choice of law and of correlation of legal orders together form "the meta order of legal systems competition".[191]

Krisch sees law as an entangled web rather than an integrated and coherent system, as depicted in the Western "standard image of law". He "shifts the focus to the ways in which actors create connections and distance between different legalities in domestic, transnational and international law". The identity of each legal order and the character of the whole can be understood only if we consider legal norms and legal systems not as "selfstanding entities", but as "tied up in relationships with others", not being separate and not integrated. Law is the product of these relations, and we face a challenge "when trying to square such practices into the frame of unitary, well-ordered legal systems". And these relations are not predefined, but "remain to be determined through the social interplay of actors". In "an order of multiplicity" of law there are temporary accommodations and inconsistences, and they should be rather "processed and navigated" than eliminated or neglected.[192]

Krisch notes that such an entanglement had been an essential feature of legal development before the consolidation of the modern national State, with its aspiration to become the only type of legal order. But many "pockets of entanglement" have survived. Now "increasing societal diversity" and the "rise of transnational and international legalities" is revitalizing entanglement as the realization of legal pluralism. Krisch suggested that a new post-national entangled law is close to pre-national legal orders.[193]

Dana Burchardt posited the norm-centered rather than system-centered transnational legal sphere formed by the intertwinement of legal spaces. The latter are understood as "the systemic structure formed by a group of legal norms" of various origin. Burchardt stresses here the path from norms (with their interaction) to order

191 Anne Peters, "The Competition between Legal Orders", *International Law Research*, III, no. 1 (2014), pp. 48, 52, 63.

192 Krisch, "Preface", in Krisch, note 166 above, pp. i, xi-xii, 1, 10, 28, 30.

193 Krisch, note 166 above, pp. 7-10, 32.

and not *vice versa*.[194] Legal order is traditionally understood as a "normatively closed system", but, in the vision of Burchardt, is no longer an exclusive "point of reference for the creation and application of norms"; its role weakened because of interrelations of norms blurring the frameworks of legal orders ("more openly designed model"), different norm-creating entities operating in parallel, and the emergence of transnational normativity.[195] Unlike certain other scholars, Burchardt is aware that her searches do not resolve "the normative question of legitimacy" of forms of coexistence and interaction of legal orders.[196]

Simon Roberts (1941-2014) defined the positive essence of legal pluralism movement as: "Law could no longer be treated as unproblematically determinative of social forms; nor could 'order' be claimed as the exclusive product of a top-down, centre towards periphery movement, the skilled achievement of those in power".[197] Roberts saw three major problems in legal pluralism: definitions of different normative orders (especially what is legal and what is not, and the unified concept of law becomes hardly possible), conceptualizing of their relations, and "the very nature of the comparative project": "Whatever the specific objective, its execution must involve a self-conscious attempt at the impossible – the establishment of a framework of analysis distinct from the 'cultures' compared".[198]

Gad Barzilai offered a critique of legal pluralism theories. Although legal pluralism is based on such strong grounds as the decentralization of State law and cultural relativism, it is missing a key concept of political power in asymmetrical legal reality. Roberts believed that States themselves are promoting and legalizing a sort of legal pluralism for better control over their constitutive parts and "non-ruling communities", preventing them from challenging the legitimacy of these States. Globalization to some extent has weakened the role of State regulation in some regions of the world,

[194] Dana Burchardt, "Intertwinement of Legal Spaces in the Transnational Legal Sphere", *Leiden Journal of International Law*, XXX (2017), pp. 305-310, 321.

[195] Ibid., pp. 308, 321-323.

[196] Ibid., pp. 307, 326.

[197] Simon Roberts, "Against Legal Pluralism", *The Journal of Legal Pluralism and Unofficial Law*, XXX (1998), p. 96.

[198] Ibid., pp. 97, 100-101, 105.

but not decisively transferred it to international and transnational actors. The State still strategizes and regulates local and global levels of legal pluralism: "At the outset of the 21st century, nation-states have not become obsolete, nor are they overwhelmingly dwindling; rather, they are transforming some of their power through local and global agents". Law is thus "transformative law", which is created by different local, national, and global agents to regulate relations of individuals and these actors.[199]

CONCLUSIONS

When a scholarly image is formed from certain fragments of reality as one interconnected complex phenomenon, a science or scientific discipline is being born. The root of this image is a certain paradigm, and the generalized image could be perceived as a subject of contemplation. In fact, there are different subject-matter or a part of the subject-matter of another science, and the very imaging of these parts of reality as a single phenomenon is the process of a new science or discipline subject-matter creation. To be sure, the real subject-matter exists independently from a researcher, whereas others are created or developed with researcher participation. Uniting (necessarily grounded in a certain paradigm) them in one interconnected complex phenomenon is itself the fundamental object rather than a subject. The consciousness of this activity of conceptualizing subject-matter in a certain way and modelling their connections, interactions, and, finally, their unity as an autonomic facet of reality – this is the genuine creation of a science.

This modelled image, already containing some paradigm – should it have a name? One possible name, quite deeply and consistently conceptualized, is the "world picture". Numerous arguments in favor of this vision of a subject-matter, object, origin of a science, and the very name of this modelled image are provided by the philosophy of science, science of science, and the history of sciences.

The ultimate aim of every autonomous general law discourse pretending to be a scholarly legal discipline is to construct

199 Gad Barzilai, "Beyond Relativism: Where Is Political Power in Legal Pluralism?", *Theoretical Inquiries in Law*, IX, no. 2 (2008), pp. 395-397, 402, 409-411, 414-416.

and realize its vision and mission as a special world picture – a conceptualized and structured model of an aspect or fragment of reality accessible with its paradigm, research program, and methods. Depending on different modes of scientific rationality, this world picture can be seen as the object, subject-matter, or aim of the scientific discipline, but still remains its core issue, even if not so formulated.

The pretension to the right to construct an own world picture as autonomic and at the same time general for all legal discourses actually has been the point of competition and dominance among legal philosophy, legal theory, and comparative jurisprudence (comparative law) for at least the last two centuries.

In the vision of many colleagues, comparative law is subsidiary scholarly discipline or even not a discipline at all, but a set of tools and a kind of activity. That is why a philosophical and theoretical legal picture of the world is taught during the first year of university studies as basic, dominating, and even the only possible view, whereas comparative law is available only on the master's level as predominantly a practical subject or general introduction to practical subjects. All is logical and clear.

Likewise logical and clear is that the essentials and the mode of thinking implied in the world picture, almost exclusively presented in the legal sciences by legal philosophy and legal theory, have consequences for the development of the legal consciousness of lawyers and for legal practice. The picture with an implied proclamation of the "nature of law" has an axiomatic character and represents a mixture of metaphysics of the Ought and speculative abstractions of the somewhere (own domestic law or some Western legal systems) or nowhere existing Is. The real experience of every concrete legal order, and especially non-Western, non-secular, non-State-centered, becomes with this picture wrongful, anomalous, exotic, or obsolete.

Moreover, the structure and elements of this world picture invisibly permeate comparative law and pervert its essence: the mode of questioning law and the *tertium comparationis* do not follow from previous research experience and conclusions, but are prescribed by this speculative construction. In many cases laws and regulatory elements are not compared with one another, but with implicit prescribed etalons. Comparative jurisprudence becomes comparative law: instead of cognition, we get ideology and means for the westernization and unification of law, a toolbox for erasing the senses.[200]

But is comparative jurisprudence (the precise and historically substantiated proper name for a later unconsciously and partly consciously distorted "comparative law") able to be not a faithful servant of other general legal discourses, branch legal studies, or practical needs, but a self-sufficient scholarly discourse with an own purely cognitive aim, own theoretical and philosophical levels? Yes, this has been so for over two centuries and remains so today.

Comparative jurisprudence did not originate as a derivative from legal philosophy and legal theory and is not their faithful servant. It was self-sufficient discipline that formed an own picture of the world once and then, so we can seek to comprehend a concise contemporary comparative-legal picture of the world now. This vision of a predominantly inductively built picture is more vital and closer to reality, worthy of further conceptualization, rethinking, and transformation, and deserving of learning and teaching in a course on comparative law as a cornerstone of legal education capable of improving the traditional semi-marginal, subsidiary, derivative status of the discipline.

The traditional and still dominant world picture of comparative law is national- and State-centered. During past centuries the long struggle to realize this in practice to some extent canonized the paradigm. This in essence modernist paradigm provided for total coverage of national-State legal orders (Individual in law), correlated in form and partly in content by international law (as General in law), and also in content by legal families, or cultures, or traditions (as Special or Particular in law).

New visions, fragmentary, but to high degree conventional and mutually corresponding to one another, of a special world picture in comparative jurisprudence (comparative law) make provision especially for: the deconstruction of national and international law, doubting the systematicity and totality of the first and the integrality of the second; and a global legal pluralism of legal orders, regimes, and their elements having different social and communicative origin. Some comparatists consider this new

[200] Similar thoughts have been expressed in various works. Among those not reducing the issue to culturalist theses is Tkachenko, note 46 above.

complex, dynamic, and highly procedural (more than material) vision of the worldbeat to be postmodern.

Only an awareness of own fundamental experience, continuity or succession, present ability, and valuable advantages in the construction of a world picture by comparative jurisprudence (comparative law) may remove it from the semi-marginal to a deserved central status among general legal disciplines in academia and the instructional curriculum. Moreover, a realistic and predominantly inductive world picture of comparative law is better placed to consider and model existing and potential profound challenges in legal development.

Chapter 3

The Legal World Picture: Concept And Epistemological-Methodological Problems Of Construction

MEHMAN A. DAMIRLI

In legal literature the expression "legal world picture", as even a cursory glance shows, is used in various ways in different discourses and contexts, and most often metaphorically. Despite the frequent use of this expression, there has been no serious conceptual analysis or definition. Accordingly, the main task is the conceptualization of the legal world picture.

Completing this task requires answering at least the following: (a) what are the philosophical and scientific foundations for conceptualizing of the world picture? (b) what is the relationship between the concepts of worldview and world picture? (c) in what meanings can the concept of world picture be understood? (d) what is the legal world picture? (e) is this a *legal picture* of the world or a picture of the *legal world*? (f) what is the "legal world" (or "world of law")? (g) what is the character of the legal world picture as an object of cognition? (h) what are the problems of cognition of the legal world as whole at present? (i) what is the role of particular legal disciplines in constructing the legal world picture? (j) what problems exist in the study of the legal world picture in comparative jurisprudence (comparative law)? The present work will address these and other related questions.

FROM THE HISTORY OF THE CONCEPT OF WORLD PICTURE: PHILOSOPHICAL AND SCIENTIFIC REFLECTIONS

Philosophical Reflections

The term of "world picture" (the English equivalent of the German *Weltbild*) was introduced into philosophical discourse about a century after the term "worldview" (*Weltanschauung*). The origin of the term *Weltanschauung* goes back to Immanuel Kant (1724-1804) in his *Critique of Pure Reason* (1790). After being used in 1807 by Georg Wilhelm Friedrich Hegel (1770-1831) this term (he defined it as "conceptual frameworks") began to be popularized. The early conceptualization of a world picture dates from the 1880s to the first quarter of the twentieth century. The discussions of the world picture occurred mainly within the framework of philosophical theories of worldview. This meant that the concept of world picture was considered to be an integral part of the said theories. Such theories are numerous. Their authors are G. W. F. Hegel, Wilhelm Dilthey, Friedrich Nietzsche (1844-1900), Edmund Husserl (1859-1938), Karl Jaspers, Martin Heidegger, Ludwig Wittgenstein, Sigmund Freud (1856-1939), Carl Gustav Jung (1875-1961), Karl Mannheim (1893-1947), Hans Georg Gadamer (1900-2002), Jacques Derrida (1930-2004), Paul-Michel Foucault (1926-1984), and others. However, not all these worldviewish thinkers have considered the question of the world picture. Here will be considered those who have also made a significant contribution to the development of the concept of world picture and its relation with the worldview.

The first systematic approach to worldview was advanced by Wilhelm Dilthey (1833-1911), a pioneer in the theory of the humanities (*Geisteswissenschaften*). He is deservedly called the "father of worldview theory"[1] and set out the first serious theoretical reflections on the concept of a world picture.[2]

Dilthey expounded his theory in a work on the types of world views and their elaboration within metaphysical systems.[3] According to Dilthey, a life world (*Lebenswelt*) in its objective manifestation and attitudes toward this world is the origin of a worldview. An important aspect of Dilthey's theory is the structure of the worldview: all worldviews have the same general structure, which is one orderly system, and they "tend towards uniformities in which the structure of psychological life is expressed". In accordance with the three-aspect structure of the latter (mind,

[1] David K. Naugle, *Worldview: The History of a Concept* (2002), p. 84.

[2] According to one statement, "world picture" as a philosophical term was coined by Wilhelm Dilthey. Benjamin Lazier, "Earthrise; or, The Globalization of the World Picture", *The American Historical Review*, CXI (June 2011), p. 606.

[3] W. Dilthey, *Die Typen der Weltanschauung und ihre Ausbildung in den Metaphysischen Systemen* (1911).

emotion, will), the worldview likewise has a three-aspect structure. As a thought process, it begins with the formation in the mind of the "cosmic picture" (*Weltbild),* which is an image of a set of concepts and judgments that adequately reflect "the relatedness and true being of reality". On this ground, the formation of the "effective value" of life takes place. On the basis of perceived value, "conditions, persons, and objects assume their importance in relation to whole of reality, and this whole itself is stamped with meaningfulness". At the next, third stage, the worldview is filled with vitality and power due to the "upper level of consciousness", containing of the highest ideals, principles and norms of behavior, and "the worldview becomes creative, formative and indeed reforming".[4]

Thus, to be concise, Dilthey reconstructs the structure of worldview as a sequence of world pictures, values, and higher ideals. These encompass the metaphysical, axiological, and ethical structural elements (level) of the worldview;[5] for Dilthey "worldview" is a broader concept than the concept of "world picture", which is merely the metaphysical level of the first.

Karl Jaspers (1883-1969) at the beginning of his work *Psychology of Worldviews* (1919)[6] poses the question "What is a *Weltanschauung*?" In response, Jaspers defined *Weltanschauung* as:

> [s]omething total and universal at the same time. For example, when we talk about knowledge: not individual specialist knowledge, but knowledge as a whole, as a cosmos. It is not a mere knowledge; it is revealed in evaluations, lifestyle, fate, in the experienced ranking of values. Or both in a different way of expressing it: when we speak of worldviews, we mean ideas, the ultimate and totality of man, both subjectively as experience, power and attitude, as well as objectively as a formed world of objects.[7]

4 Wilhelm Dilthey, "The Types of World Views and their Unfoldment within the Metaphysical Systems", in *Dilthey's Philosophy of Existence: Introduction to Weltanschauungslehre*, transl. and intro. William Kluback and Martin Weinbaum (1957), pp. 25-27.

5 Naugle, note 1 above, p. 87.

6 Karl Jaspers, *Psychologie der Weltanschauungen* (1919).

7 Ibid., p. 1.

More than a decade later Jaspers wrote:

> What we mean by a world view is indeed more than knowledge. It includes what is sometimes contrasted with it as a 'view of life': the way in which an individual will evaluate things, what matters absolutely to him and what has only relative importance, and how, in consequence, he will behave and act.[8]

It is not difficult to see that, for Jaspers, worldview has an all-inclusive character and consists of two sides (subjective and objective) of life within a larger life perspective ("the life of the spirit"). The subjective side of the worldview is composed "attitudes" (*Einstellungen*), and the objective side – "world pictures" (*Weltbilder*). If attitudes are associated with mental existence, then the world picture is not the sphere of mental existence, but mental content.[9]

According to Jaspers, "[t]he attitudes are general behavior patterns that can be objectively examined, at least in part, as the transcendental forms".[10] Basic attitudes are the product of inborn ideas or childhood experience, by means of which a person perceives and recognizes the objectively existing world and, as a result, a mental picture of the world is formed. Attitudes are varied: objective, self-reflective, active, contemplative, rational, aesthetic, and so on.[11]

In the author's definition world pictures are

> the whole of the objective content that a person possesses. We see the human being as the center, so to speak, in a circular periphery, the periphery is this world of the objective in which the human being is enclosed in the subject-object split. Or we can call the world picture the housing in which the mental's life is partly captured, which

[8] Jaspers, *Philosophie I: Philosophische Weltorientierung (*1932*)*; English transl. in Jaspers, *Philosophical World Orientation*, ed. E. B. Ashton (1969), p. 251.

[9] Jaspers, note 6 above, p. 122.

[10] Ibid., p. 38.

[11] Ibid.

> it is also partly able to create from within itself and to put outwards.[12]

Attitudes and world pictures are relatively abstract elements that isolate what actually exists together.[13] Thus, the worldview is formed by combination of attitudes and world pictures, both which are grounded in the source of "the life of spirit".

Martin Heidegger (1889-1976) in an essay "The Age of the World Picture"[14] defined *Weltanschauung* as "man's fundamental relation to beings as a whole",[15] "the position of man in the midst of beings", "the position in which he can be that being who gives to every being the measure and draws up the guidelines".[16] Whereas the world picture is "the collective image of representing production [*das Gebild des vorstellenden Herstellens*]".[17] According to Heidegger:

> Initially, the word "picture" makes one think of a copy of something. This would make the world picture, as it were, a painting of beings as a whole. But "world picture" means more than this. We mean by it the world itself; the totality of beings taken, as it is for us, as standard-giving and obligating. "Picture" means, here, not a mere imitation, but rather that which sounds in the colloquial expression to be "in the picture" about something. This means: the matter itself stands in the way in stands to us, before us ... Understood in an essential way, "world picture", does not mean "picture of the world" but, rather, the world grasped as picture. Beings as a whole are now taken in such a way that a being is first and only in being insofar as it is set in place by representing-producing (*vorstellend-herstellenden*]

[12] Ibid., p. 122.

[13] Ibid., pp. 38, 189.

[14] In fact, this is the text of a lecture given in 9 June 1938 under the title "The Establishing by Metaphysics of the Modern World Picture" before the Society for Aesthetics, Natural Philosophy, and Medicine at Freiburg in Breisgau. First published under the title "Die Zeit des Weltbildes," in Martin Heidegger, *Holzwege* (1950).

[15] Martin Heidegger, "The Age of the World Picture", in *Off the Beaten Track*, ed. and transl. Julian Young and Kenneth Haynes (2002), p. 70.

[16] Ibid., p. 71.

[17] Ibid.

> humanity. Whenever we have a world picture, an essential decision occurs concerning beings as whole. The being of beings is sought and found in the representedness of beings. Where, however, beings are *not* interpreted in this way, the world, too, cannot come into the picture – there can be no world picture.[18]

Thus, for Heidegger, a "world picture" is not so much a "painting of beings as a whole", but rather something "produced" by the person. To create the world picture, you first need to create the world, and then apply the procedure of representation, which involves thinking of the world as a picture or as a collection of objects on display.

We also find in Heidegger, in a sense, a differentiation between the "objective" picture of the world and the "subjective" picture of the world. Heidegger also points to systematicity ("To the essence of the picture belongs standing-together [compositeness], system")[19] and discreteness of the world picture as its characteristic properties. Heidegger insists on the strictly modern nature of the picture of the world. In his opinion, the production of oneself as a picture is not inherent in any other period except the modern one; there could be neither an ancient nor a medieval picture of the world:

> The world picture does not change from an earlier medieval to a modern one; rather, that the world becomes picture at all is what distinguishes the essence of modernity... But never does the being's being consist in its being brought before man as the objective. Never does it consist in being placed in the realm of man's information and disposal so that, in this way alone, is it in being.[20]

The objectivity of the world picture of the modernity means that it appears to the representative of the new European civilization as a fundamental event – "the conquest of the world" unfolding before him.[21]

[18] Ibid., p. 67.

[19] Ibid., p. 76.

[20] Ibid., p. 68.

[21] Ibid., p. 71.

Oswald Spengler (1880-1936) proposed a comprehensive conception of worldview, according to which a worldview is "a picture of the world (cosmos, universe)", a model of reality, "in which the whole of consciousness, becoming and the become, life and what is experienced"[22] is contained. In Spengler's concept, the worldview and the world picture are understood as a comprehensive model of reality, and completely coincide.

Early Ludwig Wittgenstein (1889-1951) opposed the modern conception of the worldview of naturalism, because in his words, this conception "is founded on the illusion that the so-called laws of nature are the explanations of natural phenomena".[23] He acquired his comprehensive conception of worldview from Oswald Spengler and claimed that a comprehensive "conception of a perspicuous presentation … [of things] is fundamental".[24] Wittgenstein outlined his final concept in the work of the last years of his life, *On Certainty*, where he almost abandoned the word "worldview", using it rarely, and called own philosophical outlook a *Weltbild*.

In characterizing Wittgenstein's conception of world pictures, Naugle notes four main themes that are conspicuous in this concept:

> First, a *Weltbild* forms one's way of seeing and conceiving of the world and its basic character. Second, a *Weltbild* is not chosen as a result of some verification process, but rather is inherited from one's context so that it serves as the assumed substratum for all thinking, acting, judging, and living. Third, the narratives constituting a world picture function as a kind of governing mythology. Finally, world pictures are promulgated rhetorically and are accepted in faith. Given these various characteristics, world pictures and forms of life with their inherent language games seem almost identical.[25]

[22] Quoted in Naugle, note 1 above, p. 151.

[23] Ludwig Wittgenstein, *Tractatus Logico-Philosophicus*, transl. D. F. Pears and B. F. McGuinness (1961), p. 70.

[24] Wittgenstein, *Remarks on Frazer's "Golden Bough"*, ed. Rush Rhess; transl. A. C. Miles (1979), pp. 8e-9e.

[25] Naugle, note 1 above, p. 161.

Later Wittgenstein represented a new kind of non-Cartesian world picture which he believed was the human "way of seeing" the world. On one hand, Wittgenstein defined world picture epistemologically, and on the other hand, the world picture in his conception takes the place of a worldview.

Scientific Reflections

The roots of the concept of a world picture in the natural sciences date back to Sir Isaac Newton (1642-1727) in his *De mundi Systemate* (1685). True, he was not talking about the world picture, but about "the system of the world". In doing so, he proceeded from his own field, the science of mechanics, and mathematical principles of philosophy ("the principles of philosophy; not philosophical, but mathematical"), which "are the laws and conditions of certain motions, and powers or forces, which chiefly have respect to philosophy". But "lest they should have appeared of themselves dry and barren", Newton "illustrated them with some philosophical scholiums, giving an account of such things as are of more general nature, and which philosophy seems chiefly to be founded on", and constructed "the frame of the System of the World".[26] Newton's views became the basis of the mechanical picture of the world.

For a long time, the picture of the world in the natural sciences continued to be defined descriptively, without any conceptualization. In this process, a certain milestone worthy of attention was the creative insight of Friedrich Wilhelm Heinrich Alexander von Humboldt (1769-1859) in his *Essai sur la géographie des plantes* (1805).[27] Based on a geographical approach to botany, his study thoroughly investigated the distribution of plants in the world and presented a scientific world picture of the nature based mainly on empirical methods of research.

In the natural sciences one of the first, if not first, to use the term *"Weltbild"* was the German physicist Heinrich Rudolf Hertz (1857-1894) in his book *The Principles of Mechanics: Represented in a New Form* (1894).[28] He used this term with respect to the physical

[26] Isaac Newton, *A Treatise of the System of the World* (1728; 2d corr. ed.; 1731), pp. v, vi.

[27] A. von Humboldt, *Essay on the Geography of Plants*, transl. Sylvie Romanowski (2009).

[28] Heinrich Hertz, *Die Prinzipien der Mechanik in neuem Zusammenhange dargestellt*

world picture, interpreted by him as a set of internal images or symbols of external objects, the "form which we give them is such that the necessary consequents of the images in thought are always the images of the necessary consequents in nature of the things pictured".[29] The created images must meet three requirements: (1) the permissibility of the image – they must not contradict the laws of our thinking, (2) the correctness of the image – their essential relationships must not contradict the relations of external things, and (3) the appropriateness of the image – they must reflect in addition to the essential properties things, a minimum of superfluous or empty relations, that is, be simpler. Herewith "[e] mpty relations cannot be altogether avoided: they enter into the images because they are simply images, images produced by our mind and necessarily affected by the characteristics of its mode of portrayal".[30]

The simplest picture of the things of the sensible world and the processes occurring in it which physics is able to create, according to Hertz, includes the basic principles of mechanics, from which the whole of mechanics can be derived without reference to experience, together with the principles of a lower rank connecting them. Since it is possible to state the principles of mechanics in different ways, depending on the choice of the positions underlying it, "we can thus obtain various pictures of things", which can be checked and compared with each other in respect of permissibility, correctness, and appropriateness.[31]

The term "world picture" was widely used by Max Planck (1858-1947). In a lecture given at the University of Leiden, 9 December 1908, "Die Einheit des physikalischen Weltbildes", he advocated the construction of a "physical world picture" (*physikalische Weltbild*), understanding by this concept the image of the world formed by physical science and reflecting the real laws of nature. It represented a theoretical model based on experiments. Any scientific picture of the world, according to Planck, has only

(1894), p. 30. There is an English translation: *The Principles of Mechanics: Represented in a New Form*, transl. D. E. Jones and J. T. Walley (1899). In this book, "*Weltbild*" is translated into English as "image of the universe". Ibid., p. 25.

29 Ibid., p. 1.

30 Ibid., p. 2.

31 Ibid., p. 4; Hertz, *Die Prinzipien*, note 28 above, pp. 4-5.

a relative character. He considered the creation of such a world picture, which would be something definitively real and would not need, therefore, any more improvements, an unattainable task.

The scientific picture of the world obtained from experience is a "phenomenological world," which is always only an approximation, a more or less successful model of the real world. According to Planck, "[t]he compound term '*Weltbild*' has only become common for the sake of caution, in order to rule out certain illusions from the outset".[32] In his lecture, "Sinn und Grenzen der exakten Wissenschaft", delivered in November 1941, Planck distinguished between a practical picture and a scientific picture of the world. The practical picture of the world is a holistic view of a person about the world around us, which each of us carries in ourselves in everyday life and which is developed gradually on the basis of our experience. And the scientific picture of the world (or the so-called world of phenomena) is defined as a model of the real world in the absolute sense, independent of individuals and all human thinking.

Both practical and scientific pictures of the world are not final; they are constantly changing and improving. The scientific picture of the world differs from the practical one not in quality, but in its finer structure, relating to the world of everyday life in the same way that the picture of the world of an adult relates to the picture of a child. Although the sensory sensations caused by various objects may not coincide with different people, but

> the picture of the world, the world of things is the same for all people, and it can be said that the transition from the sensory world to the creation of its scientific picture comes on then, when instead of a motley subjective diversity, stable objective order performs, instead of chance – law, instead of changeable visibility – unchanging being.[33]

Albert Einstein (1879-1955) developed the idea that the creation of a world picture is a necessary moment in human vital activity. In his speech on the sixtieth birthday of Max Planck on 26 April 1918,

[32] Max Planck, *Die Einheit des physikalischen Weltbildes* (1909) (available online).

[33] Planck, "Смысл и границы точной науки" [The Meaning and Boundaries of Exact Science], *Вопросы философии* [Questions of Philosophy], no. 5 (1958), pp. 105-106.

in the German Physical Society, entitled "Motives for Research",[34] he outlined his vision of the world picture:

> Man tries to make for himself in the fashion that suits him best a simplified and intelligible picture of the world; he then tries to some extent to substitute this cosmos of his for the world of experience, and thus to overcome it. This is what the painter, the poet, the speculative philosopher, and the natural scientist do, each in his own fashion. Each makes this cosmos and its construction the pivot of his emotional life, in order to find in this way the peace and security which he cannot find in tbe narrow whirlpool of personal experience.[35]

Einstein wonders: what place does the theoretical physicist's picture of the world occupy among all these possible pictures? In his opinion, through the use of mathematical language, this picture satisfies the highest possible standards of rigorous precision in the description of relations. On the other hand, the physicist has to limit himself severely, being content with depicting the simplest phenomena available to our experience, leaving aside all subtle and more complex phenomena. "Does the product of such a modest effort deserve to be called by the proud name '*Weltbild*'?" To this question the Einstein answers in the affirmative. The proud name is well deserved, because the most general laws on which the edifice of theoretical physics is based claim to be valid for every natural phenomenon. From these general laws, by pure logical deduction, one can derive a world picture, that is, a theory of all natural phenomena, including life. Consequently, the rejection of the completeness of the physical picture of the world is not a matter of fundamental principle.[36]

Thus, Einstein's (scientific) picture of the world is a network of general propositions about all natural phenomena, including

[34] Albert Einstein, "Motive des Forschens", in *Zu Max Plancks sechzigstem Geburtstag*, Ansprachen, gehalten am 26. April 1918 in der Deutschen Physikalischen Gesellschaft von E. Warburg, M. v. Laue, A. Sommerfeld und A. Einstein (1918), pp. 29-32. There is an English translation in Diana Kormos Buchwald (ed.), *The Collected Papers of Albert Einstein* (2002), VII, pp. 54-59.

[35] *The Collected Papers of Albert Einstein*, note 34 above, p. 56.

[36] Ibid., pp. 43-44.

life, derived in a pure logical way from the physical picture of the world, i.e. from the general laws of theoretical physics.

As can be seen from the above, Einstein connected the problems of the scientific world picture mainly with the analysis of the physical world picture, not surprising given the leading position of physics in the natural sciences. Despite the fundamental nature of the knowledge gained in physics, the physical picture of the world created on its basis could not be adequate not only in relation to the world as a whole, but also for all natural phenomena.

Volodymyr Ivanovych Vernadsky (1863-1945), a Ukrainian naturalist and historian of science, was among the first to draw attention to this circumstance. He considered that the physical picture of the world ("Cosmos") is merely one way to describe the world. According to Vernadsky, in order to obtain a complete picture of the world around us, which is a huge variety of phenomena, it is necessary to cover many elements, including living things, which cannot be explained by the physical picture of the world. He called such a picture of the world naturalistic ("the world picture of a naturalist"). This representation of the world is "more complex and more close and real for us, which is still closely connected not with the entire Cosmos, but with its part – with our planet"; this is "that representation that every naturalist who studies the descriptive sciences has about the nature around him. A new element that is absent in the constructions of cosmogony, theoretical physics or mechanics – an element of the living, always enters to this representation".[37]

In another work, Vernadsky expands his reflections:

> Separate private phenomena are connected together as parts of one whole, and in the end one picture of the Universe, Cosmos is obtained, which includes the movements of the heavenly luminaries, and the structure of the smallest organisms, the transformations of human societies, historical phenomena, the logical laws of thinking.[38]

There is every reason to believe that in these statements, in fact, we are already talking about the general picture of the

[37] V. I. Vernadsky, Живое вещество [Living Substance] (1978), p. 13.

[38] Vernadsky, Избранные труды по истории науки [Selected Works on the History of Science], ed. and intro. S. R. Mikulinsky (1981), p. 43.

world. Thus, unlike physicists, Vernadsky, not limiting the world picture only to the physical world picture and offering to build a general world picture, made an important contribution to the theory of worldview. Vernadsky also considered the question of the relationship between the scientific worldview and the scientific world picture. The scientific worldview, which exists along with the philosophical worldview,[39] was defined as:

> the representation about phenomena accessible to scientific study, which is given by science; ... a certain attitude to the world of phenomena around us, in which each phenomenon enters in the framework of scientific study and finds an explanation that does not contradict the basic principles of scientific search,[40]

and a scientific picture – as a special form of systematization and synthesis of knowledge received in separate sciences. Thus, the scientific worldview does not include all this knowledge, but only "general provisions connected to the scientific representation about the Cosmos",[41] "part of the representations prevailing at a given time",[42] as well "everything that enters the scientific worldview, one way or another, passes through the crucible of *a scientific attitude to the subject*".[43] Based on these statements, it can be assumed that Vernadsky, unlike those philosophers who completely reduced the world picture to one component of the worldview, considered only the general world picture as a part of the (scientific) worldview.

As for the development of the problems of a special scientific picture of the world in the socio-humanitarian sciences, the roots go back to the linguo-philosophical concept of Wilhelm von Humboldt (1767-1835), Alexander von Humboldt's older brother. He as early as 1801-1802 in his *Fragmente der Monographie über die Basken* noted:

[39] Ibid., p. 51.

[40] Ibid., p. 43.

[41] Ibid., p. 62.

[42] Ibid., p. 67.

[43] Ibid., p. 47.

> Different languages are not just different designations of the same object; they are different visions (*Ansichten*) of it .... Through the diversity of languages, the richness of the world and the diversity of what we recognize in it grows directly for us; at the same time, the scope of human existence expands for us, and new ways of thinking and feeling stand before us in specific and real characters.[44]

From Humboldt's point of view, each language in inseparable unity with consciousness creates a subjective image of the objective world. This idea that there is a special linguistic world vision (*sprachliche Weltansicht*) of the German philologist finds its theoretical justification in the famous report delivered by him in 1820 at the Berlin Academy of Sciences "Ueber das vergleichende Sprachstudium in Beziehung auf die verschiedenen Epochen der Sprachentwicklung",[45] where, based on the concept of *sprachliche Weltansicht,* the principles of comparative linguistics are set out.

Max Weber (1864-1920) initiated the comprehension of the phenomenon of world pictures in "understanding sociology". He claimed that it is not interests (material and ideal), or even ideas, but "the world pictures that were created by these ideas" which dominate human behavior.[46] He showed the connection of socio-cultural types with the world pictures inherent in these types. According to Weber, the three most general types, the three ways of relating to "the world", which comprise the corresponding attitude that predetermines the direction of people's social action, are (1) the Confucian-Taoist type (in China), (2) the Hindu-Buddhist type (in India), and (3) the Judaic-Christian type (which originated in the Middle East and spread to Europe (and later to the Americas). The sociologist defined the first type as adaptation to the world, the second as escape from the world, and the third as mastery of the world. Each contains a corresponding picture of the world.

Unlike representatives of the natural sciences, their colleagues in the socio-humanities sciences were not particularly involved in the conceptualization of world pictures. In the socio-humanities sciences, this concept is in most cases used as a metaphor or

[44] Wilhelm von Humboldt, *Gessamelte Schriften*, ed. Albert Leitzmann (1908), VII, p. 602.

[45] Ibid., IV (1905), pp. 1-34.

[46] Max Weber, *Gesammelte Aufsatze zur Religionssoziologie* (1986), I, p. 252.

studied in different aspects (historical, cultural, psychological, anthropological, and others) without corresponding developments of the concept of the world picture. Even those who have works on the theory of worldview omitted questions related to the world picture. Well-known works by representatives of socio-humanities sciences devoted to the problems of worldview, for example in psychology Sigmund Freud (1856-1939), "The Question of a Weltanschauung" and Carl G. Jung (1875-1961), "Psychotherapy and Weltanschauung",[47] or in sociology Karl Mannheim's (1893-1947), "On the Interpretation of Weltanschauung",[48] or in cultural anthropology Michael Kearney (1937-2009), *Worldview*[49] and Robert Redfield (1897-1958), "The Primitive World View"[50], having made a significant contribution to the development of the concept of "worldview," avoided the problems of the world pictures.

WORLD PICTURE IN ITS INTERRALATIONS WITH WORLDVIEW: SOME GENERALIZATIONS AND PERSPECTIVES

At the turn of the nineteenth and twentieth centuries and in the first half of the twentieth century, the question of the world picture had become the object of philosophical and scientific discourse. Philosophers and scientists, having made an important contribution to the theory of worldview and theoretical comprehension of the concept of the world picture, offered original solutions to the conceptualization of this concept. However, despite the enormous popularity of the concepts of the worldview and the world picture in the philosophical and scientific community, both at the philosophical level and at the scientific level, there is still no clear, generally accepted definition of these concepts, nor

[47] Carl G. Jung, "Psychotherapy and Weltanschauung", *Schweizerische Zeitchrift für Psychologie und ihre Anüendungen*, I, no 3 (1943), pp. 157-164. Translated as "Psychotherapy and Philosophy of Life", in *The Practice of Psychotherapy: Essays on the Psychology of the Transference and Other Subjects*, transl. R. F. C. Hull (2d ed.; 1966), pp. 76-83.

[48] Karl Mannheim, "On the Interpretation of Weltanschauung," in *From Karl Mannheim*, ed. and intro. Kurt H. Wolff (1971), pp. 8-58.

[49] Michael Kearney, *Worldview* (1984).

[50] Robert Redfield, "The Primitive World View", *American Philosophical Society Proceedings*, no. 96 (1952), pp. 30-36.

a clear delineation between them. At the same time, in the views of intellectuals reflecting on the world picture there are common points of contact. Many recognized the existence of an objective and subjective world picture.

The expression objective world picture means a world picture as objective reality; it dominates in a particular culture at a particular epoch, for example, world picture of each epoch of history, world picture of the modern age. The expression subjective world picture means the comprehension of this reality as a world picture in a twofold aspect: (1) as a cognitive construction, as a conceptual comprehension of the very notion of a world picture: its conceptualization, identification of its relationship with the concept of the worldview, determination of its structure and varieties (in this sense it is used in the first section of this article, and in general is the task of this study); (2) as a comprehension of the world picture in historical, intellectual, and cultural-scientific contexts (comprehension of the world picture of some thinker, people, or epochs). Examples of such works are the books of: C. Semler, exploring pictures of the world from the era of the Iliad;[51] E. M. W. Tillyard, describing the world pictures of the Elizabethan era;[52] A. Gurevich, reconstructing the medieval picture of the world;[53] D. Newsome, dedicated to the Victorian world picture;[54] J. Wamberg, tracing cultural evolution in images from the Paleolithic Period to the Middle Ages, and the early modern period'[55] articles of: W. K. C. Guthrie, dedicated to the Pre-Socratic world-picture;[56] and B. Kölver, exploring the early stages in the world picture evolution of Indian tradition.[57]

51 C. Semler, *Das Weltbild der Ilias und seine Bedeutung für unsere Zeit* (1885).

52 E. M. W. Tillyard, *The Elizabethan World Picture. A Study of the Idea of Order in the Age of Shakespeare* (1943).

53 A. Gurjewitsch, *Das Weltbild des mittelalterlichen* (1978); transl. as Aron Gurevich, *Categories of Medieval Culture*, transl. G. L. Campbell (1985).

54 David Newsome, *The Victorian World Picture: Perceptions and Introspections in an Age of Change* (1997).

55 Jacob Wamberg, *Landscape as World Picture. Tracing Cultural Evolution in Images*, transl. Gaye Kynoch (2009). 2 vols.

56 W. K. C. Guthrie, "The Pre-Socratic World-Picture," *Harvard Theological Review*, XLV, no. 2 (1952), pp. 87-104.

57 Bernhard Kölver, "Stages in the Evolution of a World Picture", *Numen*, XXXII, no. 2 (December 1985), pp. 131-168.

The objectivity of the world picture does not mean a purely objective construction, since "the subject cannot be excluded from the world"[58] picture. It includes carriers with their inherent internal subjective experiences, with their subjective views on the world around them.[59] Likewise, a subjective world picture is not a purely subjective construction, because the knowing subject, although approaching the "world" from his own point of view, comprehends the model of objective reality, which has objective carriers, empirically detectable facts that provide material for knowledge.[60] Thus, neither the objectivity of the world picture nor the subjectivity of the world picture should be absolutized.

Summarizing the experience with the conceptualization of the world picture, it may be noted both philosophers and scientists proposed different meanings of the concept of the world picture. For the sake of clarity, we list the following authoritative definitions are (not exhaustive):

- Dilthey: a depiction of reality, a set of concepts and judgments;
- Heidegger: the world conceived and grasped as a picture; the collective image of representing production;
- Jaspers: the whole of the objective mental content an individual possesses;
- Spengler: a comprehensive model of reality;
- Wittgenstein: "way of seeing" the world;
- Hertz: a set of internal images or symbols of external objects;
- Planck: the image of the world, formed by physical science and reflecting the real laws of nature; a theoretical model based on experiment;

[58] See D. Aerts, L. Apostel, B. de Moor, S. Hellemans, E. Maex, H. Van Belle, and J. van der Veken, *Worldviews: From Fragmentation to Integration* (1994).

[59] Proceeding from phenomenological sociology, "legal reality should be perceived not as external to a person reality (the subject of its comprehension), but as such, in which it itself is involved in the process of communicating with other participants of legal life". S. I. Maksymov, "What is Law? Key Points of the Concept of Legal Reality", in O. V. Petryshyn (ed.), *Щорічник українського права* [Yearbook of Ukrainian Law], no. 10 (2018), p. 53.

[60] See note 58 above.

- Einstein: a network of general propositions, derived in a pure logical way;
- Vernadsky: the ways to describe the world, a special form of systematization and synthesis of knowledge obtained in separate sciences.

Comparing and synthesizing these heterogeneous definitions, and identifying common elements and contradictions in them, allows the following three meanings of the world picture concept to be singled out:

- way of seeing, depicting the world (in this meaning it coincides with the worldview);
- images, symbols or theoretical models of the world, a set of concepts, judgments, general propositions;
- a special form of systematization and synthesis of knowledge obtained in separate sciences.

These meanings of the world picture concept will be taken into account when conceptualizing the legal world picture below.

Standing on the shoulders of giants, we turn to the present writer's vision of the relationship between the worldview and the world picture. Generalization of various understandings on this issue allows us to state that some defined the world picture without reference to worldview (Planck and Einstein), whereas others solved this issue in two aspects:

(1) *a world picture as a synonym of a worldview* (they are identified); they are understood as a comprehensive model of reality: either they completely coincide (as, for example, in Spengler), or the world picture takes place of the worldview (as in late Wittgenstein);

(2) *a picture of the world as a component of a worldview* (as, for example, in Dilthey, Jaspers and Vernadsky); in this case, the concept of worldview is broader than the concept of a picture of the world, and the latter occupies only one (metaphysical) part of the former, expressing general provisions connected to the system-structural characteristics of the world, obtained at a certain stage of historical development.

Undoubtedly, worldview and world picture are not the same thing. Their identification is incorrect, since the picture of the world coincides with the worldview only partially, in one of its layers.

Various types of both worldview and world picture are distinguished. However, for our purposes, their rational types are of interest, which are the scientific and the philosophical world pictures. Generally speaking, the scientific picture of the world is an integrative system of ideas about the world, initial assumptions of its vision, elaborated by science on the basis of worldview and systematization of the whole corpus of scientific knowledge. A philosophically comprehended and justified scientific world picture becomes a philosophical world picture that is a component of the philosophical worldview together with beliefs, values, and paradigms. The philosophical world picture (at the same time a general world picture), reflecting the world in extremely general, philosophically significant, concepts, categories, propositions, and assumptions, speculatively abstract in nature, is in the domain of philosophy. The latter builds the general world picture on the basis of the conclusions of all sciences by linking them into a consistent and complete system.

It is generally accepted to distinguish the following levels of the scientific world picture: general scientific world picture, natural-scientific world picture, social-humanitarian scientific world picture, and special (or local) scientific world pictures (within particular sciences). The general scientific world picture contains general ideas about the world (about nature, society, and man) and is formed as a result of synthesis of knowledge obtained in various sciences. It occupies an intermediate position between philosophy and science(s). Part of the general scientific world picture, including ideas about nature, the structure and development of nature, is usually called the natural-scientific picture of the world, and the other part of the general scientific picture, consisting of ideas about society and man – the socio-humanitarian scientific picture of the world. The lower level in this hierarchy is occupied by special scientific world pictures, which are confined to specific spheres that constitute the subject matter of the corresponding science.

Thus, the author's vision of the interrelations between the worldview and the world picture, and hierarchical background of the world picture at all can be graphically depicted as in the following figure.

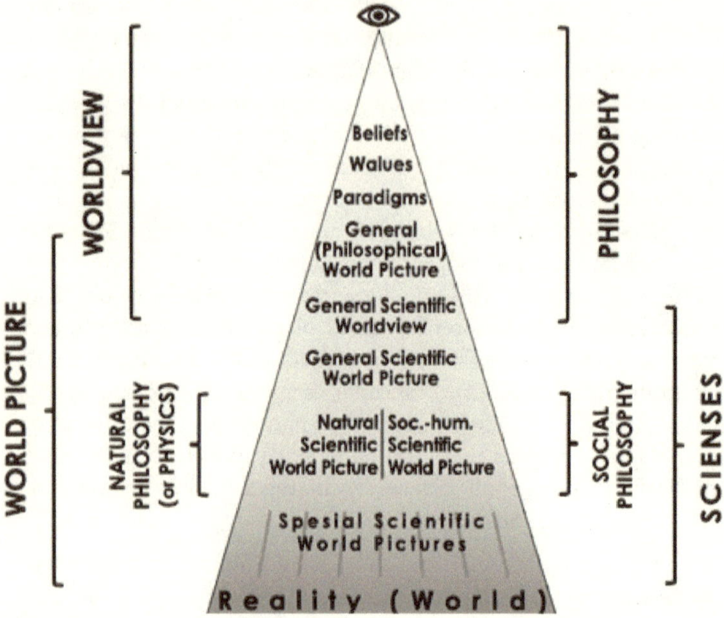

Note: Any graphic depiction allows for certain inaccuracies. The presented graphic depiction is no exception. Some inaccuracies are related to the fact that the graphic depiction reflects not only the structure of the world picture, but its connections with the worldview, and the structure and levels of the worldview and the world picture do not always coincide. And others are related to the complex relationships between philosophy and science. In the figure, natural philosophy and social philosophy are shown to be divorced from general philosophy, and so on.

THE LEGAL WORLD PICTURE: CONCEPTUAL FRAMEWORK

The next step in conceptualizing the legal world picture is a preliminary clarification of the possible distinctions and meanings of certain concepts.

Possible Interpretations of Concept of Legal World Picture: *Legal Picture* of the World or Picture of the *Legal World*?

When applying the concept of "world picture" to the legal realm, a natural and logical question arises: what is emphasized by the word "legal" in the expression "legal world picture". Does it refer to the picture or to the world? There are two possible options, which are included in the title of this subsection: (1) *legal picture* of the world or (2) picture of the *legal world*. Whereas in the first case the emphasis is on a special (legal) prism for seeing the world as a whole, then in the second case – on a special world, as a relatively detached part of the world as a whole. Indeed, does the law have a special, only his inherent prism to see the world as a whole, as is the case, for example, of philosophy?

The general world picture views the world as whole. Such autonomous spheres of social consciousness as mythology, religion, philosophy, art, and science (in general) have their own special prisms through which a person sees the world as whole. Consequently, the result of their worldview is the corresponding world picture – mythological, religious, philosophical, artistic, and scientific (some scientists include the linguistic picture of the world). All reflect the world as a whole through a special prism. But specialized branches of human activity, particular sciences, do not have a special prism reflecting the world as a whole, because these sciences focus on a limited aspect of reality. None of the world pictures developed within the framework of particular sciences reflects the world as a whole. Even physics, which claims to have a certain degree of generality, despite the unsuccessful attempts of physicists to extend the physical picture of the world to the whole world, could not (and cannot) offer a unified picture of the world.

Legal science is no exception. In the discourse of physics, reflecting the world through its special prism, all phenomena of the social world remain beyond the boundaries of knowledge, including goodness, happiness, dignity, justice, law-abidingness and similar phenomena; in the discourse of legal science, in its special prism of reflection of the studied world there is no place for natural phenomena. Therefore, legal science cannot embrace the world as a whole and is limited to its legal aspect, called the legal world. Consequently, the expression "legal world picture" should be taken as a *picture* of the *legal world*.

Concept of "Legal World" ("World of Law"): Review of Literature

In everyday and professional life, the concepts of "legal world" and "world of law" are often used metaphorically to refer to everything related to law. In special legal literature, both variants are used for different purposes and contexts: to characterize the legal perceptions of individual thinkers, certain peoples, and various social groups,[61] when interpreting certain historical epochs in historico-legal works,[62] as well as in studies on law and legal practice,[63] and others.

In such works, the said concepts are usually fixed "ostensively", that is, through the description of relevant situations or examples, without thinking about the constructs themselves. Various

[61] See Joan I. Schwarz, "Oliver Wendell Holmes's '*The Path of the Law*': Conflicting Views of the Legal World", *American Journal of Legal History*. XXIX, no. 3 (1985),pp. 235-50; David W. Louisell, "The Psychologist in Today's Legal World", *Minnesota Law Review*. XXXIX, no. 3 (1955), pp. 235-272; Ambreena S. Manji, "Imagining Women's 'Legal World': Towards a Feminist Theory of Legal Pluralism in Africa", *Social & Legal Studies*, VIII (1999), pp. 435-455; Anna-Maria Marshall and Scott Barclay, "In Their Own Words: How Ordinary People Construct the Legal World", *Law and Social Inquiry*, XXVIII (2003), pp. 617-628; Franklin E. Zimring, *The Changing Legal World of Adolescence* (2014); Stephen L. Wasbi, "The World of Law Clerks: Tasks, Uilization, Reliance, and Influence", *Marquette Law Review*, XCVIII (2014), pp. 111-130.

[62] See David A. Bell, "The 'Public Sphere,' the State, and the World of Law in Eighteenth-Century France", *French Historical Studies*, XVII (1992), pp. 912-934; Andrew M. Riggsby, *Roman Law and the Legal World of the Romans* (2010); Virginia Amorosi and Valerio Massimo Minale (eds.), *History of Law and Other Humanities: Views of the Legal World Across the Time* (2019).

[63] See Ephraim London (ed.), *The World of Law* (1960). 2 vols: 1: The Law in Literature; 2: The Law as the Literature; Niklas Luhmann, *Closure and Openness: On Reality in the World of Law* (1986), pp. 1-29 (EUI Working Paper No 86/234); Ernest Caparros, "Some Myths and Some Realities in the Contemporary World of Law", *American Journal of Jurisprudence*, XXXV, no. 1 (1990), pp. 87-104; Morris L. Cohen, "Research in a Changing World of Law and Technology", *Dalhousie Law Journal*, XIII (1990), pp. 5-19; Howard Turtle, "Text Retrieval in The Legal World". *Artificial Intelligence and Law*, no. 3 (1995), pp. 5-54; 1999 Charles L. Brieant, "Is It the End of the Legal World as We Know It?", *Pace Law Review*, XX (1999), pp. 21-31; Ossie Davis, "The Wonderful World of Law and Order", in Deborah J. Morad (ed.), *Children's Literature Review* (2000), LVI (available online); originally published in *Anger, and Beyond: The Negro Writer in the United States* (1966), pp. 154-180); John R. Reed, "Laws, the Legal World, and Politics", in Patrick Brantlinger and William B. Thesing (eds.), *A Companion to the Victorian Novel* (2002), pp. 156-171; R. van Gestel, H.-W. Micklitz, and M. Poiares Maduro, *Methodology in the New Legal World* (2012/13), pp. 1-23 (EUI Working Paper LAW, European University Institute Badia Fiesolana); D. Fassin, *The Moral World of Law Enforcement* (2013); William van Caenegem, "Ignoring the Civil Law/Common Law Divide in an Integrated Legal World", in William van Caenegem and Mary Hiscock (eds.), *The Internationalization of Legal Education* (2014), pp. 145-172; Ellen Ott Marshall, "Theological Humility in The World of Law", *Journal of Law and Religion*, XXXII, no. 1 (2017), pp. 93-97; Howard Lesnick, "Personal Fulfillment in the Changing World of Law Practice: Opportunities and Obstacles", *Temple Law Review*, no. 72 (1999), pp. 1011-1017.

meanings are attributed to them. This circumstance is well demonstrated by Andrew M. Riggsby:

> I use the phrase "legal World" to bring together a number of different things. On the one hand, it includes the law roughly as it was understood by the Romans themselves. This kind of "law" has been used and studied almost continuously from Roman times. What rights and responsibilities were assigned by the laws? What procedures could be used to enforce these substantive rules? Now, somewhat more practically, should or could you act in various situations to take advantage of the law (or at least to make sure you weren't tripped up by it)? But on the other hand, I also want to take into account the various ways in which the law interacted with the rest of the social world. How could actual people get access to the legal system? How much difference did various kinds of individual identity (age, sex, nationality, economic class, social status, ets.) make in legal matters? What kinds of cultural and economic values did the law support or assume? How much voluntary cooperation did the legal system assume or receive from individuals? How did the lawmaking and law-enforcing processes fit into the government more broadly?[64]

Along with the aforementioned circumstance, it should be noted that conceptual analysis of the concept discussed here is not completely absent. In the specialized literature, three positions on comprehension of the phenomenon of the legal world are presented: two monistic and one pluralistic. Let us dwell on them.

Positivist approach to the world of law developed by Jaap Hage. He delineates "a picture of legislation as a kind of legal transaction by means of which the world of law is (re)built", changed, and modified[65] and suggests a view of the world of law "as a specialized, institutionalized part of social reality". Following the Wittgenstein approach to the world as the collection of all facts, Hage defines the world of law as "the collection of all legal facts, where legal facts are those facts which are the result of the application of legal

[64] Riggsby, note 62 above, pp. 5-6.

[65] Jaap Hage, "Building the World of Law", *Legisprudence*, 1, no. 3 (2007), p. 359.

rules".[66] Into the ontological structure of the world of law in a broad sense, according to the author, enters "everything the existence of which is based on the application of legal rules. This includes real estate, mayors, cars, but also certain kinds of events, acts, states of affairs and rules".[67] In another work, Hage defines the structure of the world of law as "all the facts, rules and other entities that exist through the application of legal rules", "rule-based facts (and individuals), and most of these facts derive their relevance from legal rules which attach consequences to them".[68]

The idea of a legal world was the subject matter of an article by Michael Salter.[69] Although the main purpose of his work is to elucidate a series of possible differences and meanings of the legal world that can be used to make sense of the idea of lawyers belonging to this "world", of interest are some aspects of the author's understanding of the legal world, which, while avoiding traditional dichotomies (for example, subjective/objective), rejecting the model proposed by the positivist tradition, especially the behavioral paradigm, instead proposes a *phenomenological approach* to the legal world, that assumes the legal realm as a "life-world". From Salter's point of view, "our legal realm is set up in such a way as to amount to its own characteristic 'world', one whose vocabulary, symbolism, rituals, theatrical contests and modes of interpretation are quite distinct from other social worlds, especially the everyday world of the lay person".[70] Instead of treating the legal realm as an autonomous realm of formal rules, or as a socio-economically determined "effect" of "external contextual determinants", Salter deems necessary "to consider it in terms of reciprocal mediation between the interpretative horizons of a diversity of different social worlds". Among the various senses of the expression of the legal world, the Salter distinguishes the following: (1) as a particular mode of social existence; (2) as

[66] Ibid., p. 362.

[67] Hage, "A Model of Legal Acts: Part 1: The World of Law," *Artificial Intelligence and Law*, XIX, no. 1 (March 2011), p. 33.

[68] Hage, "The (Onto)logical Structure of Law: A Conceptual Toolkit for Legislators", in M. Araszkiewicz and K. Płeszka (eds.), *Logic in the Theory and Practice of Lawmaking* (2015), p. 35.

[69] Michael Salter, "On the Idea of a Legal World," *International Journal of the Legal Profession*, 1 (1994), pp. 283-310.

[70] Ibid., p. 283.

a specific "space" with intangible cultural borders; (3) as an immanent subjective milieu situating all practice; (4) as a milieu that has a social or "intersubjective" quality.[71]

Sergey Maksymov proposes a *pluralistic, integrative* conception of legal reality, also including ideas about the nature, foundations, structure of the complex world of law. In explaining his concept, Maksymov proceeds from the distinction in the legal discourse between the broad and narrow meanings of the concept of "legal reality": in the first case, as the entire set of legal phenomena, in the second – as the basic legal phenomenon: legal norms and institutions for legal positivism, legal relations for sociological jurisprudence, and legal consciousness (as reality of meanings) for the theory of natural law and the psychological conception of law. Maksymov himself suggests "an "integral" concept of legal reality as the world of law which is constructed from legal phenomena, ordered according to their belonging to the basic phenomenon "as a kind of 'primary reality' (own reality) of law".[72] He distinguishes "legal reality as an objectively existing world of law, given to an individual in practical life, and a picture of legal reality as a model of legal reality, serving as a means of cognition and construction of the world of law".[73]

Based on the methodological principles of pluralism and contradictions in the (dynamic) structure of legal reality, Maksymov distinguishes the following relatively autonomous layers, or levels (the forms of law being, or world of law): "(a) the world of ideas (the idea of law); (b) the world of symbolic forms (legal norms and laws); (c) the world of social interactions (legal life). ... The unity of these layers represents law, or legal reality".[74] According the author, such a division is traditional and generally analogous (although not completely identical) to the division into such forms of the being of law as legal consciousness, legal norms, and legal relations.

[71] Ibid., pp. 285-300.

[72] S. I. Maksymov, Правовая реальность: опыт философского осмысления [Legal Reality: Experience of Philosophical Comprehension] (2002), p. 148; id., "What is Law? note 59 above, p. 54.

[73] Maksymov, note 72 above, p. 147.

[74] Ibid., p. 177.

The three-tiered structure of the world of law in Maksymov's conception is reminiscent of Popper's "three worlds" (the existence of the physical world, mental world, and the world of ideas), but this is a superficial resemblance. Maksymov notes the possibility of comparing them (since "the status of legal reality in its reliability is similar to the status of the reality of logical and mathematical truths") and even including the world of law in Popper's "third world" – the world of ideas in general. But he also notes that "law has a nature close to the nature of moral reality. What is common to both law and morality is obligation [ought]. Therefore, the legal world is not a reality of the sensually perceived world, not a world of mental states, but a deontological reality".[75]

Of the above approaches, the integrative is the most adequate and suitable for our purpose – the purpose of conceptualization and further comprehension of the legal picture of the world, because this approach contains the opportunity to see the legal world as a complex multi-level system consisting of relatively autonomous subsystems, and allows to put in order all legal phenomena, so to speak, "on the shelves", thereby meeting the requirement a systemic nature of picture of the world, noted by Heidegger.

Concepts of "Legal World Picture" and "Legal World Map"

In the legal literature in general, and in comparative legal literature especially, to refer to broad legal spaces, scholars along with "picture" often freely use such spatial metaphors as "panorama", "map", "landscape", "empire", and others. At the same time, in comparative jurisprudence, the study of the legal world picture most often comes down to legal mapping.

According to one authoritative definition, by "mapping law" is meant all "attempts to construct overviews or total pictures of law in the world as a whole" – "sometimes figuratively, but sometimes quite literally by producing geographical maps".[76] In comparative jurisprudence, it is precisely this literal understanding of "mapping law" that prevails. Sometimes this narrow mission (creating a legal world map) is considered the subject matter of a comparative legal discipline, especially typical for some legal scholars in the post-

[75] Ibid., p. 153.

[76] William Twining, *General Jurisprudence Understanding Law from a Global Perspective* (2009), p. 67.

Soviet space.[77] In this case, there is a substitution of the subject-matter of research with the methodological tool of its research, which ultimately leads to dogmatism. Wittgenstein accused Spengler of exactly such a mistake, for the latter confused his research model (the picture of the organism) with the object under study (culture).

John Henry Wigmore (1863-1943), who first wrote about the legal map of the world,[78] took a completely different approach to this issue. He presented a "world-map of present-day legal systems" in the form of an Appendix[79] and accompanied it with the following comments:

> Since the world's legal systems can be identified in area, and are limited in number, the study of them would be assisted by a map showing the areas of the world's surface covered by the respective systems. Changes at successive periods could and should be shown by a series of period-maps (as is done for the history of national and dynastic boundaries). But here, for a first attempt, will be offered only a map of the present-day period.[80]

Thus, for Wigmore, the legal map of the world was only a means, but not the main subject matter of research, and rightly so. Nevertheless, the possibility of drawing maps of law should not be entirely excluded, as Gordon Woodman does, referring to the complexity, variability and specificity of legal systems;[81]

[77] See A. Saidov, Сравнительное правоведение (основные правовые системы современности) [Comparative Jurisprudence (Major Legal Systems of Contemporaneity)], ed. V. A. Tumanov (2003), pp. 114, 116.

[78] In comparative legal literature, the introduction of the concept of "legal world map" is mistakenly ascribed to the Russian scientist V.A. Tumanov (Saidov, note 77 above, p. 119). Tumanov used this term in the preface of the Russian edition of the Rene David's book only in the 1970s. See: V. Tumanov, "Preface," in R. David, Основные правовые системы современности (сравнительное право) [Major Legal Systems of Contemporaneity (Comparative Law)], transl. M. A. Krutogolov and V. A. Tumanov (1967), pp. 5-20.

[79] John Henry Wigmore, *A Panorama of the World's Legal Systems* (1936), pp. 1144-1146. The 1928 edition, in three volumes in pre-depression United States, was reissued in an economical one-volume version in 1936.

[80] Ibid., p. 1133.

[81] G. R. Woodman, "Why There Can be No Map of Law", in R. Pradhan (ed.), *Legal Pluralism and Unofficial Law in Social, Economic and Political Development* (2003), III, pp. 383-392 (Papers of the XIIIth International Congress of the Commission on Folk Law and Legal Pluralism, 7–10 April 2002, Chiang Mai, Thailand).

on the contrary, a comparatist will find them useful didactically and scientifically as a tool of study and analysis to help orientate the teeming waters of the diversity of contemporary legal world. However, a legal map of the world and a legal world picture are not the same thing; drawing maps of law cannot replace the creation of a comprehensive legal world picture.

LEGAL WORLD PICTURE AS BASIC CONCEPT OF LEGAL SCIENCE

Definition of Legal World Picture

It is now appropriate to turn offer the author's definition of the legal world picture. If the conclusions above in relation to the concept of the world picture in general are extrapolated to the legal world picture, and one proceeds from the conceptual frameworks of the legal world picture outlined in the previous section, we can distinguish narrow and broad concepts of the legal world picture and provide the following definitions.

Legal world picture in the narrow sense is an image of the legal world containing the most general, essential, and significant representations and assumptions about the arrangement of the legal world based on a comprehension of this world as objective reality and serving as a means of cognition and construction of the legal world.

Legal world picture in the broad sense is a comprehensive vision of the legal world expressed in theoretical models of the legal world, in a set of concepts, judgments, or provisions connected to the systemic and structural characteristics of the legal world, developed on the basis of the systematization, generalization, synthesis, and integration of knowledge obtained in separate legal disciplines at a given time.

The definition of legal world picture can be further clarified by answering the questions negatively: what the legal world picture is not?

First, legal science studies a separate sphere of being – the legal world – and creates pictures of it, not of the world as a whole.

Second, the legal world picture is not the result of a simple fixation of certain facts of the legal world, and cannot be replaced by simple mapping; in other words, with maps "showing the areas of the world's surface covered by the respective systems" (Wigmore). Creating a holistic legal world picture is a more complex procedure than creating legal maps.

Third, the legal world picture, although it is knowledge about the legal world as a whole, is not the totality, the simple sum of all available knowledge about the legal world. When a legal researcher identifies new facts, comes to new conclusions in his field, and, integrating all current scientific knowledge, seeks to link them in a consistent manner with all the knowledge of his field, he builds a picture of the legal world, forms a comprehensive view of the legal world, a view of this world through the created model.

Legal World Picture as an İnterdisiplinary Enterprise

Interdisciplinary research is carried out, first, on such an objective basis that in the reality itself, by the nature of things themselves, there are close links, certain similarities of the subject areas under study, due to which "overlapping" problems and/or boundary and complex objects are formed, which are in the intellectual field of different sciences.[82] According to one authoritative definition, interdisciplinary study is "a process of answering a question, solving a problem, or addressing a topic that is too broad or complex to be dealt with adequately by a single discipline or profession".[83] Thus, an important criterion of interdisciplinarity is multi-faceted or complexity objects of knowledge or problems.

The legal world is just such a complex, multi-faceted object because it covers the entire legal space, includes all legal phenomena without exception, embraces the full multiplicity of law. And the legal world, along with the complexity of its structure, as a subsystem of the societal system has close ties with other social worlds. Consequently, the legal world picture should be studied taking into account the complexity of the structure

[82] M. A. Damirli, "Междисциплинарность в исследовании права" [Interdisciplinarity in the Study of Law], in Розвиток методології сучасної юриспруденції [Development of the Methodology of Modern Jurisprudence] (2015), pp. 26-34; id., Сравнительное исламское право: введение в теорию и методологию [Comparative Islamic Law: An Introduction to Theory and Methodology] (2017), pp. 154-158.

[83] J. Klein, and W. Newell, "Advancing Interdisciplinary Studies", in J. Gaff and J. Ratcliffe (eds.), *Handbook of the Undergraduate Curriculum: A Comprehensive Guide to Purposes, Structures, Practices, and Changes* (1997), p. 393.

and said connections of the legal world, in a broad socio-cultural context.

Functions of The Legal World Picture

The legal world picture as a fundamental construct of legal science has important cognitive significance, which is most fully revealed in its functions. As follows from the above proposed definition, the legal world picture has various functions in legal cognition, among which the following can be highlighted:

(1) knowledge systematization function.

It is through systematization that a reasonable order is introduced into the disorderly variety of knowledge about legal phenomena obtained by various legal and non-legal sciences, by applying certain techniques and principles (for example, classification).

(2) synthetic (integrative) function.

The essence of this function is the synthesis (integration) of fragmentary or unrelated ideas, concepts, and theories, in order to ensure the receipt of integral knowledge of the world of law.

(3) knowledge generalization function.

This function consists in the development of legal concepts, categories, generalized knowledge about the world, conceptions, models, and others.

(4) methodological (or paradigmatic) function.

According to this function, the legal world picture acts as a standard for the acquisition of scientific knowledge, methodological tool (paradigm, research program, conceptual schema) that directs the formulation of empirical and theoretical tasks, as well as the choice of means for solving them.

(5) prognostic function.

This function serves to obtain advanced information about the legal world, is most clearly manifested in the foresight of certain changes in legal reality, in the determination of trends in legal development, in the advancement of hypotheses about the future of the world of law.

EPISTEMOLOGICAL-METHODOLOGICAL PROBLEMS OF CONSTRUCTING A LEGAL WORLD PICTURE

Constructing a Legal World Picture and Legal Theories: Need for an Integrative Approach

The legal world picture as a model reflecting objective legal reality cannot be identified either with the world of law itself and simple knowledge about it, or with legal theories dealing with conceptual understandings of the law (theories of legal understanding). The legal world picture, although it is a special component of theoretical legal knowledge, but at the same time differs from concrete legal theories. Any specific legal theory represents only a separate aspect of the manifestation of multifaceted legal reality. Legal theories in accordance with its purposes, unlike legal disciplines, express concepts of law that are true from their point of view; they believe that they themselves most appropriately and best understand the law.

The legal world picture becomes subject to different legal theories. Each draws the legal world picture from their own perspective. In other words, there are as many ways to depict the legal world as there are legal theories. Whatever concrete legal theory we take as a basis, a one-sided legal world picture will appear before our eyes. In other words, when proceeding from different theories we will come across various one-sided legal world pictures. Whereas the legal world, as already noted above, is multidimensional. Consequently, the construction of its comprehensive picture requires a synthesis of the propositions of all legal theories, their integration. Therefore, the integrative approach is the most adequate and suitable methodological tool for purpose comprehension and construction of the legal world picture.

As for the criticism of the integrative approach in the literature for the external eclectic compound of the possibilities of different theories (approaches), given the absence of a methodological and logical basis, we addressed the unfoundedness of this kind of criticism in a previously published article and presented the logical-ontological and logical-methodological underpinnings of the integrative approach in the light of fuzzy logic.[84]

Constructing a Legal World Picture: Cognition Levels, Aspects and Role of Separate Legal Disciplines

Many consider the creation of a comprehensive legal world picture as the task of comparative jurisprudence. Only William Twining's view differs from this widespread view. So, according to Twining, "building an accurate and coherent picture of law in the world is a central task of general jurisprudence".[85]

Unlike dogmatic legal disciplines developing within national boundaries, comparative jurisprudence does not suffer from a way of thinking limited by the scale of national legal systems; on the contrary, it deals with a holistic vision of the subject of legal science as a whole. This circumstance makes the position of comparative jurisprudence advantageous in the comprehension of the legal world picture. Another question is how successfully it is fulfilling this mission (see below).

Comparative legal science has rich potential for constructing a comprehensive picture of the legal world. Nonetheless, one cannot absolutize its role. It would also be wrong to absolutize the role of either the general theory of law or any other discipline. This is the mission of all legal science. Moreover, above-mentioned characteristics of the legal world picture as an interdisciplinary enterprise require interdisciplinary integration, close interdisciplinary links, drawing on the perspectives of both all legal and extra-legal disciplines, and ultimately integration of their insights by building of a more comprehensive perspective. Legal science will become integrative and synthesizing to achieve the goal of constructing a holistic picture of the legal world only if legal scholars learn to take into account the insights of representatives of other social sciences; moreover, legal disciplines, just as all other disciplines, do not have a monopoly on the field of study. Thus, to form a truly multidimensional understanding of the world

[84] Mehman A. Damirli, "Integrative Jurisprudence from Fuzzy Logic Perspective", in R. A. Aliev, et al. (eds.), *14th International Conference on Theory and Application of Fuzzy Systems and Soft Computing – ICAFS-2020. Advances in Intelligent Systems and Computing* (2020), MCCCVI, pp. 198-205.

[85] William Twining, *Globalisation and Legal Theory* (2000), p. 177.

of law, to create a comprehensive picture of the legal world, the legal world picture should be developed not by just one scientific discipline; it is necessary to bring together deeply disparate legal disciplines and extra-legal disciplines, "and perhaps even to use them for purposes for which they were not originally developed".[86]

Although the legal world picture is included in the field of study of different disciplines, each discipline will look at the legal world from a certain point of view, and they will draw the picture of this world in terms of its own purpose and method. This can contribute to creation of a more embossed picture, thus adding richness to this picture. Unlike legal theories, legal disciplines are not mutually exclusive, they can stand side by side and at the same maintain close interdisciplinary connections.

In the creation of a comprehensive legal world picture, three levels of cognition can be distinguished. If we take as a basis the movement of thinking from the concrete to the abstract, they can be ranked as follows: at its lowest level is the empirical level, middle level – the level of theoretical comprehension, and at the top of the triad – the metatheoretical level (level of philosophical reflection). At the empirical level, we are dealing with a study based on the collection and initial generalization of empirical data on the phenomena of the world of law. At the theoretical level, we are talking about research, in the course of which a deep theoretical generalization of the available factual material is carried out, the processes of scientific explanation and understanding through abstract thinking take place. Abstractions, in turn, come in different levels of generalization. The higher the level to which the researcher goes, the more abstract the picture of legal reality he recreates becomes. The highest level here is represented by the metatheoretical level (level of philosophical reflection).

It should also be noted that the substantive separation of the empirical, theoretical, and metatheoretical levels does not at all mean the establishment of clear boundaries between them. Although these levels have relative independence, but they are internally interrelated in the process of functioning and development of scientific knowledge as a whole; "both empirical and theoretical are always present, and one can only speak of the

[86] Note 58 above.

predominance of one or the other in scientific knowledge".[87] Thus, we can only talk about the conditionality of the demarcation line between indicated levels.

There is a certain correlation between the above-mentioned levels of cognition and separate aspects of the legal world picture, as well as aspects its cognition. Among these aspects the following can be distinguished:

(1) legal world picture as a way of seeing, depicting the legal world;

(2) legal world picture as the images or symbols of the legal world;

(3) legal world picture as a theoretical model of the legal world;

(4) legal world picture as a set of concepts, judgments, general propositions regarding the legal world;

(5) generalizations in the form of typologies and classifications of the legal systems;

(6) generalization of the intersystem legal interactions and mutual influences;

(7) pictures of separate branches of law in a world scale;

(8) provision of empirical material for creation a legal world picture.

Each listed aspect, in turn, is in the domain of various legal scientific disciplines. Thus, correlation between the levels of cognition, separate aspects of the legal world picture, and legal scientific disciplines can be formulated as follows:

1. At the level of metatheoretical, philosophical reflection, the legal world picture as a way of seeing the legal world and as the images or symbols of the legal world are included in the domain of philosophy of law.

2. At the level of theoretical comprehension:

(a) the elaboration of theoretical model of the legal world and establishment of a set of concepts, judgments, general propositions

[87] Damirli, Право и История: эпистемологические проблемы [Law and History: Epistemological Problems] (2002), pp. 291-292.

regarding the legal world are carried out by the general theory of law;

(b) the making of generalizations in the form of typologies and classifications of the legal systems and the elaboration of the theory of intersystem legal interactions and mutual influences are carried out by the comparative theory of law or comparative legal theory (which is a special theoretical comparative legal discipline that arises at the intersection of the general theory of law and comparative law);[88]

(c) creating pictures of separate branches of law on a world scale is the task of branches of comparative law (comparative constitutional law, comparative civil law, etc.).

3. Provision of empirical material for creation a legal world picture is performed by all other legal disciplines.

The same correlation can be graphically depicted as follows:

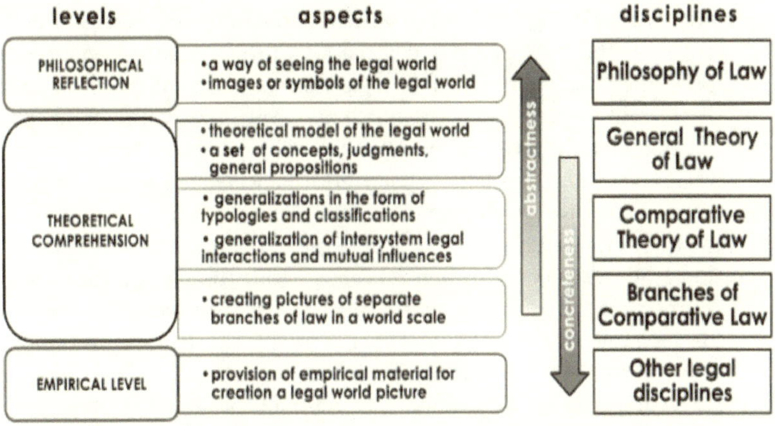

Comparative Jurisprudence and Problems of Constructing a Legal World Picture

Criticism of comparative jurisprudence has intensified over the past decades on various grounds: for being Western-oriented, Eurocentrism, black-letter-law, private-law-oriented and so

[88] Damirli, Сравнительное правоведение: Ч. 1. Статус, предмет и система [Comparative Jurisprudence: Part 1. Status, Subject and System] (2013), I, pp. 119-125.

on.[89] Among the latter, the tendency to focus on rules ("black letter rules") occupies a special place. At best, legal systems are compared only in terms of such characteristics as the sources of law, the structure of the legal system, and legal institutions. Deeper layers of the legal system, such as legal culture, legal thinking, legal mentality, and others, that deserve to become promising areas of comparative studies, remain outside the attention of researchers. Also overlooked is that "rules cannot be fully understood isolated from their legal and non-legal context".[90] Without taking into account these important considerations in comparative legal research, it will be impossible to reach, as Mark Van Hoecke put it, a deep level.

In the context of the above, among the problems of comparative legal science related to the construction of a comprehensive legal world picture, we focus attention on the following.

One main problem in comparative jurisprudence regarding to the constructing a legal world picture is that of the three structural elements of the legal world described in the previous pages of this work, at the present time, comparative jurisprudence is mainly concerned with the world of legal norms, and a little less with the world of socio-legal interactions, while the world of legal ideas generally received no attention. This leads, in turn, to an incomplete picture of the legal world. Especially if we take into account that the world picture is a world of subjective reflection of the surrounding reality, a generalized representation, some integrative system of representations about the world, then the connection between the world picture and the world of ideas becomes even more obvious. That is why this shortcoming must be corrected as soon as possible. Moreover, when studying the world of legal ideas, the focus should be on both the study of the legal thoughts of the "highbrows", that is, the professional-elite level, and the ordinary-mass level.

[89] See Ugo Mattei, "Patterns of Law: Taxonomy and Change in the World's Legal Systems", *American Journal of Comparative Law*, XLV (1997), pp. 5-44; H. Patrick Glenn, "Comparative Legal Families and Comparative Legal Traditions," in M. Reimann and R. Zimmermann (eds.), *The Oxford Handbook of Comparative Law* (2006), pp. 421-440; E. Örücü and D. Nelken, "Preface", in E. Örücü and D. Nelken (eds.), *Comparative Law: A Handbook* (2007), p. v; Mark Van Hoecke, "Do 'Legal Systems' Exist?", in S. P. Donlan and L. H. Urscheler (eds.), *Concepts of Law: Comparative Law, Jurisprudential and Social Science Perspectives* (2014), p. 53.

[90] Mark Van Hoecke, "Deep Level Comparative Law", in Mark Van Hoecke (ed.), *Epistemology and Methodology of Comparative Law* (2018), p. 167.

Another problem is the overestimation of the importance of classifying legal systems (in the literature, often referred to as the legal-families approach). Some shortcomings of this approach have already been criticized. In particular, the following were identified as key defects: the legal positivist orientation of Western law, which emphasizes formal norms, institutions, cases, and doctrines, has completely obscured the factual realities of other legal realms when it comes to cross-cultural macro-comparisons; concentration mainly on private law; petrification of classification over time; inability to take into account hybridity or *mixité* of law, and so on.[91] For these reasons the legal-families approach based on "classifications into legal families often do not provide an accurate picture".[92]

Figuratively speaking, comparative scientists are busy decorating a beautiful picture frame, leaving aside the picture itself. As though taxonomy has become a prison from which there is no apparent escape. We do not question the usefulness of these classifications for comparative jurisprudence. Obsession, too much infatuation of comparative scholars with classifications of legal systems, engenders objection. We oppose the dissipation of forces and energy in the process of scientific research which hampers their effectiveness and efficiency. The result of this obsession is the non-fulfillment or inadequate fulfillment of other important tasks facing comparative legal science.

In comparative jurisprudence, as noted above, the study of the legal world picture is reduced primarily to legal mapping, which, apparently, is the result of a literal understanding of the word "picture". Sometimes this mission is limited to the drawing of a legal world map. And these maps inevitably exaggerate some aspects of the world of law to the detriment of others, sometimes overlook some important aspects. Efforts to make maps in comparative jurisprudence have not been successful.

In comparative jurisprudence, cartographic metaphors are mainly used to represent the legal systems of the world. Such an application is a spatial view of the world of law and maps "legal systems" by using recognized political borders, not taking into

[91] Jaakko Husa, "The Future of Legal Families", in *Oxford Handbooks Online: Scholarly Research Reviews* (2016), pp. 5-6.

[92] Mathias Siems, *Comparative Law* (2d ed.; 2018), p. 109.

account other functionality of cartography. To overcome the traditional statistical and simplistic approach, it is necessary to compile atlases by branches and institutions of law (for example, crime mapping), and most importantly, to use the possibilities and recent innovations of a new direction – critical (legal) cartography, which, while criticizing traditional academic cartography, offers alternative, new cartographic methods, innovative ways of solving questions of representation.[93] According to critical cartography, the task of this field of knowledge is not just the compilation of maps. Cartography is an objective, scientific activity. Its goal is to produce more accurate and better depictions of the world. "Critical cartography is critical in that it challenges the traditional understanding of maps as objective or scientific attempts to portray reality graphically and reorients us to acknowledge that maps make reality as much as they represent reality".[94] Within the framework of critical cartography, such alternative approaches as, for example, hybrid maps, story maps, and multidimensional cartography, are proposed.

PERSPECTIVES FOR FURTHER RESEARCH

The present investigation was undertaken as a stepping-stone to more detailed research into the issues associated with creation of a legal world picture. It can be taken also as an introduction to further study of the topic.

A more or less adequate solution to the problem of conceptualizing the legal world picture has been suggested herein. The same can be said about the epistemological problems of constructing a legal world picture. However, the methodological problems of constructing a legal world picture were merely posed. These latter remain topical and await resolution urgently, which will require painstaking work on the part of critical legal scholars.

[93] Jeremy W. Crampton and John Krygier, "An Introduction to Critical Cartography", *ACME: An International E-Journal for Critical Geographies*, IV, no. 1 (2006), pp. 11-33; Jeremy W. Crampton, *Mapping: A Critical Introduction to Cartography and GIS* (2010); Nicola Lettieri and Delfina Malandrino, "Cartographies of the Legal World. Rise and Challenges of Visual Legal Analytics", in *22nd International Conference Information Visualisation, IV* (2018), pp. 241-246 (available online); N. Reiz, S. O'Lear, and D. Tuininga, "Exploring a Critical Legal Cartography: Law, Practice, and Complexities", *Geography Compass*, XII, no. 5 (2018), pp. 1-10 (available online).

[94] Reiz, O'Lear, and Tuininga, note 93 above, pp. 5-6.

Discussion of the topic can be continued by searching for answers, for example, to the following questions: does the "legal worldview" have the right to exist as a separate type of the general worldview? If yes, how does it correlate with the legal world picture? If not, can we talk about the legal aspects of the general worldview? What is influence of the legal world picture on legal consciousness and legal culture? What is its role in the mutual understanding of people in the legal space? And others.

Chapter 4

"Writing the Earth and Representing the World": The Cartographical Ambitions of Comparative Law

MATTEO NICOLINI

This article examines the special relationship between comparative law and geography. It reappraises the commonalities between the two disciplines and ascertains how the former peruses geographical features when arranging world knowledge in ways that fit into its conceptual framework. Far from being bare facts, physical geographical features are rewritten so as to allow comparative law to devise its own representation of the world's legal systems. To this end, the discipline makes deliberate use of geography, in general, and cartography, in particular. Both have supplied and still supply the practical knowledge comparative law needs to naturalize its world picture, manufacture legal spatialities, and assert the superiority of Western legal traditions. Under no circumstances were its cartographic ambitions confined to the colonial era; the practice of classifying and ranking legal systems also characterizes the current global politics of space. Through digital technology, these ambitions take the form of indexes and indicators to assess the economic performance of the legal systems of the world.

DISCIPLINARY CONSTRUCTIONS: COMPARATIVE LAW AS SPATIAL PRODUCTION

Just as any other epistemic community, comparative lawyers have their own *Weltanschauung*, which supplies a world picture consistent with their methodological approaches. A predicament like this would probably be a truism were it not for some features that have been fashioning comparative law since its inception as an academic discipline. Both methodological and substantive, these features suggest that comparative-law research be made up of (or, at least, fall under) a good dose of "disciplined subjectivity". This expression is particularly fitting for the purposes of this article, as it portrays the uneasiness of comparative scholars when describing the *disciplinary construction* of their field of scientific research.[1]

The question of disciplinary identity is pivotal in terms of comparative law delivering its world picture. The uneasiness of comparative scholars is related to the difficult-to-draw boundaries of their discipline. As it does not coincide with a set of rules applicable to a specific legal ambit, its boundaries are demarcated on methodological grounds. We have been taught – and still teach our students – that our methodology is "an intellectual activity" and "a form of study" of the law, whose boundaries are outlined by the very process of comparing and contrasting the sundry legal systems of the world,[2] which means constantly redrawing the fuzzy boundaries of comparative law.

Such uneasiness is the *distinctive trait* of comparative law, which stems from its critical, often provocative, and decisively subversive approach to legal research.[3] Indeed, it runs counter to the self-referential attitude of doctrinal legal scholars who love being "insulated within the disciplinary boundaries, intuitively presumed or authoritatively drawn", of, say, administrative, private, and commercial law.[4] The uneasiness is methodological because of the epistemologically *external* point of view adopted,

[1] See M. Nicolini, *Legal Geography. Comparative Law and the Production of Space* (2022), p. 289. On the relevance of disciplinary identity in comparative law see J. Husa, *Interdisciplinary Comparative Law. Rubbing Shoulders with the Neighbours or Standing Alone in a Crowd* (2022).

[2] Respectively: J. Husa, *Advanced Introduction to Law and Globalisation* (2018), p. 37; G. Mousourakis, *Comparative Law and Legal Traditions. Historical and Comparative Perspectives* (2019), p. 1; J. Gordley, et al., *An Introduction to the Comparative Study of Private Law: Readings, Cases, Materials* (2nd ed.; 2021), p. 1. See also Husa, *Introduction to Comparative Law* (2d ed.; 2023), pp. 20-22.

[3] See Husa, note 2 above (2023), p. 1: the lack of "generally accepted theoretical frames" and "aims" triggers a sense of "insecurity", also because comparative does not possess a "true paradigm" in Kuhnian terms.

[4] J. Gaakeer, (2020) "Interdisciplinarity 3.0: The Hub of the Universe or Fantasy Island?", *Pólemos*, XIV (2020), p. 322. This uneasiness is epitomized in F. H. Lawson, (1977) "Comparative Law as an Instrument of Legal Culture", in *The Comparison, Selected Essays* (1977), II, p. 78: "Comparative law cannot remain purely descriptive. Comparative lawyers must criticise".

which keeps the precincts of legal studies open and permeable to influxes, interactions, and pollination from the outer world.

This has substantive implications. First, it affects how comparative scholars approach the study of the law. In terms of disciplinary construction, comparative law is "disposition, not discipline".[5] It is an empirical field of legal research, whose "problem-based approach" is "the starting point of a comparative analysis".[6] Its dispositional character finds "expression in the effort to identify contingencies ... that may disrupt the order's operation", thus making our discipline well-equipped when it comes to assessing the world and its legal complexity.[7] Basic comparative legal concepts such as "law in books", "law in action", "law in context", and "legal formants" denote attentiveness to operational rules well beyond the written law.[8]

The second substantive implication refers to how comparative law devises its world picture by privileging a contextualised approach to legal studies.[9] Comparative law avoids "bracketing" the law. Far from constructing boundaries "within which interactions take place more or less independently of their surrounding context", it engages with the real world, ordering its knowledge

[5] N. Blomley, (2021) "Foreword: What is Legal Geography? Why, and Why Now?", in R. Bartel and J. Carter (eds.) *Handbook on Space, Place and Law* (2021), p. xvii.

[6] M. Siems, *Comparative Law* (2d ed.; 2022), p. 32. See, though, H. Spamann, "Empirical Comparative Law", *Annual Review of Law and Social Sciences*, XI (2015), p. 132, who prefers to term comparative law as a discipline tackling "causal" (that is, bottom-up) questions. He confines the empirical approach to the quantitative study of cross-country variations and transplants.

[7] R. Mullender, "Transmuting the Politico-Legal Lump: Brexit and Britain's Constitutional Order", *Cardozo Law Review*, XXXIX (2018), pp. 1020-1021.

[8] See, for example, R. Pound, "Law in Books and Law in Action", *American Law Review*, XLIV (1910), p. 12; K. Llewellyn, *Brumble Bush: On Our Law and Its Study* (1930), p. 3; R. Sacco, (1991) "Legal Formants: A Dynamic Approach to Comparative Law (Instalment I of II)", *The American Journal of Comparative Law*, XXXIX (1991), p. 1.

[9] See I. Spigno, "Methodologies of Comparative Constitutional Law: Contextual Approach", in *Max Planck Encyclopaedia of Comparative Constitutional Law* (2017) (MPECCoL). This approach in pivotal in comparative-legal (and geographical) studies. See A. Kedar, "Expanding Legal Geographies: A Call for a Critical Comparative Approach", in I. Braverman, et al. (eds.), *The Expanding Spaces of Law: A Timely Legal Geography* (2014), p. 95; L. Spencer, "Comparative Legal Geography. Context and Place in 'Legal Transplants'", in T. O'Donnell, et al. (eds.) *Legal Geography. Perspectives and Methods* (2020), p. 149.

in legally relevant terms.[10] This dispositional attitude is part of its disciplinary construction. Unlike the doctrinal (and bracketed) study of the law, comparative law has neither separated the human and the environmental nor interrupted the *continuum* between the subject and the object, nor turned the world into a separate entity. Indeed, it has maintained a firm grip on the geographical "reality" when mapping the complexity of the world's legal systems.

This connection with the world at large has also sparked geographical interest among comparative legal scholars. The law – particularly comparative law – has always been in a special relationship with geography.[11] This relationship has taken different forms and served several functions, as it supplies world knowledge functional to the *theatrum legale mundi,* that is, "an imagined repository that would include the entire corpus of the laws of all peoples at all places and in all times".[12]

We shall revisit this attentiveness to the materiality of the real world.[13] When coining the term "geography", indeed, Eratosthenes of Cyrene (288-205 BC) had already realized how complex "Writing the Earth" would be. Geography "writes" the earth in its complexity – even in its legal complexity, as the legal systems of the world demonstrate.[14]

We shall also see to what extent this special relationship has been subservient to the comparative-legal ambition of mapping these legal systems. In comparative law, the art of "writing the earth" and "representing the world" is far from a neutral exercise.

[10] On bracketing see Blomley, "The Ties that Blind: Making Fee Simple in the British Columbia Treaty Process", *Transactions of the Institute of British Geographers*, XL (2015), p. 169. See also M. Callon, "An Essay on Framing and Overflowing: Economic Externalities Revisited by Sociology", in M. Callon (ed.), *The Laws of the Markets* (1988), p. 249.

[11] On the special relationship between law and geography see Blomley and J. C. Bakan, "Spacing Out: Towards a Critical Geography of Law", *Osgoode Hall Law Journal*, XXX (1992), p. 661; Blomley, *Law, Space, and the Geographies of Powers* (1994). For recent assessments see the essays collected in M. Coleman and J. Agnew (eds.), *Handbook on the Geographies of Power* (2018).

[12] R. Hirschl, *Comparative Matters: The Renaissance of Comparative Constitutional Law* (2014), p. 284 (referring to Leibniz's comparative legal project of mapping the world).

[13] B. Anderson and J. Wylie, "On Geography and Materiality", *Environment and Planning A: Economy and Space*, XLI (2009), p. 318.

[14] Eratosthenes, *Geography*, transl. D. W. Roller (2010).

Cartography is essential to naturalizing this legal-geographical representation of the world. Within it, physical-human geographical features acquire a new meaning and are rewritten through the law. This new meaning reflects not the ontology of physical features, but their representation; their "existence" rather than their "essence". Owing to its cartographical ambitions, comparative law *does* "reshuffle [these features] in space", transforming "the natural environment into a cultural environment".[15] This process still conveys the idea that physical geography reflects a "neutral" reality. Yet, its representation gives rise to a new ontology, which comes into existence when it finds its place on the map. This is a mountain, a watershed, and a river – our maps say – because we have ideologically made these physical elements part of our own politico-legal discourse.[16]

Through legal mapping, comparative law has rearranged geographical features to deliver a world picture rooted in the legal and cultural superiority of the West. As an ethnocentric attitude, processing the Western legal superiority reached its heights in the nineteenth and twentieth centuries, when comparative law reinforced the colonial attitude towards non-Western (that is, inferior) conceptions of the law. The West gained the global politics of place; by virtue of its legal traditions, it ultimately imposed their allegedly superior *legitimacy* over other non-Western ones and rearranged colonial spaces through its own culture-specific "legal frame".[17]

In sum, the disciplinary construction of comparative law turns out to be a legal-spatial production of the world. Intriguing, as it is, both "construction" and "production" are consonant with the "spatial turn" that took place in cultural geography in the late twentieth century.[18] The stance was cross-disciplinary; space

[15] L. K. D. Kristof, "The Nature of Frontiers and Boundaries", *Annals of the Association of American Geographers*, XLIX (1959), p. 275.

[16] See D. Wood, *Rethinking the Power of Maps* (2010), ppp. 56-57.

[17] J.-L. Halpérin, "The Concept of Law: A Western Transplant?", *Theoretical Inquiries in the Law*, X (2009), p. 333.

[18] See H. Lefebvre, (1974) *La production de l'espace* (1974); transl.: *The Production of Space*, transl. D. Nicholson-Smith (1991). The expression became topical in cultural geography: for a comprehensive survey see N. Nayak and A. Jeffrey, *Geographical Thought. An Introduction to Ideas in Human Geography* (2012), p. 97 et seq.

was conceived as "a (social) product" made up of sundry social, political, geographical, and legal variables.[19]

Precisely because space is a social construct, its relationship with the law is a matter of representation. Before examining how comparative law rewrites the world (and the Earth's surface), we turn to the commonalities that make the relationship between our discipline and geography so special and functional to our cartographical representation of the world.

GRASPING THE WORLD INTELLECTUALLY: COMPARATIVE LAW AND "GEOGRAPHIES"

In the previous section the relationship between comparative law and geography has been called "special". It has evolved, supplying comparative law with world knowledge functional to the legal-spatial production of the *theatrum legale mundi.* In so doing, comparative law has acted as the interface between the materiality of the physical world and the spatial hierarchies, imaginative geographies, and geopolitics of Western law.

It would be simplistic, though, to reduce this special relationship to an opportunistic use of geography by comparative law. What makes it authentically special cannot merely depend on how spatial production delivers the world picture of comparative law. Something more is required. *This something more* consists of the epistemological underpinnings of both disciplines, which are traceable back to their disciplinary construction. In preserving the *continuum* between the human and the environmental, both disciplines have traditionally exhibited a peculiar attentiveness to the real world without turning it into a separate entity. This figuring out the world in its complexity has led the human geographer Alastair Bennett to assert that "geography's defining act" lies in its "ability to grasp the world intellectually".[20] Bennett could not have coined a better definition, which also reflects the ambitions of comparative law as "method of knowledge acquisition".[21]

For both disciplines, ordering world knowledge gives sense to the complex "space-place-environment nexus" present in

[19] Lefebvre, note 18 above (1991), p. 26.

[20] A. Bonnett, *What is Geography?* (2008), p. 32.

[21] Husa, note 2 above (2023), p. 64.

legal contexts.[22] Both deploy methods and practices whereby the manifold relations between law, power, and geography might be understood. In a world which has become more troubled and globalized, comparative law and geography engage in a process of co-production of law and space. This is apparent as far as the law is concerned. Far from being an unfettered, not to say extrinsic, force, the law is a performative spatial practice, the meaning of which is pragmatically enriched by socio-geographical contexts: "Law divorced from its cultural matrix is meaningless".[23] Taking the "spatialities of law seriously" means ceasing "to look upon" it "as a closed, formal, and acontextual system and see it instead as an assemblage of heterogeneous elements".[24] This resonates with another feature of comparative law, that is, its *empirical* approach, which allows scholars to grasp the "deep structures of the legal systems"; in dialogue with non-legal disciplines, it gains control of the "deep connection" of the law with its cultural and environmental contexts.[25]

The dialogue is first and foremost with geography, whose empirical pedigree stretches back to a fieldwork made up of explorations, travels, discoveries, land mapping, and surveying. As Richard Hartshorne put it in his *Perspective on the nature of geography* (1959), "geography is that discipline that seeks *to describe and interpret the variable character from place to place of the earth as the world of man*".[26] Being empirical, it is interested in "the imprint of history" with "its detailed effect on the human condition". It is an imprint, Ron J. Johnston acutely states, which "is made by individuals, acting within the structural forces and perhaps affecting them slightly".[27] Geography thus establishes a bridge

22 J. A. Matthews and D. T. Herbert, *Geography. A Very Short Introduction* (2008), p. 17.

23 E. A. Hoebel, *The Law of Primitive Man: A Study in Comparative Legal Dynamics* (1954), p. 39.

24 R. Hogg, "Law's Other Spaces", *Law/Text/Culture* VI (2002), p. 34. See also D. Delaney, *The Spatial, the Legal and the Pragmatics of World-Making* (2010), p. 7.

25 Respectively: P. Legrand, "European Legal Systems are not Converging", *International and Comparative Law Quarterly*, XLV (1996), p. 56; G. Watt, "Comparison as Deep Appreciation", in P. G. Monateri (ed.), *Methods of Comparative Law* (2012), p. 84.

26 R. Hartshorne, *Perspective on the Nature of Geography* (1959), p. 47.

27 R. J. Johnston, "Texts, Actors and Higher Managers: Judges, Bureaucrats and

between the "complex web of relations" that populate spatial contexts; it unfolds the processes of politico-legal Westernization, challenges the claims of objectivity and autonomy of the law, and recognizes "the subsistence of other legal orders and other legal possibilities".[28]

The consequences of this empirical approach are twofold. The first one accounts for the ability of both law and geography to address "*concrete* questions" and assess "a wide range of phenomena connected to the Earth" in a conversation with the world.[29] The second consequence justifies their methodological pluralism.[30]

Their interaction is special because of this variety of approaches, which "gives better opportunities for free research" and is also "open to ... insights from such neighbouring disciplines as history, linguistics, economics and social science".[31] However "messy and imperfect" and "characterized by several different and conflicting projects" they may be,[32] the methodological approaches available in comparative law and geography are often mixed and jointly applied, fitting into a wide range of legal geographical truly interdisciplinary intellectual projects.[33] They also represent a toolkit capable of enhancing a critical thinking in both disciplines and challenging the "isolationist" attitude of lawyers and geographers. In so doing, they open up both disciplines to external connections, pluralize the methodological debate, and trigger "internal critiques

the Political Organization of Space", *Political Geography Quarterly*, II (1983), p. 16.

28 Respectively: D. Massey, "Politics and Space/Time", *New Left Review* CXCVI (1992), p. 66; T. O'Donnell, et al., "An Australasian and Asia-Pacific Approach to Legal Geography", in T. O'Donnell, et al. (eds.), *Legal Geography. Perspectives and Methods* (2020), p. 4.

29 J. Agnew, et al., "General Introduction", in *Human Geography. An Essential Anthology* (1996), p. 5.

30 On methodological pluralism in comparative law see P. G. Monateri, *Advanced Introduction to Comparative Legal Methods* (2021); R. Scarciglia, *Methods and Legal Comparison: Challenges for Methodological Pluralism* (2023), p. 135.

31 Husa, note 2 above (2023), p. 1.

32 Respectively: A. Adams, "Comparing Law: Practice and Theory", in M. Adams and J. Bomhoff (eds.), *Practice and Theory in Comparative Law* (2012), p. 5; Monateri, note 30 above, p. vii.

33 I. Braverman, et al. (eds.), *The Expanding Spaces of Law: A Timely Legal Geography* (2014); Braverman, (ed,). *Laws of the Sea: Interdisciplinary Currents* (2022).

of the core principles" of both disciplines.[34] Thinking outside the box thus entails a good dose of subversion, which describes comparative law, geography, and their approaches as *critical*.

COMPARATIVE LAW, GEOGRAPHY, AND SPACE: A RELATIONSHIP ROOTED IN GENERALIZATIONS

There is a further commonality that accounts for the special relationship between comparative law and geography, that is, the process of their institutionalization.[35] "Institutionalization" refers to their emergence as academic disciplines in the second half of the nineteenth century. From that time onwards, what counted as "geography" or "comparative law" has been decided within academia to give them consistency and scientific rigor.[36]

Per se, institutionalisation does not convey anything relevant; besides comparative law and geography, the nineteenth century saw the birth of several other "academic" disciplines, such as anthropology, sociology, and ethnology. Institutionalisation affects the methodological construction of both disciplines. As mentioned above, the process has to do with the broader question of *disciplinary identity* – ultimately, with comparative law delivering its world picture. We all know that legal methods are seldom value neutral. Even in comparative law. When ordering world knowledge, they do not act as neutral forces. Their outputs are "value-laden"; in comparative law, these are usually hinted at by the cartographic representation of the legal systems of the world.

Legal mapping represents – and presents to us – a particular representation of the world. On the one hand, it establishes a relation between comparative law, power, and geography; on the

[34] Blomley, (2003) "From 'What?' to 'So What?': Law and Geography in Retrospect", in J. Holder and C. Harrison (eds.), *Law and Geography* (2003), p. 22.

[35] Geographical and comparative-law practices had been applied well before their institutionalization. See Mousourakis, note 2 above, p. 49 *et seq.*; B. Fekete, *Paradigms in Modern European Comparative Law. A History* (2021), pp. 31 *et seq.* See M.-C. Robic, "Geography", in T. M. Porter and Ross (eds.), *The Cambridge History of Science: The Modern Social Sciences* (2003), VII, p. 379.

[36] As for comparative law, see M. Ancel, "Cent ans de droit comparé en France", in *Livre du Centenaire de Société de législation comparé* (1969), p. 3; Fekete, note 35 above, p. 62 et seq. As for geography see Nayak and Jeffrey, note 18 above, pp. 11-21.

other, comparative law acts as an ideological driver. Hinted at by the cartographic representation is a set of *implicatures*. In referring to the interpretation of meaning that linguists work out in pragmatics, the term denotes "the act of meaning or implying one thing by saying something else".[37] In comparative legal studies, implicatures point to the superiority of Western legal derivatives that, on maps, are visualized as the dominant world legality.

The way maps are arranged in atlases confirms this predicament. As Jeremy Black puts it, we do not usually pay particular attention to the "disproportionate amount of space" that is devoted to "maps of Europe and North America", which "are also generally placed before maps of other continents". We assume this as a fact. "This very arrangement", Black continues, "suggests a hierarchy of importance and a Eurocentric, or rather 'Western', primacy" within geographical knowledge.[38] The way continents and countries are arranged is a matter of hierarchy, which cannot be explained merely in cartographic terms. Meaningful places are not "simply 'there' awaiting discovery and representation"; rather, their production is the outcome of a politico-legal discourse, with wider (geographical, political, and legal) implications.[39]

Black grasps the point: spatial production underpins a Eurocentric depiction of the earth. Hierarchy replicates the competition among different actors – in particular, Western political ones. In reflecting the "politics of spaces" European powers had been pursuing since the dawn of the Age of Discovery,[40] legal cartography was (and still is) subservient to these geopolitics: moving "itself outwards, [Europe's] sense of cultural", as well as political, "strength was fortified".[41] European powers were thus able to shape African, American, Oceanian, and Asian legal cartographies. Just as Western societies, communities located beyond the West might become as legally developed

[37] See D. Wayne, "Implicature", in E. D. Zalta (ed.), *Stanford Encyclopedia of Philosophy* (2019) (available online).

[38] J. Black, *Maps and Politics* (1997), p. 40.

[39] Nayak and Jeffrey, note 18 above, p. 242.

[40] A. Gordon and B. Klein, "Introduction", in Gordon and Klein (eds.), *Literature, Mapping, and the Politics of Space in Early Modern Britain* (2001), p. 5. See also D. N. Livingstone, *The Geographical Tradition* (1992), p. 32; J. Brotton, *Trading Territories: Mapping the Early Modern World* (2018).

[41] E. Said, *Orientalism* (2003), p. 117.

as Europe provided that they evolved through various stages of development that are universal and lead to the same stage of superiority envisaged by European comparative legal traditions. Through it, Europe westernized the world and superimposed its own *geopolitics of law* onto it.[42]

The main implicature is the assumption that Western conceptions of the law are a universal legal paradigm "superior" to all other legal systems. Comparative law has encouraged the search for legal uniformity by way of *generalizations*; the term indicates both a concept common to the whole of humankind and the process whereby an idea is, or is intended to be, used everywhere.[43] Generalizations reflect the methodological attitude we comparativists term *universalist approach,* whereby legal concepts were (and still are) made applicable irrespective of time and place.[44]

The widespread application of this approach has a pedigree stretching back to the institutionalisation of comparative law. Only the limited set of civilized, that is, "European", systems were considered generalisable and exportable. No wonder that legal scholars considered western law "an absolute given with universal applicability".[45] Such superiority, it goes without saying, reflects the superiority of Western culture, which favoured the fabrication of the global politics of space *also* through legal practices.

Legal cartography supplied world knowledge useful for establishing Western legal superiority. Like comparative law, geography was also rooted in generalizations. The appointment

[42] See Monateri, *Geopolitica del diritto: genesi, governo e dissoluzione dei corpi politici* (2013).

[43] On generalizations as constitutive features of comparative law, see Nicolini, "Methodologies of Comparative Constitutional Law: Universalist Approach", in *Max Planck Encyclopaedia of Comparative Constitutional Law* (2d ed.; 2023).

[44] See Mousourakis, note 2 above, pp. 8, 149. The 1900 Paris Congress paved the way for an ambitious project: entrusting comparative law with the discovery of universal principles common to "civilised" systems, that is, the laws of European nations. See A. Peters, "Universalist Assumptions and Implications of Comparative Law: Should They Be Deconstructed?", *Proceedings of the Annual Meeting (American Society of International Law),* XLIII (1999), p. 366. See also Fekete, note 35 above, pp. 77, 92; Gordley, "The Universalist Heritage:, in Legrand and Munday (eds.), *Comparative Legal Studies: Traditions and Transitions* (2003), p. 31.

[45] J. Q. Whitman, "Western Legal Imperialism: Thinking About the Deep Historical Roots", *Theoretical Inquiries in Law,* X (2009), p. 308.

of Sir Halford Mackinder (1861-1947) as Reader in Geography at Oxford University (1887) reflected the same universal (and commercial) ambitions, satisfying "the practical requirements of the stateman and the merchant, the theoretical requirements of the historian and the scientist, and the intellectual requirements of the teacher".[46] If we bear in mind that Mackinder is also regarded as the founding father of geopolitics,[47] we might conclude that geography was born to give consistency to a clear geopolitical ambition, that is, the generalization of the interests of "the modern geographical world-view" of the West, "in which access routes, markets and production dominate the way countries are represented".[48] To put it bluntly, "the *raison d'être* of colonies is *to benefit the commerce of the Mother Country*".[49]

This attitude was strengthened in the second half of the twentieth century, when a new *state of mind* emerged beneath the surface of both disciplines. In the aftermath of World War II, geographical studies dismissed the colonial and ethnocentric attitudes that had populated their institutionalisation. This, though, did not entail uprooting generalisations. In the 1950s and 1960s geography veered towards quantitative approaches, whose "rigorous scientific method" has now become so "powerful that it can determine even how we allow ourselves to imagine the world".[50]

With this shift towards spatial analysis, the quantitative turn in geography meant a revival of the universalistic approach. The incorporation of scientific techniques enabled "geographers to undertake ... research that" could "provide general explanations

[46] H. J. Mackinder, "On the Scope and Methods of Geography", *Proceedings of the Royal Geographical Society and Monthly Record of Geography*, IX (1887), p. 159.

[47] F. P. Sempa, "The Roots of Mackinder's Geopolitics", *Orbis*, LIX (2015), p. 613.

[48] Bonnett, note 20 above, p. 22.

[49] H. Egerton, *A Short History of British Colonial Policy* (1887), p. 2. (emphasis added). For more on this, see Nicolini, (2019) "Monstrosity 'Overseas'? Civilisation, Trade and Colonial Policy in Conrad's African Tales", in D. Carpi (ed.), *Monsters and Monstrosity. From the Canon to the Anti-Canon: Literary and Juridical Subversions* (2019), p. 235.

[50] B. S. Hammond, "Scriblerian Self-Fashioning", *The Yearbook of English Studies*, XVIII (1968), p. 113; G. Levine, "One Culture", in Levine (ed.), *One Culture: Science and Literature. Essays in Science and Literature* (1987), p. 3.

and predictions".[51] Space became an abstract and absolute "container" of social-environmental interactions; and geography, "the discipline concerned with place, was to become a placeless science".[52] The abstract, measurable, and geometrical conception of space also had a strongly regulatory essence, enabling geographers to generalise patterns of spatial relations; spatial laws explained and predicted space-related phenomena. These quantitative practices did not represent a neutral-laden approach to geography; generalised spatial processes were applicable everywhere triggering changes in human-environmental relations.

Comparative law did the same at the end of the previous century when it experienced its own "mathematical turn".[53] Recent studies have joined hard sciences in employing quantitative approaches giving way to what Mathias Siems labels as *numerical comparative law*. Likewise, there is "a growing field of empirical legal studies" applying "statistical methods to legal questions". Through quantitative methods, scholars assess the "quality" of the legal systems of the world and rank them according to several benchmarks. For instance, the world-famous essay *Law and Finance* by La Porta et al. measured and ranked forty-nine national legal systems: the benchmark was the quality of the shareholder and creditor protection regulation.[54]

In encapsulating the relations between society, power, law, and geography, comparative legal studies unveil the legal implicatures behind the law. In sum, comparative law decisively gives sense to the world by delivering a particular representation of it, but this is often "a direct result of the craft competences of the investigators rather than a portrait of reality".[55] The special relationship between comparative law and geography is therefore a discursive practice through which we scholars "naturalise", that is, generalize,

[51] Nayak and Jeffrey, note 18 above, p. 39.

[52] R. J. Johnston, "Human Geography as a Generalizing Social Science: Trans-Atlantic Contrasts in Local Government", *The Geographical Journal* CL (1984), p. 335.

[53] D. Restrepo Amariles, "Legal Indicators, Global Law and Legal Pluralism: An Introduction", *The Journal of Legal Pluralism and Unofficial Law*, XLVII (2015), p. 14.

[54] Siems, note 6 above, p. 207 et seq.

[55] Livingstone, note 40 above, p. 16.

our own representation of the world, gaining control of it, and entrenching spatial hierarchies.

'A MATTER OF CHOICE': ON THE CARTOGRAPHICAL AMBITIONS OF COMPARATIVE LAW

There is another generalization that populates geographical studies, which also affects the comparative-law world picture rooted in the generalization of Western law.

Within academic circles, geographical studies experience a disjuncture, which approximately coincides with the human geography-physical geography divide. Once institutionalized, the relevance of this disjuncture was not as obvious as one might have expected. Geographical research and teaching could have paved the way to different, and alternative, processes. On 31 January 1887, Sir Halford Mackinder delivered a paper "On the Scope and Methods of Geography" at the evening meeting of the Royal Geographical Society. There, he went straight to the point: "Is geography one, or is it several subjects? ... Are physical and political [i.e. human] geography two stages of one investigation, or are they separate subjects to be studied by different methods, the one an appendix of geology, the other of history?" The issue had already been a matter of scholarly disagreement. Determined, as he was, to make geography a single discipline, he proposed to define it "as the science whose main function is to trace the interaction of man in society and so much of his environment as varies locally".[56] From that time onwards, scholars had had to "focus on the relation of history and geography", which "meant that geographers must no longer treat physical geography as separate from political geography".[57] In Mackinder's view, "political questions will depend on the results of the physical inquiry"; when "Man alters his environment ... the action of that environment on his posterity is changed in consequence".[58]

[56] Mackinder, note 46 above, pp. 142-143.

[57] Sempa, note 47 above, p. 614.

[58] Mackinder, note 46 above, p. 157. "The physical inquiry includes three elements: the configuration of the earth's surface; weather and climate; and the distribution of natural resources". Sempa, note 47 above, p. 615.

It is not the intention to restore Mackinder's *geographical experiment* as the "bridge over the abyss ... between the natural sciences and the study of humanity".[59] Nor is it intended to challenge the academic distinction between physical and human geography. The purpose is limited and points to "geographies" as "integrative" of societies and environment in terms of comparative law delivering its world picture.

It is a matter of how our discipline grasps world knowledge intellectually. In this sense, physical and human geographies alike expand the scope of comparative legal research, assisting us in gaining knowledge of the variables implicated in spatial production. The idea of "integrated geography" – which is advocated by geographers[60] – must be reframed in terms that fit into our conceptual framework. The human-physical geographical nexus is part of a broader and ideological politico-legal discourse revolving around geographical features and entities (for example, mountains, forests, and rivers) that populate the natural environment. But *that* environment is also occupied by individuals who superimpose their representations onto the earth's surface. And *that* environment becomes meaningful because the discourse about it provides the practical knowledge needed by policymakers (and comparative scholars) when manufacturing legal spatialities. Being part of the interaction between natural environment and human agencies, spatial production becomes servient to the legal mapping of the world.

The cultural geographer Ronald J. Johnston raised several objections as regards the usefulness of human- and physical-geographical interactions in geographical research.[61] Reframing the idea of "integrated geography" in terms of ideological discourse helps us to sidestep these objections – at least in the field of comparative law.

Johnston terms this "quest for unity in geography" an "environmental fix". He assumes that the debate on the "separation/integration of physical and human geography" is no more "than talking across rather than at each other", without a

[59] Mackinder. Ibid., p. 145. See also Livingstone, note 40 above, pp. 189-196.

[60] Matthews and Herbert, note 22 above, p. 83.

[61] R. J. Johnston, "Four Fixations and the Quest for Unity in Geography", *Transactions of the Institute of British Geographers*, XI, (1986), p. 449.

real conversation between both (sub)disciplines. This is due to the semantic dualism of the lexical item "geography", which has two usages, namely the academic and the vernacular. The former describes both "geographies" in terms of scientific disciplines, whereas the latter refers to their practical application. The geographical experiment is far from being a form of integration; academics (physical or human geographers alike) who oversee the process of integration also govern which vernacular usage of the "other" geography is relevant for their research. In human geography, for example, human (academic) geographers use the physical (vernacular) geography in examining the transformation of spaces into meaningful places.

When delivering the map of the world's legal systems, however, it is possible to integrate physical and human geography into a whole. When emphasizing how human agencies impact on the environment, Johnston grasps "the importance of studying the human/physical interface".[62] The missing point in his arguments is the definition of what *acts as the interface.* Such a role is probably played by the third "geography" that populates spatial production, that is, imaginative geography. Through the latter, comparative law is able to process physical geographical data and naturalize its own world picture, projecting it onto the earth's surface through maps. Unlike its physical and human counterparts, imaginative geography does not have two usages. Both geographies (human and physical) provide world practical knowledge, which is nothing more than the sum of physical and human (vernacular) usages that are integrated to manufacture spatial normativies.

What matters is the practical application of physical and human geographies. Both are processed to create, rather than simply reveal, a new "practical" and ideologically motivated world knowledge. And this precisely is what comparative law does. It makes a deliberate use of physical and human geographical features, and the outcomes resemble a "reshuffling of the spatial furniture as a result of some external intervention".[63]

62 Ibid., 449. On the importance of the human/physical interface see also Johnston, "Resource Analysis, Resource Management and the Integration of Physical and Human Geography", *Progress in Physical Geography: Earth and Environment* , VII (1983), p. 127.

63 Blomley, "Text and Context: Rethinking the Law-Space Nexus", *Progress in Human Geography*, XIII (1989), pp. 512–534.

The legal mapping provided by comparative law is therefore a politico-legal "way of seeing, a way of framing and imagining the environment". It is a practice that orders the world and naturalizes its representations. Comparative law "draws lines, constructs insides and outsides, assigns legal meanings to lines, and attaches legal consequences to crossing" and disregarding them.[64] At the same time, owing to the classification of legal systems, its legal genera "acquires complexity and subtlety"; it is "intrinsically geographical". Space is "clearly far more than a passive surface", and its "specificities [...] may serve to shape the law".[65]

Human and physical geographical interactions are ultimately assessed in relation to the production of maps, in general, and legal maps, in particular; and the emphasis is placed on the rendering of spatial data, cartographic techniques, and models that describe legal-geographical phenomena and act as a "powerful imaginative act" organizing the "sensuous variety of the earth's [legal] surface".[66]

No wonder, therefore, that we consider the mapmaker a "creator rather than [a] reflector" of the world.[67] Such creativity is favored by the constraints of geographical knowledge. "Deformations and contortions, distortions and misrepresentations ... are the unavoidable consequence of attempting to display simultaneously on a plane the entire surface of the sphere" which is the earth.[68] Mapping legal systems supplies their "unchanging" and "static" spatial representations, where "frozen" legal families are displayed without any reference to the processes of creation and classification criteria that might have changed. Time is considered crucial in managing geographical data models and the examination of legal spaces; the latter are indeed socially bound, and therefore subjected to the temporalities of space. Temporally located in a particular

[64] D. Delaney, "Legal Geography I: Constitutivities, Complexities, and Contingencies", *Progress in Human Geography* XXXIX (2015), p. 99.

[65] Blomley, note 63 above, p. 517.

[66] J. Brotton, *A History of the World in Twelve Maps* (2013), pp. 7, 337.

[67] Black, note 38 above, p. 11.

[68] D. Wood, *The Power of Maps* (1992), p. 56.

position, legal systems are made static to conceal the idea of legal spaces as contingent (and colonial) practices.[69]

(Legal) map-making is, in sum, a matter of "choice", which extends over "scale, projection, orientation, symbolization, key, colour, title and caption", as well as the intentional suppression of world knowledge. As legal mapmakers, we also normally take into account factors before deciding whether to display them on maps. In so doing, we make an ideological, that is, calculated, use of cartography, turning challenges (for example, the choice of supporting Western legal superiority) into opportunities (for example, the objectivity of their cartographic representation).

COMPARATIVE SCHOLARS AS MAPMAKERS

In examining its cartographic ambitions, we have seen that comparative law is decisively implicated in the spatial production of the world. There is indeed a strong connection between legal map-making and the vernacular use of human and physical geography. On the one hand, this connection confirms that the way geographies are integrated is consonant with the cross-disciplinary stance also known as the "spatial turn"; on the other, comparative law engages with social, political, geographical variables in spatial terms, upholding that legal spaces are a matter of "construction", "production", and "choice". When acting as cartographers, comparative lawyers are *creators* of the world's legal systems.

This cartographic competence is also a cultural-cum-political competence traceable back to the "Age of Discovery". This expression points to the interweaving of voyages and explorations that led to the expansion of European geographies of power through the world in the fifteenth and sixteenth centuries.[70] This age marked the dawn of European colonialism, during which the

[69] On the extrasignificance of time to maps see Wood, note 16 above, p. 94. On how time reinforces the contingency of socially constructed legal places see F. von Benda Beckmann and K. von Benda-Beckmann, "Places That Come and Go: A Legal Anthropological Perspective on the Temporalities of Space in Plural Orders", in I. Braverman, et al. (eds.), *The Expanding Spaces of Law: A Timely Legal Geography* (2014), p. 30.

[70] See J. H. Parry, *The Age of Reconaissance, Discovery, Exploration and Settlement, 1450 to 1650* (1981); Livingstone, note 40 above, pp. 32, 41-54. See also Nicolini, note 1 above, Chapter 4.

interactions between law and geography secured the superiority of the West over the rest of the world. Being the major European powers, the Spaniards, the Portuguese, the English, the French, and the Dutch accommodated newly discovered territories into a new political order made visible through maps. In this sense, the Age of Discovery also required a new spatial order; it also made a vernacular use of physical and human features so as to fit them into the imaginative geographies of the Western interface. The production of new legal spaces soon ensued.

Non-Western legal traditions still bear the consequences of such interactions. Europe "essentialised", that is, misrepresented (or which is the same thing, produced) the rest of the world.[71] Geography had to be rewritten, and the earth mapped again. To demonstrate their legal-cultural superiority, colonial powers projected their Western imaginaries onto the whole earth, encoding newly discovered territories with the superior principles of Western legal civilization. Their pre-colonial past was erased, and their legal systems buried. The practice of settler colonialism sought to "eliminate the native presence from the land ... to build a settler society" by replacing native law and land titles with European processes of legal (and spatial) production.[72] The thorough application of legal encoding had the "material effect" of outlining "depopulated", "often void of human traces", and visually "empty" spaces,[73] which would be subsequently arranged so as to comply with "Western beliefs" – even those related to Christianity, which has undoubtedly shaped the way comparative law sees the world "in terms of views on law".[74] With irony, we may say that this was also a process of legal sanitation; once

[71] F. Driver, *Geography Militant. Cultures of Exploration and Empires* (2001), p. 7.

[72] L. Bhungalia, "Governing Banishment: Settler Colonialism, Territory, and Life in an Economy of Death", in M. Coleman and J. Agnew (eds.), *Handbook on the Geographies of Power* (2018), p. 314. See also P. Wolfe, *Settler Colonialism and the Elimination of the Native* (1999); A. Kedar, (2003) "On the Legal Geography of Ethnocratic Settler States: Notes Towards a Research Agenda", in J. Holder and C. Harrison (eds.), *Law and Geography: Current Legal Issues* (2003), p. 401.

[73] J. Crampton, *The Political Mapping of Cyberspace* (2003), p. 47.

[74] Respectively Gordon and Klein, note 40 above, p. 1; Husa, "Comparative Law Christianity – A Plank in the Eye?", *Oxford Journal of Legal Studies*, XX (2023), p. 19.

cordoned off, the non-Western world was reduced to "cartographic silence".[75]

The infusion of colonial lands with the principles of Western (civil- or common-) law reflected the narrative of property, economy, and progress secured by the civilizing mission of the West; and this proprietary narrative represented the "just" title for the acquisition of colonial lands and the "just" indiscriminate dispossession of native legal geographies. Colonial policies disregarded ancestral and non-territorial arrangements based on borderless spaces. Divided among different States, communities were arbitrarily separated and subsequently merged with other groups with the aim of creating political entities based on territorial jurisdictions.

This process still affects the way we display the world's legal systems on maps. Impressing the seal of Westernization into the fertile grounds of the colonies also explains why comparative law has traditionally focused on the similarities between former colonies and Western legal systems. By emphasizing legal-colonial links, scholars rank French, Spanish, Portuguese, Dutch, and Italian former colonies among the civil-law legal systems; former British colonies and protectorates are ascribed to the common-law legal tradition, whereas countries with a mixed colonial past join the mixed jurisdictions.[76] This perpetuates the ethnocentric approach of nineteenth-century geography and comparative law, when only the limited set of civilized, that is, "European", systems were considered generalizable and exportable. The marginalized non-Western legal traditions might progressively evolve through various stages with the Western legal paradigm as the natural end point. This entails that it is feasible to legally process even the lower stages of legal development so that they may reach the same stage of superiority envisaged by European legal traditions.

[75] J. B. Harley, *Victims of a Map: New England Cartography and the Native Americans* (Paper read at the Land of Norumbega Conference, Portland, Maine, December 1988), p. 57.

[76] R. Zimmermann and D. Visser, "Introduction. South African Law as a Mixed Legal System", in Zimmermann and Visser (eds.), *Southern Cross: Civil Law and Common Law in South Africa* (1996), pp. 7–8.

WESTERNIZING THE GLOBE: SPATIAL PRODUCTION OF THE WORLD'S LEGAL SYSTEMS

Grounded on the superiority of the West and the marginalization of non-Western legal traditions, the new "spatial model" framed during the colonial era led to a political reading of legal cartography. Located in the Global North, Western legal systems set the benchmark in relation to which all systems had to be measured. Thus, the "point of view was elevated, to the point of grasping in a single instant the convexity of the terraqueous globe". This geometrical cartographic discourse still needed a "*centre*, an *omphalos*, in order to describe, in degree of civilisations, its difference from [the] diffuse *periphery*" which was the uncivilized, that is, inferior, "rest of the world".[77]

This center was the West. Take, for example, how comparative legal handbooks dedicate chapters to, say, African and Asian legal systems. Their analyses are still affected by methodological biases, such as an Ethnocentric, and colonial, attitude towards non-Western conceptions of the law. This results in either a lack of reference to them[78] or a limited extension of chapters on non-Western law in handbooks; references to Asian, African, and Pacific legal traditions are usually limited in range and scope and are confined within either classifications of the legal systems or micro-comparative analyses.[79] The bias is also apparent even when scholars adopt new taxonomies. Patrick H. Glenn (1940-2014) advocated the establishment of chthonic legal traditions, into which several pre-colonial legal traditions (African, Asian, Polynesian, and Inuit)

[77] Gordon and Klein, note 40 above, p. 3; F. Lestringant, *Mapping the Renaissance World: The Geographical Imagination in the Age of Discovery* (1994), p. 5.

[78] K. Zweigert and H. Kötz, *Einführung in die Rechtsvergleichung* (3d ed.; 1996) and C. Valcke, *Comparing Law. Comparative Law as Reconstruction of Collective Commitments* (2018) omit references to African law.

[79] See G. Ajani, et al., *Diritto comparato. 3. Le tradizioni giuridiche asiatiche e africane* (2023); T. W. Bennett, (2006) "Comparative Law and African Customary Law", in M. Reimann and R. Zimmermann (eds.), *The Oxford Handbook of Comparative Law* (2d ed.; 2006), p. 652; Uwe Kischel, *Comparative Law* (2019); T. Rambaud, *Introduction au droit compare* (2d ed.; 2017); R. David, et al., *Les grands systèmes de droit contemporains* (12th ed.; 2016); R. Sacco, "The Sub-Saharan Legal Tradition", in M. Bussani and Ugo Mattei (eds.), *The Cambridge Companion to Comparative Law* (2012), p. 313; A. Gambaro and R. Sacco, *Sistemi giuridici comparati* (2d ed.; 2009); W. F. Menski, *Comparative Law in a Global Context: The Legal Systems of Asia and Africa* (2006); C. Ntampaka, *Introduction aux systèmes juridiques africains* (2005).

coalesce.[80] However, the legal descriptor does not account for the rich variety of non-Eurocentric conceptions of the law: within the chthonic milieu, all beyond-the-West conceptions of the law lose their own legal-specific features.

This is the ethnocentric way comparative law has always arranged legal cartography. Pier Giuseppe Monateri provides us with a clear geopolitics of law when listing some of these classifications. In his presentation to the 1900 Congress of Paris, for example, Adémair Esmein (1848-1913) referred to the legal families to which the countries of the "Concert of Europe" belonged. The Roman, German, Anglo-Saxon, Slavic, and Islamic families reflected Europe's balance of power between France, Austria, Prussia, the United Kingdom, Russia, and Turkey. The rest of the world was relegated to politico-legal irrelevance. Sanitized and essentialized, it was located in a peripheral *département d'outre-mer*.[81]

Likewise, in his 1922 comparative-law treatise, Henri-Léon Lévi-Ullman (1870-1947) categorized the legal systems into three groups: the Continental, the Anglophone, and the Islamic systems, essentializing both the Western and the Mediterranean legal cultures to the exclusion of the rest of the world. The same holds true for Georges Sauser-Hall (1884-1966), whose controversial classification around linguistic criteria reduced the law to three groups: Semitic, Indo-European, and Mongol.[82]

As they revolve around European and Asian landmasses, these classifications resonate with legal applications of geopolitics and precisely with Mackinder's *Geographical Pivot of History*. This was the center from which all legal systems of the world radiated and were arranged upon a hierarchical scale.[83] Even in the post-colonial

[80] H. P. Glenn, *Legal Traditions of the World: Sustainable Diversity in Law* (5th ed.; 2014), p. 60.

[81] A. Esmein, "Le droit comparé et l'enseignement du droit", *Revue historique de droit français et étranger*, XXIV (1924), p. 489. See Monateri, note 42 above, p. 13; Monateri, note 30 above, pp. 23-41.

[82] H. Levy-Ullman, (1923) "Observation générales sur les communications relatives au droit privé dans les pays étrangers", in *Les Transformations du droit dans les principaux pays depuis cinquante ans (1869-1919). Livre du cinquantenaire de la Société de Législation comparée* (1923), p. 85; G. Sauser-Hall, *Fonction et méthode du droit comparé* (1913), pp. 59-63.

[83] Mackinder, "The Geographical Pivot of History", *The Geographical Journal*, XXIII (1904), p. 421.

era classifications, this ethnocentric approach to legal cartography was preserved.[84] Yet, the seminal comparative-law treatise that René David dedicated to the legal systems of the world still focuses on the three major legal Euro-Asiatic legal traditions (Romano-Germanic; Common law, and Soviet law), essentializing Hindu, Eastern Asian, Islamic, and African laws under the banner "Other Conceptions of the Law and the Social Order". When proposing a classification grounded in the deep-rooted differences between all models of social organization, even Ugo Mattei[85] did not escape Western-driven methodological biases. The way he arranges systems according to the rules of *professional law, political law,* and *traditional law* clearly resonates with the hierarchical distinction between: (1) superior (that is, European) systems based on separation of powers and division between morality and the law (rule of professional law); (2) systems which either are experiencing a transition from a colonial, undemocratic regime to democracy or make the law servient to politics (rule of political law), such as China, Russia, and several allegedly Third-World countries; finally, (3) Western systems and jurisdictions where non-Western (and therefore backward) conceptions of the law are still dominant.

Last but not least, scholars in the United States also arranged Ethnocentric legal cartographies. The most relevant United States classification was devised by John Henry Wigmore (1863-1943) in 1928. His *A Panorama of the World's Legal Systems* lists five cultural contexts, which might evolve through various stages of development leading to the same stage of superiority envisaged by United States and European comparative legal traditions: the primitive, ancient, Euro-American, religious, and Afro-Asian contexts.[86] Perhaps the most intriguing of all classifications was devised by Harold Joseph Berman (1918-2007) in *Law and Revolution*.[87] Berman's assumption is that the Western world has

[84] P. Arminjon, et al., *Traité de Droit Comparé* (1950), I; Zweigert and Kötz, note 78 above, devised classifications that broadened the scope of traditional legal cartography but still had Europe as their center.

[85] Ugo Mattei, "Three Patterns of Law: Taxonomy and Change in the World's Legal Systems", *The American Journal of Comparative Law*, XLV (1997), p. 5.

[86] J. H. Wigmore, *Panorama of the World's Legal Systems* (1928). 3 vols.

[87] H. J. Berman, *Law and Revolution: The Formation of the Western Legal Tradition* (1983).

elaborated a unique legal tradition, into which the basic features of Western legal culture have coalesced, that is, the "Sagesse" of English law, the principles of French Enlightenment, and German "genius". It goes without saying that these features have come to blend in the United States, which now represents the universal model of Western legal culture.

Perhaps most paradoxical is that Berman essentialized European legal traditions. The ideological intent is apparent: he backed United States geopolitics by applying legal cartography. Not only does the law of the United States embed the principles inherited by European colonization, but it is also the dominant Western tradition. Within spatial production, Berman's reasoning supplements the United States politico-legal discourse with a sort of "counter-pivot of history". The American continent is the land where individuals enjoy their freedoms; in the classification devised by the Argentinian comparative lawyer Enrique Martínez Paz (1882-1952), this continent was also home to several liberal democracies, such as the Latin American ones in the 1930s.[88]

As a land of freedom, the American continent, in general, and the United States, in particular, sharply contrasted with Europe, the land of monarchies. Not only did the American continent inherit the superiority of the Western law, but it also ranked first within it. The victory in World War II upheld the primacy of the United States within the Western legal tradition, as well as the validity of this strategic global thinking, which definitively relegated Europe as the continuation of the Western hemisphere to the Eastern one.

MAPPING AND RANKING THE SPATIALITY OF GLOBAL LAW

The practice of ranking legal systems also characterizes the imaginative geographies of globalization.[89] It is no coincidence that the current state of world affairs is labelled "globalization". This phenomenon has generated its own spatiality of law and the

[88] E. Martínez Paz, *Introducción al estudio del derecho civil comparado* (1934), p. 155.

[89] On how global actors (the World Bank, and the EU Commission) use of such methods when promoting legal change see A. Nicita and S. Benedettini (2012) "Towards the Economics of Comparative Law: The *Doing Business* Debate", in Monateri (ed.), *Methods of Comparative Law* (2012), p. 291; Siems, note 6 above, p. 209.

inception of a new global politics of space. Just as comparative lawyers, transnational actors have their own cartographical ambitions, geopolitics of law, and spatial hierarchies. The difference lies in how implicatures are hinted at and represented. Digital technology allows them to use indexes and indicators according to which some countries are said to be more or less democratic than others, and some systems ensure more elevated economic performances than others. Indicators thus provide "an alternative source of legitimisation", that alters the geographical representation of the law through a deliberate "plan of … change based upon an imitation of laws", transplants, and borrowings.[90]

The dismantlement of colonialism in the 1960s and 1970s, the end of the Cold War, and the advent of "new world order" announced by the United States President George Bush led to the reopening of territories. The post-Cold-War, the 1994 Uruguay Round, and the World Bank advocated a new space which had to be governed under the "good governance" scheme. A true Neoliberal era begun. As well as a new spatiality of law. The ambition was that this would promote "peace and security, freedom and the rule of law" alongside economic development: indeed, the global village had already been established "from the economic ground up".[91]

We have got used to localizing trade and civilization within globalized markets; as legal scholars, we also praise global law. Our Western minds describe it in accordance with a narrative of *superiority* and *progress*. Global law possesses a liberating force that facilitates the harmonization of laws and stimulates economic development. Global markets need the production of new legal spaces to favor the smooth flows of goods, capital, and services across frontiers.

This does not mean rubbing borders out of maps. It solely requires new efforts to enforce globalization, that is, the outcome of spatial production stimulated by transnational actors. Lefebvre

[90] Ajani, "Ruling by Indicators: How the Use of Vague Notions and Quantitative Indicators Facilitates Legal Change", *The Cardozo Electronic Bulletin* (2017), p. 1. See also D. Nelken, (2018) 'The Legitimacy of Global Social Indicators: Reconfiguring Authority, Accountability and Accuracy", *Les Cahiers de Droit* , LIX (2018), p. 35. See also M. Bussani, et al. *Comparative Legal Metrics. Quantification of Performances as Regulatory Technique* (2023).

[91] S. J. Rosow, "Globalisation as Democratic Theory", *Millennium*, XXIX (2000), p. 29.

highlighted that; as it is produced by socio (and legal) practices, even space is not immune from the exercise of the hegemony of the holders of global capital. They make "use of it ... on the basis of an underlying logic and with the help of the knowledge and technical expertise, of a 'system'".[92] To this end, they create several cross-border regulatory systems that match their "private ordering in the name of party autonomy".[93] They have also found ways to generalize their interests by promoting changes in national spaces, which act as "striations and discrepancies that interrupt [the] monolithic spaces" of globalized normativities.[94] As a part of a new process of spatial production, it reflects the imaginative geographies of global and transnational actors, their geopolitics of law, and spatial hierarchies. The difference lies in how space is arranged, and the spatiality of law is manufactured.

LEGAL MAPPING; OR THE GEOGRAPHY OF INDICATORS

The practice of ranking legal systems also characterizes the current state of affairs. Globalization has favored new waves of universalism. Take, for instance, the dissemination of European constitutionalism around the world: "the basic principles of constitutional law" are now deemed to be "the same around the world", their "universal respect" and "observance" is dependent on their being "a common standard of achievement for all peoples and all nations".[95] Global law is supposed to "offer everyone the benefits of peace, human rights, representative democracy, and moderate government".[96] Over the past few decades, we have also

[92] Lefebvre, note 19 above, p. 11.

[93] H. Muir Watt, "The Relevance of Private International Law to the Global Governance Debate", in Muir Watt (ed.), *Private International Law and Global Governance* (2014), p. 9.

[94] Carpi, "The Island Metaphor in Literature and Law", *Pólemos*, XIV (2020), p. 225.

[95] D. Beatty, *Comparative Law in Theory and Practice* (1995), p. 10. See also R. Arnold, "Reflections on the Universality of Human Rights", in Arnold (ed.), *The Universalism of Human Rights* Springer (2013), pp. 12-13; T. Bingham, *Widening Horizons: The Influence of Comparative Law and International Law on Domestic Law* (2010); C. Gearty, "Human Rights Law", in R. Masterman and R. Schütze (eds.), *The Cambridge Companion to Comparative Constitutional Law* (2019), p. 291.

[96] M. Xifaras, "The *Global Turn* in Legal Theory", *Canadian Journal of Law &*

been experiencing a considerable degree of legal convergence: the comparative-law discourse is oversaturated with "transplants", "borrowings", and so on.[97] These changes have paved the way to several cartographic experiments. In our globalized world, recipient countries usually adopt Western legal paradigms as their benchmark, against which it is possible to assess whether a given jurisdiction respects human rights. In addition, the use of quantification in comparative law allows us to measure, *inter alia*, "global-transnational influences on constitutional human rights".[98]

Indexes, such as the Global Democracy Index, "illustrate the point that an instrumental part of cartography (and more broadly of scientific practice) is ideology"; and the joint application of thematic mapping and GIS creates a hierarchy of colors and jurisdictions within maps.[99] Each country is colored to reflect its rank and democratic outlook in terms of shades of blue and red. The redder the country, the less democratic it is; the darker blue the recipient, the more democratic it is. The possibility of clicking on this map to ascertain whether a country comports with a further five indicators (electoral process and pluralism, functioning of government, political participation, democratic political culture, and civil liberties) also reflects an additional pattern of normalization within the Global Democracy Index.

Whatever projection is chosen for representing the world, this space is objectivized both in geographical and comparative-law terms. And the cartographical representation is no longer limited to technicalities for recording and storing information. The imaginative geographies of transnational actors promote the change in national spaces, whose decision-making processes must adapt to the interests of transnational actors to code their own interests through the law.[100] The relationship between "spatial

Jurisprudence, XXIX (2016), p. 216. See also G. Gong, *The Standard of "Civilization" in International Society* (1984).

97 For more on these processes see Nicolini, note 43 above.

98 C. L. Beck, et al, "Constitutions in World Society: A New Measure of Human Rights", in G, Schaffer, et al, *Constitution-Making and Transnational Legal Order* (2019), p. 95 (constitutions are now "global-transnational documents as much as national ones").

99 J. W. Crampton, *Mapping: A Critical Introduction to Cartography and GIS* (2010), p. 70.

100 Nicolini, note 1 above, p. 127 et seq.

technologies" (cartography, remote sensing, and GIS, just to quote a few) and globalization marks a new "defining moment" for cartography "coming to grips with" a new function of maps – that is, the propaganda of global interests relegating the representation of the earth to a purely decorative role.[101]

This has fostered the use of both indicators and rankings, through which "the most economical solutions have been chosen and ... are permanently in control".[102] The link between law and economic performance has a huge impact on classifications. Now the ranking of legal systems depends on their performativity, which is rooted in their legal origins. The *Western legal tradition* is dominant, and, within it, the *common law* prevails over the *civil law*. Although civil-law systems have demonstrated their ability to secure a shareholder and creditor protection regulation higher than common law jurisdictions, the latter are said to ensure more elevated economic performances. Measured, as they are, through numerical indicators, legal systems now fall under "numerical comparative law", which presupposes that "legal institutions have an impact on economic growth" – and "in tune with neoclassical law and economics" – the dominant paradigm is based "essentially on the idea that law should be measured by the incentives it sets for welfare-maximizing conduct". The holders of capital have created spatial hierarchies through "cross-country comparisons including rankings of the attractiveness of different legal systems for doing business".[103]

[101] See J. Pickles, "Texts, Hermeneutics, and Propaganda Maps", in T. J. Barnes and J. S. Duncan (eds.), *Writing Worlds: Discourse, Text, and Metaphor in the Representation of Landscape* (1992), p. 193; J. Crampton, "Cartography's Defining Moment: The Peters Projection Controversy, 1974–1990", *Cartographica: The International Journal for Geographic Information and Geovisualization*, XXXI (1994), p. 16.

[102] See R. Rottenburg and S. Merry (2015) "A World of Indicators: The Making of Governmental Knowledge through Quantification", in R. Rottenburg et al. (eds.), *The World of Indicators: The Making of Governmental Knowledge through Quantification* (2015), p. 1; Oto-Peralía and Romero-Ávila, *Legal Traditions, Legal Reforms and Economic Performance. Theory and Evidence* (2017), pp. 57-83.

[103] R. Michaels, "Comparative Law by Numbers? Legal Origins Thesis, Doing Business Reports, and the Silence of Traditional Comparative Law", *American Journal of Comparative Law*, LVII (2009), 768, 766.

"STILL REPRESENTING THE WORLD"? THE CONSOCIATIONAL, THE CARTOGRAPHIC, AND THE LEGAL IN A TIME OF GLOBAL COMPARATIVE LAW

In examining how the epistemic community of comparative lawyers devises a world picture consistent with its own *Weltanschauung*, this article has drawn a connection between comparative law and geography. This connection is a "special relationship" because the disciplines at stake share several commonalities, which are rooted in their epistemological underpinnings. Both display an empirical attitude towards world knowledge, peruse a variety of methodological approaches, enhance critical thinking, and challenge the bracketing (not to say isolationist) attitude of lawyers when making sense of the complex space-place-environment nexus present in geographical contexts. In sum, they figure out the world in its complexity, showing an incredible ability *to grasp the world intellectually*.

This article has then reframed these commonalities in terms of disciplinary construction. Neither comparative law nor geography has interrupted the *continuum* between the human and the environmental nor turned the world into a separate entity. This dispositional attitude has kept the precincts of legal and geographical studies open to interactions with the outer world. But it has also highlighted how their disciplinary construction affects the way their world picture is outlined. This is apparent in comparative legal research, whose legal methods are functional to ordering world knowledge, that is, supplying a particular representation of the world's legal systems. What lies beneath this representation is a set of *implicatures* asserting the superiority of Western legal derivatives. The main implicature considers the Western conception of law a universal paradigm "superior" to all other legal systems.

Comparative law has done so by engaging in a cross-disciplinary dialogue with geography. Cross-disciplinarity has made an invaluable addition to the field of comparative law by helping it to stage its world picture in the broader geographical context. This is the "vernacular use" of physical and human geographies: the law acting as the interface between them provides its own legal mapping, orders the world, and naturalizes the representation of the latter. Undoubtedly, this has boosted the cartographical ambitions of comparative law. Map-making is indeed a matter of spatial "production", disciplinary "construction", and political "choice". By *acts of simplification* law reduces the inherent complexity of the world to a picture by stripping away whatever comparative law considers ideologically useless or dangerous. Generalizations add the finishing touches to this process of spatial production, inasmuch as "naturalizing the map has the effect of *universalizing* it" and the Western legal superiority it endorses.[104]

This approach to the world's legal systems still populates the spatiality of globalization. The purpose is the same: to uphold the superiority of a given set of legal derivatives. With huge differences, though. First, technological advancements have replaced traditional cartography with new software, GIS, and applications, thus relegating the representation of the earth to a purely decorative role. Second, the geopolitics of global spaces is governed by a constellation of non-State actors coding their interests in a coordinated way through transnational law.[105] Not only do the forces of capital impact on, and therefore reduce, the ability of States to control how multinational corporations operate, but they also propagate their global interests through further processes of legal generalization. It is not a matter of generalizing, exporting, and disseminating the limited set of civilized, that is, Western, legal systems. Rather, globalization produces a qualitative change in the world's legal systems by evaluating their efficiency and attractiveness to international investments. The new legal-geographical spaces of globalization are saturated with indexes and indicators that promise elevated performances provided that legal systems converge toward a superior stage of legal development that is universal: the more efficient the system, the more likely the investment, and the higher the economic return.

We must be held somewhat accountable for such a state of affairs. On one hand, the widespread application of the universalistic approach has encouraged the search for legal uniformity by way of generalisations even in a time of globalization. Our

[104] Respectively: Brighenti, "On Territory as Relationship and Law as Territory", *Canadian Journal of Law & Society*, XXI (2006), p. 69; Nayak and Jeffrey, note 18 above, p. 240.

[105] See G. Schaffer and C. Coye, "From International Law to Jessup's *Transnational Law*, from Transnational Law to *Transnational Legal Orders*", in P. Zumbansen (ed.), *The Many Lives of Transnational Law: Critical Engagements with Jessup's Bold Proposal* (2020), p. 126.

generalizations thus represent our major contribution to the rise of another epistemic community, that of global comparative law. Comparative law seems to have handed over the idea of producing transnational legal culture, which is now firmly in the hands of global legal scholarship. This means severing universalism as a methodological approach from the comparative-law epistemological community that created it. In encouraging, and therefore *generalizing*, the recourse to generalizations, global legal scholarship has converted them into a wide-reaching legal device. Its effects are now apparent on scholars; and "legal globalisation is [...] transforming legal culture on a global scale".[106]

This process still conveys the idea that geography reflects a "neutral" reality. Even in a time of global comparative law, which acts as the new interface between physical and human geographies alike. Just as in traditional comparative law, cartographic representations of the global politics of space give rise to a new ontology, which comes into existence when it finds its place on the map. Or, which is the same thing, the new legal-geographical features come into existence provided that they comply with the benchmarks set by indicators.

As is evident, indicators share the biases of traditional legal cartography; "through numerical representation, one always loses some aspects of the reality".[107] Their ability to reconcile scientific objectivity and measurement with real-world tests is attained by leaving out of the picture the striations that may disturb transnational derivatives wherever economic interests deem it fit to do so. As in traditional cartography, transnational actors superimpose their own nomenclatures and imaginative geographies onto the earth's surface. They have "the potential to alter the forms, the exercise, and perhaps even the distributions of powers in certain spheres of global governance" – not to mention its representation in geographical terms.[108]

Indicators deliberately omit data and variables, notwithstanding their relevance in real-world assessments. Such omissions may

[106] See Husa, note 2 above, p. 32.

[107] Rottenburg and Merry, note 103 above, p. 8.

[108] K. E. Davis, et al., "Introduction: Global Governance by Indicators", in K. E. Davis, et al. (eds.), *Governance by Indicators. Global Power through Quantification and Rankings* (2012), p. 4.

also trigger a strabismus in metrics, which unavoidably affects the reliability of their outlook. Odd as it may seem, this type of strabismus may prevent them from scratching the surface of the data and realizing that there are concrete signs of danger, if not of catastrophe. But, indicators also point to danger, which we may either ignore or take seriously. The strabismus of indicators occurred, for instance, just before the 2007 financial crisis, when "all the standard financial indicators declared that financial system was safe". It could have been sufficient to scratch the surface and realize that real economy exhibited signs of danger; and yet, there was a "collective declaration of safety being issued by the financial market indicators".[109]

This new cartography of the world is evidently unable to grasp the world intellectually. Being a generalisation of sectional interests, private orderings, and transnational financial actors aiming to maximise their own profits, cartography is not interested in representing the world. The production, construction, and choice of the global holders of capital act as a liberating force that facilitates the maximisation of profits for shareholders, capital investors, and asset owners. How it is possible that such a selfish mechanism of cartographical representation, made up of indicators and data, holds a particular fascination for us all?

It holds a particular fascination because it is *consociational*. Coined by Arend Lijpart, the expression points to those federal processes whereby highly conflictive societies, usually divided along ethnolinguistic cleavages, are accommodated and the maintenance of territorial integrity is secured.[110] The consociational argument arranges different sectionalities around a power-sharing organizing principle. It assumes the unequal distribution of wealth; but this does not prevent each member of the community from gaining access to it.

[109] W. Davies, "Spirits of Neoliberalism: 'Competitiveness' and 'Wellbeing' Indicators as Rival Orders of Worth", in Rottenburg, et al (eds.) *The World of Indicators: The Making of Governmental Knowledge through Quantification* (2015), p. 283; A. Farlow, "Financial Indicators and the Global Financial Crash", in Rottenburg, et al. (eds.), *The World of Indicators. The Making of Governmental Knowledge through Quantification* (2015), pp. 221-222.

[110] On consociational federalism, see A. Lijpart, "Consociation and Federation: Conceptual and Empirical Links", *Canadian Journal of Political Science*, XIII (1979), p. 505.

The consociational argument is also useful for propagating global comparative law as it favors its generalization. Egalitarian in its commitment, it facilitates the harmonization of laws to stimulate business and economic development. It also proposes a transnational, borderless legal geography into which heterogeneous legal systems coalesce. This occurs under pressure from economic models, which aim to make laws converge towards a common economic semantics. The alleged egalitarianism of global comparative law is thus the new cartographic projection of global financial dominance, which evaluates the efficiency of legal systems and their attractiveness provided that they positively discriminate in favor of international investors.

Chapter 5

Basic Transformation of Legal Pictures: Purpose and Method of Comparative Law

OLEG A. HALABUDENKO

Comparative jurisprudence has travelled a long way in its historical development, which, in the legal systems embraced by the Western Legal Tradition, was initiated by forms of legal communication arising between the law of the urban community (urban law, *ius civile*) and the law of nations (*ius gentium*):

> Roman law's originality lies in the fact that it has been formed as the law of a city. At the same time, in the urban centres of the ancient world, one finds peregrines for whom – with the exception of the legal institutions of the ius gentium – not the same law applies as for Roman citizens.[1]

The dialectical link between the law of the city and the law of other communities serves as a basis for the future development of law in its pragmatic understanding as a means and method of legal regulation of the behavior of a subordinate subject of law. However, more importantly for the purpose of this study is that such a dialectical relationship serves as a heuristic communicative model that allows us to explore the essence and forms of legal communication between different legal cultures without detachment from reality.

From the position of the dominant, until recently, pragmatic approach to law as an invariant way of achieving a certain result,[2]

[1] See Martin Avenarius, "Roman Law as the Law of a City. the Origins of the Concept and the Changing Conditions of its Further Development", *Proceedings of the Institute of State and Law of the Russian Academy of Sciences*. XIII, no. 3 (2018), pp. 7-47.

[2] This approach assumes a vision of law as a means of changing the world without taking into account the connection with reality, or a conception of law whose connection with reality unexplainable with the proposed methodology,

forms of legal communication, reflecting the dialectical relationship between urban law and the law of nations serve as valuable material, as a formal basis for the construction of all possible typified legal constructions (models of relations as prototypes of legal constructions in their Kantian understanding) of modern legal orders. The latter is important for legal cultures united by a common tradition at a stable stage of their existence, but it is insufficient for understanding the principles, the foundations, of legal communication between legal cultures that do not share a common tradition.

The idea of law as a pragmatic means of regulating the behavior of subordinate subjects, which once triumphed in the minds of "lawyers who were seated in a comfortable chair acquired as a result of social revolutions", turns out to be useless under the conditions of regional conflicts and the "global storm"'. In the latter circumstances, law is expected to explain patterns of communication between subjects from different cultures not bound by a common legal tradition.

Comparative jurisprudence, having a scientific status, unlike legal dogmatics, considers legal phenomena and processes in connection with reality. Accordingly, comparative jurisprudence includes only those legal phenomena and processes that have a connection with reality – we define such a connection as the transcendental basis of law. At the same time, we argue that the only transcendence for legal phenomena and processes characteristic of particular legal cultures should be considered *loci* of law – its spatial dimension.

Legal processes should be considered in the context of perception of legal communicative models (legal constructions) arising from the dialogue of different legal cultures, and transfer of the established concept of them in the course of legal communication to new *loci* – law of national States, City law, regional law, law of Virtual Worlds, emerging Global meta-law. In turn, in our opinion, legal phenomena as mental forms related to reality considered in a methodological way, through the search for their epistemic basis, allows us to understand their existence.

that is, approach legal regulation as a version of naive magical influence of legal norms on human behavior.

The subject of this study is legal communication between different legal cultures. The main task is to find an answer to the question: how under conditions of conflict between cultures is their legal communication is possible? The answer implies, in the first place, an appeal to the methodological arsenal accumulated by comparative jurisprudence during the its previous stages of development. The latter allows us to draw a number of conclusions regarding the metaepistemic vision of law and its main categories – legal culture, legal tradition, codes of legal communication, and legal constructions. The first section of this article is devoted to the methodology and epistemic dimension of comparative jurisprudence.

The second section, focused on the spatial organization of law, reviews legal communication arising in connection with the spatial localization of legal cultures as artifacts, setting the inherently transcendent existence of law at the level of national States, cities, regions, global and virtual levels.

COMPARATIVE JURISPRUDENCE IN THE CONTEXT OF CHANGE IN ITS EPISTEMOLOGICAL DIMENSION

The needs of legal communication between persons with different legal affiliations make it necessary to adopt a single code to enable biosocial interaction. In turn, the generation of the required code of legal communication becomes possible through a comparison of typical models of behavior (legal constructions).

The present writer has hypothesized that the direct object of comparative jurisprudence is legal constructions: "legal constructions reflect specific aspects, demanded by practice, of a general conceptual nucleus being the foundation of a normative material of legal orders unified by a common legal tradition".[3] It is hardly possible to dispute that initially legal communication itself is caused by the needs of dialogue between actors of law – persons belonging to different legal cultures. Various facets of social reality – such as concepts, beliefs, norms, and values – are

[3] O.A. Halabudenko, "Legal Constructions in the Focus of Inter-Temporal and Inter-Local Methods of Comparasion: The Methodological Aspect", in William E. Butler and Oleksiy V. Kresin (eds.), *The Interaction of Legal Systems: Post-Soviet Approaches* (2015), p. 86.

formed through continuous interactions and negotiations among society's members.[4]

The rhetorical question posed by Franz Wieacker (1908-1994) – "Do the traits of our legal culture outlined here have a chance to become part of a future planetary legal culture?"[5] – has an unequivocal negative answer. In this regard, Roger Cotterrell noted: "A law immersed within a culture is of necessity, and this must be emphasised, different from a law that exists in another culture".[6] However, it is the pluralism of legal cultures that gives rise to the necessity of legal communication, and in the scientific aspect, with regard to the subject and method of comparative law, such pluralism makes it necessary to cognize forms of communication through the establishment of the common and particular among legal phenomena and processes.

The practical significance of comparative law is to develop ways and means of intercultural dialogue between actors involved in different legal discourses of different legal cultures. In this case, the discourse is understood as a complex communicative phenomenon, a complex system of knowledge hierarchy, including, in addition to the text, extra-linguistic factors, the consideration of which is necessary for understanding the text.

The assertion that a con-text is the semio-socio-cultural environment in which the text unfolds, and consequently that the text and the con-text are so are so intimately related that neither concept can be comprehended in the absence of the other,[7] is undeniable. But we unable to understand the logical meaning of the discourse field without knowing the rules of its reading, which are constructed in the process of dialogue and which endow it with inter-actor meanings.

[4] See Peter L. Berger and Thomas Luckmann, *The Social Construction of Reality: A Treatise in the Sociology of Knowledge* (2011).

[5] Franz Wieacker and Edgar Bodenheimer, "Foundations of European Legal Culture", *American Journal of Comparative Law*, XXXVIII (1990), p. 27.

[6] Roger Cotterrell, "Comparative Law and Legal Culture", in R. Zimmermann and M. Reimann (eds.), *Oxford Handbook of Comparative Law* (2006), pp. 711-712.

[7] See M. A. K. Halliday and R. Hasan, "The Structure of a Text", in *Language, Context, and Text: Aspects of Language in a Social-Semiotic Perspective* (1985), pp. 52-69.

In juxtaposition with the tasks of intercultural dialogue provided by the search for ways of semantic transliteration and adaptation to the syntax of a text forms acceptable for comprehension, in other words, to the reception of the text inscribed in a different legal culture, the field of comparative legal research is narrowing. "Culture can refer not just to shared beliefs and values, and common traditions, but also to what anthropologists call 'material' culture – levels of technological development and economic interaction", and hence –

> Not to be neglected, either, are shared emotional attachments and rejections: culture can be a matter of loves and hatreds, attractions and repulsions, definitions of 'us' and 'them', that are not necessarily reducible to differences of tradition, belief or values; or to shared conditions of economic or other kinds of instrumental interaction. Thus, when people think of their cultural attachments they sometimes find that these are not entirely explicable in terms of beliefs/values, traditions or material interests (though efforts may be made to rationalise them in those terms).[8]

However, whatever the actual significance of emotions related to law, in actors representing "own" legal cultures, the transliteration of codes of "alien" legal culture is always carried out in a rational form. The starting point in this process is the rational form of legal formations understanding, which fulfils the function of transliteration of the codes of "alien" legal culture, and, accordingly, the irrational form of perception, which endows the compared legal cultures with distinctive features that do not imply any perception. Thus, dialogue between cultures is achieved through the acceptance of a common legal tradition, which serves as a code of legal communication and allows for effective communication.

In turn, the basis of a specific legal culture is the community of legal ideas (concepts), conditioned by the manifestation of a certain legal tradition and finding the appropriate embodiment (reception) in typical legal forms. Hence, the study of legal culture (taking into account its socio-cultural components) outside the context of the legal tradition involved in its formation, reduces

[8] Roger Cotterrell, "Law and Culture – Inside and Beyond the Nation State", *Retfærd Argang*, XXXI, no. 4/123 (2008), pp. 25-26.

the subject of comparative jurisprudence to the field of knowledge related to legal geography.

It is not difficult to see that the above approach to the vision of legal communication established between different legal cultures leads to a logical circle: speech is possible if a common code of communication is elaborated, which must precede the beginning of legal communication.

The adoption of a common communicative code within a certain paradigms does not mean, however, that in the process of legal communication political-legal terms are interpreted by participants absolutely identically. Thomas Samuel Kuhn (1922-1996), reflecting on commensurability, comparability, communicability, rightly noted,

> So long as the members of a speech community agree on a number of standart examples (paradigms), the utility of terms like 'democracy', 'justice', or 'equity' is not much threatened by the occurrence also of cases in which community members differ about the applicability of these terms. Words of this sort need not function unequivocally; fuzziness at the borders is expected, and it is the acceptance of fuzziness that permits drift, the gradual warping of meanings of a set of interrelated terms over time.[9]

When talking about legal culture, we should note that this concept itself outside the context of the general communicative code is devoid of connotative meaning. In other words, legal culture is a culture of value for its representatives and does not necessarily correspond to a civilizational ideal. Its real value may be learned only in consequence of perceiving by representatives of other legal cultures (not always voluntarily) and, consequently, in the process of comparing its basic constructions and institutions with those that are known for representatives of the perceiving culture. Indeed, Gustave Le Bon has convincingly demonstrated that culture is by no means an indicator of a nation's civilization, that civilizations are often led by peoples with underdeveloped, utilitarian cultures but strong character and ideals, that the power of civilization lays not in technical and cultural achievements, but in character and ideals, and finally, that even a higher culture,

[9] Thomas S. Kuhn, *The Road Since 'Structure': Philosophical Essays, 1970-1993, with Autobiographical Interwiew*, ed. Hames Conant and John Haugeland (2000), p. 57.

which is not peculiar to a nation, undermines its morals and destroys the values formed over centuries, which makes such a nation even lower.[10]

Thus, legal tradition is the common element that unites legal cultures between which there was no dialogue before, and its effectiveness is determined by the necessary epistemic authority, which, according to Jürgen Habermas (b. 1929), is achieved by the actions of the speech community. Thus, the need to establish a dialogue between the bearers of different legal cultures creates a new "legal situation" significantly different from that which existed within a particular legal culture. Such a «situation» can be characterized by special epistemic characteristics: the autonomous subject of legal communication ceases to exist, its place is taken by the named communicative community, the correspondent theory of truth is replaced by consensus theories, and the place of the epistemological subject is replaced by intersubjectivity.[11]

In other words, the question of – "is there some operation code or hidden formant we are missing that actually drives the pattern of law?"[12] – within the framework of comparative jurisprudence suggests that there is an unambiguous answer. An attempt to overcome the logical circle set by the Habermas critical conception is made by Paul-Michel Foucault (1926-1984), who freed the key concept of "discourse" from any transcendental or any psychic basis and comes to the conclusion about the omnipresence, totality of political power. For Foucault, the human person – the primary medium of communication – is absent; he/she is nothing but an ephemeral construction of a historically conditioned discourse that dictates the "episteme" of a historical epoch.[13]

Niklas Luhmann (1927-1998), who, following the principle *that if something does not create itself, it is not a system*, completely separated mental processes from social ones and perceived the

[10] See: Gustave Le Bon, *Psychology of Crowds* (2009).

[11] See Jürgen Habermas, *Theory of Communicative Action, Volume One: Reason and the Rationalization of Society* (1996); Habermas, *Between Facts and Norms: Contributions to a Discourse Theory of Law and Democracy*, transl. William Rehg (1998).

[12] Edward J. Eberle, "The Methodology of Comparative Law", *Roger Williams University Law Review*, XVI (2011), p. 56.

[13] See Michel Foucault, *Discourse & Truth and Parrēsia*, ed. Henri-Paul Fruchaud and Daniele Lorenzini; intro. Frédéric Gros (2019).

human personality in society as a communicative artefact, as a product of social autopoiesis acting in the context of an autopoietic social system.[14] Thus, at the methodological level, the well-known dispute between realism and nominalism is resolved in a new reading: epistemological realism leads ultimately to holism, which affirms the reality and primacy of society, and hence its inherent culture. For comparative jurisprudence, such epistemic paradigm, in particular, gives reason to draw the following conclusion: legal culture is not absorbed or determined by the general culture, legal culture is autonomous and capable of self-development.

Moreover, from the point of view of the analytical approach to comparative jurisprudence, legal culture is structured, and therefore, it is acceptable to distinguish different indicators of legal culture – legal formants.[15] Nevertheless, legal formants are not a simple collection of sources of law not only in their narrow sense (forms of law), but also in their broadest sense (the legal order as a whole). As Pier Giuseppe Monateri notes, "The theory of legal formants, also known as the dynamic approach to comparative law, focuses on law as a social activity: a formant of the Law is a group, a type of personnel, or a community, institutionally involved in the activity of creating Law". Accordingly, "The main idea is to substitute the model of the law as a more or less consistent system of interrelated, hierarchically connected propositions, by a model of competing formants within the unique setting and constraints of one legal tradition".[16]

Rather, it is permissible to define legal formants as a category of legal artefacts, which makes it acceptable to apply to them in such a case the relevant methodology. In this sense, the theory of legal formants

> offers a picture of laws as bundles of transplants of competing sources of law. The formant approach is then a totally comparative approach based on a kind of 'external' study of the law as a form of sociological or economic

[14] See Niklas Luhmann, *Einführung in die Systemtheorie*, ed. Dirk Baecker (5th ed.; (2009).

[15] See Rodolfo Sacco, "Legal Formants: A Dynamic Approach to Comparative Law", *American Journal of Comparative Law*, XXXIX (1991), pp. 343-401.

[16] P. G. Monateri, *Legal Formants and Competitive Models: Understanding Comparative Law from Legal Process to Critique in Cross-System Legal Analysis* (2008) (available online).

appraisal of lawyers' activities, coupled with an 'internal' analysis of documents as a kind of form criticism.[17]

The analytical approach distinguishes legal culture from other cultural phenomena, structures it on the basis of empirical data, and thus makes it possible rationally describe the links between law and other cultural phenomena. However, the analytical approach leaves a number of fundamental questions unresolved. First, it is a question of the *a priori* foundations of a particular legal discourse. Indeed, if "discourse formations are historically contingent, lacking any a priori foundation", then "every society has its own order of truth, its own politics of truth".[18] From the above assumption, we can draw the methodological conclusion that discourse patterns regulate themselves.

Foucault's attempt to abandon the idea of autonomous discourse in order to avoid autoreferentialism leads to the idea of searching for a quasi-transcendental basis for discursive practices, which he identifies with total power. For legal discourse, the norm of law is the embodiment of total power, and it is also recognized as the basic element of borrowing by the recipient culture - the "seedling norm" borrowed from the donor culture.

Ultimately, an effective way of solving the problem of the endless search for the foundation of episteme was proposed by Gunther Teubner, who develops Luhmann's theory of autopoiesis in relation to law. This concept, adopted from biology, refers to a system that reproduces its elementary components by means of a functioning network of the same elements and, thanks to this, is separated from the external environment. In a social and, as we can assume, legal system, reproduction takes place in the form of communication. Thus, autopoiesis is a way of reproduction of a certain system identical to itself, provided by replication of the code of legal communication.

Nevertheless, Teubner, reflecting on the fate of the "unified legal discourse", which, in his opinion, is being deformed by "the invasion of poststructuralism, critical theory, self-referentiality and autopoiesis in the socio-legal world", contrasts the volitional behavior of individuals with "infamous mystifications of

[17] Ibid.

[18] Gunther Teubner, "How the Law Thinks: Toward a Constructivist Epistemology of Law", *Law and Society Review*, XXIII (1989), p. 735.

collectivities".[19] Without going into polemics concerning the possibility of collective action, in reality we are talking about the dichotomy of legal discourse, its division into two components: power, on one hand, and structures of public consciousness, on the other.

In this regard the question is: what should we recognize as the "centre" of legal constructions serving as the actual content and primary legal units of each legal culture – public authority or the will of individuals expressed in relation to legal constructions that have developed through autopoietic processes? And in this regard: should public authority be seen as something opposed to the biosocial forms of existence of human communities? If the latter is true, then no less important is the question: what are the limits of deformation of public consciousness exposed to the influence of power imperatives? Umberto Eco (1932-2016), resorting to the metaphor of sport as a rule-based competitive procedure, answered the questions posed in the following elegant way:

> So, there is a deep area of the collective sensibility that no one, whether through conviction or demagogical calculation, will allow to be touched. And there is a profound structure of the Social whose Maximum Cement, if broken up, would cause a crisis in every possible associative principle, including the presence of man on earth, at least as he has been present in the last tens of thousands of years.[20]

If we cease trying to find the missing structure within the logically flawed framework of structuralism, the answers to these meta-legal questions might be obtained by changing ideas about the grounds of any legal phenomenon or process. This is a constructivist approach to understanding legal phenomena and processes: that any "legal construction does not follow, but immediately precedes the legal statement and thus conditions the development of law".[21] The compared legal constructs have three basic ontological levels:

[19] Ibid., p. 728.

[20] Umberto Eco, *Faith in Fakes: Travels in Hyperreality* (1995), p. 160.

[21] O. Halabudenko, "К вопросу становления понятия «юридическая конструкция»: методологический аспект" [Towards the Formation of the Concept of 'Legal Construction': Methodological Aspect], Закон и жизнь [Lex and Life], no. 10 (2010), p. 22.

(1) the level corresponding to public consciousness (the idea of law);

(2) the level of fixation in the form of normative statements (fixation of the legal idea in the legal text);

(3) yhe level at which, as a result, of the legally significant behavior of the actor, the legal idea reflected in the legal text is transformed into a legal reality (the form of implementation of the right).

Based on this perspective, the birth of the idea of law (a legal construct at the level of public consciousness) from law itself is logically impossible, no matter what power imperative applied in this case. On the other hand, the norm of law altogether as a normative statement, a rule of behavior and a regulatory rule – has an effective impact on individual and on public consciousness only when it is an element of a particular legal construction. Thus, an occupation regime's order is not recognized as a legitimate legal form of impact on human behavior until it will be perceived at the level of social consciousness. In this regard, it is permissible to assume that legal constructions are the basic elements of legal reality that allow us to overcome the *traps of collectivism*.

Consequently, it is not a political imperative or a normative statement that shapes public consciousness, but cultural factors – the faith that those institutions of organization of the biosocial life of a particular society are the most relevant to the tasks of its existence and, possibly, development. To what extent faith in institutions such as government, human rights, democracy, forms of organizing property rights, or, for example, shari'a law constructions, corresponds to the expected result is a question answered by the real state of affairs when we compare it with our expectations, with our beliefs.

As soon as the pragmatic aspect of this or that institution accepted by the public consciousness, it immediately becomes an object of worship based on the faith that this *idea-form* of organization of bisocial life of the community is the best for its existence. This is how the idea of a "better law" is born, which in the end is generally recognized as law of the forum (*lex fori*) exercising jurisdiction *ratione materia, ratione personae, ratione loci, ratione temporis*. Metaphorically, this idea was accurately expressed by the Ukrainian poet Taras Shevchenko (1814-1861): "Truth, strength, and will are all one's own in one's house".[22]

However, trivial it may seem, the tensions between cultures that arise during communication increase the risk of conflict. As Cotterrell aptly put it, "'law and culture' makes people angry",[23] and confrontation, as we can witness in practice, does not disappear when competing cultures are able to perceive each other's language. Doubtless "language certainly is a problem and it might be even greater then most of us expect it to be".[24] In analyzing issues related to legal communication, however, it should be borne in mind that "the legal language will follow the legal order which uses that language (and not the other way round)".[25] In turn, "Each language or discourse will necessarily filter reality through the prism of its own assumptions".[26]

On the face of it, "with the 'Return of Grand Theory', with the invasion of poststructuralism, critical theory, self-referentiality and autopoiesis in the socio-legal world, the unified discourse of law and society is falling apart again into different cultural provinces".[27] However, in reality, the problem of legal communication is rooted not in the plurality of methods of law, but in the distinctive features of legal cultures that define the idea of law in its ontological dimension. The plurality of legal cultures, in turn, is predetermined by the differentiation of the legal space, or more precisely, by the existence of multiple legal spaces.

The stability of any system, including the legal system, depends on the presence of "contours" that ensure its functioning. Law is no exception – along with power imperatives (*potestas*), its action

[22] Taras Shevchenko, Зібрання творів: У 6 т. [Collected Works: In 6 vols.] (2003), I. p. 349.

[23] Cotterrell, note 8 above, pp. 25-26.

[24] Bernhard Grossfield, "Comparative Law as a Comprehensive Approach: A European Tribute to Professor Jack A. Hiller", *Richmond Journal of Global Law & Business*, I (2000), p. 11.

[25] Danny Pieters, *Functions of Comparative Law and Practical Methodology of Comparing, Or How the Goal Determines the Road!* (2009), p. 20 (available online).

[26] Monateri, "Methods of Comparative Law", in *Research Handbook in Comparative Law* (2012), p. 69.

[27] Teubner, note 18 above, p. 728.

is due to cultural authority (*authoritas*).[28] These "contours" serve "bearings" that set the law in motion and ensure its stability. In this sense, law is a cultural artefact arising in the process of legal communication, the participant of which, sometimes invisible, is public authority. "Epistemic trap" is overcome if we take into account the point that the legal artefact absorbs all external factors related to its "creation" and subordinates legal communication to its inherent code alone. Thus, any factual phenomenon is not separated from the legal discourse, not opposed to it, but absorbed into it. That is why any legally significant fact is the "centre" of a legal construction; only when it is "absorbed" by a legal construction, in the context of a certain legal construction, does such a fact acquire a legal meaning. From this point on, the factual phenomenon acquires a noumenal dimension, and the legal construct acquires an existentiality autonomous from the world of facts.

It follows that a fruitful search for a relevant method in comparative jurisprudence is possible only on the assumption that such method acceptance is agreed by all interested participants of legal communication. What for one culture in the field of epistemology is considered meaningless speculation (Jabberwocky), in another culture is recognized as a reasonable and productive means of solving the problem at hand.

In this sense, we concur with Monateri's conclusions: "... method is not absolute ... and method is not objective ..., and any method is someone's method ...".[29] The interpretation of data obtained from a particular method depends on the metaepistemic paradigm. On the assumption that "metaepistemology takes a step back from particular substantive debates in epistemology in order to inquire into the assumptions and commitments made by those who engage in these debates",[30] in the context of solving methodological issues of comparative law, we consider the following statements acceptable:

[28] See Halabudenko, "Legal Norms in the Focus of the Constructivism Theory", *Theoretical and Applied Law*, no. 2(4) (2020), pp. 31-43

[29] Monateri, note 26 above, pp. 66-67.

[30] See "Metaepistemology", in *Stanford Encyclopedia of Philosophy* (available online).

(1) the set of specific methods or approaches to the compared legal reality corresponds to the legal culture and its underlying intentions;

(2) only within a particular meta-epistemic paradigm is it permissible to interpret the data of a particular method or approach in a relevant way;

(3) there are can be no universal methods in comparative law that are irrelevant to a particular legal culture.

Thus, the basic assumption of the functionalist approach that "incomparables cannot usefully be compared, and in law the only things which are comparable are those which fulfil the same function"[31] suggests that "the law of different countries can be compared by finding a common social issue and identifying different legal solutions thereto".[32] Hence, the application of such an approach to the development of a "particular guideline" *a priori* presupposes from the outset the existence of general social and current (common) legal issues, and thus the existence of a coherent communicative model aimed at a result perceived by all participants in the communication. The latter circumstance shows that the application of a certain approach (method) in comparative jurisprudence is only possible if there is a metaepistemic paradigm accepted by the participants in legal communication.

In turn, the claim that "law and economics can be used to build efficient models, which work as uniform terms of comparison for the concrete solutions of the legal institutions analyzed"[33] is not objectionable in principle, but only given that the proposed method is applied in the context of a culture based on "economic imperialism". In all cases, the application of the method of law and economics is based on the belief in money – symbols that, *prima facie*, "carry the maximum tolerance, uniting people of the most distant cultures and creating the conditions for globalization".[34]

[31] K. Zweigert and H. Kotz, *An Introduction to Comparative Law*, transl. Tony Weir (3d ed.; 2011), p. 34.

[32] Marta Tóthová, "Several Aspects of the Comparative Method in Law", *The Lawyer Quarterly*, 1 (2023), p. 80.

[33] Ugo A. Mattei, Luisa Antoniolli, and Andrea Rossato, *Comparative Law and Economics* (1999), p. 506 (available online).

[34] Stanislav Komarek, Європа на роздоріжжі [Europe at a Crossroads], transl. Olena Krushyns'ka (2020), p. 165.

However, such a belief is not absolute; it is heterogeneous and manifests itself in different ways in different legal cultures, usually taking a subordinate place among other, often altruistic, principles and ethical norms. The assertion that the economic result, expressed in money, is the dominant motive of every legal culture is in stark contrast to the current situation: the adoption of the "belief in money" by most legal cultures does not lead to, but on the contrary exacerbates, the conflicts between them to an extreme degree.

The above arguments and additional characterizations of the most important epistemological questions of law, fundamental to the solution of the problems facing comparative jurisprudence, allow us to pose the question of the metaepistemic dimension of law anew. As Teubner states, "Law is defined as an autopoietic social system, i.e. a network of elementary operations that recursively reproduces elementary operations".[35] Autopoietic discourse allows us to argue that the fundamental element of the legal system is not the norm of law and political power as a form of legitimate violence perceived by the actors of legal communication, but the determinate outcome of communication itself: "The law autonomously processes information, creates worlds of meaning, establishes goals and objectives, creates constructions of reality and defines normative expectations – all quite independently of the views of the world in the minds of lawyers".[36] Since the legal system is autopoietic, it is subordinate to the regulations developed in other socially connected systems such as politics, economics, ecology, medicine, and others.

The classic example of an institutional conflict between legal facts and scientific facts is then resolved according to the rules established for *res judicata*. Even if it can later be proven that what was stated in the trial was clearly wrong, the court decision and its legal, economic, and social consequences will not be overturned if the procedural requirements have been met and appeal procedures have been exhausted. It follows from the foregoing that all scientific facts, in order to be recognized as legally relevant, must be evaluated within the accepted constructions of the legal community.

35 Teubner, note 18 above, p. 739.

36 Ibid.

The autopoietic system is autonomous in the sense of operational closure and at the same time susceptible to external influences due to structural conjugation.[37] In other words, in order to recognize the surrounding reality, the system must remain identical with itself and at the same time be open to irritations and events from outside, which it uses for its own change and reorganization. Thus a system creates an inner order out of the external noise. In our opinion, the above-mentioned features of autopoietic systems characterize legal systems in the communication process precisely.

Therefore, other social discourses serve as a source for the production of legal constructions within the given coder. This applies fully to explaining the process of borrowing legal material by one legal system from another. Moreover, such borrowing often occurs through the recoding of discourses that are recognized as non-legal by one culture into discourses that are designated as legal by another.

The above remarks enable us to evaluate the significant changes that have taken place in our conceptions of society and law from a methodological point of view. Our conception of society and law is shifting further away from realism towards constructivism and away from the individual, personal towards the social construction of reality. For law, the crucial point in this transition is the combination of a change in epistemology and a new conception of individuality: epistemological constructivism eliminates the naïve assumption of reality that human actors create the basic institutions of society through their intentional actions.

Constructivist epistemology rules out the claim that the perception of law can be attributed to a corresponding socio-economic institution that lies outside of legal discourse. Law is an autonomous epistemic object that constructs its own social reality. It is not a matter of deliberate actions by individuals that create law as a cultural artefact, but on the contrary, law itself, which is a communicative process, creates actors through its legal operations.

Within the methodology of legal constructivism and the epistemic paradigm of autopoiesis, we can observe the process of rethinking the fundamental characteristics of legal communication as a form of intercultural dialogue. Whereas in the early days of

[37] See Teubner, "The Two Faces of Janus: Rethinking Legal Pluralism", *Cardozo Law Review*, XIII (1992), pp. 1444-1445.

comparative jurisprudence it was assumed that there was a legal actor associated with a particular legal culture, the constructivist paradigm suggests that an actor is a form of representation of a particular code of legal communication. In our view, this is the general outcome of the development of the understanding of law, which is fundamental to the methodology of comparative law.

We express the cautious hope that the above reflections on methodological questions of comparative law will serve as a key to understanding the processes that take place in certain local legal areas.

COMPARATIVE JURISPRUDENCE IN THE CONTEXT OF CHANGING SPATIAL DIMENSIONS

Legal space is, in our view, a transcendent dimension that is *a priori* filled with certain symbols, meanings, and implications due to the intense behavior of actors trying to establish forms of legitimate control over the circulation and appropriation of limited resources in this space. The legal map is dynamic, and any change on it is *per se* the subject of comparative legal research.

The development of comparative law as a system of knowledge about the codes of legal communication between domestic law and foreign law is connected with the formation of national legal orders (national legal space). National legal systems subordinate forms of interaction to positive law, whose symbols, meanings, and expressions do not have universal characteristics. For this reason, comparative law research was conducted outside of legal positivism, and many researchers, even in the early days of comparative law, "considered the influence of the spread of legal positivism on the development of comparative legal studies to be negative".[38] In this regard, Sacco aptly remarked: "No one who wishes to describe the law realistically can ignore the existence of sources other than those formerly recognized in the Constitution".[39]

[38] O. V. Kresin, *Comparative Legal Studies: 1750 to 1835. Approaches to Conceptualization*, ed. and transl. W. E. Butler (2019), I, p. 80.

[39] Sacco, "Legal Formants: A Dynamic Approach to Comparative Law (Installment II)", *American Journal of Comparative Law*, XXXIX (1991), p. 344.

The above-mentioned epistemic search for ways to solve the fundamental questions of comparative law is linked to the desire to go beyond legal positivism. Over a long period of time, beginning, we can assume, with the Axial Age – Achsenzeit (Karl Jaspers) to the present, the Western legal tradition and the associated legal cultures have developed within the same paradigm, despite epochal but nevertheless endogenous changes. From the point of view of the development of legal phenomena and processes, we speak of the transfer of the basic ideas of urban law to the human oikoumene with the subsequent consolidation of the corresponding legal forms in the national legal systems, which in turn establish international communication.

The spatial organization of law is changing radically. On one hand, between the establishment of the United Nations in 1945 and the *de facto* destruction of the system of international law caused by the occupation and subsequent annexation of Crimea in 2014, the number of recognized States increased rapidly. The legal system of one founder of the United Nations did not recognize the concept of nation in its traditional political and legal sense, and many later recognized States are based on institutions and legal constructs that were mechanistically transferred to the level of their "legal cultures" without regard to legal tradition. The quasi-legal culture of many such recognized States differs fundamentally from the original idea of the nation State and in practice often denies the idea of the rule of law at its core.

The attempt to achieve synthetic unity within the framework of "Greater Europe"[40] or "Pan-European House",[41] cultures based on diametrically opposed traditions of law – European and Soviet (Russian and its satellites in the post-Soviet space), ended with the actual genocide of the Ukrainian people.

The institutions and legal constructions used in quasi-legal cultures either imitate their original legal idea, or, and this is much sadder from the point of view of the consequences, these institutions and legal constructions, while retaining their authentic

[40] See Jean Thiriart, *L'Impero Euro-sovietico da Vladivostok a Dublino* (2018); Yves Lacoste, "Dans l'avenir, une très grande Europe de l'Atlantique au Pacifique?", *Dans Hérodote*, no. 3 (2005), pp. 202-212; Pierre Grou, *Vers une très grande Europe: quelle taille minimale pour l'Europe dans la mondialisation du XXIe siècle?* (2008).

[41] See Alexei G. Arbatov, Karl Kaiser, and Robert Legvold (eds.), *Russia and the West: The 21st Century Security Environment* (1999).

form, acquire a diametrically opposed meaning in the discourse of the mutated culture.[42] At a certain point, such deformed and perverted institutions and structures begin to serve as instruments for certain actors to destroy civilization, and the existence of the actors themselves becomes a problem for humanity.

On the other hand, during the same period, Non-United Nations member States recognized by at least one United Nations member State and Non-United Nations member States recognized only by other non-United Nations member States emerged under different circumstances. These territories represent anomalies in the international system, and the exploitation of such anomalies as means of manipulation in the context of international law by certain actors, as current events show on the geopolitical map of the world, not only jeopardizes observance of basic human rights but also serves as a source of regional instability for the unleashing of conflicts that threaten all of humanity.

One way or another, quasi-State entities, being located on part of the territories of recognized States, are in conflict with the latter: "states and stateless entities involved in these conflicts engage in endless legal disputes concerning the status of territories and the legitimacy of non-state actors".[43] They are usually used by actors with a mutated legal culture, who have embarked on a policy of organized terrorism, as a proxy force for undermining regional stability to carry out "false flag" operations. Unrecognized States are mostly "ticking bombs" or "black holes", and the actions of their socially irresponsible administrations are usually aimed at discrediting the basic institutions and structures of civilized communities.

This by no means implies that quasi-State or non-State entities serving as proxy organizations for actors destroying the international order should be ignored in comparative legal studies. One task of comparative jurisprudence is to identify "legal

[42] The analysis of such deformed and perverted institutions and legal constructions is a separate topic for research. All legal systems of mutant cultures based on legal perversions, which include, in particular, the institutions of elections and representative democracy, the construct of "multinational people", socialist ownership, or in the modern lexicon of nations trapped in a mutant culture, State property with the same legal meaning as its counterpart in socialist law, and so on.

[43] See Lilian Apostol, *Frozen Conflicts – in Between Jus in Bello and Jus ad Bellum. Academy of International Humanitarian Law and Human Rights* (2019) (available online).

pathologies" whose malignant growth threatens the existence of humanity. Comparison cannot be for the sake of comparison itself or for the purpose of subsequent reconciliation of defective models of biosocial organization of society with institutions and legal constructions that provide the backbone of human existence.

In any case, ignoring the factor of quasi-States as testing grounds for the development of "legal anomalies" leads to the rejection of the precedential practice of recognizing the responsibility of a State exercising effective control over such entities. In turn, ignoring the fact that behind the façade of quasi-State entities and their paramilitary terrorist units lie forces that have embarked on the path of organizing mass terror on a human scale entails legitimizing the sponsoring States of terrorism. Ultimately, if quasi-States experience legitimization by international organizations and their jurisdictional bodies, the criminal actions of States sponsoring terrorists could have tragic consequences.

In the context of the dramatic changes taking place on the geopolitical map, we can observe a certain reverse process. We are talking about the legal deformation of nationally designed spaces and, at the same time, the sharply growing crisis of international communication, which has largely lost its legal form. Furthermore, we are discussing the rapid concentration of authority and power in urban spaces and urban centers, which, in the context of the growing crisis, are an access point to basic material and social goods.

The metaphorical characterization of City-state communication with a State is vividly characterized by the following: "Over the eight or ten millennia since the couple first appeared, cities and states have oscillated between love and hate";[44] this disequilibrium tends to become unbalanced with the weakening role of national States. The model in which cities specialized in credit institutions and States engaged in warfare seems exhausted.

This trend leads to the formation of an autonomous system of City law, co-existing and in communication with the law of national States. The latter circumstance significantly changes the configuration of the legal map of the world. The legal space in this case loses its apparent homogeneity, for which there are several reasons. First, the heterogeneity of legal space is explained

[44] Charles Tilly, *Coercion, Capital and European States, AD 990 - 1992* (1993), p. 2.

by the fact that it is a part of social space that, in turn, cannot be homogeneous (the more actors are involved in communication, the denser is the social space). Second, the spatial differentiation of law turns out to be a problem that is difficult to solve using traditional legal tools, since the axiom of uniform legal influence does not allow us to determine the nature of this differentiation within the existing legal knowledge,[45] unless we take into account the fact that legal constructions are not abstractions detached from the transcendent bases of human existence as a biosocial being.

The said tendency related to the differentiation of legal space in the context of issues addressed by comparative jurisprudence suggests, in our opinion, paying attention to legal urbanism. Being an interdisciplinary research program, it at least allows us to study the city as a specific legal space. Legal urbanism enables us to find links between legal codes and codes that constitute the specificity of urban cultural phenomena, as well as to study the peculiarities of legal communication in the institutionalised organisation of urban life.

In this regard, we agree with Olha Melnychuk that "the conceptual level of the methodology of legal urbanism is closely related to the peculiarity of the methodological situation in jurisprudence in general",[46] adding that this not only in general, but also in particular, and perhaps primarily in relation to methodological issues in comparative jurisprudence. In the view of Antonia Layard, "Drawing on a wide range of legal methodologies – socio-legal, comparative, or doctrinal analysis – urban law can study the city as a distinctive legal entity".[47]

Another factor influencing changes in the legal map of the world is the rapid rise of globalism. Globalization has a strong impact on the national State, weakening its power and financial resources, directing its institutions to adapt in a globalized world.[48] At the same time, globalization and related processes of

[45] O. S. Melnychuk, Міська правова система: теоретичні та нормативні засади [Urban Legal System: Theoretical and Normative Foundations] (2015), p. 14.

[46] Ibid, p. 21.

[47] Antonia Layard, "Researching Urban Law", *German Law Journal,* XXI (2020), p. 1447.

[48] D. G. Sevriukov, Суверенітет. Генеалогія ідеї в контексті політичної та правової історії [Sovereignty. Genealogy of the Idea in the Context of Political and Legal History] (2018), p. 184.

global interaction, resulting in increased international trade and exchange of ideas, beliefs and culture, have a tangible impact on legal concepts and legal formants.

Moreover, the need for international dialogue is of particular importance in view of environmental issues and the emergence of the concept of Global Environmental Law, which should be considered from a comparative legal perspective. According to Elisa Morgera,

> A perspective informed by global environmental law, understood as the promotion of environmental protection through a plurality of legal mechanisms relying on a plurality of legal orders, thus prompts the study of environmental law at the international, regional, national and sub-national levels as *inter-related* and *mutually influencing* systems.[49]

Taking into account the factors of unification of the City legal system, on one hand, and the influence of global processes on legal life, on the other hand, the *loci* physically present on the legal map include: city legal systems, national legal systems united by a certain legal tradition, and the global meta-legal system. As Yuri Oborotov noted, "today, under the influence of globalization processes, universal ideas about the development of the world order, the formation of inter-civilisational norms are being formed, and there is a move beyond the traditional (state-centric) organization and international institutions".[50]

Societies are becoming more interdependent and hyperconnected due to globalization processes, but a "boat" that symbolizes the form of human communities' co-habitation in the modern world, divided into separate "cabins" (jurisdictions), has not become safer as a result of globalization, and testing its strength like Noah's ark, is not a good idea. The isolationism justified by overcoming the threat posed by a global pandemic and the bloody conflicts that followed, while not reversing, did put a tangible halt to the process of globalization. Under these circumstances,

[49] Elise Morgera, "Global Environmental Law and the Comparative Legal Method(s)", *Review of European Community and International Environmental Law*, XXIV (2015), pp. 254-263.

[50] Iu. N. Oborotov, «К вопросу о формировании глобальной правовой системы» [On the Question of Forming a Global Legal System], Наукові праці Національного університету "Одеська юридична академія" [Scientific Works of National University "Odessa Law Academy"], X (2011). p. 230.

according to Klaus Schwab and Thierry Malleret, "The most likely outcome along the globalization–no globalization continuum lies in an in-between solution: regionalization".[51]

Changes in the legal map of the world, influenced by the "globalization-no globalization" factor, should not be ignored by comparativism. They, in our opinion, imply a shift in the focus of attention of comparative jurisprudence from the legal systems of national legal orders to the meta-law of regional associations and, accordingly, the law of local communities. The global dimension of law has its limits, and therefore "the rule of law should not be seen as an absolute given with universal applicability but rather as a political ideal and a means to constructive international dialogue and the establishment of legitimate international organizations".[52]

The correlation of the considered trinity of the modern legal dimension with the biosocial forms of life organization intensify as it increases civilization conflicts between the determining actors of the local civilizations. The barbaric aggression against Ukraine unfortunately confirms Samuel P. Huntington's (1927-2008) prescient prediction that future wars will be between cultures, not between countries.[53] The clash of civilizations has a rationale in that "after the end of the Cold War, world politics moved into a new phase, in which non-Western civilizations are no longer the exploited recipients of Western civilization but have become additional important actors joining the West to shape and move world history".[54] The question remains whether such actors will accept the forms of civilized communication, taking into account what was been said about it above or being fascinated by perverted interpretations of institutions and legal constructions offered by the actors inciting bloody conflicts, or will join the ranks of mutant cultures.

[51] See Klaus Schwab and Thierry Malleret, *COVID-19: The Great Reset* (2020) (available online).

[52] Ellen Hey and Elaine Mak, "Introduction: The Possibilities of Comparative Law Methods for Research on the Rule of Law in a Global Context", *Erasmus Law Review*, II, no. 3 (2009), p. 288.

[53] See Samuel P. Huntington, "The Clash of Civilizations?", *Foreign Affairs*, LXXII, no. 3 (Summer 1993), pp. 22-49.

[54] S. Murden, "Cultures in World Affairs", in J. Baylis, S. Smith, and P. Owens (eds), *The Globalization of World Politics* (5th ed.; 2011), pp. 416-426.

That is why, speaking of the three-dimensional physically present loci of the modern legal map of the world, the following question is pertinent: whether it is possible in such *loci* for inclusive institutions outside the legal tradition in which they emerged as conceptual forms of the biosocial life of the members of a certain society. To answer the question posed, legal comparativism should add comparative institutional studies to its methodological arsenal.

If we take into account Huntington's view that institutions are "stable, value-based, repeatable patterns of behavior",[55] we can conclude – there are no universal forms of inclusive institutions that function equally well in all legal cultures. On one hand, we cannot ignore the fact that modern cities tend to show more common features among themselves than between them and the States where they are situated. This commonality is due to the similarity of legal institutions. The study of urban institutions developed in the Western legal tradition allows us to argue that thanks to them such features as communitarianism, constitutionalism, and secularism are added to the common features of law – objectivity, universality, and reciprocity of rights and obligations.[56] These features of urban law are enshrined in virtually inclusive economic and political institutions of open-access orders.

"The need to resolve internal elite conflicts and to guarantee that elite rights are conflict-free", seen by researchers as the main impetus for the institutionalization of orders of open-access to economic and political life, is first realized at the level of the urban social landscape and enforced precisely by the institutions of urban law. However, the continued growth of nation-states, as opposed to the stable existence of cities earlier, was actually due to the "rising cost of war" as it involved the creation of new institutions to administer and finance warfare.[57]

On the other hand, by noting the differentiation of legal orders in relation to the characteristic features of the institutions in them, the following questions arise: what are institutions as objects of

[55] Huntington, *Political Order in Changing Societies* (1968). p. 12.

[56] See Harold J. Berman, *Law and Revolution: The Formation of the Western Legal Tradition* (1983), pp. 357-403.

[57] See Tilly, note 44 above.

study? and, accordingly, can an institutional approach be useful for the purposes of comparative law?

If institutions are, as Avner Greif suggests, a set of elements (rules, norms, beliefs, and organizations), [58] or, as proposed by Douglass C. North, they are the set of the same elements but without organizations,[59] then, as they determine the characteristics of rule-based social orders, it should be recognized that institutions precede the legal order itself. This statement may seem absurd from the point of view of causality, but it makes sense if we consider that the legal formants that constitute institutions are determined by the logic of self-organizing autopoietic systems.

Institutions in this case are interpreted in the context of the research project that applies the tools of neoclassicical economics to transaction costs, property rights, and public choice, which, in contrast to institutional political economy, takes out of the field of study "the importance of political realities in the selection of public policies and highlights the role of institutions in setting the terms of human interaction", and focuses mainly on "rules of the game" or "restrictions which men impose on human interaction" that regulate the transaction costs and define the possibilities for economic development.[60]

If this hypothesis about institutions is accepted as true, it confirms the thesis that law is a self-developing system, the main element of which are legal constructions. Institutions, as interpreted by the authors who study them, are nothing other than legal constructions, with the only fundamental difference being that the set of elements in institutions – rules, norms and beliefs – is not differentiated, structurally unexplained, the connection between factual data and legal reality unexplained, systematically almost unexamined.

In turn, the theory of legal constructions, having exhausted the field of their cognitive dimension, including the issues of

[58] See Avner Greif, *Institutions and the Path to the Modern Economy* (2006).

[59] See Douglass C. North, John Joseph Wallis, and Barry R. Weingast, *Violence and Social Orders: A Conceptual Framework for Interpreting Recorded Human History* (2009).

[60] Fernando López Castellano and Fernando García-Quero. "Institutional Approaches to Economic Development: The Current Status of the Debate", *Journal of Economic Issues*, XLVI, no. 4 (December 2012), p. 924.

intensionality and causal beliefs, needs to explain the role of transcendencies that condition the spatial dimension of the relevant legal constructions. In our opinion, legal spaces as such transcendencies should be considered. Accordingly, relevant shifts in the *locus* of law deserve to be recognized as a factor of legal change.

There is no reason to deny the attractiveness of open-access models of social organization, namely: political and economic development, rich and vibrant civil societies with diverse organizations, more decentralized governments, widespread impersonal social relations, including the rule of law, secure property rights, fairness, and the treatment of all as equals.[61]

There is no reason to object North's proposed features of social institutions characteristic of open-access orders, such as a consolidated political control over violence; a widely held set of beliefs about the inclusion of and equality for all citizens; entry into economic, political, religious, and educational activities; support for organizational forms in each activity that is open to all; rule of law enforced impartially for all citizens; impersonal exchange.[62]

At the same time, the transition to open access arrangements has taken place in the West. In this regard, based on the legal world map of the modern era, and adhering to the "convergence" hypothesis that "legal systems starting from different points tend to converge toward similar solutions",[63] *prima facie*, one might agree that legal orders "did not come to open-access along the same path or using the same institutions".[64]

But were views on the institutions of open-access orders so different in the emerging national jurisdictions? And even more specifically in this context: why have institutions for the administration and financing of war emerged in the West, institutions that establish a monopoly on the use of force, modern credit institutions, and, above all, structures based on impersonal relationships? The answers to these questions are to be found in

[61] North, et al., note 59 above, pp. 11-12.

[62] Ibid., p. 114.

[63] Mattei, et al., note 33 above, p. 508.

[64] North, et al., note 59 above, p. 248.

the characteristic features of the legal tradition, the representation of which was performed by the actors at that time.

The formation of nationally organized legal orders happened in the context of modernization. However, the modern dimension of political power does not imply the rupture of relations with the institutions from which the legal tradition formed. On the contrary, modernity, realizing itself through revolutions, thus changes the cultural orientation of time, but retains the basic concepts of a certain legal tradition. In this sense, modern institutions are institutions of the same legal tradition. Outside of this tradition, as experience demonstrates, they prove to be of functionally unusable or limited functionality.

Thus, the discussion – "Do human beings share the same or similar ideas about order? Do all cultures have certain features of order in common? Is there an invisible hand that creates patterns of orders without being noticed?"[65] – is resolved with the conclusion that – "Our impetus for commonalties may not mislead us 'to proclaim sameness' and to blind our eyes to human differences".[66] The problem of the "implementation" of inclusive institutions outside the legal tradition that led to their formation cannot be solved solely by a structural analysis of the institutions themselves and their corresponding classification.

The analysis of four criteria proposed by Huntington to measure the development of institutions (adaptability – rigoricity, complexity – simplicity, autonomy – subordination, coherence – separateness)[67] without taking into account legal tradition as a factor in their formation, leads to the conclusion that institutions are nothing more than impersonal rules that perform the functions of organizing the life activity of a social organism.

The distinguishing feature of such rules, according to North, is that they are "humanly invented constraints that shape human

[65] See Grossfield, note 24 above, p. 25. See also Grossfeld, "The Invisible Hand: Patterns of Order in Comparative Law", *Journal of South African Law*, no. 4 (1997), pp. 650-651.

[66] Grossfield, note 24 above, p. 25. See also V. G. Curran and Grossfeld, "Dealing in Difference: Comparative Law's Potential for Broadening Legal Perspectives", *American Journal of Comparative Law*, LVI (1998), pp. 657-668.

[67] See Huntington, note 55 above, pp. 12-24

interaction".[68] In other words, institutions include not only formal-legal prescriptions, but also informal rules. However, if a legitimizing basis for such rules is not found, they will remain outside the purview of comparative law.

Finally, when reflecting on legal spaces as factors that are beyond the established mental legal forms and, at the same time, condition them, one cannot ignore the dynamically forming Virtual legal space and the legal constructions typical for it. The Virtual legal space is a virtually present *locus* of the actual legal map of the world. There is no doubt that Virtual Reality, which replaces the real world altogether, and Augmented Reality, which allows digital content to be layered over the real world, "like many big technological advances, will in some ways challenge legal doctrine".[69] In fact, if "societies have laws, so why should virtual societies be any different"?[70]

The problems associated with Virtual Reality exacerbate the question of the impact of the space of law on the relevant legal constructions. It is relevant for comparative law in this regard to find an answer to the question of the existence and validity of the law of the Virtual world different from the law applicable to the Virtual world.

If comparative law scholars are not to ignore the law of Virtual worlds, the next objects of comparative law research would be to recognize: constructions of artificial intelligence and related biosocial interactions; constructions of the Social Credit System, constructions of virtual property, constructions of contracts (smart contracts based on blockchain technologies), including forms of investment and exchange governed by contract law in the real world; constructions of social groups operating in the Virtual world that "in the absence of legal regulation can and should develop their own norms to govern permissible and impermissible social interactions".[71]

[68] North, et al., note 59 above, p. 3.

[69] Mark A. Lemley and Eugene Volokh, "Law, Virtual Reality, and Augmented Reality", *University of Pennsylvania Law Review*, CLXVI (2018), p. 1051.

[70] James Grimmelmann, "Virtual Worlds as Comparative Law", *New York Law School Law Review*, XLIX (2005), p. 147.

[71] Lemley and Volokh, note 69 above, p. 1135

From the point of view of comparative-institutional research programs, issues related to access to Virtual public space are of interest as well. This is about spaces created by software developers that give users a digital, virtual room where the users can socially interact with other users on the virtual platform.[72] They should be effectively explored in the context of institutionalizing the right of access.

In general, the answers to questions about the law of Virtual legal space exacerbate the problem of establishing the limits of government-imposed law's intensional interference and, in our opinion, allow us to clarify the idea of law as an autopoietic system.

CONCLUSIONS

Thus, comparative jurisprudence arises from the need for scientific reflection on the forms of legal communication established between actors who represent in certain legal forms the legal ideas of the legal culture with which such actors are associated. For civilization, the beginning of which initiated by significant changes in the forms of thinking, ways of organizing biosocial life and, accordingly, features of legal communication, chronologically defined by the Axial Age, it is initially about legal communication between representatives of urban law and those whom such representatives considered foreigners.

Intertemporal comparative legal analysis demonstrates that the entire further process of development of legal cultures up to the present time has predominantly taken place in the dialectical form of interaction between City law and the law of other cultures. City law serves as a universal form of concentration of basic legal concepts that subsequently retranslated to the legal space beyond its jurisdiction and retains this property even when it loses its jurisdictional autonomy.

The core of the legal culture that emerges from the dialectical unity of City law and the law of other communities is the Western legal tradition, which retransmits the unique code of legal communication known to us until today. During this period, a legal culture based on the Western tradition of law developed all possible forms of circulation and appropriation of goods, all

[72] See Daniel B. Koburger, "Legal Implications of Public Spaces in Virtual Reality", *Landslide,* XII, no. 1 (2019) (available online).

possible and rationalized legal constructions to meet the needs of the existence of communities based on legal communication. The study of the unique code of legal communication proposed by the Western Tradition of Law is of particular importance for legal orders declaring European identity, and at the same time serves as a methodological basis for understanding the legal processes occurring in legal spaces at the global and regional levels.

It is acceptable to assume that at present the arsenal of legal culture based on the Western tradition of law, at least within the nationally organized legal spaces, is exhausted. The real cause of the current crisis of humanity is connected with this state of affairs. There are signs of a kind of reversal (return) to the model that existed at the dawn of the formation of legal cultures united by the Western Tradition of Law, but this time at the global level, on the scale of humanity. It is about the increasing importance of the civilization of cities and, at the same time, the observed increasing crisis of national-States caused by their cultural heterotopia.

At the same time, dramatic changes in the forms and ways of organizing the biosocial life of human communities are taking place against the backdrop of the contradictory process of globalization, leading to the formation of large legal spaces (regions) united by the commonality of legal culture. In addition, Virtual Legal Space, in which legal constructions immanent to it arise and function, is being added to the allocated *loci* of the actual legal map.

In general, the examination of issues related to the changes on the legal map of the world leads to the conclusion that specific legal constructions have emerged in each of the *loci* mentioned above. However, the tensions between cultures that characterize each of these legal spaces must be overcome through legal communication in the interest of the continuation of human civilization under conditions of increasing conflict. In the current state of affairs the main question to be answered by comparative jurisprudence is to find the condition under which legal communication is possible.

The state of affairs under study is characterized by a tangible *primordial* contraversion. On one hand, dialogue between cultures is possible if the code of communication is agreed and accepted by all participants in legal communication, but this is possible only if they accept a common legal tradition. On the other hand, we should recognize that every legal culture is a culture of values only for its representatives and does not necessarily correspond to the civilizational ideal.

Comparative law should give an answer to a fundamental question: is it possible to apply its previously accumulated methodological arsenal to new realities, when it is not a question of comparing the formants of different legal families, but of ensuring legal communication of human communities in crisis?

In current circumstances perhaps we should abandon the search for universal methods of comparative law, since each specific method or approach (functionalism, law and economics, theory of legal formants, and so on) is relevant only to a particular legal culture. The effective application of a particular approach (method) in comparative law is only possible if there is a metaepistemic paradigm that is accepted by the participants in legal communication.

The problem of legal communication is not rooted in the plurality of methods of law, but in the peculiarities of legal cultures that have an autonomous idea of law in its ontological dimension. The plurality of legal cultures, in turn, predetermined by the differentiation of legal space, more precisely, by the existence of multiple legal spaces (homogeneous or heterogeneous *loci*).

Second, it should be recognized that the effectiveness of a tradition that unites legal cultures (in this case, such legal cultures are united into a homogeneous legal locus) is determined by its epistemic authority, which is achieved primarily by the actions of the communicating community. The need for dialogue between speakers of different legal cultures creates a new "legal situation" different from the one that existed within a particular legal culture prior to the communication.

Third, human communities existing within legal cultures are autopoietic social systems, identical to themselves and reproduced by replicating a code of legal communication. The actors of legal cultures, in turn, are their representatives, and the results of their actions are legal artifacts. Consequently, legal culture is not absorbed by the general culture (civilization); it is autonomous and capable of self-development. However, in conditions where there is a need for dialogue, particularly in the process of globalization or regional forms of coexistence of different legal cultures, the autonomous discourse of one or more of them, if it is based on "legal pathologies", becomes a threat to other legal cultures, and possibly to civilization as a whole.

Fourth, it is necessary to recognize that only the need to overcome a conflict situation gives rise to a dialogue of cultures. In all cases, the real cause of conflict is related to the tension between political power and the consciousness structures of a certain culture bearers. But we believe that political power does not have its own autonomous discourse; it only represents certain forms, structures of public consciousness, and therefore conflictogenicity is caused by the collision of different structures of consciousness. In other words, the "clash of civilizations" is primarily a conflict between the consciousness structures of different legal cultures. Neither linguistic identity, much less formal unification of terminological apparatus, nor even formal unification of institutions can overcome the clash of legal cultures if they are based on different legal traditions.

Fifth, the structures of consciousness, which are reflected and consolidated in the form of legal constructions that serve as the basic building blocks of legal culture – legal artifacts that absorb all other factors related to their existence. A legal norm, or more broadly – a legal formant is not an autonomous legal unit. These are merely segments of legal constructions, the existence of which have three dimensions: the level of public consciousness, the level of fixation in legal formants, the level of direct legal reality manifested in the forms of realization of the idea of law. Comparison is always a comparison of legal constructs that fulfill the same function in different legal orders. Hence, an interlocal comparison of relevant legal constructions may serve for communicative success, or at least an awareness of what is happening in the context of the need to establish a dialogue between different legal cultures.

Chapter 6
Comparative Law and its Aspirations

JAMES GORDLEY

The concept of "world picture" is a fulcrum for raising fundamental problems of comparative law. Kresin has observed:

> An opposition exists between traditional legal philosophy as one reflecting an *a priori* and metaphysical, universalist, and monist worldview and the philosophy of comparativism and comparative jurisprudence as reflecting an empirically oriented, historical, social, pluralist, spatial worldview.[1]

He concludes that "on one hand, comparative jurisprudence needs an own philosophy and creates this, using own experience and the achievements of various sciences, and, on the other – comparativism and its philosophy never can be embodied in a single discipline". In the "philosophy of comparativism", "ideas concerning law" are "elements of a legal worldview of concrete societies" which "it considers ... not as absolute, not as emanations of pure reason, but as pluralist and relative, localized in time and space".[2]

In his account, comparative jurisprudence began with the rejection of the "natural law teaching" present in the "metaphysical philosophy" of Christian von Wolff (1679-1754). The "father of comparative jurisprudence was Paul Johann Anselm von Feuerbach (1775-1833):

> Feuerbach wrote that philosophy first 'tried to gain a foothold on the ground of jurisprudence' only during the time of Christian Wolff, in the first half of the eighteenth

[1] O. V. Kresin, "World Picture of Comparative Law: 'The Courage of Your Convictions'", *Journal of Comparative Law*, XIX (2024), p. 16, citing Paul Johann Anselm von Feuerbach, "Vorrede. Blick auf die teutsche Rechtswissenschaft", in Carl August Dominik Unterholzner, *Juristische Abhandlungen* (1810).

[2] Ibid.

> century. Even the attempts of philosophy to evaluate and conceptually organize jurisprudence according to mathematical logic, leaving aside experience and historical peculiarities 'had very bad consequences': 'What it displayed was nothing more than a flimsy web of concepts that neither shed light on new truths, nor cemented old ones', translated living truths 'in a distorted and restricted form'. This metaphysical and speculative philosophy failed, but returned in a 'Kantian revolution' with even more ill-founded pretensions.[3]

The rationalist philosophy of Wolff was indeed *a priori* and metaphysical, universalist, and monist. That philosophy is incompatible with a "comparative jurisprudence" in which "ideas concerning law" are "consider[ed] ... not as absolute, not as emanations of pure reason, but as pluralist and relative, localized in time and space". Nevertheless, it was not the first time philosophy had "gained a foothold" in "jurisprudence". For centuries before the rise of rationalism, jurists had drawn on what some call the "great tradition" in philosophy which stretches back through Thomas Aquinas (1226-1274) to Aristotle (384-322 BC). This article will briefly describe that philosophy and why it is far more compatible with the comparative enterprise.

TWO PHILOSOPHIES

Natural Law: Timeless or Variable?

The philosophy of Wolff was indeed "*a priori* and metaphysical, universalist, and monist".[4] For Wolff, the natural law was a set of timeless and invariable precepts. This view was grounded in a metaphysics which he borrowed from Gottfried Wilhelm Leibniz (1646-1716) and can be traced to Francisco Suárez (1548-1617). In this metaphysics, a "possible being" is one that may exist; an "actual being" is one in which this possibility is realized. Wolff said:

> Being is what can exist, and consequently, that with which existence is not incompatible ... [A] right triangle with

[3] Ibid, p. 6.

[4] Kresin, note 1 above, p. 6.

> acute angles drawn on paper is a being, as it exists in act, but no less is a triangle that can be drawn a being, because it exists when it is first drawn, and therefore it can exist. If a stone is exposed to fire or to the rays of the sun in summer, it is hot. Therefore, a hot stone can exist, and therefore it is a being, not inasmuch as it exists in act, but inasmuch as existence is not incompatible with it. The idea of being taken generally scarcely involves existence but only a lack of incompatibility with existence, or, which is the same, the possibility of existing.
>
> Because what is possible can exist, what is possible is a being.[5]

Consequently, whatever may exist can be understood independently of whether it exists or not. Independently of whether a right triangle actually exists, it must have angles that sum to 180°, and consequently, any right triangle that does exist will have that property. Similarly, one can identify the properties of a just action independently of whether anyone is acting justly. According to Leibniz:

> The doctrine of law (*doctrina iuris*) belongs to those sciences that depend on definitions and not on experience, on demonstrations of reason and not of sense, and are matters of law, one can say, and not of fact. As, indeed, justice consists in some congruity and proportionality, we can understand that something is just even if there is no one who is acting justly, or who is being treated justly, in the same way that the concepts (*rationes*) of numbers are true even if there were no one to count and nothing to be counted, and we can predict that a house will be beautiful, a machine efficient, or a commonwealth happy if it comes into being even if it should never do so. We need not wonder, therefore, that the principles of these sciences possess eternal truth.[6]

From the idea that whatever may possibly exist is a being it was a short step to the idea that the study of whatever exists

5 C. Wolff, *Philosophia prima sive ontologia*, ed. J. Ecole (1962), §§134-135.

6 G. W. Leibniz, *Elementa juris naturalis* in G. W. Leibnitz, *Philosophische Schriften Erster Band 1663-1672*, ed. Akademie der Wissenschaften der DDR (1990), p. 460.

depends upon "definitions and not on experience" and can arrive at conclusions that "possess eternal truth".

In contrast, in the tradition of Aristotle and Aquinas, the world is composed of actual beings. Concepts such as a right triangle are abstractions formed by the human mind on the basis of experience. Justice does not exist even if there is no one acting justly.

For that reason, Suárez disagreed with Aquinas over whether the natural law varies according to the circumstances. Aquinas said that it did. His example was a situation which Marcus Tullius Cicero (106-43 BC) and St. Augustine (353-430) described in which one person promised to keep another person's sword and to give it back when that person asked for it. Should the sword be returned to its owner if he has become insane or intends to commit a crime? Cicero, Augustine, Aquinas and Suárez said that it should not. For Aquinas, the reason was that the natural law varies with the circumstances. Under normal circumstances, the sword should be returned. If the owner is insane or homicidal it should not.[7] Suárez claimed that "granted that in this case [the sword] is not to be returned, the reason is not that the natural precept has changed, for the principle was not posited for this case but for others ...".[8] "For [natural law] prescribes one thing as to the material in one situation, and another for that in another, and so in itself it remains always unchanged ...".[9]

Stated more fully, the natural law prescribes that sword should be returned unless the owner is insane or malevolent. That precept never changes although it requires the person with custody of the sword to act one way in one set of circumstance and differently in another. The natural law consists of precepts that are invariable because they take account of every circumstance that has arisen or ever could arise. Its precepts are therefore universal and eternal.

Suárez' view of natural law was grounded in his metaphysics. Like Leibniz, he believed that "something is just even if there is no one who is acting justly, or who is being treated unjustly". According to Suárez,

[7] T. Aquinas, *Summa theologiae* I-II Q. 94, a. 6

[8] F. Suárez, *Tractatus de legibus et de legislatore deo* (1612), lib. 2, cap. 13, no. 6.

[9] Ibid., no. 9.

> it is one thing to speak of the existence of precepts ... and another to speak of their actual obligation or exercise. Therefore, although one can postulate a state in which one precept is in use and another is not, nevertheless, the law of nature is always the same, and made up of the same precepts, because they are either principles or conclusions necessarily elicited from them which are not defective in any situation.[10]

In contrast, for Aquinas, the precepts of natural law exist within the mind of a person who is deciding what to do under the circumstances he is facing. Under normal circumstances, he is not deciding what to do if the person demanding the return of the sword were insane or malevolent. Under other circumstances, he is. Since the precept of natural law exists within the mind of the person who is deciding what to do, it is different in the one situation than it is in the other.

Legal Reasoning: Theoretical or Practical?

As Kresin observed, Feuerbach criticized attempts "to ... conceptually organize jurisprudence according to mathematical logic".[11] That was Wolff's approach. Conclusions about natural law were to be reached, as in mathematics, by deduction from higher principles that are self-evident, like the axioms of geometry.

In the Aristotelian tradition, some conclusions were reached deductively by theoretical reason as in mathematics. Conclusions about how to act, however, were reached by practical reason. Both required first principles.[12] For example, a first principle of theoretical reasoning is the law of non-contradiction: a proposition cannot be both true and false at the same time in the same way. There was no way to prove that proposition. Any proof assumes that the law of non-contradiction is valid.[13] The first principles of practical reason are ends that are worth achieving for their own sake: for example, preserving one's life, seeking truth, having friends. A human being understands that these ends are

[10] Ibid., cap. 8, no. 9.

[11] Kresin, note 1 above, p. 6.

[12] Aquinas, note 7 above, I Q. 79 a. 12.

[13] Aristotle, *Metaphysics* IV.4 1005^b-1006^a.

valuable without proof. Practical reason identifies the actions that best contribute to them under the circumstances in which a person finds himself. A law, according to Aquinas, is a decree of practical reason. The first principles are invariable in the sense that every human being can recognize the value of such things as life, knowledge, and friendship. As we have seen, the actions that best promote them may vary with the circumstances.

Conclusions as to how one should act may be related to these first principles or ultimate ends in two ways. It may be that under the circumstances that a person is facing, there is only one course of action that is consistent with attaining these ends. In that event, Aquinas said, the relationship between these principles and that course of action is like that between a premise and a conclusion of theoretical reason: given the premise, there can only be one correct conclusion. Or it may be that under a given set of circumstances, there is no one right course of action. There are several. Aquinas used the term *determinatio*, "determination", to describe the choice a person makes when there are many good ways to choose but they cannot be rank ordered. One cannot say that one choice is better than another.[14]

Even when there is no one right choice, the choice one makes may matter very much. For Aquinas, it matters that God created the universe, but he discussed God's freedom in the same way as that of human beings: there is no best of all possible worlds that God had to create.[15] If had never fallen and perfect human beings still inhabited Eden they would differ in knowledge and virtue, not because they had fallen into vice, but because through the exercise of their "free will" they would develop their human capacities in various ways by making different choices concerning "what is to be done or to be sought or to be known".[16]

The conclusions of mathematicians are invariably correct. The conclusions reached by practical reason are "not absolute, not as emanations of pure reason, but ... pluralist and relative, localized in time and space".

[14] Aquinas, note 7 above, I-II, Q. 95, a. 2.

[15] Ibid., I Q. 19, aa. 3, 10.

[16] Ibid., I Q. 96 a. 4.

Eclipse of the Aristotelian Tradition

The philosophy of rationalists such as Leibniz and Wolff differed so greatly from that of the Aristotelian tradition that one would have expected there to be an intellectual battle before rationalism prevailed. But the battle was never fought. Suárez claimed to be interpreting Aristotle. As Leroy Loemker noted, in the seventeenth century, "Suárez's *Disputationes Metaphysicae* had become the academic standard of doctrine for Protestant and Catholic Europe alike".[17] Wolff said that it "must be agreed, among the scholastics" that it was Suárez who "most profoundly meditated matters of metaphysics".[18] More surprising is that Wolff believed his own conception of being was that of Aquinas.[19] The actual position of Aquinas had dropped off the radar screen. As Étienne Henri Gilson (1884-1978) said, "Suárezianism has consumed Thomism".[20]

For many people, rationalism still epitomizes the natural law tradition. John Mitchell Finnis, Germain Gabriel Grisez (1929-2018), and Gilson stressed the difference between the philosophy of Aquinas and Suárez, in part, because many Catholic writers neglected it. Roberto Mangabeira Unger criticized "the metaphysical systems of ancient and medieval Europe" with their belief in "intelligible essences" which "Aquinas' theory of natural law exemplif[ies] ...". He said, in a footnote to the passage just quoted: "For the development of this view see Christian Wolff, *Philosophia Prima sive Ontologia* § 143".[21] John Bordley Rawls (1921-2002) described what he apparently regarded as the traditional approach to natural law. He called it "rational intuitionalism". It has four features, which are the very ones that distinguish the rationalist moral philosophy from that of Aristotle and Aquinas: (1) "moral first principles and judgments, when correct, are true statements about an independent order of moral values ... which does not depend on ... the activity of any (human) minds, including the activity of reason"; (2) "moral first principles are known by theoretical reason"; (3) this approach has a "sparse conception

17 L.E. Loemker, "Introduction" to *Gottfried Wilhelm Leibnitz Philosophical Papers and Letters*, ed. L.E. Loemker, 1 (1956), p. 17.

18 Wolff, note 5 above, § 169.

19 Ibid.

20 E. Gilson, *Being and Some Philosophers* (1952), p. 118.

21 R. M. Unger, *Knowledge and Politics* (1975), pp. 30-31, 31, n. 1.

of the person" which "needs little more than the idea of the self as knower; (4) "moral judgements [are] true when they are both about and accurate to the independent order of moral values".[22]

As John Philip Dawson (1902-1985) said,

> [T]he influence of Wolff was enormous even among those who reacted against it. His admirers set themselves to perfecting his system and working out its consequences; his opponents could not escape the net it cast. Its influence reached more gradually, and, in the end, incompletely to 'half-learned' or unlearned judges and practitioners; in the abundant legal literature that still poured forth, there was much that followed older styles and gave only a pale reflection of the Wolffian synthesis. The agents for the transmission of his ideas were overwhelmingly law professors.[23]

Immanuel Kant (1724-1804) said that reading the work of David Hume (1711-1776) first roused him from his dogmatic slumber. It was Christian Wolff who lulled him to sleep.

Logical Implication or Teleology?

Wolff's method fits Kresin' description: it was "*a priori* and metaphysical, universalist, and monist". The method of those who wrote in the Aristotelian tradition was also metaphysical. It was based on the metaphysics of Aristotle. Yet in contrast to the method of Wolff, it can be described as "empirically oriented, historical, social, pluralist" and "localized in time and space". The precepts of natural law were not to be deduced from timeless principles. They were formulated as human beings dealt with the problems before them. The method was teleological. It was concerned with how, by practical reason, people choose the best means to pursue an end. Because it was teleological, it could take account of the purposes that precepts of law serve. The deductive method of rationalists such as Wolff could not. Moreover, because it was teleological it could take account of continency. There might be not one right way but several different means to an end and the best might depend on the circumstances.

22 J. Rawls, *Political Liberalism* (1993), pp. 91-92.

23 J. P. Dawson, *The Oracles of the Law* (1968), p. 237.

As described elsewhere,[24] in the sixteenth and seventeenth centuries, a group of philosopher jurists centered in Spain synthesized Roman law, as interpreted by the medieval jurists, with the philosophy of the philosophy of Aristotle, as interpreted by Thomas Aquinas. They are known to historians as the late scholastics.

Their method was strikingly different than that of Wolff. It took no account of purposes. For example, according to Wolff, it followed from the definition of property that the owner had the right to exclude others from using what he owned. "The right of disposing of a thing by one's own decision, indeed, as one sees fit, we call ownership".[25] Therefore it "includes the right to exclude others".[26]

In contrast, according to writers in the Aristotelian tradition, the rights of the owner are limited by the purpose that the institution of private property serves. Private property was instituted to avoid the disadvantages of common ownership. If all things were held in common, people would quarrel, and those who did not work would receive as much as those who did.[27] Therefore, the owner did not have the right to exclude others in time of necessity.[28]

Similarly, for Wolff, it followed from the definition of promise that promises are binding. It depends on the will of the owner alone whether he wishes to transfer ownership or some right of his own or not".[29] "A promise ... is a declaration of our will to make a performance for another joined to the right to require that transfer of that which is to be performed".[30] Therefore, "Promises are to be kept".[31]

[24] J. Gordley, *The Jurists: A Critical History* (2013), pp. 82-110.

[25] C. Wolff, *Jus naturae method scientific pertracta,* published as *Jus naturae* in C. Wolff, *Gesammelte Werke,* ed. M. Thomann 17-24 (1972-), II §118.

[26] Ibid., §§ 119-120.

[27] Aristotle, *Politics* II. v. Aquinas, note 7 above, II-II Q. 66, a. 2.

[28] Aquinas, note 7 above, II-II Q. 66, a. 7 ; L. Lessius, *De iustitia et iure, ceterisque virutibus cardinalis* (1628), lib. 2, cap. 12, dub. 12 ; D. Soto, *De iustitia et iure libri decem* (1553), lib. 5, q. 3, a. 4; L. Molina, *De iustitia et iure* (1614), disp. 20.

[29] Wolff, note 25 above, III, §12

[30] Ibid., §361

[31] Ibid., §431

According to writers in the Aristotelian tradition, a promise might be made for two good reasons. One was to exercise "liberality", which meant not only to confer a benefit on another, but to do so sensibly, in Aristotle's words, "to the right people, the right amounts, and at the right time, with all the other qualifications that accompany right giving". [32] The other reason for promising was to receive something in exchange. In that event, according to Aristotle, commutative justice required that the performances exchanged be equal in value so that neither party is enriched at the other's expense.[33]

Moreover, there was no one right answer to the question of what rules would best ensure that a person who gave away money or property acted sensibly or that the parties exchanged performance of equal value. Writers in the Aristotelian tradition approved of the rule of Roman law that a promise to give away money must be made formally, which, since the Middle Ages meant that they must be notarized. They also approved some exceptions to this rule that jurists had recognized. A promise to make a gift on account of marriage (*proper nuptias*)[34] or to a charitable cause (*ad pias causas*)[35] was binding without notarization. These rules made it more likely that one made such a promise was acting sensibly.

Medieval jurists had a Roman text which gave a remedy to one who sold land for less than half it just price to give a similar remedy in sales of goods as well as land, to buyers as well as sellers, and in leases and kindred contracts such as leases.[36] According to writers in the Aristotelian tradition, the reason was to preserve commutative justice. The remedy was given only for a deviation of more than half from the just price because of practical concerns such as the stability of commerce.[37]

For these writers, there was no one right way to ensure that gifts were given out of liberality or that performances of equal

[32] Aristotle, *Nicomachean Ethics* IV.i. 1119^b-1120^a.

[33] Ibid.,V.ii 1130b-1131a; V.i 1131b-1132b. .

[34] Molina, note 28 above, III, disp. 279, no. 7 (1614).

[35] Ibid., no. 2; Lessius, note 28 above, lib. 2, cap. 18, dub 13, no. 102

[36] For example, *Glossa Ordinaria* (1581) to C 4.44.2 to *auctoritate iudicis*.

[37] See Soto, note 28 above, lib. 6, q. 2, a. 3 (1553); Molina, note 28 above, disp. 348; note 28 above,, cap. 21, dub. 2.

value were exchanged. The law in force in their day had adopted certain rules that were appropriate, but others might serve as well. They could approve of this flexibility because their method was teleological. Sometimes it is necessary to follow a rule to achieve a certain end but sometimes the relationship between following the rule and achieving the end is contingent.

THE FUNCTIONALIST METHOD IN COMPARATIVE LAW

Since the work of Hein Kötz in Germany and Arthur von Mehren (1922-2006) in the United States, one of most influential approaches to comparative law has been functional. It describes, compares, and evaluates the law of different times and places in terms of the purposes served by legal institutions, doctrines, and rules.

A teleological approach to comparative law does not presuppose that Aristotle was right. It does presuppose that laws are to be understood in terms of the purpose that they serve. In comparing the modern civil and common law, Kötz observed that "the legal system of every society faces essentially the same problems, and solves these problems by quite different means though very often with similar results".[38] If a scholar finds no functional equivalent of a rule in a foreign legal system, he should "check again whether the terms in which he posed the original question were indeed purely functional, and whether he has spread the net of his researches quite far enough.[39] It would be better to say that different legal systems face the same problems often but not always, and that they often solve them in similar ways.

Two common objections to this approach rest on misunderstandings.[40] One objection is that it presupposes a

[38] K. Zweigert and H. Kötz , *Introduction to Comparative* Law, transl. Tony Weir (3d ed.; 1998), p. 35.

[39] Ibid., p. 40, although Zweigert also noted that sometimes "the need to which institution X responds is met in foreign law by results produced by heterogeneous techniques which are impossible to compare with our institution X, or, again, quite simply, by custom". K. Zweigert, "Méthodologie du droit comparé", in *Mélanges offerts à Jacques Maury* (1960), I, p. 590.

[40] J. Gordley, "Comparison, Law and Culture, A Response to Pierre Legrand", *American Journal of Comparative Law*, LXV (2017), p. 133.

similarity among legal systems that may not be there.[41] It is true that if the legal systems of different societies faced wholly different problems, this approach would not work. But it does not assume that the problems are the same.

Sometimes, indeed, the problems that different legal systems face are alike only when they are stated in very general terms. One can still understand each institution in terms of the problems that it does address. That is true when one compares very different societies.

An example is exchange in pre-commercial societies. In these societies, when people make gifts, the recipient is often obligated to give back something equivalent but as yet unspecified. When people in these societies exchange, they often form stable trading relationships with particular partners. Each party to the relationship is obligated to exchange when the other asks, and to exchange at a price that remains stable despite changes in supply and demand.[42] It is not like our own society, where gifts are often made to enrich another party at the donor's expense, and where a person can exchange with whomever he wants and charge what the market will bear. Economically minded anthropologists have suggested that the rules of pre-commercial societies make sense given their circumstances. There are few ways to store wealth. Therefore, it makes sense to give gifts in order to have a claim for help in the future. Markets are thin or non-existent, and so supply or demand can swing wildly from day to day. Therefore, it makes sense to trade with a regular partner who will not exploit a temporary advantage and who, in return, is not to be exploited.[43] That is not to imply that people in these societies see their rules as appropriate only under certain circumstances. They might have trouble imagining it could ever be proper for a donee not to give in return, or for a person to raise the price he charges a regular customer. They have never had occasion to consider how circumstances might be different, and what it would be proper to do then.

[41] P. Legrand, "Jameses at Play: A Tractation on the Comparison of Laws", *American Journal of Comparative Law*, LXV (2017), p. 1.

[42] J. Gordley, "Contract in Pre-Commercial Societies and in Western History", in *Contracts in General*, in *International Encyclopedia of Comparative Law* (1997), VII, pp. 2-9.

[43] Ibid.

As one might expect, when societies are more similar, so are the problems they face. The same purposes are more often served by rules that are more particular. That is so, as comparative lawyers have shown, even if the rules are formulated differently.

For example, in Anglo-American common law, offers to contract are revocable and acceptances are effective on dispatch.[44] In German law, offers are irrevocable and acceptances are effective on receipt.[45] Arthur von Mehren observed:

> Although, in the past, thinking respecting offer and acceptance problems has been significantly influenced by doctrinal abstractions such as 'meeting of the minds,' the ultimate solutions seem to be based on a common policy of giving the offeree a firm basis for considering whether to accept. The German Civil Code addressed this problem directly by making offers firm in principle: the common law, because of the doctrine of consideration, had to proceed less directly and advanced the same policy by making the acceptance effective on dispatch.
>
> If this analysis is correct, the natural counterpart to the rule that offers are binding, is the proposition that acceptances are effective only upon receipt. Conversely, the view that offers are revocable calls forth the rule that acceptances are effective only on dispatch.[46]

Sometimes the rules and results are simply different. Then one must ask why. It could be that they serve the same purpose, but that in the circumstances of one society, one rule better serves this purpose than in the circumstances of the other. Or it could be that there is no one right answer to the question of which rule is best under the circumstances. For example, a rule that gives more complete protection to the freedom of speech may give less protection to privacy. As James Whitman has observed,

[44] The rule was established in Dickinson v. Dodds, [1876] 2 Ch. Div. 463 (C.A.)

[45] Bürgerlichesgesetzbuch § 145.

[46] A. T. von Mehren and J. R. Gordley, *The Civil Law System. An Introduction to the Comparative Study of Law* (1977), pp. 891-892.

there is no one right answer to which of these of values should be compromised to protect the other.[47]

The second objection is that the functionalist approach, by focusing on similarities among different societies, neglects the ways in which societies differ. A method that explains rules as aspects of the culture of a particular society is often thought to be in tension with a method that explains them in terms of the problems that different societies face.

On the contrary, many aspects of a society's culture are distinctive solutions to problems that other societies face as well. There are many situations in which German law protects privacy while the law of the United States protects freedom of speech. The reason is not that Germans do not care about freedom of speech or Americans about privacy. The German constitution protects freedom of speech, and American tort law recognizes liability for the disclosure of embarrassing private facts. The difference is in how their law responds when the two values are in tension.

Not all cultural differences are differing responses to values in tension. Some are differences in taste. Some are rooted in historical experiences or even national myths. The functional approach considers only one source of cultural difference. Yet it is an important one.

The approach would not work if the values of society were intelligible only within its own culture. In the nineteenth century, some Germans, disillusioned with universalist claims of rationalism, concluded since values were not absolute, they had normative significance only for those who share a particular *Weltanschauung* or world view. This approach lingers among comparative lawyers. Michele Graziadei has described it as "holism", by which he means "any theory by which an account, or an interpretation of a part is impossible, or at least inadequate, without reference to the whole to which that part belongs".[48] Consequently, as Graziadei observes, the "radical version of holism holds that it is impossible to know what it is like to think like an American or an Italian lawyer unless that condition is experienced in the first person, that

[47] James Q. Whitman, "The Two Western Cultures of Privacy: Dignity Versus Liberty," *Yale Law Journal*, CXIII (2004), p. 1151.

[48] M. Graziadei, "Comparative Law, Legal History, and the Holistic Approach to Legal Cultures," *Zeitschrift für Europäisches Privatrecht*, VII (1999), p. 538.

is to say, unless one actually becomes an American or an Italian lawyer".[49]

To compare the law of different societies by the functionalist method would be impossible if the purposes pursued by one society were pointless except from the standpoint of the mentality distinctive of a particular society. Were it so, to regard these purposes as worth pursuing one would have to subscribe to a set of values accepted within that society but nowhere else. Is that likely?

I think not. If the members of one society valued a purpose or end that was completely unique to that society, it would be meaningless to anyone else. We may regard Babylonian liver divination as superstitious and torture as impermissibly cruel, but we can understand the motives of those who practiced them. Otherwise, we could only regard those who did so as insane, or, perhaps, non-human.

One need not be an Aristotelian to take a functionalist approach to comparative law. Nevertheless, it is not true that to do comparative law one must reject metaphysics. The rejection of rationalist metaphysics was a precondition for the study of comparative law. The rejection of any metaphysics was not.

TWO CONCLUSIONS

If the functionalist method is appropriate for the study of comparative law, then we must qualify two of Kresin's conclusions. One concerns the sort of "world picture" that the comparative study of legal systems requires. The other concerns whether comparative law is an independent discipline.

A world picture?

The rationalists believed that the principles they established were objective and universal. They were true in every possible world. As mentioned, one reaction was to claim that values are neither objective nor universal. They have meaning only for those who share a particular *Weltanschauung* or world view.

[49] Ibid.

Kresin describes every scientific discipline as entailing a world picture which is neither objective, like the principles of the rationalists believed, nor subjective, like the elements of a *Weltanschauung*. His description of a world picture deserves to be quoted at length:

> When a scholarly image is formed from certain fragments of reality as one interconnected complex phenomenon, a science or scientific discipline is being born. The root of this image is a certain paradigm, and the generalized image could be perceived as a subject of contemplation. ... The consciousness of this activity of conceptualizing subject-matter in a certain way and modelling their connections, interactions, and, finally, their unity as an autonomic facet of reality – this is the genuine creation of a science.
>
> This modelled image, already containing some paradigm – should it have a name? One possible name, quite deeply and consistently conceptualized, is the "world picture". Numerous arguments in favor of this vision of a subject-matter, object, origin of a science, and the very name of this modelled image are provided by the philosophy of science, science of science, and the history of sciences.
>
> The ultimate aim of every autonomous general law discourse pretending to be a scholarly legal discipline is to construct and realize its vision and mission as a special world picture – a conceptualized and structured model of an aspect or fragment of reality accessible with its paradigm, research program, and methods.[50]

World pictures are like the paradigms which, according to Thomas Samuel Kuhn (1922-1996), accompany advances in the natural sciences.[51] Sir Isaac Newton's (1642-1726/27) picture of the world prevailed until phenomena were observed that it could not explain, and then it was replaced by that of Albert Einstein (1879-1955). A world picture is not wholly subjective. They "model an aspect or fragment of reality". Neither are they wholly objective. They are "construct[ed] and realized" and model only that aspect

[50] Kresin, note 1 above, pp. 53-54.

[51] T. S. Kuhn, *The Structure of Scientific Revolutions* (1962).

of reality "accessible within [the] paradigm, research program, and methods".

The study of comparative law by the functionalist method does not arrive at conclusions which are universal and demonstrable like those which the rationalist sought. Yet it does more than model an aspect of reality. Its goal is to faithfully describe that aspect of reality with which it is concerned: choices made by human beings in pursuit of ends. The description may be right or wrong depending on what these purposes actually are. But if it is right, it is not a model of what people are doing. It is a faithful description.

One might still say that the study of comparative law depends on a world picture. The picture is one in which laws are made by human beings to govern their affairs in the particular circumstances they face. This picture is selective. It does not capture every feature of these laws or of the situation of those who make or are governed by them. But if laws are made to serve purposes and can be understood in terms of the purposes which they serve, then the picture faithfully depicts a very important "aspect of reality".

An Autonomous Discipline?

If the laws of different legal systems are studied by the functionalist method, can "we assume that comparative law is an autonomous discipline"? We can do so if we are referring to the range of problems which the study of comparative law can address. It includes all the problems that arise when people govern their affairs by law. Nevertheless, it is often assumed that the study of comparative law is independent of the study of the law of a particular legal system. That assumption needs to be questioned. If it is false, then the study of comparative law is not a discipline distinct from the study of domestic law.

Nineteenth century positivists claimed that one could determine what the law is without regard to what the law ought to be. The law is laid down in authoritative texts whether they are the opinions of judge in decided cases or the provisions of civil codes. The judge must apply these texts to new cases by logical inference. The rationalists thought that the conclusions that they reached by logical inference would have the same certainty as their premises. The positivists thought that the conclusion a judge reached would have the same authority as the texts he was interpreting. Otherwise, he would not be interpreting the law but making it.

Critics of positivism such as François Gény (1861-1959) and Rudolf von Jhering (1818-1892) claimed that one could not understand authoritative texts without considering the purposes which the law serves. That claim has been widely accepted. Yet if it so, why should jurists, judges and lawyers assume that they can understand the laws in force in their own jurisdictions without looking elsewhere?

When comparative law is studied by the functionalist method, one task is to identify the purpose that laws serve. The purpose may be the same as that of laws in other jurisdictions that are formulated differently. One way to identify the purpose is by observing that similar results are reached in practice despite dissimilar formulations. How can that conclusion fail to interest a judge or scholar who is asking what the law is or should be in his own jurisdiction?

Another task is to explain why laws that address similar problems often differ not only in formulation but in result. The difference may be due to differences in circumstances. It may be that each solution has its own advantages and disadvantages. Again, how could that conclusion fail to interest a judge or scholar who is asking what the law is or should be in his own jurisdiction? When a new case arises, he can ask whether the advantages and disadvantages are like those of the cases previously decided or which the lawmaker addressed. When laws are understood in terms of the purposes that they serve, statements about what the law is have implications for what the law ought to be.

Kresin notes that according to Kötz "comparative lawyers 'compare the legal systems of different nations' and provide their reflections for 'the proper policy for the law to adopt'".[52] It does not follow he "did not provide for comparative law any sufficient and final cognitive goal" or was less interested in "discovering the truth" than in "social engineering".[53] The functional method is no less concerned with the truth about things as they are because it is useful in discerning how things ought to be.

[52] Kresin, note 1 above, p. 36.

[53] Ibid.

Chapter 7
Contested Economic Maps of Legal Systems

MICHELE GRAZIADEI
MARCO GIRAUDO

Exploring comparative legal discourses through an investigation into the shared worldviews of scholars is both an ambitious and an indispensable program. It is ambitious because a similar exercise requires fresh investigations of legal comparisons on a world scale to be valid. It is challenging because influential worldviews emerge over time and tend to exert their effects over considerable periods of time, hence the need to extend the analysis over entire epochs. Such a vast program is therefore by its nature a collaborative endeavor. At the same time, an effort to approach this topic anew is necessary because the progress of knowledge requires open debate about the central tenets of any academic discipline or branch of learning. The worldviews that underlie many comparisons are among the central tenets of the discipline. Conversely, comparisons based on worldviews that are not openly and critically discussed risk being flawed.

Starting from the antiquity, various areas of the world have emerged as cultural, economic, and political units. The division of world into States that enjoy mutual recognition under international law has prevailed in recent times. Throughout the emergence of the current world order, comparisons have been made on the basis of different worldviews. Looking at the field of comparative law, the classification of the world's legal systems into legal families has been a way to give voice to such worldviews. As evidence that worldviews are subject to change, it should be noted that the classifications of legal systems into legal families elaborated in the nineteenth and early twentieth centuries do not correspond to the later classifications associated with the classic works of René David and Zweigert and Kötz.[1] These in turn are often considered

[1] M. Pargendler, "The Rise and Decline of Legal Families", *American Journal of*

to be outdated (or are qualified) by recent classificatory efforts, or are met with outright skepticism.

To be sure, scholars based in socialist countries always presented a different map of the world. Considerations related to the prevailing socialist ideology were a dominant factor in their classification of the world's legal systems. The prevalence of a certain ideological outlook in reconstructing a legal map of the world is not an exclusive prerogative of works that adhered to that ideology. On the contrary, it underlies works that aspire to objectivity. The tendency of key comparative law works to subordinate or to marginalize those systems that do not conform to the Western canon in their ideal map of the world's legal experiences has thus become the target of lively criticism.[2] This criticism maintains that law is not separate from culture, and the culture of European ruling classes adhered to an idea of superiority vis à vis "the other" that was an essential component of imperialistic projects launched by European powers all around the world in the modern and the contemporary epochs.[3] Similar reflections have informed the call for a decolonial comparative law approach coming from leading academic institutions.[4]

The cosmopolitan outlook that emerges the aforementioned classics seems to be a reaction to the destructive nationalistic spirit that cast a long shadow over the European continent and beyond.[5] Looking back on this legacy, one has to keep in mind that the subordinate masses of Europe and those parts of the European population that were considered by the ruling classes as marginal were among the first to suffer from this state of affairs. Before undergoing democratization, on both sides of the Atlantic, the State and the ruling classes had few scruples in dealing with those deemed to be "uncivilized", whether they lived within or

Comparative Law, LX (2012), p. 1043.

[2] D. Bonilla Maldonado, *Legal Barbarians: Identity, Modern Comparative Law and the Global South* (2021); V. Corcodel, *Modern Law and Otherness: The Dynamics of Inclusion and Exclusion in Comparative Legal Thought* (2019).

[3] B. Bowden, "'Poisons Disguised with Honey': European Expansion and the Sacred Trust of Civilization", *The European Legacy* , XVIII (2013), p. 151.

[4] L. Salaymeh and R. Michaels, "Decolonial Comparative Law: A Conceptual Beginning", *Rabels Zeitschrift* ..., XXXVI (2022), p. 166.

[5] V. G. Curran, "Cultural Immersion, Difference and Categories in U. S. Comparative Law", *American Journal of Comparative Law*, XLVI (1998), p. 43.

beyond its borders. On the other hand, ethnocentric prejudice and imperialist projects cannot be considered a unique trait of a single polity or culture. The history of the world would be very different if this were the case. It is a supreme act of condescendence to imagine that the West has not borrowed much from others in the course of its history and, likewise, it is a supreme act of condescendence to imagine that there were no other projects or intentions at work in the history of modernity but those advanced by the West.

This article, a contribution to a collective, self-reflective enquiry such as the one launched herein, examines the diverging worldviews that have emerged as a result of debates over the way the law improves the general welfare. It is widely assumed that law has a major role in securing institutions that provide a firm ground for economic growth. On the other hand, exactly what type of institutions do provide such foundations has been widely debated and is still debated.[6] This debate that has not just involved lawyers. Economists have eagerly joined the discussion. Indeed, it is hard to overstate the role of economists' views on "things legal" and the nature and effects of legal change processes, given the prominent role that economics has come to play in the social sciences and policy-making circles.[7]

Law and science have been widely recognized as the leading institutional processes conducive to social progress, with economics being the prominent "science" for understanding and explaining social dynamics and change as far as the management of resources is concerned.[8] Economics in all its variants and schools of thoughts has been able to provide a number of consistent intellectual frameworks "to fill the gap" exposed in the early part of the twentieth century by legal realists such as Karl Nickerson Llewellyn (1893-1962), who confided that: "economic analysis would have provided a useful tool for understanding the nature

[6] For an assessment of the state of the art, see S. Dercon, *Gambling on Development: Why Some Countries Win and Others Lose* (2022).

[7] G. J. Stigler, "Economics: The Imperial Science?", *The Scandinavian Journal of Economics*, LXXXVI (1984), p. 301.

[8] Economists – just as lawyers – do not share a common definition of their own disciplinary boundaries: R. E. Backhouse and S. G. Medema, "Retrospectives: On the Definition of Economics", *The Journal of Economic Perspectives* , XXIII (2009), p. 221.

of law and legal change and for devising laws that would improve the social condition".[9]

The promise of economics as a leading social science discipline has long been that of providing a common analytical framework to assess the legal quality of institutions as well as to provide a *normative* term of comparison to establish more efficient solutions.[10] At the end of the twentieth century, some economists with a legal penchant have transformed their economic analysis of law agenda into a *comparative economics* program. They eventually came up with an economic map of the legal world based on the stylized dichotomy of countries whose legal system originated in the common law or civil law world, claiming that the former group can boast more efficient institutions.

These economists have contributed to designing a map of the world and to elaborating a worldview that, according to them, serves descriptive and normative purposes. Their influence has been vast and profound, shaping how law makers and investors perceive legal systems. It is this outlook on the law that we intend to reconstruct. We may frame the debate as a contest over the creation of an economic map of the legal world affecting business transactions and investments. On one hand, we have some influential economists educated in common law countries who are at work designing and promoting a global map drawn by the "invisible hand" of markets and court decisions around the world; on the other hand, we have a number of comparative lawyers educated and raised in civil law countries who reject such a map in defense of the role of statutory law and the "visible hand of the state". The creation of the worldview embedded in these maps and discussed below had lasting effects and, even when proven false, conditioned many debates on how to promote economic growth and regulate the economy.[11] Comparative law has been involved in the discussions and has spotted some cracks in the edifice that

[9] N. Mercuro and S. G. Medema, *Law and Economics: From Posner to Postmodernism* (2006), p. 17.

[10] H. Hovenkamp, "Knowledge about Welfare: Legal Realism and the Separation of Law and Economics", *Minnesota Law Review* (2000), p. 1490.

[11] On the importance of maps and the power relations they embed see in general N. Rajkovic, "The Visual Conquest of International Law: Brute Boundaries, the Map, and the Legacy of Cartogenesis", *Leiden Journal of International Law*, XXXI (2018), p. 267.

distinguished proponents of that worldview erected. This is why reflecting on this chapter of intellectual history is an instructive exercise.

This article does not intend to provide a full discussion of the contributions of economics to legal analysis, nor intend to be a roadmap to the variety of economic analyses of the law based on comparative elements. The purpose is more modest: to show the itinerary that some economists or lawyer-economists have followed to elaborate a worldview based on considerations about the comparative efficiency of the law involved in the regulation of business transactions and investments. We also discuss what criticism they encountered when their map of the world was examined more closely from a variety of disciplinary perspectives, including the comparative law perspective, as was bound to happen.[12]

THE MARKET, THE COMMON LAW, AND THE LEGISLATURE: A HYPOTHESIS

In the annals of United States jurisprudence *Lochner v New York*[13] stands out as the symbol of classical, *laissez faire* liberalism. In due time this ruling was abandoned, to recognize that the Constitution did not mandate the enforcement of a particular economic doctrine, and that government intervention in the economy could take place on a much larger scale, as the New Deal legislation demonstrated.[14] The long period of economic growth that followed the end of the Second World War provided support for the new role of the State in the economy for which John Maynard Keynes (1883-1946) had argued, amid discussions with academia and policy making circles.[15]

[12] For broader reflections on the relationship between law and economics, see G. Calabresi, *The Future of Law and Economics* (2016); Mercuro and Medema, note 9 above; A. Marciano and G. B. Ramello (eds.), *Law and Economics in Europe and the U.S.* (2016).

[13] 198 U.S. 45 (1905). The decision held that a New York State statute setting maximum working hours for bakers violated the right to freedom of contract.

[14] M. J. Horwitz, *The Transformation of American Law, 1870-1960 The Crisis of Legal Orthodoxy* (1994), pp. 34 ff.

[15] L. H. White, *The Clash of Economic Ideas: The Great Policy Debates and Experiments of the Last Hundred Years* (2012).

This intellectual and political climate favouring State intervention in the economy remained unchanged until the last quarter of the twentieth century. Beginning in the 1970s, however, public intervention in the economy was assessed anew at first in the United States, and then elsewhere. One strand of thought is worthy of attention in the present context: the school of thought that began extolling the virtues of judge-made law over legislation. This inspired a second round of debates that had their inception on the old continent, between the two world wars, and that the arrival of Friedrich August von Hayek (1899-1992) in Chicago in the 1960s contributed to revive.[16]

Public law making through political deliberation mostly serves a redistributive function, which is typically symbolized by taxation and public expenditure. On the other hand, the common law, administered by supposedly impartial judges, would have the merit of advancing economically efficient outcomes. This discourse was first presented as descriptive reconstruction of the common law, but soon was also introduced as a normative claim. The principal proponent of the latter view was Richard Posner. In the first edition of his book *Economic Analysis of Law* the claim was advanced that judges in deciding cases and in searching for "a reasonably objective and impartial standard" must necessarily pay attention to efficiency in resolving disputes.[17] Posner's hugely productive career as a legal theorist "largely consisted of piling up evidence for that argument".[18] In a relatively short time, the argument advanced by Posner thus became known as the "efficiency of the common law hypothesis".[19]

We will not retrieve here the whole debate that such hypothesis generated, as the available literature encapsulates the essential

[16] T. J. Zywicki and E. P. Stringham, "Austrian Law and Economics and Efficiency in the Common Law", in Zywicki and P. J. Boettke (eds.), *Research Handbook on Austrian Law and Economics* (2017), pp. 192-208.

[17] R. A. Posner, *Economic Analysis of Law* (1972), pp. 98-99. The book reached its ninth edition in 2014. For the normative claim see Posner, (1980) 'The Ethical and Political Basis of the Efficiency Norm in Common Law Adjudication", *Hofstra Law Review*, VIIII (1980), p. 487.

[18] D. Friedman, *What Economics has to do with Law and Why it Matters* (2000), p. 16. The author is Milton Friedman's son.

[19] F. Parisi, "The Efficiency of the Common Law Hypothesis", in C. K. Rowley and F. Schneider, *The Encyclopedia of Public Choice* (2004), p. 519.

points made by the participants in the debate.[20] However, whereas Posner recounted the evolutionary path of the law tending towards efficiency by considering judge made law as the paradigm producer of efficient rules, subsequent commentators went further. They ascribed the same function more specifically to the common law as administered by courts of jurisdictions belonging to the common law tradition. They thus set this modality of adjudication against the institutional arrangements prevailing in France, which was taken to be (right or wrongly!) the paradigmatic civilian jurisdiction. A typical statement reflecting this approach is:

> English common law developed as it did because landed aristocrats and merchants wanted a system of law that would provide strong protections for property and contract rights and limit the Crown's ability to interfere in markets. French civil law, by contrast, developed as it did because the revolutionary generation, and Napoleon after it, wished to use state power to alter property rights and attempted to ensure that judges could not interfere. Thus, quite apart from the substance of legal rules, there is a sharp difference between the ideologies underlying common and civil law, with the latter notably more comfortable with a centralized and activist government. [21]

It is perhaps ironic but, at the beginning of the twentieth century, opinions about the efficiency of the common law in the United States were quite different from those emerging in the last quarter of the twentieth century from the confident pages of scholars inspired by the Chicago approach to economics. Readers of *The Journal of Political Economy* for 1918 could, for example, find in the pages of that important publication a completely different assessment of the common law in terms of efficiency, which is at odds with those later accounts:

> The fundamental reason for the attack upon the common law is to be found in the rapid economic development of America contrasted with the relatively slow rate of change in the common law. Not only has American industrial

[20] D. Sokol, "Rethinking the Efficiency of the Common Law", *Notre Dame Law Review*, XCV (2019), p. 795.

[21] P. G. Mahoney, "The Common Law and Economic Growth: Hayek Might Be Right", *The Journal of Legal Studies*, XXX (2001), p. 503.

> revolution proceeded at a rate that surpasses all previous records of change but the common law has been held back by a load of inherited tendencies which prevented it from adapting itself to American conditions.[22]

This view of the common law is not unique to the United States. Jeremy Bentham (1748-1832), for example, often regarded as one of the forerunners of economic analysis of law, loathed and despised all "judge-made law", which he considered as bad as "priest-made religion" and believed to be motivated by the same sinister motives. In his eyes, the "English common law" was the brainchild and product of "Judge and Co", the association of lawyers and judges, and served nothing but the "sinister interests of that illicit partnership". The following excerpt gives an idea of the overall argument:

> But wherever it [the judge-made law] exists, lawyers will be its defenders, and, perhaps innocently, its admirers. They love the source of their power, of their reputation, of their fortune: they love unwritten law for the same reason that the Egyptian priest loved hieroglyphics, for the same reason that the priests of all religions have loved their peculiar dogmas and mysteries.[23]

Bentham was among the fiercest advocates of the superiority of statute law over common law. As John Stuart Mill (1806-1873) commented, Jeremy Bentham and his works: "approached all ideas as a stranger and if they did not fit this test (the test of utility), he dismissed them as vague generalities". Mill went on to say that what Bentham did not realize was that "these generalities contained the whole unanalyzed experience of the human race", which could not be obliterated lest losing touch with reality.[24]

Comparative lawyers have leveled criticisms along similar lines – with respect to the legal origins thesis and the *Doing Business in 2004 Report* (see below) – by emphasizing the role of culture and

[22] H. Hoyt, "The Economic Function of the Common Law", *Journal of Political Economy*, XXVI (1918), p. 167.

[23] J. Bentham, "General View of a Complete Code of Law", in *Works*, ed. J. Bowring (1838-1843), III, p. 206.

[24] J. S. Mill, "Bentham", in F. R. Leavis (ed.), *Mill on Bentham and Coleridge* (1980), pp. 39. 59.

other non-quantifiable cultural and legal variables to assess the nature and the functioning of legal systems across the world.

No less a figure than Max Weber (1864-1920) had reservations about the common law as an engine of economic growth. He basically argued that the economic development triggered by the Industrial Revolution in Britain in the nineteenth century occurred in spite of (rather than because of) the law emerging from the decisions of the English courts, which at the time were rather dysfunctional.[25]

Almost a century later, in the United States these conceptions were reversed. During the last quarter of the twentieth century and beyond, the prevailing approach to law and economics sought to validate the hypothesis that there was a form of law making that could be rescued (or shielded from) from a political view of the law, and that was therefore susceptible of treatment by the science of economics, essentially focussed on efficiency and wealth maximisation.

Within economics, the debate about the nature of the law gained momentum due to the initial success of the "Free Market Study" (1946-1952) and the subsequent "Antitrust Project" developed at the University of Chicago under the direction of Aaron Director (1901-2004) in the late 1940s.[26] These projects gradually evolved into a broader research program aimed at applying "economic theory— primarily microeconomics and the basic concepts of welfare economics—to examine the formation, structure, processes, and economic impact of law and legal institutions".[27] It was in the framework of the Free Market Study that von Hayek was invited to Chicago and able to develop his influential legal economic agenda.

This program eventually gained recognition in the United States as a dominant theoretical paradigm, lately dubbed as the "Twentieth century synthesis", in which: "efficiency analysis anchors both the descriptive framing and the normative assessment

[25] For an analysis and a partial correction of Weber's understanding of the English legal system and its relationship to capitalistic development see: J. Getzler, "Theories of Property and Economic Development", *The Journal of Interdisciplinary History*, XXVI (1996), p. 639.

[26] See P. Mirowski and D. Plehwe, *The Road from Montpellerin* (2015), p. 5.

[27] Mercuro and Medema, note 9 above, p. 1.

of law".[28] On this view: "law now required mainly tinkering and maintenance, casting legal scholars—not only in fields like antitrust but also critically in domains such as environmental law, administrative law, and the like—as a band of methodologically equipped efficiency inspectors".[29] Ultimately by: "analyzing legal rules and providing prescriptions for legal reforms, law and economics scholars could participate in the major areas of discourse within legal academia. They could even demonstrate the power of their coherent and rigorous theory over the confused intuitions of other legal scholars".[30]

SOME INTERDISCIPLINARY CONSEQUENCES OF A HYPOTHESIS

However fragile and later dismissed, the "efficiency of the common law hypothesis" gained considerable traction among policymakers and economists who subscribed to the idea that efficiency was an inbuilt factor and a formant of the legal system, tacitly applied and enforced by lawyers and courts themselves. Indeed, the ostensibly descriptive claim that efficiency drove legal developments in several fields opened the way for economists to exert an ever-greater influence on the legal domain. They eventually asserted their role of custodians of the body of knowledge concerned primarily with the "efficiency" of the expected behavioral effects of alternative legal solutions. This happened even though the hypothesis itself was contested, and eventually criticized as poorly supported by the evidence.[31]

[28] J. Britton-Purdy, D. S. Grewal, A. Kapczynski, and K. S. Rahman, "Building a Law-and-Political-Economy Framework: Beyond the Twentieth-Century Synthesis", *Yale Law Journal* , CXXIX (2019), p. 1784.

[29] Ibid., p. 1817; see also F. Esposito, *The Consumer Welfare Hypothesis in Law and Economics: Towards a Synthesis for the 21st Century* (2022).

[30] R. Harris, "The Uses of History in Law and Economics", *Theoretical Inquiries in Law*, IV (2003), p. 664.

[31] D. Oto-Peralías and D. Romero-Ávila, *Legal Traditions, Legal Reforms and Economic Performance* (2017) B. Depoorter and P. Rubin, "Judge-Made Law and the Common Law Process", in F. Parisi (ed.), *The Oxford Handbook of Law and Economics* (2017), pp. 129-142; N. Garoupa and C. Gomez Liguerre, "The Syndrome of the Efficiency of the Common Law", *Boston University International Law Journal*, XXIX (2011), p. 287.

Such a strong idea of efficiency being one of the asserted driving reasons at the heart of legal change offered to economists – understood as an epistemic professional group – an unusual opportunity to expand the questions that could be solved with potential success through the use of economics theoretical and empirical methods.[32] As long as economists consider economics to be "what economists do", no internal methodological constraints hamper the expansion of their analysis to laws and institutions worldwide Such an opportunity, coupled with the prominent role that economics plays among the social sciences, paved the way for a period of competition, if not confrontation, with lawyers as to which epistemic community has superior knowledge about the *actual* functioning and effects of laws around the world. This was facilitated by the reductionist paradigm upheld by Posner and other prominent figures in the law and economics movement about law's role in the economy, which suggested the idea of classifying legal systems in terms of economic efficiency alone.

The extension of efficiency claims to the common law system as a whole, rather than to its component constituted by judge-made law, morphed the entire research agenda into a comparative economics program based on a stylized understanding about why legal institutions matter. A "legally informed" comparative economics project thus took form to test the relative efficiency of civil law countries vis-à-vis common law jurisdictions in various fields. Many economists came to believe that they possessed the theoretical tool kit that could provide insights on how legal solutions differ or show uniformity around the world. The theory thus advanced intended to explain the origins of such variability, as well as to test their comparative efficiency of legal systems through empirical and statistical methods. This involved the instrumental use of legal categories such as the classification of legal systems into legal families to correlate them with statistical analysis concerning the efficiency of legal solutions prevailing in different countries. This use of legal knowledge by economists ultimately aimed at identifying rules and institutions that should be reformed rather than adopted in light of their expected impact on economic performance in terms of efficiency.[33]

[32] See R. H. Coase, "Economics and Contiguous Disciplines", *The Journal of Legal Studies*, VII (1978), p. 202.

[33] See Y. Chang, *Property Law: Comparative, Empirical, and Economic Analyses*

Such an economic analysis of law tapped the demand for new empirical research questions in the field of institutional economics and comparative economics. This became urgent as a result of the major transformations that took place in the 1980s and 1990s with the downfall of the Soviet bloc. Traditionally, comparative economics had focused on the difference between capitalist and socialist economies according to the dichotomy market economy vs centralized economic planning.[34] In the aftermath of the collapse of the Soviet Union, in a "end of history" climate of thought, many believed that institutional competition would henceforth be limited to the various models within the family of liberal institutions of the Western democracies.[35] Comparative economists faced the question whether the collapse of the Soviet Union and the satellite systems and the disappearance of the competing institutional system of capitalism meant that comparative economics was dead.[36] Their response in the negative led to a re-purposing of their discipline towards a comparative economics agenda based on the generalization of economic efficiency as a guiding hypothesis in the comparison of institutional models within the family of market economies.[37]

The legal origins literature developed into what is now known as the law and finance project. The project is still influential and is being developed by other economists. While the premises and legal insights that guide the project have changed substantially over time, the economic impact of legal institutions remains its core, driving research questions and hypotheses.[38] This was originally based on a series of articles by a group of economists who conducted cross-country studies on the relationship between legal rules and economic outcomes. These contributions explained those outcomes in terms of the legal origins of the respective legal

(2023), p. 46.

34 S. Djankov, E. Glaeser, R. La Porta, F. Lopez-de-Silanes, A. Shleifer, "The New Comparative Economics", *Journal of Comparative Economics*, XXXI (2003), p. 595.

35 F. Fukuyama, "The End of History?", *The National Interest*, XVI (1989), p. 3.

36 See Djankov, note 34 above, p. 596.

37 Djankov, et al., "The Regulation of Entry", *Quarterly Journal of Economics*, CXVIII (2002), p. 27; La Porta, Lopez-de-Silanes, and Shleifer, "The Economic Consequences of Legal Origins", *Journal of Economic Literature*, XLVI (2008), p. 305.

38 See the next section below.

systems. They thus aimed to map the different legal systems according to the criterion of economic efficiency by categorizing the legal regimes in force in different countries with regard, for example, to perceived levels of protection of property rights and investors in companies against abuse and "expropriation" by company directors.[39]

The fundamental research question aimed to evaluate the level of investor protection on the assumption that systems providing stronger guarantees would experience a correspondingly greater degree of financial development. Building on this hypothesis, a comprehensive research program was initiated, categorizing and mapping the legal landscape according to how: "legal rules protecting investors vary systematically across legal traditions or origins, with the laws of common law countries (originating in English law) being more protective of outside investors than the laws of civil law countries (originating in Roman law) and in particular French civil law countries".[40] Then they controlled for the instrumental variable of "legal families" to which they had previously assigned the different countries. This step aimed to establish a causal relationship between investor protection and the legal origins within common law or civil law countries, respectively.[41] The findings of this group of economists (often referred to by the acronym LLSV from the initials of their last names) maintained that legal traditions could be introduced as instrumental variables to explain different levels of investors protection. They also argued that countries undergoing a shift toward a market economy or aspiring to modernize their institutions and overcome underdevelopment should embrace common law models, which, in their perspective, provided the most robust protection for investors.[42]

[39] La Porta, Lopez-de-Silanes, Shleifer, and R. Vishny, "Law and Finance", NBER Working Paper No. 5661 (1996); id., "Legal Determinants of External Finance", *Journal of Finance,* LII (1997), p. 1150. For critical analysis: A. Vandenbulke, "La Legal Origins Theory: droit, économie, idéologie", *Revue internationale de droit économique,* XXXVI (2017), p. 79.

[40] World Bank, *Doing Business in 2004: Understanding Regulation* (2004), p. x.

[41] La Porta et al., note 37 above, p. 305.

[42] T. Beck, A. Demirguc-Kunt, and R. Levine, "Law and Finance: Why Does Legal Origin Matter?", *Journal of Comparative Economics,* XXXI (2003), p. 653; for a synthesis of the debate and the subsequent evolutions of the law and finance movement, see G. Schnyder, A. Grosman, K. Fu, M. Siems, and R. V. Aguilera,

The findings on the comparative economic performance of legal systems finally became a template to design an economic map of the legal world, as happened with the adoption of their model by World Bank, who supported the whole project and endowed it with additional political, normative, and professional implications, drawing also inspiration from pioneer field experiments conducted by the Peruvian economist Hernando De Soto.[43] Not surprisingly, large sectors of the comparative law community, especially those with a civil law background, reacted strongly against what was perceived as a startling encroachment on their intellectual and professional spheres of influence through the use of questionable generalizations.

AN ECONOMIC MAP OF THE LEGAL WORLD

The protagonists of the (re)discovery of the complementarity between law, finance, and economics were directly involved in the strategy of the World Bank Group for tapping private initiative to reduce poverty. Simeon Djankov and his fellow economists were directly tasked by the World Bank to design the *"Doing Business in 2004"* (hereinafter *Doing Business Report*) report to follow on their previously envisioned economic assessment of legal institutions. The World Bank launched the *Doing Business Report* project with the aim of assessing regulation through the elaboration of objective measures of business regulation and enforcement of legal provisions across the world. The approach was admittedly functional and outcome oriented, aimed at capturing the effects of regulations applicable to business activities. As the Report stated: "It covers regulatory outcomes, such as the time and cost of meeting regulatory requirements to register a business, as well as measures of actual regulations, such as an index of the rigidity of employment law or the procedures to enforce a contract".[44]

"Legal Perception and Finance: The Case of IPO Firm Value", *British Journal of Management*, XXXIII (2021), p. 88.

[43] H. De Soto, *The Other Path: The Invisible Revolution in the Third World* (1998); De Soto, *The Mystery of Capital: Why Capitalism Triumphs in the West and Fails Every Else* (2000).

[44] World Bank, note 40 above, p. ix.

The *Doing Business* project aimed to advance the World Bank Group's agenda for the development of the private sector according to the following lines:[45]

- motivating reforms through country benchmarking
- informing the design of reforms
- enriching international initiatives on development effectiveness
- informing theory by producing new indicators that quantify various aspects of regulation
- promoting the institutions and models that were found to be superior and preferable from such analyses.

The program was designed to assess how regulation affects small and medium-sized enterprises (SMEs), with the aim of identifying and helping to remove "inefficient" constraints on business.[46] The program was embedded in an economic intellectual framework and research program developed and led by economists such as Simeon Djankov and Rafael La Porta and aimed at articulating a set indicators to:

> (i) measure the ongoing regulatory reforms through countries' benchmarking; (ii) induce changes in those areas of the business regulation which adversely affect a country's competitiveness; (iii) improve the effectiveness of money aids by helping donors to monitor the quality of the institutional environment of a country; (iv) provide quantitative measures of the actual rate of regulation, in order to test the impact of existing theories.[47]

The program included 183 countries. Initially, it involved an empirical study of ten indicators relating to different stages of business activity, from "starting up" to the resolution of commercial disputes. The collection of data about each country was realized through surveys submitted to about 2,000 judges, lawyers, accountants, credit registry representatives, business consultants, and government officials from around the world.

45 Ibid., p. x.

46 Ibid., pp. ix-x.

47 S. Benedettini and A. Nicita, "Towards the Economics of Comparative Law: the 'Doing Business' Debate", *Comparative Law Review*, 1 (2010), p. 2.

Many contributors were partners in Lex Mundi law firms, or were members of the International Bar Association.[48] The local partners were selected as informers to provide an "objective" assessment of each country's business regulation as it actually takes place.[49] Upon statistical analysis of the answers to these surveys, the *Doing Business Report* published a set of international rankings of the national economies in the various domains, relating to their perceived attractiveness and competitiveness. At the same time, it marketed the conclusions drawn on the basis of the interpretations of the collected data as a substantial improvement of: "our understanding of productivity growth and the optimal scope for government in regulating business activity".[50]

Surprisingly for many, the *Doing Business Report* showed that wealthy and leading civil law jurisdictions performed very poorly in the final rankings when compared to less developed countries belonging to the common law family of jurisdictions. The case of Rwanda, with a ranking of 47 (better than Italy) in the 2015 *Doing Business Report,* despite having per capita national income under $1,000 and more than 40% of its population in poverty, was paradigmatic. Such counterfactual results added further political dimensions to the interdisciplinary row, as major civil law countries such as France set up institutionally coordinated responses to counter inefficiencies claims mounted against the civil law tradition in general and the French legal tradition in particular.

The outright disposal of legal rules and legal institutions that did not meet the efficiency criteria upheld by the *Doing Business Report* seemed aggressive to lawyers, as has long been the case when economists dub as irrational and "non-sense upon stilts" legal solutions culturally and institutionally at home in any given legal system. A notable pitfall of the report was its lack of focus on how gender related issus play out in the economy, although discriminatory policies against women surely affect economic performance. Reacting to criticism, the World Bank prepared and published a separate report on *Women, Business and the Law,* now

[48] World Bank, note 40 above, p. i.

[49] Ibid.

[50] Ibid., p. xi.

in its ninth edition, that identifies barriers to women's economic participation and encourages reform of discriminatory laws.[51]

Such use of comparative law concepts to draw a map of the world that showed a clear bias in favor of the common law system[52] did not leave the comparative law community indifferent. In addition to the response from the French and francophone legal community,[53] several comparative law scholars objected to the method and the conclusions presented in the *Doing Business* report.[54] A first order of issues raised was the normative and reductionist nature of the report aimed at classifying different systems according to questionable standards through the determination of doubtful causal relations.[55] A second source of criticism targeted the incomplete and erroneous definition of law, which ignored the plurality of legal formants and was mostly blind to the essential distinction between "law in action" and "law in the books".[56]

The superficiality with which the various countries were alternately categorized as belonging to the "civil law" and "common law" families was criticized. Such categorizations tend to overlook how the circulation of legal models and the

51 For the latest report see: The World Bank, *Women, Business and the Law in 2023* (2022) (available online).

52 M. Infantino, *Numera et impera: Gli indicatori giuridici globali e il diritto comparato* (2019), pp. 151-152.

53 See Association Henri Capitant, *Les droits de tradition civiliste en question: à propos des Rapports Doing Business de la Banque Mondiale* (2006); I. Lee, "Le marché du droit: observations néoclassiques sur les rapports Doing Business et la rivalité common law - droit civil", in G. F. Gaudreault-Desbiens, et al. (eds.), *Convergence, concurrence et harmonisation des systèmes juridiques* (2009), p. 77; C. Valcke, "The French Response to the World Bank's 'Doing Business Reports'", *The University of Toronto Law Journal*, LX (2010), p. 197.

54 The main criticisms are aptly presented in R. Michaels, "Comparative Law by Numbers? Legal Origins Thesis, *Doing Business* Reports, and the Silence of Traditional Comparative Law", *American Journal of Comparative Law*, LVII (2009), p. 765.

55 G. McCormack, "Why 'Doing Business' with the World Bank May Be Bad for You", *European Business Organization Law Review*, XIX (2018), p. 649.

56 Michaels, note 52 above, p. 776; Schnyder, Siems, and Aguilera, (2021) "Twenty Years of 'Law and Finance': Time to Take Law Seriously", *Socio-Economic Review*, XIX (2021), p. 377.

transplantation of norms complicate similar classifications.[57] Furthermore, simple recipes for the adoption of specific reforms ignore that legal transfers hardly take place in full due to the simultaneous influence of multiples factors and of conflicting policies.[58] The mere formal adoption of laws originating elsewhere does not guarantee an effortless transplanting of their interpretation and meaning, as initially established abroad, into local contexts. The legal origins literature all too often employs a concept of legal transplantation that overlooks the intricate nature of the process involved in transferring the meaning of a legal rule across borders, not to mention the challenges of transplanting a practice from one country to another.[59]

The complementarity between legal models, legal expertise, and policy transfers is well known in comparative law, as are the implications of a partial diffusion and reception of some legal formants. A simple statistical analysis based on perceptions of the impact of certain rules on entrepreneurial freedom is not an objective measurement of the applicable law, and inevitably suffers from cultural barriers that favor more understandable responses and practices closer to the culture and experience of the observer. We thus have both a problem of commensurability concerning efficiency and the concrete risk of a homeward bias.[60] Finally, data collection is a means to enhance the accountability of government, but the use of those data for the elaboration of policies should not short-circuit public debates and deliberations when legal or administrative measures are introduced to carry out reforms, or indicators are used to steer the action of the public administration, and thus become instruments of government.[61] Similar problems are a matter of concern for a range of other global indicators that

[57] N. Garoupa and C. G. Liguerre, "The Efficiency of the Common Law: The Puzzle of Mixed Legal Families", *Wisconsin International Law Journal*, XXIX (2011), p. 671.

[58] See, for instance, M. Siems, *Comparative Law* (2d ed.; 2018), pp. 229-261

[59] M. Graziadei, "Legal Transplants and the Frontiers of Legal Knowledge", *Theoretical Inquiries in Law*, X (2009), p. 723.

[60] Michaels, note 52 above.

[61] S. Cassese and L. Casini, "Public Regulation of Global Indicators", in K. E. Davis, A. Fisher, B. Kingsbury, and S. Engle Merry (eds.), *Governance by Indicators* (2012), pp. 467-469.

are utilized as soft means of governance, as a recent in-depth comparative study shows.[62]

After years of debate and some methodological improvements to the report, which led to the removal of some indicators (such as the one that rewarded legal systems that made it easier to fire workers), the World Bank decided to discontinue the Doing Business program in 2021.[63] The Bank's decision was due to the finding of irregularities regarding the data collection for certain countries and to ethical concerns about the conduct of the personnel involved in producing the reports for 2018 and 2020.[64] The World Bank instructed an international legal firm (Wilmer Hale) to investigate these irregularities and published the resulting report.[65]

Despite the scandal, the experts' criticisms, and the discontinuation of the program, the insights and the worldviews supported by this work are still highly influential and guide many conversations and policy and investment decisions. The reports have had an enormous impact on *perceptions* of the legal qualities of different jurisdictions assigned to one of the two leading legal families belonging to the Western legal tradition, and perceptions are often what counts in terms of decision making.[66]

The image, the map provided by the "legal origins" line of research and, most importantly, by the *Doing Business Report* has had a lasting impact on the way economists, policymakers, and external analysts view legal systems and discuss their efficiency. These maps of the world have won the "battle of ideas" and became

[62] M. Bussani, S. Cassese, and M. Infantino, (2023) "Quantification of Performance as a Regulatory Technique: A Comparative Appraisal", in Bussani, Cassese, and Infantino (eds.), *Comparative Legal Metrics* (2023), p. 323ff.; Infantino, note 52 above.

[63] The press release by the World Bank: World Bank Group to Discontinue Doing Business Report (16 September 2021) (available online).

[64] F. Nicola, "Scandal around World Bank's Doing Business Index Exposes the Perils of Sports-like Rankings", *The Conversation* (20 October 2021).

[65] Investigation of Data Irregularities in Doing Business 2018 and Doing Business 2020 Investigation Findings and Report to the Board of Executive Directors (available online).

[66] See Schnyder, note 42 above, p. 41. The role of (mis)perception of "legal qualities" in the making of investment decisions is not confined to legal orders as a whole. It can also affect investment decisions in innovative activities whose "legal qualities" are uncertain: M. Giraudo, "Legal Bubbles", in A. Marciano and G. B. Ramello (eds.), *Encyclopedia of Law and Economics* (2022).

part of "climate of opinion, the dominant *Weltanschauung* of a period".[67] Thus, they remain locked-in the mentality of generations of policy makers and resist change even when undermined or refuted.[68]

The World Bank's decision to discontinue the *Doing Business* program was not the end of the story, however. Almost immediately after ending it, the Bank announced a new flagship report, once more benchmarking the business environment and investment climate in most economies worldwide. The new product is labelled the B-ready report. This report, to be published in 2024, shall: "assesses the regulatory framework and public services directed at firms, and the efficiency with which regulatory framework and public services are combined in practice".[69] Once again, the focus is on providing a more favorable business environment for the private sector by delivering: "actionable evidence to promote reforms for a stronger private sector".[70] The new program was prepared by *The Doing Business: External Panel Review Final Report* delivered in September 2021. Produced by a group of academics external to the World Bank, this study suggested a major overhaul of the *Doing Business* methodology.[71] The design of the new project is set out in a *Concept Note* released in 2022, that is accompanied by a *B-Ready Manual and Guide* and *Methodology Handbook.*[72] The *Manual and Guide* describe the protocols, processes, safeguards, and resources related to the end-to-end production of the data and reports, while the *Handbook* presents the basis for the asserted transparency, quality, and integrity of the B-Ready project.

[67] This a quotation by F. A. Hayek, "The Intellectuals and Socialism", *University of Chicago Law Review*, XVI (1949), p. 423, who surely knew why intellectuals wield power.

[68] On why this happens, see A. Yalcintas, *Intellectual Path Dependence in Economics: Why Economists do not Reject Refuted Theories* (2016).

[69] The World Bank website.

[70] Ibid.

[71] The authors of the Report were: Laura Alfaro, Harvard University; Alan Auerbach, University of California (Berkeley); Mauricio Cárdenas (Chair), Columbia University; Takatoshi Ito, Columbia University; Sebnem Kalemli-Özcan, University of Maryland; Justin Sandefur, Center for Global Development.

[72] All these documents are available online.

ORIGINATE AND DISTRIBUTE

The intrinsic quality of the *Doing Business Report* and the hype dynamics typically assisting interdisciplinary vistas enabled by knowledge brokerage[73] cannot alone explain the huge resonance that it enjoyed or of the legal origins theory that underpins the whole project. The *Doing Business Report* and the legal origins research programs did not emerge out of nothing; they reflected the spirit of the time in which they were conceived and released. On one hand, they were an outgrowth of a pre-existing intense flow of legal transfers and policy diffusion waves that were unleashed by the collapse of the Soviet Union in 1991.[74] On the other hand, they were part of a wider series of attempts to provide quantifiable measures to rank the world's legal systems by assessing the local business environment through the use of legal and institutional data. Other programs were inaugurated in the same period such as the *Global Competitiveness Report* by the World Economic Forum,[75] the *Index of Economic Freedom* by the Heritage Foundation,[76] the *Business Environment and Enterprise Performance Survey* (BEEPS) by the European Bank for Reconstruction and Development and the World Bank.[77]

Why is the map provided by the *Doing Business Report* still relevant and important today, despite the criticism levelled at it? First, the very fact that it was initially so successful is a reason in itself for the endurance of the images and maps of the world that accompanied it. Given the great institutional diversity of the world, the Report soon became a focal point, gaining extraordinary saliency as a convenient way to find in a single publication data from the great majority of the countries of the world.[78] The

[73] The strategic advantage of knowledge brokerage between adjoining disciplines is highlighted by R. S. Burt, "Structural Holes and Good Ideas", *American Journal of Sociology*, CX (2004), p. 349.

[74] G. Ajani, "By Chance and Prestige: Legal Transplants in Russia and Eastern Europe", *American Journal of Comparative Law*, XLIII (1995), p. 93.

[75] World Economic Forum, Global Competitiveness Report Special Edition 2020: How Countries are Performing on the Road to Recovery (available online).

[76] Heritage Foundation, Index of Economic Freedom (available online).

[77] These surveys cover Central and Eastern Europe and the former Soviet Union, as well as Turkey (available online).

[78] For an instructive discussion of how saliency is acquired see J. W. Schiemann,

wide coverage of each edition of the report by the general and the specialized press contributed to its success. Furthermore, it provided a platform for for-profit consultancies to perpetuate the demand for their own expertise (rather than to improve the evidence base for aid allocation and the evaluation of development projects).[79]

On another level, the success of such a map is based on reasons that have long been familiar to those comparative scholars who have studied the ways in which broad ideas, legal models, and rules travel across borders. A key factor in this respect is the role played by the cultural prestige enjoyed by the "framers" of the objects in question, combined with the particular workmanship and characteristics of the cultural artifact itself. In other words, prestige and the ability to present knowledge in a simplified form, in a nutshell that is both accessible and gets to the point, turn out to be an effective means of influence.

As far as prestige is concerned, let us recall the positions held by the authors of both the main seminal articles in the legal origins research venture and of those who produced the *Doing Business Report*. These were economists based in the United States, ultimately leading a program at the World Bank. This was launched by an institution that should have spoken on behalf of the best expertise available at the global level, at a time when American power was at its height. These characteristics made their analyses and contributions almost by definition authoritative in any debate on legal reforms.

Furthermore, the *Doing Business Report* played a significant role in disseminating the worldviews inherent in the research findings on legal origins by presenting them in a format that was easily accessible to governments and policymakers. Comparative law has highlighted the importance of nutshells, defined as: "books written as teaching manuals (whether in a law school or for home study) for beginning law students or to instruct non-lawyers in the elements of the law".[80] Nutshells provide consistent and coherent

"Meeting Halfway between Rochester and Frankfurt: Generative Salience, Focal Points, and Strategic Interaction", *American Journal of Political Science*, XLIV (2000), p. 1.

[79] A. Broome, "Gaming Country Rankings: Consultancies as Knowledge Brokers for Global Benchmarks", *Public Administration*, C (2022), p. 554.

[80] A. Watson, "The Importance of 'Nutshells'", *American Journal of Comparative*

tools for interpretation and action in the legal domain. The *Doing Business Report* was a nutshell of its own kind, considering the institution that released it and the specific information provided to its readers. It had a power and an impact comparable to, if not superior to, other forms of nutshell often discussed by the comparative law literature. It served as a targeted tool for policymakers and investors, aiming to encourage the adoption of common law-inspired reforms and attract investment in countries embracing such regulatory models.

Indeed, prior to the publication of such an influential nutshell, countries wishing to borrow foreign models for legal reform tended to rely on local specialized institutions that made expert comparisons between a limited set of alternative legal solutions. By providing readily available rankings to promote model reforms, the *Doing Business Report* instead apparently invited policymakers and investors to make more independent decisions, on the basis of a vastly superior critical assessment of the domestic legal environment. The report provided a consistent, readily available set of heuristics, either for planning legal reform programs to attract investment, or for private investors seeking overseas opportunities to choose among seemingly equally distant and unknown jurisdictions. Understanding the dissemination of the *Doing Business Report* as an example of the workings of a nutshell may therefore help to explain the resilience and strength demonstrated by the map of the world it provided.

Although the discussion on the persistence and diffusion of nutshells in the comparative law literature typically concentrates on merely legal nutshells, such as the French Civil Code or Blackstone's *Commentaries*, the case of the *Doing Business Reports* shows that the same dynamic can be replicated with respect to the legal-economic and policy-making field. As it is often the case with epistemic borrowings, interdisciplinary views of legal issues can have long-lasting effects, regardless of their merits, thus shaping the academic debate and policy making debate for quite some time.[81]

Law, XLII (1994), p. 1.

[81] M. Giraudo, "Some Remarks on Lawyers' Use of Knowledge. Charting a Course", *Isaidat Law Review*, no. 2 (2021), p. 13

CONCLUSION

Each academic discipline tends to develop its own view of the law and of the world. Jurists and legal practitioners are not alone in trying to understand legal phenomena and legal institutions in all their diversity. Their worldviews may be challenged or confronted by those of other disciplines, such as sociology, anthropology, philosophy and economics. Economics in particular has taken a keen interest in law. Within economics, the search for a methodological tool that could provide a neutral assessment of the law led economists and law and economics scholars to consider the efficiency of legal rules as a means of having better laws. This search led some scholars to identify judge-made law as a form of lawmaking that leads to more efficient laws in an evolutionary way. On this assumption, legal systems that typically tend to rely more on legislation to bring about legal change are subject to reservations because legislation would entail a greater degree of interference in the choices made by private parties. Ultimately, this approach has led to the conclusion that common law systems are more efficient than civil law systems in providing guarantees to investors and a more friendly business climate. The *Doing Business Reports* produced by the World Bank by and large followed this line of thinking. The world view thus produced hierarchies of "good" and "bad" performers which instrumentalised the classical classification of the world's legal systems into different families.

This came as a surprise to the comparative law community, which had never developed these classifications for similar purposes. If used for such purposes, these classifications should at least have been analyzed by taking into account several other elements, such as the fact that the way the law was originally transplanted and received in some jurisdictions is a more important determinant of legality than the supply of law from a particular legal family (English, French, German, or Scandinavian).[82] Economists as well objected to the hypothesis that common law adjudication leads to more efficient legal outcomes.[83] Furthermore, the whole exercise based on the ranking of the world's legal systems by the World Bank's *Doing Business Reports* ignored the simple truth that

[82] D. Berkowitz, K. Pistor, J. F. Richard, "Economic Development, Legality, and the Transplant Effect", *European Economic Review*, XLVII (2003), p. 165.

[83] See note 31 above.

the more an indicator is used for decision-making, the more it is subject to corruption pressures and the more likely it is to distort and corrupt the social processes it is supposed to monitor. This ultimately led to the cancellation of the program.[84]

Comparison is about measurement, but it turns out that measuring an artefact as complex as the law is a more difficult matter than many would think, perhaps because the law rarely has the opportunity to pursue a single goal but must pursue a multiplicity of goals.[85] On their side, economists have concluded that: "Any robust policy dialogue must rely on a much broader assessment of reform than on the Doing Business rankings".[86] A new initiative by the World Bank has been announced. Will it be able to deflect the kind of criticism that the previous one attracted? Will it give us a more credible map of the world? The warning is that the law should be taken a little more seriously in the exercise than it has been.[87]

84 D. T. Campbell, "Assessing the Impact of Planned Social Change", *Evaluation and Program Planning*, II, no. 1 (1979), p. 67.

85 F. Denozza, "È possibile una misurazione delle prestazioni dei sistemi giuridici?", *Annuario di diritto comparato e studi legislativi* (2012), p. 73.

86 T. Besley, "Law, Regulation, and the Business Climate: The Nature and Influence of the World Bank Doing Business Project", *Journal of Economic Perspectives*, XXIX (2015), p. 117.

87 Schnyder, Siems, and Aguilera, note 56 above.

Chapter 8
Comparativism, Philosophy of Law, and Comparative Jurisprudence

OLEKSANDR D. TYKHOMYROV
DENYS O. TYKHOMYROV

The philosophy of legal comparativism is an adaptation of comparativism to the peculiarities of legal reality and the reflections thereof, and also includes unique properties thereof. Diverse variations of their interlinkage are formed at the "intersection" of comparativistics, philosophy, and the forms of contemplation of legal reality: comparativism, legal comparativism, philosophical foundations of legal comparativistics, comparative philosophy of law, and others. The present study addresses two of them: comparativism as the grounds of post-postmodernist philosophy of law and the philosophical grounds of comparative jurisprudence.

COMPARATIVISM AS GROUNDS OF PHILOSOPHY OF LAW IN POST-POSTMODERNIST CONTEXT

The contemporary state of globalization and differentiation of world development, the dynamism of the changes thereof, and the origin and development of new trends in the inter-civilizational dialogue require a rethinking of the traditional tenets of legal science and recourse to problems of contemplating the comparativeness of the philosophy and theory of law in the context post-postmodernism.

The advisability of such an approach is seen in the fact that in the worldview context the traditional tenets of legal science were formed basically in the era of modern, the classical and non-classical periods of the development of science in the course of a respective worldview – modernism. During the second half of the twentieth century, the worldview of postmodernism, and respectively – the post-non-classical period of the development of science – conditioned a different understanding of the fundamental grounds, criteria, evaluations, significance, and role of legal science.

Postmodernism arose as a reaction against the crisis in western culture virtually simultaneously (historically) in different countries and spheres of culture, and therefore initially had no determined content besides the fixation of a new stage of social development.

Against the background of crisis manifestations in philosophy and worldviews based on the values of European civilization and Eurocentrism, postmodernism brought hope of a way out of this situation just as in science similar hopes are linked with synergetics. The merit of postmodernism was that it forced one to view the world differently and to reassess the values and norms of thinking traditional for modernism and scientism.[1]

An analysis of the diversity of approaches to postmodernism enables one to single out: elimination of the "general" and "universal", gravitation towards the "unique", simulation of reality and other postulates thereof directed towards juxtaposition to modernism, and also attempts to overcome them by positions of "moderation" and late postmodernism, "redacted modern", "ultra-modern", and also to acknowledge its historical, spatial, and cultural limitedness.[2] Thus, on one hand, its radicalism, rejection and failure to accept much that was achieved in European civilization, although postmodernism itself was born in the bosom thereof, and, on the other, the conditions of globalization, the emergence of not only an "American" and "European", but also a "Japanese", "Chinese", "Latin" and other centrisms, conditions the understanding of the limitedness of the gnoseological potential of postmodernism, the concrete historical conditionality of the origin and existence of the postmodern era as one of the periods of development of only part of mankind inasmuch as the views of the world by different civilizations cannot be identical, and the history of mankind provides incontrovertible evidence of this.

1 A. A. Grevtseva, «Место и роль ценностей постмодеринизма в «культурной глобализации» [Place and Role of Values of Postmodernism in "Cultural Globalization"], Вестник Орловского государственного университета [Herald of Orel State University], no. 7 (2009), p. 17.

2 A. Dugin, Геополитика постмодерна. Времена новых империй. Очерки геополитики XXI века [Geopolitics of the Postmodern. Times of New Empires. Survey of Geopolitics of the XXI Century] (2007), pp. 24-26.

Just as universalism in modernism, the "different" and the "other" were absolutized in post-modernism, and the reality became virtual and depersonified. The denial of absolutization both of universalism and pluralism originate in the post-modern era, with various forms of worldview and practice (philosophy, science, religion, morals, international cooperation, and others) and ideas of comparativism based on recognition of the equality of the General and the Different, the creation of the "General" in dialogue of the "Different(s)", historical limitedness, and the "subjectivity" of all previously established programs and schemes.

Comparative thought is to a certain degree concretized in the philosophy of the post-postmodern – transmodernism,[3] transversal philosophy,[4] especially the philosophy of comparativism, but not as a subject-matter philosophy, but as a way of philosophizing.

The sources and various forms of manifestations of comparativism lie in the sphere of numerous comparative, inter-disciplinary, cross-national, and other studies of a philosophical, sociological, politological, legal, linguistic, and other character, and also in spaces of other forms of cognition: religious, mythological, day-to-day, practical, and so on.

One of the reasons for it arising is the development of a "common world" which cannot be realized only according to the benchmarks of North America or continental Europe; a "common" world is a world of existence of all countries and civilizations which build it in interaction and according to benchmarks established in this interaction, not only at the level of the United Nations and other international organizations, but in different and numerous acts of cooperation, struggle, and competition of States, non-State associations, and individuals.

Therefore, underlying comparativism is a pluralism of understandings of the world by representatives of various countries, peoples, civilizations, each of which forms its own

[3] V. A. Kutyrev, «Философия иного, или Небытийный смысл трансмодернизма» [Philosophy of the Other, or Non-existent Sense of Transmodernism], Вопросы философии [Questions of Philosophy], no. 12 (2005).

[4] A. S. Kolesnikov, Диалог философских культур и трансвервальная философия. От постмодерна к трансверсальной философии в мире мультикультурализма [Dialogue of Philosophical Cultures and Transversal Philosophy. From Postmodern to Transversal Philosophy in the World of Multi-Culturalism] (2013).

picture (or image) of the world, diversity of direct human life of the planet, creating the General with their behavior in the processes of a real transformation of the world and adaptation thereto. The real diverse world today is common to all, and everything else is various forms of the cognition thereof, understanding, transformation.

Another reason is the expansion of common information space, telecommunications, and so on which have made information accessible about any point of the planet or event previously inaccessible or known to individuals and being outside the limits of mass perception.

Of importance in the rise of comparativism is the transition to post-non-classical rationality,[5] expansion of the empirical base of research, socialization and culturalization of science, tolerance to other forms of cognition and understanding, and the like.

Taking the above into account, and relying even more on that written on this problem by representatives of various countries, professions, and specializations, one may say that today a worldview is being formed which is based primarily on the diversity of a single world of mankind in which distinction is "removed" as with commonality in a dialogue, polylog, or "polyphony" of voices of the "similar", "other", and "different" countries, and they are contemplated in concepts: multiplicity and unity of the world; forms of cognition thereof; correlation of cognition and the world; supplementarity, patience, tolerance, competition, struggle, commensurability, non-commensurability, equality, inequality, identicalty, monologue, dialogue, polylog, polyphony, and antipodes thereof; family similarities and family distinctions, collectiveness, "ensemble"; time and space; subject, life thereof, living world; situation and cycle; discontinuity and continuity; order and chaos, and others.

These conceptual ranges, in our view, enable comparativism to be interpreted as one of the worldview phenomena of the post-postmodern which rejected any absolutism, "assimilates" both a universalism of modernism and the pluralism of postmodernism, representing them through the "general and different" in the context of "one, other, different", relativity and supplementarity, presence and absence, dialogue and adialogue, and the like. Comparativism arises as manifestation of post-postmodernism if

5 V. S. Stepin, Теоретическое знание [Theoretical Knowledge] (2000).

the last is regarded as overcoming radicalness of both modernism and post-modernism and in this interpretation is a larger and deeper phenomenon having its sources in various domains of cognition and social life – art, religion, day-to-day existence, philosophy, socio-humanitarian sciences, practical activities, and so on, being distinctively transformed with respect to their features.

Comparativity is immanently peculiar to the philosophy of law, for "in the history of mankind culture lacks a single universal benchmark of philosophizing. Many schools and orientations related themselves to philosophy had and have a rather different cognitive orientation",[6] and contemporary philosophy exists "only in that understanding that certain problems of the present time interest all thinkers of our time and they all are obliged to take certain new positions into account. But from there to a notion of one single school or one single trend is an enormous distance. The philosophy of the present is astonishingly rich and diverse".[7] In this regard Lebedev noted that "in the history of world philosophy there has never existed any single philosophy of science understood identically by all (for philosophy, pluralism is an absolutely natural and essential condition of its existence)".[8]

The vision of the prospects for the development of philosophy is so multi-dimensional. Some scholars suggest to be oriented towards resolving its present topical problems and possible future ones by way of a rapprochement but not identity of philosophy and other forms of worldview;[9] others, towards an integration of philosophical positions;[10] yet others consider the creation of a

[6] K. Kh. Momdzhian, Введение в социальную философию: Учебное пособие [Introduction to Social Philosophy. Instructional Aid] (1997), p. 31.

[7] Iu. M. Bokhenskii, Современная европейская философия [Contemporary European Philosophy], transl. from German (2000), p. 12.

[8] S. A. Lebedev, «Предисловие» [Preface], in Lebedev (ed.), Философия науки: Учебное пособие для вузов [Philosophy of Science: Instructional Aid for Institutions of Higher Education] (2004), p. 3.

[9] Ibid., p. 4.

[10] V. V. Okorokov, Трансформація західноєвропейської метафізики (онтологічний зріз) [Transformation of Western European Metaphysics (Ontological Cross-Section)] (2003) (diss. doctor of philosophical sciences).

meta-philosophy to be optimal;[11] and yet others substantiate the need for a comparative philosophy.[12]

Thus, a weakening of the positions of a universalist understanding of philosophy and strengthening of the "pluralism" of philosophical schools, currents, systems, and a more precise awareness of the pluralism as a distinctive feature of contemporary philosophical development, a "recognition of equality of claims to the universality by different forms of understanding",[13] is an important feature of the philosophy of the twentieth and twenty-first centuries, because "for an objective cognition a diversity of opinions and methods encouraging such diversity is essential".[14]

A similar tendency is to be observed in the Ukrainian philosophy of law, which at the stage of the restoration of the previously acquired traditions the pluralism of approaches is inherent to the fundamental grounds thereof, in particular the determination of the subject-matter, tasks, functions, and correlation to the general theory of State and law, philosophy, philosophy of politics, philosophy of culture philosophy of science, and so on.[15]

[11] G. A. Brutian, «Философия и метафилософия» [Philosophy and Meta-Philosophy], Вопросы философии [Questions of Philosophy], no. 9 (1985), pp. 85-90.

[12] A. S. Kolesnikov, «Философская компаративтисика в истории идей» [Philosophical Comparativistics in the History of Ideas], Философский век. Альманах. Вып. 25. История философии как философия [Philosophical Century. Almanach. Vyp. 25, History of Philosophy as Philosophy] (Spb., 2003), XXV(2), pp. 22-30.

[13] V. S. Bibler, «Итоги и замыслы (конспекты философской логики культуры» [Results and Ideas (Synopsis of the Philosophical Logic of Culture)], Вопросы философии [Questions of Philosophy], no. 5 (1993), pp. 75-93.

[14] P. Feuerabend, Избранные труды по методологии науки: Переводы с английского и немецкого [Selected Works on the Methodology of Science: Translations from English and German], ed. I. S. Narskii (1986), p. 179.

[15] Iu. M. Oborotov, «Філософія права і методологія юриспруденції» [Philosophy of Law and Methodology of Science], Проблеми філософії права [Problems of Philosophy of Law] (2003), I, pp. 41-43; V. M. Bratasiuk, «Інтеллектуальна традиція постмодерну та проблеми реформування правової системи сучасної України» [Intellectual Tradition of the Postmodern and Problems of Reform of the Legal System of Contemporary Ukraine], Проблеми філософії права [Problems of Philosophy of Law] (2004), II, pp. 156-162; N. M. Onishchenko, «Аксіосфера сучасної держави та сприйняття права в суспільстві: проблеми теорії» [Axiosphere of Contemporary State and Perception of Law in Society: Problems of Theory], Проблеми філософії права [Problems of Philosophy of Law] (2008-2009), VI-VII, pp. 49-53; S. I. Maksymov, Філлософія права: сучасні інтерпретації. Вибрані праці, статті, аналіт. огляди, переклади

Having regard to the foregoing, this makes it possible to hypothetically trace certain phenomena of comparativism in the philosophy of law.

An important aspect of the contemporary philosophy of law is the detection of the "dynamics" of the general and the different in legal reality, and the methodological basis of such "dynamics" may be the presence or absence of a dialogue, polylog, or "polyphony" of legal and extra-legal cultures. In this situation the General is illuminated as derivative from the interaction of the Different(s), the general emerges in the dialogue of the different since the absence of the General is a manifestation of the absence of dialogue; that is, adialogue. Dialogue leads to the development of the General and change in the process of the dialogue of the Different(s), and therefore the more dialogue, the more General and the less different and *vice versa*. However, dialogue not only furthers the development and, respectively, the eliciting of the General in the Different(s), but also the process thereof makes one aware of the Different with respect to the General. So, adialogue is not only the presence of the Different, but also the absence of the General. The dialogue character of the General and the Different(s) makes possible the transition to their changeability, their mutual transitions, their inter-changeability; that is, to contemplation of the General and the Different(s) in the legal realities of different civilizations in the coordinates of time, space, groups of countries, nature of law, and correlation thereof with other social regulators.

The real world of law is cognized, understood, and transformed by diverse forms of behavior and thought of various subjects, and not only by philosophers, scholars, clerics, politicians, and representatives of other elites, who merely determine the directions and paths of these processes in certain domains and aspects. The forms of cognition of the world are as varied as the world, and therefore a single and true philosophy (theory, conception, doctrine) concerning the world of law is lacking. Moreover, each of the existing forms of cognition of the world (philosophy, science, religion, mythology, practical, and day-to-day knowledge) reflects and understands the world of law by means and methods inherent to it and forms as a result diverse pictures of the world

(2003-2010) [Philosophy of Law: Contemporary Interpretations: Selected Works, Articles, Analytical Views (2003-2010) (2010); M. V. Kostytskyi, Філософські та психологічні проблеми юриспруденції. Вибрані наукові праці [Philosophical and Psychological Problems of Jurisprudence. Selected Scientific Works] (2008).

of law which become regulators of behavior and thought of their proponents and through the last participate in the transformation of legal reality. Therefore, comparativism in the philosophy of law is also manifest through actualization of the significance and multiplicity of day-to-day life of all humans, associations thereof, processes and mechanisms of transfer, perceptions embodying various forms of cognition and understanding of the world of law by different subjects. In particular, for example, legal reality directly perceived in life by man and other subjects is changeable and diverse and exists in the form of concrete legal phenomena and events having individual, non-repeatable properties, limited in space and time, and so on. On the other hand, on this level of sensitive perception one observes not only the difference, but also the interlinkage of legal phenomena and fixes their similarity and commonality. This aspect may be investigated in the context of the philosophical-legal contemplation of life.

Relations of equality, tolerance, patience, justness, freedom, and others comprising the content of the comparability of law were not only developed in fundamental works on the philosophy and theory of law, but received official recognition at the international and national levels. Without dwelling on their manifestations in the law of Ukraine because they have been considered in detail in a number of monographs, it should be noted that recognition of the diversity and equality of countries, cultures, and civilizations is a progressing trend in international law and activities of the United Nations and other international organizations and is displayed in fundamental United Nations documents from the 1960 Declaration on the Granting of Independence to Colonial Countries and Peoples to the 2000 United Nations Millennium Declaration.

Subsequent international documents are imbued with recognition of the cultural diversity of peoples of the world which emphasize that although the process of globalization represents a challenge to cultural diversity, it also creates conditions for a new dialogue between cultures and civilizations on the basis of the recognition of: cultural diversity as a common heritage of mankind; the need for a transition from cultural diversity to cultural pluralism – the harmonious coexistence and interaction of cultures; cultural diversity as a factor of development; human rights as a guarantee of cultural diversity; and so on. The globality and interdependence of the world, the need to implement the global partnership of regions and countries, and the preservation of cultural pluralism have become the leading basis of many international documents, for example: the 2004 Human Development Report: Cultural Liberty in Today's Diverse World; the 2005 Human Development Report: International Cooperation at a Crossroads: Aid, Trade, and Security in an Unequal World.

The foregoing, in our view, enables one to conclude that the principles on which the comparativist context of the philosophy of law is based reflect also the substantive properties of contemporary legal reality as its comparability and the trends of development of the last.

Orienting ourselves towards the theme of the XXIII World Congress of Philosophy, "Philosophy as Inquiry and Way of Life", held at Athens in 2013,, it should be noted that the fundamental significance of the concept "life" is significantly broader in comparativism than the concept of "legal life": the concept of life reflects the existence of a subject, above all through pluralism, diversity, multiple human lives, societies, civilizations, cultures, their existence in time and space, group of individuals and forms of behavior; life as a concept requires no substantiation, verification, or evidence of its reality. It is being investigated in various aspects, by various means, is reflected and understood in various forms of worldview (science, religion, mythology, philosophy, art, morality, practical and everyday consciousness and in an unconscious); the concept of life is directly connected with the subject, his "existence – with", and coexistence with others and other subjects. The term "life" is adequately translated into all languages of the world. Life is oriented towards understanding of a man in the context of the existence thereof, living space, in the family, collective, group, class, ethnos, which do not exist beyond the life of people. Life is reflected through the concepts of "reality", "validity", "being", "system", "order", "superstructure", "sphere", and others in philosophy and in science; in essence these are specific means or forms of understanding inherent to philosophical systems and scientific approaches. Life is diverse, different, not ultimately cognizable, and therefore, unlike its reflections in concepts, it includes in itself the uncognizable.

PHILOSOPHICAL GROUNDS OF COMPARATIVE JURISPRUDENCE

Consideration of the philosophy of comparative jurisprudence is possible in various contexts or strata. One is the contemplation of the philosophical foundations of comparative jurisprudence and the spheres of comparative legal studies.

In 1991 Martynenko wrote:

> The way out to individual branch sciences outside the limits of Ukrainian law, despite difficulties of a factual nature, lead to involvement in their subject-matter domain of the objective phenomenon of inter-systemic legal links and interactions and dialectic of the general, particular, and unique, which requires involvement in these sciences of rules of a comparative-typological approach.[16]

Almost ten years later Patrick Glenn brought this thought to completion and formulated a proposition fundamental for contemporary comparative jurisprudence: the penetration of the comparative legal method and thought into various legal sciences and the expansion of disciplinary and inter-disciplinary comparative legal studies leads to "comparative law losing the character of an independent discipline, dissolving into jurisprudence, which imparted a new character to it, leaving, just as the Cheshire cat from the well-known fairy tale, only a satisfied smile: 'And the smile of the world's last comparative lawyer will be the sign of the ultimate triumph of comparative legal thinkiing'".[17]

In the post-Soviet countries special significance is imparted in the philosophy of science and the science of science to the grounds of science, which characterizes the state thereof and provides "coordinates" for its development and scientific research. Indeed, as the creator of this conception, Viacheslav Stepin, noted:

[16] P. F. Martynenko, «Порівняльне правознавство: онтологічний статус» [Comparative Jurisprudence: Ontological Status], Вісник Київського університету імені Тараса Шевченка. Серія: Суспільно-політичні науки [Herald of Shevchenko Kyiv University. Series: Socio-Political Sciences], no. 3 (1991).

[17] G. A. Bermann, P. Glenn, K. L. Scheppele, A. Shalakhany, and D. V. Snyder, "Comparative Law: Problems and Prospects", *American University International Law Review*, XXVI (2011), p. 944.

> These grounds and the individual components thereof were fixed and described in the terms 'paradigm' (T. Kuhn),[18] 'nucleus of research program' (I. Lakatos),[19] 'ideals of natural order' (S. Toulmin),[20] 'basic topics of science' (G. Holton),[21] 'research tradition' (L. Laudan).[22] The problem of differentiated analysis of the grounds of science became acute in the process of discussions between proponents of various conceptions.[23]

If the said conception is adapted to comparative jurisprudence, one may single out in the grounds thereof three basic components: ideals and norms, a special scientific picture of the world, and philosophical grounds which are interlinked; however, each of these grounds has its own content and performs certain functions. Thus, the ideals and norms of comparative jurisprudence have a regulatory orientation and, in particular, reflect notions accepted in the scientific community about purposes and means of scientific activities and the responsibility of the researcher which determine both the procedure for undertaking scientific activity and the functioning of science as a social activity and institution.[24]

The scientific picture of the world has systematizing significance for constructing scientific knowledge and scientific research. The role of a special picture of the world as a type of legal reality obtained by means of comparison is manifest in the systematization of respective scientific knowledge about legal and regulatory reality and in determining the tasks of comparative scientific studies of law and provides the selection of means for resolving them. A special scientific picture of the world is

[18] Thomas S. Kuhn, *The Structure of Scientific Revolutions* (4th ed.; 2012).

[19] Imre Lakatos, *The Methodology of Scientific Research Programs. Philosophical Papers*, ed. John Worral and Gregory Currie (1978), I.

[20] Stephen Toulmin, *Foresight and Understanding. An Enquiry into the Aims of Science* (1961).

[21] Gerald Holton, *Perspectives on the Thematic Analysis of Scientific Thought in Victory and Vexation in Science: Einstein, Bohr, Heisenberg, and Others* (2005).

[22] Larry Laudan, *The Aims of Science and Their Role in Scientific Debate* (1984).

[23] Stepin, note 5 above, pp. 185-186.

[24] N. V. Motroshilova, «Нормы науки и ориентации ученого» [Norms of Science and Orientation of the Scholar], Идеалы и нормы научного исследования [Ideals and Norms of Scientific Research] (Minsk, 1981), p. 91.

fixed from outside in the corpus of publications of the results of comparative legal studies.

The philosophical grounds of comparative jurisprudence reflect the grounds thereof as a form of culture, at the worldview level they condition the ideals and norms and the scientific picture of the world, and ensure the interlinkage of science and worldview, culture, social practices in temporal and spatial contexts; that is, in a determined historical epoch and determined space. The philosophical grounds of comparative jurisprudence are not identical to philosophical knowledge in general or to the philosophy of law just as philosophy and science are close to one another but not identical. Different variants (philosophical grounds of legal comparativistics, philosophy of law and philosophy of jurisprudence as a science, the comparative philosophy of law, philosophical-legal comparativistics, and others) exist in the general field of mutual influences of philosophy and comparative jurisprudence.

It is generally acknowledged that the significance of the grounds of science is that they perform their functions so long as ideals and norms and the special picture of the world ensure an integral and methodologically effective reflection of the subject-matter of the science. Therefore, new properties arise of the objects of comparative jurisprudence (its intra-disciplinary development) and the perception of the picture of the world of other comparative scientific disciplines and sciences which in one way or another study law (inter-disciplinary development) are conditioning the change or restructuring thereof. One in so doing may single out several variants of the future development of comparative jurisprudence, a change of the special scientific picture of the world without changing comparative methodology or a change of comparative methodology without changing the picture of the world or a change of both.[25] Analysis shows that the development of comparative jurisprudence is proceeding along the path of joint change – change of the objects of contemplation, methodology of research, and a special scientific picture of the world.

The formation and change of philosophical grounds of comparative jurisprudence are undertaken at the "juncture",

[25] V. S. Stepin, V. G. Gorokhov, and M. A. Rozov, Философия науки и техники. Учебное пособие [Philosophy of Science and Technology. Instructional Manual] (1996), p. 278.

the "limit" thereof, with philosophy, and not only by selection and adaptation of respective philosophical systems, traditions, and other knowledge to the nature and requirements of comparative legal studies; that is, the concretization, clarification, transformation, and filling with new meanings.

Traditionally, blocks of ontological, gnoseological, methodological, axiological, and anthropological grounds are separated out in the philosophical grounds of comparative jurisprudence, just as in other sciences. Whereas the ontological grounds reflect the foundations of the "existence" of an object of comparative-legal studies, the gnoseological respectively reflects the foundations of their cognition, and epistemological and methodological – the methodology, and axiological – the values aspects, and anthropological – the "human dimension".

Another variant is possible for singling out and forming philosophical grounds of comparative jurisprudence: namely, in the context of those philosophies which are separated out in general philosophy and not only, in particular, in strata of thought, worldview, general philosophy, philosophy of history (or time), philosophy of geography (or space), philosophy of science, philosophy of culture, philosophy of law, and others, but likewise the philosophy of comparativistics as the dominant philosophy of a comparative attitude to the world, namely in the comparative dimension – within the context of the different and unique between them. As has been demonstrated in studies of the philosophy of West and East, the advantage of a tradition of the West is a way out from the limits of only philosophy as being inherent in comparative thought.

In the context of the philosophy of science, the problem of the diversity of definitions of comparative jurisprudence may be explained by the fact that at different historical stages of the development of science the last also had a different substantiation:

- Ontological-gnoseological (classical), when science and scientific disciplines were linked with the subject-matter (or object) and specifics of cognitive processes;
- Activity-institutional (non-classical), when the structure of science was conditioned by change of the grounds thereof, peculiarities of the subjects of research, and methods used in science, by certain socio-organizational structures

(institutes, chairs, university faculties, and others) dependent on society;

- Synergetic-culturological (post-non-classical), when the genesis and development of science were contemplated from positions of new scientific synergetic thought and interlinkages of science and culture and other forms of worldview.

Thus, in the early twenty-first century a multiplicity of methodological and theoretical approaches for the investigation of science were formed, based on which one may conclude that research of comparative jurisprudence is possible on micro, mediate, and macro levels where:

- The micro level represents empirical studies of qualitative and quantitative changes that occur in the corpus of scientific legal publications, citation links, and other communications of legal scholars for relatively brief periods of time and characterize the problem aspect of legal science. To these, in particular, relate studies connected with innovations in legal science reflected in journal articles as an elementary unit of changeability of scientific knowledge; an analysis of the frequency of innovations arising and the modification thereof; determining the direction of the flow of scientific publications and changes thereof; a study of the substantively linked aggregates of publications, clusters thereof, and hierarchy by frequency of citations; separating out certain research groups, scientific communities, and the like;
- The mediate level comprises studies of any changes in science, such changes in socio-humanitarian and legal sciences occurring over rather prolonged periods based on convergence and divergence (merger and separation as autonomous) of research programs, scientific theories, paradigms, and the arising of more complex and changing structures of science, and so on;
- The macro level forms studies of global, civilizational changes, dependence of science on trends of the development of mankind, region, country, culture, and civilization, the place and role of science in these processes, and so on.

Comparative jurisprudence in the broad understanding is a complex amalgamation of scientific phenomena not reducible to a scientific discipline and even more to a method of research. Comparative jurisprudence may be interpreted in various aspects or strata with the assistance of different methodological approaches, being characterized by stability and changeability, "traditionalness", and "novelty", the existence of ontological, gnoseological, axiological, and other properties, interlinkage with contemporary legal, social, and cultural changes at various levels of their manifestations.

Under this approach it is advisable to abandon the dominant trend to fill "comparative law" or "comparative jurisprudence" with sometimes arbitrarily selected content and undertake the opposite operation – study the sphere of comparative legal studies and then synthesize the elements, parts, fragments, and so on thereof.

On this plane it seems topical to:

- Single out, describe, and contemplate "space" within whose limits existed and exist various comparative legal studies (theoretical, methodological, comparative, descriptive, and others);
- Determine the criteria for separating out this "space" and investigate the common and different from other similar "spaces", establish the peculiarities of the entering thereof into larger "spaces", the structuring thereof on various grounds, and so on;
- Analyze general and distinctive properties and extents of the levels or elements thereof, classify (or typologize) them, determine the character of interlinkages, undertake their formalization, and so on.

Thus, separating out the "space" of the existence of comparative legal studies with other similar "spaces" is possible within such frameworks (limits, "coordinates", understandings): juridical – legal – extra-legal; scientific – practical – cognitive (worldview); professional – non-professional; monistic – integrative (synthetic) – pluralist; methodological – subject-matter (substantive); national – civilizational – world; general – special – unique; theoretical – empirical; positivist – social – cultural; and others.

The philosophy of science is significant because it provides such an interpretation of the resolution of the problem, which entirely justifiably leads to a multi-dimensional and pluralist structuring of comparative legal studies, multiplicity of forms of their manifestation and their understanding by scholars, and also correlation of various scientific structures according to principles of dialogicity (or polyphonicity), supplementarity, and so on.

The multi-dimensionalness and pluralism of interpretations of comparative-legal studies is observed in a geographical (spatial) stratum of their contemplation. Within the framework of any national school there have existed and exist various approaches (or positions) of scholars relative to the understanding thereof, and therefore only may speak only of the dominance of a particular approach widespread among scholars undertaking comparative legal studies. Without undertaking a detailed analysis of this problem, it may be noted that in the geography of comparative jurisprudence a pluralism, multiplicity, and peculiarities of its understandings is manifest, the "conditionality" thereof by language, culture, legal orders of a particular country or region.

An even greater "range" of opinions exists among scholars belonging to different civilizations in which philosophy, science, and law occupy a different place and play a role different from their status in countries of European civilization.

Taking into account the historical and geographical pluralism in the understanding of comparative jurisprudence, the possibility of its existence as primarily a "universal" or "world" science seems exaggerated. It is more advisable in this context to speak of those forms of the organization of comparative-legal studies as international cooperation of scholar-comparatists and the communities thereof, scientific dialogue and polylogue of scholars of different countries in the course of which in a concrete-historical situation common approaches are formed to resolve urgent problems of world and national legal and cultural development. Thus, the development of the Universal in comparative jurisprudence proceeds from diverse approaches, opinions, and views to the establishment of the Universal in real cooperation and interaction of scholars, and not from theories, conceptions, or doctrines established beforehand by someone. To be sure, particular approaches may dominate in this interaction of scholars at a certain time and in certain countries, but none had and do not have a "universal" character or were not, are not, and will not be the only one.

The philosophical principles of spatial contemplation of comparative-legal studies are not confined to the said aspects, but in any variants of their interpretation condition the need for the development of scientific studies directed towards the comparative contemplation of national comparative jurisprudence.

The comparative method is not only one of the simplest and universal means of thought, methods of practical, day-to-day, and other cognition, but also a general scientific method requiring special knowledge, complex, with a complicated structure, and so on. In contemporary comparative sciences it is understood not only as a method of comparison, but as an arsenal of inter-connected methods of study "not of one" object (comparative, analogy, areal, typological, and so on) oriented towards the elucidation of the general and the distinctive, but in another interpretation than in the classical and non-classical periods of the development of rationality.

Traditionally accepted in the dialectic is the correlation of the General, Common, Special, and Individual had been formed in the philosophy of the identicality with the accentuation of the dominance of the General, which in the philosophy of distinction as postmodern philosophy is formulated through the juxtaposition – the universality of the distinction of phenomena, and in the philosophy of post-postmodernism – as the relativity of the common and different, denial of dominance of one or the other (non-universality of the general and non-universality of the distinctive).

Their contemporary interpretation is undertaken through the concepts of "one", "other", and "different", which became one of the basic in post-non-classical philosophy (philosophy of late postmodernism) within the framework of a communicative approach in philosophical studies.

Understanding of the triad "one – other – different" in comparative studies has the following distinctive features: (1) the dichotomy of "one – other" presupposes the commensurability of different objects according to the principle of conformity, the possibility of quantitative study within the limits of certain general qualities, fixation of the presence of similar qualities (common), and others; that is, everything that is inherent to comparison in its traditional understanding; (2) the dichotomy of "one (or other) – different" directed towards eliciting the non-commensurateness of objects and their correlation, according to the principle of supplementarity (Niels Bohr), reflects the possibility not of comparison, but of juxtaposition (contrast), the fixation of different qualities, ontological given of the different as contrast; (3) the triad "one – other – different" enables one to reflect, fix, and study objects in relations of commensurateness – non-commensurateness, unlike traditional comparative studies oriented only towards commensurateness, which introduces into a scientific study the identification and study of the non-comparable as unique and opposite, necessary for an integral perception and reflection of the world; (4) the non-acceptance in a comparative study of the relations of "commensurateness" and "non-commensurateness" is determined by the principle of relativity – their dependence on aspects, coordinates, grounds, and parameters of study. By virtue of these propositions, for example, the integrity of legal space will be incomplete without a study of criminality, which with respect to law acts as the "other" that supplements the lawful, and social regulators are the "different". In legal norms a violation is fixed through a prohibition; that is, through the absence thereof – as a lawful failure to act; however, action and failure to act are non-comparable phenomena only in certain correlations.

What is the methodological significance of these propositions? In academic writings, as a rule, there is suggested as the foundations of a comparative study "a withdrawal into a meta-position and the creation of a meta-language with respect to particular objects, concepts, and texts",[26] which reflects only part of the question both a meta-position and meta-language presuppose something external with respect to objects, concepts, and texts and therefore they and these meta-grounds already are different, which should be taken into account under such an approach. Moreover, contrast on the basis of meta-language is by the discovery of commensurateness, the common and differences only with respect to these grounds, not only the commonality of the different being discovered as

[26] I. Vinov, Философия как социальное действие [Philosophy as Social Action] (available online); E. V. Ushakov, «Имеет ли исследователь-компаративист логическое преимущество?» [Does the Comparatist-Researcher Have Logical Advantage?], in Современная философия как феномен культуры: исследовательские традиции и новации [Contemporary Philosophy as a Phenomenon of Culture: Research Traditions and Innovation] (2001) (available online).

such inasmuch as the commonality and divergence with respect to the previously and artificially created meta-language (theoretical scheme). The different in this event is defined only as the non-common, and difference itself is not investigated.

Thus, a meta-position is a position of the "common", for the use as grounds of one of the "different" provides an internal contract in which the common is not the "other" with respect to "one and the other" but is itself "one" and/or "second"; that is, in this instance their commensurateness is discovered, and when adding the "different" – non-commensurateness.

There arise the following additional requirements of a comparative approach: (1) the very grounds of juxtaposition should be adequate not only to the common, but to the different; (2) the use as grounds of one of the "different" removes only "half" this problem; (3) in order to investigate the "common" among the "different", the grounds themselves should be diverse so that their "set" may make it possible to reduce the different to a minimum in order to ensure the maximum "common" (in comparative jurisprudence, the more grounds for the classification of legal systems, then the larger number of legal families there will be, but they will acquire more commonality and less difference), or, on the contrary, reducing the common to a minimum and ensuring the maximum of the different (or unique).

The completeness of comparative contemplation presupposes that the grounds of contrast should be the "one", "other", and "different"; that is, the different (comparable and non-comparable), and the meta-position as a common is external with respect to them. The meta-position enables the degree of "entry" to be identified into the new aggregate of "coordinates", system, whole, and others, reflecting more the "vertical" of juxtaposition than the "horizontal" thereof.

An important aspect of the philosophy of comparativism is identification of the "dynamic" of the general and the different, the methodological basis of which may be dialogue,[27] polylogue, "polyphony", and their opposites. In this situation, the common is derivative from the interaction of the different; the common emerges in dialogue of the different while the absence of the common is a manifestation of the absence of dialogue; that is, adialogue. Dialogue leads to the development of the common and

[27] Kolesnikov, note 4 above.

a change in the process of dialogue of the different, and therefore, the more dialogue, the greater the common and the lesser the different, and *vice versa*. Dialogue, however, not only furthers the development and, accordingly, the identification of the common in the different, but in the process the different being understood with respect to the common. Thus, adialogue not only is the existence of the different, but also the absence of the common. The dialogue character of the common and the different makes possible a transition to their changeability, their mutual transitions and mutual changes; that is, to contemplation of the common and the different in the coordinates of time and space.

The turn of the twentieth and twenty-first centuries was marked by increased attention to the pluralism of cultures and the formation of world order, especially in conditions of globalization. This concerns the culture of the peace, which is regarded as a combination of value imperatives, worldviews, traditions, types of behavior and ways of life based on the principles of freedom, justice, democracy, tolerance, solidarity, cooperation, pluralism, cultural diversity, dialogue, and mutual understanding at all levels of society and between peoples. In the previously mentioned United Nations Millennium Declaration it was emphasized that whereas globalization offers great opportunities, these will be realized only if there are large-scale measures to form a common future based on a common affiliation of mankind in all its diversity and emphasis is placed on such fundamental values as freedom, democracy, equality, solidarity, tolerance, respect for nature, shared responsibility, and the rule of law, among others.[28]

Recognition of the cultural diversity of the peoples of the world has been provided for in subsequent international legal documents in which culture is regarded not only as the aggregate of distinct spiritual, material, intellectual, and emotional qualities inherent to a society or social group, but it is emphasized that in addition to art and literature, culture encompasses a way of life, the skill and knowledge to live in amity, systems of values, traditions, and beliefs. It is stressed that although the process of globalization itself represents a challenge to cultural diversity, it also creates conditions for a new dialogue between cultures and civilizations on the basis of recognition of: cultural diversity as the common heritage of mankind, the need for a transition from cultural diversity

[28] Approved by General Assembly Resolution 55/2, 8 September 2000 (available online).

to cultural pluralism – the harmonious coexistence and interaction of cultures; cultural diversity as a factor of development; human rights as a guarantee of cultural diversity; and so on. The globality and interdependence of the world, the need to undertake a global partnership of regions and countries, and the preservation of cultural pluralism have become the principal idea in international legal documents of recent years, most noteworthy:

- The significance of overcoming barriers was emphasized in the 2009 Human Development Report "Overcoming Barriers: Human Mobility and Development", which noted: "Our world is very unequal ... The 2009 HDR explores how better policies towards human mobility can enhance human development. It lays out the case for governments to reduce restrictions on movement within and across their borders, so as to expand human choices and freedoms" (available online);
- The 2010 Human Development Report "The Real Wealth of Nations: Pathways to Human Development" stressed: "Data from the past 40 years also reveal an enormous diversity of pathways to human development achievement: there is no single model or uniform prescription for success" (available online);
- The civilizational and regional advances in the world and overcoming threats were addressed in the 2013 Report "The Rise of the South: Human Progress in a Diverse World" and the 2014 Report "Sustaining Human Progress: Reducing Vulnerabilities and Building Resilience" (both available online). The 2014 Report observed: "While globalization has brought benefits to many, it has also given rise to new concerns manifest at times as local reactions to the spillover effects of events far away. Preparing citizens for a less vulnerable future means strengthening the internal resilience of communities and countries".

CONCLUSIONS

In the context of pluralism of cultures, "non-universality of postmodernism, localism and cultural conditionality of any theoretical schemes, acknowledgement of the diversity of worldviews, establishment of the common and the distinctive between them in the process of their real interaction, and the arising of comparativism as the foundation of the philosophy of law primarily in a rational way eliminates the absolutization of universality and uniqueness, determinedness and spontaneity, chaos and order in legal reality, and not only, is based on their relativity, supplementarity, cyclicity, and incidentalness of mutual transformations and through them optimizes and harmonizes a modernist and post-modernist perception of the world of law, contemplates it as pluralist, multi-dimensional, multi-polar through the diversity of forms of contemplation adequate to its nature and cultural diversity, and subject of cognition.

The comparative philosophy of law is one orientation of research of the philosophy of law proper as a sphere of its rational contemplation which at the contemporary stage of its development is confined to a description of various philosophical systems of law and in the future should be orientated towards their comparative study.

In turn, the philosophical grounds of comparative legal studies are conditioned by the substantive properties of contemporary legal reality and by developmental trends of philosophy, comparative socio-humanitarian sciences, philosophy of law, philosophical-legal comparativistics, and comparative jurisprudence proper as an autonomous legal science:

- Comparative legal studies are formed in the space of the interaction of comparative and legal sciences where comparative sciences determine their methodology, and legal sciences – the peculiarities of the objects (or legal reality); therefore their integration into a system of comparative sciences, the perception with a respective transformation of the methodological potential of these sciences enriches their methodology, ensures an adequate perception of the multi-dimensionality and multiplicity of legal reality, and on the other hand, enables a contribution to be made to socio-humanitarian comparativistics;
- In the ontological aspect, philosophical-legal comparativistics investigates law in its basic dimensions of existence – space (geography), time (history), dynamics of development; a diversity of forms of the existence of law generates also a multiplicity of forms of comparative studies: law as a worldview should be investigated by the philosophy of law, and the last by the comparative

philosophy of law, and legal texts by comparative linguistics of law, and the subjects of law by the anthropology of law, and legal behavior and relations by the comparative sociology of law, and so on;

- In the gnoseological-epistemological aspect, philosophical-legal comparativistics cannot be reduced to any one form of cognition (autonomous scientific discipline or method), but represents a complex formation encompassing various forms of cognition and the undertaking and organization of comparative legal studies;
- In the axiological and anthropological dimensions, philosophical-legal comparativistics is orientated towards the unity and plurality of universal human, civilizational, and national values, and also towards subjects of law, persons, countries, measure of human and subjective in legal realities, and everyday human existence;
- The methodology of comparative-legal studies cannot be reduced only to the comparative legal method and knowledge of the application thereof, but exists at various levels and encompasses various components, which include not only methodological, but also subject-matter knowledge in the methodological significance thereof (worldview, paradigms, types of scientific thought, and others). The comparative approach as the basis of comparative methodology contains the comparative method and other components of science having methodological significance. In turn, the comparative method combines all methods of research "not of one" ("one, other, different") object or state thereof, the subject-matter of which is to identify the different and the common, the general, the particular, and the unique, and therefore is not reducible only to comparative; its components are comparison, contrast, juxtaposition, confrontation, and others.

Chapter 9

After the "Picture Of Law": Legal Comparison as the Discourse of the Existence of Law

OLEKSANDR V. TKACHENKO

In all likelihood, Thucydides (c. 460-400 BC) more than others told us what was Europe and who may be considered to be European. When we speak of what is most important, he who speaks first usually identifies what is most important. The same was so with Pheidas (c. 480-430 BC), who had no predecessors, and all who were after him were his followers.

Thucydides wrote: "For we are lovers of the beautiful in our tastes and our strength lies, in our opinion, not in deliberation and discussion, but that knowledge which is gained by discussion preparatory to action".[1] These simple words name the *perpetuum mobile* of Europe – all-powerful discourse. The nature of power in Europe is rhetorical – all that happened and happens in European history is the embodiment of tales, of those narratives which arose as replies to other narratives. The polyphony of histories about man, his destiny and interconnection with the world.

Therefore one can hardly imagine a more anti-European judgment to which a noted modern intellectual, Yuval Harari, comes in completing a clear tale about the retrospective and prospects of human history with a suggestion to reject narratives as such – to cease construing the world with the aid of words and to return to the basic and universal level of feelings and reactions, finding in them construction designs for a new world.[2]

We cannot, however, suppress the voices of those by whose tales we are. Freedom and dignity are not achieved by deaf ontological forgetfulness. On the contrary, we must aspire to listen better to

1 Thucydides, *History of the Peloponnesian War*, transl. Rex Warner (1972), p. 146.

2 Yuval Noah Harari, *A Brief History of Humankind* (2014).

these voices and do everything to raise the level of the conversation with them, to try to become authors, to write the history about ourselves. Significantly more persuasive than Harari's thesis about the need for the elimination of textuality from human existence is the Gumbrecht thesis on the "constructivist vertigo" – an awareness that reality does not render any natural resistance to the narrative structures of our thought, and, consequently, that language in a certain sense encloses itself without permitting an objective and immutable existence to something to which signs relate; that is, the existence of referents, denoters, and so on.[3]

Was everything said about us in the words of Thucydides? Is there possibly something super-important that might explain to us the essence of what now is happening, something about our fate?

At the outset, we glance at pictures. Insofar, as Maksim Kantor correctly affirms, a picture does not illustrate the state of society, a picture itself creates society.[4] Take any European. Time and style have no significance. A matter of your taste. Simply a picture hanging in one of the European museums. The present writer would choose the "Ghent Altarpiece" by Jan van Eyck (c. before 1390-1441) – a picture embodying the Burgundy project for the unification of Europe. Or the "Haycart" by Hieronymus Bosch (c. 1450-1516), a picture in which there is an omen of the end of "Gothic Europe". And take any Chinese picture. Also adapted for its viewing.

Is there something common among all European pictures and something common among all Chinese pictures? Some *tertium comparationis* of Europeanness and Chineseness? And if so, in what respect do they stay relative to one another?

In all European pictures the frame is applied snugly to the image on canvas, and between the image and the frame emptiness, unfilled space, is not permitted in principle – this is one of the most explicit transubstantiations by means of art of the Parminedean prohibition on "nothing". The frame acts as an integral part of what the artist portrayed. A precise contour is formed.

[3] Hans Ulrich Gumbrecht, Производство присутствия: Чего не может передать значение [Production of Presence: What Meaning Cannot Convey] (2006), p. 19.

[4] Maksim Kantor, Чертополох и терн. Возрождение веры [Thistle and Thorn. The Revival of Faith] (2021).

All Chinese pictures include a broad field free of any depiction of space between the composition and the frame. The frame seemingly hangs in emptiness. The artist deliberately leaves a significant space of canvas unexploited, unfilled, untouched.

What do we say about this? In truth, much can be said, but we necessarily see in this peculiarity of Chinese pictures a hint in principle of uncompletion, an appeal to the viewer for co-authorship – to be involved in the creation and to try himself to control the open space left for us by the artist. We see the same emptiness that seeks our gaze and attempts to cope with it which Alexander Arkhipenko (1887-1964) created for us through sculpture. In Chinese pictures one can try to see his "archipenctures".

Why does emptiness surround the portrayed composition of a Chinese picture? Possibly the accent therein is, in principle, the incompletion of the world in which each of us should cultivate the ability to create something unique, creating oneself in such a creation? Possibly in us ourselves an uncompleted emptiness is present – the source of our dignity, and thus the style of Chinese pictures acts as a distinctive map of our soul? We live in the present when we not only follow the existing, but we also create the new. In everyone there is access to the source of freedom. The world is not completed; consequently, it should not be a judgment and prison for us.

We cite another example of a "picture". This is the "rock garden" in Kyoto, Japan. White sand. Black rocks on it. For Europeans taught by René Descartes (1596-1650) and the European metaphysical Moderne generated by him with its intent to control and consider the world the question arises at once: how many are there? How many black rocks on the white sand? The composition is so structured that fourteen are seen from any vantage point. Each step around the perimeter of the space removes one rock from the field of vision and another replaces it, hitherto unseen. The picture is changeable. Each movement of the viewer "enlivens" rocks, which begin a playful interaction with one another and the viewer. It is impossible to see all the rocks simultaneously. Only from above. Then one can see fifteen rocks. A view of the world from above, however, is the view had by God. And now the question is not whether this is achievable. A person may attribute it to himself, succumb to the temptation to recount all the rocks, to achieve completion and reliability. But the price is commensurate – cessation of this remarkable and intriguing game of rocks, interaction of the person with enlivened rocks, joy that each step gives a new picture of the rocks, and chagrin that the last picture is lost with each step. The Man-God glancing at the rock garden from above sees only a life extinguished and lost. He counted the rocks, having lost in return for this, reliable knowledge of the unique singularity of space and time given to him by the master who created this masterpiece of belonging to and the unity of man and the world – being-in-world – when this sand and these rocks are no longer just external to you, the curse of the subject-object dichotomy has been overcome, they become yours, echoing in you a new attitude towards the world and yourself,, a different attitude of contemplation.

What idea is embodied in the "rock garden"? The European contemplation of the world is focused on searching for fundamental principles of all that experience gives us. Each of us in this sense is a "miletec" engaged in a quest for the *arche*. We can probably talk about the manifestation of the incompleteness of our experience and knowledge, which paradoxically is transformed into joy, intrigue, interest, and involvement. The fullness of life is not only to see, but also, even to a greater degree, not to see. The unseen and the inaccessible already are present in our existence. Not to see everything is a condition of the formation of our fantasies and imagination. Imagination is more important than knowledge. An encounter with the new brings us to a greater degree to ourselves more than a reliable mathematical calculation. The adherence of a person to own existence lies not in reliability, but in the possibility of an encounter with the new. And for this one cannot stand still. It is essential to take a step, and one rock disappears from view and another appears in its place. Each loss is compensated by an acquisition. It is merely necessary to proceed and be prepared for an encounter with the new.

And here for Europeans a euphoria arises, being a mixture of fanaticism and messianism. After all, everything said above is about our European world, about the torment and dialectic of the soul of the European, about the struggle and dispute in each of us of Odyssey and Faust. This is created not by us, nor for us, but this is all about us. When looking at a Chinese picture or a Japanese "rock garden", we can visibly see what the Scottish philosopher and theologian Richard de Saint-Victor (d. 1173) called the "incommunicable existence of reasonable nature" (*existentia incommunicabilis naturae rationabilis*) – words which capture and impart to us the individuality of the person as the cornerstone of the European world.

In the empty space of the extremities of Chinese pictures or a Japanese "rock garden" we can see another means of achieving that which was done in Europe with the assistance of transforming sunlight penetrating the stained glass of Gothic cathedrals into a direct perspective of an oil painting, invented by the Flemish School at Tournai in Belgium – a transition from the individual personality of one (God) to the individual personality of each. We see ourselves, wherever we look, with that gaze of individuality, the birth of which as the language of painting was proclaimed by Rogier van der Weyden (c. 1399-1464) and Hans Memling (c. 1430-1494). And from this feeling that we are "everywhere at home" likewise two, at first glance, incompatible consequences are possible: solipsism or universalism. The entire history of Europe predetermined the second path.

A "Pythagorean faith" acts as this predetermination – a conviction that non-trivial reason may see in the world of mathematics entirely cleansed from any empiricism the fundamental structure of the universe. In order to cognize and control the world it is necessary to learn to think mathematically. "Let no geometrician enter" – this inscription above the entrance to the Academy of Plato also crowns the entrance to the European world.

Mathematics as an ideal of correct thinking leads to a dual assertion. The first is known as the "anthropic principle" – the universe is so structured that a person with the assistance of mathematics might perceive the full beauty of its structure. The universe is structured so as to make possible the emergence of life, reason, and consciousness capable of seeing and understanding its pure mathematical beauty.[5] The second assertion, using the terminology of Immanuel Kant (1724-1804), is to allow the possibility of *a priori* synthetic judgments. Allowing such links mathematics and physics – from the outset we draw from *a priori* precepts of our reason and write in the sand, on papyrus, paper, or blackboard a mathematical formula, and later, sometimes a century

[5] Aleksey Burov and Lev Burov, "Genesis of a Pythagorean Universe", in Anthony Aguirre, Brendan Foster, and Zeeya Merali (eds.), *Trick or Truth? The Mysterious Connection Between Physics and Mathematics* (2016), pp. 157-170.

after, experimentally prove the subordination of the matter to this mathematical expression.

Mathematical physics – this indestructible monastery of the Pythagorean faith – became the embodiment of the methodological and epistemological standard of a scientifically constructed world. And it also became the language which embodies the conceptual power of the western world. The temptation to see physics everywhere was too great to resist. If there is an exclusive language for understanding, explanation, and manipulation of a single and universal essence of physical matter, why would such a language not exist in the sphere of human actions and the organization of human communities? Are man and society not matter? Why here can the synthetic (relations between people) not be *a priori*?

It is important in principle to emphasize that there was no chance that everything would be confined by the sphere of nature without expansion into the spiritual, social, and legal sphere of the person. All the giddy successes of the natural sciences of the Moderna era were merely tests of faith and superstructure instruments ahead of real work, the execution by Europeans of that purpose which was the basis of their self-determination. This may be called by the language of phenomenology the European intentionality, the constituent thereof. This is more important and fundamental than even logic and rationality. This is transcendental and defines everything. This is an existential requirement to see the world as a picture. Picture in the singular. As one picture.

What is the source of this requirement? Why has Pythagorean faith in all-powerful mathematics become so important? One Eleatic is at fault for everything, which infected us with the One while prohibiting us from asking about the Nothing. This also was the point of singularity of the European world, its "great explosion" – simultaneously a blessing and a curse so that the European world became a world as such, the entire world.

The exclusive distinctive feature of the European is to scale up itself in the world by means of discourse and constantly to increase the scale. Such an increase of scale Friedrich Wilhelm Nietzsche (1844-1900) called a will to power – conceptual power to give names, to determine, and this means also to measure everything by its own measure. Protagoras (c. 490-420 BC) was absolutely right, with a minor qualification: European discourse makes the person the measure of all things, which makes sense only in a European picture of the world.

For the European the world from the outset w as confined by the walls of the *polis*. The "cosmos" was merely within the limits thereof. It is noteworthy that Remus, having desecrated the sacredness of the city boundary, was executed precisely because this became the fate of the city named in honor of his brother and that world which he founded with the assistance of law: constantly increase the scale, bring order to the world by one's language, rationality, and argumentation, give everything to the world in one's name – that is the fate which the European conferred on himself. Transform the entire world into an own discourse about it – draw the world as a picture.

Radiating epistemological optimism based on the successes of the natural sciences, the nineteenth century during the first half invented social physics, and closer to the end also the social engineer, who thenceforth became the jurist. And only inn this capacity might jurists become involved in the Pythagorean faith and finally sever law from the relativist quagmire of cultures and traditions – that chthonic quagmire which has no place in a geometrically pure world of ideas. The canvas of the world had been cleared. The brushes and paints were ready. The twentieth century began with an assurance that a single picture of the world would be created by law.

But happily problems unexpectedly arose with law. The scale of the problems demonstrates a misunderstanding expressed by Konrad Zweigert (1911-1996) and Hein Kötz – the prophets of one current of the Pythagorean faith known as the functionalism of comparative law – 150 years after the postulation of social physics. This misunderstanding is best formulated by the term "scandal". If, according to Kant, the principal scandal of philosophy, which forced him to substantively engage in it in order to gain peace and fortitude for himself and others, there was a lack of irrefutable evidence of the existence of a world outside us; for Zweigert and Kötz the principal scandal and misunderstanding in the contemporary enlightened world, where "there is no such thing as German physics or Belgian chemistry or American medicine",[6] remains the existence of a separate law in each State or jurisdiction.

[6] Konrad Zweigert and Hein Kötz, *An Introduction to Comparative Law*, transl. Tony Weir (2d rev. ed.; 1992), p. 14.

And because the European scientific canon requires generality and universality, according to them and not only to them, there so far is no science of law (which may only be a singlel science (nor subject-matter of this science_ (a single and universal law).

There is naturally no doubt that law should exist within the same conceptual framework as physics, biology, and medicine. And it is of n o interest that mathematics may serve not only as affirmation of the universal, general, and single, but also of the unique, particular, and unrepeatable. In the fugues of Johann Sebastian Bach (1685-1750) mathematics is more than anywhere else, however, speaking of them we can talk about a lot, but it is unlikely that there will be an assertion that these fugues contain music as such, and everything that is not them is not music. The maximal admissible generalization here may be the assumption of the "Miracle of Thuringia" – the special significance of this territory for the origin of classical music, but therein is more a wish to undertake a beautiful narrative than to offer a convincing explanation.

The question of the orientation when building a conceptual skeleton of law on such phenomena as, on one hand, physics or, on the other hand, music, has paradigmatic significance, and here possibly, with a large measure of conditionality, the paradigms of functionalism and culturalism are juxtaposed. But for my reflections here this is not only of no fundamental importance, but of no significance whatsoever. The "picture of the world" intentionality of European existence exceeds and includes any paradigmatic dichotomy, acquiring a metadigmatic significance.

The European world-projection is not confined by a concrete content. The picture of the world may be drawn monochromatically, as functionalism suggests. An analogy would be a "black square" by Kazimir Severinovich Malevich (1879-1935). Only shades invisible to the naked eye are allowed. Such a picture of the world is filled with grief that cultures, languages, and traditions exist in general in the world. Undoubtedly the world would have been "better" if it had become a supermarket where only identical requirements for everyone had significance and identical means of satisfying them in the spirit of a functionalist *praesumptio similitudinis*. The last is structure on the model of a simple evidentiary syllogism: (1) Law is merely a means of satisfying requirements (minor premise); (2) All people have identical requirements (major premise); (3) Law must be identical for all people. The minor and major premises of the syllogism are not logical in nature, being deeply voluntaristic and embodying an aspiration to mathematize and technicize a particular ethics multiplied by an imperial ideology. Everything non-utilitarian is removed from law.

This is a picture of the world as a uniform and monotonous time and space. Best known of its conceptualization is the thesis of the "end of history" advanced by Francis Yoshihiro Fukuyama. The ideology of liberal democracy determines entirely the content of time. The technologies mastered by and subordinated to man enable the world to be synchronized at the global level – to immerse him in a single, self-identical, and infinite "now". "Tomorrow" in its existential understanding should never come again. The same purposes, goals, and means of achieving them should unite the entire world as a single picture.

A single picture of the world, however, may be created in a contrary manner. A conceptual system always is in interaction with an opposite. Binary oppositions have been woven into the fabric of the European world-projection. Therefore, the picture of the world also may be one that does not contain the existing "colors" in order to portray the entire diversity of cultures and traditions. New "colors-concepts" are invented. In this sense Pierre Legrand also draws a single picture of the world, as have Zweigert and Kötz.

In this connection the thesis of the French philosopher, Alan Badiou, seems correct that the "logic of the common equivalent and the logic of cultural identity oof the communities or minorities form an ordered unity".[7]

To repeat, no substantive transformations, oppositions, or revolutions are capable of casting doubt on the European picture of the world and truly disturbing European reason. Classical German idealism and post-Modernism substantively, methodologically, and philosophically differ from one another as radically as is possible; however, all this is designing the world as a single picture. The discourse oof colonialism as the "white man's burden" or anti-colonial discourses. The aspiration for unification and globalization, or *vice versa*, for fragmentation. All this has been entered on the European picture of the world. Everything named,

[7] Alan Badiou, Апостол Павел. Обоснование универсализма [Apostle Paul. Justification for Universalism] (1999).

any oppositions of methodologies, paradigms, ideologies in equal measure act as projections of the conceptual power of the West.

One can believe in anything or affirm any content of human life and relations, the main thing being that this was done in European and American universities with immersion in the day-to-day life of western societies and with the use of rules of discourse and argumentation. Naturally, on the basis of the dialectic. Namely, Aristotelean, Hegelian, or negative dialectic of Theodor W. Adorno (1903-1969), the choice is not important. Important is the outcome, that there will be a world which we understand and which we can explain to ourselves and to others.

Now, however, something unusual is happening for the European perception of the world, although this novelty also has a subtext of inevitability and feeling of doom. History is returning, and we are in the midst of a breakdown, a collapse. We refer not to a picture of the world, not to a particular concrete picture, but to a world-as-picture.

The fact is that the Pythagorean faith in which Europeans have discourse, adequately involved in the principles of building a social world as such, finally encountered reality. There is no "as such". The dual "Platonic jest" – neglect of diversity of the concrete to the advantage of the single with recognition of the non-materiality of this single – created a "jargon", created a world. The problem is that we refer only to the European world (West). That the West is not the world as a whole one might have assumed earlier, but such disappointing knowledge was not necessary. The presence of power and authority deprived of the status of delusion the assertion that the next European discourse (for example, the recent discourse on human rights) was embedded in the very ontology of reality, making it universal and unified.

It turned out in the end that the ontology has some significance only within the European world. In China there are many things, but just without taking the perspective of the view which transforms what is seen into a picture. There nothing exists that Europeans call a vision of a thing – eidos, there the things reveal themselves to man differently. The absence of a direct perspective (the right of private ownership acts as the legal expression thereof) signifies the absence of an individual who by means of self-authorship works with emptiness, creating own life as a work of art. The same, but not the same, concerns Japan.

And it is not about differences in political ideologies or cultures. It is not about differences which may be overcome. In that place there are no eyes which look at the world as a picture. There is no world-as-picture in that place. And there should not be. There is no foregone conclusion and logical necessity that there was a world everywhere, and everywhere this world was a picture. From the standpoint of a European, there is nothing there. There is not even a "nothing". We cannot build an adequate ontological distinctive. "There" – is beyond existence and nothing. For us there are no supports there. They are beyond our "point of singularity" and "great explosion". There is no "One" of Parmenides of Elea (sixth-fifth century BC). They are outside the limits of our world. Totally. We do not find any common support with us going back to the beginning, to the very first rock in the foundation of our world.

Europe found the limit of scaling. The Europeans have no addressees of their narratives except for themselves. This is not a question of differences between "us" and "them". This not oeven a question of multiple worlds. Everything is much more important, and this creates a unique intellectual situation – a situation of an awareness that we do not have a language for the entire world, and that law is solely our language, a tale exclusively about us.

The collapse of the Pythagorean faith and the lack of a language for the entire world conceals within the danger of paralysis – the loss of the ability to use discourse in general. It was for us identical to the world as such; for all, one world. Europeans may lose the ability even to speak for themselves because they always spoke, turning to the world as such, to the entire world, with the world in mind.

A solipsism, despite all the efforts of philosophical thought, finally overtook the Europeans. Everywhere we see the world-as-picture, but we see only ourselves. There is no picture. No one except us sees that which we call the world. No one seeks or questions himself. Because only in us does the voice echo of that Athenian who loved to conceal himself and his view of the world-as-picture behind the figure of his teacher.

The time has come for question truly determining everything. Are we capable of controlling a world which is not a picture? Are we necessary in such a world? Can Europeanness exist in a world in which it is impossible to scale?

This is a fork from which two possible paths proceed.

The first path is the inability of European thought to re-establish itself without reliance on the One. In this event one may continue to persist in one's desire to see the world as a single picture. It is only now that the refusal to fundamentally reflect on the very foundations of the European has come to have entirely a specific price – putting oneself in the power of technologies and artificial intelligence. Ultimately, it also draws a picture not badly.[8] And ChatGPT 4 may cope with drawing up texts of laws and judicial decisions, which it will do with the irony inherent to it.

Only by such means may even the illusion of the universality and unity of the world be maintained. The question as to why something created by artificial intelligence cannot be considered law deserves separate consideration. As too the question of why something created by artificial intelligence may not be considered a world.

The second path proceeds from the fact that European thought in many ways is exactly itself thanks to a phenomenon called "transcendence". European thought is "always a way out beyond limits", "exceeding". Simultaneously, just as the difference between Europe and non-European exceeds any substantive moments, the task of today becomes the reinstallation and re-establishment of Europe, a new metadigm for its assembly. And this, in turn, assumes the raising and resolution of two fundamental questions: first, what changes must philosophical thought undergo in order to ensure the existence of the European in the world after the "picture of the world"; second, how should the relation of legal thought to philosophical thought change, and what significance does legal comparison have here.

The "return of history", after the aforesaid manifestation of its end, leads to an understanding of time as a condition of a philosophical statement. This, in turn, makes the space of philosophy a dialectic of necessity and impossibility. On one hand, philosophical thought is necessary as the sole mode of the person-as-existence. The synonymity of "humanness" and "philosophicalness" is conditioned by a distinctive feature of existence as "ec-staticness"; that is, the ability not to be an "essence" in the sense of non-substantionality, the ability not to become a thing, to be independent of any preliminarily given essence or other

[8] "An A.I.-Generated Picture Won an Art Prize. Artists Aren't Happy", *New York Times*, 9 February 2022 (available online).

affiliation. Such an understanding of the inseparable involvement of man and philosophy opens recognition of the last as the sole art of man always to remain empty – to exist, means to reveal an unfilled, open space of the possible, which embraces the configuration of existence, without becoming a part of it, maintaining the position of "being-in-the-world"; that is, leaving the possibility for existing to be different, to change, to be meaningful, opening up the prospect of something new. This means that philosophy is not an external instrument in the hands of a person, to be a person means to be ec-static space of meaningfulness, the essence of which in openness to something new, the struggle for history, so that the world is not transformed into eternal self-creation.

In view of this, the principal task is the conceptual framing of cognition as maintaining a distance with the existing, its possibility in principle of reflection as incomplete and untenable. The main question is wherein lies the possibility of speculative thinking and what is the mirror for the existing?

The second pole of the said dialectical linkage enables the new and unaccustomed content of the contemporary intellectual situation to be fixed – for all its necessity, in some significant sense philosophy proves to be impossible. We refer to a construction of intellectual space of modern times which, needing philosophical meaningfulness, rejects philosophy in its traditional European understanding. This phenomenon may be called the effect of the "delocalization of philosophy" – the impossibility of its existence as a systematic, *a priori*, transcendental, unitary, timeless, and single horizon of philosophical thoughts. Delocalization is the principal attribute of the era of "overcoming metaphysics"; it points to the exhaustiveness of the Platonic jest – a project of philosophy according to which a single gnoseological, epistemological, and methodological construction of cognition allowed changes only in the form of ontological variants. Now we speak of a change of the construction of thought itself, about a gnoseological, and not an ontological, mixture. This space may be characterized as a transition of philosophical meaningfulness from unified vertical space to horizontal space. Change occurs at the level of the principle of structuring gnoseology itself – in place of a dichotomy (the possibility oof demarcating fundamental/regional, metadigmal/paradigmal, transcendental/ empirical), gnoseological monism proves to be constitutive – philosophy is possible only as a means of processization of thinking within concrete disciplinary discourses, and not in some supra-disciplinary, metadigmal space. For jurisprudence this means that philosophy is a procedure of discursive thinking demonstrating the untenability of legal material and thereby ensuring its semantic increment, whereas actually the philosophical significance of the meaningfulness of law does not exceed the limit of jurisprudence, which also constitutes jurisprudence as an autonomous philosophical discourse.

In comparative jurisprudence such own philosophical content appears in the mixture of the content of transcendence. The interpretation by Martin Heidegger (1889-1976) of one of the basic postulates of Leibniz's monadology is of importance: "a monad has no windows". Heidegger reconstructed the logic of Leibniz in a spirit of what the present writer calls the thesis of self-sufficiency. Each monad already contains within itself the entire world as a whole. Leaving the monad is not necessary. Each monad, being an essence, a substantiation, already contains the aggregate of everything material.[9]

The construction of such thinking proves to be a pyramid in which a monad crowns the summit, acting as a *tertium comparationis* – a general and sole ontological invariant of reality performing with respect to cognition the function of ordering discourse and ensuring its semantic invariance. This is a thinking that seeks what is constantly present. Transcendence also acts as an indicator to a constantly present, the achievement of a constantly present, the foundation of all that it is possible to know. With respect to law, such thinking was brilliantly described by Varga:

> We began to see the law as a purified concept, alienated from ourselves, as if it could function without us, like the Delphic oracle or ordeals, operated as a special automaton for deciding our case, into which we could load the parameters of the case so that then it could issue a single final decision from the 'black box'.[10]

[9] Martin Heidegger, Основные проблемы феноменологии [The Basic Problems of Phenomenology] (2001), p. 399.

[10] Csaba Varga, «Природа права. Историческое сравнение правовой отнологии и правовой идеологии» [The Nature of Law. Historical Comparison of Legal Ontology and Legal Ideology], Право України [Law of Ukraine], no. 1 (2011), p. 154.

Heidegger gives a different interpretation in principle to the existential structure of the monad. It has no windows not because everything that exists is included in it and it is self-sufficient. On the contrary, the monad is always outside itself, always without, always addressed to another being, and in such recourse it is always within itself.[11] Such recourse without, going beyond the limits of self, Heidegger also called transcendence. But obviously this is another transcendence – transcendence-"between".

Legal comparison is such transcendence-"between", allowing you to overcome your law but never allows you to achieve another. Another law is never objectified because there is no direct access to it, and national law does not become an object given that comparison is directed to its untenability, to the non-existent therein, to differentiation and increment, to deconstruction. On this basis the essence of the *tertium comparationis* changes – instead of ontological invariance with metadigmal status of metaphysical thought, it acts as a "between" one's own and another law.

Rejection of the Pythagorean faith in the sphere of law enables the question to be raised of the value of another law, discourse, or experience for us. This value and significance is not scaling your law against others. It also is not to extend own conceptualization to another law. Nor is it even to ascertain the sense of differences between our and another law. In the sphere of law we never touch upon another law in any way. It is unattainable.

Why then legal comparison? The reason is not to prepare the foundation of foreign law or construct a taxonomy reaching beyond national legal orders and supposedly relevant to them. The purpose of legal comparison is to go beyond the limits of own law. Go where? To the "nothing" of own law. The meaning of legal comparison is in transcendence as an ontological distinction between existing and being. The "nothing" of own law is "between" it and another.

Legal comparison prepares the Nothing, and thanks to this receives the possibility of own philosophical expression, which only by means of recourse to the Other may remove own law from the sphere of established meaning, bring the last into movement.

Therein lies the transition from the essence of law to its existence. Insofar as existence is this essence in its relation with its

11 Heidegger, note 9 above, p. 400.

own source, the task of legal comparison consists of recourse of its own law to the source of the legal, the maintenance of its own law in the state of its existence.

Openness to another law and to another in law is the source of the legal. Legal transcendence as the transcendence-between gives to us an optic of a vision of the world that enables the Roman praetor to create that which we now call law.

In re-establishing itself, Europe should become the new Rome. Roman experience of existence should replace the Greek experience of essence. Remi Brag magnificently demonstrated this: to be a Roman means to experiment with the old as a new, something is revived, carried over to a new soil. Such a carrying over provides a principle of new development from the old. The experience of a beginning from the renewed is Roman.[12] Therefore, law, as the art of praetors, was the fullest embodiment of the Roman means of a vision of the world.

The figure of the peregrine praetor also should become an epistemological model for contemporary comparatists. Law cannot be taken or purchased from others. Law is extracted from oneself, transforming and constantly reaffirming own experience. The ability, however, to create own law arises only when there is recourse to others – the space between legal orders. Others are needed. And the distinctiveness of others is essential. Only thanks to their foreignness can the magic of the presence of law arise in us ourselves. Recourse to others is essential not for the purpose of borrowing. But for a more grand and non-utilitarian purpose – for the creation nnof self, one's world, with the assistance of one's law. Others in their non-attainability enable us to see ourselves.

Therein is the magic of legal comparison. And therefore comparative jurisprudence is more important than ever. Now. When the world ceases to become a picture, it will no longer be her. So that we can regain ourselves and our dignity. And they go their own way, the Roman way, the way of the Europeans. Yes, we see in Chinese pictures and the "rock garden" that which does not exist in China and Japan, and that which we have, and that we clearly see in that which is neither their nor ours. In the eyes of Europeans the "rock garden" is "between", in emptiness, from which we also invent our world. Yes, in this there is loneliness. But

[12] Remi Brag, Европа. Римский путь [Europe. The Roman Way] (1995).

this is not a solipsism in pure form. We see only ourselves, but, correctly arranging the optics of the glance, we can see ourselves always different, always renewed, always creating.

And indeed, the time has come for us to acknowledge the world has never been and could not be one. The world is solely a European invention.

SECTION 2.

Law: Spaces of Order and Interaction

Chapter 10

National Legal Systems in the Context of Comparative Law

AKMAL KH. SAIDOV

Following the comparative methodology and beginning with the term, it is necessary to determine the place and role of the legal system in comparative law. There is no need, however, to explain what is hidden behind the term "legal system" in modern legal science, particularly in comparative law. Language differences do not really matter here.

In what way can a legal system be discussed in the context of comparative law? That is really *ignotum per ignotius* – explaining the unknown by means of the more unknown. Numerous points of view have been expressed and defended, but their consideration is not the subject-matter of this study. It is necessary only to identify as the starting point the legal material from which some theoretical and practical conclusions about the place and role of the legal system in comparative law can be drawn. Despite national, historical, and other differences in legal systems, there are certain general patterns of development of modern legal systems.

However, the objective of this study is to define what the legal system is. The phrase "legal system" is used here to mean "national legal system". For example, the legal system of France, Uzbekistan, Italy, and so on. In order to characterize a certain set of national legal systems, which, by reason of common features and characteristics, can be attributed to one group, it is advisable to use the concept of "legal family".

The following features are assumed by the category "legal system":

- legal understanding (historical evolution of the conceptual apparatus, legal mentality, legal ideology);
- lawmaking (formation and development of sources of law);

- law enforcement (patterns of court organization, judicial interpretation).

The similarity and difference in each element is taken into account when classifying national legal systems, attributing them to one or another legal family.

Two criteria were suggested by the renowned French comparativist René David (1906-1990) as the starting points for the classification of national legal systems:

first, ideological – religion, philosophy, economic and social structure;

and second, legal – legal technique.

David distinguished between three families of legal systems using these perspectives:

the Romano-Germanic legal family,

the common law family,

and the socialist law family.

The classification criteria incorporated the conceptual frameworks of various national legal systems or the hierarchy of different sources, as well as the type of society that seeks to be established through the application of law (and the role of law in this social system).[1]

Other approaches in the comparative literature[2] can together be defined as a "breakthrough of comparative law of the XX century".[3]

The insights of comparative legal studies have found general expression in ideas put forth by legal theorists, philosophers, sociologists, and political scientists; that is, by specialist collateral disciplines. In the present writer's view, a legal system is an

[1] See R. David, *Les grands systèmes de droit contemporains* (7th ed; 1978).

[2] Numerous publications on comparative law in the Russian language, many of which were cited in Soviet and post-Soviet textbooks on the theory of state and law, made the doctrinal views of such comparativists as Konrad Zweigert, Hein Kötz, Christopher Osakwe, V. E. Chirkin, Iu. A. Tikhomirov, M. I. Marchenko, V. I. Lafitsky, and others well known.

[3] For details, see R. Legere, Великие правовые системы современности: сравнительно-правовой подход [Great Modern Legal Systems: Comparative-Legal Approach] (2010), pp. 103-110.

ideological component, or set of legal views, that is historically conditioned, interconnected (interdependent), and organized hierarchically in terms of law-making and law enforcement.

The theoretical analysis of the laws of the historical development of law, designed, in particular, to show that the path of development of law within the framework of national statehood, is not an expression of "legal provincialism" which gives way to "legal universalism", but one of the most important laws of the development of the civilization of law. All legal systems should be recognized as equal. Comparative law today rejects searching for "universal ways of development" or "optimal legal models" that are appropriate everywhere and always.[4]

The first category in comparative law is the legal system. In the modern world, each State has its own national law, and it often happens that several competing legal systems operate within the same State. For example, in India the norms of the new national legislation, Hindu law, English common law, and Islamic law coexist and interact. Non-State communities also have their own law: canon law, Islamic law, Hindu law, and Jewish law. There is also international law regulating inter-State and foreign economic and other relations on a global or regional scale.

The national legal system of each State is formulated in different languages, uses different legal terminology and legal techniques, and is created for a society with differing structures, mores, beliefs. The place and features of national legal systems reflect the legal map of the world. Moreover, the concept of "legal map of the world" is capacious and developed within the framework of comparative law. The study of all its aspects in dynamics and historical perspective is of particular interest to comparativists.

COMPARATIVE LAW IS THE SCIENCE OF THE LEGAL MAP OF THE WORLD

The legal map of the world is characterized by high dynamism. It reflects the main political and legal changes, including the formation of new national legal systems, changes in their status,

[4] See A. Kh. Saidov, «Юридическая глобалистика – новое направление правовых исследований» [Legal Globalistics – New Direction of Legal Studies], in Правовая система России в условиях глобализации [Legal System of Russia Under Conditions of Globalization] (2005), p. 33.

the impact of integration processes, processes of divergence, rapprochement, convergence, unification, and harmonization of law.

The legal map of the world in all its diversity being the subject-matter of the study of comparative law, the question of the number and grouping of national legal systems is of great scientific, theoretical, practical, and applied interest. The main components of the legal map of the world are national legal systems. According to Veniamin Evgen'evich Chirkin (1924-2019):

> The modern world already has more than 200 States. The constituent parts of almost 30 modern federations consist of approximately 400 subjects of federations, each having its own territorial public collective. In ten States of the world there are about 200 territorial autonomous entities (more than 150 in China). The number of municipalities in every major State is tens of thousands.[5]

During the twentieth century, the total number of national legal systems has been constantly increasing and almost tripled. This was caused primarily by the territorial redistribution of the world after the First and Second World Wars. In the early 1990s, following the collapse of the former Soviet Union, the former Yugoslavia, and Czechoslovakia, more than twenty independent States emerged. As of 2024, various sources estimate the total number of national legal systems at 195 (193 United Nations members and observers: the Vatican and the State of Palestine).

After 1945, 102 countries in Asia, Africa, America, Oceania, and even Europe (Malta) achieved State and legal independence, and the number of Non-Self-Governing Territories (colonies, protectorates, so-called overseas departments, and so on) decreased from 130 in 1900 to 35 in 2024. Most are small island possessions in the Caribbean Sea and Oceania.

An important guideline in determining the number of national legal systems can be membership in the United Nations. The growth in the number of United Nations members from 1950 to 1989 was mainly due to the admission of States liberated from colonial dependence. That is what they are called – liberated

[5] See V. E. Chirkin, Сравнительное правоведение: учебник для магистратуры [Comparative Jurisprudence: Textbook for the Magistraturate] (2012), p. 147.

countries. From 1990 to 2024, several more liberated countries (Namibia, Eritrea, East Timor) joined the United Nations, but the main increase was associated with the admission of post-socialist States previously part of the former USSR, Yugoslavia, or Czechoslovakia.

The scale of future changes on the legal map of the world will be determined by the further course of ethno-cultural processes in multinational States and by the nature of economic, political, and cultural relations between countries and peoples, because the formation and development of new national legal systems is a complex historical process determined by a variety of internal and external factors: political, social, economic, cultural, ethnic.

With such a large and, moreover, increasing number of national legal systems, there is an urgent need for their classification into groupings, which is usually based on several criteria. With respect to existing national legal systems the literature of comparative law makes reference to such terms as the "legal map of the world" (V. A. Tumanov), "legal geography of the world" (V. Knapp), or "community of legal systems" (J. Stalev). These terms encompass national legal systems. Attempts to present the legal map of the world as a supranational world law or as a mechanical sum of national legal systems should be rejected.

When setting out the concept of "legal map of the world", we proceed from the general laws of the development of human society. This is the most objective way to study the legal map of the world – complex, diverse, full of contradictions and confrontation of various legal trends. The principle of historicism makes it possible to explain the place of each individual national legal system on the legal map of the world by belonging to a particular legal family or legal civilization. Attributing a specific legal system to a specific legal family allows, even without a detailed acquaintance with specific legal material, to draw a number of conclusions about its characteristic features.

METHODOLOGY TO DESCRIBE MODERN WORLD LEGAL GEOGRAPHY

A key component of contemporary comparative law is a comprehensive understanding of the national legal system in the context of its specific historical genesis and taking into account the socio-economic environments in which it operates. Each legal family should be considered against the background of its historical development, then its modern structure should be described (a summary description of the leading branches and sources of law), the distinctive features of law enforcement (legal proceedings), and the approach to legal thinking.

When describing the principal legal families, the comparativist should make a meaningful selection and, above all, limit the number of legal systems under consideration. A representative approach is used. The comparativist must first determine the so-called pedigrees, or maternal, legal systems where original legal solutions were first created, and then trace their further geographical distribution by considering the so-called subsidiary (received) legal systems.

As a rule, the legal systems of large States with extensive and long-term legal experience are the parents. This experience is used by small and new States belonging to the same legal family as the mother legal system. Such was the impact of French civil law on the law of the States that appeared in Europe after the French Revolution (for example, Italy, Belgium, Luxembourg). To be sure, the ideological influence of the mother legal system varies in different branches of law.

Thus, the description of each legal family should, on one hand, be a reflection of its historical development, and on the other, be based on its essential legal properties today.

The process of forming a modern legal map of the world has been underway for several millennia. Many historical epochs have elapsed enabling the postulation of a periodization in the formation of the legal map of the world. It is possible to distinguish: ancient, medieval, new, and modern periods.

LEGAL TYPOLOGY OF NATIONAL LEGAL SYSTEMS

The legal typology of contemporary national legal systems is among the topical methodological problems of comparative law. Many comparativists are engaged in its solution. In contrast to the classification of national legal systems, their typology is based not only on legal, but also on civilizational indicia (or criteria) that allow each to be attributed to a particular legal civilization.

The type of legal civilization should be understood as objectively established relatively stable, inherent conditions and features of development that characterize its role and place in the world legal community at this stage of the world history of law. In other words, the main typological features of national legal systems that bring them closer to one and, on the contrary, distinguish them from other legal systems.

Comparative law as an autonomous legal science studies the territorial differentiation of legal systems that is the legal geography of the world. Since the law reflects not only the connection of time, but also the huge modern diversity of national legal systems and the uniqueness of the legal world, the question arises about the division of the world into legal regions based on a civilizational approach to law; that is, legal civilization.

Many ancient, medieval, modern, and contemporary scientists continued the study of legal civilizations that Herodotus actually started. They found that, during the early stages of the development of local legal civilizations, the boundaries of legal regions frequently coincided with the physical and geographical boundaries that constrained the area of distribution of a particular ethnic community. Geographical and legal boundaries have lost some former defining characteristics as a result of the development of legal civilizations, the Great Migrations of Peoples, subsequent mass migrations of the population, and the emergence of regional and even more global ties, although they still played an important role as legal boundaries.

Each national legal system has its own unique features. However, by identifying any features similar to other legal systems, it is possible to identify certain types of legal systems. The type of legal system forms a set of conditions and features of legal development, which in significant, sometimes decisive (typological), features, on one hand, make it related to a similar legal systems, and on the other hand, distinguish it from all others. The very existence of types of legal systems and their historical evolution reflect the fact that legal development is occurring in States at different rates, in different situations, in different conditions, and in different ways. At the same time, it is impossible to distinguish types of legal systems based on one or more criteria important for all national legal systems.

A legal typology may differ. Some take into account all national legal systems of the world (global typology); others are confined to the legal systems of one region (regional typology); others focus on the typological characteristics of one national legal system. Various criteria can serve as the basis of a legal typology.

A more detailed typological classification of national legal systems, proposed by David and, to a lesser extent, the German comparativist Zweigert, has been widely discussed in doctrinal literature. However, these typologies raise questions. For example, they do not take into account significant changes in the legal map of the world that have taken place over the past quarter century.

The idea of studying law through geography (geographical maps) is not new. Aristotle tried to make a map of law (by analyzing the constitutions of Greek city-polises). As a science, the legal geography of the world took shape in the early twentieth century with the publication of the fundamental treatise by John Henry Wigmore (1863-1943) of a sweeping panorama of the world's legal systems,[6] wherein the author for the first time depicted the current national legal systems on the world map. Despite being a scientific breakthrough, Wigmore's theories needed extensive revision.

This was undertaken by David, the founder of the science of comparative law. Based on the related origin (evolution) of legal norms, he introduced the concept of a legal family into scientific circulation. The foundation for the development of comparative law was comparative philology (linguistics), this term for a language family having been introduced a couple of centuries earlier by Gottfried Wilhelm Leibniz (1646-1716). By superimposing (combining) these sciences, it was determined that the development of law directly depends on the development and evolution of a particular language.

Thus, the whole world (all world law) is divided (or classified). David points to certain legal families, that is, "blocks" of law, united by a single source, the history of evolution, similar doctrines and the very concept of law. David gave the legal geography of the world the form that is now accepted as the basis.

A legal typology can be based on a geographical criterion, in which case there can be distinguished on the legal map of the world:

[6] John Henry Wigmore, *A Panorama of the World's Legal Systems* (1928). 3 vols.

- legal map of Europe;
- legal map of America;
- legal map of Asia;
- legal map of Africa;
- legal map of Australia and Oceania. A brief overview is in order.

Legal map of Europe. Europe, together with Asia, makes up a single continent – Eurasia. There are fifty national legal systems in Europe, differing in their basic legal parameters and traditions. The modern legal map of Europe in the twentieth century underwent serious changes, including the results of two world wars and the collapse of the world system of socialism.

An original legal civilization was formed in Europe that spread throughout the world. Several legal families are salient on the European legal map: English common law, Romano-Germanic law, Scandinavian law; some legal scholars point to the family of Slavic law. Europe has historically sought a single legal space. European Union law occupies an important place on the legal map of Europe. There is a strong trend toward the harmonization and unification of national laws.

Legal map of America. America as a part of the world consists of two continents – North and South America, connected by the Isthmus of Panama. The legal map of America consists of thirty-five national legal systems. Whereas the legal systems of fourteen States, namely the United States of America, Canada, and the States within the Commonwealth of Nations, belong to the family of common law, then the legal systems of twenty Latin American States[7] either belong to the family of Romano-Germanic law or constitute the family of Latin American law, and the legal system of Cuba belongs to the socialist law family.

The formation of the modern legal map of America has a long history. The discovery, exploration, and seizure of territories and States of America during the fifteenth to eighteenth centuries and their subsequent integration into the system of world economic

[7] Latin America is a common name for countries located southward of the United States, in the West Indies and on the mainland of South America, where there are twenty sovereign States, as well as possessions of the United Kingdom, France, the Netherlands, and the United States.

relations were a consequence and an integral part of one of the stages of the development of European legal civilization. The national legal systems of America have an original legal culture. Economic integration processes are usually intensive, but this cannot be said with regard to the legal development of the American States.

Legal map of Asia. Asia is the largest segment of the planet; more than half of the population of our planet lives on its territory. Up to the mid-twentieth century, over 90% of the Asian population lived in colonies and dependent countries. The main metropolitan countries were the United Kingdom, France, The Netherlands, Portugal, Japan, and the United States. The law of the colonial powers, along with the distinctive legal traditions of the East, had a significant impact on the formation of the modern legal map of Asia.

The modern legal map of Asia includes about fifty national legal systems, which can be attributed to various legal families (Hindu law, Far Eastern law, Islamic law) or to mixed legal systems.

Legal map of Africa. Africa occupies one-fifth of the land area of the globe. There are approximately fifty-four national legal systems on the modern legal map of Africa, They are a symbiosis of the norms of traditional African customary law, the legislation of former metropolitan States, and their own national legislation. The development of the law of African States was significantly influenced by English common law and Romano-Germanic law. The African Legal Map is a laboratory of comparative law.

Legal map of Australia and Oceania. Australia and Oceania are a region characterized by political, legal, and economic diversity. Australia is a country that occupies an entire continent, whereas Oceania is the largest cluster of islands on the planet (about ten thousand) in the central and southwestern parts of the Pacific Ocean. English common law occupies a predominant place on the legal map of Australia and Oceania.

TEACHINGS ON LEGAL FAMILIES

The purpose of the doctrine on legal families is to answer numerous questions facing comparative law. Is it possible to classify the legal systems of the world by dividing them into a limited number of large groups? What are the criteria for such a classification? And if it succeeds, then on the basis of what criteria should a legal system be assigned to one or another group? The task of such classification is to ensure that various legal systems, as a result of their systematization, become more accessible for scientific analysis. These questions were asked by Konrad Zweigert (1911-1996) and Hein Kötz.

The classification of national legal systems into certain groups, or families, is one of the main challenges of comparative law. In search of a detailed classification of the main legal systems, comparative lawyers took a variety of factors into account, ranging from ethnic, racial, geographical, religious, and ending with the legal technique and style of law. It was difficult to find any clear basis in the proposed classifications.

According to the French comparativist René Rodière (1907-1981), in comparative legal studies, "there are almost as many classifications as there are comparativists". [8] The participants of the First International Congress of Comparative Law, held in 1900, distinguished between the French, Anglo-American, German, Slavic, and Islamic legal families. In 1919, during the celebration of the fiftieth anniversary of the French Society of Comparative Legislation, its participants limited themselves to a classification consisting of three legal families: French, Anglo-American, Islamic.

Wigmore reduced all the principal pre-existing and modern legal systems to sixteen: Egyptian, Mesopotamian, Jewish, Chinese, Hindu, Greek, Roman, Japanese, Muslim, Celtic, Slavic, Germanic, Maritime, Ecclesiastical, Romanist, Anglican. It is difficult to find any clear basis for classification here. It is ambiguous, for example, on what basis maritime law is allocated to a separate system. However, Wigmore assembled vast historical and legal material. He extensively applied the method he called illustrative.[9] For example, when considering each basic legal system, he produced several dozen photographs of historical monuments of law, buildings of law enforcement agencies, and representatives of the legal profession. A map of modern legal systems was provided at the conclusion of the third volume.

Wigmore was correct that an understanding of earlier legal systems is necessary in order to comprehend contemporary legal

[8] René Rodière, *Introduction au droit comparé* (1979), p. 27.

[9] Wigmore, note 6 above, I, p, xi.

systems. However, he combined the synchronous and diachronic aspects of the classification of legal systems in his classification.

CONCEPTS OF DAVID AND ZWEIGERT

The classification of legal systems is becoming more important than ever before. This is demonstrated by purely quantitative indicators. In the twentieth century, the number of national legal systems almost tripled and their current number exceeds two hundred.

But the matter, of course, is not confined to quantitative changes. The complexity of legal classification lies not only in the infinite variety of national legal systems, but also in the fact that the unevenness of social and historical development makes it possible for different stages of legal development to exist on the same synchronous slice.

In comparative legal studies, there are two different concepts of the legal system – narrow and broad. If the narrow concept of the legal system is understood as national law, then the legal system in a broad sense is a group of national legal systems united by the common origin of the sources of law, basic legal concepts, and methods of development.

In this regard, the legal comparativists of the world are similar to those who compare world religions, each of which (for example, Christianity, Islam, Buddhism) is based on fundamental unity, which, however, does not exclude the presence of sects, cults, and interpretations within its framework. Terminology in the second case is diverse; for example, David uses the term "family of legal systems"; Zweigert, Kurt Hanns Ebert (1913-1992), Max Rheinstein (1899-1977) – "legal circles"; the term "legal family" is most common in comparative literature.

Few works are devoted to the actual doctrine of legal families. With all the variety and multiplicity of available positions and points of view in postwar comparative legal studies, it is possible (very conditionally) to distinguish two main directions of the classification of modern legal systems, each of which in turn has several sub-varieties with certain features. The first direction is most clearly represented in the concept of legal families of David, the second – in the concept of the "legal style" of Zweigert.

David put forward the idea of a trichotomy – the separation of three legal families (Romano-Germanic, Anglo-Saxon, socialist), to which the rest of the legal world appertains, covering 80% of the planet and called religious and traditional systems.[10] His classification is based on two types of criteria: ideological criteria (here David includes the factors of religion, philosophy, economic and social structure) and criteria of legal technique; both should be used "not in isolation, but in combination". David's classification enjoyed considerable popularity in legal science. The course "Basic Contemporary Legal Systems" in French universities is taught in accordance with the classification of David.

The best-known representative of the second direction is Zweigert. As a classification criterion, he puts forward the concept of "legal style": "Individual legal orders and whole groups of legal orders have their own specific style. Therefore, comparative law seeks to identify these legal styles, group them into legal circles and place separate legal orders in these legal circles, depending on the decisive stylistic elements, style-expressing factors".[11]

The doctrine of "legal styles" is described most fully in his work (co-authored with Kötz) "Introduction to Comparative Law: The institutions of private law". According to Zweigert, "legal style" as a criterion for the classification of legal systems consists of five factors:

1) the origin and evolution of the legal system;

2) the originality of legal thinking;

3) the specific legal institutions;

4) the nature of the sources of law and the ways of their interpretation;

5) the ideological factors.

On this basis, Zweigert distinguished the following legal circles: Roman, Germanic, Scandinavian, Anglo-American, Socialist, Islamic law, Hindu law. This classification is not original and is based on the classification put forward by Pierre Arminjon (1869-

[10] For the Russian translation, see R. David, Основные правовые системы современности [Principal Legal Systems of the World] (1988), pp. 37-48.

[11] Konrad Zweigert, "Zur Lehre von den Rechtskreisen", in Kurt H. Nadelmann, Arthur T. von Mehren, and John N. Hazard (eds.), *XXth Century Comparative and Conflicts Law: Legal Essays in Honor of Hessel E. Yntema* (1961), p. 46.

1960), Baron Boris Nolde (1876-1948), and Martin Wolff (1872-1953) in the three-volume course of comparative law published in 1950.[12]

Ebert also adhered to the classification of Zweigert. He referred to the theory of ethnohistorical formation of legal systems as one of the possible "working schemes of differentiation and ordering of legal systems". On the basis of this theory, he, just as Zweigert, identified five main grouping factors that determine the "general legal style" of a particular legal system and emphasized that, according to ethnohistorical theory, each legal system (legal circle) is characterized by the dominance of one or another legal idea, or the rule of law.

Thus, in the Romano system it is the French Code Civil, in the Germanic – the 1897 German Civil Code, in the Anglo-American – the English Common Law, in the Far Eastern – the Confucian theory of law, and so on. Further, when considering individual legal families, he drew upon the classification of Zweigert.[13]

[12] Konrad Zweigert and Hein Kötz, *Einführung in die Rechtsvergleichung auf dem Gebiete des Privatrechts* (1961-1969). 2 vols.

[13] See Kurt Hanns Ebert, *Rechtsvergleichung: Einführung in die Grundlagen* (1978), pp. 39, 44.

Chapter 11

National, Transnational, and Global Law: Trends of Development and Interaction

ALEKSEI V. EGOROV

The phenomenon of "transnationalism" was injected into social life by scientific-technical progress. The development of information technologies, transport, communications, and other components of the world infrastructure determined the possibility of survival in the contemporary world at the expense of neighboring communities and conglomerates thereof. The principal idea of transnationalism was a distribution of functions relating to the creation of material and spiritual benefits between countries and peoples which represented specialized units of a single macro-world. Gradually, the technocratic trends of the division of the world determined the formation of an autonomous type of transboundary thought popularized back in the twentieth century by the writer Bourne.[1]

ON THE DEVELOPMENT OF TRANSNATIONALISM

From the outset transnationalism was described as a new means of relations between cultures. Subsequently, the ideas of transboundary interaction of States spread to the economic sphere, for there the doctrine of transnationalism was perceived most pragmatically. Transnational corporations emerged that aspired to maximize profit and minimize expenditures by activating the movement of flows of people, goods, and even ideas across political boundaries. Economic globalization required if not the complete elimination of State boundaries, at least the rather strong

[1] R. Bourne, "Trans-National America", *Atlantic Monthly*, no. 118 (July 1916), pp. 86-97.

liberalization of political regimes relating to the free movement of labor resources, goods, and intellectual product.

On the political level, States long resisted these processes. But in the contemporary world stable and dynamic processes were discovered testifying to the growth of irreversible processes of the identification of societies. Contemporary wars and military conflicts, despite all their scale and tragedy, represent nothing more than a belated reaction to a revolution in the consciousness of past and present generations wishing to live in another world. This world assumes the presence of new global space which will have other traditions and other models of interaction of countries and peoples.

A major instrument and simultaneously variety of the new social structure is law, comprising the foundation of legal systems which for the moment are called "national". The association of contemporary legal systems with political boundaries of States is receding into the past. This trend is well substantiated by the science of comparative jurisprudence. First, never has the legal world been represented solely by territorial legal systems. Virtually all traditional religious-community systems were of a personal nature and their geographical extent depended on the migrations of the bearers of these legal cultures. Krasheninnikova somehow figuratively observed that "every Hindu carries his own law with himself".[2] The spread of Muslim law on the legal map of the world also happens irrespective of the territory of States naming themselves "Islamic". The trends in the application of traditional Muslim law testify to the strong influence of those norms, long not regarded by continental and Anglo-American jurists as legal norms. The practical activity of Muslim judges on the territory of a number of European countries showed the unfoundedness of ignoring the normative force of Muslim law. Judgments and decisions of judges were enforced by traditional means and often were in contradiction with national law enforcement practice.

The practical application of personal law on the territories of States achieved normative consolidation in national normative acts establishing rules for the application of law having a multiplicity of legal systems. When the law of a country is subject to application in which several territorial or other legal systems operate, the rules

[2] N. A. Krasheninnikova, Индусское право: история и современность [Hindu Law: History and Contemporaneity] (1982), p. 12.

or principles of application are regulated by a national law. This algorithm does not exclude the possibility of the extensive use of traditional norms of foreign origin.

One may say that personal law, just as personal legal systems as a whole, were the forerunners of the transformation of national legal systems, and also a partial rejection of State courts following solely national jurisdiction.

Second, the sphere of regulation by private international law played a large role in this process, being initially orientating the law enforcer towards the need to choose between norms of national and foreign law. The duty to apply foreign law was placed on judges in instances determined by national legislation. Such application assumed not the simple use of foreign norms in the national jurisdictional system, but taken into account foreign doctrine and practice of the application of these norms in the States of their origin. In virtually all continental legal systems the principle operates of the application of the "native" legal order, which assumes the need to use interpretative, doctrinal, and judicial practices formed in foreign States. Anglo-American practice, although limiting itself in the application of foreign law, all the same granting to the party which has petitioned concerning the need to apply foreign norms, assumes identical approaches to evaluating the content of foreign law.

It must be noted that the practice of private-law "communion" of States and subjects of legal relations cardinally "expanded" national boundaries of legal systems. The political identity of countries became a secondary in the world architectonic and today performs for the most part a negative role in integration leading to world social well-being.

The forming of global space requires the creation of so-called global law. But this phenomenon represents merely a normative link of an enormous trans-national system where in addition to law there are included: lawmaking, law-application, and legal consciousness (global legal thought). We refer to a completely new structure of legal system which, on one hand, is sufficient technologically and enables all processes of global legal regulation to be described and, on the other, preserves national identity in concrete normative regulation. The forming of a transnational legal system encompassing virtually the entire legal macro-world is happening.

Contemporary researchers and law enforcers perceive national law as an effective normative system. Even international regulators are today not deemed an active means of impact on transnational relations (the more so having regard to the contemporary crisis of authority of public international law). To be sure, norms regulating international private-law relations remain needed, as confirms the viability of the system of transnationalism through participation in the regulation of economic relations of any level – from private individuals States.[3] Private international law is not exclusively a conflicts law referring to norms of foreign legislation. It has long since become a fully-fledged link in the system of material law, both international and national.

But today within the systems of law of a number of countries an intensification is occurring of the imbalance between public and private law regulators. Private national law aspires towards integration with analogous legal regulators of international and foreign origin. At the same time, national public law norms attempt to stop this process, consolidating the priority of national law over international law in their constitutions,[4] actualizing the lost authority of the national institution of public policy which was a brake on the application of norms of private foreign law.[5]

Private international law is proceeding to a new level of regulatory signifiçance foro the entire world community. In the near future these norms will be in the fairway of the entire global legal system. Despite its initial conflicts origin, private international law is becoming material law directly determining rights and duties of subjects of trans-boundary relations, including States. This law has a common doctrinal nature. Identical legal institutions are present in virtually all national systems of law. The structure of regulated social relations is analogous. Basic approaches have formed and

[3] The contemporary sanctions policies of States has slowed down but not excluded States from the sphere of international economic interaction.

[4] Suffice it to survey the constitutional documents of the post-Soviet region: Lithuania, Estonia, Tadzhikistan, Uzbekistan and Ukraine do not recognize the priority of international treaties over national laws and call them an integral part of national legislation; Belarus and Moldova expressly prohibit the conclusion of international treaties contrary to the Basic Laws.

[5] To date there is no clear definition of what is understood by national public policy – "public interests of the Chinese People's Republic", "basic values of Austrian public policy", "general principles of the Venezuelan public policy", "constitutional order or good morals" (Estonia), and others.

trends designated to single out an autonomous procedural link of private international law.

In this connection the modeling of future normative foundation of a transnational legal system seems possible on the example of the system of private international law. One may assert at the moment that the system of global law being formed will be bi-elemental, consisting of private and public law links. These links will be in principle "divorced" because globalization does not tolerate pressure on the part of public authorities. Underlying this division will not be criteria of private interest regulated by a certain group of norms that is characteristic of national, especially Romano-Germanic, law, but the character and degree of participation of the State in the realization of the doctrine of "legal transnationalism".

The essence of this doctrine lies in the rational distribution of the volume of social relations to be regulated between the legal systems of different States. A single center is formed coordinating lawmaking and law-application within frameworks of the realization of global law norms. The United Nations may act as such a center, whose role and functional significance should be reviewed in the foreseeable future. The structure of this organization enables us to begin at once to form doctrines for the distribution of the normative volume of regulation between countries.

We do not refer to the consolidation for certain States of spheres of social relations which will be regulated solely by particular political entities. There is always a certain problem of law-comprehension in different legal families. Especially illustrative is the experience of the realization of Muslim, Hindu, Chinese, and Japanese law whose normative nature was not always acknowledged by representatives of Romano-Germanic and Anglo-American cultures. The traditional approach of European jurists came down to defining national law as the system of norms sanctioned and supported by enforcement powers of the State. Community and religious legal cultures adhered to a more liberal view of the character of legal enforcement, appealing to the consciousness of the subject-bearer of rights and duties (Muslims, Hindus, members of African communities, and others). Contemporary trends of technocratization and globalization of social life require the approximation of approaches to law-comprehension, which are becoming more international.

The philosophy of the contemporary understanding of law is formed in the sphere of comparative jurisprudence, which is transitioning from the category of a discipline simply studying foreign law and legal systems to the level of a science capable of transforming the legal foundation and social life as a whole. Contemporary legal comparativistics has two constituent foundations – comparative jurisprudence and comparative law, which is not an autonomous branch of law but represents a meta-theory (doctrine) of an integrated perception of a legal world.

Similar to the general theory of law which nonetheless considered itself to be national, comparative law consists of those doctrinal components – the essence of law, legal relations, operation of norms in time, space, and group of persons, legal responsibility, sources of law, and so on. But unlike the theory of law, comparative law has a broad view on inter—systemic legal links at the macro-level of the functioning of legal families. Comparative-legal science considers in the doctrinal aspect the same theoretical-methodological problems of legal structure, but with the participation of all legal systems of the modern day, both territorial and personal. The institution of legal responsibility is regarded not as a link of a concrete legal system, but as an inter-systemic formation with common features inherent in legal responsibility in Chinese, French, and Swedish legal cultures. The structure of a legal relation becomes international, where subjects, objects, and content of a legal relation also theoretically rest on the experience of the functioning of the most different legal cultures – from continental, Anglo-American – to traditional Muslim, Jewish, Hindu, and others. The very essence of law is regarded as the normative beginning of the life of any society irrespective of its secular or religious orientation. Contemporary conditions of a technocratic society enable this new view of law and its concomitant institutions to be formed.

The basis for forming the system of global law comprises objective criteria of the functioning of the social milieu, which today is becoming increasingly one type. One cannot say that social life in Japan differs in principle from analogous conditions of a social character in China and even in European countries. Technical progress has done its job. The normative regulator has merely to adequately and efficiently react to questions of integration practice of the interaction of States. The objective conditions of social life depend on the requirements of human society, which seeks simplicity in the ordering of legal regulators. Regrettably, national norms of law throughout human history were more a brake than a stimulus towards the forming of an open society. A new time requires completely different approaches to the regulation of national and transnational relations. Global law is becoming such a new regulator.

The doctrinal foundation thereof is comparative law, containing single-type theoretical approaches and conceptual-categorial conceptions with respect to all national components of a legal character. In essence, we refer to the forming of a universal doctrine of a legal character of one type for national legal systems. The key components of such a doctrine are the following elements: essence of law, sources of law, system of law, norm of law, legal relation, legal responsibility. The tools of the realization are of one type – interpretation of norms, technology of application of foreign and international regulators, legal technique, and others. As a result, the one-type architechtonic of legality, legal order, legal behavior, and mechanism of legal regulation as a whole is arranged. The doctrine of the general theory of global law thus is represented by three large links – integration conceptions, integration technologies, and integration mechanisms.

Integration conceptions touch upon the very basis, the heart, of the global legal world. First and foremost, problems of law-comprehension are relegated here, to which we referred to above. The integrated forming of a single approach to the definition of law as a normative means of ordering social relations already is occurring. Illustrative is the experience of Far Eastern legal systems – China and Japan – where together with the traditional perception of national law – continental European approaches have been strengthened in the legal evaluation of social phenomena and processes. Even Muslim law has been materially transformed under the impact of contemporary interpretative practice of judges and doctors of theology.

The base conception of law-comprehension is built on the doctrinal approximation of a national understanding of the nature and purposes of legal regulation. Practically all societies use normative mechanisms, identifying them with an understanding of a certain order in society. Law serves to order social relations. It acts as a guarantor that society will not become chaotic. One conception of such an understanding of the role of law is determined by the existence of law, which is called upon not to create an ideal society on earth, and not to allow it to end up in a primeval state. Even contemporary Muslim conceptions consider the shariat not to be the sole "path to follow", but as a certain normative system for ordering relations within and without Islamic society.

FORMAL COMPONENTS DEFINING CONTEMPORARY LAW

Formal indicia are important components defining contemporary law. Illustrative of the result of legal convergence is not the external manifestation of active lawmaking and law enforcement activity of special subjects, but the new nature of contemporary law being formed, being not of a profoundly national, but of an integrative, character and manifesting itself in such common doctrinal indicia of law as normativity, officialness, and formal certainty of normative regulators. The problem remains that every time they attempt to impart a national-specific hue to these doctrinal components behind which the true integrative "universal" nature of law is not visible, as well as perspectives of a large-scale convergence of national legal orders.

Normativity

The normativity of contemporary law lies in the legal typization of a certain order of things formed in a particular society. For example, in one system of law the age of marriage is age sixteen (Great Britain) and in another – thirteen and sixteen respectively for women and men (Spain), and in a third, the age of marriage is age nine years for women (Muslim law); in one society the conclusion of contracts is strictly formalized (legal systems of the continental type), and in another a rather simplified procedure exists for the conclusion of transactions at the discretion of the parties (Anglo-American practice), and so on. In any event, the norm of law reflects typical instances of aa behavioral relation formed in different societies: only such a rule of behavior is desirable for a particular society and it has or thereafter may have respective systemic expression in official forms – laws, precedents, legal customs, and so on.

The normativity of law possesses the quality of universality for all legal systems. No society can exist outside normativity. The precise content of the rules to be established will, of course, differ.

But normativity as a quality of law is immutable and is inherent to any society and every legal system irrespective of its State identity.

Officialness

Another component determining the integrative essence of contemporary law is the officialness of the established rules. The contemporary palette of legal life of countries and peoples is represented by an enormous multiplicity of multi-polar, sometimes absolutely mutually-excluding, legal components. Carious mechanisms have been formed for the functioning of the continental codified, English precedential, and Muslim traditional law. These legal formations are so different that to find common components of legal regulation in them is quite difficult. But all these normative formations are brought into operation by public power realized by State formations using an entire arsenal of means and methods of legal impact on social relations.

With regard to the impact on social relations by means of State-authoritative legal regulators, it is worth noting that authority law enforcement is not always present everywhere. Suffice it to recall the presence of traditional law enforcement in a number of African legal systems having no public presence of a State in tribal relations (for example, the application of the Malagasy codes). In secular societies recently institutions of a religious character are being introduced, especially norms of Muslim law. Moreover, English law is not merely a law of judicial practice, but also a result of parliamentary activity. The sanctioning by the State of certain standards of behavior is important inasmuch as we must investigate all aspects of the normative life of society, both sanctioned and unsanctioned by State authority. At certain stages particular models of behavior may engage "indifference" on the part of public authority, but this does not mean they are of no interest to the science of comparative law. Sometimes, borrowing "unsanctioned" rules formed in other social systems, we can provide qualitative regulation of certain relations in another country.

Formal Certainty

Closely connected with the officialness of law is its formal certainty, which represents an object which we can perceive materially. Codes and collections of precedents, systematized acts and materials of judicial practice, regulations, decrees, and ordonnances – all these and other sources have an impact on our verbal perception of forms in which rules of behavior are clothed. The trend has recently intensified for the unification of approaches for the expression of the official will of the State: optimal forms have been found for consolidating rules of behavior in the form of traditional sources of law. National normative documents are consolidated by th technologies of lawmaking and law enforcement.

But the understanding of the formalization of a norm does not always take account of the experience of legal doctrines formed in different legal families. Anglo-American practice especially goes beyond the framework of understanding of exclusively an "command character" of norms and consider rules of behavior beyond of normativist theory; Romano-Germanic doctrine, on the contrary, formalizes more the consolidation of regulatory rules; religious and community traditional law has a dual character – religious and community formalization of rules of behavior. These aspects of the formal expression of law generate the integrative theory of formal certainty of legal norms irrespective of the type of origin of a source of law. As a result, the trends of the formalization are becoming more understood: will it reduce to a mechanistic consolidation of rules by verbal means or, on the contrary, transcend the framework of a normativist understanding of a generally binding rule.

A change of format of the understanding of the essence of legal regulation is a certain trend in the forming of the contemporary integrative essence of law, which is perceived as a certain social phenomenon, an achievement of all mankind, but not of a geographical or national entity thereof. The science of comparative law is being called upon to play its own role in the scientific provision for these processes, the doctrinal component of which integrates all possible rules of societal development in the elaboration of a new macro-world of legal reality. Components of the new legal reality are finding their place within the system of "comparative law" being formed. To those components may be relegated questions of the integrative substance of law as the foundation for subsequent consideration and substantiation of such base elements of general theoretical legal science as "legal relation", "operation of norms of law", "legal responsibility", and other categories and concepts, but from the standpoint of the theory of legal comparativistics. This does not diminish the role of the general theory of law. Comparative legal science augments and enriches the general theoretical orientation of legal science, making it specialized, using the rich potential of the method of comparison applicable to the legal foundation.

ROLE OF INTEGRATIVE TECHNOLOGIES

The next level of the global law doctrine is integrative technologies. We refer too the forming of uniform technical approaches to national lawmaking and law enforcement. It must be noted that legal technique has long since had an integrative character. If one examines in principle the rules of legal technique for creating normative acts in Germany and France, they will not be very different. Even the procedures for parliamentary lawmaking of Anglo-American countries were integrated with generally-recognized technical rules for the creation of a law. If one takes into account contemporary codification trends in Anglo-American law, then the judicial "technique of distinguishing" applied by Anglo-American judges will soon cease to be relevant.

An analogous law of societal development also is present in national law enforcement. Generally-recognized approaches relating to the choice of the legal foundation of a case, the comparison of factual circumstances, the adoption of a legally significant decision --- far fr om a full list of ways of applying norms irrespective of their national-legal nature. Any law enforcer is guided by technologies of the realization oflaw which are common. Law enforcement activity cannot fail to pass through all stages – from the establishment and investigation of the factual circumstances of a case and choice of a norm to communicating the legal decision adopted to the interested subjects. As also affects the acts of law enforcement themselves, whose content differs but the technical requirements for structure and realization are identical.

The spheres of lawmaking and law enforcement from the standpoint of the realization ofo certain technologies have long developed in a uniform channel of integrative mutual understanding of countries. And although the names of certain procedures or designations of acts of lawmaking and law enforcement differ from country to country, the approaches in principle determined by uniform requirements for the creation and application of normative acts are the same.

CUSTOMARY LAWMAKING

Customary lawmaking has been consigned to the past. Even contemporary judges' lawmaking is oriented towards parliamentary acts and documents of regulatory authority. Therefore, one may say that today a single optimal path is forming for the creation of social rules to which the State attaches a generally binding character and, when necessary, ensures their performance by enforcement. On this level, integration technologies for forming global law are oriented towards a simpler mechanism for the creation of norms, which is lawmaking by parliamentary and governmental structures. Lawmaking by judges, however authoritative it was in the Anglo-American milieu, is losing its position, being acceptable to a large degree at the national level but not in the sphere of global regulation of social relations. Even René David (1906-1991) agreed that only 10% of all decisions of the High Court of the United Kingdom became precedents binding for subsequent application in judicial practice.[6] Acts of parliaments and subjects of regulatory authority engage in everything else in the regulation of social relations.

Global law doctrine is realized in the most important component of its presence on the legal map of the world. We refer to integrative mechanisms, which are not formed at once but are an illustration of the effectiveness of the entire system of global law. The principal integrative link of this level is the transnational mechanism of legal regulation. Every legal system has its own national mechanism for the regulation of social relations. Traditionally, we include in the structure of such a mechanism the norms of national law themselves, as well as acts of the realization of law, to which we relegated the actions of subjects of legal relations and law enforcement acts.

We determine the legal fact and the legal relation as doctrinal components of national mechanisms. Global law has no special position with regard to doctrinal components because these links have no national-law nature. Legal facts and various kinds of legal relations have no national coloring and do not depend on authorization for their existence from subjects of authority. Global law may fill objective categories with its own international content,

[6] R. David and C. Jauffret-Spinosi, Основные правовые системы современности [Basic Legal Systems of the World] (1997), p. 259.

which happens mostly by the emergence of new norms. Thus do we again approach the need for forming a single conglomerate of legal norms, the basis for forming which is comparative law – as an international doctrine for forming and developing a legal foundation irrespective of a national nature. Theoretical science has long since left a state of solely national recognition of doctrinal categories. To be sure, in legal science of post-Soviet countries works still appear devoted to the theory of law of their own country.[7]

CONCLUSIONS

In reality, all legal phenomena as such have an integration nature. For a long time they were formed in the bosom of national jurisprudence and filled with the normative content of a municipal character. Ultimately, contemporary categories of legal relation, legal responsibility, legal capacity, dispositive legal capacity, and a number of others may not be regarded as the legacy of some individual group of legal systems, and the more so of one national legal system. Filling the content of these concepts and categories with international norms regulating social relations as a one-type relation is the next step. In the medium term the difference between legal families will lessen, today they being in the form of Romano-Germanic, Anglo-American, and religious-community law. The task of global law is to remove normative and technological limitations between national legal systems.

The world community is seeking a new law whose conception was consolidated normatively in the United Nations Charter. According to Article 38, the power of the Court is not prejudiced to decide a case *ex aequo et bono*. The same position is adhered to in a number of arbitration courts, which on one hand testifies to the crisis of national officially-recognized law and, on the other, to extensive prospects for the creation and application of global law satisfying the principles of the new world structure in formation.

[7] M. N. Marchenko and E. M. Deriabina, Теория государства и права России [Theory of State and Law of Russia] (2019). 2 vols.

Chapter 12

The Impact of Religions on Law-Making and Classification of Legal Systems (Islamic Law)

HASHMATULLA BEHRUZ

There exist at present in the world a large number of national legal systems. 193 States are members of the United Nations, each of which has its own, reflecting normatively the historical, political, cultural, religious, and other distinctive features of each people and society.

SELECTING CRITERIA FOR CLASSIFICATION OF LEGAL SYSTEMS

The classification of legal systems has theoretical and practical importance. The theoretical significance lies in the possibility of the cognition and study of the llegal panorama of the world in order to identify the substantive aspects of legal systems that ensure their functioning. Their practical significance is explained by the need to approximate legal systems and by interaction in the legal sphere.

Various criteria are used to classify legal systems – ethnic, racial, geographical, religious, and legal technique, legal style, and others, which, in turn, explains the existence of multiple classifications. Thus, within the framework of comparative jurisprudence the classification is becoming possible of the classification of national legal systems into various groupings or families. The criteria of classification may be highly diverse.

Among the many classifications proposed of legal systems, deserving of attention of the classifications build on principles of multiple criteria and aggregates of objective and subjective factors. The classification of legal systems on three levels or on two levels of macro-classification according to legal traditions, or on one level of micro-classification according to legal families. At the first level of macro-classification on the basis of religious orientation, religious legal systems are demarcated from non-religious. To the principal religious legal systems are relegated Muslim (Islamic), Hebrew (Judaic), canon law of the Catholic Church, and Hindu law.[1]

In comparative legal literature it is commonplace to distinguish between differentiated and undifferentiated legal systems which have access to various types of law-comprehension conditioned by various legal traditions.[2] In undifferentiated legal systems the functioning of law is realized not simply in close connection with religion, morality, customs, but also under their direct impact, and within the framework of differentiated legal systems, law functions relatively independently of religion, morality, and traditions.

The religious factor is an important component of the civilizational criterion. Thanks to legal regulation, the structuring of society is ensured not last in turn and its unity is preserved, and religious doctrines, world outlooks, and dogmas facilitate the combining of people within the framework of single canons to essential for social development. The role of religion within various developmental periods of society, State, and law, as well as the legal system, is difficult to overestimate.

From the moment of the emergence of religion in one form or another, it gradually exerted a noticeable influence on all spheres of the life of society, including culture, law, State, and others. In many societies religion exerted a certain impact on the forming and development of legal systems. Virtually all legal systems to some extent are influenced by religious doctrines and beliefs which may form values or principles and influence the realization of law. Depending on the extent of the influence of the religious factor, the classification of legal systems becomes more objective.

The recent need to investigate religious law dictates the need to activate the entire methodological instrumentation available to contemporary legal science. The potential of the civilizational

[1] Christopher Osakwe, «Размышление о природе сравнительного правоведедния: некоторые теоретические вопросы» [Reflection on the Nature of Comparative Jurisprudence: Certain Theoretical Questions], Журнал зарубежного законодательства и сравнительного правоведения [Journal of Foreign Legislation and Comparative Jurisprudence], no. 3 (2006), p. 61.

[2] Iu. N. Oborotov (ed.), Общетеоретическая юриспруденция: учебный курс [General Theoretical Jurisprudence: Instructional Course] (2011).

approach is required for a complex analysis of the religious factor in the forming and functioning of legal systems.

CIVILIZATIONAL APPROACH AS METHODOLOGICAL FOUNDATION OF STUDYING INFLUENCE OF RELIGIONS ON FORMING AND CLASSIFICATION OF LEGAL SYSTEMS

In the methodology of contemporary legal science an inestimable role belongs to the civilizational theory and the civilizational approach formulated on the basis of that theory.[3] The need to use the civilizational approach in studying different social, cultural, religious, economic, political, and, of course, legal phenomena was based on the works of many scholars – Adam Ferguson (1723-1816), N. Ia. Danilevskii (1822-1885), Oswald Arnold Spengler (1880-1936), Arthur Joseph Toynbee (1889-1975), Pitirim Aleksandrovich Sorokin (1889-1968), Samuel Phillips Huntington (1927-2008). However, the use of the civilizational approach begins with Abd ar-Rahman ibn Haldun (1332-1406). He was the first thinker who assessed the historical process from a civilizational viewpoint. He noted, in particular, that the civilizational approach may serve as an explanation of various phenomena of social life.[4]

In Toynbee's view every civilization represents a distinctive attempt at a unified, great creation of mankind, and if we consider it retrospectively, this is a distinctive example of a unified, great experiment of mankind. In his perception, civilizations represent types of human communities generating certain associations in the domain of religion, architecture, painting, morals, customs; that is, in the domain of culture. Toynbee also asserted that if one goes from Greece and Serbia, endeavoring to understand their history, one comes to Orthodox Christianity or the Byzantine world. If one travels from Morocco and Afghanistan, inevitably one comes to the Islamic world.[5]

[3] H. Behruz, "Civilization Approach as Methodological Basis of Studying of Islamic Law", *Law of Ukraine*, no. 11-12 (2011), pp. 156-161.

[4] Ibn Haldun, Избранные произведения мыслителей стран Ближнего и Среднего Востока XI-XIV вв. [Selected Works of Thinkers of Countries of the Near and Middle East of the Eleventh to Fourteenth Centuries], ed. S. N. Grigorian (1961), pp. 559-629.

[5] A. J. Toynbee, Цивилизация перед судом истории: сборник [Civilization

For an objective consideration of the principal trends of the social development of State-law phenomena, including legal, the use of the civilizational approach is becoming essential. The civilizational approach makes it possible to consider the history of mankind as a multi-variant process.[6] Accordingly, the use of this approach in comparative jurisprudence enables, on one hand, our vision of the evolution of legal systems to be more multi-dimensional. On the other hand, the consistent use of this approach in studying the evolution of legal systems leads to a conclusion that they differ, in principle, in their significance on the level of cultural-historical development, and this, in turn, affects the need to study all legal systems.

Use of the civilizational approach assumes rejection of the principle of Euro-centrism, which is a narrow approach to an analysis of world history – a consequence of inadequate knowledge of the history of other peoples and a feeling of superiority over non-western civilizations.[7] On this basis the transformation of notions about law and State within the framework of the civilizational approach has a direct relationship to an objective study of the legal panorama of the world in general and of different legal systems.

This approach points to not only differences between legal traditions and systems, but also opens new horizons of legal acculturation within the framework of a dialogue of legal systems. Legal acculturation is a major characteristic of contemporary legal systems, including religious.[8] A consequence thereof is a dualism of legal systems of the religious type generating serious challenges for the religious consciousness of the individual and of religious institutes as a whole. Therefore, in practice, they are in conflict today with the complex processes of internal transformation being caused by changes within these States and by their traditions.

Before the Court of History: Collection] (2002), p. 300.

[6] Behruz, Основы цивилизационного подхода в сравнительном правоведении [Fundamental Principles of Civilizational Approach in Comparative Jurisprudence] (2007).

[7] Behruz, Порівняльне правознавство: підручник [Comparative Jurisprudence: Textbook] (Odessa, 2009), p. 25.

[8] Behruz, "Religious and Secular Norms in the Legal Systems of Islamic States", in W. E. Butler and O. V. Kresin (eds.), *The Interaction of Legal Systems: Post-Soviet Approaches* (2015), pp. 441-451.

Thus, in accordance with the civilizational approach to the forming and functioning of legal systems, social phenomena such as traditions, culture, religion, and others exert great influence.

FAMILY OF RELIGIOUS LAW ON LEGAL MAP OF WORLD

The family of religious law is formed on the basis of own specific law-comprehension based on its religious origin. Law is formed and operates on the basis of religious dogmas and norms. Divine will acts, according to religious-legal doctrine, as the principal subject of law. The most important distinctive feature of religious law is that its sphere of extent depends upon affiliation to a religious community (or, by virtue of loyalty, to determined principles, as in Hindu law) irrespective of place of residence or location.

A distinctive feature of religious law differentiating it from other legal systems is the combining therein of religious and strictly legal principles reflecting the specific nature of its sources and structure, mechanism of operation, and law-comprehension. This distinctive feature also is manifest in the fact that for the realization of legal norms their conformity is essential not only to basic legal principles but especially to religious principles and norms. Jewish law, Hindu law, and Islamic law are within this group of legal systems.

Jewish Law as Variety of Religious Law. Jewish law is the aggregate of religious, moral, and legal norms and principles formed on the basis of the religion of Judaism. The distinctive features of Judaism as a religion in general and of Jewish law in particular are explained by a complex historical fate of the Jewish people who in ancient times lost not only their own State, but also the land of ancestors and were forced to live on the territory of other States.

An important distinctive feature of Jewish law is that it is a component part of Judaism. This is especially manifest in a common origin of legal norms and the commonality of their sources. The Bible is the source of Jewish law and religion – the first five Books thereof, or the Torah. The religious precepts which determine the relationship of man to the Creator, observance of Saturday and holidays, kosher laws, and others are simultaneously both religious and legal norms. Thus, norms of Jewish law are intertwined with religious norms and primarily directed towards the determination of the duties of man as a member of the Jewish community. They regulate the relation of members of the Jewish community to God and his laws and commandments, religious rituals, State, social institutions, other members of the community, and people of another faith. In certain instances various types of social sanctions are expressly provided for a violation of the basic commandments given by God to Moses on Mount Sinai.

A distinctive feature of Jewish law is the principle of the Jewish people being chosen by God, the singling out thereof by God from among other peoples. In order to ensure the effectiveness of this principle, Jewish law establishes a prohibition against assimilation with other peoples; for example, marriages are prohibited with non-Jews, as well as recourse to non-Jewish judicial organizations, and others.

Jewish law acts as the law of a community because the extension of its norms depends on affiliation to the Jewish community formed on the basis of Judaism. It is an important component of the legal system of Israel, formed in 1948 as a secular legal system. The legal system of Israel is a mixed system where elements of Romano-Germanic and Common law are encountered, as well as religious – Jewish and Islamic law. Jewish law thus became part of the Israeli legal system, but not the basis thereof. This is to be explained by the fact that the legal system of Israel is a territorial law; that is, the operation thereof extends to all citizens who reside on that territory. This is especially manifest in the consolidation at the State level of principles and norms of Jewish law. The Declaration of the Independence of the State of Israel consolidated the principle under which Israel is deemed to be a Jewish State. Thereafter, this principle was affirmed in a number of legislative acts approved by the Knesset – the parliament. In 1992 the Knesset adopted the "Basic Law: Human Dignity and Liberty", whose purpose is to defend human rights to respect and freedom, having combined this with the basic values of Israel as a Jewish and democratic State.[9]

Jewish law today regulates certain types of social relations linked with the personal status of Jews. Issues of marriage, divorce, material maintenance of family members, alimony, and management of personal property are regulated with the assistance of Jewish law. In addition, relations are regulated

[9] The Law was adopted by the Knesset on 17 March 1992 and published in *Sefer Ha-Chukkim*, no. 1391 (25 March 1992) (available online).

concerning religious worship and charity and the interpretation of religious conceptions (marriage and divorce of foreign Jews and Jews residing in Israel). Jewish law is applied by rabbinic courts, which according to the 1984 Basic Law on the Judiciary are an integral element of the Israeli judicial system and have exclusive jurisdiction over all cases concerning marriages and divorces, together with certain other matters.

Hinduism as Foundation of Hindu Law. Hinduism is the symbiosis of philosophical, religious, and social views and doctrines. The influences could not be avoided by a single confession which existed in India: Buddhism, Jainism, Sikhism, or Islam and Christianity brought in from without.

Hindu law represents the aggregate of philosophical, religious, and social views based on Hinduism. Hindu law regulates first and foremost the private status of Hindus, especially family law relations, inheritance, certain civil law relations, and others. Hindu law is the law of communities living in India, Pakistan, Myanmar, Singapore, Malaysia, as well as in States on the east coast of Africa,, primarily in Tanzania, Uganda, and Kenya, members of which profess Hinduism.

Hindu law accepted as its philosophical foundation the teachings of Hinduism, which became the basis for legal regulation of the social and private life of Hindus. Insofar as rituals were considered an important means of the socio-cultural regulation of the life and behavior of Hindus, they left an imprint also on the formation of Hindu law.

Hindu law was formed not under the influence of other legal systems, although one cannot deny certain changes made under their impact. New branches of law appeared in colonial India under the impact of English Common Law – criminal, obligations, procedural, ownership. Thus Setalvad wrote:

> Beginning with its application in the seventeenth century to British subjects in small areas in certain parts of India which were known as the Company's factories, the common law of England with its statutory modifications and the doctrines of the English courts of equity has deeply coloured and influenced the laws and the system of judicial administration of a whole sub-continent inhabited by nearly four hundred million people. The law and jurisprudence of this vast community and its pattern of judicial administration are

> in many matters different from those of England in which they had their roots and from which they were nurtured. Yet they bear the unmistakable impress of their origin.[10]

As a result of such large-scale codification, the sphere of operation of Hindu law was strongly circumscribed.

Thus, the principal distinctive feature of Hindu law is its being intertwined with religion, which complicates it being an autonomous phenomenon because it is a part of Hinduism. In modern India trends are observed towards the replacement of traditional conceptions of law of a religious character by a contemporary secular law. The contemporary legal system of India is the aggregate of all legal norms which have general application with respect to all citizens residing on the territory of India, irrespective of religious affiliation; that is, a territorial legal system. Nonetheless, family, inheritance, land, property, and certain other relations remain basic spheres regulated by classical Hindu law, as before.

Influence of Islamic Religion on Formation of Islamic Law. Islamic law is one of the clearest examples of the influence of religion on legal systems. It is based on the teachings of the Islamic religion and has greatly influenced the legal systems of many States with an Islamic population. The influence of classical Islamic law on the formation and classification of the legal systems of Islamic States is difficult to overstate.

According to Islamic religious doctrine, the legal prescriptions are regarded as components of a single Divine order and law which governs the entire world. Only Allah is a subject of law, and Muslims are considered to be the bearers of duties established by God. Islamic law is based entirely on the religion of Islam, and therefore it is rather difficult to draw a line between legal and religious norms.

Islam as the foundation of Islamic law repeatedly has demonstrated in its historical development the ability to adapt to changing conditions of social development. The flexibility and, at the same time, the stability of Islam ensure a high capacity for a civilizational resistance to both internal and external attempts directed to weakening the religious foundations of social life.

[10] M. C. Setalvad, *The Common Law of India* (1960), pp, 1-2.

However, this adaptation is not a complete transformation of basic religious norms and principles or bringing them into conformity with dominant ideological currents. As Bernard Lewis rightly asserted, in order even to partly understand what has happened in the Islamic world in the past and is occurring now, it must be acknowledged that the religious factor is a common and central element in the life of Muslim peoples, including legal life. In addition, as Lewis noted, the Islamic religion for Muslims is:

> Something more, which has no equivalent in Western Christendom ... Is not merely a system of belief and worship, a compartment of life, so to speak, distinct from other compartments which are the concern of nonreligious authorities administering nonreligious laws. It is rather the whole of life, and its rules include civil, criminal, and even what we would call constitutional law.[11]

Dualism is characteristic of the legal systems of contemporary Islamic States, consisting of the co-existence of legal norms differing in their content and specific nature – norms of classical Islamic law and norms borrowed from other legal systems. This makes it possible to adapt the legal systems of contemporary Islamic States to the constantly changing economic andsocio-political milieu.

Basic Sources of Islamic Religion as Basic Sources of Islamic Law. The origins of Islamic law are linked with the emergence of the fundamental sources of the Islamic religion, which simultaneously are also the sources of Islamic law. Divine revelations sent to people through the Prophet Muhammad later were collected and compiled in the Koran. The Koran was sent down to the Prophet Muhammad from the year 610 – the beginning of his prophecy and until his death in 632; that is, during approximately twenty-three years. The Koran consists of 114 chapters which differ in length and are divided into two parts which are further subdivided into four parts and 6,219 verses.[12] Only some verses of the Koran contain normative-legal provisions; the majority concern religious issues, the precise number of which is difficult to ascertain because of the indivisibility of Islamic law and religion. They primarily consider questions of marriage, polygamy, dowry, alimony, rights

[11] Bernard Lewis. *Islam and the West* (1993), p. 4.

[12] *The Holy Qur'an* (available online).

and duties of spouses, divorce, wills, inheritance, contracts, loans, pledge, court procedure, and others.

The prescriptions of the Koran having a regulatory character form the source of Islamic law, the code of conduct of every Muslim from birth to death. They are the criterion which enables in any sphere of life to distinguish the true from the false, the good from the bad, and the permitted from the prohibited. To the Koran are inherent those qualities which all other normative-legal acts lack – it may not be corrected, or changed. Therefore, the prescriptions of the Koran have remained immutable for the last almost 1,400 years; that is, from the time of its appearance.

The basic provisions of the Koran came down to Muslims in oral form – commandments which illuminated many questions of their life and faith; therefore, deeds, words, and even silence of Muhammad and his disciples were accepted as commentaries on the Koran. These commentaries formed the second source of Islamic law in importance – the Sunna.

Despite the fact that the basic norms comprising the foundation of the system of sources of Islamic law have a Divine beginning; that is, were consolidated in the Koran and Sunna, this does not preclude the existence of positive law on the basis of fundamental sources and allows the formation of other, derivative, sources, additional and lesser with respect to the first.

"Islamic Law" and "Legal Systems of Islamic States". For an objective study of this correlation, of major methodological significance is the separation of two concepts: classical Islamic law and the legal systems of Islamic States. Classical Islamic law was formed almost fourteen centuries ago on the basis of the Islamic religion. The Islamic dogma became the basis of the formation of Islamic law. The legal systems of Islamic States began to be formed as independent Islamic States arose in the twentieth century.

The difference between these concepts is explained by circumstances which actually led to changes that occurred in the legal sphere in recent centuries. Among such circumstances were the process of borrowing of legal provisions by Islamic States from other legal systems within the framework of legal acculturation. This led to the so-called westernization of Islamic law. The character and degree of these borrowings by various Islamic States differed materially – to be explained by history and the developmental process of the legal systems of these States. These borrowings to a great extent affected the sphere of State, criminal, and criminal procedure law; that is, the domain of public law, and to a lesser degree – family, inheritance, and other personal legal relations; that is, the sphere of private law.

The constitutions of Islamic States consolidated a number of respective provisions showing the influence of classical Islamic law on the legal systems of Islamic States. One such constitutional provision existing in approximately twenty-eight Islamic States and reflecting the influence of Islamic institutions and norms on State law is the recognition of Islam as the State religion. Such provisions have been consolidated in the constitutions, for example, of Jordan, United Arab Emirates, Tunisia, Qatar, Pakistan, among others. Moreover, the constitutions of a majority of Islamic States contain a norm under which only a Muslim may become the Head of State.

Six constitutions were adopted during the twentieth century in Afghanistan. Islam was consolidated in all as the State religion. In addition, it was provided that legislation must correspond to the principles and norms of Islamic law. Nonetheless, one cannot speak of the total Islamicization of the Afghanistan legal system. A dualism was characteristic of the Afghanistan legal system throughout the twentieth century under which the legal norms of various systems had their place in the functioning of the legal system.

It is difficult to determine the transformation of the legal systems of Islamic States during the last decade. Throughout the twentieth century one can speak of the processes of Islamicization and de-Islamicization of the legal systems of Islamic States. The legal system of Turkey is a shining example of such transformation. Following the abolition of the Osman Caliphate in 1924, the Turkish Republic was proclaimed to be a secular State. After the Party of Justice and Development came to power in contemporary Turkey one may speak of the Islamicization of various spheres of the life of Turkish society. If one takes the legal system of Iran as an example, after the 1979 Islamic Revolution there occurred the total Islamicization of secular Iranian society.

In the legal systems of some Islamic States borrowings predominate from the Romano-Germanic legal family (for example, Afghanistan, Algeria, Egypt, Morocco, Turkey), whereas in others borrowings occurred from the Common Law family (Pakistan,

Malaysia, Nigeria). Legal doctrine has formed several conceptions with regard to the status of borrowings by Islamic law of provisions from other legal systems. According to one suggested by René David, one observes in the legal systems of some Islamic States a symbiosis of categories and concepts borrowed from western law and methods, reasoning, and approaches deeply permeated by the tradition of Islamic law.[13] According to another conception, Islamic law represents a system of legal principles and norms that are solitary from other legal systems. Although a number of similarities exist between them reflected in legislative and judicial practice, they cannot be regarded as borrowings by Islamic law of legal ideas and provisions from other legal systems.[14]

The functioning of contemporary legal systems in Islamic States, however, shows the possibilities of legal acculturation, according to which classical Islamic law is capable of adapting to new conditions requiring various spheres of social relations to be regulated anew. This shows that they are adapting to contemporary conditions not only by borrowing legal provisions from other legal systems, in particular from western law, but from the application of customs not contrary to the Koran and Sunna with the assistance of legislation and legal practice. Despite the borrowing of certain legal norms of a secular character from western law, the distinctive features of the functioning of these provisions within the said legal systems are determined by Islamic legal doctrine. The operation of this principle within the legal systems of contemporary Islamic States is limited by an important reservation not allowing its unequivocal application: only those legal norms of a secular character may be applied within the legal systems which correspond to the basic principles of Islamic law based on the fundamental postulates of the Islamic religion.

Being based on the fundamental sources of the Islamic religion and having received further substantiation and elaboration in Islamic legal doctrine, Islamic legal norms, as before, remain the most powerful factor determining the characteristics and distinctive features of the functioning of the legal systems of contemporary Islamic States.

[13] R. David and C. Jauffret-Spinosi, *Les grands systémes de droit contemporain* (10th ed.; 1992).

[14] J. Schacht, *An Introduction to Islamic Law* (1983).

The norms of Islamic law regulate, as previously, basically the personal status of the Muslim; that is, the spheres of private law, although issues of public law also are addressed. Classical Islamic law plays a certain role in the formation not only of formal, but also substantive, elements of the legal system. First and foremost, it is a legal ideology; that is, fundamental principles determining all spheres of legal reality in society. The legal ideology formed in Islamic States is of a purely religious character, emanates from fundamental sources of the Islamic religion and Islamic law – the Koran and Sunna, and also was formed in the course of the doctrinal development of Islamic law.

Islamic Religious Teachings and Islamic Legal Doctrine. Islamic legal doctrine has played a major role in the development and functioning of Islamic law and Islamic State. Ijma, considered the third most important source of Islamic law, is a clear example of such influence and represents the agreed opinion of Islamic religious teachings on religious and legal issues requiring practical application of provisions of the Koran and Sunna. However, Islamic legal doctrine developed the immutable principle that any agreed decision within the framework of ijma cannot change or eliminate provisions contained in the Koran or Sunna. The distinctive features should be emphasized of the legal force of ijma depending on its character: if any ijma rests on the texts of the Koran and Sunna, it cannot be abolished subsequently by another unanimous opinion: if a ijma is based only on social interests, it may be repealed thereafter if the public well-being requires this.[15]

A fatwa also represents oral and written views of authoritative theologians and jurists with regard to decisions of secular authorities adopted on questions of social life, and also interprets various provisions contained in the basic sources of law having a general character. This is an official view, a kind of verdict on some religious-legal or social issue rendered by authoritative religious figures in response to the inquiry of a judge or other person. A fatwa may serve as the grounds for a judicial decision or for a choice by persons requesting it of their actions. Often fatwas are a form of reaction by Islamic theologians-jurists to events of a socio-political and cultural life generating disputes both in the Islamic world and beyond its limits.

[15] Behruz, Исламские традиции права [Islamic Traditions of Law] (2006).

Islamic religious teachings play, as before, a significant role in the formation of and ensuring compliance with and the application of laws. For example, experts in the Islamic religion and judges often bear responsibility for the interpretation and application of Islamic law. In the majority of Islamic States, Islamic religious councils function which supervise compliance with Islamic principles and norms in lawmaking and law enforcement activity of the State. They possess extensive powers, up to and including suspension of the operation of laws.

According to Islamic legal doctrine, the implementation of Islamic law emanates from the consciousness of Muslims and is effectuated only in the prescribed form with observance of all aspects of strict ritual. It is ensured also by the collective responsibility of the Islamic community for the behavior of every member of the community and the individual link of the Muslim with Allah.

Islamic Conception of Human Rights. The Islamic conception of human rights was formed in accordance with the principles and norms of the Islamic religion at the beginning stage of its development. Regionalization in the sphere of regulating human rights commenced as a reaction against universal standards which required adaptation to the specific features of the cultures of different countries and civilizations. The majority of documents regulating the sphere of human rights in the Islamic world on the regional and national levels reproduce many doctrinal foundations of classical Islamic law. The adoption of these documents, however, within the Islamic world is a reaction to the contemporary vision of the conception of human rights consolidated in international legal documents; in particular, the 1945 United Nations Charter, 1948 Universal Declaration of Human Rights, 1950 European Convention on the Protection of Human Rights and Fundamental Freedoms, and others.[16]

Islamic international-legal acts concerning human rights adopted at the regional level reflect certain liberal conceptions of Islamic jurists directed towards bringing the Islamic conception of human rights into conformity with the realities of today. The

[16] Behruz, «Конвенція про захист прав людини і основоположних свобод та ісламські міжнародно-правові документи (компаративістський аналіз)» [Convention of the Protection of Human Rights and Fundamental Freedoms in Islamic International-Legal Documents (Comparative Analysis)], *Право України* [Law of Ukraine], no. 10 (2010), pp. 114-118.

contemporary vision of human rights in the Islamic world is reflected in regional international acts: the 1981 Universal Islamic Declaration of Human Rights, the 1990 Cairo Declaration on Human Rights in Islam, and the 1994 Arab Declaration of Human Rights. An analysis of norms of Islamic regional human rights acts provides a basis for asserting that their provisions are not contrary in principle with international-legal human rights standards. But the rights consolidated therein, of course, have specific features conditioned by the peculiarities of the Islamic religion and law.

Thus, according to the Universal Declaration of Human Rights (Article 29), the exercise of rights and freedoms is limited only by the requirement of securing due recognition and respect for the rights and freedoms of others. Limitation of rights and freedoms in Islam have been established by normative prescriptions of the Islamic religion and law. Any behavior of a person is assessed from the standpoint of the permitted and the prohibited within the framework of Islamic religious tenets. Such concepts as freedom to express an opinion, freedom of information, and others may serve as examples. The Universal Declaration of Human Rights grants the right to freedom of opinion and expression, and also to receive and impart information and ideas, not making any reservations relative to content, without interference and through any media (Article 19). The Cairo Declaration on Human Rights in Islam provides for the possible expression of opinion only by a means not contrary to the principles of the shariat (Article 22). Information, in accordance with that Article, may not be used to infringe upon the holiness and dignity of the Prophet, circulate doubts as to moral values, and weaken faith.

Such a concept as freedom of profession of faith consolidated both in the Universal Declaration of Human Rights and in Islamic international-legal documents has different limits. International legal documents in the sphere of human rights consolidate the freedom of conscience and profession of faith. In prohibiting compulsion of a person to change or renounce religion, the Cairo Declaration (Article 10) does not provide, as does the Universal Declaration of Human Rights (Article 19), for the possibility to change the Islamic religion to another.

The protection of motherhood and childhood is declared both in international legal and Islamic legal documents. However, there are a number of material differences between them. The Universal Declaration of Human Rights (Article 25) establishes the equality of children born in or out of wedlock. This provision is absent in Islamic legal documents. The Cairo Declaration contains the formulation "parents and those who replace them" (Article 7), which indicates the absence of the institution of adoption in Islam. The Universal Islamic Declaration of Human Rights (Article 21) establishes not only the right of a child to grow in a family, but also the responsibility of the community with respect to the child whose parents cannot perform their duties – the communitu must perform their duties. This Article consolidates the right of the mother to concern and assistance of the family and the community.

Influence of Islamic Religion on Islamic Justice. The origin of Islamic justice is linked with the process of the forming and development of Islamic State and law, the main content of which was determined by the life and activities of the Prophet Muhammad, who performed the role of chief judge in the first Islamic State. The administration of justice by the Prophet Muhammad became the basis for the further formulation of the basic principles of Islamic justice.

Islamic justice was formed finally in the tenth century simultaneously with the completion of the development of Islamic legal doctrine, which, together with judicial practice, at the time proposed a new judicial procedure and rules of proof on the basis of the following principles: the principle of justice, mentioned in many verses of the Koran, for example: "... if you judge between people, to do with justice";[17] the principle of equality consolidated by the Koran, in particular: "Believers are brothers"; the principles of publicness and transparency of a court proceeding expressed in the fact that they are held in a public place, usually in a mosque, and others. Judges are appointed to their office by the head of the Islamic State. Before appointment, the candidate is examined on his knowledge of Islamic law based on the Islamic religion; that is, the office of judge is not elective. Taking up office occurs immediately after promulgation of the edict. In the event of a change of the Head of State, confirmation by the new ruler of previously occupied judicial office is necessary.

At present, many Islamic States entirely or partly reject Islamic courts in preference to secular courts. Before 1952 in Egypt the organization of and procedure in Islamic courts was regulated by a law. Islamic courts of three levels existed – lowest, which

[17] *The Qur'an,* transl. M. A. S. Abdel Haleem (2004), p. 56.

considered ordinary cases; first instance, whose jurisdiction included the consideration of more complex cases and appeal against the decision of the lowest courts; and the Supreme Court. Special shariat courts were liquidated in 1956 and their powers were transferred to general civil courts. An attempt was made in 1954 to liquidate Islamic courts in Libya, but after four years they were restored. Despite the various degrees of influence of norms of classical Islamic law on the judicial systems of Islamic States, in the majority of these States they today continue to exert considerable influence on the administration of justice.

CONCLUSIONS

The contemporary period of the development of mankind is characterized by a strong turbulence which raises a number of questions for the humanities that, without resolution, make it impossible to study contemporary trends of the development of society and to forecast the dynamic of its development. The interaction of civilizations – and in the view of some contemporaries – the conflict of civilizations – has again moved to the center of scientific discourse. Contemporary international relations are demonstrating a complex and multi-faceted character of such interaction.

The ideology of the juxtaposition of democracy and autocracy served as the basic of contemporary relations between States and alliances thereof. They have recently combined towards a juxtaposition between the ideology of traditionalism and conservatism, on one side, and globalism, on the other. An ideology of neo-traditionalism and neo-conservatism at the contemporary stage of development of society is spreading in many regions which are not part of the West. Religion is the major component of the ideological foundations of various civilizations and communities. The religious factor, as the contemporary state of international relations shows (especially contemporary conflicts) is being transformed into a powerful trigger of tension in these relations. Accordingly, the arrangement of a dialogue of different civilizations and the formation of stable and safe international relations without taking account of these ideological changes does not seem possible.

Religion plays an important role in the forming and functioning of virtually all legal systems; however, the degree of influence of the religious factor on them differs radically. This demonstrates the importance of investigating the religious factor on the basis of the civilizational approach in the light of the intensifying influence of the ideology of neo-traditionalism and neo-conservatism.

The correct understanding of the Islamic conception of law is based on such an axiom: Islamic law is encompassed by the framework of Islam, but Islam is not exhausted by the framework of Islamic law. Consequently, the essence and content of the Islamic conception as a whole also is based entirely on Islam. Islam contains a system of norms and principles which regulate and determine the way of life and behavior of people professing this religion in all of its manifestations, including legal.

The influence of religion on the legal systems of Islamic States is multi-faceted. The legal systems of Islamic States are based on classical Islamic law; however, noteworthy differences exist between them, depending on the degree of such influence. In certain legal systems there is a more conservative interpretation of the principles and norms of Islamic law, whereas in others there is a more liberal interpretation. Differences also exist in the means of realization of the principles and norms of Islamic law in various Islamic States.

Chapter 13
Conception of Human Rights as Component of Religious Legal System (Contemporary Catholicism)

SERHIY P. RABINOVYCH

Many of the major methodological problems of comparativistics have their roots in problems of law-comprehension. The original law-comprehension is capable of both materially narrowing and, on the contrary, expanding the horizon of investigating the legal picture of the world. The last would be materially united if it consisted only of normative components forming official State-law systems, and also from some normative institutions within religious-law and traditional legal systems. The combining of the consideration of a legal systems into one normative level thereof could only serve as a not entirely deserved tribute to legal positivism which, however, despite its authority in post-Soviet space, now is neither the sole nor universal approach to an understanding of law.

The vision of the legal picture of the world today is increasingly based on a multi-tiered law-comprehension by the inclusion in the structure of legal reality and legal system of at least three components: legal ideas, norms, and relations. Having regard to this, an object of research interests of comparatists should be not only normative, but also doctrinal and behavioral components of legal reality taken in their interlinkages and inter-dependencies.

CATHOLIC LEGAL DOCTRINE AS OBJECT OF COMPARATIVE RESEARCH

There is no doubt that a significant component of the legal map of the world is legal thought (or, legal doctrine), which in the said trinity structure of the legal system is State law, religious, and traditional, and corresponds to the level of "ideas". In turn, the official legal ideology is closely connected with the normative components of the legal system, acting as a means of substantiation and legitimation of its norms and institutions.

This applies fully to contemporary religious-law systems, especially Christian, which this example illustrates.[1] The Catechism of the Catholic Church promulgated in 1992 by Pope John Paul II (1920-2005) and the Compendium of the Catechism of the Catholic Church presented by Pope Benedict XVI (1927-2022) on 28 June 2005 set out a specific theological substantiation for each of the Ten Commandments as unified and syncretic – simultaneously religious-normative and ethical-legal – principles and explains the profound spiritual reasons for following them.

For example, with regard to the Fifth Commandment, "Thou Shalt Not Kill", explanations are given of the reasons for respecting human life (§466); it is explained why the legal protection of the individual and society are not contrary to the prohibition against homicide (§467); the purposes of punishment imposed by public authorities on a criminal (§468); substantiation of the principle of commensurateness when applying punishments (§469); and offering a concrete response to the question "what precisely does the Fifth Commandment prohibit"? in a bioethical interpretation. According to the official teaching of the Catholic Church, proceeding from the Fifth Commandment there are prohibited: direct and intentional homicide and accessory thereof; conscious interruption of pregnancy (abortion); and likewise complicity therein; conscious euthanasia; suicide and voluntary assistance therein (§470). Also indicated are what medical procedures are admissible when the ensuing of the death of a person is irreversible (§471); whether the transplant or donation of organs are allowed before or after death (§476); what acts are contrary to respect for the integrity of the body of a human person (§477). The Compendium explains what are the moral requirements for earthly peace (§482), when precisely the use of armed force by States is morally justified

[1] When preparing the present article the monograph Права людини у природно-правовій думці Католицької церкви (за матеріалами соціальної доктрин католицизму) [Human Rights and Natural-Law Thought of the Catholic Church (Materials of the Social Doctrine of Catholicism)] (2004) was used, revised and augmented to take account of later changes in the social doctrine of Catholicism during the periods of Pope Benedict XVI and Pope Francis. Special attention is given to the views of the Vatican on issues of war and peace expressed after the armed aggression of the Russian Federation against Ukraine. Additional editorial changes were made in individual instances in the 2004 text. All Vatican documents cited are available online.

(§483), and so on. These illustrations show the close interlinkage among religious-normative, ethical-theological, and natural law elements of the transnational socio-normative system of contemporary Catholicism.

The interlinkages between systems of canon law of the Catholic Church (so-called positive canon law), Catholic moral theology, and secular law of the Vatican City-State are noted in official documents of the Holy See:

> Canon law is the primary source of the laws of VCS and the primary criterion for interpretation; however, it should be noted that not every aspect of canon law is applicable in the temporal governance of VCS (cf. Law of 1 October 2008, N. LXXI, art. 1 (1), on the sources of law, in force 1 January 2009, amended the Law of 7 June 1929, N. II as regards the sources of law). Canon law, in comparison with the laws of other States, is *a complex unity of divine natural law, divine positive law, and human law* which reflect and express the Catholic Church: its origin, means, spiritual and moral mission, organizational structure, supernatural end, and spiritual and temporal goods. *The divine natural law (also referred to as simply "natural law") and divine positive law indicate the primary and essential norms regulating the moral life, as interpreted by the Church's teaching authority and set out in the Catechism of the Catholic Church (CCC).* In confronting particular circumstances, purely human laws are developed which are mutable. They may include elements borrowed from the civil law, but human law can never breach divine natural law or divine positive law (italics added).[2]

The common roots and essential unity of the canon law systems as a "complex digest" of norms belonging to qualitatively different but nonetheless substantively interconnected religious-ethical, religious-legal, and State law socio-regulated systems called here respectively "divine natural law", "divine positive law", and "human law" harmonized with the first two systems.

Hereinafter this study will explore the official legal, namely "human law", ideology of the Catholic Church presented in

[2] Committee on the Elimination of Racial Discrimination, Consideration of reports, submitted by States parties under article 9 of the Convention Sixteenth to twenty-third periodic reports of States parties due in 2014. Holy See, p. 10.

its official documents (encyclicals, messages, and other acts of the Popes of Rome and the Roman curia. Works of leading theologians and philosophers will be taken into account, together with commentators on the social doctrine of Catholicism. The purpose is to identify the specific nature of the inter-linkage of value and normative (religious-theological, religious-ethical, and religious-legal) components in the legal ideology of contemporary Catholicism.

EVOLUTION OF CATHOLIC HUMAN RIGHTS DOCTRINE IN NINETEENTH TO TWENTY-FIRST CENTURIES

The development of the European philosophy of human rights is closely tied to Christian theology. Suffice it to recall Francisco de Vitoria (c. 1483-1546), Francisco Suarez (1548-1617), Miguel Servetus (1509/1511-1553), Sebastian Castellio (1515-1563), and others. From the late nineteenth to the end of the twentieth centuries the principal branches of Christianity (Orthodox, Catholicism, and Protestantism) elaborated own conceptions of human rights as responses to social challenges of the twentieth century. The theological and philosophical-anthropological basis of all Christian conceptions of human rights is the biblical idea of the creation of man in God's image and similarities and the spiritual and religious understanding of the existential foundations of such rights.

The Catholic teaching about human rights is the most developed in contemporary Christianity. The Catholic Church considers human rights in the context of own social doctrine (special form of the expression of a social ethic) – the aggregate of socio-economic, socio-political, and ethical-legal conceptions consolidated in official documents of the Catholic Church and other sources (works of Catholic theologians, philosophers, sociologists, and economists). Neo-thomism acts as the general philosophical-ideological foundation of the Catholic conception of human rights – the most authoritative orientation of Catholic philosophy based on the teachings of Thomas Aquinas (1226-1274).

Two stages are traditionally singled out in the development of the Catholic conception of human rights: (1) from the issuance of the first social encyclical by Pope Leo XIII (1810-1903), "Rerum Novarum", in 1891, to the mid-twentieth century (gradual coming together of Catholic human rights doctrine with international human rights ideology); (2) from the reign of Pope John XXIII (1958 to 1963) and II Vatican Conclave (1962 to 1965) to the present (acceptance of system of human rights recognized in international law, their adaptation to postulates of the Catholic social ethic, and elaboration of specific theological substantiation of such rights).

Natural Law as Human Rights

The crucial stage in the evolution of natural-law Neo-Thomist thought begins with the election to the Papacy of John XXIII. This is a period of *aggiornamento* – renewal or modernization – as a reaction against the deepening crisis in which the Catholic Church found itself. The essence of the crisis was an aggravation of contradictions between traditions, norms, and criteria concerning the past of the Catholic Church and its preceding organization and structure, on one hand, and the new conditions of existence of the church in the contemporary world, on the other.[3] The Church faced the task of imparting to its doctrine an essential dynamism in order to adapt to the changing social reality. It was necessary to move on from confrontational relations with non-Christian socio-political formations to a dialogue with them, without, however, renouncing own worldview precepts.[4]

In the period here considered, a distinctive codification occurred of the social doctrine of the Church in four documents: encyclicals of Pope John XXIII, "Mater et magistra", 15 May 1961, and "Pacem in terris", 11 April 1963; another adopted by the II Vatican Conclave, "Gaudium et spes", 7 December 1965, and an encyclical of Pope Paul VI, "Ropulorum progressio", 26 March 1967.

The principal topic of the encyclical "Pacem in terris", addressed not only to Catholics but to all people of good will, was the doctrine on human rights. Pope John XXIII affirmed therein the idea of the equality of nature of all people and man's personal dignity and spoke against racial and sexual discrimination (PT, 86). The basic provisions of the document are the idea of natural

[3] A. Kazanova, Второй Ватиканский собор. Критика идеологии и практики современного католицизма [Second Vatican Conclave. Critique of Ideology and Practice of Contemporary Catholicism] (1973), p. 9.

[4] A. S. Vatoropin, «Религиозный модернизм и постмодернизм» [Religious Modernism and Post-Modernism], Социологические исследования [Sociological Studies], no. 11 (2001), p. 87.

law in its Thomist understanding and the thesis of the highest transcendent dignity of "each individual man". These thesis be come the basis for the formulation of "man's rights", "rights of individuals", which are "universal and inviolable". A systematized list of human rights is presented that includes rights recognized in preceding church documents. Moreover, the catalog of human rights is materially expanded of both civil and political and of socio-economic rights.

For the first time in the Catholic tradition the encyclical recognized a universal right "to worship God in accordance with the right dictates of his own conscience, and to profess his religion both in private and in public" (PT, 14). The phrase "the right dictates" with respect to the indications of conscience introduces a certain ambiguity into the formulation of the right.

The list of economic rights is augmented by the right "to engage in economic activities suited to his degree of responsibility" (PT, 20). Each of the rights proclaimed is accompanied by explanations which, in turn, point to additional rights and freedoms; socio-economic rights often act as guarantees of the exercise of civil and political freedoms.

Thus, natural human rights were presented by Pope John XXIII within the framework of a systematized theoretical model. Among its important distinctive features were: specific "dual argumentation" of human rights; the complex of human rights is presented as an integral phenomenon whose elements are inextricably connected; human rights are presented as a constitutive element of the social and State-law order; within the framework of conception of such an order human rights are combined with its moral duties; and significant importance is given to State and international guarantees of human rights.[5]

Pope John XXIII created a distinctive turning point in Catholic legal thought, recognized today by researchers virtually unanimously.[6] At this stage, first, an attempt was undertaken to

[5] S. Rabinovych, «Права людини і соціальна доктрина католицької церкви» [Human Rights and Social Doctrine of the Catholic Church], Вісник Академії правових наук України [Herald of Academy of Legal Sciences of Ukraine], no. 1 (2001), p. 167.

[6] A.-M. Baggio, «Християнське соціальне вчення: ідентичність та методологія» [Christian Social Doctrines: Identity and Methodology], Соціальна доктрина церкви: Зб. Статей [Social Doctrine of the Church: Collection of

contrast the fundamental principles of natural law with concrete historical conditions, and, second, the group of problems illuminated in social doctrine was expanded.[7] This fully emerged in the results of the II Vatican Conclave, rightly considered one of the major events of the twentieth century.[8]

On 2 October 1962 the General Congregation of the Conclave adopted a Message, "Ad universos homines", which said that God loved all (!) people and that this circumstance determines the relation of the church to the world, especially the poor, humiliated, and rejected.[9] This document, also touching upon problems of universal justice and peace, became a distinctive prototype for a truly grandiose act – the Pastoral Constitution on the Church in the Contemporary World "Gaudium et spes", approved by the Conclave on 7 December 1965. The analysis of soc ial problems in the Constitution rests on methodological principles which emerged as a result of a perception by the Catholic hierarchy of modernist theological-philosophical conceptions, especially existential personalism.[10]

Articles] (1998), p. 70; Iu. S. Pyvovarov, «Демократическая утопия социального христианства (Идеи и судьба непрочитанного классика католической мысли)» [Democratic Utopia of Social Christianity (Ideas and Fate of Unread Classic of Catholic Thought)], Политическая наука (1999 – 2). Проблема демократии в политической мысли XX столетия: Пробл.-темат. сб. [Political Science (1999-2). Problem of Democracy in Political Thought of the Twentieth Century: Problem-Thematic Collection] (1999), p. 103; B. A. Filippov, «Папы и проблемы прав человека» [Popes and Problems of Human Rights], Православие и католичество. Социальные аспекты: Пробл.-темат. сб. [Orthodoxy and Catholicism. Social Aspects: Problem-Thematic Collection] (1998), p. 210; A. A. Krasikov, «Религия и общество в Европе» [Religion and Society in Europe], Европа: вчера, сегодня, завтра [Europe: Yesterday, Today, Tomorrow] (2002), p. 124.

7 Iu. Maika, Социальное учение Католической церкви. Опыт исторического анализа [Social Doctrine of the Catholic Church. Experiment of Historical Analysis], transl. from Polish (1994), p. 452.

8 Kazanova, note 3 above, p. 9; K. Falconi, Ватиканский собор и причины его созыва [The Vatican Conclave and Reasons for Convoking It] (1964), p. 24; Pyvovarov, note 6 above, p. 103; J. Omenn, Христианская духовность в католической традиции [Christian Spirituality in the Catholic Tradition] (1994), pp. 354-355.

9 Maika, note 7 above, p. 391.

10 Among those observing this were: A. Bogomolov, V. Garadzha, B. Gubman, A. Krymskii, M. Korotkov, D. Hollenbach, F. Ovsienko. See F. Ovsienko, Эволюция социального учения католицизма: Философско– критический анализ [Evolution of Social Doctrine of Catholicism: Philosophical-Critical Analysis] (1987), p. 196; V. I. Garadzha, «Католический модернизм и неотомизм»

The Conclave confirmed the legal conception of Pope John XXIII, devoting special attention to human rights in nurturing, education, culture, and family life. The last, in addition to the Pastoral Constitution, found reflection in the Decree on the Media of Social Communications, "Inter Mirifica", of 4 December 1963; the right to religious freedom, in the Declaration on Religious Freedom, "Dignitas Humanae", of 7 December 1965; in the Declaration on the Relation of the Church to Non-Christian Religions, "Nostra Aetate", of 28 October 1965. An important innovation in "Nostra Aetate" was acknowledgement of violations of the right to religious freedom permitted by the Church in the past (NA, 4).

The Declaration on Religious Freedom contained a theological-anthropological substantiation prepared by the American theologian, John Courtney Murray, SJ (1904-1967), of the natural and civil right of man to religious freedom (DH, 2-8, 9-14). As noted in the literature, such a bold step in the history of the Church was unknown.[11]

The right of workers to strike in the event of extreme necessity became an important addition to the list of socio-economic rights recognized by Catholicism. Also meriting attention was consolidation of the principle that "If one is in extreme necessity, he has the right to procure for himself what he needs out of the riches of others" (GS, 69). These human rights were considered by

[Catholic Modernism and Neo-Thomism], in: A. Gaidis, et al. (eds.), Католицизм и современная идеологическая борьба [Catholicism and Contemporary Ideological Struggle] (1975), p. 171; N. D. Korotkov, «Модернистские тенденции в католическом социальном учении» [Modernist Trends in Catholic Social Doctrine], ibid., p. 165; David Hollenbach, *Claims in Conflict: Retrieving and Renewing the Catholic Human Rights Tradition* (1979), cited in D. Hollenbach, «Розвиток римо-католицької теорії прав людини» [Development of Roman Catholic Theory of Human Rights], in: Релігійна свобода і права людини: богословські аспекти [Religious Freedom and Human Rights: Theological Aspects] (2000), I, pp. 173-175; B. L. Gubman, Современная католическая философия: человек и история [Contemporary Catholic Philosophy: Man and History] (1987), p. 57.

[11] Krasikov, «По пути обновления Церкви и защиты прав человека. Новое прочтение документов II Ватиканского Собора» [En Route to Renewal of the Church and Protection of Human Rights. New Reading of the Documents of the II Vatican Conclave], Русская мысль [Russian Thought], 17 June 1999, p. 6; Hollenbach, note 10 above, pp. 177-179. It is worth noting that the Lateran Pacts of 1929 concluded between the Italian State and the Holy See continued in force; they provided that the sole religion of Italy is Catholic and introduced the study of this religion in State schools.

the Conclave within an evangelical person-centric approach: "the Sabbath was made for man, and not man for the Sabbath" (GS, 26).

As is evident from the foregoing, the doctrine of the Conclave consolidated the most important revolution in the entire history of the development of Catholic legal thought concerning the conception of inalienable and equal rights of all people. The direct manifestation thereof was the fact that since approximately the mid-twentieth century the category of human rights had become the "very heart of the social doctrine of the Church" (J. I. Calvez).[12] A number of Catholic commentators (J. Höffner, J.-M. Aubert, O. von Nell-Breuning, J. Maritain, J. Messner) drew attention not so much to the material changes which occurred in the legal ideology of Catholicism in the 1960s as in the identity of natural law and human rights in the doctrine of the Church.[13] Johannes Messner declared that "natural law is the totality of natural human rights, rooted in the man's moral responsibility for himself". Elsewhere he pointed out that "no ethical skepticism has as yet succeeded in showing that the moral conscience with its knowledge of original human rights, rooted in man's moral responsibilities, is merely a self-deception of the human mind".[14]

Such a position is correct from the standpoint of an analysis of the general philosophical-methodological precepts characteristic of Catholic law-comprehension. In and of itself, however, it does not an opportunity to analyze the evolution of what occurred in Catholic legal thought at the stage here considered nor an answer to the question of the substantive-conceptual foundations of these changes. In this respect the approach of Baggio is more fruitful; he points out that an openness of the traditional natural law to new

[12] Baggio, note 6 above, p. 69.

[13] J. Höffner, Християнське суспільне вчення [Christian Social Doctrines] (2002), pp. 65-75; J.-M. Ober, Моральне богослов□я [Moral Theology] (1997), p. 24; Jacques Maritain, "On the Philosophy of Human Rights", in: *Human Rights: Comments and Interpretations: A Sympsoium edited by UNESCO with an Introduction by Jacques Maritain* (1950), p. 73; Maritain, *Man and the State* (1951), pp. 80-107; Iu. S. Pyvovarov, Естественное право и социальная этика в XX столетии. Вводные замечания: Обзор [Natural Law and Social Ethics in the Twentieth Century. Introductory Comments: Survey], in: Право XX века: идеи и ценности [Law of the Twentieth Century: Ideas and Values] (2001), pp. 190-191.

[14] J. Messner, *Ethik: Kompendium der Gesamtethik* (1955), p.. 273; Messner, "Postwar Natural Law Revival and Its Outcome", *The Note* (1959) (Natural Law Forum. Paper 41) (available online).

elements is apparent in the Catholic conception of human rights.[15] He notes that the conception of human rights in the social doctrine of the Church is evidence of the development of the traditional theory of "natural law" at the expense of the component of historicity (dynamism), which indicates the *development* of man and, accordingly, the content of natural law – values and rights perceived by consciousness in the process of such development (italics added).

Commentators have expressed various views on the evolution of Catholic legal thought in the mid-twentieth century as to which elements of the Conclave conception of human rights should be considered to be the most significant.[16] On this issue it seems those commentators closest to the truth are those who emphasize the new character and content being acquired by natural law in the Conclave documents. Leist believed that the Catholic theory of law in the twentieth century accepted the idea of the "renaissance of natural law" being formed outside theology, as well as the "significantly expanded notion of the content of human rights and freedoms in the spirit of contemporary civilization". This became possible only thanks to the material renewal of the philosophy of neo-Thomism.[17]

Ovsienko notes that in the doctrine of the II Vatican Conclave the ideas of Pope John XXIII are developing so that natural law does not cease to be "uni-directional", although a "biological law" is predetermined by God.[18] Gubmen and Ovsienko emphasize the personalist character of the interpretation of natural law by the Conclave. In the view of neo-Thomist philosophers, this is achieved thanks to an emphasis on the special significance of the human conscience, "in the depths of which man discovers his right". Thanks to this, the emphasis is placed on the "active role of the individual in the establishment and even enrichment of the

15 Baggio, note 6 above, p. 76.

16 Kazanova, note 3 above, p. 246; Hollenbach, note 10 above, p. 170; Cz. Strzeszewski, *Katolicka nauka społeczna* (1994), p. 412; B. A. Filippov, note 6 above, p. 213.

17 O. E. Leist (ed.), История политических и правовых учений [History of Political and Legal Doctrines] (1997), p. 86.

18 Ovsienko, note 10 above, p. 123.

content of natural law".[19] One must concur that one may identify in the evolution of the Catholic conception of natural law as a whole a movement from the "naturalist" position towards a "personalist" one.[20] The reservation should be made, however, that it would be in principle incorrect to reduce the Catholic understanding of natural law to some purely "biological" naturalism, which, it seems, Chetvernin does.[21] Catholic "naturalism" is based on divinely revealed biblical grounds, in accordance with which all nature is the creation of God and is not merely a biological reality, autonomous as a whole with respect to the sphere of the transcendent but, on the contrary, a reality filled with the highest divinely revealed thought.

Thus, the first and determining distinctive feature of the legal conception of the Conclave is the personalism (theological person-centrism). The second characteristic feature of this conception is egalitarianism, which is rightly emphasized by the Polish commentator, T. Jaroszewski and the American, Ch. Curran: "'equality' does not mean, as before, just one equality of all people before the holy sacraments, God, and death; it now also acts as a requirement of equal chances to receive economic benefits and access to political life, culture, and education".[22]

The significance should be specially stressed of the substantive differences which Catholic doctrine has undergone concerning natural law in the period here considered. The argumentation based on an objectivist conception of the "natural order of things" is both a methodological means and an ideological instrument used for apologists of the existing socio-legal precepts.[23] Undertaking the transition to a conception of natural human rights

[19] Gubman, note 10 above, p. 176.

[20] Ovsienko, note 10 above, p. 123.

[21] V. A. Chetvernin, Современные концепции естественного права [Contemporary Conceptions of Natural Law] (1988), p. 33.

[22] T. Jaroszewski, *Личность и общество: проблемы личности в современной философии – марксизм, экзистенциализм, структурализм, христианский персонализм* [The Individual and Society: Problems of the Individual in Contemporary Philosophy – Marxism, Existentialism, Structuralism, and Christian Personalism](1973), pp. 347, 135, 354-355.

[23] Not only such secular commentators as L. Velikovich, A. Gaidis, M. Kowalski, M. Korotkov, and T. Jaroszewski indicate this, but also the Austrian theologians A. Knoll and J. Dobrensberger. See A. M. Knoll, *Katolishe Kirhe und Scholastisches Naturrecht* (1962), p. 169.

required an anthropocentric revolution in law-comprehension and recourse to the idea of the universal nature of man as an existential basis of the equal rights of all people. Taking this into account, it is noteworthy that during the tenure of Pope Pius XII (1876-1958), from 1939 to 1958, and especially during the tenure of Pope John XXIII from 1958 to 1963, the Catholic Church turned not so much to sociological ("natural order" of social relations) as to anthropological ("dignity of the human individual" and "nature of man") legal argumentation. As a consequence, this also became the substantiation by the Conclave of the "excluding any discrimination" of universal legal equality finding its fullest revelation in the conception of natural human rights.

The moral-theological substantiation of the full equality of all people was consistently elaborated by the Vatican during subsequent decades. In the Report provided by the Holy See to the United Nations Committee on the Elimination of Racial Discrimination in 2014 it was emphasized that:

> the Holy See promotes four fundamental principles: "1) The unique, divine, origin of mankind postulates unity between all men so that no one is alien to the creative design of God; 2) The brotherhood which exists between all members of the human family, created by the Father in His own image and redeemed by the Son, is ontological in nature; 3) It is this particular bond which gives rise to the eminent dignity of human nature, both in the person and in the species, and it is on this dignity that individual and collective rights and duties are founded; 4) The natural equality of all human beings with respect to their dignity implies an absolute rejection of discrimination, which would be an offence to the fundamental rights of the person.[24]

The equal dignity of every human being and the rejection of any form of racism and racial discrimination is founded on a transcendent basis:

[24] CERD/C/118/Add.11, p. 5, citing "The Holy See and the International Convention on the Elimination of All Forms of Racial Discrimination", in L'Osservatore Romano, 1 May 1969. See: Committee on the Elimination of Racial Discrimination. Consideration of reports, submitted by States parties under article 9 of the Convention Sixteenth to twenty-third periodic reports of States parties due in 2014. Holy See, p. 15.

> Since something of the glory of God shines on the face of every person, the dignity of every person before God is the basis of the dignity of man before other men ... [it]is the ultimate foundation of the radical equality and brotherhood among all people, regardless of their race, nation, sex, origin, culture, or class (Compendium §144).

The said document referred to the preceding positions of the Vatican. In 2011 the Holy See declared that "the Church rejects racism in any form as a denial of the image of the Creator inherent in every human being... From this common origin in fact, stems a common destiny of humanity that should inspire in one and all a strong sense of solidarity and responsibility".[25] In that same year, the Holy See stressed that "racism is a sin. It is fundamentally a lie" and "creates division in humanity".[26]

During the 1960s, as a result of the second wave of national-liberation movements, a number of new States emerged which had, as did the majority of countries in the Third World, a weak economy. As a result, economic and cultural inequality between States and peoples intensified in the contemporary world.

Attempting to resolve "the social question [that] ties all men together, in every part of the world",[27] Pope Paul VI (1897-1978), having replaced Pope John XXIII during the work of the II Vatican Conclave, concentrated on two main themes: first, on the idea of building a genuinely humane "civilization of love" and, second, the elimination of socio-economic under-development of countries of the "Third World". Both themes he addressed in the encyclical "Populorum progressio", of 26 March 1967, where he spoke of the development of the individual person in the context of the development of the "whole family of man". The human right to the creation of social conditions for man's complete development is the basic right underlying the consideration of social questions in the encyclical.[28]

[25] Statement of the Holy See at OSCE/SHDM, 10 November 2011. Ibid., p. 16.

[26] Ibid., p. 16.

[27] The official French version of the encyclical opens under the rubric: "La question sociale est aujourd'hui mondiale".

[28] In French, "un développement intégral de l'homme". See also: Ludovic Bertina, "The Catholic Doctrine of 'Integral Human Development' and its Influence on the International Development Community", *International*

The Catholic conception of private ownership was further developed in the "Repolorum progressio". This encyclical most precisely in comparison with other church documents set out the view of the need to limit the right of private ownership and pointed to the moral substantiation of the nationalization of objects of this right. One must agree with Jaroszewski that such desacralization of the right of ownership became a distinctive "return to the sources" – to the biblical conception of the universal purpose of earthly goods.[29]

The crisis phenomena iin the early 1970s (energy and financial crisis, crisis of traditional political institutions, in turn clearly demonstrated crisis of values based on an "uncritical faith in science and "uncritical faith in science and the progress of civilization" (B. Filippov) created new favorable conditions both for the activity of the Church as a whole and for drafting the Catholic Church problematic of human rights.[30] In 1974 Pope Paul VI declared that relations of mutual permissiveness should exist between the evangelization of the world and human progress: human rights were deemed by the Pope to be a task not contrary to the evangelization of the world.[31]

A consequence of the new situation both throughout the world and in the Catholic Church itself were the documents "De iustitia in mundo" and "The Church and Human Rights", adopted respectively by a Synod of Bishops in 1971 and by a Pontifical Commission "iustitia et pax" in 1974, and also by an Apostolic Appeal of Pope Paul VI of 8 December 1975, "Evangelii nuntiandi".

Development Policy, no. 4 (2013) (available online). Contemporary commentators note that «development» serves as the denominator for the philosophical and theological concept of "life". See Iu. Chernomorets, Учение о любви – фундамент социального учения папы Бенедикта XVI [Doctrine on Love – Foundation of Social Doctrine of Pope Benedict XVI], in: Религиозно-информационная служба Украины [Religious Information Service of Ukraine], 24 April 2010 (available online).

29 Jaroszewski, «Изменения в социальной доктрине Ватикана и социальные проблемы современности» [Changes in Social Doctrine of the Vatican and Social Problems of Today], in: Katolicysm'77: Сборник статей [*Katolicysm'77*: Collection of Articles] (1977) p. 44.

30 Filippov, note 6 above, p. 214.

31 G. A. Gal'tseva, «Католическая панорама» [Catholic Panorama], in: Социальные идеи христианства в XX веке: Сборник обзоров [Social Ideas of Christianity in the Twentieth Century: Collection of Surveys] (1989), p. 19.

The document "De iustitia in mundo" was a contribution to the further development of the Catholic doctrine on human rights. The Synod expressed the inter-connectedness of all human rights by using the "right to participation" and the "right to development". The last was defined by the Synod as "a dynamic interpenetration of all those fundamental human rights upon which the aspirations of individuals and nations are based".

The document "The Church and Human Rights" (1974) not only formulated for the first time the fullest systematized catalogue of human rights in social doctrine, but also proclaimed that the Church extended its activity to the defense of Christianity throughout the human community in order to defend the rights of each person. Moreover, the Fathers of the Synod declared that henceforth the Catholic Church sees as its primary task the nurturing of the people of the entire world in an awareness of their inalienable rights and in the protection thereof against any forms of violation.

Thus, the Conclave and post-Conclave stages of the development of Catholic legal thought were noteworthy for these distinctive features:

(1) the anthropological revolution ("natural social order" cedes place to the "nature of man");

(2) man and his rights are deemed to be the basis, the cause, and the purpose of the activity of all social structures; the principle of egalitarianism extends to all spheres of social relations;

(3) the conception of natural human rights becomes the heart of social doctrine of the Church;

(4) the scale of the consideration of human rights (idea of "civilization of love" of Pope Paul VI) is globalized;

(5) freedom is deemed to be one of the grounds the Christian social system (Pope John XXIII, II Vatican Conclave), which makes dialogue of the Church possible with opposition doctrinal trends; religious freedom also is recognized and doctrinally substantiated;

(6) the catalogue of human rights and the systematization and codification thereof is further expanded in individual documents: "Pacem in terris" (1963) and "The Church and Human Rights" (1974);

(7) the conception of "development" is elaborated (II Vat ican Conclave, Pope Paul VI) and "participation" (Synod of

Bishops, 1971), as system-forming principles, integral objects and purposes of the exercise of human rights; the Christianological argumentation is deepened of human rights and the philosophical-anthropological basis of this argumentation is expanded, which becomes methodological instrumentation of existentialism (G. Marsel), philosophical anthropology, phenomenology, Christian evolutionism (M. Sheler, P. Teilhard de Chardin), Catholic social personalism (J. Maritain, E. Mounier), and existential hermeneutics. The traditional rationalist natural-law argumentation recedes to the second plane comparatively with biblical argumentation;[32]

(8) the dynamic historico-conceptual approach for the consideration of the social conditions for the realization of human rights (II Vatican Conclave).[33]

According to the commentators, the tenure as Pope of John Paul XXIII commenced in a period of the most "profound crisis" in which the Church and the Papacy had ever been.[34] The historical circumstances of that time were characterized by the growth of political tension between East and West and the intensification of world socio-economic contradictions (economic chasm between North and South). In this period the further elaboration of methods of psychological impact on the mass consciousness in combination with information-technological progress made possible the manipulation of man on a large scale. Such a multi-aspectual interlinkage of mankind received the name "globalization", one of whose major features becomes the threat of universal dehumanization. These circumstances explain why the anthropological problematic was constantly in the center of attention of Pope John Paul XXIII.

The distinctive features of Pope Paul II's doctrine on human rights may be adequately understood by taking into account the philosophical-methodological grounds of his doctrine

[32] Gubman, note 10 above, p. 181; A. A. Radugin, «Модернистские тенденции в послесоборной католической теологии» [Modernist Trends in Post-Conclave Catholic Theology], in: Эволюция идей II Ватианского собора [Evolution of Ideas of the II Vatican Conclave] (1987), pp. 59-60; V. Serhiyko, «Проблеми розвитку соціального вчення католицизму» [Problems of Development of Social Doctrine of Catholicism], Українське релігієзнавство [Ukrainian Science of Religion] (1999), pp. 58-64; B. Sutor, *Politische Ethik. Gesamtdarstellung auf der Basis der Christlichen Gesellschaftslehre* (1991), p. 350.

[33] Jaroszewski, note 29 above, p. 45.

[34] Filippov, note 6 above, p. 207.

on man. While still a young theologian, Wojtyla elaborated a line commenced by Pope Pius XII and Pope John XXIII on the subjectivization of the Catholic social ethic with, however, the essential distinction that the future Pope expressly recognized the inadequacy of classical Thomism as the philosophical foundation for a genuinely personalist conception of man.[35] Therefore, the worldview-methodological basis of the social doctrine of Pope John Paul II is characterized as Christian personalism combined with the extensive use of the achievements of existentialism, phenomenology, structuralism, and philosophical anthropology.[36] In this context Wojtyla's works "Love and Responsibility" (1962), "Participation or Alienation?" (1975), "The Individual and the Act" (1969), and "Subjectivity and the 'Irreducible' in Man" (1994).[37]

The theological-legal positions of Pope John Paull II and especially views on human rights in the most systematized form were set out in encyclicals issued under his signature: "Laborem exercens" (14 September 1981), issued on the ninetieth anniversary of "Rerum Novarum"; "Sollicitudo rei socialis" (30 December 1987), issued on the twentieth anniversary of the encyclical "Popularum progressio"; and the encyclical "Contesimus annus" (1 May 1991), issued on the hundredth anniversary of "Rerum Novarum".

The encyclical "Laborem Exercens" is devoted to human labor in the context of new technologies and economic and political conditions. Pope Johnn Paul II believed that human labor is "no doubt the basic key to the entire social question". The Pope proclaimed in this document the principle of the priority of labor over capital, appealing to the categorical opposition noted by the existential philosopher, Gabriel Marcel (1889-1973). Pope John Paul II insisted that internal justice and equity might be only that

[35] K. Wojtyła, *Ocena możliwości zbudowania etyki chrześciańskiej przy załozeniach systemu Maxa Schelera* (1959), pp. 5-12.

[36] M. Novachik, Социальная мысль К. Войтылы [Social Thought of K. Wojtyła], Современный католицизм [Contemporary Catholicism] (1982), p. 34.

[37] Wojtyła, «Суб'єктність і «те, що не піддається редукції» в людині» [Subjectivity and the 'Irreducible' in Man], in: Досвід людської особи: Нариси з філософської антропології [Experience of the Human Individual: Essays from Physical Anthropology] (2000), pp. 19–29; Wojtyła, «Участь чи відчуження?» [Participation or Alienation?], ibid., pp. 245–259; John Paul II, «Фрагменты из трактата «Любовь и ответственность» [Fragments from the Treatise «Love and Responsibility»], in: John Paul II, Мысли о земном [Thoughts on the Earth] (1992), pp. 5-23; Wojtyła, *Osoba i czyn oraz inne studia antropologiczne* (1994); Wojtyła, note 35 above.

system of labor is which the antimony between labor and capital is overcome.[38] In addition to the universal purpose of earthly goods, in the conception of Pope John Paul II the right of ownership is juxtaposed also to the universal right to work inasmuch as only through labor can man enter into the possession of the right of ownership of earthly goods. The restrictive understanding of the right of ownership by the Pope especially concerned ownership of the means of production. Pope John Paul II insisted on the need to review "artificial and static conceptions of ownership and the imparting of a dynamic character to them".[39]

The Encyclical of Pope John Paul II "Centesimus annus" expressed the most mature and contemporary view on the social doctrine of the Catholic Church. This document, according to the Ukrainian religious specialist P. L. Iarots'kyi, is a distinctive "Papal requiem to Marxism, communism, and socialism".[40] With regard to human rights, principal attention in the Encyclical is devoted to the social purpose of the right of ownership and the socio-economic rights of workers and rights to the creation of private associations, thanks to which the "subjectification" of society occurs. The Pontiff reminds us of the Christian duty to share our "surpluses" with others and, in certain instances, even "vital necessities". The Pope also defined the moral duties of owners with regard to choosing the spheres for placing their capital. The "Centesimus annus" relegated to the fundamental human rights: the right to life; the right to live in an amiable atmosphere enabling the development of own personality; the right to bring to maturity one's reason and

[38] A. A. Radugin, «Модернистские тенденции в послесоборной католической теологии» [Modernist Trends in Post-Conclave Catholic Theology], Эволюция идей II Ватиканского собора [Evolution of Ideas of the II Vatican Conclave] (1987), p. 92.

[39] G. Baum, «Приоритет труда: Комментарий к энциклике папы Иоанна Павла II «Лаборем экзерценс»» [Priority of Labor: Commentaries on the Encyclical of John Paul II «Laborem exercens»], Социально-этические проблемы в религиозном правосознании [Socio-Ethical Problems in Religious Legal Consciousness] (1987), pp. 152-156; Ovsienko, Критический анализ католической теологии труда [Critical Analysis of Catholic Theology of Labor] (1984), pp. 55-58; V. Osipov, «Христианство и проблемы собственности: Статьи» [Christianity and Problems of Ownership: Articles], Наш современник [Our Contemporary], no. 12 (1990), p. 165.

[40] P. L. Iarots'kyi, «Соціальна доктрина католицизму (на матеріалах папських енциклік 1892 – 1992 pp.)» [Social Doctrine of Catholicism (On Materials of Papal Encyclicals 1892-1992)], Філософська і соціологічна думка [Philosophical and Sociological Thought], no. 12 (1992), p. 73.

freedom in quests for cognition of truth; the right to participate in labor processes in order to properly value the goods of earth and create from them everything necessary for maintaining oneself and near ones; the right to freely create a family, not prevent the birth of children, with responsibility for manifesting sexuality; the right to nurture children.

Religious freedom is named as the foundation for all human rights. The Encyclical also defined the general ethical-economic and politico-legal prerequisites of a Christian social structure: a society of free labor, entrepreneurship, and creative activeness of man in an economy in which freedom is "placed in a reliable legal context of genuine democracy" possible "only in a rule-of-law" State and on the basis of a true conception of the individual. The rule-of-law State, in turn, provides for the principle of separation of powers.41 In the view of the Pope, though, all the said prerequisites, although essential, are insufficient to ensure human rights, possible only en route to radical moral renewal of the individuals and communities. The Pope believed that the source of replenishing the social question with moral thought is his own spiritual religious contemplation.42

Thus, in the substantiation of human rights by Pope John Paul II a Christological theological approach dominates expressively. This is especially because of the requirement of contemporary Catholicism for self-identification – a requirement especially needed in the post-Conclave period.[43] In addition, as Gaidis noted, the "references of John Paul II to the historical personality of Jesus Christ give the Church in its struggle for man and his rights possibilities which in their concreteness and fullness are impossible to achieve with the assistance of argumentation based on "natural law": the natural-law base concerns super-temporal "essentialia"

[41] This principle, however, is proclaimed by the Pope only as a wish, possibly because the Basic Law of the Vatican provides that the Pope as the supreme head of the Vatican city-State possesses the full plenitude of legislative, executive, and judicial power (Article 1). See La nuovo Legge fundamentale dello Stata della Cittá del Vaticano.

[42] T. Borutka, J. Mazur, and A. Zwoliński, *Katolicka nauka społeczna* (1999), pp. 170-171.

[43] K. G. Ballestrem, «Церковь и демократическая культура: проблемы адаптации и конфликты» [The Church and Democratic Culture: Problems of Adaptation and Conflicts], Вопросы философии [Questions of Philosophy], no. 1 (2002), p. 76.

and, at the same time, "minimalia", the social minimum of joint human life. And with the assistance of a theological-Christocentric argumentation the Church is attempting at a new level to manage human life, to act as a teacher and vanguard on issues of human rights.[44] Speaking in Kyiv on 24 June 2001 at a meeting with representatives of the All-Ukrainian Council of Churches and Religious Organizations, Pope John Paul II turned to the conception of theo-centric humanism of Paul VI.[45] The Pope observed that the defense of human rights "emanates from the Gospels" where the truth is contained that Christ is in a determined way connected with each person (Gaudium et spes).

The Catechism of the Catholic Church promulgated by the Pope (§1955) set out the traditional elements of the Catholic teaching in the renewed post-Conclave interpretation. It is asserted in particular that the Decalogue reflects the basic tenets of natural law. Turning to Christian revelation, the Pope endeavored not only to substantiate individual human rights, but also to confirm that alternatives to a religious path of ensuring these rights does not exist.

Family relations are a sphere of operation of natural law engaging the primary attention of Pope John Paul II. The special significance imparted to human rights in these relations is attested by a number of church documents: the V Ecumenical Assembly of the Synod of Bishops (26 September-25 October 1980) on the subject "Mission of the Family in the Modern World"; such acts of Pope Johnn Paul II as the Apostolic Exhortation "Familiaris consortio" (22 November 1980); the Apostolic Letter Mulieris Dignitatem (15 August 1988); the Letter "To Families Gratissimam Sane" (2 February 1994); the Letter to Children in the Year of the Family (13 December 1994); the Letter to Women (29 June 1995); the Letter to the Elderly (1 October 1999); and others. It should be recalled that the Charter of the Rights of the Family was proclaimed by Apostolic Letter (22 October 1983); and documents of the

[44] Gaidis, Католический клерикальный антикоммунизм: критический анализ философской и социально-политической проблематики [Catholic Clerical Anti-Communism: Critical Analysis of Philosophical and Socio-Political Problematik] (1982), p. 173.

[45] Промови і проповіді, виголошені Святішим Отцем під час візиту на Україну 23–27 червня 2001 року [Speeches and Sermons Delivered by the Holy Father During a Visit to Ukraine on 23-27 June 2001], Агенція Релігійної інформації [Religious Information Agency], no. 6 (2001), p. 27.

Pontifical Council for the Family: "Truth on Human Sexuality and its Essence" (8 October 1995); "Preparation for the Sacrament of Marriage" (13 May 1996); and "Family, Marriage, and 'De Facto' Unions (20 July 2000).

Together with religious freedom, fundamental is the right to life in the human rights conception of Pope John Paul II. We note that life is regarded as an all-embracing program appearing as a path to a "civilization of love" (Paul VI) and, in turn, contrasted to a "civilization of death".[46] Considering this right in a bio-ethical aspect, the Pope defined the content thereof as the right of a person to develop in the womb of the mother after conception, the right to birth, and then to existence until a natural death (CA, 46). In the Encyclical "Evangelium vitae" (25 March 1995), Pope John Paul II declared that the "direct and voluntary homicide of an innocent human existence always is profoundly immoral" and affirmed the succession of the bio-ethical positions of the Church set out previously by Paul VI and the Congregation of Faith – the absolute inadmissibility of performing an abortion, euthanasia, and suicide.

It should, however, be noted that the right to life as treated by Pope John Paul II has certain limits. The Pope did not exclude the possibility in principle of depriving a person of life in a situation of self-defense or the application of the death penalty by States (EV, 55).

On 26 November 2001 the Holy See in a communique decisively condemned experiments conducted in the United States to clone a person, pointing to the "inhumanity of laboratory reprogramming of the nucleus of a cell for the purpose of obtaining a new individual". Thus, the Catholic Church today upholds the human right to a natural means of birth.[47]

In the Apostolic Letters "Tertio millenio aveniente" (10 November 1994) and "Novo millennio ineunte" (6 January 2001) the "Smiling Pope" suggested to acknowledge repentance through

[46] Filippov, note 6 above, p. 219.

[47] Релігійна панорама [Religious Panorama], no. 4 (2000), p. 29. We note that several international legal documents adopted by the European Union also prohibit the cloning of a human. See the Convention for the Protection of Human Rights and Dignity of the Human Being with Regard to the Application of Biology and Medicine (ETS No 164), opened for signature on 4 April 1997 in Oviedo (Spain).

the Vatican Conclave by the Catholic Church for sins against human rights committed by it in the past.

Specialists in the modern development of Catholic legal thought single out different aspects of Pontificate doctrine as the most important. The Swiss theologian, Patrick de Laubier, believes that the distinctive contribution of Pope John Paul II to the social doctrine of the Church was the ascertainment of a link of principle between the philosophical approach (human rights) and the "light of Revelation" (biblical ideals) in an eschatological context.[48] In the view of an American theologian, N. Novak, the most important points in which John Paul II went beyond the existing framework of legal doctrine were to consider freedom as a "basic category of the social doctrine of the Church together with justice in the world; emphasis on the role of democracy as an essential condition of genuine development, the high assessment of law for economic initiative and accentuating the significance in principle of religious freedom".[49] The Catholic social doctrine was becoming open for dialogue with liberalism recognizing eternal Christian values,[50] to democracy as a State regime creating conditions for observance of human rights within the framework of a conception of an "objective moral order".[51] Filippov, in describing the approach of Pope John Paul II to human rights, attached key importance to the right to life and the "spirit of initiative" as an immutable condition of human development.[52]

The diversity of views cited can be summed up in the conclusion that at present the legal conception of the Catholic Church has the following distinctive features:

[48] P. de Laubier, Столетие христианского социального учения: от Льва XIII до Иоанна-Павла II [A Century of Christian Social Doctrine: From Leo XIII to John Paul II] (transl. from French; available online).

[49] N. Novak, *Liberalizm – Sprzymierzeniec czy wróg kościoła? Nauczanie społeczne Kościoła a institucje liberalne* (1993), p. 227.

[50] M. Zięba, "Kościoł wobec liberalnej demokracji", in: *Chrzescijańименно, demokracja, kapitalizm* (1993), pp. 113-155.

[51] Samuel P. Huntington, "Religion and the Third Wave", *The National Interest*, no. 24 (Summer 1991), pp. 29-42; J. Bryan Hehir. Catholicism and Democracy: Conflict, Change, and Collaboration", in: John Witte (ed.), *Christianity and Democracy In Global Context* (1993).

[52] Filippov, note 6 above, pp. 220-221.

(1) the category of human rights is acquiring the most multi-dimensional and extensive application during the existence of the social doctrine of the Church;

(2) the combination of spiritual (religious-moral) and institutional (socio-economic and politico-legal) is being proposed as a social mechanism for the realization of human rights through a renewal of society: ecumenical on one hand, and "proper" capitalism, democracy, and rule-of-law State, on the other;

(3) serious significance is being devoted to the principle of freedom as one of the major existential grounds of human rights;

(4) the right to religious freedom is recognized as the basis of the other human rights;

(5) the conception of socio-economic rights is developing;

(6) in addition to the universal purposes of earthly goods, the right of ownership in the conception of Pope John Paul II aalso confronts the right to work;

(7) the further subjectification of the conceptual grounds of natural-law doctrine is occurring;

(8) the theological Christological argumentation of human rights is being actively elaborated;

(9) the existential-phenomenological approach is being extensively used, on one hand, and socio-economic analysis, on the other;[53]

(10) human rights are contemplated in a synthetic ethical-axiological key on the basis of the priority of religious-spiritual values over material. Pope John Paul II substantiated these rights not so much in *lex naturalis* as in *lex divinae*, and in their specific human individual and transcendent essence.[54]

Thus, commencing in the 1960s the Catholic conception of human rights became in essence a personalist (subject-centric) reinterpretation of the Thomist theory of natural law traditional for Catholicism. Both natural law and human rights act as normative moral-legal formations. Whereas, however, the first is

[53] B. Kuzmitskas, Философские концепции католического модернизма [Philosophical Conceptions of Catholic Modernism] (1982), pp. 126-151.

[54] John Paul II, Закон божественный и человеческий [Divine and Human Law], Российская юстиция [Russian Justice], no. 3 (2001), p. 58.

treated as the objectification of a "natural" social order, human rights are interpreted as the manifestation of the individual nature of man and his supranatural divine dignity. It is evident that the Catholic conception of human rights testifies to a subjectification of a natural law in which the individual principle is emphasized.[55]

We dwell briefly on an analysis of the positions in the literature on the reasons for the evolution considered herein of Catholic jusnaturalism. The following groups of approaches may be singled out: (a) recognition of the dominant influence of "internal" doctrinal and "ecclesiastical"-praxiological factors (Hehir, de Laubier); (b) institutional requirements and interests of the Catholic Church in concrete-historical social conditions (conception of "adaptation") – Gubman, Curran, Mal'tsev, Ovsienko, Jaroszewski, Filippov);[56] (c) evenness of "internal" requirements and "external" – socio-political factors (Hollenbach).

The approach suggested by Hehir rests, not obviously, on a distinctive methodological tautology.

The aforesaid position of de Laubier, Maika, Mazurek, and Ianetski[57] demonstrates an insufficient objectivity in the approach to the problem caused, in our view, by a certain engagement in the protection of the institutional interests of the Catholic Church. The view proposed by Hollenbach, although it refers to those factors which it seems actually influenced the development of Catholic legal thought, unjustifiably equates their significance, leading to a single list of "political events, economic realities, ideological

[55] Rabinovych, note 5 above, p. 166.

[56] Gubman, note 10 above; G. V. Mal'tsev, Понимание права. Подходы и проблемы [Comprehension of Law: Approaches and Problems] (1999); Ovsienko, note 10 above; T. Jaroszewski, Личность и общество: проблемы личности в современной философии – марксизм, экзистенциализм, структурализм, христианский персонализм [The Individual and Society: Problems of the Individual in Contemporary Philosophy – Marxism, Existentialism, Structuralism, Christian Personalism] (1973); C. Curran, Релігійна свобода і права людини у світі та церкві: християнська перспектива [Religious Freedom and Human Rights in the World and the Church], Релігійна свобода і права людини: богословські аспекти [Religious Freedom and Human Rights: Theological Aspects] (2000), I, pp. 342-370.

[57] P. Ianetski, Правы чалавека ў грамадскім вучэнні каталіцкай царквы [Human Rights and Social Doctrine of the Catholic Church], Адкрытае грамадства. Інфармацыйна-аналітычны бюлетэнь [An Open Society: Informational-Analytical Bulletin], no. 1 (1999), p. 16.

conflicts, and institutional interests of the Church itself".[58] No doubt the concrete interests of the Church as a participant of ideological conflicts changed, depending on political events and economic realities. Therefore, most convincing seems to be the position explaining the reasons for the evolution of the legal doctrine of Catholicism which rests on socio-historical and requirement approaches.

In the context of a historical survey of the evolution of Catholic natural-law thought it is advisable to also consider the influence of "human rights" doctrine of Catholicism on the socio-political practice of the twentieth century. As was shown above, until the tenure of Pope Pius XII, from 1939 to 1958, Catholicism was in ideological opposition to political and civil rights and freedoms. The full theoretical recognition by Catholicism of the "secular" conception of human rights reflected in the 1948 Universal Declaration of Human Rights comes during the tenure of John XXIII and the II Vatican Conclave, from 1958 to 1965. As for the real introduction of the human rights doctrine proclaimed by the Church, it should be noted that the practice of catholic churches in individual regions of the world where authoritarian political regimes ruled (Spain, Portugal, Latin America) continued to be contrary to this doctrine almost until the 1970s. An analysis of the literature on this issue enables the conclusion of a general positive influence of Catholicism on the development of the social State and a civil society in the postwar Federal Republic of Germany and Austria, on the course of democratization processes during the 1970-80s in Europe and in South and Central America (Chile, Argentina, Brazil, Dominican Republic, El Salvador, Guatemala, Panama, and Paraguay), Eastern Asia (South Korea and Philippines), and Republic of South Africa.

Individual commentators (Auer, Rauscher, Kerber, Mazurek) point to the interconnection between legal thought of postwar Germany and Austria and the social doctrine of German and Austrian Catholicism.[59] This is explained on one hand, by the specific nature of the historical fates of Germany and Austria and,

[58] Hollenbach, note 10 above, p. 191.

[59] Pyvovarov, note 6 above, pp. 186-189; F. J. Mazurek, "Integralnie rozumiane prawa człowieka podstawą personalistycznego porządku gospodarczego", *Zeszyty Naukowe KUL*, nos. 1-2 (1996), p. 53.

on the other, by distinctive features of German-Austrian Catholic social doctrine.

The interlinkage between Catholicism and the democratic movements of the 1970-80s is considered by such authors as Huntington, Hehir, and de Laubier. Huntington noted that after 1970 Catholicism, thanks to changes within the Church, was transformed into a moving force of democracy. Approximately three-quarters of the countries moved on to democracy between 1979 and 1989, among them Portugal, Spain, Poland, Hungary which were Catholic.[60]

Huntington, Hehir, de Laubier, and Mazurek also cite evidence for confirmation of the influence of Catholicism on the movement for human rights in South America. Mazurek, referring to many commentators, noted the activeness in defending rights by the Catholic Church in the post-Conclave period: the addresses of Paul VI and John Paul II during international visits, the activities of local Latin American churches, especially anti-totalitarian statements of the Bishop conferences in Medellin (1968) and Pueblo (1979), and the creation of social organizations and movements for the protection of rights in Chile, Peru, Bolivia, and Brazil.[61] Moreover, he cited other facts in confirmation of the political activeness of the Holy See in the protection of human rights in Europe and the world. During the tenure of Paul VI, the Papal Curia began to collaborate with many international intergovernmental organizations. The delegate of the Vatican took part in drafting the Final Act of the OSCE, submitting a proposal to consolidate in that document the principle of respect for human rights and the obligations of parties to the Act to guarantee the right to religious freedom to religious communities and individuals. Mazurek relegated to activity relating to the protection of human rights the signature by the Vatican on 26 June 1972 of the non-proliferation treaty.[62]

We note, however, that on the whole the practical activity of the Catholic Church in defending human rights during the tenure of Paul VI was evaluated variously in the literature. Ladyvirova observed that Paul VI, although he "did not make a material

[60] Huntington, note 51 above.

[61] Mazurek, *Prawa człowieka w nauczaniu społecznym Kościoła (od papieża Leona XIII do papieża Jana Pawła II)* (1991), p. 277.

[62] Ibid., p. 271.

contribution to the theoretical elaboration of human rights but perceiving them as an integral part of the struggle for peace and justice, actively favored their observance".[63]

Filippov adhered to a different position, pointing out that Paul VI, who signed the documents of the II Vatican Conclave and sanctioned the decisions of the Synods and the "Iustitia et Pax" Commissions, nonetheless did little to defend human rights in practice.[64] This last view, however, is based, it seems, primarily on a narrow-practical approach to the defense of human rights, underestimating the power of this identical and specific spiritual and pastoral mission of the Holy See on one hand, and the special significance of natural law on life from the moment of conception upheld by Paul VI, on the other.

In our view, one should agree with Kovalskii and Ivanova that the position of the Vatican testifies to support for the pan-European process, although, of course, the Church favored ensuring security and cooperation on the continent, considering these problems through the prism of its specific interests.[65] On the whole, it seems, with regard to the vitality of the social doctrine of Catholicism in the economically-developed countries of Europe the assessment of the French historian, Thibaud, is illustrative; he was skeptical in evaluating the influence of the Christian values propagated by the Catholic Church on the contemporary "consumer" society.[66]

As for Pope John Paul II, according to the unanimous testimony of commentators, this period is distinguished by the greatest activism of Catholicism in the human rights movement.[67] This is

[63] S. Ladyvirova, Проблеми та тенденції розвитку соціальної доктрини католицької церкви [Problems and Trends in the Development of the Social Doctrine of the Catholic Church], Права людини в Україні [Human Rights in Ukraine] (1996), XV, p. 25.

[64] Filippov, note 6 above, p. 216.

[65] N. A. Kovalskii and I. M. Ivanova, Католицизм и международные отношения [Catholicism and International Relations] (1989), p. 202.

[66] P. Thibaud, Релігія прав людини [Religion of Human Rights], "Ї". – Незалежний культурологічний часопис, no. 21 (2001), p. 269.

[67] Huntington, note 51 above; Hehir, note 51 above; Krasikov, note 6 above; Laubier, Три града. Социальное учение христианства [Three Cities. Social Doctrine of Christianity] (2000); Filippov, «Иоанн Павел II» [John Paul II], Вопросы истории [Questions of History], no. 3 (1993), pp. 49-67; Mazurek, note 61 above.

confirmed especially by the data cited above on the significance of the papal visits to countries in which democratic transformations occurred. Huntington, Hehir, and de Laubier emphasize the "Catholic" democratization significance of the visits of John Paul II to Poland in 1979 to 1987.[68] During his addresses and speeches at the United Nations and other international organizations and during trips to various countries John Paul II constantly had recourse to urgent problems of the protection of human rights and set for local churches the task of propagandizing these rights among the population. Thus, the Pope's Message for the World Day of Peace on 1 January 2002 was a distinctive answer to the terrorist acts in New York on 11 September 2001. In that document the Pope declared that the right to self-defense against terrorism, just as any other, should be consistent with the moral and legal rules when choosing both the purposes and the means. On 24 February 2002 the Pope appealed to all heads of State and governments with a Letter "Ten Commandments. The Decalogue of Assisi for Peace", which contained the obligation of the Church to "stand in defense of those who suffer need and deprivation, stand up for the disenfranchised, take concrete steps to prevent any injustices, being guided by the conviction that no one may be happy in isolation".

A detailed and multi-dimensional socio-philosophical and theological elaboration of "human rights" issues of protecting the entire human environment – natural and social – was set out in the "ecological" Encyclical of Francis, "Laudato Si", in 2015. The distinctive features of this document are illustrated by the logical meaning of the structure of the Encyclical as reflected in the titles of its chapters:

Chapter one. What is happening to our common home;
Chapter two. The Gospel of creation;
Chapter three. The human roots of the ecological crisis;
Chapter four. Integral ecology;
Chapter five. Lines of approach and action;
Chapter six. Ecological education and spirituality.

Especially illustrative of the distinctive features of the papal approach to ecological issues in the Encyclical is chapter four on

[68] Huntington, note 51 above; Laubier, note 48 above, pp. 183, 218-223; Hehir, note 51 above, p. 213; Laubier, note 67 above, pp. 220, 248.

"integral ecology", which identifies the problems of ecology in inextricable interaction with the various spheres of their emergence – the environment, economy, and social spheres:

> When we fail to acknowledge as part of reality the worth of a poor person, a human embryo, a person with disabilities – to offer just a few examples – it becomes difficult to hear the cry of nature itself; everything is connected (LS, 117). Human ecology also implies another profound reality: the relationship between human life and the moral law, which is inscribed in our nature and is necessary for the creation of a more dignified environment (LS, 155).

Turning to Saint Francis of Assisi, the Pope propagated the idea of love and an attitude of care towards everything living, worshiping life as a Divine creation. The idea of mankind as a universal community and universal purpose of earth's goods substantiate a requirement for "justice between generations" (idea of Paul VI), limitation and self-limitation of consumption, subordination of the interests of transnational business to ensuring the rights of the poorest countries and peoples and eliminating the existing global inequality.

Speaking of the environment as "rather than a problem to be solved", Pope Francis avers that "the world is a joyful mystery to be contemplated with gladness and praise". Pope Francis echoes the pastoral call for "a global ecological conversion":

> Christian spirituality proposes an alternative understanding of the quality of life, and encourages a prophetic and contemplative lifestyle, one capable of deep enjoyment free of the obsession with consumption. (LS, 222). An adequate understanding of spirituality consists in filling out what we mean by peace, which is much more than the absence of war (LS, 225).

From Conception of Just War to Principle of Non-Coercion: Evolution of Catholic Approaches to Law of War and Peace

The development of the law-comprehension of the Catholic Church in the twentieth and twenty-first centuries is starkly represented on issues of the law of war and peace. On these issues the social doctrine of Catholicism is evolving from the traditional doctrine of the just war in the direction of a position of active non-coercion. The specific link of the Catholic ethic of war with problems of philosophy of law is traced through the substantiation of the natural right of man to life, principles of retributive justice, and the conception of a "natural moral law".

Historically, official Catholic doctrine developed two ways of considering the military issue; these may be called, respectively, the transcendental (primarily individual and ideal-perfectionist) and socio-immanent (practical-social, oriented towards the realities of military conflicts.

The first document containing an expanded human rights substantiation of peace was the Encyclical "Pacem in terris" of Pope John XXIII, involved in resolving the 1963 Caribbean Crisis. His successor, Paul VI, proclaimed the idea of creating a "civilization of love" and "integral humanism" combined with the requirement of unconditional respect for human life from the moment of conception ("Human Vitae", 1968).

The life-creation of Pope John Paul II was an organic amalgam of theology, social philosophy, ethics, and the practice of active non-coercion. Theological grounds of the "culture of life" and simultaneously the natural-law grounds of the deontology of contemporary Catholicism are revealed in the doctrine of this Pope. The said grounds are set out in systematized form in the Encyclical "Evangelium vitae", 1995).

The Catholic ethic of non-coercion is Christ-centric in principle and soterilogical, being based on the Gospel history of salvation: "The commandment 'Thou shall not kill', included and more fully expressed in the positive command of love for one's neighbour, is reaffirmed in all its force by the Lord Jesus" (EV, 41). The correlation of the commandment of mercy and the principle of justice is resolved in the dialectical removal of the last in the commandment of love: the last, including in particular the principle of love thine enemies, appears here already as a commandment of perfect justice.

The traditional rigor and moral absolutism of Catholic natural law deontology expresses the following principle of the Encyclical: "No circumstance, no purpose, no law whatsoever can ever make licit an act which is intrinsically illicit, since it is contrary to the Law of God which is written in every human heart, knowable by reason itself, and proclaimed by the Church" (EV, 62). Thus, the

"Gospel of life" proclaimed by Pope John Paul II becomes the basis for cultivating the "culture of life" juxtaposed to the "culture of death" present in the contemporary world.

However, the categorical nature of the aforesaid moral-legal prohibition does not exclude a traditional natural-law substantiation "of legitimate defence", which as stressed in the Catechism of the Catholic Church (§2265) "can be not only a right but a grave duty for someone responsible for another's life, the common good of the family or of the State" (EV, 55). "Unfortunately, – John Paul II recognized, – *it happens that the need* to render the aggressor incapable of causing harm sometimes *involves taking his life.* In this case, the fatal outcome is attributable to the aggressor whose action brought it about, even though he may not be morally responsible because of a lack of the use of reason ..." (EV, 55; italics added).

The ideas of active non-coercion were developed by John Paul II's successor, Benedict XVI, in 2007 on the basis of the moral-theological commandment of love:

> The capacity to accept suffering for the sake of goodness, truth and justice is an essential criterion of humanity, because if my own well-being and safety are ultimately more important than truth and justice, then the power of the stronger prevails, then violence and untruth reign supreme. the capacity to accept suffering for the sake of goodness, truth and justice is an essential criterion of humanity, because if my own well-being and safety are ultimately more important than truth and justice, then the power of the stronger prevails, then violence and untruth reign supreme. Truth and justice must stand above my comfort and physical well-being, or else my life itself becomes a lie ... <...> Love simply cannot exist without this painful renunciation of myself, for otherwise it becomes pure selfishness and thereby ceases to be love (Encyclical "Spe salvi", 38).

The natural "right of extreme necessity" already had been combined with Christian deontology by Pope John Paul II. Hence the combination of the principles of non-coercion with the principles of just war having been included in the Catechism of the Catholic Church in 1992 (§2302-2330). The Catechism specially stresses:

> The strict conditions for legitimate defense by military force require rigorous consideration. the gravity of such a decision makes it subject to rigorous conditions of moral legitimacy. At one and the same time:
>
> - the damage inflicted by the aggressor on the nation or community of nations must be lasting, grave, and certain;
>
> - all other means of putting an end to it must have been shown to be impractical or ineffective;- there must be serious prospects of success;
>
> - the use of arms must not produce evils and disorders graver than the evil to be eliminated. the power of modem means of destruction weighs very heavily in evaluating this condition.
>
> These are the traditional elements enumerated in what is called the "just war" doctrine.
>
> The evaluation of these conditions for moral legitimacy belongs to the prudential judgment of those who have responsibility for the common good (§2309).

At present, the above provisions of the Catechism are being rethought by Pope Francis, having regard to the moral, theological, and international-political realities of modern times:

> War can easily be chosen by invoking all sorts of allegedly humanitarian, defensive or precautionary excuses, and even resorting to the manipulation of information. In recent decades, every single war has been ostensibly "justified". The Catechism of the Catholic Church speaks of the possibility of legitimate defence by means of military force, which involves demonstrating that certain "rigorous conditions of moral legitimacy" have been met. Yet it is easy to fall into an overly broad interpretation of this potential right. In this way, some would also wrongly justify even "preventive" attacks or acts of war that can hardly avoid entailing "evils and disorders graver than the evil to be eliminated". "We can no longer think of war as a solution, because its risks will probably always be greater than

> its supposed benefits. In view of this, it is very difficult nowadays to invoke the rational criteria elaborated in earlier centuries to speak of the possibility of a "just war". Never again war! (FT, 258, 240-243).

The ideas of Christian pacifism receive further elaboration in documents of Pope Francis directed to "all peoples of good will". In the Message for the Celebration of the Fiftieth World Day of Peace (1 January 2017), the Pope called upon all to build a world of non-violence: "make active nonviolence our way of life», «in the most local and ordinary situations and in the international order, may nonviolence become the hallmark of our decisions, our relationships and our actions, and indeed of political life in all its forms".

According to Francis, "whoever accepts the Good News of Jesus is able to acknowledge the violence within and be healed by God's mercy, becoming in turn an instrument of reconciliation". The general religious and institutional dimension of non-violence Francis in his Message identified with Mother Theresa, Mahatma Gandhi, Abdul Ghaffar Khan, Martin Luther King, and Leymah Gbowee.

In the Encyclical "Fratelli tutti" (2020), Pope Francis declared:

> In the name of innocent human life that God has forbidden to kill, affirming that whoever kills a person is like one who kills the whole of humanity, and that whoever saves a person is like one who saves the whole of humanity (FT, 285). [Francis proclaimed that] the first victim of every war is the human family's innate vocation to fraternity, [and therefore] every threatening situation breeds mistrust and leads people to withdraw into their own safety zone (FT, 26). War is a failure of politics and of humanity, a shameful capitulation, a stinging defeat before the forces of evil. [Consequently], we will be able to grasp the abyss of evil at the heart of war. Nor will it trouble us to be deemed naive for choosing peace (FT, 261).

It is noteworthy that, unlike his predecessors, "Pope Francis does not use the conception of natural law as the basis of the doctrine of the Church on war and peace, but instead turns directly to the Gospels".[69]

It should be stressed that beginning from March 2022 Pope Francis consistently condemned the Russian-Ukrainian war, using the terms "aggression" and "invasion". The number of statements of the Pope with respect to the war in Ukraine and the extent of detail with which they were made are unprecedented in comparison with those with which the Pope approached other armed conflicts.[70] He never expressly excluded the right of Ukrainians to self-defense, although he indirectly made it understood that theh correct response to aggression cannot be armaments, sanctions, or strengthening of military alliances. In September 2022 Pope Francis stated that the arming of Ukraine in certain instances may be moral and amoral, depending on the true reasons for providing weapons to Ukraine. Important in the context of evaluating the Russian-Ukrainian war was his statement that "self-defense is not only legal, but even more also an expression of love for the country. If someone does not defend himself, someone is not capable of coming to the defense of something, which means he loves no one and nothing, whereas that who defends, loves".

Pope Francis thus "struggles between pacifism and an understanding that non-violence is not in a state to defend the weakest". Despite the fact that in contemporary Catholicism the "traditional presumption against injustice" de facto ceded place to the "presumption against war and force", Catholic theology and ethical-legal doctrine demonstrates a formal coexistence of moral-legal principles of active non-violence with the traditional ethic of the just war. Such coexistence is possible thanks to the ontologism of Catholic natural law enabling the withdrawal f rom one existential source both absolute moral prohibitions of homicide of the innocent and conditional authorizations and prohibitions of just war. The historical-hermeneutic and theoretical-axiological resolution of this problem consists of placing both ethics in provisional consistency and moral-value hierarchy: the ethic of

[69] R. Zaviys'kyi, *Від тиші до тиші папи Франциска. Або чому не варто топити істину в милосерді. Лівий берег* (4 травня 2022 року) [From Silence to Silence of Pope Francis. Or Why You Should Not Drown the Truth in Mercy (4 May 2022)] (available online).

[70] P. Smytsniuk, Католицька реакція на російсько-українську війну [Catholic Reaction to the Russo-Ukrainian War], Наукові записки УКУ, Серія «Богослов›я" [Scientific Notes of the UKU, Series "Theology"], no. 10 (2023), p. 214.

a just war is a step on the path towards an ethic of non-violence similar to how the Jewish "Law and Prophecies" become the "Old Testament" – a normative step towards the commandments of the New Testament.

CONCLUDING OBSERVATIONS

During the twentieth and twenty-first centuries, the social doctrine of Catholicism developed by leading Catholic theologians and social philosophers underwent a number of material changes. The most important manifestations of these evolutionary changes became:

(a) personalist humanization of the normative content of natural law. The social thought of the Catholic Church was reoriented with conservative legitimation of existing social and State institutions to the sacralization of the human individual as the "grounds and purpose of the entire social system". If *lex naturalis* traditionally was an expression of the existing social order, then natural human rights are treated as a manifestation of his personal nature and god-given dignity.

The external reasons of priority significance for such changes were the necessity of dialogue between the Catholic Church and the liberal and totalitarian political ideologies and its adaptation to existence under a secularized social reality. The universal language of human rights is becoming an important means of renewal of the image of the Church and its communication with the contemporary world. At the same time, "internal" factors exist that are undergoing evolution: among these are unique personal qualities of the Popes of Rome elected from the middle of the past century: openness to the world and the neo-classical philosophical doctrines of Johon XXIII and Paul VI, the active humanism of John Paul II and Francis, and also the theological-phenomenological approach of Carol Wojtyla towards contemplation of the problematik of human rights;

(b) universalization of the doctrine concerning human rights manifest in the transition from the protection of the rights of individual social groups (especially Catholic believers) to acknowledgement of the equal dignity of all people and the universality of human rights;

(c) modification of the theological argumentation of human rights, the manifestation of which became emphasis on the moral essence of natural law and on its unity with divine law;

(d) expansion of the catalogue of human rights at the expense of a number of socio-economic, political, and personal rights. Among the last, the most essential are religious freedom recognized by John XXIII in 1963 and substantiated by the II Vatican Conclave as the source and synthesis of all other rights (Declaration on Religious Freedom, 1965); human right to participation (Synod of Bishops, 1971) and also bio-somatic human rights (John Paul II); and ecological rights of future generations (Francis);

(e) changes in the interpretation of basic socio-economic rights (right to work and rights of capital), consisting of an expansion of the list and content of the rights of working people at the expense of limiting the rights of owners of means of production. The right of private ownership is juxtaposed to the principle of the universal purpose of earthly goods and the universal right to work (John Paul II);

(f) gradual expansion of the catalogue of human rights, combining of human rights into groups in accordance with the requirements and spheres of human activity; codification of these rights in the Encyclical of John XXIII "Pacem in terris" (1963) and documents of the Pontifical Commission "Iustitia et pax", the "Church and Human Rights" (1974), and the "Compendium of Social Doctrine of the Church" (1974);

(g) the addition of historical-social analysis to the metaphysical anthropology traditional for Thomism;

(h) statements concerning the need to rethink the conception of just war and movement in the direction of a conception of active non-violence (Christian pacifism), although the right to self-defense also is not denied (Francis);

(i) the actual transition from natural-law argumentation of the human right to life and the right of peoples to peaceful coexistence to a primarily Gospel substantiation thereof (John Paul II, Francis).

A multi-dimensional understanding of the essence of human rights is characteristic of the social doctrine of contemporary Catholicism. Human rights are identified as:

(a) a specific anthropo-legal reality requiring social recognition, State-legal consolidation, and real moral respect;

(b) moral requirements directed towards ensuring justice in all spheres of human existence;

(c) an objective value purpose of social order – a universal good;

(d) means of creating on earth a person-centric social order corresponding to a divinely established order;

(e) the condition of genuine peace on earth;

(f) the basis for the unification of all mankind and criteria for evaluating the humaneness of all socio-political phenomena.

Specific to Catholicism is a synthesizing value-normative and ontological point of view enabling on the basis of combining a theological natural-law, anthropological-philosophical, and socio-philosophical paradigm an expanded substantiation to be provided of the interlinkages of all properties of human rights recognized today. From the inviolability of a divine-established natural law, of which human rights are a manifestation, flows the necessary inviolability of these rights. The anthropic dimension of human rights reflects their affiliation to an essence common to all people, to "nature". This feature of human rights conditions their universality, the legal equality of all people without exception as members of a single human species, and also the inalienability of human rights.

From the conception of man as an individual and as a psychosomatic integrity, the unity of soul and body, it follows that natural rights, in turn, form a unity, and their purpose is the integral development of man (Paul VI). Thus is argued the mutual-conditionality of all human rights and the inadmissibility of asserting some human rights at the expense of other rights. From the theological-ethical understanding of human rights follows, first, that truths concerning the dignity and rights of man are becoming an object of Christian teaching. Second, the introduction of human rights in the context of moral theology leads to the inextricable link of these rights with religious and moral duties of man. The existential foundation of human rights is man's supranatural and transcendental dignity, respect for which in social practice must be expressed in conditions of his life and development worthy of a man. The absoluteness of the dignity of a man also conditions the absolute character of the rights emanating therefrom.

In proclaiming the eternal immutable and transcendental grounds of human rights and the principles of their social exercise, contemporary Catholic doctrine recognizes the need for constant analysis of social changes occurring. This enables the content of human rights to constantly be concretized, clarified, as moral requirements permanently present in changing social conditions. The human rights themselves are interpreted as values determining the concrete-historical, ethical-legal content of a universal good of the contemporary world and each community individually.

There follows from this, in particular:

(a) recognition of the need to realize individual private and group interests on the basis of their evaluation undertaken by having regard to the concrete-historical content of the dignity and rights of the human individual;

(b) establishment of the moral duties of all subjects of social life with regard to promoting the common good;

(c) necessity of the real ensuring of the possibility of the exercise of rights and performance of duties of each person as a member of society;

(d) establishment of the basic purpose of activity of the State – ensuring the rights and duties of a person and limitation of this activity by one only for this purpose.

Catholic social doctrine also notes that excessive affirmation of the principle of equality in society may prejudice individualism under which each demands observance of his rights without aspiring, however, to assume responsibility for the common good.

The contemporary Catholic conception of human rights is characterized by several distinctive features, among which there are:

(a) emphasis on the anthropological and transcendental grounds of human rights and on the religious-spiritual basis of ensuring them;

(b) combining a sacral substantiation of human rights with attention to the anthropological and social prerequisites of violations thereof (such prerequisites include the "structures of sin" – anticipation of profit and aspiration for power; exploitation of man by man; social inequality; poverty; marginalization, corruption, armed conflicts; terrorism, "globalization of indifference", and others).Wars and other forms of coercion are deemed to be violations of human rights: genocide, mass deportations, dissemination of new forms of slavery on the global level, and so on. The principle operates according to which the proclamation by the Church of Christian principles of human rights is more important that unmasking the violations of these rights;

(c) working out socio-ethical principles of the realization of human rights – justice, solidarity, subsidiarity, common good, integral development finding its fullness in God, the principle of participation as the antithesis of social alienation, and others;

(d) addition to an international catalogue of human rights of the right to "integral development", to participation in social life, to peaceful life, to a natural means of birth, the right to die naturally, the right of a conceived person to birth, the right to economic initiative, to just participation in the use of material goods, the rights of single persons to necessary assistance, the "rights of the needy" to receive, in the event of extreme need, the necessary material goods from the wealth of others.

Socio-economic rights have been most detailed in the social doctrine of contemporary Catholicism: the right of ownership, right to work, to just payment for labor, and to an adequate standard of living. The value-hierarchical correlation is argued between individual human rights (priority to "exist" over to "have", spiritual in comparison with the material, universal use of material goods with respect to private ownership thereof, priority of labor over capital, and so on).

Beginning with the tenure of Pope Paul VI, the human rights concerning personal and family life are being elaborated: especially bio-somatic rights; the fundamental rights of a people (or nation) to existence, to own language and culture through which a people displays and develops its own "spiritual sovereignty"; the right to live according to own customs without oppressions of minorities and violations of other human rights; the right of a people to form its own future through nurturing the young generation; upholding the rights of migrants and proposing principles of State legal regulation of migration flows (Benedict XVI and Francis); rights of the poorest and marginalized groups of individuals and peoples, and the rights of future generations (Francis);

(e) juxtaposition of a deeply "negative" liberalist understanding of freedom to its substantive religious-moral interpretation: realization of freedom assumes recourse to a divine natural moral law preceding all rights and duties and combining them; an emphasis on the ntegral priority of the spiritual calling of man when he exercises his rights ("human freedom must be liberated");

(f) theological substantiation of the moral limitations of individual freedoms (in the spheres of personal freedom, medical practices, and scientific research, family life, bio-ethical prohibitions: inadmissibility of abortions; euthanasia; suicide; use of artificial contraception; artificial heterological fertilization, human cloning, and others);

(g) balancing in questions of war and peace between principles of active non-violence and the traditional ethic of a just war. Beginning with the tenure of Francis, the views of the Catholic Church on these issues are being transformed in the direction of Christian pacifism.

Thus, the value-ethical positions of the Catholic Church here considered organically augment and materially expand the sphere of impact of positive-law regulation realized by norms of canon law. The social doctrine of Catholicism thus in appealing to all people of good will and the doctrine on the dignity and rights of man as the most important component thereof is a fine example of an organically integral-synthesizing, powerful spiritual-moral and, simultaneously, "natural-law" motivating impact on legal consciousness – an impact transnational and universal by its socio-regulatory nature.

Chapter 14

Universality and Non-Universality in International Law: Comparative Reflections and Implications

WILLIAM E. BUTLER

In January 2023 the Danish Independent Research Fund invited applications for postdoctoral positions to investigate the role that Russia and China "played" in the process of regionalization of international law and the impact that such process exerted on the stability of the international legal order.[1] Fifteen months previously Springer Singapore released of a volume of collected essays devoted to "the international law of the Association of South East Asian Nations".[2] In March 2023 the annual meeting of the American Society of International Law devoted a panel to "Non-Western Approaches to International Law"; the panelists addressed Latin America, Russia, Third World, Pacific islands, and China – a somewhat peculiar perception of "western". Countless other examples could be given of an emphasis on the "Particular", or the "Special", dimension of the law of nations in juxtaposition to the "Universal" or the "General".

THE QUEST FOR UNIVERSALS

"Universals" are not readily identified in human affairs. Given that *homo sapiens* are considered to be distinct from those creatures

[1] The Conception of Foreign Policy of the Russian Federation confirmed by Edict of the President of the Russian Federation on 31 March 2023, No. 229, would not appear to pursue a regional thesis, although it signals a different orientation in Russian foreign policy strategies. Paragraphs 20 to 23 are devoted to the "supremacy of law in international relations".

[2] Eric Yong Joong Lee (ed.), *ASEAN International Law* (2021). For these purposes ASEAN international law consists of more than 1,300 "laws and legal measures" which collectively are the corpus of ASEAN community law. Ibid., p. 2.

that preceded us (Neanderthals, Denisovans, and possibly others unidentified); we share universally whatever it is that constitutes our being *homo sapiens* – a determination we reach partly by the application of the comparative method and the creation of a nomenclature responsive to the classification or grouping of similarities and differences.

Within the category of *homo sapiens*, we are all different; that is, diversity as measured by DNA is universal.[3] The same would appear at this stage to be true of Neanderthals and Denisovans. We need not "create" diversity: we all differ from one another, always have, and, it would seem, always will. Our challenge is not to create diversity, but to manage diversity.

We do not know the origin of law, when it came into being among *homo sapiens*,[4] whether it existed among Neanderthals or Denisovans. This to date is a complete blank in our worldview of the human and pre-human past. Whenever law originated, it was and is an intangible, non-material, intellectual creation. If one accepts or believes in natural law of non-human origin, the human intellect is capable of cognizing, or perceiving, or postulating its existence. Logic usually compels the view that such law, inhering in a non-human source, is universal by definition or by affiliation to a respective religion.

Human or man-made law is associated with communities or polities of humans, prompting the Latin expression *ubi societias, ibi jus*.[5] As a metaphor, this expression is stated as a universal, but one which needs to be proven to be such. A product of the human intellect, whether a single lawmaker (ruler) or collective, we associate the origins of law with the formation of human communities, the capacity to communicate by speech or symbols, later the emergence of writing as a form of communication. We do not know how Neanderthals and Denisovans communicated with

3 Johannes Krause and Thomas Trappe, *A Short History of Humanity: A New History of Old Europe* (2021).

4 A monumental achievement in the application of the comparative method, the hierarchical taxonomy of all organic and inorganic naturalia developed by Carl von Linné (1707-1778) at Uppsala, Sweden, first included the category *homo sapiens* in 1758, when the tenth edition of *Systema naturae* appeared. See Gunnar Brobert, *The Man Who Organized Nature: The Life of Linnaeus*, transl. Anna Paterson (2023).

5 "A maxim meaning that law may be found in all forms of stable political organization arising from social collaboration". Aaron X. Fellmeth and Maurice Horwitz, *Guide to Latin in International Law* (2009), pp. 281-282.

one another or between one another, or whether they were unable to do so. We are not confident that the family, even the extended family, qualifies as a human community for these purposes, but groups of families seem to satisfy the threshold. Those who investigate the human physiological capability to utter sound or who trace the origins of language in written form keep pushing back in time what they consider to be the likelihood of humans possessing these abilities.[6]

These considerations have implications for comparative legal studies. Given that law is either of non-human origin but cognized by humans or is created by humans, is intangible, non-material, a product of the mind, a distinction must be drawn between law and non-law. Comparative legal studies do not effectively address this issue, but concentrate instead upon the "Westphalian syndrome" and take, it will be argued below, the path of least intellectual resistance in addressing the subject-matter of comparative legal inquiries.

LAW OF NATIONS: LAW OR NON-LAW

International lawyers who teach the subject in educational institutions commonly begin their course by indulging in contrastive comparison: distinguishing international law from "municipal" law, as domestic national law is often labeled. They are right to do so, for although those laws and legal systems interact, they are quite distinct. There has been a strong legal current in comparative legal circles, however, to exclude international law from comparative legal studies on the grounds that the law of nations, later called international law, was not and/or is not real law; that is, international law is non-law.

Harold Cooke Gutteridge (1876-1953), who devoted a chapter of his treatise on comparative law to the law of nations, wrote that "so far as it exists at all, any relationship or kinship between comparative law and the law of nations must … be of a very shadowy nature"; by law of nations Gutteridge understood "… the *principles* of justice, which, by the common consent of mankind, *should* govern relations between states or nations"

[6] S. Mithen, *The Language Puzzle* (2024).

(emphasis added).[7] Analogous doubts were echoed by Konrad Zweigert (1911-1996) and Hein Kötz: "At first sight there is little in common between comparative law and public international law, for public international law, or the law of nations, is essentially a supranational and global system of law".[8]

The view that there is "little in common", of course, is a comparative legal conclusion of sorts, largely achieved by definitions, but one that far from exhausts what comparative analysis might contribute.

Whether law is perceived as non-human natural law or manmade law, it regulates interpersonal relations at various levels of organizational hierarchy: interpersonal relations directly between or among human beings; relations between corporate entities formed directly or indirectly by human beings, including juridical persons established under national or international law, up to and including States or other polities or international organizations. All have a human foundation, and all rely on human beings, directly or indirectly, to create them and the rules under or by which they function. States and international inter-governmental organizations are no exception.

No State or pre-State formation is known to have denied or rejected as matter of State practice the existence of rules governing their relations *inter se*. Disagreements exist between communities as to whether a particular norm may exist, or what the substance of a rule is, but the absolute denial of the existence of norms, if this occurred in the past, has not been demonstrated and, in any event, has not endured. Insofar as such denials may occur, they emanate from exclusory definitions of law advanced by legal thinkers rather than from analyses of State practice.

COMPARISON AS UNIVERSAL

"Comparison" as a "method" of perception and identification is, however, a "universal" characteristic at its highest level of *homo*

[7] H. C. Gutteridge, *Comparative Law: An Introduction to the Comparative Method of Legal Study and Research* (1949), p. 60: Gutteridge, "Comparative Law and the Law of Nations", in William E. Butler (ed.), *International Law in Comparative Perspective* (1980), pp. 13-24.

[8] Konrad Zweigert and Hein Kötz, *Introduction to Comparative Law*, transl. Tony Weir (2d ed.; 1992), p. 7.

sapiens. We are "hard wired" to perceive, identify, and distinguish among phenomena with all of our sensory mechanisms. Visual, auditory, touch, smell, taste, and intellectual classification are among the characteristics of humankind that are expected to be present; if some are absent or truncated or disabled, that is considered to be impairment. Some may excel in their command or possession of these senses.

At the level of groupings (families, clans, tribes, peoples, and others) or polities, or communities, at some point in our remote past we began to articulate abstractions, orally expressed and later in writing, called rules or laws. Increasingly complex, these rules or laws were subjected to internal ordering and systematization, operating both within polities and between polities. The universal component is that apparently *homo sapiens* did become aware of the need for regulation of their affairs, but the substance, nomenclature, vocabulary, and most other components of this need were expressed differently – a form of regionalism or fragmentation.

The classifications, categories, definitions, and systemic differences identified or used in comparative legal analysis should not be overstated. The science of comparative law, for example, has devoted considerable attention to classifications of national legal polities into families or clusters of legal systems based on, usually, legal criteria. These classifications should be treated as perspectives, or angles of vision, and not as factual realities as they are in the material sciences. They are intellectual creations, and they offer valuable insights into the factors that make national legal polities similar and different. The question is whether the same approach applied to regional or fragmentary systems of international law works in the same way. Is one dealing with intellectual doctrinal distinctions, as is the case on some occasions, or the assertion by some subjects of international law of the existence of separate and distinct systems of international law as a matter of State practice, and/or differences in approaches to international law embedded in concepts of national law.

Nothing is by definition beyond the comparative method, which is as interested in contrasts as in similarities. The fact that the comparison of two objects/ideas/concepts shows that they may differ in absolutely every respect is nonetheless a comparative finding. The proposition that the law of nations cannot be compared by definition with aspects of national legal system is anti-scientific and untrue.

UNIVERSALISM AND FRAGMENTATION

Distinctions were drawn between the regulation within the polity or community and that lesser degree of regulation between polities or communities. Or so we restructure our past when we attempt to identify the origins of the history of the law of nations back to its earliest times.[9] The dispersions and migrations of mankind dictated over eons of time a transition from the Particular or Special to a larger awareness of the human community and a greater appreciation of, if not the Universal, then of multiple polities or communities and the formation of empires which were larger Particulars.

Regionalism or fragmentation dominated as polities or communities nurtured and developed their own cultural, linguistic, and ethnic coalescences and differentiations, accompanied in each case by the generation of rules of behavior for inter-polity or inter-community relations. Advances in the natural and social sciences enable us to identify and document individual polities or communities, many unknown to our history, trace migrations and other interactions, commerce, diplomacy, wars, armistices and peace, exploration, treaties, alliances, the formation or disintegration of regional empires – what at a minimum may be

[9] Comparative legal studies are as challenged by " prehistory" at least as much as other natural and social sciences. Comparative national lawyers associate the temporal origins of their respective national legal system with more or less certain temporal boundaries, and well within the parameters of written law. The law of nations has no determined temporal beginning; treaties are known to have existed at least five millennia back. Nothing in the law of nations precludes relevant early practice being adduced as good authority for the formation and existence of at least fragmentary norm-creation. Of considerable relevance to international and comparative legal studies is the critique advanced in Stefanos Geroulanos, *The Invention of Prehistory: Empire, Violence, and Our Obsession with Human Origins* (2024): "Over the two centuries since Europe's 'discovery' of the Americas, the indigenous peoples of the New World had been slaughtered, tyrannized, enslaved, pushed into alien lands. ... By the 1700s, the concepts of nature, for example, had established a peculiar position for the 'savages' in European thought. If they were in 'nature' and not in 'civilization', this had consequences because 'nature' was a fairly plastic concept. For jurists and political thinkers, 'nature' offered ... a supposed basic condition of humanity. 'Natural' could mean 'lacking culture', a wild situation without a state, police, or civilization" (pp. 16-17).

considered human-created institutions and practices for inter-polity or inter-community contacts and relations.

The early evidence of inter-polity practice seems to be universal in the sense that there (a) was such practice or experience; (b) patterns of practice appear to have emerged that we can identify with the presence of what in modern terms we call the law of inter-polity or inter-community relations; and (c) the surviving evidence demonstrates a high level of fragmentation or "regionalization" but a certain resilience over time. We may be at the stage of scientific discovery where we think in terms not of the discovery of material evidence that such inter-polity relations and interaction existed, but that we should assume such and look for evidence to the contrary. In short, we work from the presumption rather than the assumption.

"Sovereignty", an abstract legal concept that is associated with fragmentary human communities that came to be called "States", is partly a doctrine of "*vires*"; that is, a confirmation that a particular human community has achieved recognition of its identity in the form of territory, population, governance, and sufficient cohesion to demarcate itself in the world system of similar communities. States which conclude treaties with one another or join international organizations are said to "surrender" part of their sovereignty in the interests of achieving desirable goals or outcomes. Their respective national legal systems are an expression of sovereignty, as is the law of nations as a regulator of human-formed inter-community relations. The conception of sovereignty serves to reinforce fragmentation but simultaneously to lay the foundations for inter-community relations and institutions; that is, serve as a General and a Particular.

WORLDVIEW OF THE PLANET

A challenge of the search for "universals" in international law is the question of when conceptions emerged of systemic laws regulating a planetary community of inter-polity relations.

This is partly a question of determining when the human consciousness became aware of the desirability of the existence or the actual existence of values, principles, or concepts of some form of international community bound together by "Universals" whose importance or magnitude exceeded that of the "Particulars". These were found in notions of the unity of mankind, religious beliefs, mythologies, ideologies, natural laws, or other ideas that posited or emphasized the generality of Universals. Most such notions were rooted in perceptions of overriding Particularity, a limited perception or understanding of the spatial dimension of polities extant on the planet. Even the most far-reaching conceptions of natural law distinguished between the elect and the non-elect, conceptions rooted in the "Particular".

Whatever appeal to conceptual "Universals" may have existed, the realities of polity or community interaction reflected understandings of hierarchy usually based on power but reinforced by related notions of cultural, religious, ideological, philosophical, or other primacy or priority. The presumption is that ideas and actual policies nearly always flowed from the Particular (individual polity-level as polity-practice or individual thinkers, jurists, philosophers, statesmen, rulers, and so on) rather than from the general level downwards. This pattern is inherently "anti-Universal"; it rests on the power and influence of a fragmented planetary community and is reflexively sceptical of "Universals" or "generalizations".

TRENDING TOWARDS UNIVERSALS

To a significant extent, the practice of States-polities since the adoption of the United Nations Charter has moved in the direction of establishing or accepting more, rather than fewer, "Universals". This is evident in the number of States-parties to the United Nations Charter and several near-universal multilateral treaties, resolutions of the United Nations General Assembly that have become declaratory of customary international law, the emergence and acceptance of the principle of *jus cogens,* concepts of general international law, a higher degree of State comfort with customary international law generally, the expansion in the concept of "subjects of international law", the greater degrees of protection afforded by international law to polities which are not subjects of international law and to natural persons.

But these are steps towards "near-Universality", not "actual Universality", and they have proceeded at their own pace. It is entirely possible that complete Universality in international law will never be achieved, and need not be – that the world community will live with "approximate Universality", which, of course, is not Universality at all but rather "large-scale participation". The aspiration for Universality in international law may come at the cost of less flexibility, innovation, and suppleness that often can be used to advantage in reaching arrangements acceptable to the parties.

Powerful anti-Universalist forces and influences continue to operate within and among polities. These sometimes undermine or reconfigure Universals and remain the major component affecting the achievement or failure to achieve the formation of Universals in the domain of international law. In the views of some, they represent residual fragmentation of the international order, whereas others see them as the primary feature of the international order and whatever Universals may exist as minor and fragile exceptions.

Regional international laws or approaches to international law have always been characteristic of the planetary interaction of polities. It could not have been any other way, given the historical patterns now known of human migration and human limitations of knowledge of the spatial dimension of the planet. All communities existed within spatial boundaries with limited awareness of others. Whatever sense of "otherness" existed was subject to limitations on travel, hostility, communication, literacy, and the like; although modern archaeology and archeo-genetic research is documenting far greater interaction among polities than known or assumed in the past, the pattern is nonetheless regional rather than global. This means that regional laws of nations were the norm rather than the exception. "Universals" are the exception, and a "Universal" or general international law is a new phenomenon.

THE COMPARATIVE METHOD AND INTERNATIONAL LAW

Given the regional origins and nature of the law of nations and its continual powerful impact upon theoretical conceptions and State practice, the comparative method is a primary method for the study and analysis of international law. It could not be otherwise. An understanding of the past of the law of nations is inherently an exercise dependent upon a perception of similarities and differences over time, between regions, of concepts and languages, of distinctions between international or inter-polity law and municipal or domestic law, and the like. One cannot work with international law absent the application of the comparative method.

International law consists of rules interpreted and applied differently by the subjects of international law, and one would not expect otherwise; the same applies to rules generated by national legal systems. But arguably until recently international law has never been a universal body of rules, but rather a fragmentary, incomplete system generated primarily by various species of "regions" or of regional application. A refusal to acknowledge the comparative dimension of international law has been intellectually disingenuous on the part of international and comparative lawyers.

The application of the comparative method to the law of nations and the notion of comparative international law are two different matters. So far as can be determined, the term "comparative international law" dates from 1850 and first appeared in the French language.[10] The comparative method has been applied in international legal doctrine and inter-polity practice since earliest times but seldom recognized as comparative analysis. The essence of the comparative method is the perception, identification, description, analysis, and generalization of similarities and differences. The law of nations by its very nature cannot avoid the application of the comparative method.

"Comparative international law" is used in a multitude of meanings. Some understand by this expression simply the application of the comparative method to international law in what may be an infinite number of situations. Others use the term to indicate the study of multiple systems of international law: some based on ideological affinities (socialist); some based on theology (Islamic); some based on geographical location (Latin America); some based on alliance structures (Russia/China); some based on philosophical principles (natural law); among others. Other structures include the Universal (general international law) and the Particular (regional in some form) on the basis that the Particular may be local elaborations which are consistent with the general principles.

[10] See the present writer's review of Anthea Robert, Paul B. Stephan, Pierre Verdier, and Mila Versteeg (eds.), *Comparative International Law* (2018), in: *The Journal of Comparative Law*, XIII (2018), pp. 242-249; *Ukrainian Journal of International Law*, no. 2 (2018), pp. 148-153.

INSIGHTS AND CHALLENGES OF COMPARATIVE INTERNATIONAL LAW AND COMPARATIVE NATIONAL LAW

The proper subject-matter of comparative legal studies is all law (as opposed to non-law). This statement is a Universal, but so general as to be close to meaningless. Comparative Law needs itself to be sub-categorized into as many subdivisions as desirable: at a minimum, Comparative International Law, Comparative National Law, and Comparative Sub-National Law. What of Comparative Canon Law (those who are occupied with canon law seem to be preoccupied with the role of the Vatican and to ignore the Protestant and Eastern Orthodox churches and the canon law of non-Christian religions)? Comparative Natural Law (multiple natural laws are posited, each claiming to be Universal)?

All jurists are comparatists. They cannot fail to be. The terminology and science of law are based on abstractions expressed in symbols and/or words and can be meaningful only if distinctions are drawn between them; that is, differences and similarities. An international lawyer can no more distance himself/herself from the process of comparison than any other jurist, irrespective of whatever disciplinary distinctions or subdivisions may be erected.

If international and comparative law are viewed as two fields or disciplines, they are united by the extensive use of a single method: the comparative method. But beyond that, comparative national lawyers have developed knowledge and experience over past centuries upon which international lawyers can usefully draw to enhance their understanding of the international legal system. Do comparative international and comparative national lawyers confront common issues whose resolution can draw upon one another's experience? We venture to offer some candidacies for consideration:

Legal pluralism. Notions of legal pluralism, so trendy in national comparative legal circles for the analysis of multiple legal systems within national polities, may be useful in understanding the international legal system. On this basis, there is a general or Universal (?) international legal system originating at some time in the past which constitutes an aggregate of more or less coordinated and entangled "pluralist" international legal systems of more limited range or jurisdiction. Sometimes the pluralist international legal systems are solitary, isolated (early China); on other occasions they coexist or overlap (general international law/ Islamic international law). This would seem to be a domain where pluralist legal thinking in general might have something to offer the international lawyers. In this sense international law might also be termed a *mixité*.

Comparative legal inquiries into the interfaces between international and municipal laws, or into the seemingly infinite ways in which the comparative method and comparative legal knowledge can enrich our understanding of the nature, substance, and processes of law, are at best secondary or auxiliary approaches and not themselves, under the existing system, rule-creative or law-making.

The emphasis on pluralism and diversity leads to "relativism" in law. The international human rights documents are a good example. As noted above, having been adopted before the discovery of DNA and long before archaeo-genetic research, the major postwar human rights documents could not take into account the scientific finding that the human species is characterized by absolute diversity: no human being ever has been or is identical to another. The principle of the "natural rights" of humankind as determined, for example, in the 1948 Universal Declaration of Human Rights is ceding place to exceptions to universalism on the grounds, *inter alia*, that alternative cultural patterns long established within particular groups should be deemed consistent with the Declaration and treaties. In some quarters relativist considerations are being applied to international investment protection treaties. What passes for some as a legitimate accommodation of diversity or exceptionalism becomes for others a violation of the treaty.

Decolonization. Reference is sometimes made to "decolonizing comparative international law", a characterization that is temporally inconceivable and historically inaccurate.

"Colonization" and "decolonization" are phenomena that reach far back into human history and may prove to be linked with many patterns of human migration. Arguably, all patterns of human migration may constitute "colonization" – movements and settlements. Hunters and gatherers were supplanted by sedentary agricultural populations. However, one defines Comparative International Law as a concept in temporal terms, it did not precede patterns or practices of colonization via migration. But, to be sure, the comparative method is applicable to and may be productive of useful insights in the study of colonialism in all its forms and manifestations. Colonization did not originate in Europe. It is appropriate for Comparative International Law to ask where and when versions of colonization did originate in relations among legal polities.

TRANSMISSION OF LEGAL CONCEPTS AND NORMS

Law is an intangible routinely expressed in verbal form and commonly in writing. Comparative national lawyers are absorbed in a discussion of the impact of language on legal comparison: whether the substance of law in one language is capable of being accurately and fully expressed in another language. A negative conclusion not only renders comparison impossible; it also nullifies the accuracy of legal translation and most of the assumptions underlying proof of foreign law in courts and arbitrations. The present writer has been outspoken in the view that legal translation is the foundation of comparative law.[11] Language would also appear to be a Universal of law, which reveals itself or is created in the form of language,

Our ignorance still of the origins and migrations of the human species and the predecessors thereof, the emergence of inter-polity contacts and of usages or rules that emerged in consequence of such contacts, the terminology developed to describe or characterize such usages and rules, the patterns of movement of such terminologies, and their respective nuances in national legal terminologies are all matters that can be profitably understood through the application of the comparative method.

The notion that rules within polities would have been unknown to other polities, would not have been borrowed, or adapted, or rejected by other polities, or evaluated by other polities for their respective worth or lack thereof (comparative advantage) is simply implausible. Pure "intra-polity" legal orders, untouched by the

[11] See W. E. Butler, *Russian-English Legal Dictionary* (2d rev. ed.; 2023), p. viii. When the present writer as a 2L at the Harvard Law School applied by invitation to act as Research Assistant to Professor Harold J. Berman (1918-2007), the interview was conducted in the Russian language. Berman closed the interview by pulling from his bookshelf the Russian language text of the just adopted Civil Code of the Ukrainian SSR and set as my first task to prepare an English translation. No one, he said, is a legal comparatist unless and until they have translated a foreign code.

ideas of others, are unlikely. This proposition suggests that our periodization of the development of comparative law understates human awareness and knowledge of the law of other polities and implies that what we understand by the fruits of legal comparison were addressed earlier than the mid-eighteenth century.

But this is an observation based on the movement of legal principles, norms, institutions, ideas, and concepts from one national legal system to another – a question comparative national lawyers are asking, which is curious because a more interesting example, and perhaps more insightful, is available. International lawyers commonly say that they "speak a common language". They do not, but they share a substantially uniform terminology in their respective national languages. This is the real test for the question of language and the law: to what extent do the respective numerous languages approximate identity of concepts when addressing legal issues in what they consider to be a shared legal system, whether Universal or fragmented?

Approached historically, when, whence, and how did the vocabulary of international law move about the globe, in what languages did such terminology originate, and what is the evidence. What comparative international law needs – and such an undertaking would be of immense interest to comparative national law – is a historical dictionary, multilingual, based on evidence of State practice and appropriate doctrinal works, of international law. Follow the words, and you simultaneously follow the transmission of legal concepts from earliest recorded history at the inter-community level and with it, legal consciousness and legal change.

CONCLUDING OBSERVATIONS

The comparative method is a neutral method. The quality and objectivity of its application depends upon the sophistication of the questions being investigated, the quality of the data being considered, and the quality of the analysis. Sometimes comparison is described as much art as science. The inability to accommodate the "art" dimension of comparison is a weakness of the machine translation of legal materials and likely to be a significant drawback of artificial intelligence in its early stages, if not forever.

The goals and ultimate quality of comparison are another matter. These lie with the comparatist and may be as distorted and value-laden as the comparatist may choose. Therein lie the differences between valid or insightful comparison and mediocre comparison, between a scientific and unscientific result. Given the intangible and abstract essence of law, this comparatist has repeatedly suggested that legal translation is the foundation of comparative law. This is so irrespective of whether municipal law, regional law, international law, sub-State or other law is being examined. The comparison of law is not impossible because of language differences, but language differences are the challenge of valid comparison that have to be recognized and appropriately dealt with.

Chapter 15

The Private and Public Law Dichotomy as the Paradigm of Global Law: Reality or Myth?

EVHEN O. KHARYTONOV

OLENA I. KHARYTONOVA

Globalization is relegated by many to the arterial direction of the development of mankind. As Kononenko noted, "Globalization inspires us to believe in the integrity and indivisibility of the world community, and integrity and indivisibility are primary, preceding any divisions (political, economic, racial-ethnic, geopolitical, cultural, and others)".[1] Thus, globalization is simultaneously both the primary and ultimate form of the unity of mankind in the process of its historical development. The development of mankind, occurring in an upward "spiral" with the removal" at each turn of the "spiral" of the achievements of the preceding period, not only assumes the forming of a single global society (or civilization) with all the elements peculiar thereto (including law), but also the forming of conceptions of the "law of a new quality". To the last, in particular, is relegated the concept of "global law", understood as the aggregate of verbally expressed notions of law as a social phenomenon designated by this term.

The suggestion of a possible existence of a single concept of the "global law" is based on permitting synchronization (possible synchronization) of identical (or related) values. It is advisable to investigate these by having regard to the dichotomy "private law – public law" because as Domitus Ulpianus (c. 160-226) emphasized: "The study of law is divided into that which affects common interests (public law) and that which concerns the interests of individual persons (private law)" (Digest 1.1.1.2). Moreover, such

[1] S. V. Kononenko, Форми політологічного розуміння міжнародних відносин [Forms of Politological Understanding of International Relations] (2012), pp. 496-497.

an investigation of an "ideal" dichotomy makes sense in an "ideal – single" global society.

The "unity" and "uniqueness" of a global society, however, causes serious doubts. As Henry Kissinger (1923-2023) noted,

> With the end of Roman rule, pluralism became the defining characteristic of the European order ... Yet although it was comprehensible as a Single civilization, Europe never had a single governance, or a united, fixed identity. It changed the principles in the name of which its various units governed themselves at frequent intervals, experimenting with a new concept of political legitimacy or international order.[2]

Hopes for the establishment over time of a new world order under which the "civilization" line of demarcation would make no sense have not been justified. Whereas in 1990 President George W. Bush expressed the hope that the crisis in the Persian Gulf might lead to the emergence of a new world order in which all the countries of the world – West and East, North and South – would prosper and live in harmony, a quarter century later it is evident that "no benign new world order materialized. What exists in many parts of the world as well as in various venues of international relations resembles more a new world disorder".[3]

This chaos has manifested itself differently in democratic and authoritarian States or societies: in developed democracies populism and extremism scored points, and in other countries, authoritarianism. A "vicious circle" arose as a result: the challenges of globalization were transformed into domestic problems, and domestic problems prevented the State from coping with the challenges of globalization.[4]

In such a context the choice of type of legal means (private or public) became urgent for counteracting the threat of chaos. We understand the dichotomy "private and public law" as a concept reflecting the vision of the place of man in society, his values and interests, the possible behavior of individuals in society in interac-

[2] Henry Kissinger. *World Order. Reflections on the Character of Nations and the Course of History* (2014).

[3] Richard Haas. *A World in Disarray. American Foreign Policy and the Crisis of the Old Order* (2018).

[4] Ibid.

tion with one another. From this angle of vision these questions become vital: "is the scheme "private law – public law" global in nature?" and "is this dichotomy appropriate in any type of society?".

To begin, it is necessary to set out our position relative to the insufficiently argued thesis concerning the "general or global universality" of private law. Private law is peculiar only to Europe and types of societies derivative from European democratic (or open) societies (European + derivative + followers). Closed societies do not recognize private law.

Here a problem exists that an open society at present forms (or considers) the conception of international law "on the model of private law". This makes a certain sense because private law and international law are a "law of good will". Closed societies, however, ignore this approach (recognition of legal norms and rules of behavior as the binding result of the consensus of participants of particular relations). Therefore, such will may exist only in democratic countries, where this is the wish of the majority, unlike authoritarian countries, where the will of the leader is determinative.

The present article attempts to answer these questions with the use of materials from earlier studies.[5]

TYPE OF SOCIETY, POLITICAL SYSTEMS, PRIVACY AND RIGHT OF PRIVACY

Proceeding from the division of societies into "open" and "closed" (democratic and "non-democratic), as the basis for understanding the essence of an open society we have taken the conception of George Soros, according to whom the concept "open society" combines three different meanings: (1) a balanced state; (2) ideal type of organization to which one may strive, but never achieve; and (3) a special purpose for which to strive.[6]

When considering private law and the rights of an individual in an open society, we understand private law as: (1) a power

[5] E. O. Kharytonov and O. I. Kharytonova, Приватне право як концепт. Том V. Протистояння відкритого та закритого суспільств і приватне право (Частина II. Закрите суспільство vs. приватне право) [Private Law as Concept: Confrontation of Open and Closed Societies and Private Law (Part II. Closed Society vs. Private Law) (2023), V(2), pp. 7-50.

[6] George Soros. *Open Society: Reforming Global Capitalism* (2d ed.; 2000).

capable of achieving a balance and of ensuring and defending against imbalance; (2) the foundation and means of achieving an ideal type of organization and an element of the last; (3) a means of regulating social relations which is simultaneously an element of a worldview basis of a democratic society, the legal consciousness of members of such a society, an element of the socio-political structure of an open society; (4) as a guaranteed possibility of the invariable behavior of a private individual in his interests and limited only by the interests and possibilities of other private individuals.[7]

Each of the aforementioned essences is important, although in anomalous circumstances any one of them may come to the forefront.

Inasmuch as under contemporary circumstances the confrontation of the Open and Closed worlds is becoming more acute, when the Open world preserves means of communication and sanctions as the paradigm of avoiding a Third World War, it is important to ascertain the possible existence and effectiveness of the concept of "private law" in a closed society. It is important to establish whether private law has the same meaning for a closed society, whether it is a reality or imaginary. In other words, the means of impact used by one party to a conflict should be accessible to the other party to the conflict.

Hereinafter we proceed from the fact that a generalized vision of mutual relations between open and closed societies is as follows. An open society is creative and dynamic, based on ideas of liberal pluralism, flexible with regard to various changes and impacts, imbued with a spirit of individual initiative, rational contemplation of the world, criticism and self-criticism. A closed society is influenced by stagnation, authoritarianism, dogmatism extending to magical forms, and has as a basis the clear predominance of the social over the individual.

An open society is a type of society whose main principle is the freedom and responsibility of the individual, or as Sir Karl Raimund Popper (1902-1994) expressed it: "the society in which individuals are confronted with personal decision".[8] The closed society in one in which "social life is determined by social and

[7] Kharytonov, note 5 above, V(I), p. 8.

[8] Karl Popper. *The Open Society and Its Enemies* (1947), I, p. 152.

religious taboos; everybody has his assigned place within the whole of the social structure; everyone feels that his place is the proper, the 'natural' place, assigned to him by the forces which rule the world; everyone 'knows his place'".[9]

Popper emphasized the individual and the anthropocentric, in counterbalance to theories affirming the priority of the community over the individual, his aspirations and needs.[10] According to Popper, the sole form of the existence of an open society is democracy, which is open for changes. Political freedom and law are the basis thereof. In an open society any truth is open to criticism and quest, and the State recognizes that different people have different views and interests. The basic values of an open society are freedom, dignity, responsibility, tolerance, and equality. Such a society may have internal limitations and guarantees, but only to ensure equal opportunities for all members of this society.

The paradox of the moment is a growing demand for sovereignty and a simultaneous growth of a demand for international cooperation together with the objective dependence of countries on a choice of values made by society. This dependence is a plus because it shows the maturity of society and the clarity of its historical claims.[11] In totalitarian ideologies the individual is merely an instrument, a cog in a mechanism, which must bring historical progress closer. A cog which may be sacrificed for the sake of this progress. History, however, according to Popper, has no logic or sense, and only people impart a particular meaning to it. People are responsible for how society develops. If there is no determined scenario of development beforehand, any sacrifices made to protect it are in vAin.

CLOSED SOCIETY AND METAMORPHOSES OF DEMOCRACY

A closed society stands on a foundation of prohibitions and strict rules which cannot be doubted. Any behavior may be interpreted

[9] Ibid., I, p. 10.

[10] M. Iu. Riabchuk, «Відкрите суспільство» [Open Society], Енциклопедія Сучасної України [*Encyclopedia of Contemporary Ukraine*] (2005) (available online).

[11] O. Sushko and O. Kul'chyts'kyi, В голові у Сороса [In the Head of Soros], Дзеркало тижня [Mirror of the Week], 12 August 2020 (available online).

as unequivocally correct or incorrect. Arrangements are reached not through dialogue, but through the monopoly right of leaders or the "majority" to determine what is "natural" for such a society and what is not. Individuals do not take part in the creation of society and merely support the functioning thereof.

We in turn put questions, answers to which we already have received: can being closed be more effective than open? The Covid-19 pandemic forced States to use secrecy as a means of defense. Totalitarian countries better know how to organize a strict quarantine and were able to combat the pandemic more rapidly than democratic States, which is again an occasion to speak of the competitive advantages of closed socio-political systems? Once more the question arises of the balance between freedom and openness, on one hand, and security and stability, on the other.[12]

An open society is therefore a synonym of freedom and individualism, and the basic characteristics of a closed society are an orientation (or determination) and collectivism. These two positions represent extremes which acutely exist today in pure form. Differences became evident in the postwar period when the United States, countries of Western Europe, and other democratic countries represented primarily open societies, and the Soviet Union, its satellites, and the majority of Arab and African countries might serve as examples of more closed societies.

Henri-Louis Bergson (1859-1941) distinguished society and mankind (closed society and open society). The gradual transition from the first to the second by expansion of the social whole to which man belongs is impossible. It remains closed, however we expanded it, because expansion and opening, large and open, are completely different things. At the same time, this does not mean that the transition from a closed society to an open one is impossible in general. In Bergson's view, this is possible. Insofar, however, as these are in principle different essences, the transition from one to another is abrupt for man and requires special efforts. Each requires special paths, techniques, and orientation for consciousness and will; each is based on a certain state of mind: closed or open, static or dynamic. Hence two types of morality and

[12] Ibid.

religion. Closed morality is based on pressure, coercion, habit. It emanates from impersonal social norms and prescriptions.[13]

According to Bergson, human sociality is natural. Man by his or her nature is a social essence: nature created him as an instinctive collectivist (similar to an ant or bee). But this creation of nature was intended to live in small, closed, and non-mobile groups which in fact, like an ant nest or beehive, are ruled by instinct. Solitariness, cohesion, hierarchy, absolute power of the leader, and discipline are characteristic and immutable features of a "natural" society. War between these societies is no less "natural". However powerful was the cultured stratum, it could not destroy the natural base which it conceals: the last continues one way or another to influence it.

Bergson's "naturalness" is not only positive: on the contrary, human nature may be harmful for man. But in his interpretation, nature is as ambivalent as society, and the duality thereof underlies the dichotomy of the closed and open, the static and the dynamic, in society, morality, and religion. Bergsonn distinguishes two types of nature: wild and creative. The first nature is the source of the closed society, closed morality, and static religion; the second is the source of the open society, open morality, and dynamic religion.[14]

DICHOTOMY OR TRICHOTOMY?

Thus, in the "classical" conceptual scheme the distinction between these models is based on a different attitude to historical changes. As Soros noted, in practice there only remains for us a choice between an open and closed society, distinguishing: the critical type of thought which fully investigates ways of changes (open society); the dogmatic type of thought intolerant of uncertainty (closed society).

Both the open and closed societies are imperfect, which assumes a search for solutions in a society of another type. A closed society offers security and constancy, which an open society does not

[13] A. B. Gofman, *«Общество, мораль и религия в философии Анри Бергсона» [Society, Morality, and Religion in the Philosophy of Henri Bergson]*, in H. Bergson, *Два источника морали и религии* [The Two Sources of Morality and Religion], transl. with preface and notes A. B. Gofman (1994), p. 70.

[14] Ibid.

have in sufficient amount, whereas an open society offers freedom, which the individual does not have sufficiently in a closed society. As a result, these two principles of social organization are opposite to one another. An open society acknowledges our inclination to err, whereas a closed society denies this.[15]

The position of Soros changed after the dissolution of the Soviet system; he noted that the collapse of a closed society did not necessarily lead to the formation of an open society. Collapse also might lead to the destruction of authority and the collapse of society. A weak State might be as dangerous for an open society as for an authoritarian one. Therefore, in his view it was advisable to modernize the dichotomy of "open society – closed society" and move on to a classification consisting of three elements of space in which history is mobile: open society (close to balanced); closed society (static and unbalanced) and chaos or revolution (dynamic imbalance).[16]

The description of a closed society is supplemented by his characterization of it as an order of limited access. This enables power in society to be viewed from the standpoint of an institutional approach (that is, as institutions structuring the organization and relations of individuals, models of social organization which are called social orders), differentiating the limited access order and the open access order.[17]

The basis of social organization in a limited access order (some analogue of the category "closed society") is personal relations; that is, who the individual is and who he knows. They determine individual interactions, in particular, personal relations between bearers of power. Both these types of social order assume the existence of social and private organizations, but natural societies limit access to these organizations, unlike open access societies.[18]

Such an approach from the viewpoint of the significance and specific gravity of the legal foundations of the existence of society enables, with the assistance of the category "limited access order"

[15] Soros, note 6 above.

[16] Ibid.

[17] Douglass Cecil North (1920-2015). *Violence and Social Orders. A Conceptual Framework for Interpreting Recorded Human History* (2009).

[18] Ibid.

to additionally characterize the correlation among the concepts of open society, closed society, private law, and public law.

Under contemporary circumstances, as paradoxical as it may seem, one of the most widely-encountered varieties of closed society is the totalitarian society. Friedrich August von Hayek (1899-1992) noted:

> Probably it is true that the very magnitude of the outrages committed by the totalitarian governments, instead of increasing the fear that such a system might one day arise in this country, has rather strengthened the assurance that it cannot happen here. When we look to Nazi Germany [this written at the end of the 1930s – ed.] the gulf which separates us seems so immense that nothing that happens there can possess relevance for any possible development in this country. And the fact that the difference has steadily become greater seems to refute any suggestion that we may be moving in a similar direction. But let us not forget that fifteen years ago the possibility of such a thing happening in Germany would have appeared just as fantastic, not only to nine-tenths of the Germans themselves, but also to the most hostile foreign observers (however wise they may now pretend to have been).[19]

We note that Hayek called not only the system of Nazi Germany totalitarian but also "all the consequences with which we shall be concerned in this book follow from the methods of collectivism irrespective of the ends for which they are used". It is worth recalling, Hayek cautioned, that socialism is the most influential form of collectivism or "planning", with whose assistance liberal people once more subject themselves to a regime of economic life which they previously rejected because, using the words of Adam Smith (1723--1790), it places governments in a position that "to support themselves they are obliged to be oppressive and tyrannical".[20]

[19] F. A. Hayek. *The Road to Serfdom. Text and Documents. The Definitive Edition,* ed. Bruce Caldwell (2006), pp. 186-187.

[20] Ibid., p. 35.

THE CLOSED SOCIETY AND POLITICAL SYSTEMS

Whereas an open society can exist without special institutions of power, apparatus of State coercion, and so on, the closed society cannot avoid political institutions that engage in the formation of respective ideological, political, and cultural values, realize the chosen ideology, and exercise control over the public consciousness.

In turn, the influence of the political system of the economy is undoubted, as is the fact that the replacement of the way of government entails social consequences. Observing this, Charles F. Andrain drew attention to the fact that political systems include three analogous components: socio-political structures, cultural values, and determined lines of behavior.[21] Taking this into account, he distinguished four types of political systems depending on an assessment of their orientation towards democratic freedoms, socialist planning, or capitalist accumulation: folk (tribal), bureaucratic-authoritarian, reconciliation, and mobilization. Three parameters are the basis of the classification: (1) value hierarchies and interpretations of cultural values exerting decisive influence on the forming of political priorities; (2) influence on the political process of such structures as government, political parties, social groups within the country, various foreign institutions; (3) behavior of leaders and masses.[22]

In evaluating such a classification of political systems from the standpoint of the problems of interest here, we note that only one of the aforesaid types (reconciliation system) may be practically deemed to be an open society, whereas the remaining types (folk-tribal, bureaucratic-authoritarian and mobilization systems) fully or primarily have the indicia of a closed society. Considering, however, the link of these systems with the concept of private law, we can ignore the folk-tribal political system as one not concerned with the status of the "private person" and in general with the recognition of the existence of such a construct.

In order to determine the type of political system and the characteristics thereof the cultural aspect is important for

[21] Charles F. Andrain, *Comparative Political Systems. Policy Performance and Social Change* (1994).

[22] Ibid., p. x.

establishing the degree of fused or differentiation of the spiritual-moral and ideological values, on one hand, and material values, on the other.

From the structural viewpoint, the degree of power of the State over social groups and the population as a whole is important. Strong power assumes monopolization of the mechanisms of coercion, centralized administration, effective coordination of various aspects of State activity, and the granting of merely a small amount of autonomy to social groups.

The behavioral aspect between those who govern (effective policies) and those whom they govern (advocates of particular policy) is characterized by the scale of distance between the first and second: an insuperable chasm is an indicator of an elite type of interaction, and a small political distance, an indicator of a large or small "egalitarian" character of relations.[23]

Also to be noted is the existence of a number of problems which Hayek anticipated when responding to the question: "why do the worst come to power?" (when recognizing the values of collectivism). Analyzing this problem "from the very beginning", from a State which precedes the emergence of the suppression of democratic institutions and the creation of a totalitarian regime, he observed that in the countries of Central Europe socialist parties accustomed the masses to the existence of political organizations of the militarized type, the structure of which provides for maximal transparency of the private life of the members thereof:[24]

> Although the socialist parties had the strength to get anything if they had cared to use force, they were reluctant to do so. They had, without knowing it, set themselves a task which only the ruthless, ready to disregard the barriers of accepted morals, can execute. ... others had already learnt the lesson that in a planned society the question can no longer be on what a majority of the people agree, but what is the largest single group whose members agree sufficiently to make unified direction of all affairs possible;

[23] Ibid.

[24] Hayek, note 19 above, p. 138. In this connection the question arises of their recognizing "privacy" and the "right of privacy", to which we shall return below in another context.

> or, if no such group large enough to enforce its views exists, how it can be created and who will succeed in creating it.[25]

The candid statements of Mao Tse-tung (1893-1976) during his stay in Moscow at the International Conference of Communist and Workers' Parties well explained why totalitarian societies are a breeding ground for the coming of the worst to power and, more broadly, one of the main conditions for the formation and existence of a totalitarian society: "Poverty – is good. It is awful to imagine what would be when all people become wealthy".[26]

Therefore, we take into account the influence of the "pair" of factors on forming the type of political system: "purpose – means", not forgetting that ignoring this system is fraught with the danger of which Hayek cautioned:

> There are many people who call themselves socialists although they care only about the first, who fervently believe in those ultimate aims ofsocialism but neither care nor understand how they can be achieved, and who are merely certain that they must be achieved, whatever the cost. But to nearly all those to whom socialism is not merely a hope but an object of practical politics, the characteristic methods of modern socialism are as essential as the ends themselves. Many people, on the other hand, who value the ultimate ends of socialism no less than the socialists, refuse to support socialism because of the dangers to other values they see in the methods proposed by the socialists. The dispute about socialism has thus become largely a dispute about means and not about ends ...[27]

The consequence of ignoring such a threat became not only the arising of the Third Reich, which is what Hayek had in view, but also of the Soviet Union, where the

> system of the Soviet social system and State system was formed as a result of the attempt to realize an abstract worldview idea of a just and humane society, whose real

[25] Ibid., pp. 141-142.

[26] «Маоизм без прикрас». Сборник. [Maoism Without Embellishments. Collection], transl. from Chinese (1980), p. 118.

[27] Hayek, note 19 above, p. 34.

> structure, regrettably, was based on ignoring the principle of the continuous millennial spiritual development of mankind, national shrines, universal mechanisms of a multi-dimensional natural-historical process, and confirmation of the idea of the complete rationalization of all processes happening in society.[28]

Elaborating on this thesis, Selyvanov emphasized that the

> aspiration for the complete rationalization of society of which the classics of Marxism dreamed and which the Bolsheviks and their successors sought to implement leads not only to socialism (or communism), but also to the total dominance of power over man and society as a whole, to the deepening of contradictions between the laws of development of the Universe and the functioning of society, opposing the latter, thereby threatening the existence of the individual person and society as a whole.[29]

In order to defend his position, Selyvanov cites the view of Petr Berngardovich Struve (1870-1944) on the nature of the rationalization of socialism which it is appropriate to quote:

> Socialism requires not partial rationalization, but that which would encompass at the root the entire domain of social life. Therein is the principal difficulty of socialism, because it is evident that neither individual nor collective reason is in a position to subject all the processes happening to a single plan.[30]

If we characterize the types of political systems on such a methodological basis, having regard to the aforementioned propositions and reservations, and correlate them with the concept of law, we get the following rough picture:

first, the folk (tribal) system is a stateless society (one does not speak of law because the authority of force suffices – *authors*);

[28] V. M. Selyvanov, Право і влада суверенної України: методологічні аспекти [Law and Power of Sovereign Ukraine: Methodological Aspects] (2002), p. 22.

[29] Ibid.

[30] P. B. Struve, Patriotica. Политика, культура, религия, социализм. Сборник статей за пять лет (1905-1910) [Patriotica. Politics, Culture, Religion, Socialism. Collected Articles for Five Years (1905-1910)] (1911), pp. 549-550.

second, in the bureaucratic-authoritarian system the State exercises strict control over social groups. A person has practically no possibility to resist the authorities. Material interests and moral values are precisely delimited (public law dominates – *authors*);

third, in the elitist mobilization system the leaders of mobilization systems have no common material interests – waging war, industrialization of the nation, and so forth, ideological values; the character of a "sacred act" is imparted to these "worldly" tasks. Agencies of mobilization systems are governed by a strong State; social groups receive only slight autonomy from the State; a large political distance exists between the leaders and the governed. The authorities direct the political activity of the people. Private persons have little possibility of participating in the process of the realization of policy (law is subordinate to administration, including outside the law; there is no distinction between public and private law – *authors*);

fourth, the reconciliation system realizes a pluralist model. The State has limited control over independent social groups. The distance between political leaders and ordinary citizens is very small, and the last participate in politics. They receive certain advantages for themselves with the assistance of market relations and the State, and attachment to spiritual values is linked to religious institutions and social movements. The demarcation of material interests and moral values is reflected in the structural separation of church and State[31] (division of law into public and private law; there is no dominance of the public interest – *authors*).

The bureaucratic-authoritarian system differs in a number of fundamental principles, methods of administration, and strategies for achieving economic aims. The method of ordering by means of a precise organization systematizes the process of adopting political decisions, transforming it into a process of achieving concrete purposes. Almost always in the bureaucratic and industrializing authoritarian regime material interests – acceleration of economic development, increasing productivity, reducing inflation – prevail over spiritual-moral values. A strong State relegates to the second plane the political preferences of certain social groups. The leader

[31] Andrain, note 21 above.

at the apex of the administrative hierarchical ladder and lower technocratic elites are actually a collegial organ of administration possessing the full plenitude of power. The rulers rely on strong political institutions: civil bureaucracy, military, police, technocrats. Limited pluralism enables certain groups – business associations, parts of the intelligentsia, student body, clergy – to advance their demands to governmental officials, who may change their policy if their directives encounter group resistance.[32]

The essence of the reconciliation system is to find a path towards the reconciliation of various interests. It separates spiritual-moral values and material interests. State policy is directed towards assisting various social groups. In such pluralist societies the organization of a civil society is in significant degree independent of State control. A collegial leadership distributes power among State agencies. Politicians together with jurists – legislators and judges – reconcile conflicting interests, act as mediators in agreements, arbitrators in political discussions, and establish the rules of the political game.[33]

From the end of the twentieth century the reconciliation system is being regarded by some scholars as a distinctive window to the future. In the view of Francis Fukuyama, a certain fundamental process is ahead of us which dictates a uniform path to all societies of an evolutionary development – in essence, whether the universal history of mankind is moving towards liberal democracies.[34] Liberal-democratic ideas – freedom, equality, human dignity, elections, supremacy of law, universal suffrage – have occupied a dominant position in world culture. Economic liberalism based on the market and private ownership carries the day over State socialism.

Other analysts assess more pessimistically the prospects for the universal adoption of reconciliation systems, noting that ideals of liberal democracy prevail in the superstructure; however, in the majority of countries the process of adopting political decisions, as before, is under the influence of bureaucratic-authoritarian trends.

[32] Ibid.

[33] Ibid.

[34] Francis Fukuyama. *The Origins of Political Order: From Prehuman Times to the French Revolution* (2011); Fukuyama. *Political Order and Political Decay: From the Industrial Revolution to the Globalization of Democracy* (2014).

Reconciliation systems have little chances of survival in conditions of declining economic growth, increased inequality of incomes, intensified fragmentation of society, and domestic imbalances as a result of foreign interference. It is assumed that in this case mobilization systems are necessary in order to carry out social transformations, as was so in Russia, Germany, China, Vietnam, Korean People's Democratic Republic, Iran, and Cuba. Strong States having organs of coercion have destroyed the *ancien regime* and are striving to carry out their own policies by methods denying liberal-democratic principles of the reconciliation system.[35]

As the experience of Russia and North Korea shows, the mobilization system functions in accordance with inherent principles political styles, and methods of social transformations. The participation of the masses is, as a rule, the moving force, spontaneously, through populism. The leaders (populists-mobilizers) combine material interests and adherence to radical ideological transformations. Moral aspirations are advanced by activists, but not the wish to conclude political agreements. It is worth noting that a common ideology defining populism does not exist. Leftist populism accepts fundamental antagonism between the people and the elite as the essence of its policy. Rightist populism, in its American and Western European versions, operates in a democratic context.[36] However, rightist populism is possible also in totalitarian States (Stalinism in the Soviet Union and Putinism in the Russian Federation).

Mobilization changes are directed towards the achievement of social changes by means of constitutional transformations. Changes iin the political system, however, lag behind social. Therefore, elitist mobilization systems, as a rule, are not long-lived. After the death of a charismatic leader, they are transformed into another systemic type – as a rule, bureaucratic-authoritarian regime.

Many experts are skeptical about the ability of totalitarian societies to undertake a radical restructuring of the existing system. In the view of Hannah Arendt (1906-1975), however, totalitarian elites possess sufficient will and power to transform socio-

[35] Ibid.

[36] John B. Judis, *The Populist Explosion: How the Great Recession Transformed American and European Politics* (2016).

political structures: "Wherever it [totalitarianism] rose to power, it developed entirely new political institutions and destroyed all social, legal and political traditions of the country".[37]

In connection with the special place of a charismatic leader in these systems, the question arises of the significance of his or her personality or ideology, and also the real interconnection between radical rhetoric and the real realization of policy. But an even more important factor of changes in a totalitarian society or State is the "anti-privacy" purpose of the existence of such closed societies in the activity of their leaders. Madeleine Jana Korbel Albright (1937-2022) and Bill Woodward were correct in saying: "Communists and Nazis both thought it their calling to forge a 'new man,' a creature of modernity who would rise above the individual quest for money, property, and pleasure that pitted workers against one another and, in their view, made of democracy a moral cesspool".[38]

The receding into the past of many dictators and the dissolution of the Soviet Union and the socialist camp provided a basis for the conclusion that totalitarian systems no longer exist, leaving only "post-totalitarian" in which nothing remained other than dogmatic jackets. Consent was not needed from the population, only obedience; not a chorus of approval of the words of the leader, but silence. Even where the establishment of communist rule was an outcome not only of the introduction of Soviet forces, this regime had long since lost any legitimacy.[39] This position had as a consequence a certain complacency which, in turn, entailed an underestimation of the threat to the contemporary world on the part of totalitarian regimes.

Having regard to the foregoing, we consider the conclusions of Andrain concerning the dynamic of political systems in the contemporary world and believe they may be useful to ascertain the link between this factor and the status of the individual in society. At the end of the twentieth century:

> All systems, whatever their type, reveal a contradiction between policy intentions and consequences. Political development has scarcely brought paradise on earth. In the

[37] Hannah Arendt, *The Origins of Totalitarianism* (1951).

[38] Madeleine Albright and Bill Woodward, *Fascism: A Warning* (2018).

[39] Andrain, note 21 above.

> elitist mobilization system, revolutionaries lost faith in the possibilities of attaining their utopian vision. Bureaucratic-authoritarian officials forswear any policy efforts to realize paradise. For most reconciliation leaders, paradise has been postponed. In every political system, people still await public policies that ensure greater individual rights, economic abundance, and human development.[40]

In these hopes, values, and interests a key place is allotted to the concept of "privacy" in the context of studying the possible existence of and meaning of private law.

CONFIDENTIALITY AND ANTI-PRIVACY

Having chosen "anti-privacy" as the key word to characterize a closed society from the standpoint of the essence of its relation to the individual, it is necessary to present the principles of this understanding. A better means to achieve this, however (as in any dichotomy, including "closed society – open society", "public law – private law", and so on) is contrasting the concepts according to the principle "this is not like this". And so we view "anti-privacy" as an indicator of the closed society in its contradiction with the concept "privacy".

The first observation is that, in the view of Brian Fagan and Nadia Durrani, before the industrial revolution privacy was not a priority in any society in the world. The need for solitude came after money, prestige, security, and convenience.[41] Such an assertion is rather unexpected: in patrimonial societies it seems entirely logical insofar as the need for warmth and defense prevailed over the aspiration for seclusion, whereas in the case of ancient Rome, to which were are indebted for the creation of the concept of private law, it seems rather strange. The more so that the evaluation by the said authors of the existence and state of private life in ancient Rome is not entirely clear because they remark: "Even the Roman word *privatus,* from whence our word *private,* was typically used simply to mean a citizen without public office and derives from the word *privo,* or "I bereave, deprive" but also "I free, release".

[40] Ibid., p. 191.

[41] Brian Fagan and Nadia Durrani, *What We Did in Bed: A Horizontal History* (2019).

Thus, Fagan and Durrani in stating that "then, as now, privacy was a contradictory concept" in fact conclude that the concept is differentiated depending on what countries one is referring to and what strata of the population. They quote Socrates, who condemned people who avoid taking part in social life thanks to seclusion: "No man will ever rightly gain either his due honor or office".[42]

In our view, this vision of privacy is indefinite, as too the criteria for delimiting the last. The question arises: what kind of service to the State are we talking about: political activity, holding State office, performing functions for the protection of public order, free performance of work to State benefit, and so on. It is further incomprehensible why "privacy" is evaluated either as a criterion of service or non-service to the State or depending on the presence or absence of the wish "to flaunt one's wealth". Finally, the main question: can one consider "anti-privacy" an equal "virtue" as evidently follows from Socrates quoted above.

These observations lose their severity when it follows from further comments by Fagan and Durrani that they regard "privacy" and "openness" as phenomena of the same order.[43]

Christianity became a powerful catalyst of the western interpretation of privacy. Seclusion inspired by the epochal forty-day sojourn of Jesus Christ in the desert became a central principle of Christian ideas, augmented by moral dogmas and notions of the sinfulness of a world imbued by evil, pious admiration through renunciation of worldly life and even from monastic communities, and contemplation of God and human existence outside this world. But their seclusion was not a search for privacy, but "a form of atonement for Christ's suffering on the cross. There was ... no Latin nor indeed medieval word for privacy".[44]

Material changes occurred in the nineteenth century. In December 1890 the *Harvard Law Review* published an article[45] by Samuel Dennis Warren II (1852-1910) and Louis Dembitz Brandeis

[42] Ibid.

[43] Ibid.

[44] Ibid.

[45] Samuel D. Warren and Louis D. Brandeis, "The Right to Privacy", *Harvard Law Review*, IV (1890), p. 193.

(1856-1941), who in 1916 became an Associate Justice of the United States Supreme Court. The authors spoke of a right to privacy and that because of the intensity and complexity of the development of civilization, solitude and seclusion had become more important for man.[46]

Having regard to the not very long century of the existence of his concept, we see what privacy means at present. In the national legislation of Ukraine the right to privacy is guaranteed by the Constitution of Ukraine. Article 30 of the Constitution defends the territorial privacy of private life (inviolability of the dwelling); Article 31, communicative privacy (secrecy of correspondence, telephone conversations, telegraph and other correspondence); Article 32, privacy of private life; and Article 28, individual aspects of physical privacy (no one may be subjected to medical, scientific, or other experiments without the voluntary consent thereof).

The security of so-called "sensitive data" should be emphasized. This is data which is basically kept in non-governmental organizations and often concerns the health of a person, or the religious or political views thereof, and others. The data does not always fall under the definition of personal data, but the leakage thereof may cause significant reputational, moral, and sometimes physical harm to a person.

Considering "privacy" from this point of view, it should be noted that in the context of this article privacy should be evaluated as a subjective right (private or public). Without dwelling on this issue in detail, we draw attention to one aspect of the understanding of "private law" of importance to this study.

According to Carl Friedrich von Savigny (1779-1861), in public law a whole (the State) is a whole, and the individual is subordinate, whereas in private law each individual is a self-whole, and every legal relation concerning his existence or special status is merely a means.[47] This is reflected in the fact that private law defends private interests of individual persons, and public law defends the interests of the State, public interests. In the view of August Thon (1839-1912), however, from the very beginning every norm is directed towards furthering the well-being of society, stimulating

[46] Fagan and Durrani, note 41 above.

[47] F. C. von Savigny, Система современного римского права [System of Contemporary Roman Law] (2011), I, pp. 286-287.

better knowledge and aspirations in the interests of the last. In this sense there is no difference between rules creating public rights and those which create private rights.[48]

The excessive, in our view, "publicization" of this position is compensated for by the following assertion: "... The interests of society will coincide with the real interests of individuals. Because society consists of individuals, it is not distinct from them inasmuch as all legal norms are directed to the defense of the interests of natural persons without distinction of public and private law".[49] Hence it follows that norms of "private law" may be considered such only conditionally, above all with respect to subjective (civil) rights.

We emphasize, in addition, that in closed societies, especially totalitarian, where the "totalitarian regime violates the harmonious coexistence of the public and private spheres", the concept "public" reflects those aspects and characteristics of society which have transparency, empirical openness, and publicness. As for the individual, the private, this sphere is reflected in closeness, the absence of others, involvement only in this person, and therefore bears a certain imprint of intimacy.[50]

When determining the criteria for delimiting the private-law and public-law ensuring of interests, it is important to take into account the provisions of the "will theory" of Georg Jellinek (1851-1911), according to which law in the objective sense is understood as the priority of human will directed to a certain good or interest. This priority is recognized and defended by the supremacy of law. The dominance of will is a formal element, and the good or interest as a material element of a subjective law. In turn, individual interests are subdivided into those which are established in priority for individual purposes (that is, purposes of individuals), and those which are established primarily for social purposes.

[48] August Thon, Правовая норма и субъективное право. Этюды по общей теории права (часть третья) [Legal Norm and Subjective Right. Studies on the General Theory of Law (Part Three)], *Вестник гражданского права* [Herald of Civil Law], XII, no. 3 (2012), p. 273.

[49] Ibid., p. 274.

[50] Ханна Арендт о тоталитаризме: политический и моральный дискурс (по материалам книги «Истоки тоталитаризма») [Hannah Arendt on Totalitarianism: Political and Moral Discourse (Based on Materials of the Book 'Sources of Totalitarianism")], Вестник Санкт-Петербургского университета [Herald of St. Petersburg University], series 6, no. 1 (2006), p. 68.

An individual interest recognized first and foremost as a public interest comprises the content of public law. A subjective public right in its material aspect is a right belonging to an individual on the basis of his status of a member of the State.

As for the formal element of law, the priority of will, Jellinek distinguished two types of laws: dürfen (wish, aspiration, striving) и können (possibility). Dürfen translates literally as "to have a wish, to dare to do something". In so doing, "public policy recognizes respective actions of an individual as permissible; that is, allows the will of the individual to exercise his freedom in certain directions". Können means "to be capable, to be able", and here the "supremacy of law may add to the natural ability of the individual to do what does not belong to him by nature ... namely, to give him the right so that certain of his actions would be deemed to be legally valid and subject to performance". Thus, a private subjective right contains both dürfen and können, whereas a public subjective right contains only können. And so in private law as aspiration (dürfen) is always present, but in public law there is only a possibility (können). Public rights are based not on those which have been authorized, but only on those which have been granted by the authorities. Consequently, they are not part of natural freedom regulated by a law, but a continuation of the rights thereof.[51]

In the sphere of public law this is first and foremost a question of the subordination of one person to another, the competence of State agencies and officials, on one hand, and, on the other, passive legal personality, as a rule, of the subordinate persons, their duties and responsibility arising from power acts of State agencies and officials. Within the domain of private law, the legal personality of participants of civil law relations is identical and based on principles of legal equality, freedom of will, and initiative when establishing legal relations, and then the realization by them of respective subjective rights and duties.

These propositions have the character of scientific abstraction inasmuch as they relate to private and public law as abstract categories which are singled out for the purposes of scientific analysis. In order, however, to identify the real position of a person in accordance with norms of legislation in force in a State, such an

[51] Georg Jellinek, Общее учение о государстве [General Doctrine on the State] (2004), p. 376.

approach is not correct because it reflects a competition between principles of public and private law.

But it also should be noted that the aforesaid concerns "privacy" especially, which is regarded as a "right". As already observed, "anti-privacy" is the antonym of this term and the antithesis of the respective concept. The question arises in this connection whether "anti-privacy" is a legal construct or conception or a real status of affairs or relations? The answer, in our view, is as follows.

To be sure, the concept "anti-privacy" may be defined by "pushing off" from the opposite category "privacy" (or right of privacy). But it should be noted that "privacy" in this sense also may be regarded as opposite in meaning but connected by a list of values, with the concept of "publicness". Then it would be better to proceed from the definition of this right in leading international documents mentioned above. If one proceeds from the fact that the aforesaid norms are relegated to "privacy and right of privacy", then "anti-privacy" in the most general sense of this concept means that this is arbitrary or illegal interference in the personal and family life of a person, arbitrary or illegal infringement on the inviolability of the dwelling thereof or secrecy of correspondence of a person, or illegal infringement against the honor and reputation thereof.

This is not simply a violation of the "right to privacy", but a denial in principle of the existence of the rights and values of members of society which in their time were constituted as "Victorian values – privacy" and which, taking into account their significance, sometimes are described as a "Victorian obsession with privacy (private life)".[52]

"Anti-privacy" is a certain state inherent to closed societies, to which societies with a certain type of political system are relegated: tribal, bureaucratic, authoritarian, mobilization. To this should be added certain important emphases. Totalitarianism limits freedom and impinges on inalienable human rights. As Arendt emphasized, it makes no difference how these political values were defined somewhere (as the right to life, liberty, and pursuit of happiness according to the American formula, or as equality before the law, liberty, defense of ownership – according to the French formula). Totalitarian States in which systemic limitations

[52] Fagan and Durrani, note 41 above.

of freedom are daily practice have departed completely from humanist principles. Having repealed legislation typical of pre-totalitarian power, totalitarian regimes do not reflect principles of equal sovereignty and self-determination of individuals and their freedoms in normative acts, freeing themselves from any moral responsibility to their own people and the world community. The assertion of Adolf Hitler (1889-1945): "Law is that which is good for the German people" – is merely a vulgarized form of the concept of legislation. Having rejected the institutionalization of moral requirements and their consolidation in norms of political organizations, totalitarianism placed itself outside morality and law.[53]

CONCLUSIONS

As a result of the present study, we have come to the conclusion that the response to the question "is the scheme 'private law – public law' global in its nature"? must be negative. The substantiation of this view is set out in the following theses:

First, law in general and private law in particular is understood as a concept; that is, an idea, containing a certain approach to a vision of reality which, when the content thereof is revealed within a system of judgments, forms a concept. In other words, this is an aggregate of models, constructs, ideas, emotions, sensations which arise in connection with the use of the term "private law'.

Second, law as a concept is regarded as an element of culture (or civilization), which determines the advisability of using the civilization approach when studying it.

Third, law as a supranational element of civilization under conditions of globalization should be studied with an assumption of the existence of the dichotomy "private law – public law".

Fourth, private law as a concept is a phenomenon organically inherent in western European culture (or civilization), and also an awareness perceived by societies sharing democratic civilization values (open societies). Closed societies do not recognize private law as such.

Fifth, recognition of the concept "private law" as the foundation of a national legal order is a consequence, condition, and element

[53] Arendt, note 50 above, p. 68.

of an open society. This makes possible and advisable the combining of a "civilization" and "anthropological" approaches when investigating the significance of the concept of private law in an open society.

Sixth, it is advisable to study the concept "private law" by taking into account the dichotomy "private objective right" – "private subjective right" because the last ("rights of the person") is relegated to the base values of an open society.

Seventh, private law exists as a concept in the legal traditions of Western and Eastern Europe. But whereas for the former private law is an immanently inherent phenomenon, in the second instance the terms "private law" and "civil law" often are identical.

Eighth, the system "Open – Closed Society", creating the possibility of taking account of the different nature and different proportions of social and individual values, is a paradigm of the civilizational (or cultural) construction "East – West" (or western religions – eastern religions, and so on) under conditions of integration (or globalization) processes.

Ninth, the concepts "private law" and "open society" correlate because underlying them is the same meaning: recognition of the leading place of man, as a private person, within the system of social relations. In addition, they have the same purpose: ensuring and defense of human rights as such and ensuring the realization of the rights and interests thereof as a private person.

Tenth, in societies of a transitional type the concept "private law" may be adjusted because exceptional circumstances arising in such a society condition the need to depart from "classical" principles of private law in favor of using a number of principles of public law and increasing the share of imperative method in the regulation of civil relations. Such adjustment is temporary, and the ultimate result depends on the predominance of the vector of development towards an open or closed society.

Eleventh, the state of "privacy" may serve as the criterion for the level of "openness" of a society and the potential for the reform thereof, having regard to the paradigm of political system: (1) "privacy" is not denied (legally recognized), but is violated (reconciliation system); (2) "privacy" is not denied, but is not legally recognized (authoritarian-bureaucratic system); (3) "privacy" is denied as such and not recognized ideologically or legally (mobilization system). It follows that the concepts "privacy" and "open society" are correlatives, just as the concepts "anti-privacy" and "closed society" are correlatives.

Twelfth, with regard to the idea of "global law" one may conclude that a single global system (or understanding) of law does not exist, and instead it is advisable to refer to "private" and "public" means (or legal means) of ordering social relations, the choice of which depends upon the type of society (open or closed).

Chapter 16

The Concept of "Imitation" and its Epistemological Relevance in Comparative Law and Comparative Legal History

MANUEL GUTAN

In the last decade, comparative law and legal history have encouraged greater interdisciplinarity. Comparative legal scholars are building numerous bridges to the humanities and social sciences, seeking methodological inspiration or offering their services.[1] In contrast, legal history has become more purposively comparative, to the extent that a hybrid discipline was born: comparative legal history.[2] Under the umbrella of interdisciplinarity, comparative law and (comparative) legal history may share challenging areas of research and fruitful methodologies, but they share the same shortcomings. Both were and are interested in law circulation in space and time. The legal transplants/diffusion studies inevitably looked in the past for cross-border movement of law; the (comparative) legal historians are looking beyond the nation-state's legal space to discover its external sources. Despite certain advantages of pooling knowledge and wisdom, their power of cross-fertilization has evident limits. The concept of "imitation" may be a relevant example. Both disciplines mention the imitation (copying) of big or small amounts of legal ideas, norms, institutions, and codes by a particular society from different

[1] See M. Adams and M. van Hoecke (eds.), *Comparative Methods in Law, Humanities and Social Sciences* (2021).

[2] A European Society of Comparative Legal History, established in 2009, organizes biennial congresses; a *Journal of Comparative Legal History* was published since 2013 with Taylor and Francis, and a book series of Studies in Comparative Legal History was launched in 2021 with Routledge. A prominent handbook was published in the field: O. Moréteau, A. Masferrer and K. A. Modéer (eds.), *Comparative Legal History* (2019).

foreign legal models for a diversity of purposes, but none have a proper theoretical framework to address it.[3]

THE INNOVATION-IMITATION PATTERN OF THINKING IN COMPARATIVE LAW

Comparative law scholarship detects imitated law in addition to transplanted, imported/exported, transposed, or borrowed law. The concept is frequently present in legal transplant studies, but nowhere is it made the object of a thorough epistemological clarification. Spectacular instances of law diffusion, such as the cases of Japan[4] and Turkey,[5] were the object of extensive comparative analyses, but an in-depth theorization of legal imitation has yet to occur. As suggested, comparative legal history may assume an ambitious agenda of "critical transnationalism" centered on "the complexity of (legal) transfers", and "the jurisprudential mentality" of the legal actors.[6] Katharina Isabel Schmidt's invitation to focus on the legal actors' endeavor to "construct and reconstruct their legal identities" is very welcome. One may add that "the construction and re-construction of legal identity" may involve, besides "providing national legal imagination with

[3] In *The Oxford Handbook of European Legal History*, for example, the concept of "imitation" is used repeatedly concerning the spread of codifications in the modern era, sometimes contraposed to "copying", but without explaining what it means. See H. Pihlajamäki, M. D. Dubber, and M. Godfrey (eds.), *The Oxford Handbook of European Legal History* (2018), pp. 907 ff. *The Oxford Handbook of Legal History* (2018), edited by M. D. Dubber and C. Tomlins, is in the same situation.

[4] Painter uses the concepts of transplantation, borrowing, and imitation to assess Japan›s public administration›s modernization, but the difference between them needs to be clarified. See "Legacies Remembered, Lessons Forgotten: The Case of Japan", in M. Painter and B. G. Peters, *Tradition and Public Administration, Palgrave-Macmillan* (2010), pp. 84 ff; J. Toye, *The Many Faces of Socioeconomic Change* (2017), pp. 43 ff.

[5] Of particular attention are the excellent works of Esin Örücü about the legal modernization of Ottoman and Republican Turkey. See E. Örücü, "A Synthetic and Hyphenated Legal System: The Turkish Experience", *Journal of Comparative Law*, I (2006), pp. 261-281; see also A. Rubin, "Legal Borrowing and its Impact on Ottoman Legal Culture in the Late Nineteenth Century", *Continuity and Change*, XXII (2007), pp. 279-303.

[6] See K. I. Schmidt, "From Evolutionary Functionalism to Critical Transnationalism. Comparative Legal History, Aristotle to Present", in Dubber and Tomlins, note 3 above, pp. 283-284.

innovative content (meaning)"[7] taken from abroad, the interest in replicating others' legal meaning. Schmidt sees the legal transplant studies in comparative law as playing the role of methodological and epistemological beacon for (comparative) legal history,[8] but, as far as the subject matter of imitation is concerned, comparative law has lost itself in a dense conceptual fog.[9]

In a much-quoted paper published two decades ago, William Twining constructed a sophisticated critique against the so-called "country and Western" approach, too much focused on country-to-country and Western-to-non-Western legal diffusion.[10] We may also remark too much focus on the "country, Western and innovation" in comparative legal studies. Legal comparatists are tempted to focus on the national legal systems, western legal traditions, and powerful innovators (original creators) of law. The "country and Western" paradigm determined the critical comparative scholars to repudiate the exceptionalist legal diffusionism preached by the proponents of the "major legal families" and to blame the excessive emphasis on the quality of the Western law as a model for the non-Western.[11] However, moving beyond the classical "legal origins" approach or encouraging micro-comparison in the diffusion of law studies entails ongoing investigation of the conceptualization and categorization endeavor in comparative law that is still addressing the worldwide circulation of law using fuzzy concepts

[7] Ibid., p. 284.

[8] Ibid., pp. 281-282. See also the interesting book edited by Thomas Duve, *Entanglements in Legal History: Conceptual Approaches* (2014); S. Soleil, "Les pièges, les méthodes, les ressources. Introduction", *Historia et ius: Comparer les droits dans une recherche historique: les pièges, les méthodes, les ressources* [special issue], XIII (2018), pp. 2-12; M. Dyson, "Comparative Legal History: Methodology for Morphology", in Moréteau, Masferrer, and Modéer, note 2 above, pp. 110-138.

[9] This chapter aims neither to establish all possible points of convergence and divergence between comparative law and legal history nor to discuss the opportunity of comparative legal history as a distinct discipline. It simply acknowledges that comparative legal history needs comparative law to reach its scientific objectives and purposes. Legal transplants studies in comparative law gathered considerable theoretical, mainly methodological, wisdom that may help legal history become more comparative. The envisaged micro-comparison, centered on the law in time, space, and minds of the legal actors, may be an excellent point of confluence.

[10] W. Twining, "Diffusion of Law: A Global Perspective", *The Journal of Legal Pluralism and Unofficial Law*, XXXVI (2004), pp. 1-45.

[11] For a detailed discussion, see J. Husa, *Interdisciplinarity in Comparative Law. Rubbing Shoulders with the Neighbours or Standing Alone in a Crowd* (2021), pp. 127 ff.

like "imitation". This concept goes uncritically in contemporary comparative law, regardless of the increasing interest in diversity, pluralism, and interdisciplinarity.

Merely splitting the legal world into models and imitators has limited epistemological relevance without an insightful (critical) theoretical background. The concept of imitation traditionally places the receiving countries in a peculiar position against the exporting ones, transformed into superior/exceptional/extraordinary/prestigious national legal systems. The classical comparative law scholarship made clear that the law is regularly circulating from the prestigious "mature" legal models (usually Western) towards the "immature" imitating ones (usually non-Western) in specific historical (frequently colonial) circumstances and producing legal sameness.[12] The legal world was mapped around the pillars or parents of the major legal families, for example, England, France, Germany, approached as supreme centers of legal expansion.[13] However, the concept of imitation did not have its maximum occurrence in the realm of these taxonomic efforts.

Right before World War I (1911), Raymond Saleilles (1855-1912) was eager to move comparative law studies beyond "the pure historical conception" much appreciated in the nineteenth century. He appreciated the imitation of one legal system by another as a subject matter capable of anchoring comparative law in the future. No wonder he made a case about following Jean-Gabriel de Tarde

[12] Konrad Zweigert and Hein Kötz were among the comparative law pioneers of the unbalanced approach of the mature legal systems "extensively imitated by others" to the detriment of "the affiliated" legal systems. See K. Zweigert and H. Kötz, *An Introduction to Comparative Law*, transl. Tony Weir (3d ed.; 1998), p. 41. See also J. H. Merryman, "On the Convergence (and Divergence) of the Civil Law and the Common Law", *Stanford Journal of International Law*, XVII (1981), pp. 357-388.

[13] The considerable weight the classical legal families taxonomy still has in contemporary French comparative law is fascinating. The concepts such as "expansion", "prestige", and "imitation" are still making the French law a hard case of legal exceptionalism. See R. David and C. Jauffret-Spinosi, *Les grandes systèmes de droit contemporain* (2002), pp. 56 ff.; G. Cuniberti, *Grandes systèmes de droit contemporain* (2007), p. 32; R. Seroussi, *Introduction au droit comparé* (2000), p. 21. See T. Rambaud for the use of the syntagm "juridical patriotism", in *Introduction au droit comparé. Les grandes traditions juridiques dans le monde* (2014), p. 67. The impressive *comparative law* synthesis published by the German comparatist Uwe Kischel and translated into English [2019] follows the same old pattern of law diffusion from West to East. For critical analyses, P. Legrand, "Kischel's Comparative Law: Fortschritt ohne Fortschritt", *Journal of Comparative Law*, XV (2020), pp. 292-346.

(1843-1904), *Laws of Imitation,* which was highly influential at that time.[14] We may not be sure this was when the concept of imitation entered modern comparative law. However, it is a pertinent period to start with.[15] Saleilles was not interested in reproducing the whole complex theory of imitation developed by Tarde. Instead, he was attracted by the idea that imitation is the ineluctable way the law circulates from one society to another. This perspective became highly popular in the following years, even if Tarde's theory was mentioned only occasionally.

After World War II, the concept of "imitation" spread among legal comparatists, as much as the interest in cross-border circulation of law gained a new methodological insight in comparative legal studies. In a series of works published between 1949[16] and 1956, Marc Ancel (1902-1990) addressed the cross-border movement of penal codes using the paradigm innovation-imitation borrowed from Tarde. In his opinion, imitation of legislative innovations is either conscious or spontaneous, justified by the desire of the legislator to improve the legal system.[17] Ancel wrote about "the international exchange or imitation of [legal] ideas" but had no in-depth theoretical approach. He followed the then-French view on migration/circulation of law, interested in the expansion, rapprochement, and uniformization of the national legal systems. Addressing, in 1957, state of the art in the reception of foreign law studies in the frame of comparative law, the Hungarian comparatist Imre Zajtay (1912-1983) agreed with the latter aim, but he deplored the paucity of the theoretical debates. He was critical of the excessive focus on the reception of Roman Law and the French

[14] R. Saleilles, "Droit civil et droit comparé", *Revue internationale de l'enseignement,* LXI (1911), p. 27.

[15] In the same period, the American comparatist Roscoe Pound published his series of articles dedicated to sociological jurisprudence, where he proved to be a good connoisseur of Gabriel Tarde. See R. Pound, "Scope and Purpose of Sociological Jurisprudence", *Harvard Law Review,* XXV (1911-1912), pp. 489-516. He frequently used imitation in all of his subsequent scientific work.

[16] M. Ancel, "La fonction judiciaire et le droit comparé", *Revue internationale de droit comparé,* I (1949), pp. 57-66; Ancel, "Rapport général, présenté : L'organisation et les buts des l'instituts de droit comparé", *Revue internationale de droit comparé,* VII (1955), p. 100.

[17] Ancel, "Collection of European Penal Codes and the Study of Comparative Law", *University of Pennsylvania Law Review,* CVI (1958), pp. 329-384, translating in English his introduction to the massive four volume *Les codes pénaux européens* (1956).

Civil Code and called for more methodological theorization and broadening of the scientific inquiry.[18] Of maximum interest is his conceptual analyses, preceding the future battle over metaphors. Zajtay manifested a predilection for "reception" but also used the concept of imitation, although as a marginal occurrence.[19] Thus, imitation would become an explanation (among others) for the legal sameness between the national legal systems discussed inside the classical methodological paradigm of legal comparison.

In 1979, René Rodière (1907-1981) explained the uniformization of the legal systems also using Tarde's "law of imitation", but avoided his diffusion of innovations (as original creation) pattern.[20] Instead, he made some valuable distinctions and introduced some explanations which will mark latter the diffusion of law studies, that is, the imitation is either imposed or voluntary; "prestige" is the leading cause of the latter.[21] The French anthropological and sociological legal scholarship had their visions about the European and trans-European cross-border movement of law but avoided the concepts of innovation and imitation. By contrast, they used a plethora of specific concepts like *circulation, emprunte, transferts, expantion, and acculturation*[22] while ignoring the intense exchange of ideas on legal transplants that started to trouble the English-speaking comparative law in the 1970s. The legal historian and sociologist Jean Gaudemet (1908-2001) was preoccupied in the same period with assessing the causes, mechanisms, and effects of the legal transfers[23] but did so independently of the North-American methodological debates in comparative law studies.[24] Nevertheless, Jean Rivero (1910-2001) used by 1972 the

[18] See I. Zajtay, "La réception des droits étrangères et le droit comparé", *Revue internationale de droit comparé*, IX (1957), p. 695.

[19] Ibid., p. 600.

[20] R. Rodière, *Introduction au droit comparé* (1979), pp. 11 ff.

[21] Ibid., p. 15.

[22] Ibid., pp. 669 ff. See also E. Agostini, *Droit comparé* (1988), pp. 243 ff.; N. Rouland, *Anthropologie juridique* (1988), pp. 337 ff. However, Agostini uses the concept of imitation in his subsequent works. See Agostini, "La circulation des modèles juridiques", *Revue internationale de droit comparé*, XLII (1990), pp. 461-467.

[23] See J. Gaudemet, *Sociologie historique de droit* (2000), pp. 91 ff.

[24] See J. W. Cairns, "Watson, Walton, and the History of Legal Transplants", *Georgia Journal of International and Comparative Law*, XLI (2013), p. 670.

syntagm *"greffe d'organes"*, beside *echange, emprunte,* and *imitation.* His angle of approach was unclear, but he seems to have been influenced by the same Tardeian diffusion of innovations through imitation perspective when he wrote:

> [T]he entire history of constitutions, from a few rare original prototypes, is made up of imitations, adaptations, and rejections. Civil rights, too, offer classic examples, whether Ataturk's Turkey importing the Swiss Civil Code, or the diffusion of Code Napoleon.[25]

Beyond emphasizing the greatness of the law exporter, the inferior position of the importer, and the unidirectional flow of legal civilization between them, this concept of imitation explained nothing about the process of imitation *per se*. The unique and complex relationship between the model and imitators was ignored. All these legal comparatists were not interested in explaining the process of legal change in terms of diffusion of innovations but in assessing the causes of similarity between the national legal systems. At best, imitation was a conscious endeavor driven by prestige; at worst, it pointed to a dubious uncritical state of mind of the receivers, mirroring the worldwide expansion of some "mature" exceptional national legal systems (especially the French) and the objectified phenomenon of legal uniformization.[26] Imitation, wrote Mario Sarfatti in 1951, occurs when one State adopts the legislation of another and is regularly undertaken by States with an inferior civilization from the State that reached the peak [of civilization].[27] Despite Zajtay's appeal and Rodière's theoretical exercise, the cross-border transfer/circulation of law remained highly undertheorized, and the concept of imitation too.

In the mid-1970s, a methodological change occurred in comparative law studies. Alan Watson (1933-2018) seemed to do justice to all "imitators" by making legal transplantation/borrowing

[25] J. Rivero, "Les phénomènes d'imitation des modelés étrangers en droit administrative", in A de Laubadère, A. Mathiot, J. Rivero, and G. Vedel, *Pages de doctrine* (1980), II, pp. 459-460. [my translation].

[26] North-American comparative law had a similar approach. See V. Corcodel, *Modern Law and Otherness. The Dynamics of Inclusion and Exclusion in Comparative Legal Thought* (2019), pp. 120 ff.

[27] M. Sarfatti, "Le droit comparé en fonction de l'unification du droit", *Revue internationale de droit comparé,* III (1951), p. 70 [my translation].

a non-demanding mass endeavor accessible to everyone. Thus, he unchained comparative law from the old differences/sameness paradigm and turned it into a historical inquiry for legal transfers. Watson did not need imitation as a key concept of his heuristic approach and was not interested in the meeting between the legal model (the original creator) and her/his imitator. He focused mainly on the "transplant bias" and the cross-border circulation of legal ideas by the legal actors looking to bolster their authority at home. However, it cannot be ignored that Watson uses concepts like "innovation" and "invention" to pinpoint the extreme rarity of law's creation and the ordinary character of legal transplants/ borrowings.[28] One may notice a clear pattern of legal change: from the exceptional innovation/invention as original creation to the ordinary diffusion through transplantation/borrowing. While his concept of "transplant" was disseminated in comparative law, legal sociology, and legal history, facing constant critique,[29] the concept of imitation had its path in the diffusion/transfer of law studies.

The idea of innovation (original creation) diffused through legal imitation inspired the Italian comparatist Rodolfo Sacco (1923-2022) in about the same period. Since the mid-1970s, he used the pattern innovation – imitation of law to explain the circulation of legal models. The influence of Watson on Sacco is not fully evident. In 1974, Sacco had outlined his theory about innovation and imitation.[30] If my insight is correct, he was influenced by the French use of imitation in the previous debates about the legal transfers inspired by the seminal work of Tarde. Later, he copiously quoted Watson and used his innovation (original creation) – diffusion approach, but wrapped it in "the original legal model versus imitators" conceptual framework.[31] In my view, Watson's

[28] As Watson puts it: "Just as very few people have thought of the wheel yet once invented its advantages can be seen and the wheel used by many, so important legal rules are invented by a few people or nations, and once invented their value can readily be appreciated, and the rules themselves adopted for the needs of many nations". See A. Watson, *Legal Transplants. An Approach to Comparative Law* (1993), p. 100.

[29] See Cairns, note 24 above, pp. 658 ff.

[30] See R. Sacco, "Les buts et les méthodes de la comparaison du droit", in Associazione italiana di diritto comparato, *Rapport nationaux italiens aux ix congres international de droit comparé* (1974), pp. 127-130.

[31] See Sacco, "Les mutations de modelés", in *La comparaison juridique au service de*

and Sacco's diffusion of innovations as original creation through borrowing/imitation has become very influential in the last five decades in comparative law.[32]

Historically speaking, we may discover behind these viewpoints a modern pattern of thinking recalibrating the old, premodern balance between innovation and imitation. Niccolo di Bernardo dei Machiavelli (1469-1527), for example, used the concept of imitation in his "Discourses" in the sense of innovation by imitating the great man of the past and returning to ancient institutions.[33] Innovation by imitating the past was the key to political stability. A negative approach from the seventeenth century onwards replaced this positive approach. The innovators became the number one enemies of the monarchies and church, of the entire social establishment, because they were threatening the social, political, and religious order and discipline. The innovators were the proponents of free will, the revolutionaries, the preachers of change. In the modern era of socio-economic progress and industrialization, innovation changed its meaning again. It became the equivalent of originality and novelty.[34] As such, it was opposed to imitation and entered sociology, anthropology, economic, and political studies. Many have inevitably noticed that the mass of imitators outnumbered the original creators/inventors. "We ourselves are infinitely more imitative than inventive", wrote Tarde in 1890.[35] This thinking pattern gave birth to the extended theoretical inquiries of Watson and Sacco about the process of legal change.

la connaissance du droit (1991), pp. 113 ff; id, "Rapport de synthèse: La circulation des modèles juridiques", in Travaux de l'Association Capitant, XLIV (1993), pp. 1-19; A. Gambaro, R. Sacco, and L. Vogel, *Le droit de l'occident et d'ailleurs* (2011), pp. 23-26.

[32] In 1990, E. M. Wise rejected the Watsonian theory of legal transplant and offered an innovation/invention–imitation perspective built on the body of knowledge produced by the early school of diffusionism, apparently not noticing that the same pattern was underlying Watson's approach. What makes Wise's viewpoint a particular case is his focus on the innovative function of diffusion/imitation. See E. M. Wise, "The Transplant of Legal Patterns", *American Journal of Comparative Law Supplement*, XXXVIII (1990), pp. 1-22.

[33] See B. Godin, "Why is Imitation Not Innovation?", in B. Godin and D. Vinck (eds.), *Critical Studies of Innovation* (2017), pp. 18 ff.

[34] B. Godin, *Innovation Contested. The Idea of Innovation over the Centuries* (2015), pp. 226 ff.

[35] Tarde, *Laws of Imitation* (1903) [1890], p. 98.

All these may explain why, in many comparative/historical approaches, the non-Western law is recognizable only as far as it is an imitation or copy of the West.[36] Unfortunately, it is not clear what exactly imitation of law means and which is the difference between imitation and, for example, influence, importation and borrowing of law. Undertheorized, the concept of imitation may become, in Veronica Corcodel's terms, a strange inclusive approach of non-coercive domination[37] in comparative law studies and (comparative) legal history. The innovation-imitation paradigm of law diffusion discussed above comes with well-established inbuilt epistemological prerequisites: it necessarily entails two sides, that is, a model (the original creator of law), her/his imitators, and a specific relationship. The legal model is unique and visible; the imitators are numerous and anonymous. The considerable weight the innovation has in modern thinking makes the flow of wisdom regularly unidirectional: from the model to imitators. Regardless any subsequent original re-creation in the receiving society, the focal point will always be the original creation. Looking for the originality of law in Latin America, after one hundred years of intensive imitation, René David (1906-1991) discovered that

> [t]he abyss that separated Latin America and European nations is now filled in. After manifesting during a century a defensive standpoint [against the Occident] and being able to preserve the achievements of the West, the jurists of Latin America may now go forward along with the Europeans to make more justice and a better world.[38]

The imitators are not tolerated but needed, no matter their motivations, to mirror the greatness of the model. Either way, the original creator (innovator) has a particular epistemological advantage in comparative legal studies. In "the diffusion of innovation through imitation approach", the imitator will always

[36] Giorgio Fabio Colombo deplores that Japan is addressed only as an importer of Western law in comparative law, with flagrant disregard for its contribution as an exporter of law. See G. F. Colombo, "Japan as a Victim of Comparative Law", *Michigan State International Law Review*, XXII (2014), pp. 731-753. See also S. Kalantry, "Reverse Legal Transplants", *North Carolina Law Review*, XCIX (2020), pp. 49-99.

[37] Corcodel, note 26 above, pp. 172 ff.

[38] David, *Le droit comparé. Droits d'hier, droits de demain* (1980), p. 171 [my translation].

be incapable of original creation, and the accent will usually fall on the diffusion process itself. Not accidentally, the imitator counts only as the trigger of the process, not as its principal actor. All these explain why diffusionists are, at best, interested only in the imitator's psychological-cognitive causes/motivations of imitation.

No wonder many allegations about the imitated or copied character of particular legal norms, institutions, or texts in some importing countries were made from the perspective of legal exporters. This frequently implied a standardization process of some legal principles, values, and institutions and their projection as legal models.[39] The epistemological endeavor of model-making entails both a previous and a subsequent process of imitation. The processes of regional political-legal convergence and legal globalization[40] become the perfect environment for expected "learning"[41] from self-promoted (global) constitutional models and sincere constitutional imitation. At the beginning of the 1990s, constitutional standardization was backed by the alleged lack of alternatives to socialist "constitutionalism" and Marxism-Leninism. "The wind of change" was blowing from the West to the East in the matter of the post-communist constitution-making process.[42] Some are attempting to grasp this large-scale change in

[39] See D. S. Law, "Constitutional Archetypes", *Texas Law Review*, XCV (2016), pp. 153-244; A.-M. Slaughter, *A New World Order* (2004).

[40] See Sacco, "Diversity and Uniformity in the Law", *American Journal of Comparative Law*, ILIX (2001), p. 171-189; B. de Witte, "New Institutions for Promoting Equality in Europe: Legal Transfers, Normative Bricolage, and European Governance", *American Journal of Comparative Law*, LX (2012), pp. 49-74; M. Bussani, "Deglobalizing Rule of Law and Democracy: Hunting Down Rhetoric Through Comparative Law", *American Journal of Comparative Law*, LXVII (2019), pp. 701-744.

[41] See B. Goderis and M. Versteeg, "Transnational Constitutionalism – A Conceptual Framework", in D. J. Galligan and M. Versteeg (eds.), *Social and Political Foundations of Constitutions* (2013), pp. 115-119.

[42] Here, one should record the impressive scholarship on the post-communist transition to democracy and the rule of law in Central-Eastern Europe. See, for example, J. Elster, "Constitutionalism in Eastern Europe: An Introduction", *University of Chicago Law Review*, LVIII (1991), pp. 447-482; R. R. Ludwikowski, "Mixed" Constitutions-Product of an East-Central European Constitutional Melting Pot", *Boston University International Law Journal*, XVI (1998), pp. 1-70.

terms of imitation.[43] As Krastev and Holmes explain,[44] the weak States (that is, the Central-Eastern European ones) did nothing else but acting ordinary when they imitated the powerful and successful States (the Western ones). They may be right, as no other way seems more proper to achieve constitutional convergence and globalization than imitation. Beyond the deterministic exercise in exceptionalism, placing the complex process of post-communist political and constitutional transition towards liberal democracy and the rule of law under an overarching concept of imitation has inner perils. Above all, it may be too reductionist, especially when the concept of imitation is poorly and unconvincingly theorized. Not all constitutional change in Central-Eastern Europe implied full-scale imitation or the mimicry the authors are trying to credit.[45] Overall, it should not have necessarily implied the unconditioned constitutional change by imitation expected by some Western scholars. In the Romanian case, a process of imitation occurred to a certain extent, but the "aspirational constitutionalism",[46] which boosts imitation, was intimately intertwined with the "aversive constitutionalism" and the expressivist ones, which reject the idea of imitation.[47] It results that the temptation of zooming-out too much is counter productive and a proper ground analysis is needed when imitation is involved. As this article will argue below, the social sciences-inspired models explaining the diffusion of (legal) institutions/policies and sameness are reducing imitation to a simple objectivated, sometimes automatic, social mechanism of (institutional) transfer and instead do injustice to the legal

[43] See M. Rosenfeld (ed.), *Constitutionalism, Identity, Difference, and Legitimacy Theoretical Perspectives* (1994), for the contributions of L. Henkin and A. Arato; J. Elster, C. Offe, and U. K. Preuss, *Institutional Design in Post-Communist Societies. Rebuilding the Ship at Sea* (1998), especially p. 15.

[44] I. Krastev and S. Holmes, *The Light that Failed. Why the West Is Losing the Fight for Democracy* (2020), pp. 20 ff.

[45] See also C. Offe, "Designing Institutions in East European Transitions", in R. E. Goodin, *The Theory of Institutional Design* (1996), pp. 199-226.

[46] The concepts of aspirational and aversive constitutionalism are herein borrowed from K. L. Scheppele, "Aspirational and Aversive Constitutionalism: The Case for Studying Cross-Constitutional Influence through Negative Models", *International Journal of Constitutional Law*, I (2003), pp. 296-324.

[47] See M. Guţan, "Romanian Constitutional Identity in Historical Context", in L. Csink and L. Trócsányi (eds.), *Comparative Constitutionalism in Central Europe* (2022), pp. 109-128. See also I. Lungu, "Romanian Constitutional Nationalism", *Polish Sociological Review*, CLX (2002), pp. 397-412.

imitation *per se*. It ignores the imitator and her/his underlying psychological-cognitive process aiming at typical outcomes and goals. The same conclusion may be drawn about the application of the paradigm innovation-diffusion-imitation in diffusion-oriented legal history aiming to explain legal pluralism in non-western societies[48] or to merely record the diffusion of legal innovations through imitation in time.[49]

A variant of this external approach stresses the perils of copying Western legal models, but its negative emphasis does not approach the process of imitation in its own right. Treating imitation as a wrong political and legal change strategy only tells a little about imitation *per se*. It may be not only an exercise in wise legal diffusionism but also a sign of "hierarchical transnationality" emphasizing "the legal inferiority", paradigmatic "legal failure", and the need for more external legal aid.[50] Thus, the focus on imitation as new innovation does not necessarily put the imitator in a more advantageous position. Nevertheless, no matter how ill-inspired and ill-directed would be the imitation of a foreign legal model, it deserves a full assessment as an extraordinary psychological-cognitive encounter between the imitator(s) and its model.

In their turn, the legal comparatists and legal historians from the "imitators" side sometimes have entirely different approaches to the same (kind of) legal phenomenon. Some see the post-communist constitutional transition in Central-Eastern Europe as a process of rational selection and borrowing of legal models.[51] The Belgian legal historians consider the Romanian 1866 constitution-making process a matter of imitation and copying (see below). However, the same authors are approaching the making of the Belgian 1831 Constitution as a mere influence, although only about

[48] See D. Heirbaut, "Europe and the People without Legal History: On the Need for a General History of Non-European Law", *Legal History Review*, LXVIII (2000), pp. 269-280.

[49] See J. Bouineau, *Traité d'histoire européenne des institutions. Tome II : XVIe – XXe siècle* (2009); J.-L. Halperin, *Histoire des droits en Europe de 1750 à nos jours* (2020).

[50] See J. L. Esquirol, "The Failed Law of Latin America", *American Journal of Comparative Law*, LVI (2008), pp. 112 ff.

[51] See A. Rapaczynski, "Constitutional Politics in Poland: A Report on the Constitutional Committee of the Polish Parliament", *University of Chicago Law Review*, LVIII (1991), pp. 595-632; V. Perju, "The Romanian Double Executive and the 2012 Constitutional Crisis", *I•CON*, XIII (2015), pp. 246–278.

5% of its text was original.[52] The Romanian (legal) scholars consider the Romanian Constitution of 1866 the outcome of an original process of re-creation. Many Western scholars are approaching the modernization of Meiji Japan and Turkey in terms of imitation.[53] In contrast, Japanese and Turkish scholars are more circumspect about this concept.[54] Esin Orücü uses the concept of imitation in the case of Turkish legal modernization during the nineteenth century and the beginning of the twentieth but favors the concepts of transposition, tuning, and infusion. The comparatist of Turkish origin accepts the dichotomy between the powerful Western-European legal models and the weak Turkish one but prefers to concentrate her analyses on the socio-cultural effects of legal imitation and borrowing.[55]

Thus, the concept of imitation is handled with methodological serendipity by many legal comparativists and (comparative) legal historians. It is deeply embedded in the unchallenged dichotomy "powerful (original) creator/innovator" versus "weak

[52] Jean Gilissen carefully avoids concepts like "imitation" and "copy" in his quest for the sources of the Belgian Constitution, favoring concepts and words like "borrowing", "taken", or "coming directly". See J. Gilissen, «La Constitution belge de 1831: ses sources, son influence», *Res Publica*, X (1968), p. 132.

[53] See J.-L. Halpérin, "Transplants of European Normativity in India and in Japan: A Historical Comparison", *Rechtsgeschichte - Legal History. Journal of the Max Planck Institute for European Legal History*, XXII (2014), p. 150; Toye, note 4 above, pp. 43 ff.; P. J. Magnarella, "East Meets West: The Reception of West European Law in the Ottoman Empire and the Modern Turkish Republic", *Journal of International Law and Practice*, II (1993), pp. 281-306; P. R. Luney, Jr., "Traditions and Foreign Influences: Systems of Law in China and Japan", *Law and Contemporary Problems*, LII (1989), pp. 129-150.

[54] See Ō. Takeharu, "Ono Azusa and the Meiji Constitution: The Codification and Study of Roman Law at the Dawn of Modern Japan", *Transcultural Studies*, I (2013), pp. 101-144; S. Ono, "Comparative Law and the Civil Code ff Japan (II)", *Hitotsubashi Journal of Law and Politics*, XXV (1997), pp. 29-52; E. Ikegami, "Citizenship and National Identity in Early Meiji Japan, 1868-1889: A Comparative Assessment", *Review of Social History*, XL (1995), pp. 185-221; T. Kinoshita, "Legal System and Legal Culture in Japan", *Zeitschrift für Japanisches Recht*, XI (2001), pp. 1-35; G. Bozkurt, "The Reception of Western European Law in Turkey (From the Tanzimat to the Turkish Republic, 1839-1939)", *Der Islam*, LXXV (2009), pp. 283-295; Y. Özcan, "The European Transformation of Turkish Bureaucratic Elites", *Journal of the Academic Elegance*, II (2015), pp. 147-189; U. Ozsu, "Receiving the Swiss Civil Code: Translating Authority in Early Republican Turkey", *International Journal of Law in Context*, VI ((2010), pp. 63-90.

[55] E. Örücü, "Infusion of the Diffused: Four Circles of Diffusion Infusing the Legal System of Turkey", in S. Farran, J. Gallen, and C. Rautenbach (eds.), *The Diffusion of Law The Movement of Laws and Norms Around the World* (2016), pp. 7-24, especially at p. 24.

barren imitator" and, for that matter, undertheorized. Imitation is a word that some discover accidentally and find pleasing and valuable. Others find it unpleasant after carefully seeking it. Thus, imitation is in peril of becoming an empty word ready to be filled in with different content about the circulation of law, mirroring the legal comparatists'/historians' scientific idiosyncrasies. In some cases, imitation may be the wrong word: the (Western) legal comparatists and legal historians may see imitation where it is missing. In other cases, notional sensibilities and legal pride tend to overlook it where it exists or underestimate its magnitude. In other words, the concept of imitation has a poor epistemological value in contemporary comparative law and comparative legal history, if it has any. One would be perfectly entitled to wonder if replacing this concept with a much more suitable one would be a wise decision. If imitation is only another all-encompassing word besides the circulation/movement/diffusion/transfer/migration of law, it would be better to avoid it. It should be kept if it is related to the mindset of the imitator and its intimate linkage with the model. However, it is obvious that a neutral meaning is needed, one capable of moving the attention from the objectified innovation-to-imitation process to the subjective imitator.

Twining urged the legal comparatists interested in "diffusion studies" not only to go interdisciplinary[56] but also to go empirically, especially by focusing "on actual behaviors on the ground". Moreover, he said, "one can study the diffusion of law on one's own doorstep".[57] This advice would be followed with great circumspection by a legal comparatist researching at the confluence with comparative legal history. Nevertheless, to a legal comparatist coming from a peripheral ordinary European legal culture, this invitation may represent a relief from the frustration of not belonging to one of Örücü's extraordinary places of legal comparison/diffusion.[58] Twining argues that the scholar of legal diffusion may learn from the study of law's circulation across small geographical areas, like the intra-national one. The (comparative) legal historian may be very sympathetic to that. The peripheral

[56] See W. Twining, "Social Sciences and Diffusion of Law", *Journal of Law and Society*, XXXII (2005), pp. 203-240.

[57] Ibid., p. 235.

[58] Örücü, "Comparatists and Extraordinary Places", in P. Legrand and R. Munday, *Comparative Legal Studies: Traditions and Transitions* (2003), pp. 467-489.

legal comparatist may need to adhere to her/his transnational approach; however, her/his small case-based perspective on the diffusion of law could be much better situated, especially when imitation is involved.

Romania is not an exotic, exceptional place of legal imitation; however, it is the object of many misconceptions as regards its legal modernization during the nineteenth and twentieth centuries. This explains why this Eastern European country may be a good starting point for the following theoretical discussion. The Romanian instances of legal transplants are numerous, especially during the nineteenth century. We focus on one relevant Romanian case of alleged constitutional imitation.[59]

This article will not attempt to discard the concept of imitation from comparative legal studies or comparative legal history. On the contrary, one cannot but agree that imitation frequently occurs in the process of legal change. However, it should be released from the traditional pattern of thinking – glorious innovation (original creation) versus embarrassed imitation – which is dominating the thinking of legal comparatists and historians. At best, addressing imitation as the transfer of something that one did not initially create herself/himself and possibly re-create it may explain its causes and socio-cultural effects. At worst, the diffusion of legal innovations (original creation) through imitation theory may transform the process of legal change in some social automatism that justifies inclusive strategies of intellectual governance in comparative law. Nonetheless, this pattern obscures or ignores the hardcore of the imitative process, that is, the special relationship between the imitator and her/his model.

The Romanian case is a starting point in reassessing the epistemological relevance of this concept against its current acceptance and use in comparative law and comparative legal history scholarship. It helps to build a proper theoretical framework. For this purpose, the next section will start with an overview of the literature on the circulation of law or the so-called theory of legal transplants. It will discuss how far the comparative

[59] The case-study literature in legal transplants studies is impressive, and there is no room here for its exhaustive account. For analytical and exemplificative purposes, the Romanian case of constitutional imitation and worldwide cases of imitation discussed in comparative constitutional law and (comparative) constitutional history will be used. Where necessary, cases of legal imitation relevant to other branches of law will be used also.

law scholars are making clear distinctions between concepts like imitation, copy, transplant, import, borrowing, transfer, and transposition and pinpoint their epistemological shortcomings. Building on the body of knowledge produced by the social sciences, especially diffusion studies, social psychology, and developmental psychology, a narrower interdisciplinary meaning of "imitation", but more relevant from the epistemological point of view, will be advanced. The accent will fall on a process that unfolds in space, time, and the minds of the legal actors.

Finally, the imitation of legal models will be theorized against its proper psychological-cognitive meaning. From this point of view, one should concomitantly address the imitated quality of a constitution or any other legal text or practice against the following four coordinates: imitation as intention, that is, the conscient voluntary intention to imitate an "idealized" legal model; imitation as (textual) product, that is, observing how far the receiver is effectively replicating the model's legal texts during the law (constitution) - making process; imitation as tendential practice, that is, observing how far the receiver is tending to faithfully replicate at home the legal behaviors and practices of the legal model(s) in order to achieve the same outcomes and goals; imitation as ongoing reproduction of the model, that is, assessing how far and with what psychological consequences the imitator is interested/capable of perpetually replicating the legal model.

In conclusion, we would be in the presence of imitation only when one legal actor consciously intends to imitate one or more legal models she/he particularly values, when she/he tends to fully and faithfully replicate the means (texts, behaviors, practices) of the legal model(s) in order to reach the same outcomes and, possibly, goals and when she/he is willing to ongoing replicate the legal model despite the obvious impossibility to replicate it faithfully. This exercise in interdisciplinary micro-comparison may bring more conceptual clarity to comparative law and make legal history more comparative.

THE MAKING OF 1866 CONSTITUTION: A ROMANIAN INSTANCE OF CONSTITUTIONAL 'IMITATION'?

On 30 June 1866, Prince Carol I (1839-1914) of Romania promulgated the first Romanian modern constitution. Its text was bargained over by the Liberal and Conservative political factions of the Romanian constitutional assembly and became a masterpiece of Romanian liberal-ethnocentric constitutionalism. Adopting the 1866 Romanian Constitution was quite a geopolitical achievement as the suzerain power, the Ottoman Empire, had second thoughts about permitting the birth of the Romanian unitary nation-state in 1862. The Constitution not only strengthened Romanian State autonomy and fostered its independence (1878) but also put Romanian society on the road towards political modernity.

The detail mentioned time and again by foreign constitutional historians and comparatists about the Romanian 1866 Constitution was the strong influence of the Belgian 1831 Constitution. The former built a parliamentary monarchy with a hereditary and powerful monarch, a bicameral parliament elected upon a high electoral census, enshrined the principles of national sovereignty, separation of powers, juridical (not political) governmental responsibility, independence of the judiciary and a rich package of human rights by closely following the Belgian text. A simple comparison of the Romanian and Belgian constitutions reveals that approximately 59% of the Romanian constitutional articles were, more or less, faithful textual translations of the Belgian ones. The percentage was high enough to capture the attention of those interested in the circulation of legal models. From various theoretical perspectives and claiming different methodological goals, foreign (legal) historians and comparatists observed in the interwar period the imitated character of the Romanian 1866 Constitution.[60] In 1924, the English (of Hungarian origin) historian and political theorist David Mitrany (1888-1975) made of the Romanian 1866 Constitution a case of irrational copy-pasting and unchallenged constitution-making process:

> They [the Romanians] wanted a written Constitution; and, of course, they wanted the most attractive Constitution that had so far blossomed in the experimental nations of Western Europe (...) Two of the more radical leaders set to work and within twenty-four hours produced a slightly adapted translation of the Belgian Constitution. The special Assembly then sitting made the draft its own, unanimously

[60] A. Tibal, *Problèmes politiques contemporains de l'Europe Orientale* (1930), p. 2.

proclaiming it there and then to be the fundamental law of Romania.[61]

This perspective soon became popular in the United States and in English-speaking historical literature.[62] In the second half of the twentieth century, Belgian legal historians and comparatists manifested a natural interest in Romanian constitutional history. In 1968, John Gilissen (1912-1988) awarded the Romanian Constitution of 1866 the title of "la plus fidèle des imitations de la Constitution belge de 1831".[63] Following the same approach, Raoul van Caenegem (1927-2018) introduced Romania into a group of European imitators, along with Spain, Greece, Piedmont-Sardinia, and Bulgaria,[64] making of the Belgian 1831 Constitution a story of successful constitutional exceptionalism. Besides "the imitators", a group of "considerably influenced" countries was detected by van Caenegem: Prussia, Poland, Hungary, and Czechoslovakia, giving a complete picture of the Belgian Constitution spread all around Europe.[65]

As an analytical concept, "imitation" implied further taxonomic endeavor. Van Caenegem distinguished, on one hand, a "more or less literally" copying of the Belgian text and, on the other hand, a "taking over" of the Belgian fundamental idea of parliamentary monarchy.[66] The author is not giving an in-depth insight of this dichotomy between imitation as copy-pasting of the text and imitation as transfer of fundamental ideas. It is unclear where Romania stands, but the inner logic of the book places it somewhat in the first category.

[61] D. Mitrany, "The New Rumanian Constitution", *Journal of Comparative Legislation and International Law*, VI (1924), p. 111.

[62] See J. S. Roucek, *Contemporary Romania and Her Problems. A Study in Modern Nationalism* (1932), p. 218; R. W. Seton-Watson, *A History of the Roumanians: From Roman Times to the Completion of Unity* (1934). Seton-Watson's book was translated into French and spread the same canon. See *Histoire de Roumains* (1937), p. 357.

[63] Gilissen, note 52 above, p. 138.

[64] R. C. van Caenegem, *A Historical Introduction to Western Constitutional Law* (1996), pp. 237-238.

[65] Ibid., p. 238.

[66] Ibid., p. 237.

Günter Frankenberg has observed that "the Belgian text was reproduced as a 'modified copy' in Romania".[67] Unique about the approach of the German legal scholar is its complex theoretical framework about the transferability of law across societies. Frankenberg is interested in what happens when the legal (constitutional) items "travel" from their initial "original" occurrence to the (side) effects they may have at the end of their voyage in a different society. He builds a multi-stage pathway of transfer which entails de-contextualization, that is, the item is stripped of its historical, socio-cultural, and legal-political contextual connotations, reduced to mere text and filled in with new idealized meaning; their inclusion as standardized (constitutional) items in the IKEA-like global market of legal commodities; finally, re-contextualization, that is, the standardized constitutional items are "bought" by the interested shoppers, adapted to a new cultural and political context, and charged with new specific meaning. Focused on legal texts and acting selectively, the shopper does not bring the same product at home. This is why re-contextualization does not imply genuine copies but modified replicas.[68] Moreover, the simple "repetition of the original propositional formula" has no relevance as long as a new meaning is added.

Following this pattern, the Romanian constitution-makers of 1866 entered the "global" market of constitutional standardized items; they selected and acquired the ones they needed, which, while unpacking and assembling, considerably resembled the text of the 1831 Belgian Constitution. However, the Romanian constitution-makers added new meaning reflecting their national-cultural background.

[67] G. Frankenberg, *Comparative Constitutional Studies. Between Magic and Deceit* (2018), p. 182. For the Romanian 1866 Constitution as a copy of the Belgian 1831 Constitution, see also J. Rupnik, "Eastern Europe: The International Context", *Journal of Democracy*, XI (2000), p. 117. Scholars of Romanian-origin are spreading nowadays the same canon about the Constitution of 1866. See C. Parau, "Romania's Transnational Constitution", in Galligan and Versteeg, note 41 above, pp. 509 ff.

[68] Frankenberg, note 67 above, pp. 118-135, especially p. 132. See also Frankenberg, "Constitutional Transfer: The IKEA theory revisited", in *I-CON*, VIII (2010), pp. 563-579; Frankenberg, "Constitutions as Commodities: Notes on a Theory of Transfer", in Frankenberg (ed.), *Order from Transfer. Comparative Constitutional Design and Legal Culture* (2013), pp. 1-25; Frankenberg, "Legal Transfer", in M.- C. Foblets, M. Goodale, M. Sapignoli, and O. Zenker, *The Oxford Handbook of Law and Anthropology* (2022), pp. 333-351.

All allegations made regarding the imported or copied character of the Romanian 1866 Constitution mainly consider the constitutional text and the quantity of "the transferred" constitutional norms and institutions. The numerous Belgian constitutional values, principles, and institutions faithfully replicated in the Romanian Constitution of 1866 are easily noticeable to every external comparative observer. However, one may doubt that this focus on imitation or copying as a textual product in the Romanian case may help to properly understand what happened in Romanian constitutional and political life before during and after the year of 1866.

The making of the Romanian 1866 Constitution was the outcome of a longer and more complex process of constitutional reception undertaken by the Romanian political elites until the end of the 1860s. The French constitutional model has been highly influential since the early nineteenth century, and many Romanian constitutional projects considered French constitutional values and institutions. Nevertheless, during the 1850s and 1860s, the French model lost its prestige in the eyes of the Romanians, being replaced with the Belgian one. The French constitutional authoritarianism of the Second Empire persuaded Romanian liberals and conservatives to seek inspiration elsewhere. The small Belgian nation, fighting for national liberty and building its national State against the surrounding European powers, amazed the Romanian elites. The Romanian interest in transforming Romania into "the Belgium of the Orient" heralded the rise of Belgian prestige in Romanian society. A significant Belgian legal influence came with the territory, but the Constitution of 1866 was not its climax, as many believe. In 1859, the so-called Romanian Central Commission of Focşani intensely debated the first Romanian constitutional project. The Belgian Constitution of 1831 was effectively on the table, and the intention to imitate it was expressly articulated. It was not integrally and faithfully transferred, but its influence in terms of values and institutions was considerable.

The constitutional project of 1859, although never promulgated, was used as a starting platform to make the Constitution of 1866. Surprisingly, the idea of faithfully imitating the Belgians completely disappeared. The Belgian Constitution was just a constitutional source among the "civilized" other. As a matter of fact, the Romanian constitution-makers considered a wide range of possible constitutional models. Belgium, the Belgians, and the

Belgian Constitution had at least 47 mentions during the debates; France and the French constitutions 44; England and English constitutionalism 33, Greece 20; Polish constitutional experiments 14; United States constitutional system 11, Italy 7, Prussia 5, Spain 2, and Portugal 2.

At first sight, the philosophy of the constitution-making process had considerably changed since 1859: back then, the faithful imitation of the Belgian prestigious text guaranteed the quality of the product; in 1866, the Belgian Constitution was a constitutional model like any other. Neither the rapporteur of the special committee nor the deputies mentioned or explained the use of the Belgian constitutional text as the primary source of the Romanian constitution.

However, imitation was not out of discussion. On the contrary, many deputies admitted that imitating Western Europe was the key to a modern constitution. Replicating foreign "civilized" constitutional ideas, values, principles, and institutions was the necessary step towards European "civilized" constitutional and political outcomes: having a functional parliamentary system of government, making the parliament the true representative of the nation, having a workable and balanced legislative procedure, limiting monarchical power, making the government juridically and politically responsible, making the judiciary an independent body, broadening political rights, endowing the citizens with equal human rights. Shared European goals were also envisaged: nation-building, national independence, political and social modernization, rule of law, social justice, and economic prosperity.

Nevertheless, the constitutional debates were aggravated by the opponents of the constitutional imitation. Some deputies understood the constitution-making process as a (Herderian) cultural expression of the people. As D. Tacu put it,

> Gentlemen, a constitution is to the life of a people what character is to a man. That is why, since we have to vote for a constitution, we must look at the people's senses and thinking and work in such a way as to respond to all their expectations and all their significant needs.[69]

G. Știrbei declared:

[69] Al. Pencovici, *Desbaterile Adunărei Constituante din anul 1866* (1883), p. 115.

> [I]t is very easy and comfortable to speak only about the human liberties, about the imprescriptible natural liberties (...) but it is harder to think about the nature of those liberties, to discover the differences between them and see which liberties a society may have, considering its culture and advance of its civilization, for example to see which liberties may effectively enjoy our country, not only on paper; because each country has its liberty: there is the French liberty, the Italian one, the English one, etc., there is also the liberty of the Mormons, but this one I do not want for my country.'[70]

Other deputies openly contested the need to imitate. "If [an institution] exists in other countries, should we have it?", rhetorically asked A. Sihleanu.[71] At stake were Romanian national (ethnic) character and "Romanian way of being". No wonder Article 2(1) stated, "The Romanian territory is inalienable"; Article 3 forbade the colonization of the Romanian territory with populations of foreign race; Article 7 granted citizenship only to Christians, and Article 21(3) proclaimed the Christian Orthodoxy the dominant religion of the Romanian State.

In a nutshell, the Romanian founders considerably and faithfully transferred the Belgian constitutional text but wanted to replicate the sound outcomes of Western European liberal constitutionalism. They were interested in reaching goals belonging to all European "civilized" nations. Moreover, different Romanian constitutional-political outcomes and goals were pursued, primarily related to the need to express and protect in the constitutional text the objective elements of the Romanian ethnic majority, that is, its national territory, the collective biological roots (ethnic purity), the (Orthodox) Christianity, and its constitutional traditions. The final version of the constitutional text was a mix between liberal and ethnocentric constitutionalism. Most constitutional values, principles, and institutions were destined to replicate the Western European political and constitutional civilization the Romanian elites admired and desired. The Constitution mirrored the need of Romanian legal and political actors to become Europeans. The rest mirrored their need to protect their Romanian national identity.

[70] Ibid., p. 117.

[71] Ibid., p. 50.

Against this backdrop, what is the value of the above-mentioned allegations about the Romanian 1866 Constitution? The Belgian authors have the exporter's external look and are naturally focusing on the textual product of the Romanian constitutional-making process. They are not interested in noticing both the unique imitative bias of the Romanian fathers of the constitution (imitation as intention) and some different axiological outcomes and goals of the Romanian constitution-making process (imitation as outcome). Their concepts of imitation and copy may reflect a parochial constitutional pride related to Belgian constitutional exceptionalism.[72] Mitrany focused on imitation as intention, but this approach has false premises and lacks scientific rigor.

Frankenberg's approach, embedded in the narrative of legal transplants/transfer studies, is more rigorous. His four-step IKEA explanatory model reconciles the similarity of constitutional texts with the contribution of the constitutional importer. The former assesses the source of the constitutional transfer and its quantity; the latter captures the particular cultural context of the receiver. Overall, he seems to be right. The making of the Romanian Constitution of 1866 looks like a selective shopping of constitutional standardized items from the Western-European market followed by cultural re-contextualization in the Romanian society and an involuntary sameness with the Belgian Constitution of 1831.

Nevertheless, as with any comprehensive theory, Frankenberg's is prone to reductionism. First and foremost, this theory of legal transfer unveils conceptual issues. Why, one may ask, should the outcome of the transfer be labeled "copy" if the accent does not fall on the transfer of the texts but on the process of re-contextualization / adaptation that occurred in the receiving society? In the Romanian case, why should the 1866 Constitution be labeled as a "modified copy" if the Belgian-like constitutional items suffered some recontextualization? At the same time, why should one focus on the textual sameness between the constitutional product of the constitution-making process and a tertium constitutional text, whether the ingredients were shopped on the free market as standardized items (commodities)?

Above all, this theory makes no room for imitation as a legal diffusion/transfer path. On one hand, it does not accept a special

[72] See also C.-E. Lagasse, «Le modèle constitutionnel belge», *Studia Politica. Romanian Political Science Review*, VIII (2009), pp. 13-14.

relationship between an imitator and a model, and, on the other, the textual sameness between two constitutions is an accidental (unpredictable) side-effect of the shopping process. However, the imitation of legal models exists, entails a textual sameness that is not accidental, and has an entirely different logic.

Was the Romanian constitution-making process of 1866 a case of constitutional imitation? Answering is a difficult task, although an imitator-model connection is discernable at first sight, that is, Romanian imitators and the Belgian constitutional model. The researcher of Romanian constitutional history must face a series of challenges: how to assess the selective choice of constitutional models against the interest to imitate foreign constitutional models?; how to approach the desire to replicate the outcomes and (partially) the goals of Western European constitutional "civilization" against the massive reproduction of the Belgian constitutional text?; why the Belgian strong influence was hidden?; how to address the intricate competition between the Western European and national ethnocentric-oriented constitutional outcomes and goals?; how to explain the ongoing obsession with Western-European "civilized" constitutional and political standards unfolding long after 1866 despite their distorted application by the Romanian political elites?; how to capture the identitarian tension among the Romanian elites? Are all these fully answered by addressing the Romanian Constitution as a textual "faithful imitation" or "modified copy" of the Belgian Constitution? The answer is no. IKEA theory of legal change has limited resources to make more comparative historical analyses of Romanian constitutional modernization through imitation in the nineteenth century. Would the other perspectives on legal imitation in comparative law be more successful?

IMITATION AS SYNONYM AND ANTONYM

While surveying the scholarly account of the diffusion/migration/circulation of law worldwide, one may observe the imitated law category in dozens of academic works. The legal comparatists detected national legal actors, especially legislators, deeply engaged in imitating the law of other nations. From this point of view, the legal world was divided into creators of original law (the models) and their imitators.

Sacco was a pioneer of legal transplants / legal diffusion studies who used the concept of imitation on a large scale. Like Watson, he had the same holistic approach to legal change in space and time. Unlike Watson, who drew his theory of legal transplants/ borrowing on the diffusion of legal innovations (original law), Sacco particularly emphasized "imitation of innovations". The latter was not new in comparative law, but Sacco intended to exploit it more thoroughly. To Sacco, innovation and imitation represent a logical unit of interdependent elements that fuels the mutation of legal models: the creation of legal models gives birth to imitation, while repeated imitations legitimize the source as a legal model. From the theory of innovation and imitation, Sacco borrowed the idea of innovation as original creation. He used the concept of "original" to draw quantitative conclusions: the imitators are global, while the creators of models are but few. This explains why the legal change generally manifests as mutation or circulation of legal models through constant imitation. Mirroring Sacco's structuralism, the legal world and national legal systems are populated with various law imitators; not only the national legislator imitates, but also the practitioners (the judges) and the legal scholars. This gives a true complexity to Sacco's concept of imitation. However, he did not take full epistemological advantage of the diffusion of innovations theory's reach body of knowledge advocating the innovation as creative imitation.[73] Nevertheless, this is not the major weakness of his approach in the logic of this paper's central argument.

Using an all-encompassing concept of imitation to designate the movement of the legal models toward their receivers, Sacco introduced a series of synonyms, that is, reception, influence, and borrowing, without further logical complications. However, the same comprehensive concept made him propose oxymoronic syntagms when he deals with the causes of the imitation. "Imposed imitation" sounds strange in the context of his argumentation, even if Sacco carefully accepts that its occurrence is shallow. Maybe the most valuable contribution of Sacco is his analysis of prestige as the supreme cause of imitation. He attempted a definition of the latter through the prism of his primary cause, with an interesting psychological emphasis: "[The imitation] is the desire to appropriate the features of other, when these features

[73] See also Sacco, "The Romanist Substratum in the Civil Law of The Socialist Countries", *Review of Socialist Law*, XIV (1988), pp. 65-86; id, "One Hundred Years of Comparative Law", *Tulane Law Review*, LXXV (2000-2001), pp. 1162-1163.

are enriched by a quality which we cannot label otherwise than prestige".[74]

This understanding of "imitation" as a quasi-irrational but conscious (not reflexive) addiction or obsession for a model, which, Sacco admitted, must be deeply analyzed by other disciplines, seems to be the most appropriate meaning of imitation in comparative legal studies. The desire of the imitator to be like her/his model is the most pertinent goal of any imitative endeavor. Thus, as Monateri rightly noticed, Sacco switched the attention from the exporter to the imitator.[75] Unfortunately, Sacco did not fully picture legal imitation as a particular relationship between an imitator and a model. He did not address important issues like the process of replication, the quantity of legal concepts, ideas, norms, or institutions that would count as imitation, how faithful should be the reproduction of the legal model's means and outcomes. However, this kind of inquiry is not relevant to his theory.

Sacco's thinking on imitation was quoted by many other legal comparativists,[76] but his "diffusion of innovation through imitation" theory did not gather many adherents. After all, imitation as a general label for all that is not original creation in law is difficult to handle in legal transplant studies. At the same time, his distinction between imposed imitation and voluntary imitation went on without in-depth theoretical endeavor.[77] Instead,

[74] Sacco (1991), note 31 above, p. 123.

[75] P. G. Monateri, "Critique et différence: le droit comparé en Italie", *Revue internationale de droit comparé*, LI (1999), p. 997.

[76] See X. Blanc-Jouvan," Centennial World Congress on Comparative Law: Closing Remarks", *Tulane Law Review*, LXXV (2000-2001), pp. 1237-1238; M. Cohn, "Legal Transplant Chronicles: The Evolution of Unreasonableness and Proportionality Review of the Administration in the United Kingdom", *American Journal of Comparative Law*, LVIII (2010), p. 586; Örücü, "Infusion of the Diffused: Four Circles of Diffusion Infusing the Legal System of Turkey", in S. Farran et al. (eds.), *The Diffusion of Law: The Movement of Laws and Norms around the World* (2015), p. 24. Sacco's approach had sound reverberations among the Italian comparatists, but without his appetite for theorization. See A. Cardone, "Protection of Fundamental Rights and Constitution-Amending Process: A Theoretical Hypothesis About Constitutional Borrowing", *European Review of Public Law*, XXVII (2015), pp. 1601-1626.

[77] See M. Graziadei, "Comparative Law as the Study of Transplants and Receptions", in M. Reimann and R. Zimmermann (eds.), *The Oxford Handbook of Comparative Law* (2019), p. 448.

the critique of Watson gave the legal transplants / legal diffusion studies a different impetus and direction.

Imitation and transplantation gradually coalesced and were frequently replaced in the process of seeking more suitable, more comprehensive, and, if possible, more neutral concepts or metaphors.[78] The debates about trans-border movement, legal influence, inspiration, mutation, circulation, transfer, diffusion, reception, migration, and acculturation multiplied in comparative law scholarship. Besides, the theoretical inquiry knew different particular accents: on causes, actors, sources/models, objects, quantity, modalities, mechanisms, advantages, risks, and effects, fabricating a variety of concepts that capture not the whole process, as Watson and Sacco did, but only pieces of it.

Thus, imitation (copying) became only one type of law diffusion beside importation, borrowing, transposition, tuning, irritation, cross-fertilization, gardening, inspiration, seeping, bricolage, and mixing.[79] Unfortunately, more terminological debates did not bring more clarity. The case studies dedicated to the imitation/copying of law are not numerous, at least in comparative constitutional law/history,[80] and do not construct a clear concept of imitation. The plethora of handbooks, (research) companions, encyclopedias, and journal articles interested in synthesis are not more helpful.[81]

[78] See D. Nelken, "Legal Transplants and Beyond: Of Disciplines and Metaphors", in A. Harding and E. Örücü (eds.), *Comparative Law in the 21st Century* (2002), pp. 19-34.

[79] D. Nelken, "Comparative Law and Comparative Legal Studies", in E. Örücü and D. Nelken (eds.), *Comparative Law. A Handbook* (2007), p. 3; id, "Defining and Using the Concept of Legal Culture", in Örücü and Nelken, above, p. 118; A. Orgus, Competition between Legal Systems, in Örücü and D. Nelken, above, p. 160; E. Örücü, "Legal Families' and 'Mixing Systems'", in Örücü and Nelken, above, p. 181; Örücü, "Law as Transposition", *International and Comparative Law Quarterly*, LI (2002), p. 214; G. Mousourakis, *Comparative Law and Legal Traditions. Historical and Contemporary Perspectives* (2019), p. 3; Husa, note 11 above, p. 120.

[80] The most explicit examples are J. M. Miller and M. Gordon's thorough accounts of the Argentinian imitation of United States Constitution during the nineteenth century: J. M. Miller, "The Authority of a Foreign Talisman: A Study of U.S. Constitutional Practice as Authority in Nineteenth Century Argentina and the Argentine Elite's Leap of Faith", *American University Law Review*, XLVI (1997), pp. 1483-1572; M. Gordon, "Don't Copy Me, Argentina: Constitutional Borrowing and Rhetorical Type", *Washington University Global Studies Law Review*, VIII (2009), pp. 487-519.

[81] Some leading handbooks in comparative law avoid the concept of imitation, which may be a welcomed honest oblivion. The chapter dedicated to legal

All these abound in value judgments about the imitated character of different legal items. Nowhere is purposefully explained what imitation exactly means. Synonyms of imitation are frequently used, but the analytical background is still fuzzy. Equating "imitation" with "large influence", "translation", "replication" or "reproduction",[82] copy,[83] borrowing[84] or mimesis[85] tells nothing relevant about the causes, mechanism/process, quantity, and goals of the imitators. "Resisting the temptation of terms"[86] or "looking for the best metaphor"[87] does not seem to be the best answer to this conceptual mayhem, as far as terms/concepts matter and imitation of law is a socio-legal and socio-psychological phenomenon in its own right.

Much clarity seems to bring the differentiation between "imitation" and "borrowing", relying on the degree of similarity between the model and the imitation.[88] Thus, taking only a few legal items from the constitutional model would be "borrowing"; taking many would be "imitation". However, this emphasis on imitation as a textual product ("imitated constitution") calls for further clarification. How much should a legal imitator take from the foreign legal model(s) to be in the presence of an "imitation"? Is the whole body of a code, constitution, or legislative act, a half (50%) or 30% sufficient? Is an entire ideology or theory sufficient,

transplant in the *Oxford Handbook of Comparative Constitutional Law* does not mention imitation as a possible "metaphor" for the cross-border movement of law. See V. Perju, "Constitutional Transplants, Borrowing, and Migrations", in M. Rosenfeld and A. Sajo, *The Oxford Handbook of Comparative Constitutional Law* (2012), pp. 1304-1327.

[82] See Graziadei, note 77 above, pp. 448-449; 460.

[83] J. Husa, *A New Introduction to Comparative Law* (2015), pp. 105-108.

[84] S. Choudhry, "Migration as a New Metaphor in Comparative Constitutional Law", in S. Choudhry, *The Migration of Constitutional Ideas* (2006), pp. 17 ff; Gordon, note 80 above, pp. 487 ff.

[85] S. Holmes and I. Krastev, "Explaining Eastern Europe: Imitation and Its Discontents", *Journal of Democracy*, XXIX (2018), p. 118.

[86] See T. S. Goldbach, "Why Legal Transplants?", *Annual Review of Law and Social Science*, XV (2019), pp. 583-601.

[87] See H. P. Glenn, "On the Use of Biological Metaphors in Law: The Case of Legal Transplants", *Journal of Comparative Law*, I (2006), pp. 358-364.

[88] D. S. Law and M. Versteeg, "The Evolution and Ideology of Global Constitutionalism", *California Law Review*, XCIX (2011), pp. 1173-1174.

or only a few relevant ideas? In the same context, some scholars are interested in the fidelity of the imitation. Discussing in the frame of "innovation and imitation" theory, Albert Kocourek (1875-1952) proposed back in the 1930s a distinction between "imitation" as "literary transplantation" and reception as "non-literary transplantation".[89] No matter how opportune these approaches may be, they gave birth to a supplementary series of concepts. "Copy", "slavish imitation", "faithful imitation", mimicry,[90] "faithful word-for-word copying",[91] "blind imitation"[92] were used to reflect a total and accurate/addictive reception. Partial imitations, quantitatively and qualitatively, were captured by "modified copy",[93] "selective imitation",[94] "selective copying".[95] The terminological effort is applaudable, but an important question remains: which quantity of legal items and how accurate the reception (translation) of foreign legal texts should be in order to be in the presence of an imitation?

A sensitive issue is the motives/goals of the legal imitation. Many legal transfers have been labeled "imitations" or "copies" considering their large quantity and high fidelity, even if it was clear from the beginning that their authors had their agenda and different interests at home and effectively used foreign law to accomplish them. This is an evident focus on the immediate visible (textual) product of the so-called imitation/copy. Some scholars may be interested in this product, but how relevant is it to label it "imitation"? This is like naming imitation the act of asking her/his neighbor for her/his fancy high-tech lawnmower, known and appreciated by the entire neighborhood, to groom her/

[89] A. Kocourek, "Factors in the Reception of Law", *Tulane Law Review*, X (1935-1936), pp. 209-230.

[90] Örücü, *The Enigma of Comparative Law* (2004), p. 88.

[91] Husa, note 11 above, p. 53.

[92] D. J. Galligan and M. Versteeg, "Introduction. Theoretical Perspectives on the Social and Political Foundations of Constitutions", in Galligan and Versteeg, note 41 above, p. 15.

[93] M. Siems, *Comparative Law* (2018), p. 251.

[94] A. Jettinghoff, "State Formation and Legal Change", in D. Nelken and J. Feest (eds.), *Adapting Legal Cultures*, (2001), p. 102; M. Graziadei, "Legal Transplants and the Frontiers of Legal Knowledge", *Theoretical Inquiries in Law*, X (2009), p. 732.

[95] Husa, note 11 above, p. 117.

his dog. Perhaps some would notice that "borrowing" implies not only quantity but also the idea of purpose. Would not be much more inspired to label "borrowing" a large quantity – high fidelity reception of law made for particular purposes at home?

Last but not least, a distinction between imitation and borrowing may be suggested considering the mindset of the imitator. Nobody purposively theorized this approach, but one's account of legal transplantation/diffusion may have an underlying distinction between imitation as an irrational reception of law and borrowing as a rational reception of law. This viewpoint eliminates the rational choice as a trigger of imitation, which is debatable.

Any distinction between imitation and borrowing relying on the quantity and fidelity of the legal items transferred from the legal model in the receiving society is highly unsatisfactory. Considering the legal imitators' goals could be a solution, but only inside the proper theoretical framework. Krastev and Holmes, followed by Graziadei,[96] distinguish between "imitation of goals" and borrowing as "imitation of means". Limiting imitation to mere goals is problematic as it makes it difficult to capture the "true" imitative behavior. Without imitation of the means, the legal transfer may become, as the authors themselves pointed out, mere shallow mimetic behavior. Limiting imitation to irrationality has the merit of placing a particular emphasis on the imitator's mindset but considerably simplifies the process of imitation himself. At this point, it is clear that the state of the art in legal transplants/ diffusion studies in comparative law has no valuable answers, that a different perspective is necessary, and that interdisciplinarity would be the proper solution.

THE CONCEPT OF "IMITATION" IN SOCIAL SCIENCES

The concept of imitation does not belong only to comparative law or (comparative) legal history. On the contrary, it entered comparative legal studies from neighboring social sciences, especially anthropology and sociology. Sacco's approach is much indebted to the innovation and imitation theories developed, among

[96] Krastev and Holmes, note 44 above; M. Graziadei, "What Does Globalisation Mean for the Comparative Study of Law?", *The Journal of Comparative Law*, XVI (2021), pp. 527 ff.

others, by sociologists and philosophers of culture like Gabriel Tarde. This section intends neither to establish the paternity of the concept of "imitation" nor to survey its circulation in and between social sciences. Rather, it proposes an interdisciplinary theoretical framework for its use in comparative law and comparative legal history. It is doubtful that both these disciplines have the inner resources to provide the needed theoretical background. Despite Twining's appeal for interdisciplinarity and some limited use of methodological wisdom collected from diffusion studies, imitation is still undertheorized.

To Bandeira Galindo, comparative law studies legal transplants in space, whereas legal history may add specific epistemological value by studying legal transplants in time.[97] No matter how this sounds, this idea entails that both legal history and comparative law investigate the past. However, he is wrapping this interplay between space and time in Koselleck's ideas about history as "experience and expectations". While the experiences of legal transplantation are geolocated, the expectations put a different emphasis on future progress and prognosis. The author is linking this "subjective perception of how time flows" with the necessity to thoroughly understand the role of individual actors in the transplantation process.[98] This perspective may have a seminal impact on this discussion about imitation.

Imitation of legal models occurs both in space and time. However, one could not agree more with Sacco's emphasis on the multiplicity of individual actors of legal imitation. Imitation of foreign legal models is not primarily undertaken by societies, peoples, or countries but by legislators, legal scholars, judges, and even practicians of law. More than once, the accent was on the constitutional founders' capacity to learn from and entirely assume foreign constitutional models.[99] At the same time, many legal comparatists have discussed the mindset of these importing legal actors, that is, their motivations, their obsession and admiration for prestigious legal models, their strategies, their public discourse and publications about the necessity to imitate a particular foreign code

[97] G. R. Bandeira Galindo, "Legal Transplants between Time and Space", in Duve, note 3 above, pp. 134 ff.

[98] Ibid., p. 144.

[99] Law and Versteeg, note 88 above, pp. 1173-1175.

or constitution, their hopes and expectation vis-à-vis the imitation *per se*. Accordingly, we may accept that imitation of law has a spatial and temporal dimension, but a psychological-cognitive one should be added. Legal imitation occurs in time, space, and minds and is undertaken by specific legal actors. This certainly shows the direction of the proper interdisciplinary approach.

A quick look in the direction of social sciences allows the interested researcher to discover a considerable amount of works covering a wide range of methodological approaches to imitation or using the concept of imitation to explore the encounters between humans, societies, and cultures. Above all, the most appealing (inter)disciplinary area is, as Twining himself noticed,[100] the impressive body of knowledge produced by diffusionists. At first sight, the theories of innovation and diffusion are worth exploring, considering their impact on the thinking of leading legal comparativists like Watson and Sacco. The diffusionists working on the grounds of anthropology first emphasized that the civilizational/cultural similarity between societies is less caused by independent/parallel cultural innovation and uniformity of societal development and more by diffusion of innovations. Since the early stages of this approach, imitation of innovations was cornered as the driving force behind the cultural change.[101] Imitation was a conceptual construct necessarily used in balance with innovation: imitation is inevitable and predominant because genuine innovation is rare. Those who are not innovators are simply condemned to imitate. Interestingly, imitation was not understood as a model-imitator relationship, and the idea of replication was of secondary importance. On the contrary, the accent frequently fell on cultural diversity: diffusion of innovation by imitation is prone to new innovation in the imitating society. This explains why societies are still culturally diverse. In this theoretical context, the concept of "acculturation" has been introduced to highlight that diffusion (by imitation) is actually innovation. The early sociologists had the

[100] Twining, note 56 above, pp. 217 ff.

[101] B. Godin, "Invention, Diffusion and Linear Models of Innovation: The Contribution of Anthropology to a Conceptual Framework", *Journal of Innovation Economics & Management*, III (2014), pp. 11 ff.

same emphasis on imitation as an innovation,[102] and the work of Tarde, among others, is considered seminal in this direction.[103]

The dichotomy between innovation and diffusion (imitation) spread from anthropology and sociology to various social sciences like economics and industry innovation, marketing, political sciences, psychology, and history. However, as Godin remarks, the interest in imitation constantly diminished during the twentieth century and the beginning of the twenty-first. It was replaced by concepts like acceptance, adoption, contagion, and transfer as the focus on invention and innovation increased. This trend means the diffusion of the innovation theory may be irrelevant to the central argument of this article.

The diffusion of innovation (by imitation) explains the cultural change and may also explain the legal change. Some theoretical standpoints are useful for grasping the process of legal imitation. Following Tarde's line of thinking, diffusionists such as Everett M. Rogers and Elihu Katz accepted the individuals and the interaction between them as the main unit of analyses and discussed their voluntaristic character of the transfer/imitation.[104] At the same time, the emphasis on imitation as new innovation / new invention[105] may reinforce the idea that nothing is faithfully replicable. The imitation of law makes no exception.

However, it is unsatisfactory as a theoretical framework in comparative law and comparative legal history. First, it eventually goes beyond the binomial model-imitator conceptual background, which is epistemologically needed for any fruitful discussion about legal imitation. Second, it cannot fully explain the psychological-cognitive process behind the decision to imitate or why the legal actors of the imitating society are eager to faithfully and perpetually replicate the legal means, outcomes, and goals of their legal model. The Romanian political elites of the mid-nineteenth century did not desire to innovate, even if they did

[102] Godin, note 33 above, pp. 17 ff.

[103] See E. Katz, "Theorizing Diffusion: Tarde and Sorokin Revisited", *The Annals of the American Academy of Political and Social Sciences,* DLXVI (1999), pp. 144-155; J. Kinnunen, "Gabriel Tarde as a Founding Father of Innovation Diffusion Research", *Acta Sociologica,* XXXIX (1996), pp. 431-442.

[104] J. Srivastava and J. J. Moreland, "Diffusion of Innovations: Communication Evolution and Influences," *The Communication Review,* XV (2012), p. 295.

[105] E. M. Rogers, *Diffusion of Innovations* (2003), pp. 175 ff.

it involuntarily. They wanted to perpetually replicate Western European legal institutions and political mechanisms to achieve its modern political-legal standards and civilization.

Perhaps the main disadvantage of the diffusion of innovation theory is the negative shade it throws on imitation. The dichotomy innovation-imitation, the identification of the innovation with creativity, not only lets the imitation undertheorized but, as Godin puts it, projects imitation "as a second-rate strategy and policy"[106] and, as emphasized above, the imitator of legal innovations as a second-rate legal actor.

Other viewpoints may be more relevant to the central argument inside the broad frame of diffusion studies. Some scholars of policy diffusion focus on specific mechanisms of diffusion across States or municipalities (city-to-city diffusion) driven by individual actors, that is, the policy-makers. For example, C. R. Shipan and C. Volden[107] discuss four policy diffusion mechanisms: learning, economic competition, imitation, and coercion. Learning means observing the experiences of other governments and choosing proven successful alternatives, whereas economic competition triggers learning about the benefits of adopting others' economic policies. Imitation is opposed to learning and involves "copying the actions of others to look like the other". Coercion may trigger diffusion directly or indirectly, horizontally or vertically between States or intra-States. Z. Elkins and B. Simmons,[108] in turn, propose adaptation (to altered conditions) and learning as classes of mechanisms of policy diffusion. In their view, learning also means observing and assessing others' actions in terms of benefits and perils. Adaptations may be reputation-sensitive and prone to imitation.

It is important to remark on the interest of the policy diffusion theorists in diffusion as a process triggering specific outcomes. However, this approach is only partially enlightening to the central argument. On the brighter side, their findings may help to unveil the policy-makers' decisions backstage. The desire to be

[106] Godin, note 33 above, p. 25.

[107] C. R. Shipan and C. Volden, "The Mechanisms of Policy Diffusion", *American Journal of Political Sciences*, LII (2008), pp. 840-857.

[108] Z. Elkins and B. Simmons, "On Waves, Clusters, and Diffusion: A Conceptual Framework", *The Annales of the American Academy*, DXCVIII (2005), pp. 38 ff.

like others or sensitivity to the reputation of others may explain the imitational behavior of the legal actors. On the darker side, the focus on outcomes channels the analyses towards costs and benefits. Diffusion mechanisms are assessed against each other, and imitation/adaptation is not the winner. All mentioned authors concur in accepting the harmful effects of imitation/adaptation. Having a less rational impetus,[109] ignoring the consequences of their decisions, the imitators are perfectly positioned to transfer ill-suited policies[110] whereas reputation-driven adaptors "are likely to lead to the adoption of suboptimal institutions".[111] These scientific standpoints are not interested in clarifying the whole process of imitation in its own right.

Since Twining's urge for interdisciplinarity in comparative law, a relatively small number of empirical inquiries attempted to assess the process of law diffusion using research tools and concepts borrowed from policy diffusionists. Their great merit again relies on their focus on the motivations and cognitive mechanisms of the legal actors in the diffusion of the legislative innovation process.[112] The latter may be driven by emulation/acculturation/imitation, social learning, competition, and coercion. Behind emulation/imitation may exist a valuation process (the best legal solution) or the desire for acceptance and legitimacy. The competition entails "strategical imitation" for economic reasons. Their interest in individual legal actors had fruitful results in understanding judicial behavior, a field which the discussants of judicial transplants neglected.[113] The interest in "individual parties", for example, colleges, universities, public corporations, law firms, lawyers, as diffusors of legal innovations, is increasing.[114] Diffusion of innovation theory has intrinsic value for its contribution to the study of law migration,

[109] See also Shipan and Volden, "Policy Diffusion: Seven Lessons for Scholars and Practitioners", *Public Administration Review*, LXXII (2012), pp. 788-796.

[110] Shipan and Volden, note 107 above, p. 854.

[111] Elkins and Simmons, note 108 above, p. 47.

[112] See C. Engel and K. Weinshall, "Diffusion of Legal Innovations", *Annual Review of Law and Social Science*, XVIII (2022), p. 145. The authors are recording all contributions in law diffusion until 2022.

[113] See L. Epstein, U. Sadl, and K. Weinshall, "The Role of Comparative Law in the Analysis of Judicial Behavior", *American Journal of Comparative Law*, LXIX (2021), pp. 689-719.

[114] Engel and Weinshall, note 112 above, pp. 148 ff.

for emphasizing the relevance of "micro-perspectives" (centered on individuals), for grasping the psychological and cognitive mechanisms underpinning it, for assessing imitation's impact in terms of success or failure.

However, all these address imitation as a mechanism of law diffusion without explaining what it means and without treating it in its own right. This is more obvious in the law/policy diffusion approaches based on quantitative research. Addressing imitation as a mechanism of law diffusion in order to discover patterns of legal-textual sameness at the regional or global level may have its rationale but does not explain legal imitation itself.[115]

The institutional transfer approach[116] on imitation could be more relevant, for it critically draws on diverse theoretical threads focused on the meeting and institutional change between societies. Wade Jacoby, for example, is building his methodological blueprint by distancing from the theoretical standpoints of comparative political economy, diffusion of innovations, and policy borrowing.[117] From his point of view, comparative political economy is too focused on diversity and neglects the convergence by imitation, the diffusion tradition approaches imitation as automatism,[118] and policy borrowing is poorly addressing the necessary linkage between the policymakers' interest in borrowing and their subsequent strategies in replicating the model. Instead, Jacoby addresses imitation heuristically by focusing on the causes/motivations, the actors, the models to be imitated (emulated), and the process of imitation, including, most importantly, the strategies of the model's replication in the receiving society. Thus, institutional transfer, as "a key mode of imitation" involves

[115] See B. Goderis and M. Versteeg, "The Diffusion of Constitutional Rights", *International Review of Law and Economics*, XXXIX (2014), pp. 1-19; C. G. Couto and G. L. Absher-Bellon, "Imitation or Coercion? State Constitutions and Federative Centralization in Brazil", *Brazilian Journal of Public Administration*, LII (2018), pp. 321-344.

[116] See also H.-J. Wagener, "Institutional Transfer", in W. Merkel, et al. (eds.), *The Handbook of Political, Social, and Economic Transformation* (2019), pp. 526-530.

[117] W. Jacoby, *Imitation and Politics: Redesigning Modern Germany* (2001), pp. 1 ff.

[118] One cannot but agree. We may have in mind Philip Bobbit's book *The Shield of Achilles - War, Peace and the Course of History* [2003], which addresses the history of international relations and constitutional development across the European continent in terms of innovation and mimicry. The latter is an automatic response of the non-innovative States in the harsh international competitive climate.

three necessary conditions: "state elites refer explicitly to a model prominent in another place; they try to identify the foreign model's legal framework and the actors that help its function; finally, these elites build a replica of all or part of the model (either from scratch or by remodeling indigenous institutions to approximate the foreign model)".[119]

We may identify a particular definitional pattern: imitation means the identification, understanding, and valorization of the model followed by its more or less faithful replication in the receiving society. Jacoby places an essential emphasis on the motivations and goals of the policy-makers interested in imitation. Imitation is an intentional and purposive endeavor. This institutional transfer theory could also provide interesting insight into the strategies of particular actors of imitation (policymakers) to reproduce and insert the copied institutions in their home society.[120] Nevertheless, Jacoby strategically avoids the discussion about the success and failure of the institutional imitation, even if he is aware of the cultural challenges the institutional transfer meet in the receiving society. Instead, he prefers the concept of "effectiveness". "Effectiveness occurs when the transferred institutions acquire a legal framework, when it performs in the new society in ways broadly consistent with the aims (...) that led to the transfer attempt, and when it persists by being reproduced over time (though presumably not without some subsequent changes)".[121] The continuing attempt to reproduce the model is essential to understand institutional transfer as an imitation.

Eleonor Westney's sociological approach to (political) organizational transfer may be grasped in the same theoretical framework. She unfolds her analyses of Japanese political-statal modernization during the Meiji era against the general dichotomy between innovation and imitation. However, she also discusses topics common to institutional transfer: the motives of imitation/emulation, the encounter between the imitator (emulator) and the model, the observation and understanding of the model, the voluntary and rational (or not) selection of the model(s), the role played by prestige. Her debt to the diffusion of innovation theory

[119] Jacoby, note 117 above, p. 2.

[120] Ibid., p. 3.

[121] Ibid., p. 12.

makes Westney highlight the innovative character of the imitation (emulation), but the idea of continuing imitation of the model is not entirely absent.[122]

No matter how applicable these theories of transfer/diffusion are, they are naturally (following the pattern innovation-imitation-new innovation) focusing on political and institutional/organizational change in the receiving society. Their view may disqualify imitation as a path to (legal) change. As the sociologist and political theorist A. Arato put it: "Imitation of anything is a poor reason, due especially to the fact that (...) concrete models have a way of turning into something quite different when adopted under dramatically different circumstances".[123] This particular focus may be counterbalanced by the sociological theory of institutional isomorphism. This one uses the concepts of "voluntary imitation" and "mimesis" to explain the social mechanisms underlying the phenomenon of institutional change towards greater homogeneity.[124] It explains imitation by attraction as a learning process that integrates the decision-makers in specific socialization networks. Successful institutions are attractive,[125] which may contribute to our general discussion about prestige as a cause of imitation. Mimesis is a more straightforward form of imitation or, we may say, not imitation. It is rather a shallow imitation developed as a strategy of legitimation by the decision-makers.[126]

Institutional isomorphisms may be helpful to assess the linkage between imitation and institutional sameness, but, like any focus on objectified sameness, it has poor epistemological relevance. For example, it ignores the perpetual interconnection between the imitator and the model: it cannot correctly answer why the legal actors continue to imitate a legal model despite the evident

122 D. E. Westney, *Imitation and Innovation The Transfer of Western Organizational Patterns to Meiji Japan* (1987), p. 25.

123 A. Arato, "Forms of Constitution Making and Theories of Democracy", *Cardozo Law Review*, XVII (1995), p. 219.

124 See J. Beckert, "Institutional Isomorphism Revisited: Convergence and Divergence in Institutional Change", *Sociological Theory*, XXVIII (2010), p. 150.

125 Ibid., p. 155.

126 Ibid., pp. 157 ff.

institutional and behavioral discrepancy between the model and imitating society.

Overall, we may keep from the diffusionists their focus on the role played by the individual (leader, policy-maker) in social change. At the same time, we may remark on their interest in giving imitation the proper attention as a complex cognitive-decisional and behavioral occurrence of intersocietal (cultural) diffusion. However, our interdisciplinary approach is more interested in the psychological-cognitive process intimately linking the actors of legal imitation with their legal models regardless of the political-institutional consequences of their endeavor of (legal) change. For this purpose, a more in-depth psychological inquiry is necessary.

Of maximum interest is the body of knowledge produced by social psychology that inherited Tarde's psychological insight.[127] In the mid-twentieth century, N. E. Miller and J. Dollard[128] made imitation a hard case of learned cultural diffusion between groups (societies). On the same line of thinking, W. M. Hurh proposed at the end of the 1960s a definition of imitation as an object-directed motivated action of re-enacting the action of a model.[129] As such, imitation belongs only to humans and is an integral intentional process. Considering the then state of the art in social sciences, Hurh differentiated imitation from mere "similar behavior" or "organic impulse". Hurh's accent is relevant to the conscious relationship between the imitator and her/his "model-image": the former constantly directs her/his action toward the latter. This is why she/he is not a simple follower but an emulator, that is, the imitator is not distancing from her/his model. On this definition, Hurh constructs a five steps process of imitation: (1) the predisposition to imitation determined either by "because-motivation" or "in-order-to motives"; (2) the preacquaintanceship or contact (voluntary or involuntary) with a possible model; (3) the evaluation of the new objective entity; (4) idealization of the new

[127] V. C. de la Torre, "Imitation and Distinction. History of Two Theoretical Concepts in Social Psychology: The Legacy of Simmel, Tarde and Bourdieu", *Revista de Historia de la Psicologia*, XLII (2021), pp. 15-20; M. Blute, "Gabriel Tarde and Cultural Evolution: The Consequence of Neglecting our Mendel", *Journal of Classical Sociology*, (2022), pp. 1-19.

[128] N. E. Miller and J. Dollard, *Social Learning and Imitation* (1945).

[129] W. M. Hurh, "Imitation: Its Limitation in the Process of Inter-Societal Cultural Diffusion", *International Journal of Comparative Sociology*, X (1969), pp. 271-272.

objective entity as a desirable model; (5) ongoing re-enactment of the idealized model's action in order to reach the desired goal, for example, "a better living condition".[130]

However, the author is aware of the action of replication's limits in complex human interaction. Despite the imitator's re-enactment, the imitation is always prone to "new-enactment" in the inter-societal diffusion process. With this conclusion, Hurh falls under the influence of Rogers' theory of imitation/adaption as innovation. However, his approach has two merits: on one hand, he establishes a clear cognitive-psychological pattern of imitative action, and on the other, he clearly emphasizes the decisive weight of continuing re-enactment or replication in the whole process.

Hurh is building his theory on an "ideal-type" imitation that explains the interaction between individuals and between groups. Understanding the basic imitative behavior in humans allowed him to properly asses the cross-societal imitation and its inner limits. The diffusionists helped Hurh to understand that faithful replication is impossible and, necessarily, imitation leads to innovation. Nevertheless, does the impossibility of faithfully replicating the model occur only in cross-societal imitation? Hurh's strategic concept of imitation must be improved.

An interesting effort of conceptual clarification and theoretical synthesis has come from developmental psychology. Working on Tomasello's ideas, Ellen Fridland and Richard Moore[131] attempted to construct a meta-theory of imitation. In their view, an imitation is an intentional act of one subject to reproduce "the very same behavior" and outcome of another subject (demonstrator) without necessarily fully understanding the intentional content of its goals. On one hand, whether the imitator recognizes the demonstrator's behavior as intentionally produced and goal-directed is sufficient.[132] This does not rule out the possibility that the agent of imitation can understand the intentional content of the demonstrator and of her/ his goals. The authors point out that the imitator does not always understand the intentions and goals of the demonstrator and is not expected to do so necessarily. On the other hand, the imitator

[130] Ibid., pp. 274-275.

[131] E. Fridland and R. Moore, "Imitation Reconsidered", *Philosophical Psychology*, XXVIII (2015), pp. 856-880.

[132] Ibid., p. 857.

must intend to reproduce faithfully the behavior/techniques of the model. The last point is considered the minimum criteria and unique mark of human imitative behavior.[133]

All these may be accepted as the basic schemata of imitative behavior in humans. Of maximum interest for a workable concept of imitation in comparative law and comparative legal history are two aspects: first, the imitator is not necessarily expected to replicate the goals of the model, and, second, the imitator is not expected to replicate precisely the techniques/means of the model. The imitator may have her/his own goals, and the faithful replication of the means is tendential. Faithful imitation of the means (methods), outcomes, and goals (intentions) is impossible because, as Emma Flynn puts it, "imitation brings with it an element of change even for those who wish to copy with exact precision; [a]doption of a behavior that one has witnessed has critical differences to the original performance".[134]

One may gain valuable conceptual guidance from the theoretical approaches to imitation discussed above. Above all, we must remember that comparative law and comparative legal history approach legal imitation as an inter-societal transfer undertaken by specific individual social actors. At the same time, the object of this particular transfer is not a basic human behavior but a sophisticated mix of ideas, institutions, and practices. Legal imitation does not mean an instant reflexive reaction to external stimuli but a timely identification, valuation, and reproduction process. Replicating a legal model implies translating ideas and concepts, making legal texts before any visible legal conduit, and aiming toward complex outcomes and goals. Last but not least, it implies psychological and complex socio-cultural conditionalities. Against this backdrop, this article approaches the imitation of foreign legal models as a cognitive endeavor undertaken by specific legal actors, in particular socio-cultural, (geo)political and economic contexts, underpinned by a complex psychological process.

[133] See Fridland, "Imitation, Skill Learning, and Conceptual Thought: an Embodied, Developmental Approach", in L. Swan (ed.) *Origins of Mind* (2012), pp. 203-224.

[134] E. Flynn, "Imitation is the Sincerest Form of … Cultural Evolution, or Is It?", *Journal of Cognition and Culture*, XX (2022), p. 438.

The emphasis on individual psychology is not hazardous. Imitative behavior in humans is a natural component of social (cultural) learning and cultural development that must be understood in its own right,[135] not addressed in terms of superiority and inferiority. Assessing the positive or negative impact of imitation as a diffusion mechanism between societies is only of secondary relevance. This may downgrade the imitation to a mere unfortunate mechanism of legal change available to weak legal cultures/traditions. This is not germane to our argument to assess the imitation of the Western-European constitutional means and outcomes by the Romanian elites in and after 1866 as a wrong political step, even if the impact on the Romanian constitutional-political life was negative. In the logic of this article, the imitation of foreign legal models is a process of social interaction that is born, unfolds, and ends in the minds of the legal actors.[136]

The psychological approach is better situated to explain the need to imitate, the preference for particular foreign legal models, the amount and fidelity of textual transfer, the intricate linkage between the means, outcomes, and goals, the interest to faithfully and continuously replicate the model and the possible identitarian crisis that may occur. It narrows the imitation of law to a straightforward endeavor of legal change by making a necessary distinction from borrowing. Accordingly, an operational concept of imitation in comparative law and comparative legal history must entail:

(a) the discovery, observation, and (possible) understanding of the model's means, outcomes, and goals followed by "evaluation", "idealization", and transformation of the other in "model-image";[137]

(b) a voluntary and conscious intention to reproduce the means, outcomes, and (possibly) the goals of the model;

135 See H. Farmer, A. Ciaunica, and A. F. de C. Hamilton, "The Function of Imitative Behaviour in Humans", *Mind and Language*, XXXIII (2018), pp. 378-396.

136 This approach must not be confounded with Ewald's "law in minds" as comparative jurisprudence. See W. Ewald, "The Jurisprudential Approach to Comparative Law: A Field Guide to 'Rats'", *American Journal of Comparative Law*, XLVI (1998), pp. 701-707. This article's perspective is purposively psychological.

137 Hurh, note 129 above, p. 274.

(c) the tendency to reproduce the model's means, outcomes, and (possibly) goals as faithfully as possible in order to achieve the expected change;

(d) as long as a perfect imitation is impossible and any "re-enactment is a new enactment",[138] the continuing intention of the imitator to reproduce the model's means, outcomes, and (possibly) goals is essential.

POSSIBLE THEORETICAL BACKGROUND FOR LEGAL IMITATION

Both comparative law and comparative legal history need the concept of "imitation" to capture a particular movement of law in space, time, and minds from one society to another. The properly speaking phenomenon of imitation exists in the cross-border circulation of law. For that matter, the concept of "imitation" needs clarification and special epistemological assessment. It needs not only case-by-case research but also a clear theoretical framework. In what circumstances may a legal/constitutional text be labeled an "imitation" of another? When would one be entitled to speak about legal imitation and not legal borrowing?

The concept of imitation advanced above should not be used to explain either the causes of some particular type of law diffusion, its mechanisms, or its purposes. It should explain the causes, mechanisms, and purposes as a single logical unit. The movement of law across societies should meet four criteria in order to be labeled imitation: (a) the imitation of a legal model must be a conscious, intentional action of the legal actors oriented toward a foreign legal model and driven by particular goals; (b) the actors of legal imitation are transferring in various combinations between quantity and quality (fidelity) the legal ideas, ideologies, concepts, norms, institutions, and texts of the legal model; (c) the actors of legal imitation are tending to reproduce in their home society the legal behaviors/practices/techniques of the legal model in order to reach the same outcomes and (possible) goals; (d) the intentional process of reproducing the legal norms and practices must be ongoing, despite its inevitable cognitive and socio-cultural limitations.

[138] Ibid., p. 275.

These four criteria are not isolated progressive stages of the same imitative process, although a particular timeline may be detected: the intentional, voluntary decision to imitate is followed by the reproduction of the legal texts, succeeded, at its turn, by the ongoing reproduction of legal behaviors and practices. They are inevitably overlapping and cannot be understood otherwise but as a whole: the voluntary intention to imitate a particular legal model does not qualify as imitation unless it is followed by the ongoing reproduction of texts, behaviors and practices, outcomes, and (possibly) goals; the mere reproduction of legal texts, behaviors, and practices does not qualify as imitation, no matter how faithfully they are reproduced unless the imitator intends and tries to reproduce the outcomes and (possibly) the goals of the legal model ongoingly; the ongoing reproduction of legal model's outcomes and (possibly) goals do not qualify as imitation unless the texts, behaviors and practices are reproduced as faithfully as possible; the intentional reproduction of texts, outcomes and goals does not qualify as imitation unless it is a tendential ongoing process.

This approach does not contribute to the classical topics of the legal transplants studies, for example, the possibility of legal transplants; how legal transplants work; the conditions for a successful transplant. It does not intend to add to the impressive body of knowledge on the cultural and economic effects of legal transplants in the receiving societies that have been the favorite concern in comparative law in the last two decades. Those interested in finding conclusions regarding the process of legal mixing at large or legal globalization will be disappointed, although the viewpoint this article advances may have relevance for these topics. As far as legal imitation is approached as a psychological-cognitive process, the scientific interest goes toward the actors of imitation's hopes, strategies, and behaviors vis-à-vis their 'idealized' legal model. As the imitator of a foreign legal system is interested in the perpetual replication of the model's outcomes, goals, and means, the accent falls neither on the legal culture, legal hybridization or legal globalization. The aim is to establish the meaning of legal imitation in its own right, not to assess its impact on the receiving society or the global legal standards. At most, it may be considered, in terms of Graziadei,[139] an exercise in deepening the micro level of legal

[139] Graziadei, note 94 above, pp. 730 ff.

change through legal transplantation. Imitation of foreign legal models may be surveyed as a complex unit of "mediated action" driven by individual legal professionals.

Imitation as intention

The intention of legal actors to imitate a particular legal model exists at the beginning of every legal imitation. Three factors determine intentional imitation of law: (i) the dissatisfaction of legal actors with the legal, social, economic, and political status of their society overall, with the current governmental policies or the lack of policies, the content, coherence, quantity of legislation, the quality and efficiency of the legislation in force or the lack of any solution, with their professional skills and standards, particularly; (ii) the need to change, and (iii) the knowledge about legal solutions in other societies.

Dissatisfaction is contextually determined and may be distinguished from observing other legal solutions only for analytical purposes. It usually implies a process of (reflexive) comparison with other societies. The need for change posits a distinct cluster of sensitive issues: would it mean the rejection of the domestic socio-cultural context or its complete ignorance?; how interested are the dissatisfied legal actors in preserving and protecting the local culture or legal (national) identity during the process of imitation? Clearly, a strong sense of dissatisfaction triggers the need to be different, the need to completely identify with something else.

Knowing about the existence of a proper legal solution in a foreign society prompts the question: how did the legal actors come to acknowledge its existence? The problem was not ignored in legal transfers studies but was usually hidden behind the binary voluntary – involuntary/imposed transfer of law. In the logic of our central argument, cross-border imitation of law cannot be but conscious and intentional. There is no such thing as a spontaneous or imposed legal imitation. Imitation is deliberate because it is based on observing the legal model and learning about its outcomes, goals, and means.

A unique valorization and idealization of the envisaged legal model must occur. In Sacco's terms, legal imitation usually implies admiration for specific legal models and a desire to have them at home. Sacco's account is simplistic, and his concept of "prestige", like the instrumental concept of prestige belonging to Watson,[140] is undertheorized. The concept of efficiency was advanced as a replacement,[141] but its focus on rational selection and choice could not fully explain the meeting between the imitator and the model. However, the efficiency of the legal model in its socio-cultural and economic environment may be part and parcel of its prestige. The actors of legal imitation desire a particular legal model because its efficiency (economic or not) is widely recognized and appreciated. This happens because prestige is not an intrinsic value of a legal model. As Miller suggests,[142] prestige (as efficiency) is a matter of subjective perception. We may add that it results from the encounter between the actors of the legal imitation and the legal model, followed by a psychical process of valorization and idealization. Driven by prestige, admiration[143]/veneration, and desire or talismanic authority,[144] the imitators naturally tend to faithfully assume the legal model(s) as a whole. This is why syntagms like blind copy or slavish imitation are tautological.

A meaningful discussion concerns the role of the rational choice. Legal imitation is not primarily a process of equilibrate evaluation of alternative legal models followed by the choice of the best working legal model to imitate.[145] However, the awareness of one's backwardness or lack of proper legal solutions and the decision to make a positive legal change may lead to a process of searching, comparative evaluation and choice of the possible models.[146] It remains to establish how rational a process of legal

140 Watson, "Aspects of Reception of Law", *American Journal of Comparative Law*, XLIV (1996), p. 346.

141 U. Mattei, "Efficiency in Legal Transplants: An Essay in Comparative Law and Economics", *International Review of Law and Economics*, XIV (1994), pp. 3-19.

142 J. M. Miller, "A Typology of Legal Transplants: Using Sociology, Legal History and Argentine Examples to Explain the Transplant Process", *American Journal of Comparative Law*, LI (2003), p. 855.

143 See Sacco, "Modèles français et modèles allemands dans le droit civil italien", *Revue internationale de droit comparé*, XXVIII (1976), pp. 228-229.

144 Miller, note 80 above, p. 1488.

145 R. Dixon and E. A. Posner, "The Limits of Constitutional Convergence", *Chicago Journal of International Law* XI (2011), pp. 411-413.

146 For an optimistic approach to rational imitation, see Jettinghoff, note 95 above, p. 106; E. A. Posner and C. R. Sunstein, "The Law of Other States", *Stanford Law Review*, LIX (2006), p. 163.

reception actually could be when imitation is involved. The Japanese process of legal modernization during the Meiji dynasty was apparently a rational selective imitation (rational shopping). However, the process may not have been as rational as it was proclaimed to be.[147] The apparent rational decision to imitate may be constrained by variable factors diminishing its rational imprint.

The legal comparatists and comparative legal historians may gain a thorough insight by appealing to the impressive body of knowledge gathered by the diffusionists. Policy diffusion theorists were particularly interested in assessing the decisional mechanisms of the policy-makers. Elkins and Simmons[148] make a beneficial and insightful distinction between mechanisms of diffusion where the policy adopted (transferred) by other policy-makers alters the conditions under which policy-makers make their decisions, on the one hand, and mechanisms of diffusion where the policy adopted (transferred) by other policy-makers impart information, on the other hand. The distinction replicates the one made in comparative legal studies between prestige and rational choice. The authors do not approach "the adaptation to altered conditions" (prestige) in terms of imitation but have seminal conclusions about the extrinsic value of the policy-makers' decisions. Prestige is a matter of "threshold" (the more adapting the same policy, the merrier), and the decision to join a reputed group of policy-makers offers legitimation and immunity. This reinforces the empirical data and conclusions of the legal comparatists. Much more interesting is the assessment of policy-makers' diffusion mechanism by learning. It theoretically implies a decision based ("under the best of circumstances") on "problem recognition in the organization, development of some basic theory about how to solve the problem, review of the best solutions available and attempt to ascertain the effectiveness of these solutions".[149] This sounds like a rational legal transfer based on evaluation of the existing foreign legal solutions in order to choose the best (most efficient) one. However, the authors circumstantiate the apparent rational process of decision to the extent where the line between diffusion by adaptation (reputational) and diffusion by learning (rational) becomes very blurry.

147 Westney, note 122 above, pp. 5-23.

148 Elkins and Simmons, note 108 above.

149 Ibid., p. 42.

The policy-makers have a series of cognitive constraints that transform them into "cognitive misers".[150] They are "limited by the available data, their resources to undertake analyses, and their own cognitive faculties". First and foremost, policy-makers are constrained by the information available, focusing on the familiar models and those belonging to the reputed nations. Last but not least, the available model may be the most diffused one (implicitly highly visible) for its quality of being successful. Thus, looking for effectiveness (the best solution) means acknowledging one model's success.[151] The so-called rational choice may become so disproportionate and biased that it eventually relies on prestige. The empirical data proved that the diffusion by learning is also strongly determined by geographical and cultural proximity. Cultural similarity, especially, is fostering the policy diffusion and, generally, any process of diffusion by imitation.[152]

Rational imitation may entail discussing the quantity of the ideological and institutional transfer. If the replication of the legal model's outcomes and goals is at stake [see below], then the imitators must transfer neither too much nor too little. In 1859, discussing the first Romanian constitution-making process, the politician Mihail Kogălniceanu contested the partial transfer of the 1831 Belgian Constitution's 7th Article regulating the individual liberty, emphasizing that the obligation to provide a warrant issued by a judge (as Belgian Article 7(3) stated) was the genuine guarantee against the abuse of power. As he put it: "You said you followed the Belgian Constitution; but if you copy it, do it well, especially where it protects the liberties of the citizens".[153] Following the same logic, G. Pasquino is critiquing "the superficial imitation" or "half-baked institutional imitation" with regard the Italian reception of the United States model of primary elections.[154] Last but not least, rational imitation cannot exclude the idea of a vertical process of imitation, when the legal actors are sensitive

150 Ibid., p. 43.

151 Ibid., p. 44-45.

152 Ibid., p. 45. See also Goderis and Versteeg, note 41 above.

153 M. Kogălniceanu, *Opere III. Oratorie I 1856-1864. Partea a II-a 1861-1864* (1987), p. 170.

154 G. Pasquino, "Primary Elections in Italy. An Episode in Institutional Imitation", *Journal of Modern Italian Studies*, XVI (2011), p. 682.

to the standardized global legal assets. Voluntary replication of a global / regional legal model may be driven by a functionalist (better law) and formalist (text only) approach,[155] but we must accept that legal globalization may be not only an effect of legal imitation but also a natural cause of it.

Regardless of its causes, no legal imitation is at stake if the actor of the legal change does not intend to faithfully reproduce the institutions, practices, and outcomes of the legal model, no matter whether the legal model was chosen for its prestige, following an exercise of admiration and reification, or as a consequence of a seemingly thorough comparative quest for the best (most efficient) legal solution. Otherwise, both admiration (prestige) and rational choice of a foreign legal model may lead to merely borrowing.[156] This is why we cannot accept the need for internal and international legitimation, competition, time and cost saving, or the emergency of legal change as causes (motives) of legal imitation unless they fit in the above-established paradigm of legal imitation.

The imitation could not be the direct effect of chance in terms of Watson, as long as the imitation implies a particular mindset of the imitator. Chance may be one possible uninspired name for the contact occurrences that make some legal models more available and facilitate the imitation, for example, military conquest (the Romanian elites have imitated the French culture after the Russian military aristocracy spoke French in the Romanian parlors), diplomatic agency, personal acquittances, scholarships, commercial exchanges, tourism, mass-media, proximity. The fact that Argentina was in the geographical proximity of the United States or Romania in the proximity of France and Belgium could have made the difference. This explains why some legal imitation

[155] See R. Michaels, "'One size can fit all' – some heretical thoughts on the mass production of legal transplants", in Frankenberg (2013), note 68 above, pp. 36-78.

[156] See Örücü, "Critical Comparative Law. Considering Paradoxes for Legal Systems in Transition", *Preadvies Nederlandse Vereniging voor Rechtsvergelijking*, LIX (1999), pp. 82-83. Elisabetta Grande is following Sacco's account about prestige as a source of Italian imitation of the United States adversarial system of criminal justice. She may successfully assess why Italians chose the USA as a model, but ultimately, she reveals merely an instance of legal borrowing. The Italian legal actors were not interested in as faithfully as possible and ongoingly replicating the United States model outcomes, goals, and practices. See E. Grande, "Italian Criminal Justice: Borrowing and Resistance", *American Journal of Comparative Law*, XLVIII (2000), pp, 227-259. See also Grande, *Imitazione e diritto: ipotesi sulla circolazione dei modelli* (2000), pp. 43 ff.

actors may imitate one society's law in a subsidiary because they admire its culture and civilization. In many cases, the domestic actors of legal imitation have had previously thorough and prolonged cultural contacts with the model society, reading its literature, exchanging ideas with their elites, and spending long periods abroad.

The abovementioned concept of imitation entails that the imitator purposively intends to replicate the outcomes produced by the legal model. Thus, one political elite may imitate the laws of a particular society to produce the same effects they produced at their origin according to the goals of the local political elites, for example, the same functional parliamentary system of government, the same election system, and the same protection of human rights. The actors of the legal imitation may assume the same goals the legal actors of the legal model are pursuing. This may happen when the imitating and model societies are united by the same (geo)political, social, economic, or cultural (ideological) contexts. However, the imitating legal actors may have their complex goals. The best known motivation (goal) for imitating the law of others in modern and contemporary legal history was/is the need for modernization: filling the gap between the domestic backward society and foreign models perceived as high civilizational standards. The Romanian elites imitated the French (civil) and Belgian (constitutional) law because they could have eliminated the feudal remnants in Romanian society. Other goals may be national security, national independence, gaining international recognition and appreciation, social justice, economic prosperity, professional (academic) excellence, institutional efficiency, and others.

Acknowledging the existence of a proper legal solution in a foreign society implies another particular question: how do the actors of imitation grasp the means, outcomes, and goals of their idealized legal model? Above all, the whole process may be rendered as a communication of ideas. The imitator is learning about the legal texts, legal practices, and behaviors, their particular outcomes and goals in the model society, and their particular contexts. Of maximum importance is their capacity to understand the unique linkage between the means, outcomes, and goals, i.e., what exactly is the role and weight of the legal texts, behaviors, and practices in producing specific legal, social, political, and economic effects and reaching particular aims? The imitator may assess the model's goals against her/his own goals; the former may be rejected, fully or partially assumed. Of maximum importance is to respond to another delicate question: how far would the imitator be capable of understanding the meanings and cultural context of the legal model? Law and culture studies thoroughly discussed this issue in the frame of comparative law, and there is no room to resume the whole debate. Meeting the model entails explicit cognitive constraints discussed above and limits, briefly considered below.

Much depends on the degree and type of contact between the imitator and the model. A prolonged and vivid live interaction between the actors of imitation and the model, the intense exposure to the foreign society's culture, the direct discussions with their counterparts, the close observation of mentalities, behaviors, and practices, discovering on the spot the shortcomings and pitfalls may help the imitator to gain a certain degree of knowledge about her/his model. The Romanian political elites, for example, were educated in France from the 1820s. They spent considerable time there, and many graduated from the French law faculties and defended their PhD theses there. Their excellent command of the French language facilitated their interaction with the French-speaking Belgian society. Many Romanian revolutionaries of 1848 found the ideal refuge in Belgium after being disappointed by the authoritarian politics of Napoleon III (1808-1873). Living in Belgian society was enlightening for many of them. They found there the liberal spirit and institutions that the Second French Empire discarded.

A short interaction or learning about the model's meanings, means, outcomes, and goals from the books may be disadvantageous. Undertaking a so-called rational imitation may be helpful. Imitating a legal model because it is admired and imitated by others may be deceiving. A lot also depends on the object of imitation: imitating constitutions and codes is much more challenging than imitating judicial style or the style of academic textbooks. However, one should remember that a process of imitation usually implies idealization to the extent the model becomes an emotional-cognitive construct of the imitator. The latter may powerfully project her/his meanings on the model so that the hardcore of any learning process may be reduced to merely apprehending the surface causal relations between the legal means and outcomes. For sure, this is not an ideal situation.

All issues discussed above unveil the limits of Frankenberg's IKEA theory. The legal imitators do not "purchase" standard legal items in universal or specialized stores. They have a vivid focus on some particular legal model(s). A receiver of foreign legal models does not imitate a de-contextualized standardized constitutional item; it imitates particular constitutional items produced by a particular constitutional model. In Frankenberg's terms, an imitator is not interested in the mass-production-like wardrobe found on the IKEA shelves but in the one-of-a-kind wardrobe crafted by a famous artisan. The legal imitators are looking for legal models to imitate, but for this reason, no purposive process of de-contextualization occurs. The (legal) imitation is driven by admiration and appreciation of (a) particular legal model(s). The latter is/are followed for its/their contextual benefits.

The admiration and obsession of the Argentinian 1860 Constitution's fathers for the United States Constitution is a perfect example.[157] Reducing the legal norms and institutions of the legal model to simple commodities circulating on the legal market would strip it of its very qualities as a model. The Romanian elites debating the constitutional project of 1859 manifested the desire to import the Belgian Constitution of 1831 because it belonged to the Belgians and had a particular functionality in Belgian society. They did not want to imitate only the Belgian constitutional norms and institutions but also the Belgian social, economic, geopolitical, and political context. Many members of the Romanian political and intellectual elites imagined Romania as "la Belgique de l'Orient" meaning, in terms of Boia, "a replica, at the other end of the continent, of real Belgium, of a minor, partially French-speaking country (...) prosperous and benefiting from the neutrality guaranteed by the great powers".[158]

Imitation as (textual) product

Imitation entails reproducing the model's means to reach the same outcomes and, possibly, the same goals. Replication of the means primarily focuses on legal texts: constitutions, codes, statutes, judgments, doctrinal treatises, and textbooks. All these are the

[157] See Gordon, note 80 above, p. 506 ff.

[158] L. Boia, "Idéologie et mythologie dans la conscience historique roumaine des XIXe et XXe siècles", *Der Donauraum*, XXXIX (1999), p. 18. [my translation from French]

(textual) products of the imitation process undertaken by the legal actors in the receiving society. Some difficulties come with the territory. Reproducing legal texts is not the same as reproducing someone else's gestures, basic behavior, or simple techniques to achieve unsophisticated outcomes. It is a complex cognitive endeavor that meets inherent obstacles, limits, and perils. Some pertinent questions should be asked: how thoroughly should the reproduction of a legal text be to reach the outcomes of the legal model and, possibly, the same goals? Should a constitution or a code be entirely copied? Or is it sufficient to reproduce a small part? Should the legal text be faithfully reproduced (a faithful translation), or may it be extensively changed? In other words, how far should its imitators quantitatively and qualitatively replicate a model legal text?

The concept of imitation advanced above produces a tendential faithful reproduction of the model. What exactly could this mean? A possible response may come from the theory of "over-imitation" in social sciences:[159] the reproduction of means should not be unnecessarily faithful; it must be replicated as much as is needed to reproduce the outcomes and, possibly, the model's goals. The over-imitation may also exist in legal imitation because the imitator usually tends to replicate the model as faithfully as possible. However, we may expect the legal actors to reproduce as much legal text and faithfully as they need to achieve the same outcomes and goals as their model. This unique linkage between the (re)production of legal texts and the expected outcomes and goals, between imitation and over-imitation, is the key to understanding why the replication of foreign textual legal models may vary quantitatively and qualitatively.

More often than not, legal norms (constitutions, codes, statutes) are preferred for imitation. As the Romanian case of constitutional reception highlighted, the (comparative) legal historians and scholars of comparative law are particularly interested in the "imitation" as a mere product of the constitutional transfer. For many, constitutional imitation is equivalent to its readable result: the constitutional text. This reminds us that foreign constitutions are texts, and like any other text, the optimist translator may

[159] See the entry "Imitative Learning in Humans and Animals", in N. M. Seel (ed.), *Encyclopedia of the Sciences of Learning* (2012), p. 1499.

quickly reproduce them.[160] However, this approach has little scientific relevance to (comparative) constitutional history and comparative law without further inquiries. What is the scientific impact of a (comparative) historical research that concludes that the "constitution x" was an imitation or copy of the "constitution y"? At worst, it may encourage "the textual and normative reductionism"[161] and overestimate the need for taxonomy and typology in (comparative) constitutional history.[162] At best, it may help to map the worldwide influence of a particular constitutional model or to corner an apparent cultural weakness of the importer following its deficit in constitutional innovation.

The Romanian political elites of 1866 copied a large quantity of articles from the Belgian Constitution of 1831. The Argentinian elites faithfully copied in 1853 and, especially in 1860, almost the entire text of the United States Constitution as of 1878. However, the large quantity-high fidelity textual transfer of the legal model(s) is not a precondition for a properly speaking imitation. Imitation also occurs when a small number of ideas, norms, and institutions are transferred from one or more legal models, and the textual fidelity is low, if this is sufficient to reach the outcomes of the legal mode(s). For example, after the fall of communism, the Central-Eastern European States made their political and constitutional transition towards liberal democracy and the rule of law with the help of transfers of constitutional values and institutions from the Western liberal constitutional models. The Romanian constitutional transfers of 1991 were selective and relatively numerous, but the textual fidelity was low. Nevertheless, as Krastev and Holmes put it, "they wish their countr[y] to become 'normal,' which meant like the West".[163] This large amount – low fidelity replication of textual

[160] The quantitative comparative analyses, especially, are relevant for the magnitude of constitutional imitation. See E. J. Engstrom, M. T. Pietryka, and J. T. Scott, "Constitutional Innovation and Imitation in the American States", *Political Research Quarterly*, LXXV (2022), pp. 244-258.

[161] L. Zucca, "Montesquieu, Methodological Pluralism and Comparative Constitutional Law", *European Constitutional Law Review*, V (2009), p. 484.

[162] See the interesting conclusions of M. J. Prutsch drawing attention to the peril of oversimplification induced by "the formal transfer concepts" incapable of "describing transfer and reception phenomena in all their complexities", in *Making Sense of Constitutional Monarchism in Post-Napoleonic France and Germany* (2013), p. 213.

[163] Krastev and Holmes, note 44 above, p. 118.

means helped the Romanian political actors' attempt to reproduce the outcomes of their legal/constitutional model(s). They desired to reproduce the liberal-democratic constitutionalism grounded on human rights, separation of powers, and the rule of law. This still qualifies the Romanian constitutional transfers as legal imitation.

The existence of legal imitation depends not only on the quantity and degree of similarity of the transferred constitutional/legal items but also on their object. In the case of a constitutional imitation, we must clarify not only how much and how faithful but also what exactly the makers of a constitution transferred from the foreign constitutional model. Was it only about concepts, values, principles, institutions, and mechanisms, or were the ideas (ideology) lying behind also considered? Van Caenegem believed the European constitution-makers imitated either Belgian institutions or fundamental ideas. This allegation should be understood twofold: on one hand, we must accept that the constitutional concepts, institutions, and mechanisms may circulate without their original ideological background and, on the other, we should accept that the constitutional (fundamental) ideas may circulate without their original institutional background.

Some constitution-makers may enshrine a constitutional idea using different or slightly different institutional arrangements than the constitutional model, for example, the idea of parliamentary monarchy may imply a wide range of institutional combinations beyond its basics; at the same time, the same concepts or institutions may contribute to express a different constitutional idea in the receiving country. The institutions are more suitable for imitation than the constitutional ideas, which are likely to suffer considerable changes in meaning.[164] However, imitation entails reproducing the outcomes of the constitutional model and, possibly, its goals by observing, understanding, and assuming their moral and axiological substance. When both institutions (texts) and constitutional ideas (ideology) of a constitutional model are transferred, we are in the presence of imitation. The imitators are expected to meet their constitutional model in the writings of its intellectual and political elites, in the voice of the public opinion, in the exchange of ideas with its proponents.

[164] W. Osiatynski, "Paradoxes of Constitutional Borrowing", *I.CON*, I (2003), pp. 245 ff.

However, fully understanding the intricate intellectual, emotional, and cultural strings that bind constitutional architecture and outcomes/goals and replicating the meanings of the constitutional model remains a matter of wishful thinking. As Jōrg Fedtke correctly put it, "even mere translation will thereby often increase the difference between the original and the 'imitated' provision".[165] Thus, the key of the imitative process is the tendential approach: the imitator must be constantly, intellectually, and psychologically oriented towards and open to her/his model. Either way, the mere reproduction of institutions (texts), be it large quantity-high fidelity, for different ideas (ideology) and outcomes cannot be qualified as imitation. Thus, depending on the nature and complexity of the transferred constitutional items, the intellectual contribution of the constitution-makers may be more or less critical and decisive. In this context, it may be established whether the transfer was an imitation or a simple borrowing process.

Assessing the existence of the intention of legal actors to reproduce the ideas, outcomes, and (possibly) goals of the constitutional model(s) may be difficult for any researcher. One must not forget that the replication of a foreign constitutional text was/is a part of a broader endeavor: the constitution-making process. The process of imitation must be assessed against the backdrop of the intellectual effervescence, the richness of meanings, the diversity of constitutional sentiments (frustration, anxiety, anger, prejudice, passion,[166] hope), the fabric of constitutional strategies, the particularity of the cultural, political and social contexts existing in the constitutional moment(s) of the receiving society. The imitation should be understood against the need of the citizens to "participate in self-rule",[167] the need of the local elites or even an autocrat to develop strategies of self-legitimation and dominance,[168] and the need of a nation to prove itself on the

[165] J. Fedtke, "Legal Transplants", in J. M. Smits (ed.), *Elgar Encyclopedia of Comparative Law* (2006), p. 435.

[166] See J. Elster, "The Political Psychology of Constitutional Making", in J. Elster, R. Gargarella, V. Naresh, and B. E. Rasch (eds.), *Constituent Assemblies* (2018), pp. 207 ff.

[167] Gordon, note 80 above, p. 515.

[168] P. G. Monateri, "The 'Weak Law': Contaminations and Legal Cultures", *Global Iuris Advances*, I (2001), p. 9.

international scene[169] to produce a meaningful discourse about its own identity, constitutional values, and goals and express them in the constitutional text.

The constitution-making process is different from any other process of legal change. The making of a statute or a code does not have at stake what the making of a constitution has. The constitution-making process is a delicate moment when the makers bear considerable responsibility regarding a specific community's political future. It is not simply about discussing and voting constitutional texts; it is about founding a political community, deciding the basics of the political and legal order, about social equilibrium and trust, bargaining and taming contrasts, and making an enduring and functional institutional architecture; it is about building civic communities or survival and protection of an ethnic group, about cherishing particular values, beliefs, and principles, about meeting social and political hopes. Constitutional models are frequently needed in this process, and the tendency to imitate is more than natural. A constitutional choice may reflect a sincere need of political change. However, it may unveil a preference for constitutional identity, pride, and the need for constitutional insulation or may compensate for constitutional weakness. The decision to "imitate" may be rational or irrational, "aversive" or "aspirational", naïve[170] or highly pragmatic. Grasping all these sophisticated nuances needs an in-depth approach and, above all, full access to sources.

The constitution-making process is sometimes undertaken against an open and thorough public intellectual effervescence. Numerous public meetings, conferences, and debates occur. Newspaper and academic journal articles are published and disseminated. Monographs and specialized juridical analyses are published and trigger cross-fired critical replicas. The constitutional assembly debates are public, and almost everything is on the table. The admiration for a particular constitutional model is proclaimed in plain sight. The constitutional model texts are put forward, and the intention to imitate is not a secret. In other cases, all or significant parts of these are missing or difficult to access. Hidden political agendas may exist. However, nothing guarantees at this

[169] F. Schauer, "On the Migration of Constitutional Ideas", *Connecticut Law Review*, XXXVII (2004-2005), p. 912.

[170] Frankenberg, note 67 above, p. 130.

stage that a so-called "perfect imitation",[171] where the constitution-makers are openly transferring the whole text and loudly adhere to the ideology of their constitutional model, is expressing a sincere intention to imitate.

This constitutional text and the public discourse of the founders may cover the interest in reaching different constitutional outcomes and goals. This is why a simulated legal/constitutional imitation made, for example, to gain the acceptance of some internal or external pressure groups or international recognition, is not a properly speaking imitation as far as the other criteria of imitation are not fulfilled.

It is doubtful that the Romanian elites of the 1860s were directly influenced by the Belgian constitutional ideas and political philosophy of the 1830s. The different approach to the nation and nation-state is relevant. Romantic historicism contributed to the building of the national identity in both Belgian and Romanian cases;[172] however, in terms of Marnix Beyen, while the Belgian had to build a "Romantic version of civic nationalism",[173] the Romanians built a Romantic version of ethnic nationalism. Accordingly, the considerable ethnic homogeneity of the Romanians imprinted a decisive ethnocentric touch on the Romanian constitution-making process. On the contrary, with its ethnic and linguistic heterogeneity and different political and philosophical backgrounds, Belgium was finally committed to liberal constitutionalism in the elitist framework of the nineteenth century.[174] The Romanians grounded

[171] Graziadei, "Comparative Law as the Study of Transplants and Receptions", in M. Reimann and R. Zimmermann, *The Oxford Handbook of Comparative Law* (2008), p. 469.

[172] See S. Marteel, *The Intellectual Origins of the Belgian Revolution* (2018), p. 306. See also E. Cloots, "Constitutional Identity in Belgium", in C. Calliess and G. van der Schyff (eds.), *Constitutional Identity in Europe of Multilevel Constitutionalism* (2020), pp. 76-77; B. Deseure, "From Pragmatic Conservatism to Formal Continuity. Nineteenth-Century Views on the Old Regime Origins of the Belgian Constitution", *Journal of Constitutional History*, XXXII (2016), pp. 257-277.

[173] M. Beyen, "Belgium: A Nation That Failed to Be Ethnic", in L. Eriksonas and L. Muller (eds.), *Statehood Before and Beyond Ethnicity* (2005), p. 344. On the distinction between national identity and national spirit and the difficulties of building national identity in Belgium, see Marteel, above, pp. 255-259. For a civic nation(alism) see id, p. 305. See also C. Strikwerda, "The Low Countries Between the City and the Volk", in T. Baycroft and M. Hewitson (eds.), *What is a Nation. Europe 1789-1914* (2007), pp. 81 ff.

[174] Strikwerda, note 173 above, p. 88 ff.

their modern constitutionalism on the primacy and shared values of the majoritarian ethnic group, while the Belgians grounded their modern constitutionalism on the primacy and liberty of individuals. In Romania, the national/popular sovereignty belonged to the nation understood as a historical ethnic group united by objective elements like language, biological origin, religion, and territory; in Belgium, the national/popular sovereignty belonged to a concrete civic community. Building the nation-state had no integrative function in Romania, like in the Belgian case,[175] but exclusive and protective ones. The intermingling between ethnocentric and liberal thinking gave Romanian modern constitutionalism its particular philosophical flavor.

However, Belgians contributed to Romanians falling in love with Western European liberal political and constitutional culture. An ideological Belgian influence may be noticed at the end of the 1850s, although it is difficult to be thoroughly grasped. Considering the predominant French-origin ideological background of the Romanian intelligentsia and the paucity and fuzziness of the written sources, it is hard to say which political-philosophical approaches or constitutional ideas came strictly via the Belgian channels of acculturation or the French ones. The Romanian academic writing on constitutional issues was deficient in the 1860s; the only reliable information about constitutional ideas and doctrine is accessible in the then newspapers and parliamentary debates. Moreover, the powerful influence of Herder's "*kulturnation*" and Romantic historicism,[176] underpinning Romanian ethnocentrism in the second half of the nineteenth century, made tracking down any external origin of the Romanian constitutional idea more challenging.

In the absence of modern-like Romanian traditions, they were invented. Some constitutional values and institutions transferred from Western Europe were frequently projected in the past as Romanian constitutional traditions. All these explain why the constitution-makers of 1866 sent confusing messages about their models and their appetite to imitate. We may think of a

[175] See P. A. J. Van Den Berg, "Liberalism, Modern Constitutionalism and Nation Building in the Belgian Constitution of 1831: A Comparative Perspective", *Journal of Constitutional History*, XXXV (2018), pp. 49-67.

[176] V. Neumann, *Conceptually Mystified: East-Central Europe Torn Between Ethnicism and Recognition of Multiple Identities* (2004).

camouflaged constitutional imitation, but the constitution-making process was neither about hiding an obsessive admiration for the Belgian constitutional model nor about faithfully imitating foreign constitutional models.

The existent data unveils the presence of a French ideological influence that reached the Romanian elites using French and Belgian channels. The Romanian elites read the French scholarship on constitutional law and philosophy of the 1820s-40s. The Belgian scholarship of constitutional law in the 1830s-50s was influenced, to a certain extent, by the same French literature. The Romanians read Belgians, too. The Belgian constitutional law scholars were sporadically quoted by Romanian elites in 1859 and intensely after the 1860s. It is hard to believe that the Belgian influence suddenly vanished in 1866. However, it would not be wise to give the Belgian or any other foreign national scholarship excessive credit. From the French, Belgian, and English scholars and political philosophers, Romanians apprehended the basics of liberal constitutionalism. The latter was identified with the Western constitutional and political modernity that Romanian elites admired, desired to acquire, and eventually imitated. From the ideological point of view, the Romanian elites identified themselves with the Western Europe, not with the Belgians.

Approximately 59% of the Romanian 1866 Constitution text was almost identical to the Belgian one. In the logic of our main argument, we may be in the presence of a similar textual product of constitutional transfer but not in the presence of a properly speaking process of imitation from the Belgian Constitution of 1831. The mere translation and copying of foreign constitutional models may be a pragmatic technique of the constitution-making process but not an imitative exercise. However, although they did not expressly manifest the intention to imitate the Belgians, the fathers of the Romanian 1866 Constitution imitated. But, paradoxically, not directly the Belgian constitutional model. The Belgian constitutional text became the epitome of the European civilization and constitutional modernity the Romanians admired and desired to acquire. The Belgian constitutional provisions were de-contextualized from their general Belgian cultural background and officially re-contextualized as an expression of the Western European liberal-democratic culture. The admiration for the Belgian society and constitution may have remained the bottom layer of the Romanian fascination for Western Europe, but it was encapsulated in an all-encompassing desire to become Western European. This explains why the significant sameness between the Romanian and Belgian constitutions was not accidental.

A mere constitution-making process through imitation of the Western European ideas, outcomes, and goals was not at stake. The Romanian Constitution of 1866 was a political compromise meant to balance European and Romanian constitutional outcomes and goals: the need to cover as rapidly as possible the civilizational backwardness against the need to follow an organic and slower process of modernization; the need to use on a wide scale the Western European constitutional models against the need to preserve the Romanian constitutional (alleged) traditions; the need to have enshrined Western constitutional ideas against the need to express the Romanian national identity, the principles and values of liberal constitutionalism against the ethnic nationalism, the human rights against the need to protect the majoritarian ethnic group, the liberal against conservative politics; the need to considerably limit the monarchical power against the need to place the prince in a perfect balance of power with the parliament.

Last but not least, the constitution was a compromise between the need to make a massive constitutional transfer but a functional constitutional design, on the one hand, and the need to make a selective constitutional transfer, assuming the risk of a dysfunctional constitutional design, on the other hand. Imitating the Western-European constitutional model and preserving and giving constitutional expression to some critical features of the Romanian national identity were the overarching goals of the Romanian founders in 1866. In other words, the Romanians strongly desired to imitate and replicated the Belgian constitutional text to become Western Europeans, but only as long as their elements of national identity, that is, their common biological origin, their shared religious belief, language, and territory, were constitutionally preserved and protected.[177] Thus, the Romanian constitutional identity became bipolar: on the one hand, the Western-European centered pole was built on imitation of the West, on the other hand, the ethnocentric pole was built on the objective elements of the Romanian ethnic group.

[177] See M. Guțan, note 47 above, 2022; Gutan, "Romanian Tendential Constitutionalism and the Limits of European Constitutional Culture", in M. Belov (eds.), *Global Constitutionalism and its Challenges to Westphalian Constitutional Law* (2018), pp. 103-132.

Imitation as tendential practice

As Graziadei nicely put it, "the meaning of the import will be determined by the sense that the local user gives it".[178] This means that the legal actors of a specific society may decide whether they are undertaking a legal imitation or a simple act of borrowing. Quantity and fidelity of the transfer are not relevant. The actors of the legal transfer would only intend to borrow (not to imitate) if the large quantity-high fidelity reception is certainly destined to specific needs of the receiving society and, therefore, programmatically adapted to its socio-cultural background.

As far as the legal imitation is not mechanical but conscious and voluntary, it is always purposive. Social impact is regularly considered, but for specific goals: the imitated legal institutions are expected to reproduce in the imitating society the same sound effects they produced in their society of origin.[179] Imitation is a highly authoritative transfer of law and, as Rosenkrantz put it, implies that "one wants to be different from what one is".[180] The actors of imitation usually feel discomfort about their home legal system, traditions, mentalities, and practices and hope to replace them with better, superior, or prestigious ones taken from abroad. Above all, this means applying the replicated (normative) texts while constantly keeping its model in mind to achieve its outcomes and, possibly, goals. This may start with the legal hermeneutics of the textual products. The massive imitation (copy) of the United States amended as of 1878 Constitution by the fathers of the 1853 Argentinian Constitution and the quarrel over the interpretation of the letter in the spirit of the former is a perfect example. As the future president of Argentina, Domingo S. Sarmiento, put it: "[I]t would be monstrous, if not to say ridiculous, to pretend that the same ideas, expressed with the same words, for the same ends, might produce different results in our Constitution or have a different meaning".[181]

[178] Graziadei, note 77 above, p. 569.

[179] See Gordon, note 80 above, p. 510.

[180] C. F. Rosenkrantz, "Against Borrowing and Other Nonauthoritative uses of Foreign Law", *I-CON*, I (2003), p. 283.

[181] Quoted by Gordon, note 80 above, p. 503. See also Miller, note 80 above, p. 1516.

Questioned about some obscure provision of the Argentinian 1860 Constitution, more identical with the United States constitutional texts, the same Sarmiento said it was sufficient "to know that it [was] literally copied from the Constitution of the United States, and [because it is an exact copy,] if there is anything which is clear and luminous, it is this part which seems nebulous and obscure to us right now".[182]

Not surprisingly, the proponents of legal imitation may be convinced that the mere faithful reproduction of the most-admired legal model is the sufficient precondition for a successful top-to-bottom transformation of legal mentalities and practices. Like the Argentinian constitution-makers a few years before, the Romanian constitution-makers of the 1866 Constitution believed that merely textual replication of the constitutional values and institutions belonging to civilized European constitutional models would transform Romania into a civilized European country. As A. Pascal, the rapporteur of the special committee, put it:

> When we borrow from the nations whose system of government we envy, if we want to gain the same utility and benefit they had, we must introduce that system of government with all accessories which those nations thought necessary and indispensably to endow it with. (…) All (…) provisions regarding the prince and the ministers conform with almost all constitutional provisions belonging to the states that have the constitutional monarchy as a form of government.[183]

However, it is more than evident that the outcomes and goals of the legal model can only be reached by attempting to faithfully replicate its legal behaviors and practices beyond its legal texts. This is not about merely mimicking legislative, judicial, administrative, commercial, academic, political, or another kind of praxis existing in the model society. It entails understanding their inbuilt rationale.

This idea is reopening the sensitive discussion about the imitating legal actors need and capacity to understand the legal model meanings and contexts. For example, would it be necessary

[182] Gordon, note 80 above, p. 508.

[183] Al. Pencovici, note 69 above, p. 31.

for the imitators of the United States presidential system of government to understand its meaning in American society and all socio-cultural, economic, and political mechanisms that grant it success? Was it necessary for the Romanian political elites to fully understand the West European functional parameters of the parliamentary system of government in the nineteenth century? Or would it be sufficient to understand that a particular institutional architecture and specific constitutional-political practices build the helpful link between the means and outcomes/goals? How far are interested and capable the imitators to understand the pitfalls of their legal model's means? In specific conditions of socio-cultural compatibility, the imitated legal institution may function (almost) like in their origin society,[184] but the intention and capacity of the legal actors to faithfully reproduce meanings and contexts must be carefully assessed against their epistemological constraints. Nevertheless, regardless of the intentions and possibilities, the actors of legal imitation should aware that the imitating society's mentalities and socio-cultural background must considerably change to reach the legal model's outcomes and, possibly, goals.

For operational reasons, the accent may fall on the importer constant attempts to replicate the model's non-textual means (behaviors and practices) to reach what they consider to be the same meanings, contexts, and outcomes, which is provocative enough. The reflection of legal imitation on the day-to-day legal practice may be more difficult than expected. Much depends on the object and actors of the legal imitation. The legislators would have a more difficult task as long as the imitated laws may encounter the (cultural) resistance of the political class and population. The government members may try to (re)create as much as possible at home the proper functional parameters of the imitated legal institutions through top-to-bottom legal-cultural engineering. This would imply a public discourse about the virtues of the imitated legal ideas and institutions and a strict survey and regulation of the legal practice.

This is a difficult and time-consuming task: for example, only after more than forty years of public dissemination among the illiterate Romanian peasantry and control of the old Romanian legal customs in the rural areas, did the Romanian Civil Code of 1865, massively copied from the French Civil Code of 1804, start

[184] Siems, note 93 above, p. 239; Cohn, note 76 above, p. 592.

to be widely applied. Instead, the task of the legal scholars, law professors, and judges interested in imitating legal ideas, theories, ideologies, style, and structure of the law textbooks or the case law belonging to their legal model(s) is much easier. All these are imitated and applied by a reduced number of legal professionals.

In this theoretical framework, everything that cannot fit the paradigm "we sincerely want a foreign-origin legal item functioning at home like in its origin society" is not legal imitation. This distinct subsection has a clear conclusion: imitation means to replicate as faithful possible the legal model's behaviors and practices. The authoritarian replicator of the foreign legal models may not be actors of legal imitation. They are most and foremost interested in the immediate textual product of their legislative process and neglect its subsequent replication in practice. Reproducing prestigious and functional legal concepts, norms, institutions, and texts from abroad is the core rationale of their endeavor. All apparent process of imitation is about self-image and self-legitimation.[185]

Imitation as ongoing reproduction of the model

Legal imitation is exclusively about the intention and strategies of the imitators to perpetually replicate the legal model's ideas, norms, and practices at home to achieve the same outcomes and (possibly) the same goals. In the logic of the central argument herein, the one-time replication of the legal model's texts, behaviors, and practices is not imitation.

From this definitional-analytical stance, addressing legal imitation in terms of success or failure is of secondary relevance. The capacity of the imitator to integrally and faithfully reproduce a model legal text does not mean that the imitation was successful: the model and imitator become relatively identical. Merely copying foreign legal texts is only a part of the imitating process and is full of inbuilt problems. Likewise, it would be wrong to address the distortion of the legal model's meanings, texts, behaviors, and practices during replication as failure. Law and culture studies in legal sociology and comparative law emphasize the impact of

[185] Here may also include the strategies of "covering cases" and "prestigious propaganda" theorized by Monateri. Borrowing is the proper concept for this process of self-legitimation belonging to competing legal and political elites. See Monateri, note 168 above, p. 93 ff.

the local cultural background on every transferred legal item. The theories on social learning through imitation are correct about both imitative and creative social learning functions. The diffusionists point to the same inevitable creative occurrence in the receiving society.[186]

Developmental psychology emphasizes the impossibility of faithful replication. These are standard inevitable consequences of imitative behavior in humans. One society cannot completely reproduce the meanings and social-cultural background of the legal model(s) while eliminating its old cultural traits. An undesired and unexpected process of legal-cultural mixing occurs in the receiving society.

What matters is the imitative mindset of the legal actors. Consequently, the relevant questions are different: what keeps the imitating legal actors continuously interested in imitating a legal model?; how far the actors of the legal imitation are ready and capable of attempting the perpetual replication of the legal model?; is the intention to ongoing replicate a legal model conditioned by the successful replication of the model's outcomes?; which factors of resistance may trigger in the receiving society the attempt to replicate the legal model perpetually?

A purposive imitation of a foreign legal model keeps its name regardless of whether the receiving society's legal actors succeeded in producing the desired change of legal thinking and practice as far as the legal actors attempt to reach the outcomes of the legal model. As far as the actors of legal imitations have the foreign legal model(s) as their constant point of reference and try to reproduce it perpetually, we are in the presence of imitation. The need of the legal (political) actors to legitimate their role and power, the high-scale process of modernization, or the authority of the foreign legal model, like in the case of Western European liberal constitutionalism of the nineteenth century, are among the valuable reasons for the continuing attempt to replicate it. Even when the desire to replicate the legal model(s) in the day-to-day legal practice despite the evident cultural resistance of the receiving society may lead, in Romanian terms, to mere "forms without substance",[187] we may be in the presence of imitation. By

186 Westney, note 122 above, p. 25.

187 See Guțan, "Legal Transplant as Socio-Cultural Engineering in Modern

the same logic, an imitation of a foreign legal model loses this label if the legal actors at home start at some point in time to consider it a mistake and try to adapt it purposefully to the legal culture of their home. At that moment, it would be an error to label the transferred legal text, even identical with its legal model, an imitation, or a copy. Instead, it is a purposive adaptation or transposition.

Imitation as an intentional, tendential faithful replication of one legal model's means, outcomes, and goals is caused by a need for change acknowledged by the legal actors of the receiving society. This entails a process of identification between the imitator and its model, followed by an attempt at painful identitarian engineering. The imitator wants to be like her/his model and get rid of her/his old (legal) self. Faithful replication of the legal model is impossible, and an inevitable adaptation process occurs. However, unlike diffusionists, which are centered on imitation as a re-invention (adaptation) in the socio-cultural context of the receptor, the psychological-cognitive approach is focused on the effects of imitation at the same mental level. The main consequences of legal imitation may be a considerable or partial change in the legal identity of the receptor or a deep identitarian crisis.

The call for a considerable change of identity may trigger harsh reactions in the receiving society, no matter how necessary and opportune. As David Westbrook puts it, "the [new] normative shades into the politically existential; [i]f our ways were inadequate and must be changed, who we are?; [w]hat are we, as a polity and so as citizens, becoming?"[188] The identity of belongingness constructed through imitation of foreign models may be intensively challenged by an identity of difference constructed on tradition. In terms of Monateri, the attempt of ongoing imitation of a legal model may trigger a war of competing identitarian narratives between the legal elites looking for "non-neutral projects of governance".[189] In the presence of an identitarian crisis, the process of imitation may

Romania", in M. Stolleis, G. Bender, and J. Kirov (eds.), *Konflikt und Koexistenz. Die Rechtsordnungen Sudosteuropas im 19. Und 20 Jahrhundert. Band I: Rumanien, Bulgarien, Griechenland* (2015), pp. 481-530.

[188] D. A. Westbrook, "Theorizing the Diffusion of Law, Conceptual difficulties, Unstable Imaginations, and the Effort to Think Gracefully Nonetheless", *Harvard International Law Journal*, XLVII (2006), p. 495.

[189] See P. G. Monateri, "Methods in Comparative Law: An Intellectual Overview", in Monateri (ed.), *Methods of Comparative Law* (2012), p. 9.

be rejected and stopped or camouflaged. As long as the recovery of the old (now lost) legal self may be at stake, the legal actors may develop strategies of (re)building a national legal identity by incorporating the already transferred legal model into a domestic legal fabric. This happened during the Japanese Meiji era,[190] and also in Romania not long after 1866.

Many Romanian scholars of constitutional law accepted the idea of a "copied/imitated Constitution of 1866" only against the background of an intense critique condemning the weakness of the Romanian constitutional culture. Many accused the ruling elites of constitutional mimicry, aping (monkey-like imitation), and uncritical reception against the real Romanian needs.[191] Moreover, existed, especially in the period between the world wars, a powerful Romanian intellectual counter-current defending the opposite: the Constitution of 1866 was a process of rational choice and selection, the outcome of an intellectual turmoil in the Romanian society during the first six decades of the nineteenth century, an indirect reception and successful adaptation of the Belgian constitutional text to the Romanian needs, constitutional traditions and political particularities.

The idea of a faithful imitation was out of discussion. After the end of World War II, Alexandru Tilman-Timon concluded the Romanian quarrel over the origins of the Romanian Constitution. While acknowledging that the Belgian Constitution was, indirectly or directly, the primary source of the Romanian Constitution, he stated: "the Romanian Constitution of 1866 was not a simple imitation of the Belgian Constitution of 1831 (...) it contains dispositions inspired by the historical realities of the Romanian people (...) and by the current innate necessities of this people".[192]

Until the mid-twentieth century and even during the communist rule, Romanian legal historians made a significant effort to prove that the making and application of the 1866 Constitution eventually was a matter of original re-creation of law mirroring the Romanian

[190] See S. Yamauchi, "Civilization and International Law in Japan During the Meiji Era (1868-1912)", *Hitotsubashi Journal of Law and Politics*, XXIV (1996), p. 14.

[191] See N. Iorga, "Istoricul constituției românești", in *Constituția din 1923 în dezbaterea contemporanilor* (1999), pp. 25-53.

[192] Al. Tilman-Timon, *Les influences étrangères sur le droit constitutionnel roumain* (1946), p. 329 (my translation from French).

legal-cultural exceptionalism.[193] However, this intellectual turmoil did not eliminate the Romanian appetite for legal imitation. After the fall of the communism, the tension between the Eurocentric and ethnocentric poles of the Romanian legal/constitutional identity was again present, upon the need of the Romanian politicians to imitate the Western (European) liberal-democratic constitutionalism.[194]

CONCLUSIONS

Both comparative legal history and comparative legal studies need a clear theoretical framework to assess the phenomenon of cross-border imitation. This is not only about epistemological relevance but also about giving the special attention it deserves. The imitation of foreign legal models occurs in the process of legal change, and it needs a proper theoretical assessment. The admiration for some particular foreign legal model, the genuine desire to bring it at home, partially or entirely, the effective complex process of transferring it, and the intention and efforts to have it reproduced in legal practice deserve a closer look.

Comparative law scholarship is currently dominated by a "country, Western, and innovation" paradigm of legal thinking. The divide between glorious innovation and embarrassed imitation is splitting the legal world into creators of original law and their imitators. Against this backdrop, the concept of imitation knows biased, subjective approaches belonging both to the exporters and importers of law. The former are tempted to overuse the concept of imitation in scholarly approaches of "non-coercive domination". The latter are tempted to avoid the concept for reasons of national legal pride and national legal identity. New perspectives borrowed from diffusion studies try to explain the causes and effects of legal imitation. However, they are focusing either on the production of sameness (constitutional globalization) at the international level or on the adaptation (re-creation) at the national level. Their focus is not on the imitator but on the objectified process of legal change. Instead, legal imitation needs to be grasped in its own right.

[193] See Guțan, "The Legal Transplant and the Building of the Romanian Legal Identity in the Second Half of the 19th Century and the Beginning of the 20th Century", *Romanian Journal of Comparative Law*, VIII (2017), pp. 62-99.

[194] See Guțan, note 47 above.

Guided by the body of knowledge produced in social sciences, especially in social psychology, developmental psychology, and diffusion studies (policy diffusion, institutional diffusion, diffusion of innovations), this article tried to propose a neutral, narrower, but operational concept of imitation for internal use both in comparative law and comparative legal history.

The imitation of foreign legal models occurs when the legal actors of the receiving society voluntarily intend to replicate, ongoingly and as faithfully as needed, the means, outcomes, and, possibly, the goals of one model they particularly value. This concept may adequately capture the process of legal imitation undertaken by constitution-makers, legislators, politicians, judges, scholars, and lawyers, and it is sufficiently broad to render their mindset. It may explain why the imitation occurred, why a particular legal model was valued and how, which is the intimate linkage between the means, outcomes, and goals of the imitation, why the imitator must necessarily replicate the outcomes but not the goals of the model, which is the relevance of the low or high fidelity – big or small quantity replication of the legal texts, why the imitators tend to faithfully replicate the legal texts, behaviors, and practices of the model, why they are tending to replicate the legal model perpetually in time, even if the effective legal change did not (yet) occur, why we imitation still occurs even if the legal actors have no time, interest or capacity to understand the meanings and cultural embedment of the legal model's means, outcomes and goals. Last but not least, it may explain the complex identitarian challenges involved: on the one hand, the desire to get rid of their old identity and be like the legal model; on the other hand, the identitarian crisis and the quest for the 'old' legal self. This concept is also helpful to properly discern the masked imitations and the sham ones. A legal actor may claim she/he is not imitating while she/he is doing it; a legal actor may claim she/he is imitating while not doing it.

At the same time, it is sufficiently narrow to clearly differentiate it from other instances of law diffusion/transfer, especially the borrowing process. Any forced imitation is not a properly speaking imitation; it is a legal imposition or legal imperialism. A simple (declarative) intention to imitate or a simulated one is not a legal imitation; a voluntary, sincere intention to imitate not followed by a more or less faithful transfer of legal texts is not a legal imitation. The sincere and faithful transfer of a large quantity of legal norms and institutions from the admired legal model(s) followed by an intentional cultural recontextualization of goals and practices is not imitation. Any massive and faithful taking of legal items from the legal model(s) to be adapted to the importer's particular interests and purposes is a case of legal borrowing. Generally speaking, any voluntary transfer of law, be it large quantity-high fidelity or small quantity-low fidelity, that is not meant to ongoing replication of the legal model(s)' ideas, institutions, and practices in the receiving society is merely borrowing.

Against this theoretical background, there is no need for further terminological debates. Imitation is clearly distinguished from the concept of borrowing; "copying" becomes only a technique of the imitating process. Partial, selective, modified, slavish, blind, faithful, and identical were usually related to the textual product of the imitation process; they may now define the magnitude of the imitating process itself or may be cast apart. Both large quantity-high fidelity and small quantity-low fidelity textual transfers from the legal models deserve to be labeled imitations as far as the desire to imitate and the intention to replicate in the legal practice exist.

Considering all these, the Romanian constitution-making process of 1866 has a particular meaning. It was a case of constitutional imitation. However, the considerable textual similarity between the Romanian Constitution of 1866 and the Belgian Constitution of 1831 is irrelevant to this conclusion without further inquiry. An in-depth psychological-cognitive approach to the Romanian historical context is needed to see the whole picture. The Romanian constitution-makers and political elites were interested in nation-state building, political modernization, economic prosperity, and international legitimacy. The desire to give up the old feudal-like Romanian political-legal self was manifested against the intense admiration for the French and Belgian societies the Romanian elites were thoroughly acquainted with. The desire to become "the Belgium of the Orient" was frequently expressed since the 1850s. Nevertheless, French and Belgian constitutional models were encapsulated in an idealized Western European political and constitutional civilizational model worth imitating. The intention to replicate it was explicitly mentioned.

At the same time, the desire to imitate the Belgians was preserved as the hidden bottom layer of the Romanian idea of legal and social change. Against this backdrop, a large quantity-high fidelity replication of the Belgian constitutional text occurred.

However, the intention to imitate was counter-balanced by the Romanian founders' interest in giving the constitution-making process a Romanian national identitarian imprint and pursuing particular national political goals. The Constitution was applied after 1866 in a defective manner. However, the perpetual intention to replicate the Western-European (Belgian) constitutional-political means, outcomes, and partially, goals were constantly assessed against the valued constitutional model. The tension between the need for identity change and identity preservation, manifested during the constitutional debates, soon became the focal point of the intense debate about the possibility and strategies to conciliate the pro-European identity of belongingness and the ethnocentric identity of differentiation.

This approach of legal imitation was neither about the meeting between the imitated institutions and practices and the legal culture of the receiving society nor about the failure or success of legal imitation. It has been broadly and repeatedly discussed in the legal transplant/diffusions studies that legal transfers driven by prestige (imitation) are somewhat prone to fail. Instead, this paper focused on how long and under which conditions the actors of the legal imitation are interested in replicating the legal models at home and which consequences trigger this endeavor in their minds. The identification with the legal model entails a change in the legal actors' self-perception, mentality, and behavior that may produce a severe identitarian crisis. Imitation of foreign legal models, legal change, and legal identity of the legal actors may be a fruitful point of research confluence between comparative law and comparative legal history.

Chapter 17

The Business Judgment Rule in Anglo-American and Civil Law Systems: An Underlying Worldview

CARMELO MASSIMO DE IULIIS

In general, an individual's or a culture's worldview influences how they interpret and apply legal concepts. Worldviews can vary significantly from person to person and from culture to culture. This can lead to different interpretations of legal concepts. This article attempts to identify the worldview that underlies the Business Judgment Rule in the Anglo-American and European legal systems. The conclusions reached confirm that the Business Judgment Rule in common law countries is based on an accusatorial view of contractual liability, whereas the said Rule in civil law countries maintains an inquisitorial perspective of the same.

These two cultural legacies clearly emerge from the allocation of the burden of proof when corporations (or shareholders) bring liability actions against the directors. Despite their apparent incompatibility, such cultural heritages can effectively converge through a mutual jurisprudential reconsideration of the onus of evidence, without the need for international treaties. Before turning to this thesis, however, an overview is necessary of the Business Judgment Rule in the said legal systems and what interactions have occurred between them with respect to this Rule.

ORIGIN OF THE BUSINESS JUDGMENT RULE

The Business Judgment Rule originated in Anglo-American law. One of the earliest cases in past century that defined the Business Judgment Rule was the Dodge v. Ford Motor Co.[1] In this lawsuit,

[1] Supreme Court of Michigan, Dodge et al. v. Ford Motor co. et al. No. 47. Feb. 7, 1919, 204 Mich. 459, 170 N.W. 668, 3 A.L.R. 413 (italics added).

minority shareholders sued Ford Motor Company, alleging that its founder, Henry Ford (1863-1947), had breached his fiduciary duty by choosing to reduce the company's dividends and invest in new facilities and employee benefits instead.

The court held that the Business Judgment Rule was "grounded on the *presumption* that, when making business decisions, corporate directors acted on an informed basis, in good faith, and with the honest belief that their actions were *in the best interests of the company*".[2]

This landmark case established the Business Judgment Rule as a fundamental principle in corporate law, underpinning corporate decision-making, and shielding directors and officers from legal challenges, as long as their actions were in good faith and in the company's best interests.

A more recent example of the application of the Business Judgment Rule comes from an opinion issued by the Supreme Court of Delaware:[3]

2 The requirement to pursue the best interest of the company was introduced in *Companies Act 2006*:

> Section 172. *Duty to promote the success of the company.*
>
> (1) A director of a company must act in the way he considers, in good faith, would be most likely to promote the success of the company for the benefit of its members as a whole, and in doing so have regard (amongst other matters) to —
>
> (a) the likely consequences of any decision in the long term,
>
> (b) the interests of the company's employees,
>
> (c) the need to foster the company's business relationships with suppliers, customers and others,
>
> (d) the impact of the company's operations on the community and the environment,
>
> (e) the desirability of the company maintaining a reputation for high standards of business conduct, and
>
> (f) the need to act fairly as between members of the company.
>
> (2) Where or to the extent that the purposes of the company consist of or include purposes other than the benefit of its members, subsection (1) has effect as if the reference to promoting the success of the company for the benefit of its members were to achieving those purposes.
>
> (3) The duty imposed by this section has effect subject to any enactment or rule of law requiring directors, in certain circumstances, to consider or act in the interests of creditors of the company.

3 Supreme Court of Delaware, Grobow v. Perot, 15 March 1988.

> As previously noted, the Business Judgment Rule is but a *presumption* that directors, when making business decisions that do not involve self-interest, act on an informed basis, in good faith, and with the honest belief that their actions are in the corporation's best interest. See Aronson, 473 A.2d at 812 (italics added).

In the civil law system, a presumption is typically a legal inference regarding the existence or truth of a fact not certainly known, drawn from the known or proved existence of some other fact. However, in Anglo-American context, it functions as a rule of judgment established and applied by the judge[4] in the absence of contrary proof. The burden of proving the contrary *lies with the claimant*.

In civil law countries, a presumption, as a specific rule of judgment, must typically be explicitly provided by law: for example, Article 2486.6 of the Italian Civil Code concerning the dissolution of a company provides:

> When the liability of the directors is established in accordance with this Article, *and unless proven otherwise*, the compensable damage *is presumed* to be equal to the difference between the net assets as of the date when the director ceased to hold office or, in the case of the commencement of insolvency proceedings, the date of the commencement of such proceedings, and the net assets determined as of the date when a cause for the dissolution occurred [...] (italics added).

The Business Judgment Rule in the common law is a presumption in favor of the board and is sometimes referred to

[4] "Judge makes law" is the traditional formula to indicate the specificity and difference between the common law system and civil law countries. The sentence seems have been deduced from Sir William Blackstone's work *Commentaries on the Laws of England* (1765-1769), where he extensively discussed the role of judges and the concept of judge-made law in the common law system. In Volume I, Blackstone introduced the concept of common law and its origins. He emphasized the importance of judicial decisions in shaping and interpreting the law. However, William S. Brewbaker III, "Found Law, Made Law and Creation: Reconsidering Blackstone's Declaratory Theory", *Journal of Law and Religion*, XXII (2006), pp. 255-286, points out that in the introduction to the Commentaries Blackstone states that the judge's job is to determine the law "not according to his own private judgment, but according to the known laws and customs of the land"; the judge is "not delegated to pronounce a new law, but to maintain and expound the old one".

as the "business judgment presumption". Most generally, the business judgment rule acts as a presumption in favor of corporate managers' actions.[5]

DIFFERENT MEANING OF BUSINESS JUDGMENT RULE IN ENGLISH AND CIVIL LAW

The Business Judgment Rule takes on a different meaning in the English and European legal systems: in England this principle means nothing more than the non-reviewability of director management decisions. The legal precedent that contains this principle is In Re Smith and Fawcett Ltd.[6] The court stated: "Directors must exercise their discretion *bona fide* in what they consider – *not what a court may consider* – is in the interests of the company, and not for any collateral purpose" (italics added).

The English meaning of the Business Judgment Rule seems to have taken hold more than the American one in Italy. Italian jurisprudence has indeed embraced the English principle since 1965,[7] especially concerning managerial discretion, which remains exclusive to the director when exercised in *bona fide*.[8] This means the judgment on diligence can never invest the directors' management choices, but at most *the manner in which they were made*.[9]

French judges appear to be "immune" to interactions with the Anglo-American Business Judgment Rule. They distinguish

[5] Douglas M. Branson, "The Rule that Isn't a Rule – The Business Judgment Rule", *Valparaiso University Law Review*, XXXVI (2002), p. 631.

[6] In Re Smith and Fawcett Ltd. [1942] Ch. 304 CA (306).

[7] Cass., 12 November 1965, n. 2359, *Giur. It.*, 1966, I, 462: "The judge handling a liability action against the directors of joint-stock companies cannot review the merits of the acts carried out by the directors. In other words, the judge cannot make judgments based on discretionary criteria of suitability or convenience but must assess the behavior of the directors according to the general principles governing contractual obligations in a broad sense and compensation for damages". Also, in accordance, Cass., 16 January 1982, n. 280, *Giust. civ.*, 1983, 602.

[8] One recent judgment of the Italian Supreme Court uses the English term (business judgment rule) to emphasize the non-reviewability of management decisions. Cass. 22 June 2017, n. 15470, Banche dati Foro It. 1987-2017, "... the non-reviewability of the merits of his management choices (so-called business management rule) finds a limit in the assessment of reasonableness ...".

[9] Cass., 28 April 1997, n. 3652, *de jure*.

between inexcusable fault (management fault) and excusable error (simple negligence). In the interest of pragmatism, French courts do not penalize every unfortunate decision, recognizing that even a perfectly diligent manager can make a mistake. A conviction will only occur in cases where behavior deviates from that of a conscientious, honest, and respectful manager who adheres to the normal rules of commercial company management. For example, the fact of lending company funds in circumstances making repayment unlikely,[10] as well as certain acts of abstention such as lack of supervision and concealment of irregularities have been qualified as management errors.[11]

As for Germany, a cornerstone in jurisprudence regarding the Business Judgment Rule and the assessment of entrepreneurial decisions made by the management board is the ARAG/ Garmenbeck case.[12] The official guiding principle states:

> [...] b) The supervisory board, by virtue of its duty to supervise and control the activities of the executive board, has the duty to examine on its own responsibility the existence of claims for damages of the AG against members of the executive board. In doing so, it must take into account that the executive board must be granted *a wide scope of action for the management* of the AG's business, without which entrepreneurial action is absolutely inconceivable. [...]
>
> c) If the supervisory board comes to the conclusion that the executive board has incurred liability for damages, *it must assess, on the basis of a careful and proper risk analysis,* whether and to what extent legal action will lead to compensation for the damage incurred. Certainty that the action for damages will be successful cannot be demanded (italics added).

As we can deduce from these legal principles, *none* approaches the *presumption* of correct management of American origin.

10 CA Paris, 25th ch., 4 Feb. 1994: JurisData No. 1994-600148.

11 Cass. com., 9 May 1995, No. 92-20.746.

12 BGH, 21.04.1997 - II ZR 175/95 - ARAG/ Garmenbeck.

In 2005, the German Stock Company Act (Aktiengesetz or GePuCa) incorporated, in section 93.2,[13] the standard of care drawn from the Principles of Corporate Governance of the American Law Institute from 1994, Recommendations § 4.01(C) (1994).[14] The standard of care itself is the cornerstone of European legislation that does not introduce any presumption of good administration but rather specifies to the judge on the basis of which standards they should assess the actions of the directors.

Thus, we can observe that

> in France, Article L225-251 of the Commercial Code stipulates that directors and the general manager may be held individually or jointly liable, as the case may be, to the company or third parties. This liability can arise from violations of legal or regulatory provisions applicable to public limited companies, breaches of the articles of

[13] *Stock Corporation Act* of 6 September 1965 (Federal Law Gazette I, p. 1089), as last amended by Article 7 of the Act of 22 February 2023 (Federal Law Gazette 2023 I no. 51) (available online); Sec. 93 *Duty of the members of the management board to exercise skill and care; liability and responsibilities* (1) In managing the affairs of the company, the members of the management board are to exercise the due care of a prudent manager faithfully complying with the relevant duties. No dereliction of duties will be given in those instances in which the member of the management board, in taking an entrepreneurial decision, was within their rights to reasonably assume that they were acting on the basis of adequate information and in the best interests of the company. The members of the management board are to respect the secrecy of any confidential information and secrets of the company, particularly trade secrets or business secrets, of which they have become aware in the context of their activities in the management board. […].

[14] ALI *Principles of Corporate Governance*, Section 4.01

> (a) A director or officer has a duty to the corporation to perform the director's or officer's functions in good faith, in a manner that he or she reasonably believes to be in the best interests of the corporation, and with the care that an ordinarily prudent person would reasonably be expected to exercise in a like position and under similar circumstances. This Subsection (a) is subject to the provisions of Subsection (c) (the business judgment rule)* where applicable. * § 4.01(c):
>
> (c) A director or officer who makes a business judgment in good faith fulfills the [duty of care] if the director or officer: (1) is not interested in the subject of his business judgment;
>
> (2) is informed with respect to the subject of the business judgment to the extent the director or officer reasonably believes to be appropriate under the circumstances; and
>
> (3) rationally believes that the business judgment is in the best interests of the corporation

association, or faults committed in the course of their management;

in Italy: Article 2392, Italian Civil Code. [Directors] are jointly and severally liable to the company for damages resulting from the failure to comply with such duties [provided by law and by-law, and acting with the diligence required by the nature of the office], unless these are attributions proper to the executive committee or functions concretely attributed to one or more directors;

in England we have already seen the standard of care provided in Sec.172 CA.

TRANSNATIONALITY AND INTERACTION OF THE BUSINESS JUDGMENT RULE IN ANGLO-AMERICAN AND EUROPEAN LEGAL SYSTEMS?

From the comparison above, we cannot speak of transnationality and interaction between the two legal systems regarding the American-style jurisprudential Business Judgment Rule. This is for historical reasons. In the legal culture of continental Europe, judgment rules based on presumptions can only be legislatively mandated. No judge has the power to presume, unless it involves deducing an unknown fact from a known one based on strong, precise, and converging clues. We can, however, discuss transnationality and interaction between the two systems, especially English and Italian, concerning the rule of non-reviewability of the merits of the director's management choices, unless they are manifestly unreasonable.

A more pronounced interaction between the United States and Germany is found at the regulatory level concerning the standard of care, which, however, remains the generic "general negligence".[15] The *most significant difference*, however, between the Anglo-American and European Business Judgment Rule lies in the *burden of proof*: in the United States and England, the burden

[15] Andreas M. Fleckner and Klaus J. Hopt, *Comparative Corporate Governance* (2013), p. 128: "The standard of care is still general negligence".

lies with the plaintiff; in Italy, France, and Germany, it falls on the defendant (the director).

In Europe, indeed, the performance of the director towards the company is considered contractual in nature. Therefore, according to the general principles governing contractual liability (for example, Article 1218, Italian Civil Code),[16] the director is obligated to fulfill the obligation to administer with the required professional diligence.

In France essentially the same rule applies. Article 1353 of the Civil Code[17] states that once proof of the required performance, that is, the obligation, has been provided, the counterparty, in our case the director, must demonstrate that they have correctly fulfilled it.

In Germany, Section 93.2 of the German Public Companies Act (GePuCa) expressly prescribes that in the case of a corporate action for liability, the burden of proof is upon the directors.[18]

The only European State that, in its jurisprudence, appears to have aligned itself with the United States approach is Lithuania,[19]

[16] Article 1218, Italian Civil Code. The obligor who does not perform exactly the performance due [1176, 1181] is obliged to pay damages, unless it proves that the non-performance or delay was caused by an impossibility of performance resulting from a cause beyond its control. [my translation].

[17] Article 1353, Code Civil. Celui qui réclame l'exécution d'une obligation doit la prouver.

Réciproquement, celui qui se prétend libéré doit justifier le paiement ou le fait qui a produit l'extinction de son obligation.

[18] Markus Roth, *The Business Judgement Rule* (2012)

[19] Decree of the Supreme Court of Lithuania, 9 January 2014, adopted in civil case UAB "Mitnija" and UAB "MG Baltic Investment" v. V. G. and E. R. (Case No. 3K-7-124/2014). This Decree stated that "such a rule presuming directors' bona fide actions in the best interests of the company (i.e., Business Judgment Rule) should be applied to protect them against claims arising from loss-making decisions ex post ... the purpose of this presumption was to protect company directors against the imposition of personal civil liability for bona fide decisions taken when acting in compliance with the reasonable duty of care. Therefore, any person seeking recovery of damage suffered due to such an action or decision must not only prove the fact that such damage has been suffered, but also provide sufficient evidence that the director acted in breach of his duties (such as the duty of loyalty, fairness, reasonableness, etc.), exceeded reasonable business risk limits, committed obvious negligence, or otherwise misused his powers", See Virginijus Bit and Gintar Gumuliauskien, "The Business Judgment Rule in Lithuania", *European Business Organization Law Review*. XVII (December 2016), pp. 555-576.

whose Supreme Court "adopted" the rule of presumption of *bona fide* actions in the interest of the company.

THE UNDERLYING WORLDVIEW OF THE BUSINESS JUDGMENT RULE IN COMMON AND CIVIL LAW SYSTEMS

After this perhaps tedious but necessary comparison of the current law, we can attempt to identify the underlying worldview of the Business Judgment Rule in both types of legal system.

Common Law Jurisdictions

As for common law countries, their Business Judgment Rule implies the protection of the following aspects of economic and social life:

Shareholder Primacy and Economic Efficiency: The Business Judgment Rule reflects a worldview that places a strong emphasis on shareholder primacy and economic efficiency. In the Anglo-American legal tradition, corporations are often seen as entities whose primary purpose is to maximize shareholder wealth. This worldview is rooted in a belief that promoting economic efficiency and wealth creation benefits not only shareholders but also society at large.

Presumption of Good Faith and Expertise: The Business Judgment Rule is based on the presumption that corporate directors and officers are acting in good faith and with the expertise and diligence that one would expect from individuals in their positions. It assumes that these individuals have a deep understanding of the company's business and that they are making decisions in the best interests of the company.

Board Discretion and Non-Interference: The rule also reflects a worldview that respects the discretion of the board of directors and the management of a corporation. It is generally hesitant to second-guess their decisions unless there is evidence of bad faith, conflicts of interest, or a complete failure to exercise reasonable care.

Risk-Taking and Innovation: The Business Judgment Rule encourages risk-taking and innovation in business decisions. It recognizes that business decisions inherently involve uncertainty and that corporate managers should have the latitude to make choices that they believe will benefit the corporation in the long run, even if some decisions do not pan out as intended.

Laissez-faire Capitalism: The Business Judgment Rule aligns with the laissez-faire capitalist worldview, which emphasizes limited government interference in the affairs of private enterprises. It assumes that the market and shareholders will discipline corporate managers, and the law should not unduly interfere unless there is clear evidence of misconduct.

Limited Judicial Intervention: The worldview underlying the Business Judgment Rule tends to limit the role of the judiciary in corporate decision-making. Courts are generally reluctant to substitute their judgment for that of corporate directors and officers unless there is clear evidence of a breach of fiduciary duty.

All these aspects, here empirically identified, of the underlying worldview of the Anglo-American Business Judgment Rule can only be expressed and summarized by the accusatorial principle, especially in civil proceedings and particularly in matters of contractual liability. Referring to the judgments in Dodge v. Ford Motor Co.[20] and Grobow v. Perot,[21] it becomes evident that the American judiciary strongly emphasizes its duty to assume impeccable managerial conduct unless the accuser proves otherwise. This presumption mirrors the presumption of innocence, a fundamental principle in the American mindset and, of course, throughout the entire Anglo-American legal system, not only in criminal matters but also in civil cases. It allows for no exceptions, even within the realm of contractual liability.

Civil law systems

These tend to give more importance to the social impacts of economic activity. Here are some aspects of the worldview underlying Business Judgment Rule in Civil law systems:

Codified Law: Civil law systems are characterized by comprehensive and detailed legal codes that often provide specific rules and regulations for corporate governance. These codes lay

[20] Note 1 above.

[21] Note 3 above.

out the duties and responsibilities of corporate directors and officers with a focus on statutory compliance.

Legal Formalism: Civil law systems tend to emphasize formal legal structures and strict adherence to the letter of the law. The legal rules are typically codified and applied in a straightforward manner, with less emphasis on judicial interpretation and discretion.

Protection of Stakeholders: While common law systems often prioritize shareholder primacy, civil law systems may have a broader perspective that emphasizes the protection of various stakeholders, including employees[22], creditors, and the broader community. This reflects a social and communitarian worldview.

Independent Oversight: Civil law systems may place a greater emphasis on the appointment of independent supervisory bodies, such as supervisory boards,[23] to oversee corporate management. These bodies help ensure that management decisions align with the best interests of the corporation and its stakeholders.

Less Emphasis on Shareholder Litigation: Civil law systems tend to have fewer shareholder lawsuits and a lower level of litigation[24] compared to common law systems. The legal framework is designed to resolve corporate disputes through alternative means, such as arbitration and administrative procedures.

Government Regulation: Civil law systems may rely more on government regulators to oversee corporate behavior and enforce compliance with corporate governance rules. This reflects a

[22] For example, consider the typical German dualistic system, which grants employees the right of co-determination on the supervisory board [haben ein Mitbestimmungsrecht im Aufsichtsrat]. This right is regulated by the Act on the One-Third Participation of Employees in the Supervisory Board, Gesetz über die Drittelbeteiligung der Arbeitnehmer im Aufsichtsrat (Drittelbeteiligungsgesetz – DrittelbG: Date of issue: 18 May 2004. This is the most recent law on the topic; nevertheless, the right of co-determination has its origins in the late nineteenth century.

[23] See sec. 95 (GePuCa) ff. about the supervisory board; but also, Article 147.4 of the Consolidated Law on Financial Intermediation, Legislative Decree No. 58/1998, concerning the number of independent directors on the board of directors of listed companies.

[24] For example, in the Italian legal system, a joint-stock company (società per azioni) can initiate an action for liability against its directors only if the shareholders' assembly has approved such a legal action through a specific resolution, passed with a majority representing at least 1/5 of the share capital (Article 2393, Italian Civil Code).

regulatory worldview that believes government intervention is necessary to ensure responsible corporate behavior.

Continental Philosophy: Civil law systems often draw from continental philosophy and traditions, which may place a stronger emphasis on ethics, social responsibility, and a sense of duty toward society.[25]

In summary, civil law systems tend to have a more codified and formalistic approach to corporate governance, emphasizing the protection of a broader range of stakeholders and relying on government regulation and oversight. Their worldview reflects a communitarian perspective that places social interests and ethics at the forefront. As a result, the Business Judgment Rule as understood in common law systems, with its emphasis on shareholder primacy and judicial deference to corporate decisions, is not a central feature of corporate governance in civil law systems.

Legal formalism, protecting interests external to the social contract, and granting the right to pursue legal action for liability only when such action is approved by a qualified majority of shareholders at a general meeting, are all facets of a societal perspective that privileges those in positions of power. Those subject to this authority always bear the burden of proving that their actions align with the demands of the prevailing authority.

In the governance relationship between a corporation and a director, the corporation has the power to appoint the director. Upon acceptance of the appointment, the director is obligated to continually demonstrate to the company, rather than the shareholders who nominated them (a fundamental distinction from the Anglo-Saxon system), that they have consistently acted correctly in fulfilling their duties.

As a result, they must prove the baseless nature of the accusations against them, similar to an inquisitorial process. Essentially, the company or the shareholder, acting on behalf of the company, assumes the role of the director's inquisitor. The judge's role is limited to evaluating the evidence presented by the director in their defense, not the evidence supporting the accusation.

[25] All listed companies and banks must adopt an internal code of ethics.

JURISPRUDENTIAL REEVALUATION OF BURDEN OF PROOF DISTRIBUTION IN LEGAL SYSTEMS: A COMPARATIVE LAW PERSPECTIVE WITHOUT THE NEED FOR TREATIES

The significant difference in the application of the Business Judgment Rule between European and Anglo-American legal systems, particularly the opposite allocation of the burden of proof, appears to stem from seemingly irreconcilable judicial worldviews. The question arises whether this differing allocation of the burden can be addressed through transnational regulation without relying on treaties.

The philosophy of law of Gottfried Wilhelm Leibniz (1646-1716) can provide valuable insights. Although philosophers often place the burden of proof on those contesting a claim, no such universal agreement exists among States in court proceedings. The determination of the burden of proof, according to Leibniz,[26] should fall upon the party for whom discharging it is easier. In our context, whether the company demonstrating a liability claim against the director or the director demonstrating their proper

[26] Gottfried Wilhelm Leibniz, *Specimen Quaestionum Philosophicarum ex Jure collectarum* [Specimen of Philosophical Questions Collected from Law] (1664), in AA VI Berlin Academy of Sciences, Willy Kabitz, and Heinrich Schepers (eds.), *Leibniz. Philosophische Schriften 1663-1672* (1990), I, pp. 76-77, *Quaestio II*: "3. Among philosophers who engage in academic debates, it is certain (by tacit agreement, one might say, by an implicit contract) that the Respondent, as such, neither proves nor seeks the foundation [of their thesis]. Among disputing parties in court, it is not universally determined whether the burden of proof falls on the Plaintiff or the Defendant, as no tacit agreement has been reached between the parties on this matter. Moreover, unlike what happens among contemplative philosophers, one cannot forego the judgment or decision of the judge without prejudice to the other party. 4. Thus, there is a consensus that if the judge refrains from issuing a judgment, the case shall be deemed to have lapsed implicitly, meaning that the plaintiff does not obtain what they request. Therefore, it is necessary to extract the truth from the records and evidence, by any lawful means, so that the case can be decided. As a result, the burden of proof is imposed on the one for whom it is more convenient to fulfill it, so that the case does not conclude without a decision. 5. And since, as a rule, the one who relies on something must prove the accusation as much as possible (*Freder. Schenck, tractatus del probationibus, n.1 and 2*), it follows that the burden falls on the plaintiff or the defendant who first presents either an assertion or a denial, if they are able to provide evidence. If they cannot, for the compelling necessity of seeking the truth, the burden is transferred to the other party, and this is the commonly known Negative proof: I deny this; let the one who asserts it prove it. *Cravetta Consilia. 1. n. 10.2.* [author's translation]

fulfillment of duties is easier depends on the nature of the violation with which the director is charged.

For instance, if the violation pertains to a specific obligation, such as timely tax payment, the company must provide evidence, often in the form of the tax authority's demand. However, in cases involving general mismanagement during the director's term, the burden of proof leans towards the director as they have better access to evidence for their defense. The company, in such cases, need only demonstrate the damage and allege the facts contributing to that harm. This approach respects the principles of both the accusatorial and inquisitorial systems.

This distribution of the burden of proof can be accepted in both types of legal system without necessitating formal treaties, with the comparative method serving as a valuable tool to harmonize and align their principles in practice.

Chapter 18

Harmonization, Uniformity and Comparative Law: Latin American Experience

JORGE SÁNCHEZ A. CORDERO

It is commonplace to speak of the phenomenon of globalization facilitated by recent technological and economic changes which are expected to result[1] in a more refined globalization. However, it is not so commonplace to systematically analyze this process in legal systems that coexist in free trade areas where trade and social permeability are particularly intense.[2] It is therefore useful to compare recent experience with harmonization and uniform legislation at a global level.

In the Americas, the emergence of a significant number of trading regions is evident with the recent United States-Mexico-Canada Agreement (USMCA),[3] Central American Free Trade Agreement (CAFTA), and MERCOSUR,[4] among others. However, the unsteady work of the Inter-American specialized Conference of International Private Law (CIDIP), operating within the Organization of American States (OAS) and their lack of influence in the region should also be kept in mind.

In a synoptic perspective, the international community is a complex mosaic of legal systems that reflect different legal traditions. If notions of uniformity and harmonization of law are perceived as different historical episodes, this will provide more insight into and understanding of their changing nature. These notions are substantially different according to an analysis

[1] J. Basedow, "General Report. Worldwide Harmonization of Private Law and Regional Economic Integration», *Uniform Law Review*, VIII, nos. 1/2 (New Series, 2003), p. 36.

[2] Ibid., p. 36.

[3] The USMCA entered into force 1 July 2020 (available online).

[4] Mercosur was established by the treaty signed in the city of Asunción, 26 March 1991, between Argentina, Brazil, Paraguay, and Uruguay.

undertaken at the turn of the twentieth and the twenty-first centuries. The concepts of harmonization and legal uniformity have distinct legal consequences in radically different historical scenarios.[5]

In the late-nineteenth and early-twentieth centuries we had a mosaic of fiercely independent countries in the Americas, whilst the culturally homogeneous had close commercial ties. Similarly, in the region, from the outset, two clearly defined legal subsystems existed, both with deep and common European roots, but substantially different in their legal composition.[6]

ORIGIN OF THE CONCEPT OF HARMONIZATION AND UNIFORMITY

The tradition and the need for harmonization and uniformity of law are not recent. The first signs emerged in the second half of the nineteenth century in certain specific geographic regions. In fact, the initial impetus for the unification of law can be clearly identified in the legal subsystem of Latin American countries in the 1878 Treaty of Lima,[7] which never entered into force. This treaty comprehensively codified subjects such as private law, private international law, and civil procedure, among others.[8] In the Montevideo Conference of 1889, organized as a sequel to the diplomatic conferences held in Paris in 1883, and in Berne in 1886, eight conventions were signed on private international law, international civil procedure, copyright, intellectual property, trademarks and patents, international criminal law, legal practice, and international trade law.[9]

[5] Herbert Kronke, "Unidroit 75th. Anniversary Congress on Worldwide Harmonization of Private Law and Regional Economic Integration: Hypotheses, Certainties and Open Questions", *Uniform Law Review*, VIII, 1/2 (New Series, 2003), p. 11.

[6] Ibid.

[7] The Lima Congress 1877-1978, concluded with the Treaty of Lima signed by Argentina, Bolivia, Chile, Costa Rica, Ecuador, Peru and Venezuela but never entered into force and was only ratified by Peru. See Leonel Pérez Nieto, *La tradition territorialiste en droit international privé dans les pays d'Amérique Latine* (1985), p. 369.

[8] Ibid.

[9] The participant countries in this congress were Argentina, Bolivia, Brazil, Chile, Paraguay, Peru and Uruguay. Only Chile and Brazil did not ratify these treaties. Ibid.

Notwithstanding that these events must be considered isolated cases; they can be interpreted as the first indications of a uniform law movement in the Americas.[10] Therefore, the evolutionary trends of uniform law before World War II were an essentially regional and localized first step, either in Europe or the Americas.

One element of the analysis is the nationalist component that steered the spirit of the Latin American countries. Indeed, in Latin American States in the late-nineteenth and early-twentieth centuries, the conception was that their active participation in European-based international organizations would significantly limit their sovereignty and undermine their principles of national law. This nationalist view dominated their spirit[11] and persisted for a prolonged period, having a significant international impact. Latin American countries primarily sought to strengthen their political independence through the unification of law and the development of national legislation. The application of law within the limits of the State was a *conditio sine qua non* in safeguarding national sovereignty and consequently of excluding the application of foreign law.

In spite of the pretensions of formal universal international organizations, their performance in practice was merely regional, as shown by the minimum amount of ratifications of or accessions, if any, to international instruments by Latin American countries.[12] In support of this thesis one should recall the conclusions of the 1889 Montevideo Congress, which are undeniable proof of this nationalist sentiment. The central discussion was that the power and influence of international economic agents prevailed in international trade and any other approach to the problem that tends to obviate this reality, it was argued, "threatens the national interest".[13]

This period of time deserves a final thought; the traditional conception was that the form of "international conventions" was the most appropriate technique for the uniformity of private law

[10] Basedow, note 1 above, p. 32, in the same sense.

[11] Ibid.

[12] Ibid., p. 33

[13] Ibid., p. 33.

and private international law".[14] Indeed, in a relatively small and "civilized" international legal community,_the ratification and approval by the legislative bodies were foreseeable. It should be added to the analysis that the attitudes in international negotiations in different fields, such as the entry into force of international conventions, were quite predictable.[15] This contrasts greatly with the current situation, in which a real explosion of active nation-state participation in international forums and consequently in the construction of international business environment, can be easily perceived. The quantitative element substantially modified the role of the international convention as the suitable vehicle for drafting conventions containing conflicts or substantive rules.

After the Second World War, the concept of uniform law took on a greater degree of universality, particularly since the 1970s. There are various causes: the decline in the influence of European powers at the global level, the emergence of other powers, the blossoming of dozens of newly independent States, among others.[16]

To place the analysis in perspective, the international community has grown from 58 members, which was the largest number of nation States recorded in the heyday of the League of Nations in 1937 to 193 members in the United Nations in May 2024. In the vast majority of new States, the sense of nationalism prevails and is reflected in legislation, regardless of their legal legacy, yet much of their private law systems comes from former colonial powers.

Just after World War II Latin American countries and the United States of America accessed specialized international agencies such as the Hague Conference on Private International Law[17] and the International Institute for the Unification of Private Law (UNIDROIT)[18]. It was an era when new *ad hoc* international organizations were created, such as the International Maritime

[14] Basedow, "Uniform Law Conventions and the Unidroit Principies of International Commercial Contracts", *Uniform Law Review,* V, no. 1 (New Series, 2000), p. 129.

[15] Ibid.

[16] Basedow, note 1 above, p. 33.

[17] For more information, consult the site www.hcch.net.

[18] For more information, consult the site www.unidroit.org

Organization[19], International Civil Aviation Organization (ICAO)[20], and the United Nations Commission on International Trade Law (UNCITRAL) in the United Nations system.[21] This last forum, at Vienna in 1980, approved the United Nations Convention on Contracts for the International Sale of Goods.[22] This Convention is presently in enforce in 97 countries, and extends to more than two thirds of all world trade. It also constitutes the first major effort in the universal systematization of the general principles of contracts[23] with the last international organization being the World Trade Organization (WTO).

Finally, in the last quarter of the twentieth century and the beginning of the twenty-first, the emergence of free trade areas has been recognized; some have been perfectly well-defined and others are in the process of becoming so. The pattern of the European Union, eponymous as a free trade region, is one major model to be followed. Nevertheless, uniformity appears as a basic notion in new organizations such as the Organisation pour l'Harmonisation en Afrique du Droit des Affaires (OHADA).[24]

The free trade trilateral or bilateral conventions or agreements prevailing in the Americas, such as USMCA,[25] CAFTA, MERCOSUR,[26] better known as the "commercial spaghetti", merit a profound analysis. At this late stage there is, in commercial institutional regions, a clear trend in the transfer of business legislative powers to supranational bodies,[27] whose effects in the near future will provoke a redefinition in trade negotiations, and the reconstruction of the *ad hoc* international bodies, among others.

[19] For more information, consult the site www.imo.org.

[20] For more information, consult the site www.icao.org

[21] For more information, consult the page www.uncitral.org;_

[22] Available online.

[23] Basedow, note 1 above, p. 35.

[24] Note 7 above.

[25] Note 5 above.

[26] Note 6 above.

[27] See in this respect Article 61 of the Amsterdam Treaty which entered into force 1 January 1999. *Official Journal of the European Community*, No. C340, 10 November 1997.

It is precisely in legal integration where the transfer of State powers to an international organization, endowed with powers of decision and supranational competition is more clearly seen.[28] Insofar as this legal integration process is intensified, trade negotiations are strengthened with the representative bodies of trade regions. They are beginning to have a greater weight in international organizations themselves; at the same time, there is a significant decline in the interest of trade negotiations isolated with nation-States belonging to these commercial areas. The concepts of harmonization and uniformity of law in this new context are also a transformation of substance.

In the European Union the community institutions have been vested with legal authority[29] to conclude international agreements with one or more nation-states or international organizations.[30] The European Court of Justice has even extended powers of negotiation of the Union through the mechanism of "implicit" powers.[31] Henceforward the European Union has the competence to conclude international agreements even in the absence of an explicit mandate in the Treaty of the European Union,[32] if it has jurisdiction at all in these specific areas.[33] Moreover, the European Court of Justice has held that treaties concluded by the European Union with either third-party countries or international organizations are part of community law. [34] These conventions are considered "acts of the European Community institutions" and thereby fall under the jurisdiction of the European Court of Justice

[28] Gerard Cornu, *Vocabulaire juridique* (8th ed.; 1987), p. 468.

[29] See in this respect Article 281, Constitutional Treaty of the European Community Publisher in the Official Diary of the European Community, C325, 24 December 2002, which states: "The community shall have legal personality".

[30] See Article 310, ibid.: "The Community may conclude with one or more states or international organizations agreements establishing an association involving reciprocal rights and obligations, common actions and special procedures".

[31] Basedow, note 1 above, p. 36.

[32] Available online.

[33] Ibid., p. 36.

[34] Ibid., p. 47.

which is responsible for ensuring their uniform application[35] in the entire territory of the community.[36]

Therefore, in certain cases, the nation-states that belong to well-defined commercial areas and agree to international trade commitments with third States might even be acting *ultra vires*.[37]

THE DEBATE OVER HARMONIZATION AND UNIFORMITY.

A consequence of the phenomenon of globalization is the increased intensity of the debate on the basic notions of harmonization and uniformity of legislation which are inextricably linked to interstate or cross-border trade.[38]

In this regard, one of the main debates is whether legislative harmonization or unification fosters economic prosperity.[39] It has been argued that uniformity significantly reduces the competition between legal systems and regulatory provisions and that competition between legal systems deters the formation of harmful fossilized legal inefficiencies that could be perpetuated by a legal system because of a lack of competition brought about by harmonization or uniformity.[40]

Currently, the transplantation or borrowing of legal mechanisms is not attributed to elements of nationality but to convenience and necessity.[41] In any analysis it must be considered that uniform law is not an end in itself, but a response to practical

[35] See Article 234, Constitutional Treaty of the European Community Publisher in the Official Diary of the European Community, C325, 24 December 2002.

[36] Basedow, note 1 above, p. 47.

[37] Ibid., p. 41.

[38] There are, therefore, some authors that argue that harmonization does not necessarily result from economic imperatives or statutory mandate. See Kronke, note 8 above, p. 15.

[39] Arthur S. Hartcamp, "Modernization and Harmonization of Contract Law: Objectives, Methods and Scope", *Uniform Law Review*, VIII, nos. 1/2 (New Series, 2003), p. 82.

[40] Paulo Borba Casella, "Economic Integration and Legal Harmonization, with special reference to Brazil", *Uniform Law Review*, III, nos. 2/3 (1998), p. 293.

[41] Ibid., p. 293.

needs.[42] On a more general basis, it should be pondered that the law, and more specifically commercial law, is not a value in itself,[43] but it contributes to strengthening economic and cultural values of a society. Still, the unification of law not only responds to economic or financial interests but also recognizes political and cultural interests.

In any process of legal integration as is *verbi gratia* the directives of the European Union, legislative harmonization has an undeniable political and social value. In summary, harmonization and unification of legislation, when they occur, are cultural assets of great importance.[44]

To enable a better understanding of the intended scope of this analysis, we must first consider the notions of harmonization and uniformity, though it must be admitted that they themselves are subject to controversy.[45]

Despite their constant semantic changes, it can be argued that the notion of harmonization is to unify the enactments of legislative assemblies, either through the development of a new law, or through the design of rules and principles that enable an approximation between two or more legal systems. Harmonization entails a legislative process that make rules compatible. These rules come from different backgrounds and often from different periods of time. Harmonization modifies legislation in force in order to make it more consistent with new provisions.[46] The immediate effect of harmonization is to reduce the differences and divergences between the laws.[47] It is considered that the harmonization process should refer exclusively to the conflict rules inherent in private international law that do not alter substantive law.[48]

42 Ibid., p. 304.

43 Hartcamp, note 39 above, p. 84.

44 Ibid., p. 84.

45 In this context it has been postulated that the basics are harmonization, standardization, and uniformity. Borba Casella, note 40 above, p. 288.

46 Cornu, note 28 above, p. 423.

47 Joseph Issa-Sayeh, "Quelques aspects techniques de l'integration juridique l'exemple des actes uniformes d'Ohada", *Revue de Droit Uniforme*, IV, no. 1 (1999), p. 6.

48 Borba Casella, note 40 above, p. 288.

In the process of legislative uniformity, some concern has arisen to conceptually distinguish unification from uniformity. Unification replaces national legislative standards with rules previously agreed; the purpose is to eliminate any conflict of laws by having an identical text. The conflict of law problem, however, cannot be completely overcome since it is difficult to reach absolute unification or universal interpretation or enforcement.[49]

Unification replaces dissimilar laws previously in force with a single text. The notion of unification is more comprehensive as can be seen in substantive legal integration, for it tends to eliminate differences in legislation. This is achieved through the introduction of a single text written with identical terms by the member States of a specific free trade area or by an international organization. The feasibility of the legal text's identity depends on a number of diverse elements: the degree of economic integration, the legal nature of the member states' system within one economic region,[50] the nature of the subject that is intended to be made uniform, among others. Finally, as Professor Tallon puts it, integration at its height will end up undermining the legal autarchies.[51]

Uniformity for its part has two aspects: it can refer to both conflict and substantive rules. Uniformity is more profound than harmonization, but less profound than unification.[52]

In these processes, the weighting of the origin of the harmonization or uniformity is crucial. They should give answers to basic questions such as the origin of the rules subject to harmonization or uniformity, the economic reasons which prompted its creation, whether these rules belong to a traditional set of rules and to what extent, and whether they should be adapted to satisfy new economic conditions,[53] among others.

It is also compulsory to consider if rules to be harmonized or made uniform are designed to meet new social expectations or remain «neutral» to these.

[49] Ibid., p. 288.

[50] Cornu, note 28 above, p. 884.

[51] Denis Tallon, "Quel droit comparé pour le XXIème. Siècle?", *Revue de Droit Uniforme*, III, 2 and 3 (New Series, 1998), p. 704.

[52] Borba Casella, note 40 above, p. 291.

[53] Ibid., p. 159.

Harmonization and uniformity can have different foci; they can be universal or simply regional as in Mercosur. A multitude of elements of diversity ultimately converge; in fact the differences in a given region may well be geographical, economic, cultural or be specific to a legal system which belongs to a socio-economic reality of a specific nation.[54] Harmonization can have various levels: it can be aimed at the elimination of the main differences between national regulations, or induce only a minimum of common solutions, and its scope can also be very different: to create common rules in specific areas.

One crucial aspect of the harmonization process is the choice of the legal area to be considered. It has been frequently observed that at the universal level this choice can be attributed to academic and intellectual leaders,[55] who presided over decision centers either in governmental or international organizations. While the legal area could have academically seductive options it was a case of rejection, if not a frank indifference on the part of market agents.

The result is predictable; international instruments either do not enter into force, or the market agents do not consider them as a legal reference to regulate their contractual relations. In many cases the parameters of study areas are subject to constant change.

Professor Goode[56] expressed this well:

> treaty collections are littered with conventions that have never come into force, for want of the number of required ratifications, or have been eschewed by the major trading States. There are several reasons for this: failure to establish from potential interest groups at the outset that there is a serious problem which the proposed convention will help to resolve; hostility from powerful pressure groups, lack of sufficient interest of, or pressure on, governments to induce them to burden still further an already over-crowed legislative timetable; mutual hold-backs, each State waiting to see what others will do, so that in the end none of them does anything ...

54 Ibid.

55 Kronke, note 5 above, p. 17.

56 Roy Goode, "International Restatements of Contract in English Contract Law", *Uniform Law Review*, II, no. 2 (New Series, 1997), p. 232.

The final approach is to emphasize that although the choice of a feasible specific legal area for harmonization or uniformity is important, it is just as important to consider whether the policies of States are also reconcilable in these specific areas.

It would, however, be wrong to associate the fate of the harmonization or unification of private law in the interests of market operators or to try to draft flexible rules or principles of *soft law,* in highly sensitive areas. Aspects related exclusively to legal culture in the processes of harmonization should be addressed and its nature must be drafted with great detail to ensure consistency.[57]

To be successful, international conventions of private international law or private law, must be innovative and provide solutions to the needs of both individuals and economic agents involved in international trade.[58] In this context, more than a century ago Mancini [59] argued that in order to be effective, even if limited to certain areas, a universal legal system should be confined to general principles and rules regardless of specific national circumstances. It seems that this argument would be accurate today: uniformity requires shared cultural identities and values.[60]

Though the above arguments are meaningful, recent experience also needs to be considered. At the global level[61] *hard law* international conventions, whose orthodoxy comes from the past, have not been efficient enough in the harmonization of private law and private international law. The causes are varied and beyond the scope of this analysis. Some are often mentioned: preparation of a multilateral convention requires a significant amount of time and is generally expensive, if one adheres to the obtained results. In trade negotiations there are compromises,[62] and they are reflected in prevailing international conventions as the lowest

[57] Kronke, note 5 above, p. 17.

[58] Ibid., p. 20.

[59] Cited by Borba Casella, note 40 above, p. 291.

[60] Ibid.

[61] Andrzej Calus, "Modernisation and Harmonization of Contract Law: Focus on Selected Issues", *Uniform Law Review*, III, nos. 1 and 2, (New Series, 2003), p. 159.

[62] John Goldring, "Globalisation, National Sovereignty and the Harmonization of Laws", *Uniform Law Review,* III, 2/3 (New Series, 1998), p. 448.

common denominator[63] of national interests, which international negotiators are willing to grant.[64] This compromise has been aptly described as a "minimalist" approach.

The term "minimalist" has the following distinctive features: *a)* a list of equivalent terms in the nation-states whose legislation it is intended to standardize; *b)* classification codes and statutory provisions that correspond to these terms; *c)* identification of the common denominator of these rules; and finally *d)* the formulation of new rules consistent with those common denominators.[65] This «minimalist» approach that prevails in *hard law* conventions is summarized in the drafting of «official» or «binding» rules. In this approach, other types of rules are considered too uncertain to be made uniform. This approach overlooks the disparity of conflicting interpretations of those laws or that of their common denominators by courts, arbitrators, and contracting parties. Needless to say, it ignores the law created on a daily basis within contractual or legal practice.

These characteristics of *hard law* international conventions severely limit its innovative potential and ratification also causes a unique problem: few conventions come into force because a certain number of ratifications are required.[66] Finally, when one considers that the multilateral convention should be modified, it is necessary to reinitiate the same process. Updating these conventions is not easily done. The international community has shown little ability to update international instruments even if they have undergone changes of substance.[67]

The «minimalist» approach contrasts with the approach of achieving the best business rule. The agents in international trade

[63] Michael Joachim Bonell, Towards a Codification of the Unidroit Principles? (2007), p. 94 (available online).

[64] Goldring, note 62 above, p. 448.

[65] Boris Kozolchyk, "The Unidroit Principles as a Model for the Unification of the Best Contractual Practices in the Americas", *The UNIDROIT Principles: A common law of the contracts for the Americas? Interamerican Congress. Valencia, Venezuela, 6 to 9 November 1996. Uniform Law Review. Acts, p. 98.*

[66] E. Allan *Farnsworth,* "Modernization and Harmonization of Contract Law: an American Perspective", *Uniform Law Review, V111,* nos. 1/2 (New Series, 2003), p. 106. In the same sense see Calus, note 61 above, p. 160.6

[67] Kronke, note 5 above, p. 18.

long for maximum uniformity. This approach maintains that uniformity must be supported by business practices and habits.[68]

Other forms in the creation of the procedures and requirements for international business have been explored. In those legal systems or free trade regions which do not have of organic institutions the form of "model law" must be discussed, either prior to its adoption by the legislative bodies of each nation-state, or prior to the formulation of international instruments encompassing conflicts or substantive law that attempts to systematize trade practices such as International Commercial Terms (INCOTERMS) developed by the International Chamber of Commerce of Paris, model contractual clauses, restatements, or legislative and contractual guidelines.

> In this context, model laws and arbitration rules should be mentioned, as these endeavors developed within UNCITRAL[69] have had markedly successful results.[70] The importance of INCOTERMS is its acceptability to a large number of States. This is a clear example of legal instruments subject to the regime of *soft law.* The effect of its uniformity on relevant legislation in the international community is not only formal, but a legal framework that serves as reference for the settlement of disputes in arbitration as accepted terms and practices. In dispute settlement it provides the necessary legal uniformity that allows a high degree of predictability in foreign trade transactions and thus legal certainty.

As for the merits of legislative guides, the balance of legal and economic content is crucial. Indeed, from the outset, the legislative guides consider the diversity of legal systems to offer alternative solutions for provisions or clauses in specific contracts in order to overcome the adverse consequences arising from differences in legal standards.[71]

The legislative guide provides important foundations for economic valuations of contractual elements in specific

[68] Kozolchyk, note 65 above, p. 94.

[69] Available online: www.uncitral.org

[70] Mexico incorporated the model arbitration law into its Commercial Code according to the Diario Oficial de la Federación, 22 July 1993.

[71] Calus, note 61 above, p. 161.

transactions. The legal elements introduced in the legislative guide are not exhausted by the prospect of eliminating the consequences of differences in domestic laws. They constitute a method to single out contractual terms which are of great legal relevance[72]. All these are forms of non-binding legal texts that have been called "narrative rules" and have become the core of the legal regime of *soft law*.[73] The legal texts subject to this system, though devoid of a binding legal character, are exerting an enormous influence over market players' conduct and result in significant changes in business practices.

This construction of "narrative rules" or *soft law* has been challenged in the recent past. The process of removing barriers to international trade has led States to amend their contract law and adopt or adapt these model laws, restatements, or legislative or contractual guides developed by prestigious international organizations such as UNIDROIT and UNCITRAL.

These instruments also meet other objectives: advising parties in international transactions and offering diverse solutions to national laws, both in training and in the implementation of contracts. In these cases, the importance of this "indirect" harmonization lies in the adoption of uniform solutions, especially in the optional or additional rules that differ significantly from one legal system to another[74]. Equally, in a marked way, similar to narrative standards subject to the legal system of *soft law*, the Principles of International Commercial Contracts (UNIDROIT Principles), adopted in May 1994 by the Governing Council of Unidroit, may be cited.

Apart from the discussion of the particulars of each provision of the UNIDROIT Principles, it generally could be argued that this body of law offers a "neutral" legal system of rules. The UNIDROIT Principles could overcome deficiencies or omissions in private law conventions. But they equally mean that the Principles offer an alternative to national laws that are designed to resolve local disputes without which international or even national trade transactions would barely be solved.[75]

72 Ibid.

73 Eric Jayme, *Rechtsbegriffe und Kunstgeschichte: En neues Recht zum Schutz von Kulturgut* (available online).

74 Calus, note 61 above, p. 161.

75 Basedow, note 14 above, p. 137.

The above arguments encounter one of their supporting points in the origin of the UNIDROIT Principles. The initial working group was composed of distinguished jurists pertaining to different jurisdictions. Their diverse law perspectives were essential in a transnational debate and therefore excluded any priority of binding law from a particular legal system and ensured its international character. The convergence of different legal minds and their reconciliation in obtaining the best business rule are some of the greatest contributions in this collective work that was enriched significantly in 2004.

It can be debated whether the UNIDROIT Principles are general enough to conclude that they are indeed general principles of law. It can be argued in this context that the general character does not come from its content but from its acceptability by different States.[76] In sum, it is safe to say that the UNIDROIT Principles can be considered as general principles of law to the extent that there is evidence of their acceptance by the international community. The debate over legal nature is summarized by Professor Basedow:[77]

> "... Their normative quality can only be assessed by a new theoretical reflection. It has to cross the traditional borderline between law and fact, between precepts and habits, and it must overcome the positivist concept that lawmaking is the exclusive prerogative of the State, to the effect that normative texts can only produce a binding effect if they have been approved in the proper constitutional manner ...".

From a different perspective, the adoption of the form has been upheld as one basic approach in this process of harmonization and is part of the dilemma between, on one hand, the legal certainty and on the other, flexibility, and adaptability. The form of convention, which generally should be understood as a legal codification, satisfies the first proposition, as the various forms of the system of *soft law* satisfy the requirements of the second proposition.[78]

With the previous approach the convenience of elaborating conflict or substantive rules in the process of harmonization has

[76] Ibid., p. 132.

[77] Ibid.

[78] Kronke, note 5 above, p. 19.

been expressed. In this regard, it is thought that the extent to which conflict rules provides solutions for disputes is less satisfactory, therefore strengthening the need for uniform law conventions.[79]

Finally, legislative harmonization or uniformity requires a policy of harmonization or uniformity, and consequently, a rethinking of the notion of national sovereignty. Legislative harmonization or uniformity can only be reconciled with national sovereignty when the State legislature agrees to adopt a law that could be identical or similar to the one of another or more States. This is only possible if the State obeys societal interests, and one of the substantive interests would be the elimination of barriers to international trade.[80] By harmonizing or making its internal law uniform the State declines the right to implement different objectives in its domestic policy.

CONCLUSIONS

Conflicts of law impede the course of average daily life. Therefore, the various reasons for endorsing uniformity or harmonization are straightforward. Uniform law signifies cultural unity, that is to say, it removes obstacles and misunderstandings in a society that strives for harmony. Uniformity means that comparable cases are not handled differently; it implies the elimination of uncertainties and avoids nuisances inherent to conflicts of law in a certain space and time.

In sum, the employment of uniformity for the purpose of drawing together national legal systems or making them compatible is the pathway that represents great possibilities for moving forward. The abstract nature of the law demands uniformity. Uniformity is hindered if multiple solutions are formulated for two identical hypotheses. These are the possibilities of uniformity. But uniformity has no intention of ignoring the existence of languages, knowledge, and habits – in sum, the culture of humankind.

National traditions are deeply rooted in a society that continually seeks diversity. The challenge consists not only of selecting new elements or advanced ideas that can ensure a positive result in law improvement, but also to skillfully weave

[79] Ibid.

[80] Goldring, note 62 above, p. 449.

these new elements into the texture of domestic legislation and into the traditional environment of law activity.

Legal solutions are numerous because they are the result of variation. The huge scientific advances of the West can be explained by their diversity, in contrast with other societies. The notion that law is invariable must be excised from juristic rhetoric. Long gone are the times when laws were etched in stone in an attempt to render them eternal. Advocating diversity does not bring the elimination of uniformity, and the undertaking of uniformity does not result in the eradication of diversity. This is the symbiosis of uniformity and diversity, which alas, demonstrates the limits of uniformity. These considerations are especially valid in Latin America.

SECTION 3.
At the Margin or in the Centre? Teaching and Doing Comparative Law

Chapter 19

Can Methods from the Social and Human Sciences be of Value in Understanding Comparative Law Methodology?

GEOFFREY SAMUEL

A joint symposium (Drawing Legal Pictures) and workshop (Strategies in Comparative Legal Research) held at Lausanne in May 2023 posed a number of questions about theory, method and practice in comparative law. How are methods regarded within comparative law theory? Is there a system, or is it a matter of pluralism or indeed just anarchy? Is there a hierarchy of methods? What are the types of scientific rationality employed? Perhaps all these questions can be reduced to a general epistemological one. How do researchers and scholars engage with the objects of their research and (or) their scholarship? In the sciences and the social sciences this question has been, and remains, much discussed, usually under the general topic of epistemology (theory of knowledge). Yet, in some of the humanities this question, while not ignored, has, arguably, not been well discussed. Or, if discussed, it is often under the general label of "theory", and this can prove problematic. Comparative law, unlike perhaps legal studies in general, cannot, nowadays, be accused of ignoring the engagement question as the Lausanne, and other conferences over the past two or so decades, bear witness. However, given that much scholarship in law and comparative law involves texts, ought these theory and method issues to be considered in isolation from other disciplines such as literary and film studies (assuming a film to be a text)? Might it not be said that comparatists ought to be interested in comparison in general? Given the emphasis on "pictures", this present contribution will examine "theory" and "method" in comparative legal studies within this interdisciplinary context, with reference in particular to the visual arts.

INTRODUCTION: SETTING THE SCENE

All disciplines involve the engagement with something. In the natural sciences this engagement is normally with an external phenomenon – although mathematics is an exception – and this external phenomenon is often inert in the sense that, for example, atoms, volcanoes and the planets do not think or have a free will. However, scientists will not engage directly with these phenomena; they will construct models that will hopefully both explain the external object (or whatever) and predict its future behaviour.[1] The scheme of intelligibility is normally a causal one. Social scientists aim to do the same, although their external object – humans – are more problematic because humans can think and have (seemingly) free will. Applying a causal scheme thus becomes difficult because of the sheer complexity of trying to explain human behaviour in the context of social grouping.

In many of the human sciences (humanities) the external object is not some external phenomenon but a text. Many humanities scholars are thus engaging with a text, and this requires rather different schemes of intelligibility. It could be said that students in the natural sciences also engage with texts, at least to some extent, in that they use introductory books and textbooks as a major source for the acquisition of scientific knowledge. Yet, in the end, their research does not focus on texts as such. However, law and theology are particularly textual, as are literature and film (if one treats films as texts). One difference between the literature scholar and the legal scholar is that the former can use reasoning and methods that are not always open to the jurist. The two groups of scholars are working within different "paradigms". Literary theorists are not restrained in their enquiry; they can bring to bear on their texts political, evaluative, economic, social, cultural and other programs when analyzing and interpreting a novel, a poem, a film or (for a fine arts scholar) a painting. Many jurists, although by no means all, have considered themselves not to have the same liberty. They are restrained in the reasoning programs that they can bring to bear on legal texts. Indeed, in the past, manuscripts that strayed beyond a doctrinal or "black-letter" approach would not be published in some of the leading law journals.[2]

[1] See generally G,-G, Granger, *La science et les sciences* (2[d] ed, ; 1995).

[2] See on this point G. Samuel and P. Legrand, "A Conversation on Comparative

Accordingly, it might be useful to examine, from a social science and humanities perspective, the various methods and techniques by and through which the mind (*intellectus*) can engage with an object (*res*) that forms the basis of the reasoning and reflection. The point to be emphasized at once is that there is not just one method. There are a whole range of different possibilities, and they are often to be found under headings such as theories, programs, paradigms, schemes of intelligibility, reasoning techniques, and the like. It is arguable that those working within the discipline of law have not traditionally been particularly good or receptive to sophisticated reflection on methodology. Quite a few introductory books have been rather bland and (or) superficial in their handling of legal methods and legal reasoning. Moreover, the employment of broad terms such as "theory" and "jurisprudence" have, perhaps, discouraged a more precise vocabulary or terminology within the discipline of law in general and in comparative law. This has not acted as an obstacle to the production of skilled lawyers and jurists, but often there is a lack of self-awareness about methodology and its epistemological (knowledge) implications when one sets out to study law.[3] This is in contrast to students working in some of the other social sciences where methodology is regarded as an essential aspect of the knowledge training. How, then, do social scientists view the various ways and means by which the mind can engage, for reasoning and reflection purposes, with an object? How do those in the humanities – especially literature and the arts – engage with the objects of their scholarship?[4]

LEVELS OF OPERATION

Probably the first and most important general point that needs to be made about understanding reasoning and method in the natural sciences, social sciences, and humanities is that there are different levels of operation. No doubt many comparatists, even before embarking on their chosen research projects, will have

Law", *Journal of Comparative Law*, XV (2020), p. 371.

3 R. Van Gestel and A. Lienhard (eds.), *Evaluating Academic Legal Research in Europe* (2019), p. 449.

4 Methods in history, and their relationship with law, have been discussed elsewhere: G. Samuel, "Methods of Legal History and Comparative Law", in M. Adams and M. van Hoecke (eds), *Comparative Methods in Law, Humanities and Social Sciences* (2022), p. 11.

heard the term "paradigm". It was fashioned during the last century by the historian and philosopher of science, Thomas Kuhn (1922-1996).[5] In fact when he first employed the term, he used it in a number of rather different ways (which attracted criticism) that made a unique definition difficult. But broadly speaking, he meant by the term that "it stands for the entire constellation of beliefs, values, techniques, and so on shared by the members of a given community".[6] Most comparatists will probably appreciate that this term is important when it comes to method and reasoning but that, of itself, it is far too general to be of much help in understanding the actual techniques of analysis and reasoning in disciplines. At the other end of the spectrum, comparatists will also be aware of actual reasoning techniques such as induction, deduction, and analogy, even if they do not have a deep learning of the literature concerning these methods. On reflection, even students embarking on a law program will probably appreciate that they, themselves, have used these techniques in their own everyday lives. A student – to give a banal example – out driving might find herself overtaken by an ambulance and a police car and, later, find that the road she is on is closed by the police. From these facts (ambulance and closure) she may well reason (induce) that there has been a serious road accident.

Yet in between "paradigm" and (say) "induction" there are various intermediary kinds of engagement and reasoning levels. For example – and this is an example given by a leading (but now late) French social science theorist[7] – a student out mountain hiking sees a pile of stones shaped into a pyramid. He or she will probably ask themselves two questions. First, how did these stones get to be here and to end up as this pyramid shape? And second, what does this object – or sign – mean? These two questions actually involve rather different types of engagement scheme. The first scheme is a causal one: what caused this pyramid of stones phenomenon? And the second is one of interpretation and understanding – the answer, it would seem, to this latter question being that the path is a safe one. The two types of scheme are very different. A causal analysis is one that usually lends itself (in theory anyway) to

[5] T. Kuhn, *The Structure of Scientific Revolutions* (2d ed,; 1970).

[6] Ibid,, p. 175.

[7] J.-M. Berthelot, "Épistémologie des sciences humaines", in S. Mesure and P. Savidan (eds.), *Le dictionnaire des sciences humaines* (2006), p. 380.

being definitively falsified whereas the second one is often more ambiguous. Thus, the philosopher of science Karl Popper (1902-1994) asserted that the statement that "all swans are white" can be falsified by the appearance of a black swan.[8] However, the meaning inherent in a work of artistic creation – a question of interpretation – cannot be falsified in the same way. One critic may produce one interpretation, while another perceives a very different meaning. It cannot be said definitively that a new interpretation falsifies or nullifies previous ones (although it might be more convincing than previous interpretations). In addition to causal and hermeneutical (interpretation) schemes of engagement, we shall see that there are other forms as well.

A different level issue is the level of observation. Another French social science theorist uses the good example of a map to explain how, when the level changes, the knowledge gained changes.[9] Imagine a student who wishes to travel from London to a specific address in Manchester but knows nothing, geographically, about how to get to his destination (and does not have a GPS, Satnav, or Waves). One map will not contain the information that he needs to achieve his objective; he will need at least three – a road map, a more detailed route map of the Manchester area, and finally a street map. Each map operates at a different level and thus exhibits its own particular but vital information. This level of observation becomes most evident in a subject such as history. A work focusing on a particular battle in a World War will not reveal information about the causes and perhaps course of the war itself; that will require a different work operating at a different level and perhaps employing some different methodological engagements. Take another example. Statistics might well reveal certain patterns say with regard to university education; but the sociologist will need a different set of methods in order to discover the individual reasons why particular people from certain social classes do not go on to higher education.[10]

These different levels of reasoning and method are relevant to all disciplines. Some disciplines, however, are particular in that their primary focus is not, for example, on natural phenomena

[8] See generally Karl Popper, *The Logic of Scientific Discovery* (1959; reprint 2002).

[9] D. Desjeux, *Les sciences sociales* (2004).

[10] See R. Boudon and R. Fillieule, *Les méthodes en sociologie* (14th ed.; 2018).

– the object of investigation for the natural sciences – nor social phenomena such as human beings in society. The focus is largely on texts. This is obviously true of a humanities subject such as English literature and may indeed be partly true of history where the only evidence available might be documents. It is certainly true of law whose history, at least on the continent, has been on a particular text, namely the corpus of Roman laws which were rediscovered in eleventh century Italy and became the focus of scholarship from this period right up until today.[11] To what extent, then, do the various levels of methodology apply to legal scholarship? As we shall see, the different levels are relevant. However, before investigating this point any further, there is something particular about law which does not apply to other disciplines, save perhaps theology.

AUTHORITY PARADIGM

This particular characteristic might be labelled the "authority paradigm". Whether employing Kuhn's "paradigm" is epistemologically valid is, it must be said at once, open to debate, because Kuhn fashioned this term for the natural sciences and not for the social sciences.[12] Yet it does fulfil a certain characteristic inherent in this paradigm notion, namely that lawyers and jurists all (or most) share the same world view when it comes to legal texts. This view is that a legal text – in particular a statute and a judgment – can be criticized, perhaps severely, but never questioned in terms of its authority.[13] Such a view has impacted on methodology in that there are certain approaches to these texts that are, so to speak, out-of-bounds. Accordingly in many, but in fairness by no means all, law schools certain works about law may not feature, or, if they do, only perhaps in specialized courses.[14] The

[11] See P. Stein, *Roman Law in European History* (1999).

[12] On the relevance of Kuhn to legal history see Samuel, *Rethinking Historical Jurisprudence* (2022).

[13] See further Samuel, "Interdisciplinarity and the Authority Paradigm: Should Law Be Taken Seriously by Scientists and Social Scientists?", *Journal of Law and Society*, XXXVI (2009), p. 431.

[14] One thinks, for example, of Jerome Frank, *Law and the Modern Mind* (1949). The late Peter Birks said that the "realists and post-realists have done a good job of debunking legal science", and it was in the United States "where Jerome Frank and his intellectual successors did their most serious damage" which resulted in

reason for this is the authority paradigm which, with regard to all the positive or "black-letter" (doctrinal) law subjects, decrees that only certain approaches will be acceptable to those who exercise authority in law, that is to say, the judiciary and the practitioners. Not all law academics will operate within this kind of authority paradigm and so research students studying for a doctorate in many common law faculties will not necessarily be constrained by such a paradigm. But this is not so true in many continental law faculties; indeed, to venture outside the authority paradigm, even at doctorial level, will not enhance the academic career of research students in France.[15]

One reason for this situation on the continent is that the law faculty plays a central role in the formation of professional lawyers and thus the professors tend on the whole to be closely connected to practitioners and the judiciary. History, also, has a role here. The university law faculty has a centuries old tradition on the continent and is bound up with the development of the legal profession itself.[16] This is not true of England and Wales where law faculties teaching the common law are mainly a late nineteenth century, and primarily a twentieth century, phenomenon. One does not need a law degree to become a solicitor or a barrister, and some in the professions have actually displayed hostility towards the law degree.[17] A candidate with a first-class degree in physics could prove more attractive to some firms of solicitors than a candidate with an upper-second – or perhaps even a first – in law. One wonders whether the authority paradigm might have

letting "in floods of law and economics in the hope of filling the broken vessel". P Birks, "Equity in the Modern Law: An Exercise in Taxonomy", *University of Western Australia Law Review*, XXVI (1996), p. 4. An Oxford student following one of Professor Birks' courses would have surely thought twice before discussing in an examination either the work of Frank or the relevance of an economic analysis of common law or Roman law cases. Perhaps this is to be a little unfair, for Birks no doubt would have given credit to a well thought out argument; yet many students would surely have not taken the risk. A student following a course on jurisprudence (legal theory and philosophy) would of course have been expected to read and comment on Frank's work.

[15] P. Legrand, *Negative Comparative Law: A Strong Programme for Weak Thought* (2022), pp. 307-308. See generally P. Jestaz and C. Jamin, *La doctrine* (2004).

[16] See generally J. A. Brundage, *The Medieval Origins of the Legal Profession* (2008).

[17] Such hostility was recorded for example by Peter Birks, "A Decade of Turmoil in Legal Education", in Birks (ed.), *Examining the Law Syllabus: Beyond the Core* (1993), p. 17.

an influence here. Has it resulted in graduates with more closed minds, and with a limited appreciation of methodology and its epistemological (knowledge) implications? Certainly many law graduates will not come out of their faculties with a sophisticated appreciation of the difference between functional, structural, causal and hermeneutical schemes of intelligibility, despite the fact that these schemes – as will be seen – are fundamental to social science and humanities disciplines.

No doubt there will be some law academics who object strongly to these observations. But take this passage from a "taster" introduction to law by a team of prestigious law professors:

> When asked to list the skills needed to make a good lawyer, few people would think of putting 'imagination' on their list – the law seems far too technical to need such a creative skill. But in fact lawyers need to use their imagination all the time.[18]

This statement in itself is a little puzzling since it has long been recognized that even in the hard sciences – technical subjects most would think – imagination has a fundamental role. Imagination is, in other words, an essential feature in all research and scholarship. But stating the obvious probably does no harm. More interesting is what these authors say later. They examine a particular case involving a foster mother under whose surveillance a child was injured and who was sued for damages in the tort of negligence.[19] The authors describe the arguments of counsel in the following way:

> The claimant's lawyer had a relatively easy task, detailing why it was dangerous to leave a two-year old child in the vicinity of the hot tap, as it only takes a moment to turn it on. But the defendant's lawyer retorted with lots of very imaginative arguments as to why the foster mother had *not* acted unreasonably. These included the fact that she was looking after lots of other children, so if she carried the claimant around everywhere she would have neglected the others; that it is not necessarily a good idea to cushion

[18] C. Barnard, J. O'Sullivan and G. Virgo, *What About Law? Studying Law at University* (3d ed,; 2021), p. 27.

[19] *Surtees v Kingston Upon Thames BC* [1991] 2 FLR 559.

> children from *all* risks, because that way they grow up with no idea of how to assess risks and therefore might end up more seriously injured in the future; that carrying the child out of the bathroom might itself have been more dangerous; and that demanding too high a standard from foster parents might put people off volunteering for the role, which would be detrimental to more children in the long term.[20]

These are, of course, good legal arguments when seen from a lawyer's point of view, though one wonders why the claimant's lawyers did not strongly advance an argument that there was a lack of any safe system of child care and work environment given the defendant's counsel's account of the facts. Yet one wonders, also, whether a social scientist would regard these defence arguments as "very imaginative". Were they not just functional arguments? Was not the defence lawyer simply applying a functional scheme of intelligibility to the facts and the implied norms that governed them? If jurists think that these arguments are "imaginative", one has to ask whether the authority paradigm is still imposing a quite restrictive limitation on the law syllabus with respect to the possibility of gaining a sophisticated understanding of reasoning and method. Certainly comparative lawyers, one might think, would need to be more sophisticated.

Another problem with these "imaginative" arguments is that they appear to have been advanced without any support from thorough research. How does one know that cushioning children from all risks will result in them growing up with no idea how to assess risk? Perhaps they will, but no properly trained social scientist would make such an assertion without empirical research. Indeed, a social scientist might find these arguments not so much "imaginative" as rather simplistic (to say the least). One advantage of the authority paradigm is that there is no expectation that lawyers need indulge in sociological research, save perhaps in some family law cases involving children (although even in these cases there is the sharp distinction between "law" and "evidence"). The foundation of law is authority, and the focus is not on inquiry.

[20] Barnard, note 18 above, p. 28 (emphasis in original).

TENSIONS

Another important insight offered by Thomas Kuhn is the existence of what might be termed tensions within the scientific community that can ultimately lead to a scientific revolution. These tensions function at the level of paradigms but usually express themselves at the level of scientific theory and methodological models when these theories and models do not seem to reflect the "objective" factual phenomena. One puts "objective" in quotes here simply to emphasize the point that many scientists – including Kuhn – believe (or believed) that one can access reality only through constructed intellectual models. This idea can lead to the following question: does data shape our preconceived models or do our preconceived models shape the data?[21] This is a point that is fundamental to legal analysis and reasoning as well.

Accordingly, one tension in science is between realists and anti-realists. As Adrian Currie explains:

> Recall that both realists and anti-realists believe that there are facts about the past; however, anti-realists think the narrative events – the structure their explanations lay onto the world – are projections, cognitive tools, not representations of how things were. Realists agree that narratives are cognitive tools for generating understanding, but go further to say that successful narratives in fact reflect the structure of the world.[22]

Do we create reality or is there a reality out there that humans can directly perceive? This tension cannot be answered definitively and, at least with respect to the sciences, it is not the purpose of this present investigation to try to do this. The point to emphasize is the importance of the tension itself. Moreover this is not the only tension to be found in the sciences. Kuhn himself provoked a more general question about the importance of history in the understanding of scientific models and theories. This is the tension between a diachronic (historical) approach and a synchronic (timeless) view of science.[23] Another tension is between

[21] Adrian Currie, *Scientific Knowledge and the Deep Past* (2019), p. 15.

[22] Ibid., pp. 58-59.

[23] See generally ibid.

a structural approach to say palaeontology or a functional one.[24] Does one understand evolutionary change in terms of the function that attached to these changes or in terms of an internal structural development isolated from the functions that might or might not result from the changes? As will be seen, this is a question that has arisen regarding legal evolution. A more general tension centers around the notion of "truth". Are scientists involved in an activity in which the purpose is to reveal the "secrets" of nature – to reveal truths about the physical world and universe?[25] And, if so, what is the role of mathematics, the language of physics, in this search? Are not mathematical deductions undeniable truths? Are there non-refutable axioms? Or are scientists simply involved in an instrumental exercise of explanation and prediction, with mathematics just being a helpful tool? As one can appreciate, these tensions in science are about how the *intellectus* can and should engage with the *res*. They are also about refutability of theories and models, which is, in itself, a scheme of intelligibility – dialectics – which was once viewed with scepticism because of its association with medieval scholasticism.

But why raise these tensions in science? Do they affect everyday methods employed by scientists? In fact the reason for raising them is that, whatever the position in the natural sciences, they are of major importance in the social sciences. Here tensions are so fundamental that they are the defining focal point of social science epistemology (theory of knowledge).[26] Why are tensions so fundamental here? There are several reasons.

The first are the problems associated with the causal scheme of intelligibility. In the natural sciences explaining phenomena is largely a causal exercise. A typical area is medical science. What is the cause of this or that symptom? What is the cause of cancer or this type of fever? The method, therefore, is the research for a causal link between a phenomenon and another phenomenon which acts as it cause.[27] This is a bit simplistic, but it does illustrate the primary scheme of intelligibility in play in many of the natural

[24] Ibid., p. 36.

[25] See generally A. Boyer, "Réfutabilité", in D. Lecourt (ed.), *Dictionnaire d'histoire et philosophie des sciences* (4th ed.; 2006), p. 958.

[26] Berthelot, note 7 above.

[27] A. C. Masquelet, *Le raisonnement médical* (2006), pp. 94-118.

sciences (there are other schemes, for example structuralism in the form of taxonomy is vital in the biological sciences). When social scientists try to use the causal scheme in understanding social phenomena, they are immediately confronted with the fact that humans are not like inert objects. Humans have a will of their own which means that causal issues immediately become confused with human behaviour and actions making the isolation of a clear causal relationship between phenomenon A and phenomenon B extremely complex and often debatable.

In addition, some notions used to describe social phenomena are ambiguous. What, for example, are the causes of crime? Two general problems immediately arise with this kind of question. First, attempting to isolate a single cause will itself be highly ambiguous because of the tension between human liberty and intention, on one hand, and objective social phenomena, such as the level of unemployment, on the other. Which of these two are the cause? Second, labels such as "crime" are themselves ambiguous because the boundaries are fluid. Behavior that was criminal a century ago is not criminal today; equally behavior that was not criminal a century ago is criminal today. In short, the language used to describe and to understand in the social sciences is itself problematic.

The assertion that humans are not like inert objects leads to a second tension. This is the distinction between cause and reasons.[28] Thus, for example, in a situation where A shoots and kills B one will need to distinguish two "causes" so to speak.[29] What was the cause of B's death? In strictly objective terms the cause was the gun and the bullet. However, such a statement is unlikely to be satisfactory to a social scientist who will want to know why A shot B. One can talk again in causal terms: A shot B because B had made a blasphemous comment which A felt entitled him to take action. But really what one is identifying is not so much a cause but a motive; one is identifying a reason for A's behavior. This motive or reason is of interest to the historian and social scientist because behind such motivations are a whole set of social beliefs linked to the culture and mentality of the society being examined. This in

[28] D. Guillo, "Naturalisme et sciences humaines", in Mesure & Savidan (eds), note 7 above, p. 817.

[29] R. Ogien, "Sciences cognitives et sciences humaines", in Mesure & Savidan, note 7 above, p. 1052.

turn creates a tension because, as one can see with the A shoots B example, there are two levels of observation. There is A's action as an individual actor, and there is the culture and mentality that attaches to the community or society as a whole. The methods and schemes of intelligibility that come into play in this situation are different from the causal scheme used primarily in the natural sciences. One is trying to comprehend both A's motive and behavior and the cultural beliefs, and how they developed, of the community in which A acted.

A third reason is that in certain social and human science subjects understanding can only be obtained, indirectly, through texts, which will involve interpretation (hermeneutic method, as will be seen). One is no doubt looking for causes in history – what was the cause of this or that event? But the causal issue becomes entangled with the hermeneutical understanding and leading to a conflict of methods of a type which do not exist, with quite such an intensity at any rate, in the natural sciences.[30] Not just history is faced with what has been termed the "textual paradigm".[31] All attempts to understand in the social and human sciences are mediated through models and categories which themselves involve metaphors, comparisons, analogies, and so on; there is no world save the one reduced to a text. And this means that language, with its ambiguities and biases, cannot be ejected from the engagement between the *intellectus* and *res*. There is a continual tension between the means of description and the thing being described. In theory this is just as true, with the natural sciences; but a science such as physics or astrophysics uses mathematics as much as ordinary language as the foundation for its models. Moreover, as Popper asserted, many scientific assertions can be tested and are potentially falsifiable. How does one test an assertion made by a historian? How does one test an assertion made by a professor of literature with respect to a novel by Jane Austen?

REASONING IN THE SOCIAL SCIENCES

Before examining this Jane Austen question, more needs to be said about reasoning in the social sciences. It would be idle to say that

[30] Ibid., pp. 1052-1053.

[31] Gosselin, "Sociologie Interprétative", in Mesure & Savidan, note 7 above, p. 1110.

the term "theory" is not employed by social scientists, but the term is, perhaps, used more sparingly and alongside other notions such as methods, ideas, schemes of intelligibility, concepts, programs, and paradigms. There is, in other words, an *armature intellectuelle* which can be mobilized within the epistemological and ontological relationship between *intellectus* and *res*.[32] This *armature* is both pluralistic and hierarchical in the sense, first, that different approaches result in different kinds of knowledge and, second, that there is a certain hierarchy between some terms employed. For example, the notion of "paradigm" operates at a higher level than "theory", and both terms – or languages – function at a higher level than schemes of intelligibility or *grilles de lecture*.

Jacques Herman, in his introductory book to the languages of sociology, explains that, contrary to a theory, sociological language (*un langage*) is not testable in the same way as a theory. It is only relevant to deal more or less with a given problem in turn more-or-less relevant to such-and-such class of objects.[33] A scientific theory is, then, more precise; it is a conceptual device which satisfies the relevant requirements vis-à-vis a problem and given objects and is coherent vis-à-vis the concepts and propositions employed, being in addition testable vis-à-vis the empirical procedures concerning the body of data.[34] As for a paradigm, this is a mixture of philosophical presuppositions, theory models, key concepts, and prestigious research results which constitute a habitual universe of thought for researchers at a given moment in the development of a discipline.[35] Herman goes on to make the point that in sociology paradigms tend to attach themselves more to the languages than to theories in that they are not testable; they are "research programmes", fields of methodological possibility, ontological, and epistemological which each have their own scope.[36]

Theory and paradigm operate at a higher level of abstraction than method. Herman describes methodology as a collection of

[32] Berthelot, "Programmes, paradigmes, disciplines: pluralité et unité des sciences sociales", in Berthelot (ed.), *Épistémologie des sciences sociales* (2001), p. 458.

[33] J. Herman, *Les langages de la sociologie* (2d ed., 1988), p. 4.

[34] Ibid., pp. 3-4.

[35] Ibid., p. 4, referencing Kuhn (1970).

[36] Ibid., pp. 4-5.

guiding ideas which orientate scientific investigations.[37] He goes on to say that there are four poles of scientific research which can be distinguished analytically: the epistemological pole, determining the construction of the scientific object and the delimitation of the research problem; the theoretical pole where the hypotheses are organized and the concepts defined; the morphological pole where the various theories and levels of explanation are articulated; and the technical pole where the empirical investigation is carried out together with the fine tuning of the observation devices and the collection of data.[38] And so:

> If methodology is the practical art of scientific research, general epistemology is the study of the conditions of validity of theoretical knowledge. Epistemological problems are those concerning validity of the forms of scientific explanation, of the relevance of rules of logical inference, of the conditions of utilisation of concepts and symbols in the theories.[39]

Herman then goes on to contrast epistemology with ontology:

> Scientific ontology is the philosophical discipline which deals with the problem of the reality of objects which carry within them knowledge. What is the level of reality of social phenomena (individual, group, organisation, class, role, institution, society and so on)? What is a social process, an historical event, a social system a social actor and so on? Does a social group have a reality in itself different from that of the sum of its composing parts (holism), or is the reality only in the individual? Is culture an area of autonomous symbolic objects (culturalism) or are the cultural meanings only phenomena of the conscience (psychologism)? In the explanation of social facts is it legitimate to explain the social through the biological, the psychological or the economic (reductionism)?[40]

[37] Ibid., p. 5.

[38] Ibid.

[39] Ibid., pp. 5-6.

[40] Ibid., p. 6.

The principal, and vital, point that Herman wishes to make with respect to this discussion is that each sociological paradigm – that is to say, each complex of theories, of doctrines, of key ideas, of methods such as positivism or structuralism – operates as a means of selection of specific epistemological schemes, of ontological conceptions and of methodological devices. Each privileges some epistemological aspect (description, prediction, causation and so on) or some ontological position (holism, individualism).[41] The paradigms, Herman says, offer different types of sociological explanation according to their mode of structuration and respect for a certain coherence between their epistemological, ontological and methodological options.[42]

What, then, are the various methodological schemes of engagement? Herman himself discusses six such schemes, although he employs the term "paradigm":

- **Positivism** (this term describes a scientific approach emphasizing causal explanations, testability, and logical deductionism within a context of axiological neutrality).
- **Dialectics** (this scheme describes argumentation, negation and critical evaluation, often employing analogy).
- **Understanding** (this engagement is opposed to explanation and whose principal scheme is hermeneutics).
- **Structuro-functionalism** (this scheme is employed to describe systematization combined with a teleological analysis).
- **Structuralism** (this scheme is used to describe a symbolic order forming an anti-subjectivist totality in which society is viewed in terms of a formal structure of interrelating elements).
- **Praxeology** (this term puts the emphasis on the individual actor, the *homo sociologicus*, as a rational individual pursuing his or her own interests and society itself is a matter of interactionism between these actors).

[41] Ibid.

[42] Ibid.

The summaries outlined above are, evidently, too general to begin to capture the richness and depth of each scheme but they do, hopefully, indicate the orientations of each method of engagement.

Herman, however, is not the only social science epistemologist to set out different *grilles de lecture*. Claude Giraud, in his introductory book on the history of sociology, identifies a number of *grilles de lecture* or *types de lectures du social* used in contemporary sociology:[43]

- **Functionalist reading** (emphasizing the teleological).
- **Interactionalist reading** (emphasizing the role of individuals and the interaction between such social actions).
- **Structuralist reading** (emphasizing the interior relations of a social system conceived as a whole).
- **Individualist reading** (emphasizing the individual as the ontological basis of society).
- **Social strategy reading** (emphasizing the individual but in terms of a game in which individuals regularize their power relations and their liberty).
- **Actionalist reading** (emphasizing social actors in relation to work which is seen as the major source of social action, orientated towards transformation, in an industrial society).

Giraud sees these *grilles de lecture* as reflecting the modern tendency to examine segments of social reality rather than approaching the social in terms of grand global theories such as structuro-functionalism (which emphasizes the function of society as a holistic system).[44] They are, then, methodological schemes more than grand theories. Each reading may be embedded in a contextual paradigm, but the point is that these readings reflect the tendency to undertake empirical research founded upon precise questions.

In addition to these *grilles de lecture,* a notable attempt to isolate a number of schemes of intelligibility was by the late social

43 C. Giraud, *Histoire de la sociologie* (3d ed.; 2004), pp. 86-123.

44 Ibid., p. 122.

science theorist Jean-Michel Berthelot (1945-2006).[45] He isolated six schemes:

- **Causal scheme** (if x, then y).
- **Functional scheme** (phenomenon X is analyzed by its function within a system).
- **Structural scheme** (X is the result of an established system based, like a language, on disjunctive rules, A or non-A).
- **Hermeneutical scheme** (X is a symptom whose signification is to be discovered through interpretation).
- **Actional (*actanciel*) scheme** (X is the result, within a given space, of intentional actions).
- **Dialectical scheme** (X results from a contradiction internal to a system).

These schemes are, arguably, the most accessible in terms of their clarity and perhaps should serve as one of the central schematic methodological models for comparatists. Nevertheless, other authors and approaches include a collaboration of several authors for recent work on key ideas in an anthropology. Each author sets out a mode of analysis:

- **Causal explanation** (this engagement is an examination of the history and the problems associated with this scheme in anthropology, together with a detailed discussion of the various theories).
- **Functionalist perspective** (this perspective examines, in particular, the distinction between a functional analysis and functionalist theory; and also examines the history and the principal individual theories).
- **Structure and form** (this scheme examines the origins and history of structuralism together with the debate as to whether a structure is the product of the mind or of reality itself).
- **Historical models of intelligibility** (this topic examines, *inter alia*, how the approach to history by anthropologists differs from the approach to history by historians).

[45] See Berthelot, *L'intelligence du social* (1990). See also Berthelot, note 32 above, p. 484.

One further book deserves attention: an introductory work to methods in sociology by Raymond Boudon and Renaud Fillieule.[46] They divide the methods into three groups:

- **Causal analysis** (this approach permits the description of relations of cause and effect between macro sociologic phenomena; it emphasizes in particular statistics and causality).
- **Methodological individualism** (this is an approach which in principle explains causal relations in exposing the system of individual actions which underlies them; it emphasizes the shortcomings of statistics and causal analysis leading to an individualistic analysis focusing on the social actor).
- **Cognitive rationality** (this is an approach which emphasises the beliefs of all kinds which motivate social actors).

These three broad categories might at first sight give the impression that other schemes of intelligibility are ignored. This is not the case. Functionalist explanations are discussed in the chapter on cognitive rationality (a belief in a "good" outcome acts as a motivating factor) while hermeneutics is regarded as having a role in the interpretation of causal relations arising from the real actions of social actors, and thus is discussed in the chapter on methodological individualism.

More generally, Boudon and Fillieule make an important point about methodology, a term that has come in for criticism from some comparative lawyers.[47] They argue that to think of method as simply a matter of the techniques of observation or analysis of data is too narrow. Beyond these techniques, they say, methods are also, and above all, collections of principles which guide scientists in the elaboration of new theories and in providing the means for critical analysis of existing theories. Thus to know methods requires the deep study of sociological theories, especially those which have come to explain major phenomena whose explanation is not of itself evident in any *a priori* sense.[48] Perhaps, then, it

[46] R. Boudon and R. Fillieule, *Les méthodes en sociologie* (14th ed.; 2018).

[47] See for example S. Glanert, "Method?", in P. G. Monateri (ed.), *Methods of Comparative Law* (2012), p. 61.

[48] Boudon and Fillieule, note 46 above, p. 3.

would be tempting always talk in terms of "theory and method" rather than just method. However, such talk brings with it some epistemological disadvantages in that it suggests that there are "theories" that can be disassociated from "method", that is, from schemes of intelligibility or *grilles de lecture*. Such a disassociation can be useful, but a term like "theory" must be treated with caution. Why this is so might be better explained in looking at method and theory in literature and the arts.

REASONING IN LITERATURE AND FINE ART STUDIES

If one returns, then, to the Jane Austin question concerning the testing of an assertion made by a literary scholar examining a novel, it could be said that literature, and, as will be seen, to a great extent film, is a bit like law. The objects of analysis are texts (expanding this term to cover films). No doubt the authority paradigm restricts the kind of arguments that can be employed by the lawyer and law student, but law and literature do share a similar "object", namely a canon of textual material which, for the most part, acts as the sole focus of attention. What kind of methods are employed by literary critics? What are the ways in which such critics and academics can engage with their texts? These questions are arguably valuable for eventually understanding the reasoning methods employed by lawyers and jurists because literary (and cinema academics) have since the middle of the last century (earlier in the case of literature), if not before, been forced to think and to articulate what they do. In saying this, it is not to claim that academics working in the domains of literature and the arts have been particularly sophisticated in their descriptions of methodology and theory. Yet there are some contributions that are worth close examination.

One contribution in particular is the Terry Eagleton introductory work on literary theory, first published in 1983.[49] This work sees itself as an introduction to theory rather than to methodology and reasoning as such, but it soon becomes evident that schemes of intelligibility – functionalism, hermeneutics, and structuralism in particular – are a fundamental bedrock upon which certain theories are founded. Moreover, the author himself has much to say on methods and their relation to literature and literary

[49] See now T. Eagleton, *Literary Theory: An Introduction* (2008).

criticism. Theory and method are, then, not easy to disassociate in this discipline and this no doubt is a lesson in itself. In fact Eagleton does make an important point which alludes to the difficulty that the term "theory" presents in that it is not always an adequate level, so to speak, of operation:

> To place a course of theory alongside a course on moon symbolism in DH Lawrence is to commit what the philosophers would call a category mistake. It would be like studying Marxism simply as one variant of sociology, rather than grasping the point that Marxism is among other things a critique of the very concept of sociology. Academia, by its structure, tends to encourage these sorts of conceptual mistakes. Like the marketplace, it lays out sometimes incomparable things side by side.[50]

Later he gives an example operating at a lower level of abstraction:

> Even so, to speak in the same breath of, say, post-structuralism and post-modernism, or semiotics and post-colonialism, is another category mistake. The first two items of these pairs are bodies of theory, while the second are cultural and political realities. To imagine that they are more or less the same thing would be like thinking that Heidegger's philosophy is the same sort of thing as global warming. This, too, is the kind of error that academia sometimes tempts us into making.[51]

It might be worth adding here that a similar point about the level of operation has been made by a specialist on the theory of art. Anne Cauquelin suggests in her introductory work on the theories of art that theories should be divided into two kinds: foundational theories and accessory or secondary theories (*théories d'accompagnement, théories secondaires*). This might imply at first sight that secondary theories are just secondary, but she explains that secondary theories are just as important as foundational ones, for they are theories not about the nature of art itself but about how one engages with works of art. In other words, they are theories orientated towards analysis and method which seems to bring them closer to the idea that they are schemes of engagement

[50] Ibid., p. viii.

[51] Ibid., p. ix.

– of intelligibility – rather than theories *per se*.[52] At this secondary level Cauquelin identifies what she calls two "axes". There is a hermeneutical axis which is founded upon making sense of the artistic object and a semiological axis which engages with the organization of the signs through which the artistic object manifests itself.[53] The first axis is thus founded on understanding, that is to say on understanding how one understands (*comprendre comment on comprend*), whereas the second is centered on the logic of the sign.[54] To talk in terms of "understanding how to understand" is, then, more of an epistemological issue and so to label it "theory", while understandable, is perhaps to blur the important distinction that she actually makes. If, therefore, one understands Cauquelin's secondary theories as schemes of engagement with art she identifies, as we have just seen, two such schemes:

- **Hermeneutical axis** (founded on the idea that meaning is hidden and needs to be researched and revealed by the interpreter).
- **Semiological axis** (focuses on the logic of the sign and consists of an analysis of its elements).

Returning to Eagleton's book, this work is valuable because it adopts an historical approach tracing the various theory movements from the early days of English literature (at the beginning of the last century) to contemporary times. This journey starts with the Romantics and then takes us through Russian formalism, moral ideology (Leavis), American New Criticism (functionalist), hermeneutics, structuralism and post-structuralism. And it is a journey that is particularly enriching even for those who do not share Eagleton's Marxist stance; for the author offers both real insights into and quite devastating criticisms of the theory and methodological pretensions associated with the discipline of literature. How, then, does Eagleton go about engaging with literature? From his historical viewpoint he identifies the following "theories":

52 A. Cauquelin, *Les theories de l'art* (4th ed.; 2010), pp. 65-66.

53 Ibid., p. 67.

54 Ibid., pp. 70 and 84.

- **Phenomenology** (an approach where all reality must be treated as pure "phenomena", leading to a discussion of Husserl and Heidegger)
- **Hermeneutics** (this is the art of interpretation, leading to a discussion from Heidegger to Gadamer).
- **Reception theory** (an engagement which examines the role of the reader in literature, leading to a discussion of Iser, Barthes, Jauss, and Fish).
- **Structuralism** (a scheme which is concerned with structures and the laws by which they work, leading to a discussion on Frye, Saussure, Jakobson, and others).
- **Semiotics** (an approach which studies the system of signs, leading to a discussion of Lotman).
- **Post-structuralism** (a "theory" which represents a deconstruction of the established theories of meaning whereby such meaning is scattered across a whole range of signifiers and cannot be pinned down, leading to a discussion of Derrida, Barthes, and others).
- **Psychoanalysis** (a "theory" that is stimulated by the work of Freud, and so a psychoanalytical engagement focuses on the unconscious motivations of authors, characters and/or readers or on the psychological significance of objects and/or events, leading to a discussion of Lacan and others).
- **Political criticism** (an approach in which the ideological nature of literary theories is discussed).

These different forms of engagement – and it must be stressed that the above summaries do not reflect the actual in-depth discussions to be found in Eagleton's book – do not all work on the same level in that, for example, reception theory is generally considered to be an important part of hermeneutics whereas some psychoanalysis could just as easily fall under the heading of post-structuralism. Equally, a category such as political criticism seems too general to be regarded in itself as a scheme, perhaps being more of a theory or, better still, a program (for example, a Marxist approach). Nevertheless, they are useful categories to compare with the schemes of intelligibility used by social scientists: for example, hermeneutics and structuralism would appear to be forms of engagement that function across the social and the human sciences and so should be of particular relevance for comparative lawyers.

It might be a general category, yet more does need to be said about the chapter on political criticism because Eagleton makes notable observations about methodology. He argues that there are two ways in which any theory can provide itself with a distinct purpose and identity.[55] It can, first, define itself in terms of its particular methods of enquiry; one can see this merging of "theory" with "method", one might add, in schemes of engagement such as hermeneutics or structuralism. Second, a theory can define itself within terms of the particular object that forms the focus of enquiry. Yet, he says, any attempt to define literary theory in terms of a distinct method is doomed to failure. The reason, he asserts, is this:

> Literary theory is supposed to reflect on the nature of literature and literary criticism. But just think of how many methods are involved in literary criticism. You can discuss the poet's asthmatic childhood, or examine her peculiar use of syntax; you can detect the rustling of silk in the hissing of the s's, explore the phenomenology of reading, relate the literary work to the state of the class-struggle or find out how many copies it sold. These methods have nothing whatsoever in common.[56]

And he continues:

> In fact they have more in common with other 'disciplines' – linguistics, history, sociology and so on – than they have with each other. Methodologically speaking, literary criticism is a non-subject. If literary theory is a kind of 'metacriticism', a critical reflection on criticism, then it follows that it too is a non-subject.[57]

This is an interesting observation in the way that it indicates, as no doubt a social science epistemologist such as Jacques Herman or the late Jean-Michel Berthelot would confirm, that different schemes of intelligibility can produce different kinds of

[55] Eagleton, note 49 above, pp. 171-172.

[56] Ibid., p. 172.

[57] Ibid.

knowledge. It equally indicates how these differing methods can produce within a discipline various fundamental tensions. What perhaps is odd is why it should follow that a critical reflection on criticism is a "non-subject". Could it not be a sub-discipline within literary studies labelled, say, "literary epistemology" or, indeed, just "methods in literary criticism"? The problem no doubt is the insistence on the term "theory" which demands an all-embracing unity.

In fact Eagleton's response to this non-subject question would be that such an "epistemological" or "methodological" characterization of literary criticism is simply a pluralist vision which, he asserts, brings its own problems. "For one thing", he writes, "not all of these methods are mutually compatible" or those critics who do advocate pluralism "are usually able to do so because the different methods they have in mind are not all that different in the end". Indeed, "some of these 'methods' are hardly methods at all".[58] He concludes that the "true reason why the pluralists are wishful thinkers is that what is at issue in the contention between different literary theories or 'non-theories' are competing ideological strategies related to the very destiny of English studies in modern society".[59] The problem, then, for Eagleton is that a label such as "epistemology" would be simply a fancy "neutral" or "scientific" word concealing what actually should be labelled "ideology". This is a serious critique, and one that comparative lawyers would do well to absorb. Equally one must bear in mind that Eagleton has an agenda – or a program – and that is an attack on "liberal humanism".[60] In the end, for him, departments of literature "are part of the ideological apparatus of the modern state". As for the literary theorists themselves, he says:

> Literary theorists, critics and teachers, then, are not so much purveyors of doctrine as custodians of a discourse. Their task is to preserve this discourse, extend and elaborate it as necessary, defend it from other forms of discourse, initiate newcomers into it and determine whether or not they have successfully mastered it.[61]

58 Ibid.

59 Ibid., p. 173.

60 Ibid., p. 174.

61 Ibid., p. 175.

Any jurist reading this ought, no doubt, to feel uncomfortable. Is this not what law schools are doing?

More disturbing is when Eagleton goes on to suggest that there is something of an authority paradigm operating within literary criticism. He argues that:

> The power of critical discourse moves on several levels. It is the power of 'policing' language – of determining that certain statements must be excluded because they do not conform to what is acceptably sayable. It is the power of policing writing itself, classifying it into the 'literary' and 'non-literary', the enduringly great and the ephemerally popular. It is the power of authority *vis-à-vis* others – the power-relations between those who define and preserve the discourse, and those who are selectively admitted to it.[62]

Much the same has been said by critical lawyers (critical legal theorists) about their own discipline, but, as Eagleton goes on to observe, there is no such thing as "literary theory" with its own particular methods and schemes. These methods and schemes are just, he says, "a branch of social ideologies, utterly without any unity or identity which would adequately distinguish it from philosophy, linguistics, psychology, cultural and sociological thought".[63] Literary theory is, then, for Eagleton, an illusion.[64] It is about different methods and schemes – ideologies for Eagleton – which transcend the discipline rendering the discipline itself as non-existent because these methods could just as well be applied to the analysis of a bus ticket.

Yet is the same true of law? If these methods and schemes of engagement exposed in the social sciences and in literary analysis are equally applicable to the discipline of law (as will hopefully be seen), does this mean that the discipline of law is an "illusion"?[65] And if law is an illusion, what of comparative law? Is one comparing two non-existent objects? One way to escape from this conundrum is to reconsider the ontological basis of disciplines

[62] Ibid., p. 177.

[63] Ibid., p. 178.

[64] Ibid., p. 180.

[65] See further S. Glanert, A. Mercescu and G. Samuel, *Rethinking Comparative Law* (2021), pp. 1-30.

such as literature and law. Might it not be said, following Hans Vaihinger (1852-1933), that disciplines themselves are fictional creations? Vaihinger did not use fiction here in a pejorative sense; what he meant was that one should not worry about whether they exist as a matter of "truth".[66] What matters is their pragmatic value.[67] Moreover, as Eagleton himself says, structuralism, semiotics, psychoanalysis, deconstruction, reception theory, and the like all "have their valuable insights which may be put to use". And so what methods you adopt or reject "depends upon what you are practically trying to do".[68]

REASONING AND METHOD IN FILM STUDIES

Given Eagleton's view that the methods and schemes which he discusses transcend the discipline of literature (to its detriment as a discipline, he says), it would not be surprising to learn that some have found their way into the discipline of film or cinema studies. One more immediate reason for this transfer is that many film academics in England, at least in the early days of film studies during the last century, had read English literature at university. This meant, especially for those who had studied at Cambridge, that they came under the influence of some of the pioneers of literary studies in England – "revolutionaries" in the view of Terry Eagleton[69] – which was to have a major impact on the way films were viewed and analyzed, at least by one early writer whose work is worth considering. Of course, academic writing on film was not confined to England (far from it) and so influences from continental Europe and the United States was equally influential.

However, before looking more closely at this one writer's work, it might be valuable to consider, at a general level, the schemes and methods identified by writers on film "theory". Many of these theories and their authors can be found in Eagleton's book, thus

[66] H. Vaihinger, *The Philosophy of "As If*, transl. C. K. Ogden (1924; reprint 2021). On fiction theory and law, see G. Samuel, "Is Law a Fiction?", in M. Del Mar and W. Twining (eds.), *Legal Fiction in Theory and Practice* (2015), p. 31.

[67] For a discussion of Vaihinger's thesis, see C. Bouriau, *Le 'comme si': Kant, Vaihinger et le fictionalisme* (2013).

[68] Eagleton, note 49 above, p. 184.

[69] See Eagleton, *Critical Revolutionaries* (2022).

confirming the connection between literary and film theories. And so at the end of the last century the position could be summed up in the following way:

> What we call Theory is an abstract body of thought which came into prominence in Anglo-American film studies during the 1970s. The most famous avatar of Theory was that aggregate of doctrines derived from Lacanian psychoanalysis, Structuralist semiotics, Post-Structuralist literary theory, and variants of Althusserian Marxism.[70]

According to David Bordwell, one of the most enduring of these theories was structuralism, which was used as a scheme of intelligibility within the more general intellectual context of auteur theory.[71] This latter theory asserted that films had "authors" and such an author of a film was the director. This structural engagement could, as Bordwell goes on to point out, take the form of a binary – one might say dialectical (although Bordwell does not say this) – oppositions in the films of directors such as Don Siegel, John Ford, and Howard Hawks. Equally structuralist approaches could take the form of engaging with a whole mass of films operating within genre theory, a theory which classified movies according to categories such as Westerns, gangster films, musicals and so on. One particular notable example of this latter approach is Will Wright's structural analysis of Westerns.[72] As Bordwell says, much of this structural engagement focussed on myth and the resolving of oppositions:

> The emphasis which Hollywood filmmakers place upon the resolution of the narrative indicates the importance of key thematic oppositions such as man/woman, individual/community, work/play, order/anarchy. In order to resolve these contradictions, a mediating figure arises. Arguably, this binary approach to interpreting narrative structure is the most enduring legacy of 'cine-structuralism'.[73]

[70] D. Bordwell and N. Carroll, "Introduction", in Bordwell and Carroll (eds.), *Post-Theory: Reconstructing Film Studies* (1996), p. xiii.

[71] Bordwell, "Film Studies and Grand Theory", in Bordwell and Carroll, ibid., p. 5.

[72] W. Wright, *Sixguns and Society: A Structural Study of the Western* (1975).

[73] Bordwell, note 71 above, p. 6 (footnote omitted).

During the 1970s, Bordwell notes that structuralism started to give way to new theories such as psychoanalysis (Lacan), deconstruction (Derrida and Foucault) and feminist approaches. There was, if Bordwell is to be believed, also an element of functionalism reflected in the question about the social and psychic functions of cinema.[74] Hollywood "was seen to gratify desire by offering socially acceptable satisfactions through cinematic codes and enunciative practices" which "fulfilled ideological purposes".[75] One function of cinema, then, was to influence, maybe manipulate, its audience in particular ways.[76] This functionalism was in turn to influence what might be termed a paradigm orientation in which film was to be understood uniquely within a cultural theory. This theory "holds that pervasive cultural mechanisms govern the social and psychic functions of cinema".[77] He also adds that such a "culturist trend has also been resolutely hermeneutic",[78] a point that, as will be seen, has resonance in comparative law. In the end, Bordwell's overall view of cinema theory, in the 1990s at least, is that it relied heavily on "ideas from France" which led him to observe, first, that there was a problem of "inadvertent narrowness" arising from the fact that few film scholars read many European languages and so had to rely on translations. This meant that other European discussions were left untranslated and unconsidered.[79] Second, he observed that the French writers such as Lacan, Althusser, Baudrillard became "authorities" whose ideas were not subject to critical rigor.[80] One might say, in other words, that film studies had become subject to a kind of authority paradigm.

As for Bordwell's own contribution to theory, it is openly hermeneutical: it gives interpretation a "starring role".[81] He argues

[74] Ibid.

[75] Ibid., p. 7.

[76] Ibid., p. 9.

[77] Ibid.

[78] Ibid., p. 26.

[79] Ibid., p. 20.

[80] Ibid., pp. 20-21.

[81] Bordwell, *Making Meaning: Inference and Rhetoric in the Interpretation of Cinema* (1989), p xiii.

that there is a conceptual distinction within the interpretation model, namely between *ars intelligendi* and *ars explicandi*. This is the distinction between understanding and explaining, often in fact associated in social and human science thinking with the distinction between hermeneutical and causal schemes.[82] Bordwell, however, sees it as a distinction between comprehension and interpretation: "comprehension is concerned with apparent, manifest, or direct meanings, while interpretation is concerned with hidden, nonobvious meanings".[83] Yet, and this is his principal thesis, meanings are not found but made. Thus "to assume that sense is 'in' the text is to reify what can only be the result of a process".[84] As he explains:

> Comprehending and interpreting a literary text, a painting, a play, or a film constitutes an activity in which the perceiver plays a central role. The text is inert until a reader or listener or spectator does something to and with it ... Understanding is mediated by transformative acts, both 'bottom-up' – mandatory, automatic psychological processes – and 'top-down' – conceptual strategic ones. The sensory data of the film at hand furnish the materials out of which inferential processes of perception and cognition build meanings. Meanings are not found but made.[85]

As we shall see, this thesis is relevant to comparative legal studies, but it might also be controversial for some comparatists. When faced with a foreign legal text, is the meaning to be found 'in' the text itself or uniquely 'in' the mind of the comparatist? If the latter – if meaning is to be found in the reader or film or fine art spectator – how does this construction operate methodologically? According to Bordwell both comprehension and interpretation "require the spectator to apply conceptual schemes to data picked out in the film".[86]

[82] R. Makkreel, "Expliquer et comprendre", in Mesure and Savidan, note 7 above, p. 441.

[83] Bordwell, note 81 above, p. 2.

[84] Ibid.

[85] Ibid., pp. 2-3 (footnote omitted).

[86] Ibid., p. 4.

What, then, are these conceptual schemes? Bordwell himself, in emphasizing the centrality of interpretation, would seem to be advocating hermeneutics. As Bordwell says of literary interpretation, it "seldom acknowledges the degree to which it models itself … upon mythological and scriptural exegesis" and thus "is in many ways a secular version of biblical criticism".[87] In fact what one discovers is that "interpretation" is employed in a wide sense that embraces other schemes of engagement such as structuralism and dialectics, with further schemes like causality and functionalism being mentioned in passing. One is tempted to say that interpretation itself is a matter of different *grilles de lecture*, although this is not in fact what Bordwell goes on to say. The interpretive processes that he examines tend to be far more diffuse often combining psychoanalytical approaches, dialectical contrasts, image and behavioural metaphorical interpretations, feminist readings, structural frameworks and so on. Yet his central message is that these lower-level schemes are the most important focal point:

> Note that no mastery of theory need play a part in this [interpretation] process. A critic trained in the proper assumptions, hypotheses, schemata, and routines should be able to produce an acceptable interpretation without the benefit of theoretical knowledge. This is not to say that these activities do not have theoretical implications; they do in any realm of reasoning ... I claim only that skill in creating, understanding, or defending theoretical arguments is neither necessary nor a sufficient condition for the solving of interpretive problems.[88]

Bordwell sees this dichotomy between "theory" and "critical interpretation" as being based upon the distinction between "propositional knowledge" and "procedural knowledge".[89] This procedural knowledge, he later claims, was in some ways reminiscent of medieval scholasticism in that it has become focused on the text:

[87] Ibid., p. 24.

[88] Ibid., p. 144.

[89] A leading French work on the analysis of films makes a similar distinction but sees it as a matter differentiating between "theory" and "analysis": J. Aumont and M. Marie, *L'Analyse des films* (4th ed.; 2020), pp. 276-282.

> Academic legitimation has helped film interpretation turn into a new scholasticism complete with a canon (Hollywood and some venerated oppositional works), received truths (Theory), highly regulated interpretive moves, and guaranteed points of arrival. Underlying all these features is an appeal to authority.[90]

Bordwell does seem to regard this scholasticism as "narrowness", and he is right to see medieval methods – as many jurists who are familiar with the *mos Italicus* will more than appreciate – as operating with a strict textual and authority paradigm.[91] Yet the "procedure", being casuistic and textual, is likely to be primarily dialectical and narrowly hermeneutical until other schemes such as functionalism and reception theory (that is a more sophisticated hermeneutical approach) can break this mould. This, arguably, has not happened in the discipline of law which, as several legal historians have observed, is still governed by scholastic methods (but tempered by some functionalism and conceptualism).[92]

Yet, whatever one might think about this textual scholasticism, Bordwell is not the only film theorist to argue that critical analysis does, and should, operate at a lower level of abstraction than "grand theory". In fact Noël Carroll offers what is arguably, at least from an epistemological viewpoint, a more sophisticated analysis of methodology in cinema studies. He starts by making a point that is not at all dissimilar to the one made by Bordwell:

> Instead of thinking of film theory as a unified, single theory, it might be better to think of it as a field of activity, perhaps like sociological theory, where many different projects – theories of homelessness in America, of generic social coherence, of class conflict in India, of the resurgence of religious fundamentalism worldwide – of different levels of generality and abstraction coexist without being subsumed under a single general theory. Similarly, film theorizing today should proceed at varying levels of generality and abstraction.[93]

[90] Bordwell, note 81 above, p. 262.

[91] See further Samuel, *Rethinking Historical Jurisprudence* (2022), pp. 104-112.

[92] See, for example, J. Gordley, *The Jurists: A Critical History* (2013), pp. 42-43.

[93] Carroll, "Prospects for Film Theory: A Personal Assessment", in Bordwell and

It is tempting to think that Carroll seems more familiar with the social science epistemologists (mentioned earlier in this contribution) than other film writers like Bordwell. Indeed, Carroll goes on to state not just that film theory "should be interdisciplinary",[94] but that many film writers are contriving interpretations of individual films that are "in arcane, 'theoretically' derived jargon".[95] Carroll attributes this habit to the fact that most film writers "have exclusively hermeneutical training, as opposed to education in theoretical disciplines such as the natural or social sciences, or philosophy".[96] He goes on to say that much of this film theorizing involves "causal reasoning" in the way that it uses theory as a causal process – subject positioning – "by hermeneutically alleging to find the allegory of the Imaginary retold in a selected film". Such an engagement, given enough latitude, can lead to a situation where one "can probably allegorize anything to say whatever you wish, but that won't establish causal connections where there are none". This suggests, he concludes, that "the prospects for causal research are bleak".[97]

Carroll's reference to sociological theory is, unfortunately, not developed in a way that one might have expected. He does not examine the different schemes of intelligibility or *grilles de lecture* that are surely the key to appreciating how film analysis could function free from the kind of "authority paradigm" dictated by the types of grand theory that he (together with Bordwell) finds arcane or oppressive. Instead he prefers to look to the natural sciences for insights.[98] This leads him into claiming that his approach "is consistent with trends in the postpositivist philosophy of science" which "respects the Kuhnian, antipositivist emphasis on the importance of historical and social contexts for inquiry".[99] However he then does something of an about turn in claiming that Kuhn

Carroll, note 70 above, p. 39.

[94] Ibid., p. 40.

[95] Ibid., p. 42.

[96] Ibid.

[97] Ibid.

[98] Ibid., p. 59.

[99] Ibid., pp. 58-59.

does not compel film writers "to become social constructivists".[100] This is odd because the whole basis of Kuhn's thesis is that scientific thought is founded on model building and that these models change over time, sometimes so drastically as to amount to a "scientific revolution". One explanation for this rejection of social constructivism is to be found in his discussion of the notion of truth and interpretation.[101] Are there "true" interpretations of a text? Carroll thinks that there are, although there may be more than one and that it is necessary to distinguish between "truth" and "absolute truth". He is perfectly entitled to raise this debate, which has a real relevance for comparative lawyers as well; but given his interest in the natural science epistemology one would have thought that he would engage with the issue of falsification, associated with Karl Popper.[102] Can an interpretation of a text ever be falsified? Can it be tested? Kuhn's, and Vaihinger's, point is that it is probably not that helpful to think in terms of "truth" since the concepts and models are located in the *intellectus* rather than the *res* and that the better question is to ask whether the model is pragmatically useful. Moreover, the lesson from social science epistemology is surely that different schemes of engagement provide different kinds of knowledge.

CLOSE READING

How, then, might the insights from social science epistemology be employed to provide knowledge about films? Before exploring this question two preliminary points might usefully be made. The first is that an important distinction, identified in literary theory, needs to noted. This is the distinction between what might be termed a "close reading" and (for want of a better term) a more "grand reading". A comparatist might use the expressions "micro" and "macro". Close reading, says Terry Eagleton, means a "detailed analytic interpretation";[103] it "means the kind of reading which clings tenaciously to the shape of the sentences – to their rhythm, sound, tone, texture, syntactical form and so on – and comes up

100 Ibid., p. 59.

101 Ibid., pp. 52-56.

102 See Aumont and Marie, note 89 above, p 278.

103 Eagleton, note 49 above, p. 38.

with judgments and interpretations on this basis".[104] It is associated with the "revolutionary" (according to Eagleton) literary critics Ivor Richards (1893-1979) and William Empson (1906-1984).[105]

The second point is that one critic who ought to earn the approval of both Bordwell and Carroll is Raymond Durgnat (1932-2002), who studied English literature at Cambridge in the 1950s – at the same college in fact where Sir Henry James Sumner Maine (1822-1888) had been educated – and who was much influenced by the Richards and Empson. Durgnat not only rejected the kind of grand theory which so displeases Bordwell and Carroll but also became one of the most important (arguably) close reading film writers.[106] Equally, however, Durgnat was a writer who wrote at the level of grand reading (not grand *theory*) and who produced several remarkable books and articles, embracing vast numbers of films, on various stylistic (*films noirs*) and social (populism and everyday labour for example) themes.[107] Perhaps his most celebrated work on cinema and social themes is his analysis of English films in the two decades following the Second World War.[108] This work was extended into the decades that followed in two major articles.[109] One film writer, contributing an introduction to a reprint of Durgnat's book on English cinema, said that "if you think that you have an 'original' approach to a film or a director's work ... you generally discover that Raymond Durgnat has said it already".[110] This writer also made the point that Durgnat "avoids classification and perhaps applies no single method consistently, but it is worth observing that it hinged on a form of working-class scholarship: the use of public libraries and serendipity, more than

[104] Eagleton, note 69 above, p. 135.

[105] See generally ibid.

[106] See in particular R. Durgnat, *A Long Hard Look at 'Psycho'* (2002).

[107] Durgnat, "Paint It Black: The Family Tree of Film Noir", *Cinema*, nos. 6-7 (1970), p. 48; Durgnat, "Genre: Populism and Social Realism", *Film Comment*, XI, no. 4 (1975), p. 20; Durgnat and J. Bloch, "Attention: Men at Work", *Film Comment*, XV, no. 6 (1979), p. 18.

[108] Durgnat, *A Mirror for England* (1970).

[109] Durgnat, "Britannia Waves the Rules", Film Comment, XII, no. 4 (1976), p. 50; Durgnat, "The Great British Phantosmagoria", *Film Comment*, XIII, no. 3 (1977), p. 48.

[110] K. Gough-Yates, "Forward", in Durgnat, *A Mirror for England* (2d ed.; 2011), p viii.

on traditional academic research techniques".[111] This may be very true, yet it is this methodological pluralism that makes his close readings valuable since one does not necessarily have to be fully conscious of the formal schemes of engagement employed in one's analysis.[112]

In order to illustrate this point one might turn to one of Durgnat's early close readings: his dissection of the Hollywood Western *Johnny Guitar* (1954) directed by Nicholas Ray. Johnny no-gun (Sterling Hayden) arrives at a gambling house and bar just outside of a town situated close to where a railway is being constructed; the place is owned by Vienna (Joan Crawford) and her customers include a gang of outlaws and some other outcasts. There is hostility between the townsfolk and Vienna since she supports the railway construction, and they do not, and this leads to a serious confrontation as a result of the outlaws – two of whom have emotional relationships with Vienna – robbing the local bank. Another matriarch, Emma Small (Mercedes McCambridge), detests Vienna and convinces the sheriff that she was involved in the robbery; Emma manages to rouse the townsfolk into lynching Vienna, but she is saved by Johnny, ultimately to outgun Emma in a final showdown. Johnny himself was not all he seemed; it transpires that he is the former lover of Vienna and was once a vicious gunman himself, only to renounce such a life when he realized that one day he would be outgunned. This short summary does not do justice to the complexity of the relationships between all the principal characters, and it is this complexity which is essentially the focal point of Durgnat's reading of the film.

After a detailed description of the narrative, one of the first observations made by Durgnat is that "there are really three Viennas – Vienna the bad (wo)man in black, Vienna the scarlet (Scarlett) woman, and virginal Vienna [wearing white], made to be martyred".[113] He then comments on the psychological characteristics and obsessions of some principal characters and on the moral dilemma facing Johnny when he has to choose between saving Vienna or Turkey (Ben Cooper), an outlaw double-crossed by Emma who had promised him his life if he implicated Vienna

[111] Ibid., p. xxi.

[112] On close readings (analysis) in general see Aumont and Marie, note 89 above.

[113] Durgnat, *Films and Feelings* (1967), p. 189.

in the robbery. Moving on, Durgnat looks at the "patterns" of the relationships between the characters and notes, in particular the "emphatic antagonisms" in the film between Black Bart (Ernest Borgnine), the leader of the outlaws, and Johnny, and between Emma and Vienna.[114] However "the obvious dramatic conflict, between Johnny and the Dancin' Kid, is by-passed until the near end, when their gunfight is stopped by Vienna". The Dancin' Kid (Scott Brady) is one of the other outlaws and the prospective lover of Vienna. Thus, says Durgnat, "Johnny Guitar is 'patterned' not only by Black Bart, but also by the Dancing Kid", whereas "his encounter with Turkey has another undertone".[115] Durgnat discusses these relationships using a Freudian "authority figure' framework and concludes this part of his close reading in saying:

> We have presented these patterns in terms of similarities – but only so as to show that these patterns do exist. None the less, the first impression they give is that of strong contrasts. The similarity is there to establish the tension of the dissimilarity. We don't feel Black Bart and Johnny Guitar, or Vienna and Emma, or Emma and Black Bart, as being 'the same, but different' – quite the reverse, it's a case of 'similar poles repel'. Our patterns of similarities are also patterns of differences ...[116]

Durgnat adds that while there is the traditional "goodies-baddies" polarity, "the pattern of emotional shocks and paradoxes is both involved and nuanced".[117] It works at various levels. The characters can be grouped into three categories: the outlaws; the townsfolk; and the people who live at the gambling house (Vienna and Johnny); and these categories experience splits within them (for example, decency versus vindictiveness). But each principal character is also split within himself or herself (for example, Johnny as ally versus antagonist). The film is, therefore, not a simple melodrama, for "it has a lively and stimulating chop and change of emotional permutations".[118] In addition, says Durgnat,

[114] Ibid., pp. 190-191.

[115] Ibid., p. 191.

[116] Ibid., pp. 191-192.

[117] Ibid., p. 193.

[118] Ibid., p. 194.

the "emotional pattern is further variegated by the 'infrastructure' of the audience response".[119] Sympathy for Turkey is an early response but this changes, claims Durgnat, when his weaknesses lead to the betrayal of Vienna.

The audience itself, continues Durgnat, becomes an invisible character in the film, and while "this may seem to be getting us into very deep waters", the fact is that "scriptwriters swim happily about them every day".[120] Durgnat gives a range of examples from literature and drama concluding that dramatic relationships can generate a "bundle of feelings" which in turn incorporates the audience experiencing these feelings as an "invisible character". One could, he says, produce an "inside-out" version of *Johnny Guitar* in which, for example, there might be three women – or indeed just two – instead of the one Vienna; this would substantially alter the bundle of feelings on the part of the audience.[121] Another possibility, says Durgnat, is to throw out obvious symmetries by symmetrical surprises so as to create an "imbalance" which will effect the "bundle of feelings" on the part of the audience. This effect can be enhanced by the places in which people are located. "Feelings snowball around it", he says, "just as they snowball around the *human* characters".[122] In short, it "creates a pattern, is part of the orchestration of feelings, of the very structure of the film". Similarly, props have their role:

> A gives B a ring, swearing eternal love; B tires of him and gives it to C; C ... and so on, back to B, who is now ninety years old and just hoards it in a box of trinkets. At each appearance, the ring is 'the same, transformed'. There is no pattern of cause-and-effect; the idea is communicated by the simplest and crudest intellectual process, the 'association of ideas'.[123]

In examining this close reading it is not being asserted that one should agree with Durgnat's analysis. The point of the exercise is to identify the schemes of engagement and the *grilles de lecture*

[119] Ibid.

[120] Ibid.

[121] Ibid., p. 196.

[122] Ibid., p. 198 (emphasis in original).

[123] Ibid.

implicated in this "pluralistic" methodology, with an ultimate aim of reflecting whether there are insights for comparative law. What schemes can, then, be identified? Arguably there are several:

- **Hermeneutical** (Durgnat engages at two levels of interpretation: the first is the symbol (*signans*) of the clothes worn by Vienna, the colors of which represent the three Viennas (*signatum*). The second level is that of reception theory: the audience as an "invisible character" incorporated into the film itself).
- **Structural** (Durgnat's emphasis on the patterns of relationships itself related to the infrastructure of the audience response. A further structural engagement can be detected in the relationships identified between humans, places and props).
- **Dialectical** (Durgnat's identification of the oppositions to be found within groups and within individuals).
- **Psychoanalytical** (Durgnat's reference to Freud and authority figures).

Durgnat himself does not use these terms. Yet they are worth identifying because they can be employed – no doubt along with further schemes – in the examination of other close reading exercises in film studies. In some of these other close readings Durgnat employs different approaches. For example, his discussion of *This Island Earth* (1955) and *Forbidden Planet* (1956) focuses largely on the moral patterns and, in respect of the 1955 film, he looks at "its resonance with certain psycholpathological traits in American political thought".[124] The moral-political investigation is particularly detailed, and analogies are made both with American and with English political and cultural psychology, some Freudian analysis being added as well. Moreover, Durgnat contrasts the styles in the 1955 film with those to be found in other science-fiction movies of the same period. Much of this analysis – and some of it will not appeal to all – could be regarded as involving primarily a hermeneutical scheme of engagement, but there are structural and psychoanalytical analogies which, when combined, can produce a quite diffuse methodological pattern.

124 Ibid., p. 256.

STYLE

Style is particularly difficult because it is not something that lends itself easily to a social science analysis, although, as will be seen, it is not irrelevant to comparative law. Yet clearly image style (including composition) is a fundamental element in the visual arts, just as writing style is relevant in literary analysis. There is, equally, acting style. How, then, does the close reader (or even the more general level reader) engage with the issue of style? Certainly there can be an important hermeneutical engagement: a particular style of clothes can be used as a sign (*signans*) indicating a psychological or mental trait (*signatum*) in a film character; the state of the weather can be used to similar effect. As Durgnat said, a "fundamental equation of the cinema's is: landscape = state of soul".[125] Yet it is not just a matter of weather and landscape. Discussing Carl Dreyer, *La Passion de Jeanne d'Arc* (1928), Durgnat explained the importance of what he called sensation, shape and shade:

> Dreyer's visual flair is very strong, very simple, very strange. The 'low angle' in Welles [*Touch of Evil* (1957)] makes the character seem proud, as he looks down at others. The 'low angle' in Dreyer makes Falconetti [the actress playing Joan] humble (often because from this angle even her *level gaze* seems to be looking imploringly upwards). He photographs Falconetti from a low angle, so as to increase the slight downward curve of her very vigorous mouth, giving her an air of tragic dejection – he uses perspective to change the shape and 'meaning' of her features. He lets on to the faces a white light which seems to grind them down, to scrape them clean, to impart to them the permanence of stone … Maybe he can't chip and chisel away at his actors' bodies to get the right shape and pose he wants, so he arranges their clothes – flowing monks' robes, which can 'compose' quite freely. Some into sharp, mean crooks and cranks, others into billowing explosions of their wrath.[126]

125 Ibid., p. 102.

126 Ibid., pp. 47-48 (emphasis in original).

Architecture, too, is vital. Indeed "Carl Dreyer has argued that the cinema's closest relative is architecture"[127] and Durgnat spends many pages illustrating this observation. If one wants to create a feeling of alienation, or sinister atmosphere, or visions of oppressive totalitarianism, modern architecture is there to help; equally if the sinister disorientation is to be located beyond the rational world, the baroque pavilion (*Carnival of Souls*, 1962), the ruined abbey (*La maschera del demonio*, 1960, *Tomb of Ligeia*, 1964) or of course the Old Dark House can be useful settings to describe a "between two worlds". Moving from the outside of a building to its inside, décor can be used to tell us about an individual's character, something that may not be able to be expressed in words and thus needs to be indicated through image.[128] It may also be employed, for example, to create a heady mixture of debauchery, sado-eroticism, sensuous luxuries, and cold cruelty – as in the Hammer films of the 1950s and 1960s. As Durgnat said of these films, "the colour sings".[129] And he subsequently added that "Hammer's 'grand series' owed their success to a chemistry of moods: physical atrocity interacting with moral irony + dandy coldness + sensuousness + Victorian nostalgias + Victorian materialism".[130] Roger Corman's Edgar Allan Poe adaptions, largely set within colour-rich gothic interiors, built on the style of these early Hammer productions, confirming, equally, that the actors themselves were part and parcel of the style – Peter Cushing and Christopher Lee for Hammer, Vincent Price for Corman.

How, then, can style be analyzed? Raymond Durgnat proposed the use of the French expression *mise-en-scène* in a particular way, namely "to refer to the creative arrangements of things *within* the screen".[131] And so a "sensitive response to *mise-en-scène* means paying just as much attention to make-up, lighting, décor, costumes, gesture, and other "technical", "stylistic" details of a film as to dialogue and plot – noticing them not for their own sakes, but for their emotional meaning, their psychological impact".[132] John

[127] Ibid., p. 99.

[128] J. Gibbs, *Mise-en-Scène: Film Style and Interpretation* (2002), p. 69.

[129] Durgnat, note 108 above, p. 226.

[130] Ibid.

[131] Durgnat, note 113 above, p. 35 (emphasis in original).

[132] Ibid., pp. 36-37.

Gibbs is much more "analytical" in that he specifically takes these elements identified by Durgnat (although there is no reference to this earlier writer) and examines each in turn.[133] His list identifies, then, the following:

- **Lighting** (Gibbs discusses Hitchcock's *Notorious* (1946) but a comparatist might compare the two versions of *The Killers* (1946 and 1964) whose contrasting lighting styles are one of the most distinguishing features).
- **Costume** (Gibbs uses *Rebel Without a Cause* (1955) as his example, but a more striking film is surely Hitchcock's *Vertigo* (1958) where the styles of particular clothes have a central role; and Durgnat, of course, focused on Vienna's costumes in his close reading of *Johnny Guitar*).
- **Color** (the author uses *Home from the Hill* (1959) for his discussion of color, but one might also reflect on the rather subtle use of colour in *Vertigo* or its garish use in some Hammer productions).
- **Props** (Gibbs focuses on the chairs in *Late Spring* (1949), a good example, but, again, one might note the role of the brooch in *Vertigo* or indeed even sunglasses as props in movies such as *Psycho* (1961), *The Killers* (1964) or the *Tomb of Ligeia* (1964)).
- **Décor** (Gibbs' example is Renoir's *La Règle du jeu* (1939), a sophisticated use of décor in one particular scene, but less sophisticated examples abound in the Hammer and Corman horrors; one might also mention the surrealist or expressionist settings in a film such as *Marguerite de la Nuit* (1956) and in fact in many other movies, sometimes as dream sequences).
- **Action and performance** (the author uses Max Ophül's *Caught* (1949) and Hitchcock's *North by Northwest* (1959) to explain how certain movements can indicate patterns of thoughts on the part of characters in a film).
- **Space** (Gibbs rightly says that space can be used in a number of ways, in particular the personal space between actors placed in groups as in *The Lusty Men* (1952); one might also recall how Hitchcock, in *North by Northwest*,

[133] Gibbs, note 128 above, pp. 5-26.

places his actor at a bus stop in the middle of nowhere in order to create a puzzling tension slightly soothed, for a while, by a small crop-spraying aeroplane in the far distance).

- **Position of the camera** (Raymond Durgnat, as has been seen, mentions Dreyer's camera position as a means of expressing the feelings of a film's character, while Gibbs himself continues to examine *The Lusty Men* in order to emphasize how the position of the camera can profoundly affect the way an audience will experience a performance).
- **Framing** (Gibbs uses the Buster Keaton film *One Week* (1920) to show how the film frame can limit information for the audience thus leading to surprise on their part when something out of the frame suddenly intrudes; in *The Killers* (1964) a high angle shot shows the two professional hit-men leaving their hotel but the audience can only feel a vague sense of apprehension because the cause of what is about to happen is out of the frame).

These, accordingly, are for Gibbs, and doubtless for Durgnat, the individual elements that create the style of a particular film. Of course, as Gibbs concludes, "each of the examples we have looked at depends for its effect on a combination of elements". They have to be considered "in terms of their *interaction* rather than individually".[134]

This is where the close reading of a film becomes important, for each film's style will usually be the result of a particular combination. This is not to say that particular filmmakers lack their own individual style; the films of Josef von Sternberg (1894-1969) or of Michelangelo Antonioni (1912-2007) are very distinctive. Yet there are individual films by directors that stand out from the rest of their work. As Raymond Durgnat said of Robert Aldrich's *Kiss Me Deadly* (1955): it "is his one great film", a result of the interaction of a range of stylistic elements.[135] The "colour" (a steely monochrome highlighted by dark shadows), the architecture ("modernist"), the props (fifties sports car, tape-recording telephone and the like), the crisp and nihilistic dialogue (not mentioned by Gibbs), the music ("I'd Rather Have the Blues", again an element not mentioned by

[134] Ibid., p. 26.

[135] Durgnat, *Eros in the Cinema* (1966), p. 84.

Gibbs), the narrative structure (with its references to literature and myth) and the personalities of the characters (the "hero" detective not such a "hero") – all of these elements combine to create a film that "has the cold atrocity of a Greek tragic myth" and whose "bleak nihilism … is its terrible beauty".[136]

Nevertheless, despite seemingly being able to reduce style to its constituent elements, care must be taken because it is not always easy to distinguish style from content. As Durgnat said:

> The distinction between *'literary* content' and 'visual style' is particularly misguided because even in the work of literature much of the 'content' comes from the 'style'. Suppose we call someone 'slow but thorough' we feel this is, on the whole, a compliment. His slowness is a trifling disadvantage, the last word acts as a summing-up, an assertion of his value. But if we call him 'thorough but slow' there is an implication of criticism. The ideas and the words are exactly the same – but to change their order is like inserting some invisible words.[137]

Thus, in film, changes of order, sound, narrative, color, and so on – indeed changes in any of the elements set out by John Gibbs – do not just affect the surface style so to speak. They affect the content as well.

GRAND READING

Moving from a close reading to a more general one – that is to say, to a more macro approach – one might describe this higher level as a "grand reading". This of course suggests that there are just two categories, but "poles" would be a better term since there are intermediary levels. Rather than just focusing on one film, one might examine five or six together, as indeed Raymond Durgnat did, for instance, with respect to a selection of science fiction films.[138] The different levels of observation so to speak are connected to film "theory". At the general level there are, very broadly, three kinds of "critical method" approach; there is auteur

[136] Ibid.

[137] Durgnat, note 113 above, p. 26.

[138] Ibid., pp. 251-267

theory, genre theory, and, what for want of a more technical term, one might call thematic analysis. "The *auteur* principle", writes Andrew Tudor, "directs our attention to groups of films having in common one thing – the director".[139] Genre theory has its roots in literary studies – the classifying of works into various categories – and is a "theory" that divides up films into a number of generic categories such as the Western, the musical, the horror film, gangster movies, science fiction and so on. It is, as Tudor says, to "fit it into a class of films about which we presumably have some *general* knowledge".[140] As for thematic analysis, this is not a question of any definable category as such. It is to take a common denominator such as violence, eroticism, sadism, sexual alienation, otherness and so on.[141] Such themes, for some at least, can sometimes "harden" into a genre, although often the problem is that generic categories are themselves hard to define.[142]

This difficulty of definition is one problem that arises from labelling genre as a "theory". "What is normally a thumb-nail classification for everyday purposes", notes Andrew Tudor, "is now being asked to carry rather more weight".[143] This leads to several serious problems, one being the circularity that arises when one attempts to turn a common "theme" into a taxonomical category. As Tudor says:

> To take a *genre* such as a 'Western', analyse it, and list its principle [sic] characteristics, is to beg the question that we must first isolate the body of films which are 'Westerns'. But they can only be isolated on the basis of the 'principal characteristics' which can only be discovered *from the films themselves* after they have been isolated. That is, we are caught in a circle which first requires that the films are isolated, for which purposes a criterion is necessary, but the criterion is, in turn, meant to emerge from the empirically

[139] A. Tudor, *Theories of Film* (1974), p. 131.

[140] Ibid., p. 132

[141] See, for example, L. Alloway, *Violent America: The Movies 1946-1964* (1971); Durgnat, note 135 above; G. De Coulteray, *Le sadisme au cinéma* (1964); Durgnat, *Sexual Alienation in the Cinema* (1972); M. Richardson, *Otherness in Hollywood Cinema* (2010).

[142] See Durgnat, note 107 above, p. 20.

[143] Tudor, note 139 above, p. 133.

> established common characteristics of the films. One is to classify films according to *a priori* chosen criteria depending on the critical purpose.[144]

As will be seen, this is a type of problem for some legal theories as well. Perhaps one of the difficulties is that films – and in fact works of literature and art in general – do not lend themselves to the kind of taxonomical framework employed by biologists and zoologists. Films can be classed into different categories, but there are too many cross currents to turn these categories into watertight and axiomatic models. Take *Mildred Pierce* (1945) and *Imitation of Life* (1959): both films could be said to be about a difficult relationship between mother and daughter and both could be classed as "melodramas". But it is not easy to see how either the relationship or the class of melodrama could act as the basis for top-down "theory" analysis because there are so many other currents running through each film. One cannot really start out from "mother and daughter" relation or "melodrama" in order to analyze either of these films in any logical way. One actually has to start from the films themselves – or a particular work of art – and work towards some common denominators.[145] In other words, there is no general *theory* of melodrama or mother-and-daughter films.

Other issues arise from genre theory. One is the relationship between a film and its audience: what expectations does a viewer have regarding the genre of film that she is watching? Tudor talks of a genre such as a Western having certain rules; he cites films that stick to these rules, no doubt satisfying those viewers who are themselves conscience of the rules and do not expect them to be broken. Yet some leading westerns do exactly that: they break the rules. This can be done in several different ways. What if a motor vehicle appears in a "western"? This has happened in westerns by Sam Peckinpah, as Tudor notes.[146] What if one parodies the rules? Tudor thinks that the Italian Westerns did this in using particular Hollywood B-actors (ultimately turning some of them into A-actors) and in using stylistic techniques (clothes, landscapes, weapons,

[144] Ibid., pp. 137-138.

[145] Cauquelin, note 52 above, p. 39. As two French authors note: "analysis is often the antechamber of theory": Aumont and Marie, note 89 above, p. 282.

[146] Tudor, note 139 above, p. 144

framing and the like) associated with some of the leading western directors such as John Ford.[147] Tudor describes Sergio Leone's *Once Upon a Time in the West* (1968) as verging on self-parody – not, perhaps, an unreasonable comment in 1974.[148] Yet, today, the film is regarded by many, including filmmakers themselves, as a Western masterpiece.[149] The audience, in other words, is having a key role in determining what is and what is not to be incorporated into a generic category. Again, this is not a matter of "theory" – or, if it is, it is a matter of reception "theory" – and so it would be more appropriate to talk in terms of a hermeneutic relationship between *auteur* (who may not actually be a single individual), audience, and the film itself. Such a relationship can shift and change over time.

Certainly, as Tudor says, generic categories are not useless.[150] Such categories can be useful in the way they "direct our attention to sublanguages within [a film]". But "it is not a way in which a critic classifies films for methodological purposes, but the much looser way in which the audience classifies its films".[151] Raymond Durgnat, for his part, has examined in some depth the difficulties associated with the notion of genre and concludes by making an analogy with types of dog:

> Ultimately, the idea of genre corresponds to that of a breed, or of a species. Some films are pure Westerns just as some dogs are pure Dalmatians. But many films are hybrids, just as most dogs are mongrels. Mongrels may have breed-specific parts (Dalmatian ears and bulldog legs) or merge characteristics more smoothly and unidentifiably. Most mongrels – or litters! – are one-offs, but if enough one-offs of a particular kind are in demand it becomes a new breed. A genre, like a species, responds to changes in its

[147] On which see C. Frayling, *Sergio Leone: Once Upon a Time in Italy* (2005), pp. 59-63.

[148] Tudor, note 139 above, p. 138. Note that this Leone film uses the same construction of a railroad theme as Johnny Guitar; it also casts Henry Fonda as a vicious villain in a complete reversal to his traditional image in American Westerns. For a full discussion of this film, its background and its visual, narrative and dialogue references ("quotations"), see Frayling, *Sergio Leone: Something To Do With Death* (2000), pp. 247-301.

[149] See also Frayling, note 148 above, pp. 247-301.

[150] Tudor, note 139 above, p. 144.

[151] Ibid., p. 145.

> environment. It may evolve, or acquire a new ecological niche (the Western briefly becomes a hicktown-and-children's genre), or become extinct.[152]

Tudor, in fact, sees genre as not being a method in itself. Instead its has imported "methodologies from other disciplines, in particular techniques borrowed from structural linguistics and anthropology".[153] He later adds that genre thinking "will inevitably be led to sociological and psychological theories of film".[154] No doubt the same is true of the other "grand theory", namely, the *auteur* analysis, for this "theory" has as many problems as "genre theory".[155] In other words, there will be a merging of close and grand reading at the level of methodological schemes of engagement, which, importantly, brings one back to the point that "methodology" is often a more useful term than "theory".[156]

Durgnat's own "grand readings" tend, then, to be more thematic than genre-oriented and this, arguably, is their great strength. Three, in particular, are noteworthy. The first is his article on *film noir* in which he states that it is "not a genre, as the Western or gangster film is" but "takes us into the realms of classification by motif and tone". Thus, he said, only some crime films are *noir* while other films – melodramas, Westerns, war films and so on – can be classed as *films noirs*.[157] This permits him to construct an *arbor* much in the same way that medieval Roman law jurists constructed an *arbor actionum,* and such a tree in turn allows the reader to appreciate not just that much subsequent writing on

[152] Durgnat, note 107 above (1975), p. 23. Dogs seem to feature in comparative law as well: C. Valcke, *Comparing Law: Comparative Law as Reconstruction of Collective Commitments* (2018), p. 214.

[153] Tudor, note 139 above, p. 150.

[154] Ibid., p. 152.

[155] On which see Durgnat, note 113 above, pp. 61-86. Durgnat does not say that one cannot or should not look at the work of particular directors – he himself wrote books on Franju, Bunuel, Renoir and Hitchcock, plus articles on Vidor and Hawks. His point was that there are many films where others such as the actors, photographers and (or) scriptwriters deserve as much credit as the director. Equally, there are some directors who have made bad movies as well as good ones.

[156] As has been seen, Aumont and Marie, note 139 above, prefer the term "analysis" rather than "methodology".

[157] Durgnat, "Paint It Black: The Family Tree of Film Noir", *Cinema,* nos. 6-7 (1970). p. 48.

film noir is founded upon Durgnat's seminal piece (not always acknowledged) but also that the tree itself can act as a *passerelle* between cinema and social reality, this latter expression embracing social and sexual pathology and social and political corruption. It provides a plan for future scholarship and research.

This link between film and social reality is explored in two other articles, one taking populism as its theme the other (a jointly authored article) focusing on everyday work and labor in films. In his article on films and populism, Durgnat again adopts a family tree (*arbor popularis*) approach which brings together a vast range of films from a variety of countries and from nearly all of the genres.[158] The net he casts is huge thanks to his vision of what counts, and also what does not count, as "populist", but the chosen theme has an important message. Even nearly half a century ago, when he wrote the article, he was warning that the exclusivist elitism of many film writers was masking the resurgence of "populism/ social realism/middle-class realism" as a dominant stream in cinema.[159] If he were alive today, he would probably add that the same elitism masked a resurgence in political ideology as well. A third article is along similar lines in that its theme is on everyday work, especially of ordinary people doing, on the whole, ordinary, sometimes painstaking, work (*arbor laboris*).[160] What does *Tree of the Wooden Clogs* (1978) – a film on the art-house circuit – and *Escape from Alcatraz* (1979) – on general release – have in common? Both films are "dominated by hands at work" say the authors. One can, as the authors do, go on to make further comparisons between often unlikely bedpartner films, and this results in an analysis that indicates how a good many films – especially Westerns – really are fictions and need to be to keep the story going. Indian tactics in cowboy films cannot be shown as anything other than idiotic because the alternative would mean that the film "would have to become anthropological".[161] Had real Indian tactics been employed in John Ford's *Stagecoach* (1939) the movie would have ended well before schedule.

158 Durgnat, note 107 above (1975).

159 Ibid., p. 63.

160 Durgnat and Bloch, "Attention: Men at Work", *Film Comment*, XV, no. 6 (1979), p. 18.

161 Ibid., p. 22.

This said, there are other films whose fascination with objects as things can sometimes result in a scene where "the practical is blended with the formal, one being somewhat tempered by the other".[162] One is reminded of the formal (and fundamental) distinction in Roman law between *persona* and *res* which merged with the hard labor of the slave, not something dwelled upon in the *Corpus Iuris Civilis*. No doubt Durgnat and Bloch were right to conclude that "film is subject to prohibitions against the depiction of physical or practical details of all kinds",[163] yet sometimes in mainstream commercial films there are the odd insights. There is a scene in Don Siegal's *The Killers* (1964) (not mentioned in the article) where the two hired assassins, normally dressed in their sharp suits, are in their hotel room and the senior of the two, while engaged in story advancing dialogue with his partner, is washing his white shirt in the bathroom basin. This rather extraordinary act does not in itself advance the story one iota, yet in a way it suddenly reminds us of the mundane details of life on the move. Again, in Antonioni's *Blow-up* (1966) (also not mentioned in the article), the formalist imagery of London's luxury lifestyle led by the shallow young wealthy elite suddenly gives way to the detailed work involved in processing one weekend a 35m film in the darkroom when the photographer's staff are not there. This is where classification by theme can prove more insightful than auteur or genre theory; it is a grand reading that certainly indicates, as one might say, the forest, yet it can equally point out some very detailed trees or even the branch of a tree.

LESSONS FOR COMPARATIVE LEGAL STUDIES?

Does this exhaustive survey and discussion of methodology in the social sciences and the humanities hold lessons or insights for comparative lawyers? No doubt, at least if Dan Priel is to be believed, a good many doctrinal lawyers will be horrified.[164] But some comparatists may be more sympathetic.[165] However, the way

[162] Ibid., p. 25.

[163] Ibid., p. 26.

[164] D. Priel, "Two Forms of Formalism", in A. Roberstson and J. Goudkamp (eds.), *Form and Substance in the Law of Obligations* (2019), p. 165.

[165] J. Husa, *Interdisciplinary Comparative Law: Rubbing Shoulders with the Neighbours*

to test the relevance of the schemes and programs identified in the discussions so far is to take each one (if not all of them) and to examine the scheme, programme or approach in relation to law and in particular to comparative law. Do they provide insights?

1. Positivism. One might start with positivism, for if there is one term that is shared by law with other disciplines it is "positivism". However the term does not mean the same thing in law as it does in the social sciences; in the latter it expresses a desire to pose social problems as scientific ones and thus subject to rigorous procedures taking their inspiration from methods in the natural sciences.[166] Its central scheme of intelligibility is a causal one, that is to say, the emphasis is on the cause of a phenomenon and the procedures for testing whether a proposed causal assertion can be falsified.[167] It is equally a form of objectivism in that normative notions must not be confused with descriptive ones and judgments of value must be kept separate from judgments of fact.[168]

In law "legal positivism" has some of these characteristics. It developed historically as a theory in opposition to natural law, the fundamental assumption of the latter being founded on the idea that there was a dualism in the realm of law.[169] This dualism was expressed, at least from the twelfth century onwards, by the terms *ius positivum* and *ius naturale*; there was the positive law of each community and there was a natural law that was common to all mankind (*Omne enim ius aut naturale aut positivum*).[170] In the nineteenth century positivism acquired the more scientific meaning of something essentially objective.[171] "There was", Walter Jones said, "no room in a positivist philosophy for ideals, except to the extent that they received concrete embodiment in rules actually in force". Moreover "law must be free from contradictions and complete in itself" and since "a monistic philosophy can recognize

or Standing Alone in a Crowd (2022).

166 Herman, note 33 above, pp. 9-10.

167 Ibid., pp. 23-24.

168 Ibid., p. 25.

169 J. W. Jones, *Historical Introduction to the Theory of Law* (1940), p. 205.

170 S. Kuttner, "Sur Les Origines du Terme 'Droit Positif'", *Revue Historique de Droit Français et Étranger*, XV (1936), p. 731.

171 Jones, note 169 above, p. 205.

no sources of law which are not rules of law, there can be no gaps in the law".[172]

Such a theory is a way of conceiving law as an abstract concept and as such it is not actually a methodological scheme of engaging with a legal text. What, then, are the schemes or *grilles de lecture* that a positivist comparative lawyer might employ when engaging with foreign law? The scheme usually associated with positivism in the social sciences is, as already mentioned, a causal one. Such a scheme has been employed to suggest that common law systems are economically more efficient than civil law ones. This thesis has been described as "legal origins" (LO) theory and has, as one might imagine, attracted a huge literature.[173] In fairness there is more, methodologically speaking, to this theory than a mere causal relationship, but in essence the underlying scheme is that there is a causal connection between economic outcomes and legal traditions. Establishing a quantitative link between law and economic outcomes helps endow comparative law with the status of scientificity.[174] It is all about the investigation of causal relationships among phenomena.[175] However, as Jaakko Husa pointed out, this whole causal thesis has been put into question as a result of China's undoubted economic success, which seems to have occurred without the help of the Western style of law.[176]

Associated, at least to some extent, with a causal link between law and outcome is the functional method. This has been, and remains, a central scheme of engagement in comparative law. It has the effect, also, of affirming a positivist view of law in that to talk in terms of something having a function is to imply that there exists, ontologically speaking, a "thing" (law) separate from its "function", the latter being located outside or beyond the concept of law itself. This way of thinking may or may not be of value to the comparatist, but it is not without value generally in that cause and function are key elements in the minds of lawmakers. Politicians may hope to tackle particular social problems through the drafting

[172] Ibid., p. 206.

[173] See generally S. Glanert, A. Mercescu, and G. Samuel, *Rethinking Comparative Law* (2021), pp. 250-275.

[174] Ibid., p. 254.

[175] Ibid.

[176] J. Husa, *An Introduction to Comparative Law* (2d ed.; 2023), pp. 170-171.

of laws, and the mind-set of those charged with actually drafting the particular laws is likely to be one where legal positivism, cause, and function is dominant. The same mind-set may be found among comparative lawyers engaged in formulating transnational codes and other harmonization projects.

Nevertheless, the link between positivism and functionalism in comparative law is not necessarily inevitable. In one of the most impressive essays ever written on comparative law,[177] Otto Kahn-Freund (1900-1979) saw an important separation between the two notions. Positivism, he said "is a utopia". For "the positivist theory fails to yield a practical guidance to the judge, to the advocate, to the administrator".[178] Yet, he continued, it cannot be ignored. "Every legal system", he said, "requires an element of ideological unity", and however "much one may be aware that the application of the legal norm is, in many cases, a policy-making process one cannot dispense with a principle which links one decision with another, which raises the judicial act beyond the level of the realm of sheer expediency".[179] In short, positivism in law is a fiction.[180]

2. Functionalism. As for functionalism itself, this is another term shared by all the social science disciplines, including law. Much has been written on this scheme of intelligibility and its role in comparative law,[181] and so rather than repeat what has been said elsewhere it might be more useful to return to Kahn-Freund's essay. Writing well over seventy years ago, this comparatist said that to "repeat the arguments which have been advanced in favour of a functional approach to law itself would be equivalent to kicking at a door that is already open".[182] He then proceeded to undertake a functional comparative analysis of the institutions of private law – ownership, sale, marriage and so on – in the German model, as expressed in Karl Renner's work, and in the common law, his

177 An essay often completely ignored by those supposedly writing histories of comparative law.

178 O. Kahn-Freund, "Introduction", in K. Renner, *The Institutions of Private Law and their Social Functions* (1949; reprint 1976), p. 8.

179 Ibid., pp. 8-9.

180 Ibid., pp. 9-10.

181 For an overview see G. Samuel, *An Introduction to Comparative Law Theory and Method* (2014), pp. 65-78.

182 Kahn-Freund, note 178 above, p. 8.

overall question being this. Given a set of legal institutions, how can they change their functions without changing their norms?[183] Function here is the economic substratum and the empirical interests that drive change in this substratum while leaving the forms of law unchanged. "This development", said Kahn-Freund, "can be summarised as the functional transformation of the untransformed norm".[184]

Kahn-Freund then illustrates how the common law differs from the civil law. It is, *inter alia,* in its ability, through the concept of the trust, to do things that the civil law cannot do: "it can separate the power to protect the thing against the outside world from the right to have its economic benefit".[185] In the civil law, in contrast, the right to enjoy "economic property" can be achieved only by resorting to fictitious legal constructions which recognize economic function while preserving the form of ownership and "property".[186] Functionalism, in other words, helps explain why there is no real need in the common law to have a defined "law of property" or a defined "ownership", for functional "economic ownership" can be achieved through a range of other rights not necessarily falling within categories such as "property".[187] Of course, those jurists who reject interdisciplinarity – economic functionalism and the like – might want to focus only on the formal rules and norms. Be that as it may. But the importance of functionalism in the kind of reading undertaken by Kahn-Freund is that it provides a particular kind of knowledge that other schemes of engagement might fail to expose.

This macro approach – grand reading one might say – is just one way in which functionalism can be employed in comparative law. More often it is associated with closer readings which focus either on a particular concept or rule – does for example English law have the notion of a "natural obligation" or "abuse of rights"? – or on some specific factual situation – how do different systems deal with traffic accidents or exploding washing machines? Sometimes

183 Ibid., p. 16.

184 Ibid., p. 6.

185 Ibid., p. 22.

186 Ibid.

187 Ibid., p. 23.

this latter exercise is carried out through the comparison of cases.[188] In these situations, if there is no obvious equivalent, one looks for the function that a rule or concept has in the home system and then asks how such a function is legally achieved in the foreign system (or vice versa). This is not, it must be said, any kind of sophisticated functional scheme of engagement. "Functionalism in comparative law", writes Husa, "is heavily tailored so that it has been rendered understandable for legal scholars without research methods skills in non-legal fields of knowledge".[189] Indeed Husa does not consider functionalism in comparative is even a method; it is, for him, "a legal theoretical metaphor".[190]

3. Structuralism. Husa also points out that functionalism "is closely related to its rival structuralism",[191] a point reflected in Herman's chapter on functionalism which is entitled "structuro-functionalism". Yet structuralism is less visible as a method of engagement in comparative law when compared to functionalism. It is not mentioned, for example, either by Zweigert and Kötz in their well-known textbook nor by Balázs Fekete in his paradigm history of comparative law.[192] This is no doubt in part due to the sorry state of comparative law scholarship when it comes either to social science epistemology or to a serious investigation of comparative law writing in the modern history of the common law. Nevertheless, structuralism as a scheme of engagement is hiding in plain sight. For a start one only needs to return to Kahn-Freund's long introductory essay to Renner where he compares the highly structured conceptual model of property law in the German model to the diffusely structured "seamless web" of the common law.[193]

188 B. Markesinis, "Comparative Law – A Subject in Search of an Audience", *Modern Law Review*, LIII (1990), p. 1.

189 Husa, note 165 above, p. 169.

190 Ibid., p. 167.

191 Ibid., p. 153.

192 K. Zweigert and H, Kötz, *An Introduction to Comparative Law*, transl. Tony Weir (3rd ed., 1998); B. Fekete, *Paradigms in Modern European Comparative Law* (2021).

193 On which see F. H. Lawson, "Comparative Conclusions", *International Encyclopedia of Comparative Law*, VI (Property and Trusts), Chapter 2 (Structural Variations in Property Law), Part VIII (J. C. B. Mohr) (completed 1973), para. 274.

But structure there is in English land law, and such a "structural analysis is of general interest".[194]

This structural point regarding English property law was also reflected in Frederick Lawson's comparative contribution to the *International Encyclopedia of Comparative Law*.[195] "The more coherent a conceptual system is", wrote Lawson, "the easier it is to understand and explain its contents once one has been properly educated in it, but the more difficult it is to understand another coherent system built on different lines".[196] In fact, said Lawson, a civil lawyer looking at the common law of property would "be well advised to put out of his mind for the time being all that he has learnt about his own system and start afresh".[197] In other words, conceptual structure matters if one is to understand aspects of foreign law. Even at a more general level – a grand reading one might say – questions of taxonomy turn out to be fundamental for the comparatist. Thus "[n]ot only the general development of the various legal systems, but also their actual contents are greatly influenced by classification and the attitudes that lawyers take towards it".[198] Classification in the civil law is a matter of logical importance, whereas in the common law it is "essentially a matter of convenience for the writers of law books, whose freedom is not seriously constrained by logical, though unpractical distinctions".[199] Attempts have been made to change this structural situation and to impose the "map" of Gaius' *Institutes* on the common law.[200] But the structural history of the common law indicates that this is probably a doomed exercise.[201]

194 Kahn-Freund, note 178 above, p. 35.

195 Lawson, "Common Law", note 193 above, Part II (J. C. B. Mohr) (completed 1972).

196 Ibid., para. 24.

197 Ibid.

198 Ibid.

199 Ibid.

200 See, for example, Birks, "Definition and Division: A Meditation on Institutes 3.13", in Birks (ed.), *The Classification of Obligations* (1997), p. 1.

201 J. Hackney, "More than a Trace of the Old Philosophy", in Birks, note 200 above, p. 123.

This is not to say that the Gaian map is not of importance to comparatists. Alan Watson (1933-2018) argued that it was Justinian's *Institutes,* which was based on the plan employed by Gaius, which facilitated with ease the transplanting of Roman law into Europe from the eleventh century onwards.[202] In other words, it was the structure that mattered. "Its structure", wrote Watson, "and the structure of no other law book, allowed the beginner to learn law easily".[203] Moreover, Watson argued, it was this structure that permitted Roman law to be so easily absorbed into later Europe, for "without the *Institutes,* the Reception would have been incomparably more difficult, hence much slower, and it would have occurred in a very different way".[204] Watson may have been right or wrong in this thesis, but its substance is not what is in issue here. His method of engagement is important. Right or wrong, this Watson contribution is a work of comparative legal history, and his method of engagement should be of interest. In fact, Watson went further and argued that even at a lower level of abstraction structure mattered. "Roman law", he said, "as it appears in the sources, divides naturally into self-contained and self-referential blocks" and what got transmitted to later Europe "has often been of individual blocks, not Roman law itself".[205] Watson's thesis was taken up by Gunther Teubner, who saw in this "structural phenomenon" the ability for "legal rules to take on a 'life of their own'".[206] Law is a self-referencing system in that what has been said "about legal structures (legal norms) applies equally to other components of the legal system (elements, processes, boundaries, and so on)".[207] Structures, in other words, are capable of their internal evolution; and a "theory of legal evolution will be able to explain or even predict general structures of the law" even if it will

202 Alan Watson, "The Importance of 'Nutshells'", *American Journal of Comparative Law,* XLII (1994), p. 1.

203 Ibid., p. 5.

204 Ibid., p. 10.

205 Watson, *The Making of the Civil Law* (1981), p. 15.

206 G. Teubner, *Law as an Autopoietic System,* transl. A. Bankowska and R. Adler (1993), p. 40.

207 Ibid., p. 41.

not "be able to explain individual legal acts, court verdicts, laws, and administrative acts".[208]

4. Hermeneutics. Watson did not emerge unscathed. His structural thesis, as Teubner notes, led to him to casting a skeptical eye on the relationship between law and society. "In what sense", asked Watson, "does Gaius' *Institutes* reflect the society of pagan Rome and with some modifications Christian Byzantium?"[209] The whole idea that law is a structural system independent of social conditions and capable of its own internal evolution in effect suggests that it is a science that transcends different cultures. There are, no doubt, comparatists sympathetic to this idea, but, equally, a hermeneutical engagement with legal texts – particularly one embedded within a cultural paradigm – is capable of offering a very different view of legal knowledge.

Pierre Legrand is probably the leading comparatist advocating a deep hermeneutical engagement with foreign law texts. He does not consider this hermeneutical engagement as simply a method because *"la culture n'est pas soluble dans la méthode"*.[210] One has to disassociate a hermeneutic engagement from some kind of methodological one;[211] it is a matter of thinking in terms of a *pensée diagnostique*.[212] Moreover, this hermeneutical engagement with a foreign legal text is a linguistic exercise because comparison itself is a language experience; and, since language is a cultural phenomenon, it must itself intersect with all the other cultural phenomena such as tradition and institutionalization.[213] In short, comparison is a cultural engagement and only a cultural engagement. And because engagement with a foreign text is a cultural engagement with the language in which the text is written there can be no legal text that transcends particular languages and texts. There can be no "cultureless" law because law itself is a product of culture. It follows, accordingly, that the notion of a "legal transplant" – the lifting of a rule, concept, or structure from one

[208] Ibid., p. 49.

[209] Watson, note 202 above, p. 21.

[210] P. Legrand, *Le droit comparé* (5th ed, ; 2015), p. 58.

[211] Ibid., p. 59.

[212] Ibid., p. 61.

[213] Ibid., p. 54.

legal system and the implanting of it into another – is a false image since the rule, concept, or structure "must transform itself along the merry way" and thus is not the same thing when implanted in the other.[214] Watson's thesis is, from this hermeneutical and cultural paradigm viewpoint, untenable. Not all comparatists, even those with a sympathy for legal culture, accept this Legrand thesis. Yet, whatever one's view, the point to be made is that Legrand is offering a rich, even if controversial, hermeneutical philosophy (a term he prefers to method).

There are weaker forms of hermeneutical engagement. Each time a comparatist looks at a foreign law text (*signans*) and asks what does this or that word mean, the comparatist is involved in an interpretation exercise where she is searching for the *signatum*. Works on Roman law are full of statements telling the reader what this or that word or phrase means or does not mean, and the whole notion of interpretation in law has attracted a vast literature over the centuries. *Diffinitio vero proprie sumpta est que rei substatia per essentialia explicat*, wrote Pietro Gammero (1480-1528).[215] One is searching beyond the word itself (*verbum*, the *signans*) to its substance and essence (*signatum*). Such comparative exercises can be trite, but they can also be doctrinally sophisticated. There is work, for example, on comparative property law which indicates that many terms that seem to present one set of meanings on examination turn out to have rather different and often more complex senses.[216] Such work can involve a functional orientation, yet there is equally a hermeneutical engagement in that one is asking what do terms such as "ownership", "fee simple", or "possession" actually mean. How should the comparatist understand such expressions in their actual substantial and essential sense? No doubt the level at which such "understanding" is to operate – doctrinal, economic, cultural or whatever? – depends upon the epistemological expectation of

214 Legrand, *Negative Comparative Law: A Strong Programme for Weak Thought* (2022), p. 302.

215 P. A. Gammero, *Legalis dialectica in qua de modo argumentandi et locis argumentorum* (1522), Book I, § De loco Diffinitione.

216 See, for example, M. Graziadei, "The Structure of Property Ownership and the Common Law/Civil Law Divide", in M. Graziadei and L. Smith (eds.), *Comparative Property Law: Global Perspectives* (2017), p. 71.

the comparatist; that is one reason why one can talk, as one has done with functionalism, about different degrees of sophistication.[217]

Another domain where a weak hermeneutical approach is to be found is the interpretation of statutes and other legal texts such as wills and contracts. In describing such hermeneutical interpretation as "weak", one is not being dismissive of an exercise that is both technically difficult and well covered in the legal literature. It is "weak" in the sense that one does not find the judges or doctrinal lawyers quoting philosophers like Gadamer or Derrida when undertaking an exercise in, or writing about, textual interpretation in law. Interpretation is central to law because much legal analysis involves the interpretation of texts. Here the approach is usually an emphasis on one of the long-standing focal points of interpretation in law.[218] Does one focus on the words (*verba*), the intention of the author of the text (*mens legislatoris* in the case of statutory interpretation), or the rationality and coherence of the text (*ratio legis*)?[219] Often, however, other schemes are brought into play in order to aid the hermeneutical exercise. One might employ a dialectical contrast to limit the scope of a word (an "ingress of water" is not a "flood"), a functional approach (what is this statute intended to achieve?) or a structural analogy (does the structural pattern within the text match the pattern within the facts)? Sometimes a judge can actually be quite specific about the scheme of intelligibility brought into play:

> ... The trend in the cases, as I see them, is to shift the focus, or the emphasis, from structure and components to function and appearance — what a family does rather than what it is, or, putting it another way, a family is what a family does. I see this as a functionalist approach to construction as opposed to a formalist approach.[220]

However, as noted, it is rare to find in legal interpretation cases any references to serious hermeneutical specialists, other than occasional citations from a legal philosopher such as Herbert

[217] Legrand, note 214 above, p. 288.

[218] On which see I. Maclean, *Interpretation and Meaning in the Renaissance* (1992).

[219] Samuel, *Rethinking Historical Jurisprudence* (2022), pp. 115-118.

[220] Ward LJ (dissenting) in *Fitzpatrick v Sterling Housing Association Ltd* [1998] Ch 304, p 337.

Hart or Ronald Dworkin. Indeed, if a judge were to quote from a philosopher of hermeneutics, it could well be in the following manner:

> The appellant's grounds of appeal are set out in three and a half pages of lucid and articulate reasoning, as might be expected of someone who, at the time, was in the final throes of a masters degree in philosophy (though as it was in Paris that he studied I might reasonably have expected something a little more impenetrably post-structuralist in the manner of, say, Derrida, but fortunately not).[221]

5. Reception theory. One particular aspect of hermeneutics also of relevance to comparative law is the role of the reader of a text. As has been seen with Bordwell's work on film interpretation, there is a thesis which emphasizes the role of the reader in that meaning is not found in the text but made by the reader or (in the case of film) the viewer. On this point it might be valuable to return to the work of Pierre Legrand. This comparatist, in the course of explaining his hermeneutical and cultural philosophy, draws an analogy with painting. He takes as his example a canvas by Jacques-Louis David, namely *Le Serment des Horaces* (1784), and asks why are the characters dressed in a certain way and not in another way and goes on to pose a number of other questions about the image. The point he makes is that these are cultural traits and that these traits are "in" the painting. A legal text is similar; it has cultural elements embedded in the text itself just as a painting does.[222] Bordwell, reading this passage, might well pose the question whether these traits are actually "in" the painting: might they not be "in" the mind of the viewer who is reflecting them back into the image? Is not the viewer, rather than the canvas, constructing the interpretation?

Legrand does seem to agree that there is a certain constructive exercise on the part of the reader of a legal text in that each jurist who interprets will bring his or her own cultural mentality to bear on the text. As Legrand himself says, "the comparatist is drawing the traces out of the text" and "he does so as an encultured

[221] Judgement in Newton v Revenue & Customs [2017] UKFTT 874 First-Tier Tribunal (Tax Chamber) Case TC/2015/00517 at para 18.

[222] Ibid., pp. 297-298.

being."[223] The point is developed by this author in arguing that it is a matter of negotiation between the *intellectus* and the *res*, for there "is certainly no such dynamic as a 'subject' here and an 'object' there". Instead "it is about two enculturations – the comparatist's and the foreign law's – effectively entering into a negotiation with a view to meaning-making".[224] This view also explains why, for Legrand, there is no such thing as a genuinely transnational or global law. There may be texts purporting such a status, but each jurist engaging with the text will bring their own cultural interpretative framework into play, thus ensuring that each interpretation will be localized. Recalling that, for Legrand, law is embedded in language and that there no such thing as a "universal" language, it must follow that for example Japanese, German, French, Iranian, and English lawyers will read the text differently. It is a matter of "glocalisation".[225]

6. Individualist (actional) reading. If the role of the reader of a law text is fundamental to the interpretation of the text, what kind of ontological engagement will such a reader bring to this interpretation? Margaret Thatcher (1925-2013) once said that there was no such thing as society, only individual men, women, and families.[226] A French reader, in contrast, may well see society existing as an entity. What of the law reader? Legrand would no doubt see this difference as cultural, yet what of law itself? Is there an ontological "culture" that attaches to, for example, Roman law? When one looks at Roman law the ontological position is ambiguous. The institutional system which forms the basis of Gaius' *Institutes* suggests a kind of structural holism, but this system appears to be based upon relations between individual persons and individual things. There are of course discussions about collectivities (*universitates*) being separate from the individuals that form the group and once such a group – a town for example – could bring and defend actions one is moving from the individual actor towards more corporate thinking.[227] However, the *universitas* seems to be based on the idea that it is to

[223] Ibid., p. 296.

[224] Ibid.

[225] Legrand, note 210 above, pp. 84-90.

[226] M. Thatcher, "Interview", *Women's Own*, 31 October 1987.

[227] See generally P. Duff, *Personality in Roman Private Law* (1938).

be regarded "as if" it is a person. Much depends upon the area of law in issue. Criminal law places the emphasis on the individual actor but other areas of the law such as contract and tort (delict), while appearing individualist, actually involve for the most past commercial corporations. The fiction of individualism is, however, maintained by the law assuming that a corporation is simply an individual.

This distinction between individualist and collectivist approaches is highly relevant for the comparatist. For example, the Professor Tony Jolowicz (1926-2012) in his discussion of an English case involving the question of whether the police were to be liable for the destruction of the claimant's shop made the point that had the same facts occurred in France the claimant would not have had to allege and prove fault.[228] The French public law principle of equality of burdens would have ensured that the owner would be compensated as a matter of strict liability.[229] In other words French administrative law is ontologically orientated towards a holistic view of society, whereas English tort law is more individualistic. The police were to be treated as an individual "person" and thus to be liable only if they had been at fault. One key notion helpful for the comparatist is that of an "interest". Interests can attach to the individual, to the family, to a defined corporate person, to a collective class such as the consumer, to the State itself or, more loosely, to fragmented groups.[230] The liability of the State in French administrative law is of obvious benefit to an individual's interest, but there is also in play the public interest, which insists that a burden must be carried by society as a whole in certain circumstances where an individual has suffered injury as a result of an act that was undertaken for the public benefit.

Another example of an individualist, or agent, approach in comparative law is when the comparison focuses on individual players such as particular judges or, to give another example, particular members of legal institutions such as the jury or law faculty. John Bell's study of the judiciary in a comparative context

[228] *Rigby* v *Chief Constable of Northamptonshire* [1985] 1 WLR 1242.

[229] John Anthony Jolowicz, "Public Interest and Private Damage", *Cambridge Law Journal* [1985], p. 370.

[230] Jolowicz, "Protection of Diffuse, Fragmented and Collective Interests in Civil Litigation: English Law", *Cambridge Law Journal* [1983], p. 222; see also Samuel, *Rethinking Legal Reasoning* (2018), pp. 285-328.

largely takes as its ontological basis the judiciary as an institution, but, as he indicates, one really has to start with "the experience of the individual *judge*".[231] John Cairns in his history of the development of comparative law in Great Britain has a section on individual "pioneers", and even when he discusses more general topics he generally focuses on individuals and their contributions.[232]

Rights are another domain of interest to comparative lawyers. The notion of a "right" is one that attaches to the individual actor, often in conflict with the power of the collective. There exists a large body of literature on the individual and the State, but the whole issue is one where law soon merges with political theory and ideology. Social contractarianism finds itself in conflict with corporate theories emphasizing the State or nation. As Jones observed all those years ago, Roman law came under attack by fascists because "its strongly marked individualism makes it an easy butt to those who believe that the State or the Nation is everything and the individual nothing".[233] The Nazis even indulged in some crude comparative law in lauding English law "for having successfully defied all attempts to confine it within the strait-jacket of Roman abstraction".[234] This latter point was developed by Jones in a footnote where he quotes a German author who finds that England is a *Führerstaat*. There is "a realism and a fusion of legal and political thought, which, together with the absence of a written constitution and of 'constitutional constructions', bring it in his view in line with the present German régime".[235] It is true that English law has not developed any sophisticated notion of *le droit subjectif*,[236] and, at present, there are some in government who would like the United Kingdom to withdraw from the 1950 European Convention of Human Rights and Fundamental

[231] J. Bell, *Judiciaries within Europe: A Comparative Review* (2006), p. 3.

[232] J. Cairns, "Development of Comparative Law in Great Britain", in M. Reimann and R. Zimmermann (eds.), *The Oxford Handbook of Comparative Law* (2d ed.; 2019), p. 111.

[233] Jones, note 169 above, pp. 294-295.

[234] Ibid., p. 295.

[235] Ibid., p. 295, footnote 3, quoting O. Koellreutter, *Deutsches Verfassungsrecht* (1938).

[236] Samuel, "'Le Droit Subjectif' and English Law", *Cambridge Law Journal* [1987], p. 264.

Freedoms. Yet the idea that England is a *Führerstaat* is an interesting thesis, perhaps still of some relevance today.

7. Dialectics. Returning to the notion of an interest, it is possible to envisage law as a question of conflicting interests. Litigation decisions, in other words, are a matter of settling dialectical conflicts between two competing interests. As a scheme of intelligibility employed by lawyers, dialectics has a long history stretching back to the Roman texts themselves where legal reasoning can be seen on occasions to involve an either/or analysis.[237] This method was developed during the medieval period of Roman law, in particular to solve apparent contradictions in the Roman texts. The whole legal process remains founded on the idea of a dialectical court procedure where the principle *audi alteram partem* is fundamental in Europe.[238]

In comparative law a form of dialectical analysis can be detected in the idea that comparison in law involves the search for 'better solutions'. According to Zweigert and Kötz, after a comparatist has done his research, he must proceed to a critical evaluation which will involve the search for a legal solution that "is clearly superior to all others".[239] No doubt this equally involves a functional engagement as the "better" must be judged against something more than what is set out in the legal texts themselves.[240] Ralf Michaels makes the point that the "sociologist cannot deduce an 'ought' from an 'is'; comparative law material gives no guidelines; even commonality has no independent normative force".[241] In short, Michaels argues that functionalism provides a poor guide to "better solutions". Perhaps a better guide is, again, to examine the interests in play. Is, for example, a liability without fault regime for personal injury arising out of traffic accidents (France) "better" than one based upon proving fault (United Kingdom)? Much depends upon whether you are viewing it from the position of an

[237] See, for example, D.9.2.52.2; D.41.1.55. See generally Samuel, *Rethinking Historical Jurisprudence* (2022), pp. 53-54, 72-74.

[238] See, for example, the principle of contradiction in French law: Article 16, *Code de Procédure Civile.*

[239] Zweigert and Kötz, note 192 above, pp. 46-47.

[240] Michaels, "The Functional Method of Comparative Law", in Reimann and Zimmermann, note 232 above, p. 379.

[241] Ibid., p. 380.

insurance company, or a firm of solicitors specialising in personal injury cases, or a victim.

At a more general level one might ask whether comparative law itself is a discipline founded upon internal dialectical tensions. There are debates about functionalism versus hermeneutics (as we have seen), about a presumption of similarity versus a presumption of difference, about internal versus external perspectives, about genealogical versus analogical comparison, science (nature) versus culture and so on.[242] These tensions have proved problematic for those comparatists keen to develop a unifying theory of comparative law. According to Valcke, "the malaise of comparative law, if any, boils down to a bifurcation overload".[243] And so what is needed is "some kind of synthesis".[244] Valcke proposes that this synthesis will involve a sort of dialectical process between facts and ideals which will ultimately result in drawing together all the various dichotomies in that it would "allow comparatists to embrace both sides of, and hence move beyond, the traditional dichotomies that have long divided them".[245] The way that this is to be achieved is to employ different methodological schemes in an overall comparative framework, moving for example from functionalist analysis to a hermeneutical one. Then it "will involve dialectically relating the functionalist (what legal actors *in fact do*) and expressivist (what they *say* they do) manifestations of the law in question".[246] Thus comparison is about relating facts to ideals and vice-versa permitting the comparatist to gauge "the extent to which each system has in fact lived up to its own, peculiar ideas".[247] It is, she says, rather like a dog context where one dog is declared "best dog" despite the contestants being of different breeds. The key is "dog-ness", for it "provides a perfectly valid *tertium comparationis* for comparing fox terriers and poodles despite there being no single dog-ness metric running across them both".[248] It

[242] Samuel, note 181 above, pp. 173-179.

[243] Valcke, note 152 above, p. 6.

[244] Ibid., p. 7.

[245] Ibid., p. 217.

[246] Ibid., p. 216 (emphasis in original).

[247] Ibid., p. 217.

[248] Ibid., p. 214.

is a matter of proportional comparison in that each legal system "is then assessed as against *the peculiar set of collective commitments it has (internally) set for itself*".[249] Unity is achieved via this *tertium comparationis*. It is not evident that this "best dog" – that is to say, "best legal system" – thesis will convince all those advocating a hermeneutical and cultural approach since system ranking is not what some (many?) comparatists think is an appropriate activity.[250] But Valcke would argue that it is possible to assess a system in terms of its own declared ideals and the extent that it lives up to them. In other words, there is a dialectical engagement in play, that between declared ideal and factual reality, which can be used as a unifying framework.

8. Style. Turning from schemes associated with both social science and humanities epistemology to approaches that are largely those to be found in the humanities, one is tempted to think that these schemes would be of much less relevance to comparative law. Yet this is not true of style, or indeed of some of the other "theoretical" issues that are associated with style such as genre, grand reading. and close reading. At the level of grand reading – macro-comparison – Zweigert and Kötz argue that in their "view the critical thing about legal systems is their *style*, for the styles of individual legal systems and groups of legal systems are each quite distinctive". And so what the comparatist must do is to "strive to grasp these *legal styles*, and to use distinctive stylistic traits as a basis for putting legal systems into groups".[251]

This style manifests itself in a number of ways: the historical background of a legal system; its mode of thought; its distinctive institutions; its legal sources; and its ideology.[252] Comparing continental legal systems with common law ones, Zweigert and Kötz claim that a difference of style is particularly evident in the modes of thinking:

> On the Continent lawyers think abstractly, in terms of institutions; in England concretely, in terms of cases, the relationship of the parties, 'rights and duties'. On the

[249] Ibid., p. 215 (emphasis in original).

[250] See, for example, Legrand, note 214 above, p. 116, footnote 29.

[251] Zweigert and Kötz, note 192 above, p. 67 (emphasis in original).

[252] Ibid., p. 68.

> Continent, the system is conceived as being complete and free from gaps, in England lawyers feel their way gradually from case to case. On the Continent lawyers delight in systematics, in England they are sceptical of every generalization. On the Continent lawyers operate with ideas, which often, dangerously enough, take on a life of their own; in England they think in pictures; and so one could continue.[253]

Such a grand reading is reminiscent of genre theory in cinema studies: one is grouping legal systems, just as one groups movies, into generic categories supposedly complete as between themselves and accounting for all the world's legal systems. Yet such groupings, as in film studies, are not problem-free and might well fail to give expression to tensions and cross-currents that are not confined to the generic groupings.

There is also the danger of exclusion in that the generic categories themselves are founded upon a theory about what amounts to "law". What if a normative regime does not fulfill the conditions asserted in the various theories of law to qualify as "law"? Valcke, for example, stipulates a set of conditions, although in fairness they are open-ended in their scope.[254] Nevertheless, she argues that comparative law is about comparing laws and if a regime does not qualify as "law" then comparison, for her, is not meaningful because you cannot compare law with non-law.[255] There is certainly a logic to this argument, but the danger is that the notion used to identify law is of Western origin with the result that "there is a long tradition of Western scholarship on East Asia that tends to associate the latter, negatively, with a relative *absence* of law – or, as two contemporary comparatists put it, with 'a dim view of law'".[256] This can lead to what Teemu Ruskola has labelled "legal orientalism".[257] In fact this is a problem – that is to say,

[253] Ibid., p. 69.

[254] Valcke, note 152 above, pp. 18-59.

[255] Ibid., pp. 66-70.

[256] T. Ruskola, "The East Asian Legal Tradition", in M. Bussani and H. Mattei (eds.), *The Cambridge Companion to Comparative Law* (2012), p. 261 (emphasis in original and footnotes omitted). The two comparatists referred to by Ruskola are Zweigert and Kötz: see note 192 above, p. 287.

[257] Ruskola, *Legal Orientalism: China, the United States, and Modern Law* (2013).

orientalism is a problem – encountered in cinema studies and it popular literature as well.[258]

Style can equally be of relevance in closer readings in comparative legal studies. Using the metaphor of a "portrait", Mitchel Lasser offers us two "portraits" of French law, one official and one unofficial.[259] In the official portrait, the role of the judges is to apply in a syllogistic manner the rules of the French *Code civil* (and other pieces of legislation) and thus:

> The decisions are famously short: those of the Cour de cassation (the French supreme court in private and criminal law matters), for example, tend to run to less than a single typed page. The decisions also lack any serious description of the facts, almost never refer to past judicial decisions, and contain absolutely nothing that could be described as serious interpretive or policy analysis. Finally, the decisions are rendered by the entire court as a single unit, without concurrences or dissents.[260]

There have been some changes since Lasser's description of a Cour de cassation judgement – they have become more detailed in that past decisions, for example, are cited[261] – but in general the official portrait remains largely as he described it. They are still set out in the form of a syllogism. Lasser goes on to look in detail at a French Cour de cassation decision: that is, he undertakes a close reading which illustrates in some detail the formal structure of the judgment. This official portrait conforms, in other words, to a very particular and very formalized style. But, as Lasser says, "it is quite hard to imagine how any legal system could function if its judiciary actually behaved in accordance with the official portrait of the judicial role".[262] Accordingly, he then goes on to describe an unofficial portrait which shows that behind the formalized style of the actual judgment there are the notes to cases written by law

[258] Frayling, *The Yellow Peril: Dr Fu Manchu & The Rise of Chinaphobia* (2014).

[259] M. Lasser, "Judicial (Self-)Portraits: Judicial Discourse in the French Legal System", *Yale Law Journal,* CIV (1995), p. 1325; Lasser, *Judicial Deliberations: A Comparative Analysis of Judicial Transparency and Legitimacy* (2004).

[260] Lasser, note 259 above (2004), pp. 30-31.

[261] Available online: Cour de cassation.

[262] Lasser, note 259 above (2004), p. 38.

professors (*la doctrine*) and the reports (*rapports, conclusions*) of the reporting judges and Advocate Generals in which the actual details of a case, together with discussions about precedents, doctrinal opinions, and policy issues, are set out in the kind of detail that one might find in a Supreme Court judgment in a common law system. Style, in short, has a particular formal role to play in French law.

Style also applies to the language employed in French law. As Zweigert and Kötz say, "the Code civil is a masterpiece from the point of view of style and language" and it "has often been praised for its clear and memorable phrases, and for the absence of cross-references and jargon". This is in contrast to the German civil code in which the language is "dry and dogmatic" and thus "very unattractive in comparison".[263] There are historical reasons for this difference. The humanist jurists interpreted the word *elegantia*, found in the Roman law texts, to mean, amongst other things, the ability to express law in a clear and accurate way. This was taken up by the French jurist François Hotman (1524-1590), who asserted that French law should be expressed in language that was both understandable (*simplicité*) by ordinary people and eloquent; it was a matter of *le style véritablement français*.[264] This particular French style does not mean that other legal traditions lack style, as indeed Zweigert and Kötz imply when they talk about the language of the German code. This whole question of legal style is closely interrelated to the cultural paradigm (and hermeneutics), as Donald Kelley indicates in his discussion of the Italian humanist jurist Lorenzo Valla (1407-1457). He noted that Valla "believed also that a cultural style embraced non-literary arts as painting, sculpture, and architecture".[265] Some comparative lawyers are perhaps reawakening the humanist spirit.

9. Genre. Associated with style, as we have seen, is the attempt to classify legal systems into families or traditions. This is analogous to efforts in film studies to class films into different genres. However, the Zweigert and Kötz use of style as the means of classification is not the only one on offer. René David employed ideology while law and economic theorists – particularly the Legal

[263] Zweigert and Kötz, note 192 above, p. 91.

[264] S. Geonget, "Prolégomènes à l'édition crtique de l'Antitribonian de François Hotman", in X. Prévost and L-A. Sanchi (eds.), *L'Humanisme juridique* (2022), p. 304.

[265] D. Kelley, *Foundations of Modern Historical Scholarship* (1970), p. 35.

Origins school – use economic efficiency.[266] Monateri argues that David's mapping "is of particular importance, and received great approval, because it succeeded in combining history, legal analysis, and policy considerations into a picture capturing the essence of the world order at the time".[267] Nevertheless, as Monateri goes on to say, the Germans were not happy with David's "genre" thesis and this led to the Zweigert and Kötz style approach. This newer taxonomy thus broke the family connection, based on Roman law, between France and Germany. As Monateri says, if "we emphasise [the style] element, the Romano-Germanic family must necessarily be split between two models".[268]

There are other possibilities besides these two. Legrand sees law as a product of culture and language and thus, by implication, he would seemingly divide up legal traditions into cultural blocks. Great care must be taken here because Legrand is rightly suspicious of this whole "genre" (not his word) approach on the basis that it is little more than legal tourism. "A digest of the world's laws", he writes, "appears to entice comparatists like pheromone draws bees, and it seems to have become an unassailable institutional fact of life in comparative law that one feels able and entitled to hold forth on any heliocentric law whatsoever irrespective of competence or expertise".[269] As for Monateri, he is suspicious of the whole idea that legal systems can be classified according to culture. "Culture", he says, "is a rather prescientific concept" which "is often used as a proxy for an unknown black box where differences are originated or dissolved". He asserts: the "fact that even today reasons for divergent legal systems based on culture still appeal to some only exhibits the poor evolution of the discipline".[270] The problem, one might argue, with the idea, implicit in Monateri's criticism, that comparatists should be working only with "scientific" concepts (and not "prescientific" ones) is equally problematic when one comes to examine the

[266] See generally P. G. Monateri, *An Advanced Introduction to Comparative Legal Methods* (2021), pp. 22-47.

[267] Ibid., p. 36. See also David, *Les grands systèmes de droit contemporains* (1964) (and subsequent editions).

[268] Ibid., p. 38.

[269] Legrand, note 214 above, p. 57, footnote 29.

[270] Monateri, note 266 above, p. 30.

kind of causal thesis underpinning the Legal Origins efficiency categorization. The notion that law – especially comparative law – is a "science" is surely problematic?[271] Nevertheless, Monateri sums up the situation with regard to "genre" (not his word) in comparative law and the foundations upon which it is based in the following way. He says that "style becomes a very fuzzy word with an imprecise contour and is almost equivalent to 'culture' or 'ideology' as slippery concepts adopted by other authors".[272] These words recall the kind of language Durgnat used regarding genre theory in cinema studies. Yet just because they are fuzzy does not mean that style or culture cannot be insightful themes, even if such themes are not "scientific". Certainly, in film studies, style has provided important analytical insights, as has been seen.

10. Ideology. Perhaps this notion of "ideology" deserves further investigation with respect to engagement with texts by comparatists. On this notion again a quote from Durgnat might be valuable. He observed that he did not "think that every film is political", but he did "think that every film is ideological".[273] One might say the same for law. Even if one believes that law and politics are separate – and it is not being asserted here that they are – it cannot be denied that law is ideological, as indeed René David thought with regard to his legal families. Here the difficulty is to distinguish between ideology and culture, always assuming that a distinction is possible. At the micro-level, when one compares, say, a set of facts which might be decided as giving rise to liability without fault in a French administrative law court with how one would have to prove fault if they arose in an English court, one is dealing with ideological difference if not actually political difference. Every legal utterance, rule, judgment or whatever will be ideological in one way or another because legal concepts and institutions like ownership, contract, fault and so on are themselves ideological. The difficulty for the comparatist is in trying not just to separate ideology from culture. There is equally the problem of trying to draw a line between ideology, epistemology and ontology and thus to avoid the kind of general assertions such as ownership "is one of the characteristic institutions of human society" and so

[271] See, for example, Legrand, note 214 above, pp. 56-57.

[272] Monateri, note 266 above, pp. 106-107.

[273] Durgnat, "Durgnat vs. Paul", *Film Comment*, XIV, no. 2 (1978), p 66. See also Aumont and Marie, note 89 above, pp. 21-23.

a "people to whom ownership was unknown ... would live in a world that is not our world".[274] It hardly needs to be pointed out that such people do in fact live in our world, although not perhaps in our ideological world. Such ownership comments take one close to the kind of thinking that Ruskola criticized; one is dealing with a regime that is "not law".

Different schemes of intelligibility might also reflect different ideologies. An emphasis on an individualist reading rather than a holistic one has ideological as well as ontological and epistemological implications. "There is no such thing as society' is hardly an ideologically free statement. This ideological aspect is reflected in rights-theory debates which pitches the individual against the State, often in turn merging with economic doctrines such as economic liberalism.[275] Here causal schemes, and no doubt structural ones as well, may enter into the debate. Is economic success a result of an individual's own enterprising capacities (rights theory and economic liberalism) or is such success determined by holistic social factors (determinism)? Questions like these are of importance to comparatists keen to rank, or at least assess, legal systems in relation to economic outputs. Or, put another way, what are the economic functional outcomes of legal systems that are individualist in their orientations (rights) as contrasted with those systems more holistic orientations? Perhaps, then, the comparatist needs to reflect on Eagleton's view of methodological pluralism. "The true reason why the pluralists are wishful thinkers", he says, "is that what is at issue in the contention between different literary theories or 'non-theories' are competing ideological strategies related to the very destiny of English studies in modern society". Eagleton is not talking about comparative law, but does not his comment, by way of analogy, apply just as much to comparative legal studies as it does to literary (and film) studies?

Another dimension of ideology is representation.[276] This is of particular relevance to film studies, where how characters

[274] A. M. Honoré, "Ownership", in A. Guest (ed.), *Oxford Essays in Jurisprudence* (1961), p. 107.

[275] A. Leroux and A. Marciano, *La philosophie économique* (1998), pp. 114-121. See also J. Cobbe, "Legal Singularity and the Reflexivity of Law", in S. Deakin and C. Markou (eds.), *Is Law Computable? Critical Perspectives on Law and Artificial Intelligence* (2020), p 125.

[276] See generally, for cinema, H. Bacon, "Representation", in E. Branigan and W.

are represented on screen can have – perhaps always have – an important ideological impact, whether conscious or unconscious in the mind of the viewer and maybe the authors of the film. One fundamental question, for example, is: how are women represented in the cinema?[277] As many feminist writers have asserted, the answer is often dispiriting to say the least, particularly in Hollywood films of the past. An identical question can be asked by jurists in respect of judgments: how are women represented in legal judgments in various courts of the world? One particularly dispiriting case from the English courts has been discussed elsewhere.[278] Similar questions can be asked about other categories of humans. How are Chinese people represented in Hollywood and British films such as *The Mask of Fu Manchu* (1932), *Terror of the Tongs* (1960) and *Dr No* (1962)? As various film writers have noted, again often in a negative manner.[279] How are they represented in judgments or doctrine? Again, according to Ruskola, not very positively.[280] As a "theory", representation possibly extends beyond these clear ideological aspects – how is law "represented" by the comparatist studying a foreign legal regime? – but it also embraces certain schemes of engagement, in particular, in film studies, hermeneutics since the image in a film is a sign to be interpreted. Thunderstorms can represent more than just the weather, whereas landscape or architecture can (as has been noted) equally provide indirect insights into the psychological state of a character.

11. Psychoanalysis. Hermeneutics blends into psychology one might say. Eagleton, it may be recalled, also considered psychoanalysis as one of the principal literary theories. Is this a scheme of engagement equally of relevance for the comparative lawyer? It was, for Walter Jones, an important legal theory category. "If we define psychology broadly as the study of men's mental processes", he wrote, "it is apparent that law lends itself to examination from various psychological angles".[281] This, he

Buckland (eds.), *The Routledge Encyclopedia of Film Theory* (2014), p. 402.

277 D. Pozo, "Feminist Film Theory: Core Concepts", in Branigan and Buckland. Ibid., p. 187.

278 See Samuel, *Rethinking Legal Reasoning* (2018), p. 276.

279 See in particular Frayling, note 258 above.

280 Ruskola, note 257 above.

281 Jones, note 169 above, p. 187.

went on to say, is because "law is purely a creature of the mind – something intellectual or ideal and not a perceptible or sensible phenomenon".[282] How, then, might a psychological engagement operate? Eagleton says that a psychoanalytical approach to literary criticism "can be broadly divided into four kinds, depending on what it takes as the object of attention".[283] These objects of attention are the author of the work, the contents of the work, the formal construction of the work, or the reader of the work.[284] These categories do not easily transplant themselves into the discipline of law or into comparative law, but two objects of attention that do stand out are the notion of a legal mentality and the idea of the comparatist as a reader.

Legal mentality is closely associated with the cultural paradigm, yet it evidently has a psychological dimension as well. The search for a legal mentality is a search for the cognitive structure of a particular legal system.[285] Whether this is actually a psychological matter is open to question; the factors that are said to make up the mentality seem just as much objective as subjective. They include the nature of legal reasoning, the role of systematisation, the character of rules, the role of facts and so on.[286] If there is a legal mentality in a psychological sense, this sense seems to attach as much to the society-as-culture as to the individual's mental state as such, although this societal mentality is implanted in the individual psychologies. But this is a holistic approach. In fact, the starting point of a psychological analysis, at least in social science thinking, is the individual because a psychological engagement is one that privileges the individual thinker as the source of production; the mentality of society results from the intentions, motives and thought structures of the individual agents (methodological individualism).[287] According to this thesis, a legal mentality is simply the sum of the mentalities of all the individual legal actors in any given culture. If this is the case, then, as Jones noted, it is the actions of all these legal actors that count;

[282] Ibid.

[283] Eagleton, note 49 above, p. 155.

[284] Ibid.

[285] Husa, note 176 above, p. 141.

[286] Fekete, note 192 above, pp. 142-143, footnote 20.

[287] Herman, note 33 above, pp. 49-50.

the "actions of all these public officials, it is said, are the outcome of peculiar mental processes, and to understand what is meant by law we must approach it through the minds of these officials".[288] The comparatist must become a psychologist. "The empirical core beneath such 'fictions' as legal rule, legal duty, legal right, is discovered by the psychologist in the conduct of individuals", said Jones, "which in these matters is a reflex of the anticipated action of an official".[289]

As for the comparatist herself, her engagement as reader of a foreign law text or institution is one of perception. Two particular issues are, first, the comparatist's own legal mentality and, second, the problem of perception itself. The first is a problem that is often associated with hermeneutics which brings into play two *grilles d'intepretation*: "the *grille* of the reader and the *grille* of the author".[290] In the social sciences, a psychoanalytical engagement sees the individual researcher constructing her own social world (*le rêve du chercheur*) rather as the literary critic constructs her own interpretation of a text; it is a kind of "psychoanalytical vision".[291] It is, says Herman, a subjective vision – *une notion psychologique mentaliste* – and not an epistemological category.[292] There is not the separation between subject and object necessary for a causal scheme of engagement nor is there the to-and-fro of a dialectical approach, for the researcher is reconstructing his intelligible world in the context of a particular socio-cultural setting where he himself is inserted.[293] Is the comparatist in an analogous position? When trying to understand the "other" in comparative law, can one ever escape one's own legal mentality – one's own cognitive structures? Can the comparatist ever escape from her own cultural and psychological context? Does she end up constructing, herself, the other? Legrand does not approach this question from a psychoanalytical perspective as such, but his conclusion regarding the comparatist is that while "he remains sensitive to the singularity of otherness and aware of the fact that he cannot

288 Jones, note 169 above, pp. 196-197.

289 Ibid., p. 197.

290 Herman, note 33 above, p. 57.

291 Ibid., p. 59.

292 Ibid., p. 61.

293 Ibid.

occupy the other's horizon on account of his own singularity", he "cannot therefore eschew a misunderstanding of the other".[294] The best one can do – for "one must resign oneself to one's cognitive limits" – is not to abdicate, but, following the advice of Samuel Beckett, to "fail better".[295]

The second problem, that of perception itself, is psychological to the extent that it is a general cognitive issue. The role of the comparatist, says Roberto Scarciglia, is to perceive "reality in its actuality with greater intensity". Yet this "form of perception is not always possible and often requires a long period of study, such as the input of plural contributions".[296] The author's point here is that perception underlies everything we think, we know and we believe, for the brain constructs the world.[297] Yet, as he goes on to show, perception is problematic because the brain has different ways of seeing, a point that he illustrates by reference to the duck-rabbit image, Necker cube, and other illusions. The brain, in other words, is capable of multiple interpretations.[298] This perception issue can be problematic when, for example, one views legal institutions as formal structures; as with the Necker cube, such formal structures can result in different cognitive patterns and thus different interpretations.[299] And divergences between perceptions means that two comparatists "can no longer use a common language", Scarciglia ends up reflecting the points made by Jones in his chapter on psychological theories. That is to say, he warns about the actions – the "cognitive illusions" – of individual legal actors, in particular judges, who make decisions based upon "an erroneous perception of reality", perhaps causing the comparatist to make errors as well.[300] One might add another problem. Might not certain legal theories, or epistemological assertions, if represented by visual schemes such as Hans Kelsen's

294 Legrand, note 214 above, p 18.

295 Ibid., p. 36.

296 R. Scarciglia, *Methods and Legal Comparison: Challenges for Methodological Pluralism* (2023), p. 65.

297 Ibid.

298 Ibid., p. 66.

299 Ibid., pp. 67-68.

300 Ibid., p. 76.

pyramid of norms have the effect of closing off alternative ways of visualising law? A constitutional law committed to a Kelsenian model makes any kind of pluralistic alternative difficult to envisage without a complete rejection of the model itself. In other words, it is a matter of cognitive patterns and perceptions. It is a matter of psychological imperialism.

12. Historical models. Kelsen's model is, or should be, of interest not just for its cognitive imperialism, but also for its ability seemingly to transcend history. Yet when one abandons a synchronic epistemological approach for a diachronic one, it becomes possible to see how such a model gradually took shape.[301] History may not be of itself a scheme of engagement – it is too wide-ranging – but it is an epistemological approach. It offers a means by which one can see how a synchronic model took shape so to speak.[302] But there is a downside – or perhaps one should say a danger – associated with historicism and that is that such historicism "is nearly always haunted by the spectre of evolutionism".[303]

Comparative lawyers will be aware of this problem since nineteenth century comparative law was, thanks to jurists such as Friedrich Carl von Savigny (1779-1861) and Henry Maine closely associated with legal evolution.[304] This is not to question Maine's importance in the history of comparative law studies nor of the broader value of his work, yet the problem with the nineteenth century theories of legal evolution was the underpinning notion of progression. As Peter Stein (1926-2016) concluded, the term legal evolution is associated with "a group of theories which claim to explain legal change not merely in historical terms but as proceeding according to certain determinate stages, or in a certain pre-determined manner".[305] It did not survive because the "idea of legal evolution appealed to conservative legal thinkers, perhaps to academic conservatives who liked to think of themselves as

[301] See, for example, O. Jouanjan, *Une histoire de la pensée juridique en Allemagne* (1800-1918) (2005).

[302] R. Blanché, *L'épistémologie* (3d ed.; 1983), pp. 36-39.

[303] A.-C. Taylor, Les modèles d'intelligibilité de l'histoire", in P. Descola, G. Lenclud, C. Severi, and A-C. Taylor, *Les idées de l'anthropologie* (2022), p. 258.

[304] See generally P. Stein, *Legal Evolution: The Story of an Idea* (1980).

[305] Ibid., p. 122.

progressive".[306] Moreover, it was closely associated with Roman law, even in the hands of English writers such as Maine, and by the nineteenth century such Roman law scholarship was associated with the image of science which, in the twentieth century, became "tarnished".[307] In particular it became tarnished for comparative lawyers, as Peter Stein explained:

> This distrust of the methods of traditional science has been accompanied by a rejection of general schemes designed to provide explanations of institutional change on a universal basis. We now concentrate more on the unique character of particular societies, on the factors which made certain societies change in one way and others in different ways. In view of the complexity of different cultures, it hardly seems feasible to try to explain the origin and development of the basic institutions of any private law system, independently of the social circumstances peculiar to particular societies.[308]

Grand historical models would seem, then, to have ceded to investigations that are cultural and local. This is to say that hermeneutical methods operating within a cultural studies programme have replaced the scientific progression paradigm that was dialectical and structural in its schemes of engagement.[309] Yet, as Stein went on to say, reality can nevertheless be complex and "a model enables us to see the wood from the trees".[310] This point was developed by Gunther Teubner who, as has been mentioned earlier, argues that "a theory of legal evolution has great analytical and practical power if it stops claiming to be able to explain individual events and concentrates instead on explaining structural patterns".[311] Such a theory "will be able to explain or even predict general structures of the law" even if it will not "be able to explain individual legal acts, court verdicts, laws, and

306 Ibid.

307 Ibid., p. 124.

308 Ibid.

309 As in anthropology it would seem: Descola, note 303 above, p. 317.

310 Stein, note 304 above, p. 126.

311 Teubner, note 206 above, p. 49.

administrative acts".[312] As Teubner says, critics of this evolution model fail to appreciate that one is "dealing with two different levels of analysis".[313] Just because a hermeneutical approach is able to produce valuable cultural and other insights at a micro level, this does not mean that an evolutionary and structural model is unable to produce insights at a macro-level. It is a question of levels of observation.[314]

Take for example Blanché's assertion that a diachronic view of science sees it as passing through four stages, namely descriptive, inductive, deductive and axiomatic.[315] Such a model seems applicable to the history of Roman law in Europe as well.[316] If it is applicable – but of course there are real historiographical issues in imposing a contemporary model on the past – one can surely say that it provides methodological insights, even if the framework is unable to account at a causal level for these evolutionary developments. One insight for the comparatist is that it explains why the common lawyers seem methodologically closer to the Roman jurists than to the Pandectists: both sets of jurists were (and are) 'trapped' in an inductive stage and seemed (seem) to want to remain there. Perhaps this is a weak insight, but it is surely an improvement on the 'inner relationship' thesis.[317]

Historical models also have a role – perhaps an important one – in comparative public law. This is a topic that is often ignored by those writing a history of comparative law, yet the work of Walter Ullmann (1910-1983) and his successors is of importance to comparative legal studies. Ullmann's focus of attention was medieval political theory, but, as he said, "the medieval period stretches well into modern times" because it is "the impact of medieval political ideas" that have given shape to "those political concepts which only in the modern period have come to full

[312] Ibid.

[313] Ibid., p. 51.

[314] On which see Desjeux, note 6 above.

[315] Blanché, note 302 above, p. 65.

[316] See G. Samuel, *A Short Introduction to Judging and to Legal Reasoning* (2016), pp. 148-149.

[317] See F. Pringsheim, "The Inner Relationship Between English and Roman Law", *Cambridge Law Journal* [1935], p. 347.

fruition".[318] Of importance to the jurist is that these medieval political concepts were legal ones because medieval law "was, one might say, applied political doctrine".[319] It was in the rediscovered Roman law that these legal concepts were to be found and thus "the significance of Justinian's codification can hardly be exaggerated".[320]

The comparative model that Ullmann developed was both legal and political and it consisted of the metaphorical image of the pyramid in which there were two conceptions of government and law. There was the ascending thesis where "original power is located in the people, or in the community itself" and thus "power ascended from the broad base of a pyramid to its apex, the king or duke".[321] Opposed to this conception was the descending thesis where "original power" was located in a supreme being. "One can here also see", said Ullmann, "a metaphorical pyramid but it was at its apex that a sum-total of power was located".[322] Ullmann went on to demonstrate that the Roman and canon law model could be used to favor the descending thesis of government. The post-classical Roman law as set out in the Code, "set forth an unadulterated monarchic form of government in the guise of law".[323] The feudal model, in contrast, "proved itself an important harbinger and incubator of ideas which later could be developed on the basis of a theoretically conceived populist ascending theory of government".[324] For, in legal terms, "feudal society was governed by the law of contract".[325]

Two other fundamental constitutional models emerged from medieval legal thought. The first was the importance of the legal corporation or *universitas* which became the means by which the institutions of society were able to be envisaged through a legal

[318] W. Ullmann, *Medieval Political Thought* (1975), p. 11.

[319] Ibid., p. 15.

[320] Ibid., p. 46

[321] Ibid., p. 12.

[322] Ibid., p. 13.

[323] Ibid., p. 47.

[324] Ibid., p. 148.

[325] Ibid., p. 147.

framework, including not just cities and other social groups but the Church itself.[326] Popes could err, but the Church could never err.[327] Humans die but the *universitas* does not; it remains as a permanent institution finally becoming the model by which the State itself is envisaged.[328] The second was hierarchy. "Medieval minds", wrote Brian Tierney (1922-2019), "were fascinated, captivated by … the vision of hierarchy". Even the whole universe was perceived "as a great hierarchical chain of being".[329] Indeed, "everything from the celestial hierarchy of the heavens to the pecking order of chickens, not to mention the king of the bees" were seen as hierarchical.[330] And, as Tierney goes on to say:

> It is tempting to dismiss such argumentation as mere gothic fantasy – beasts and bees and birds (chickens indeed) as the basis for serious political theory! But now scientists have again taken to studying the social insects and dominance hierarchies in birds and animals for insights into the natural bases of human behaviour.... The argument from animal hierarchies to human hierarchies may be mere nonsense; probably it is nonsense; but it is not just medieval nonsense. The human mind has never ceased to be fascinated by natural hierarchy; and the point that hierarchical ordering is a near-universal manifestation among human cultures seems self-evident.[331]

In setting out these historical models, the purpose is not to enter into a critical discussion about the history of constitutional law and political theory. The purpose is to indicate how some of the models that are taken for granted today – Kelsen's pyramid of norms for example, or the legal corporation or genus and species taxonomy – have deep historical roots in terms of their form even if in substance there has been much change. The legal mind, one might say, has never ceased to be fascinated by the forms to be

[326] B. Tierney, *Religion, Law, and the Growth of Constitutional Thought 1150-1650* (1982), pp. 11, 19-28.

[327] Ibid., p. 15.

[328] Ibid., pp. 12, 22.

[329] Ibid., p. 42.

[330] Ibid., p. 44.

[331] Ibid.

found in the texts of Roman law. But their meanings are not necessarily Roman in that when, say, an early modern writer cited Roman texts – one thinks of the famous phrase *quod omnes tangit ab omnibus approbetur* (what touches all must be approved by all)[332] – he "was attributing to the ancient texts meanings that had been imprinted on them by medieval experience".[333] One might note, also, that these medieval constitutional models are not irrelevant to the earlier historical discussion about legal evolution. Once we abandon the idea of progress from legal evolutionary ideas,[334] comparative legal historians might be able to appreciate that they could often be thinking medieval thoughts. Or, as Jones put it, "[e]ven to-day so many roads in the law lead us back to Rome by way of the [medieval] Commentators on the Roman law".[335]

13. Programs. Rather than a model of engagement, perhaps an historical approach might equally be seen as a program of research. The term "program" was employed by the French social scientist Jean-Michel Berthelot as an alternative to terms such as "paradigm", "theory", or "school".[336] These latter terms come with epistemological baggage (so to speak) – even although they are in common use – and the advantage of an expression like "program" is that it is more precise, epistemologically and in terms of research projects, than say "theme". Yet it does not carry the same exclusivity as "theory". What differentiates a "program" from a scheme of engagement or *grille de lecture* is that it operates at a higher level of abstraction; it provides a point of view operating within a discipline in which there is the possibility of many different such views.[337]

One such program, of particular relevance to legal studies, is a feminist analysis, or, for lawyers, feminist jurisprudence. Eagleton incorporates such an analysis (with regard to literature)

[332] C.5.59.5. As Tierney says: the expression "is a genuine phase of classical Roman law but in its original context in the Code it had no constitutional significance and was not even applied to corporations; it was a mere technicality of the private law co-tutorship": Tierney, note 326 above, p. 24.

[333] Ibid., p. 104.

[334] Ibid., p. 108.

[335] Jones, note 169 above, Preface.

[336] See Berthelot, note 32 above, p. 457.

[337] Ibid., p. 461.

in his chapter on psychoanalysis, and there is no reason why jurists cannot do the same. In film studies feminist film theory embraces a range of approaches, but key among them, as has been seen under ideology, is representation. Many other programs can be mentioned in legal studies: one thinks of gender studies, postcolonial approaches, law and literature, and so on. In describing these approaches as "programs" rather than "theories" is by no means to downgrade them or to suggest that somehow they are less important than, say, natural law theory. The point is that they are not "theories" in the classic sense of an all-embracing definition, description or explication of the notion of law; a feminist jurisprudence researcher might well classify herself as a positivist or as a socio-legal "theorist", as well as a feminist "theorist". Berthelot suggested that one think in terms of moving from theories, to programs, and then to schemes of intelligibility, although a movement in the opposite direction is of a different order. If one moves from a scheme to a program, it may or may not be viable to move onwards to a higher level. The ontological and epistemological complexities encountered at these different levels may or may not permit the formulation of a rigorous theory.[338] And so the overall point to note is that schemes, programs, and theories operate at different levels, more analytical at the lower end and more descriptive at the theory end.[339]

14. Concluding Remark. Hopefully these different schemes identified in the work of social science and humanities theorists are to be seen as relevant to comparative law. Not all of them can actually be described as epistemological and ontological schemes of intelligibility, but even the more thematic ones such as style are, perhaps surprisingly, of real value to comparative lawyers. Many jurists will complain, as has been seen, that they cannot be expected to become specialists in the social sciences and (or) the humanities, and perhaps this should be respected as an argument, especially given the complexity and rapidly changing nature of some areas of legal studies. However this is not an argument that can be employed by serious comparatists because methodology – or, if one prefers, philosophical forms of engagement – is (are) fundamental to the two questions underpinning comparative law, namely the "what is comparison" and "what is law" questions.

[338] Ibid., pp. 484ff.

[339] Ibid., p. 517.

Comparative law is highly epistemological and ideological in its orientation and this aspect to the sub-discipline demands an interdisciplinary sensitivity. Such a sensitivity need not necessarily demand that one becomes a specialist in sociology, economics, English or French literature and film studies, but it does demand a knowledge of epistemology and ontology as a meta discipline. A comparatist can no longer, in any research application, simply state that he or she is going to employ the "comparative method" – at least not if they wish their applications to be treated seriously by a panel that may well include, say, sociologists, anthropologists, literature specialists, film researchers, and historians. Maybe jurists in general should up their game so to speak. Faced with colleagues from other disciplines, can they really respond to questions about their methods in talking just in terms of the "dogmatic", or "doctrinal", or "interpretative" methods?

GENERAL CONCLUSIONS

Are there, then, lessons for the comparative lawyer from theorists and thinkers in other disciplines? The answer must surely be resoundingly positive. Certain schemes, or methods, such as functionalism, structuralism, and hermeneutics appear undoubtedly to transcend subject areas and disciplines and their relevance for comparative law – indeed for law in general – seems undeniable. Some judges might consider such epistemological reflections as "grand theory" and express a wish that legal academics return to a role of doctrinal commentary[340] – an activity also justified by some academics distrustful of too much interdisciplinarity.[341] Put another way, one might say that for some grand theory and interdisciplinarity are threats to the authority paradigm.

Be that as it may. Perhaps a more pertinent argument is one aimed at the extent to which the comparative lawyer needs to examine the literature in other disciplines in order to appreciate the different methods and schemes of engagement possibly relevant to

[340] See, for example, A. Burrows (Lord), "Judges and Academics, and the Endless Road to Unattainable Perfection", The Lionel Cohen Lecture 2021 (available online).

[341] M. Bódig, *Legal Doctrinal Scholarship: Legal Theory and the Inner Workings of a Doctrinal Discipline* (2021).

comparative legal studies. Many might be sympathetic to a certain engagement but feel that there are limits. This question puts the emphasis on legal knowledge, which in one sense is completely understandable. Yet, in another sense, there ought also to be an emphasis on comparing – on the activity of comparison itself – and while attention is on comparing law it needs to be asked why one should not be extending the comparison dimension in other directions as well. The comparatist who spends time researching into social science and humanities methodology is indulging in comparison. She is comparing methods in different disciplines. Why should this not be anything other than part and parcel of comparative legal studies? One is acquiring knowledge about comparing. One is, through comparison itself, attempting to become a sophisticated comparatist. Given that there are other disciplines such as literature, theology, and politics in which comparison is a well-established sub-discipline within these disciplines, might there not one day be a meta subject – perhaps part of epistemology – devoted entirely to comparative studies?[342]

Were this ever to be the case, it would surely be desirable that comparative lawyers would be able not just to import learning from this comparative studies discipline, but also to export learning to such a discipline. Comparative lawyers would hopefully be seen as key players so to speak. And they would, arguably, be so much more effective if they were highly knowledgeable not just about their own discipline and its comparative law learning but also about the strengths and weaknesses of social science and humanities theorists as well. They would, in other words, be fluent in social science, humanities, legal methodology, and epistemology. They could, hopefully, engage in a sophisticated way with methodologists and theorists from all these other disciplines, perhaps even displaying an intellectual rigor that could be of value, say, to film studies.

Another issue to emerge from this examination of schemes of engagement in other disciplines is plurality. The idea that different schemes or *grilles de lecture* result in different kinds of knowledge is an epistemological position adopted by some comparatists.[343] However, it is a position in literary studies that attracted severe

[342] See C. Vigour, *La comparaison dans les sciences sociales: Pratiques et méthodes* (2005).

[343] Samuel, note 181 above; Scarciglia, note 296 above.

criticism from Terry Eagleton who, it will be recalled, said that the "true reason why the pluralists are wishful thinkers is that what is at issue in the contention between different literary theories or "non-theories" are competing ideological strategies related to the destiny of English studies in modern society".[344] One could say the same for comparative legal studies.[345] However Eagleton's conclusion has to be considered in the context of his overall Marxist program which, as has also been noted, is highly critical of "liberal humanism",[346] and this is what leads him logically to conclude that literary theorists are simply asserting and preserving a particular ideological discourse. Yet Eagleton does accept that structuralism, semiotics, psychoanalysis, deconstruction, reception theory, and the like all "have their valuable insights which may be put to use" and that what methods one adopts or rejects "depends upon what you are practically trying to do".[347]

A comparative lawyer approaching the issue of methodology from a Marxist perspective might, then, arrive at a similar view as Eagleton. And one can certainly argue, even from a non-Marxist position, that doctrinal writers are preserving a particular discourse about law, and they do this partly by maintaining a strict authority paradigm. Yet if one adopts a program that is non-Marxist, one can focus on Eagleton's other comment that different "theories" (methods) have their valuable insights and practical uses. As for Eagleton's associated comment, that literary theory is a non-subject because it draws so much from other disciplines,[348] one could assert that this is true of law. Interdisciplinary scholarship equally turns law into a non-discipline. Indeed, many legal scholars hold this view, and they may include some comparative lawyers.[349] There is no answer to this tension. It all depends upon one's paradigm and program orientations and, of course, on one's often unexpressed *grille de lecture* when undertaking an exercise in legal scholarship. To the outsider, law may seem a solid and independent discipline, but it is actually underpinned by methodological and epistemological

[344] Eagleton, note 49 above, p, 173.

[345] See Monateri, note 266 above.

[346] Eagleton, note 49 above, p. 174.

[347] Ibid., p. 184.

[348] Ibid., p. 172.

[349] See, for example, Priel, note 164 above, p. 165.

tensions which can become more evident when one spends time looking at disciplines other than law.

Chapter 20
Units of Comparison Beyond (National) Law

ALEXANDRA MERCESCU

All disciplines engage in determining their respective boundaries; that is. meta-theoretical, self-reflective exercises conducted in order to determine what it is that they study.[1] Together with other identitarian narratives, such as those that pursue a discipline's relation to its own history, this type of self-appraisal constitutes a powerful indicator of a healthy, worthy-of-the-name, discipline. Indeed, if they are to be taken seriously, disciplines are expected to justify their scope and delineate themselves from other fields. Comparative disciplines, in particular, must explain what it is that they compare, or in other words to deal with the conceptualization of their "units of comparison".

How comparative disciplines understand their mission will have had affected how these units are to be devised. A product of the nineteenth century, at least in its institutional, disciplinary, manifestation, "Comparatism" emerged at the intersection of several intellectual concerns of the time: the development of scientific methods, the investigation of cultural diversity within humankind, and the power relations at play between countries,[2] each being given different weight in different national contexts[3] (let us recall that "*[e]pistemology is geo-epistemology*").[4] The propensity

[1] For an extensive discussion on disciplines and their boundary work, see Alexandra Mercescu, *Pour une comparaison des droits indisciplinée* (2018). See also Thomas Gieryn, "Boundary-Work and the Demarcation of Science from Non-Science: Strains and Interests in Professional Ideologies of Scientists", *American Sociological Review*, XLVIII (1983), pp. 791-792.

[2] Joep Leerssen, "Comparing What, Precisely? H. M. Posnett and the Conceptual History of 'Comparative Literature'", *Comparative Critical Studies*, XII (2015), pp. 197-212.

[3] Ibid.

[4] Pierre Legrand, "The Guile and The Guise: Apropos of Comparative Law as We Know It", *Asian Journal of Comparative Law*, XVI (2021), p. 170.

to focus on one specific driver of comparison over others continues to shape differently the many comparative endeavors. Thus, while comparative sociology still seems interested in comparison as a means to introduce science in the realm of social reality, comparative literature has moved towards a more explicitly political approach whose mission lies in decolonizing its traditional outlook, with anthropology remaining faithful to a cultural differential framework.

These epistemological orientations are reflected in the respective disciplinary discussions concerning units of comparison. Starting from the premise that "[t]he general aim of comparative analysis [...] is to generate logically rigorous explanations of regularities and variations in empirical phenomena", Neil Smelser, writing in the social sciences, identifies the following five criteria as suitable for judiciously choosing one's units of comparison[5]:

> [f]irst, the unit of analysis must be appropriate to the kind of theoretical problem posed by the investigator", "[s]econd, the unit of analysis should be *causally* relevant to the phenomena being studied", "[t]hird, the units of analysis themselves should in fact be empirically invariant with respect to their classificatory criterion – their "society-ness" or their "culture-ness" – so as not to conceal significant sources of variation", "[f]ourth, the choice of the unit of analysis should reflect the degree of availability of data referring to this unit.[6]

While some of these criteria, such as the last, are merely intuitive or common-sense, others betray a clear preference for a type of research informed by the belief in the possibility of a proper scientific treatment as regards social phenomena. To add another example, in a contribution discussing sub-national units of comparison, Richard Snyder contends "that a focus on subnational units strengthens the capacity of comparativists to accurately code cases and thus make valid causal inferences".[7] For its part, comparative literature, speaking from a post-colonial perspective, has been preoccupied in recent years with expanding its units of

5 Neil Smelser, *Comparative Methods in the Social Sciences* (2013), p. 174.

6 Ibid., pp. 172-174.

7 Richard Synder, "Scaling Down: The Subnational Comparative Method", *Studies in Comparative International Development*, XXXVI (2001), p. 93.

comparison so as to encompass both authors from non-Western backgrounds and works of a non-strictly literary kind[8] with the consequence that some theoreticians expressed their concern over such a wide inclusiveness: "the result of both moves, going global and going cultural, is a discipline of such overwhelming scope that it no longer sounds like an academic field at all: the study of discourses and cultural productions of all sorts throughout the entire world".[9]

Thinking in terms of the three main drivers of comparison in general (science, culture, and politics), comparative law has emerged as an expression of the first (science) and the third (politics); the second factor (culture) is a recent driver of comparative legal studies that remains marginal and heavily contested ("culture by itself has dubious methodological value").[10] It is sufficient to recall that Hein Kötz and Konrad Zweigert (1911-1996), the two figures who undoubtedly influenced comparative law the most in the second half of the twentieth century, wanted to resort to comparison as a means, *inter alia*, of elevating the discipline of law to the status of science: "[c]omparative law[...] is [...] a method excellently suitable for putting legal science on a sure and realistic basis".[11] As regards the politics behind legal comparatism, through their work on legal families, comparatists contributed their part to mapping a picture of the world's legal systems that corresponded to the specific ideological reconfigurations of the time. As Pier Giuseppe Monateri put it, we need to be aware that "[i]deas do not coalesce by themselves. They are assembled by real, time-bound people, with actual needs and strategies".[12] As such, "classifications of legal systems are in their own turn narratives that contribute to shaping the world order".[13] To take one example from Monateri's research, Esmein's classification was shown to have been not so

[8] David Damrosch, *Comparing the Literatures* (2020), p. 6: "we have compelling ethical and practical reasons to move beyond business as usual".

[9] Jonathan Culler, "Wither Comparative Literature?", *Comparative Critical Studies*, III (2006), p. 87.

[10] Pier Giuseppe Monateri, *Advanced Introduction to Comparative Legal Methods* (2021), p. 48.

[11] Konrad Zweigert and Hein Kötz, *Introduction to Comparative Law*, transl. by Tony Weir (1998), p. 44.

[12] Monateri, note 10 above, p. 67.

[13] Ibid., p. 35.

much the result of a sound scholarly narrative as a "portrait of power relations among empires and spheres of influence".[14]

Therefore, an analysis of units of comparison largely depends on what prompts lawyers to engage in comparative enterprises in the first place. The followers of the orthodoxy established by Zweigert and Kötz more than half a century ago and continued today in the work of Uwe Kischel[15] emphasize those units of comparison that appear to them as amenable to proper scientific inquiry. For instance, initially private law institutions only, not public law, were deemed to be suitable units of comparison precisely because of their presupposed scientificity, public law being regarded as too enmeshed in politics.[16] It is no wonder that comparatists driven by the logic of power relations in the world will readily engage in macro-comparisons choosing traditions or entire regions as their relevant units of comparison. As for comparatists who recognize the diversity of legal cultures, they too will advance specific conceptualizations as regards the units of comparison even when they might not directly refer to this notion. The task here is to explain how a culturalist comparatist would conceive of "units of comparison" from the perspective of geography, scale, number, and, most importantly, kind, remaining aware that not all comparatists who pledge allegiance to a culturalist epistemology will agree with the conclusions.

UNITS OF COMPARISON FOR CULTURALIST MINDS

To begin, the concept of unit of comparison, bearing a scientific resonance, is not a frequent presence in the culturalist comparatist's toolbox. In the past, it was natural that comparative law should be concerned with the question of what it is that one can or should compare. When few comparative studies existed it made scholarly sense to raise the question of "units of comparison", not so much in a descriptive manner ("what does one compare?"), but rather in a prescriptive manner ("what should one compare?"). Various

[14] Ibid., p. 38.

[15] Uwe Kischel, *Comparative Law*, transl. Hammel (2019).

[16] Balázs Fekete, *Paradigms in Modern European Comparative Law: A History* (2021), p. 94; Veronica Corcodel, *Modern Law and Otherness: The Dynamics of Inclusion and Exclusion in Comparative Legal Thought* (2019), p. 150.

authors gave different answers, but generally there used to be a consensus that a certain degree of comparability is needed before one engages in comparison. Thus, many comparatists eventually adopted the formulation of Catherine Valcke: namely, that comparability requires both a certain degree of unity and at the same time a certain degree of plurality.[17]

The number of successful comparative studies produced since comparative law was in its infancy more than a century ago disproves the excessive concern for comparability and proves that all sorts of units of comparison are capable of yielding interesting results. This realization resonates with reflections from other comparative fields: "you truly can compare everything with everything".[18]

When it comes to *geography*, one has compared international law regimes, regions, national laws, and sub-national laws.[19] When it comes to *scale*, one has compared units as large and abstract as the judicial reasoning of judicial systems or as small and concrete as the outcome in two judicial decisions. There are intermediate units of comparison: a specific legal doctrine or regulation on a specific topic.[20] When it comes to *kind or type of units*, comparative law was slow to detach itself from a set of preferred subjects, typically classical institutions belonging to private law. However, it is evident that comparative law is expanding to include non-conventional units of comparison: examples are the established field of comparative constitutional law and emerging fields such as transnational regulatory processes by public and private bodies.[21]

[17] Catherine Valcke, "Comparative Law as Comparative Jurisprudence – The Comparability of Legal Systems", *American Journal of Comparative Law*, LII (2004), pp. 713-740.

[18] Angelika Epple and Walter Ehart, "Practices of Comparing", in Angelika Epple, et al., *Practices of Comparing* (2020), p. 15.

[19] William E. Butler, "Comparative International Law", *Journal of Comparative Law*, X (2015), pp. 241-250; Başak Çalı, Mikael Rask Madsen, and Frans Viljoen, "Comparative Regional Human Rights Regimes: Defining a Research Agenda", *International Journal of Constitutional Law*, XVI (2018), pp. 128–135.

[20] See, for instance, Claudia Geiringer, "When Constitutional Theories Migrate: A Case Study", *American Journal of Comparative Law*, LXVII (2019), pp. 281, 283, 285.

[21] Rozen Noguellou and David Renders, *Uber & Taxis. Comparative Law Studies* (2018); Mathilde Cohen, "Regulating Milk: Women and Cows in France and the United States", *American Journal of Comparative Law*, LXV (2017), pp. 469–526; Ryan Hediger (ed.), *Animals in War* (2012).

Indeed, subjects as diverse as ubers and taxis, the regulation of milk, or animal rights in cases of war have been compared, to mention more non-conventional ones.[22] When it comes to *numbers*, comparatists have restrained themselves to two legal systems, but have felt confident enough to explore as many as one hundred jurisdictions[23] or even all the world's legal systems.[24]

Realizing that almost "anything goes", even comparatists generally attached to the theoretical commitments of the orthodox epistemology have become less concerned with explicitly theorizing the question of "units of comparison". For instance, Mathias Siems discusses the "position that there are certain units that comparative law should not address, while other units firmly belong to comparative law" to then conclude that "this binary approach [is] too restrictive and out of line with the diversity of comparative law today".[25] Moreover, for culturalist comparatists the concept of "units of comparison" carries undoubtedly an unnecessary scientific connotation that they are not ready to accept. However, the aim here is to imagine and reconstruct a culturalist discourse on the topic of units while conceding that such an analytical investigation is not among the main epistemological preoccupations of culturalist comparatists.

Geographically speaking, culturalist comparatists will be inclined to choose nation-states as their main units of comparison, for they are the obvious expression of cultures. However, alternatives can spring from other sources. Culturalist comparatists will not shy away from shifting the lenses of comparison as long as they can read culture into what they are comparing. Despite their attachment to national legal cultures, there is nothing in culturalist comparatists' understanding of comparative law that would prevent them from including in their studies other units (supra- or sub-national). For

[22] Francesca Bignamini and David Zaring (eds), *Comparative Law and Regulation* (2018).

[23] Tom Ginsburg and Mila Versteeg, "The Bound Executive: Emergency Powers During the Pandemic", *International Journal of Constitutional Law*, XIX (2021), pp. 1498-1535.

[24] Dimitry Kochenov and Justin Lindeboom, *Kälin and Kochenov's Quality of Nationality Index: An Objective Ranking of the Nationalities of the World* (2020).

[25] Mathias Siems, "The Power of Comparative Law: What Kind of Units of Comparison Can Comparative Law Compare?", *American Journal of Comparative Law*, LXVII (2019), p. 888.

instance, John Bell has argued that there is no single legal culture in France, but that French law is a matter of cultures.[26]

Nor should there be specific constraints regarding the choice of units on the grounds of *scale* according to a culturalist apprehension of comparative law. Indeed, culturalists would embrace equally enthusiastically a comparison between two judicial decisions from two different jurisdictions, as well as a comparison between two legal traditions. Geoffrey Samuel stresses that the differential approach to be found, for instance, in Legrand's works generally leads to macro-comparisons.[27] In comparing two legal traditions or two branches of law, for example, administrative law or the law of evidence, in two different jurisdictions, one can more easily identify differences for there will be a vast realm of specificity on which the comparatist can draw. It is not that two judicial decisions (even converging on the legal solution) will not sufficiently differ from each other in order to be insightfully compared, but rather that the unearthing of differences will require more intellectual effort on the part of the comparatist. Ultimately, the scale of the comparison depends not on the epistemological approach taken, but the type of question the researcher asks.

Comparatists of all hues have paid attention to the appropriate *number* of units to be compared. In line with similar claims encountered in other comparative fields, culturalists praise small-scale comparisons, that is, comparisons limited to one (foreign law), two or three legal systems (one cannot exclude borderline situations when a bigger number could actually be epistemically justified, the more systems included in a study, the less likely a significant interpretative yield): "the more examples compared, the more superficial and peremptory is the analysis of each. [...] The deception and self-deception involved in such ventures is of the same sort that typifies all ideology: misrepresenting a part for the whole".[28] While a bipolar comparison needs not much justification (after all, "meaning is constructed through contrast"),[29] the specific

[26] John Bell, *French Legal Cultures* (2001).

[27] Geoffrey Samuel, *An Introduction to Comparative Law Theory and Method* (2014), p. 97.

[28] Bruce Lincoln, *Apples and Oranges: Explorations In, On, and With Comparison* (2018), p. 26.

[29] Ibid., p. 25.

benefits of a single-jurisdiction or a three-cultures comparison should be acknowledged more. If a lawyer takes an interest in a law other than the one in which they have been trained, if they therefore find themselves in the situation to have to ascribe meaning to foreignness for practical or theoretical purposes, they will inevitably do so through a passage, a filter, a yardstick (that of their mentality, their culture, their experience, ultimately of their "being-in-the-world").[30] Comparison will thus make itself implicit, but it will not be non-existing. Rather, one might need to find it between the lines, to be a careful reader in order to bring it to the surface. From the point of view of the writer, their task might be alleviated by the fact that they will not feel compelled to provide points of contrast at every stage of the comparison. In not visibly imposing a *comparandum*, the foreign law under investigation will be allowed to express itself on its own terms to a larger extent while still being challenged from the outside.

A three-prong comparison has specific merits as well. The comparatist will be encouraged to think in terms of relative differences. A law that appears unwelcoming to a specific category of subjects when seen from the perspective of a foreign law could be re-apprehended when set against another foreign law. Difference is then more easily understood as constructed which entails a greater responsibility placed on the shoulders of the researcher. As has been argued, a three-way comparison is more susceptible to steering clear from instituting hierarchies and declaring one of the pair as "'normal', 'natural', the standard against which the 'other' is seen as a deviation or somehow inferior".[31]

Coming to the question of the *kind or type* of units – and this constitutes the main focus of the argument –, heterodox comparatists will want to emphasize above all that "the object of analysis does not simply 'exist' or 'speak for itself'"; consequently, "the comparatist must recognize that she selects what to describe, decides what to focus on and edits the description and analysis accordingly".[32] With this in mind, comparatists who respond

[30] For a discussion on the relevance of the Heideggerian *Dasein* for comparative law, see Pierre Legrand, "Negative Comparative Law: The Sanitization Enterprise", *Revista de Investigações Constitucionais*, X (2023), p. 10.

[31] Alan Macfarlane, "To Contrast and Compare", in Kumar Srivastava (ed.), *Methodology and Fieldwork* (2004), pp. 94-111.

[32] Mitchel de S.-O.-l'E. Lasser, "The Question of Understanding", in Pierre

to calls from the perspective of legal culture must be prepared to welcome non-legal units in their comparison. Mathias Siems provides a useful, yet in my view insufficiently critical, inventory of such new, non-conventional, units. He identifies fourteen possible new units, split into five categories: new and old law of different countries, old laws of different countries, law and non-law of different countries, law and non-law of same country, existing law and fictional law, fictional laws, foreign law implicit, local laws, private lawmaking, different areas of laws, domestic and international law, different international laws – same topic, different international law – different topics.[33] The majority of new units continue to emanate from the field of law with only four categories touching on other disciplines. The law and non-law comparison builds on sociological knowledge and echoes the functionalist urge to look outside the law occasionally,[34] whenever foreign law does not provide a concrete, legal, official, solution to the legal issue at stake. The two other non-legal categories, both implying fictional laws, draw on literary and cultural studies. Indeed, in this article, Siems contends that "[t]he inclusion of research on non-law units in comparative law is not a matter of course".[35]

To the contrary, however: any meaningful comparison will eventually lead to the inclusion of non-legal knowledge and that, in at least some cases (let them be called "*extensive comparisons*"), this non-legal knowledge will be displayed comparatively (and will make all the difference). In order to make this claim, following Pierre Legrand's work, it is legal cultures that we are comparing. Culture is by no means an easy concept. How culture is to be understood is problematic. No matter the definition, it is important to avoid dangerous connotations that support ideas of fixity, conservatism, or nationalism, for cultures are always on the move. Understood as a "framewor[k] of intangibles within which ascertainable interpretive communities operate and which have normative force for these communities, even though not coherently

Legrand and Roderick Munday (eds.), *Comparative Legal Studies: Traditions and Transitions* (2003), p. 216.

33 Siems, note 25 above, pp. 880-888.

34 Zweigert and Kötz, note 11 above, p. 39: "the comparatist must *sometimes* look outside the law" (emphasis added).

35 Siems, note 25 above, p. 869.

and completely instantiated",[36] culture is ascribed in Legrand's arguments not an overriding but a constitutive role. Thus, it is not that culture comes before law or that culture would somehow place itself above law. Rather, law is "encultured"; "there is law-as-culture".[37] Simply put, French law has something to do with French culture no matter how technical – purely rational in its response to purportedly universal needs – the majority of lawyers claim or would like it to be.

The recognition of law as culture does not automatically lead to conceptualizing difference in essentialist terms. Christoph Brumann argues convincingly that those scholars who tend to view culture negatively have built for themselves in retrospect a strawman which they could afterwards easily debunk.[38] These skeptical authors' re-presentation of the manner in which culture has been employed throughout time would in fact be conveniently fabricated according to their contemporary epistemic predispositions, so that they can now congratulate themselves on the progress obtained by their distancing from the problematic connotations of the concept. Every new generation of thinkers tends to rationally reconstruct the past. As Richard Rorty claims, if this happens it is to convince ourselves that we do not simply differ from our ancestors but that we differ for the better, that is, in ways that would be recognized as being superior even by our forebears were they brought into the present.[39] It is unsurprising then that some authors have hastened to perform a not very charitable interpretation of older utilizations of the idea of culture. But has anyone ever seriously professed that the notion unequivocally reflects homogeneity, fixity, legalism, holism, coherence, a-historicity, primordialism or hierarchies?

Nonetheless, for those who remain sceptical of the notion of "difference", useful are the ideas of French philosopher and renowned sinologist François Jullien on cultural identity. In a book audaciously intitled *There is No Such Thing as Cultural Identity (Il*

[36] Pierre Legrand, "Comparative Legal Studies and the Matter of Authenticity", *Journal of Comparative Law*, 1 (2006), p. 374.

[37] Pierre Legrand, "Foreign Law: Understanding Understanding", *Journal of Comparative Law*, VI (2011), p. 110.

[38] Christoph Brumann, "Writing for Culture: Why a Successful Concept Should Not Be Discarded", *Current Anthropology* S1, 40 (1999).

[39] Richard Rorty, "The Historiography of Philosophy", in Richard Rorty, J. B. Schneewind, and Quentin Skinner (eds), *Philosophy in History* (1984), p. 51.

n'y a pas d'identité culturelle) Jullien asks the following question: "should we account for the different cultures in differential terms or according to specific traits, held to be characteristic, from which it would follow that there is an identity of each culture thus distinguished?"[40] Jullien first draws a distinction between the concept of distance (*écart*) (between cultures) and difference and argues that we should embrace the former. Both entail the idea of separation, according to Jullien. However, he argues that difference is too closely linked to the fallacious concept of identity. When we say difference, we either imply that there is some sort of a common, original identity from where the process of differentialization started or we defend the idea of fixed identities that exist in isolation from each other. On the other hand, when one speaks of *distance* one does not seek to range the object of study in any way; one simply suggests that there is a space between two or more entities that calls upon us to reflect on it, to fulfil it conceptually as one thinks fit.

Difference hints to classification, and distance, by contrast, to confrontation. There is no such a thing as identity, but only a set of resources (or fecundities) made available by each culture by virtue of the distance existing between the participants in that culture. Distance allows the conversation to continue and, thus, a culture to be built precisely in the interstices, between (entre) the various resources. Indeed, Jullien reminds us that transformation is what makes the cultural cultural when he asks: "How could we characterize European culture, how could we fix its identity? At the time when we wanted to draw a Constitution for Europe we asked ourselves whether Europe was Christian or secular. A proper answer would have been: Europe is 'at the same time Christian and secular (and other). It developed itself *in the distance* between the two'".[41] To be sure, one can take the view that the distinction between *distance* and *difference* is merely a question of language. Those who emphasize differences in comparative law are usually aware of its colonial heritage and do not attribute any hierarchical connotation to the word. But one can think of specific contexts in which the vocabulary employed by Jullien represents a useful nuance applied to the idea of culture.

40 François Jullien, *Il n'y a pas d'identité culturelle* (2016), p. 34.

41 Ibid., p. 49.

For instance, in the case of Central and Eastern European legal scholars, who come from a region that was typically belittled and left to one side in international and comparative law,[42] the concepts proposed by Jullien could be very appealing. Central and Eastern European scholars are accustomed to working in and belonging to a space that does not count in international and comparative law nor in the post-colonial discourse.[43] As Fowkes and Hailbronner have eloquently put it: "Eastern Europe was too Eastern to just become part of the West, too European to be part of the South or the Rest, and too late to join equally in anything except the West's increasing uncertainty about what, in coming first in the Cold War, it had actually won".[44] It is unsurprising that Central and Eastern European scholars are prone to reject a theoretical model insisting on differences. In an understandable strategic move, immediately after the fall of communism, Central and Eastern European legal scholarship sought to emphasize the Western roots of Central and Eastern European legal systems and therefore the prospective success of legal transplants. Moreover, differences between immensely different countries in terms of language and culture were once again effaced as one started to speak of a common Central and Eastern European legal culture, the supposed product of a single totalitarian past. Indeed, many Central and Eastern European legal scholars tend to assume similarity across Central and Eastern European countries, thus neglecting the countries' respective singularities. In a subservient gesture of self-censorship, the various countries in Central and Eastern Europe have often compared themselves to the West but generally failed to engage in intra-regional comparisons. As a consequence, they failed to engage with the whole spectrum of

[42] Momchil Milanov, "The Region without Qualities: Fiction, International Law and the Internalized Irrelevance of Central and Eastern Europe", in Cosmin Cercel, Alexandra Mercescu, and Mirosław Michał Sadowski (eds.), *Law, Culture and Identity in Central and Eastern Europe: A Comparative Engagement* (2023), pp. 63-82.

[43] Rafał Mańko, Cosmin Cercel. and Adam Sulikowski (eds.), *Law and Critique in Central Europe* (2016); Alexandra Mercescu, "Introduction: From Country to Country, From Time to Time, Questions and Answers of Self and Other", in Alexandra Mercescu (ed.), *Constitutional Identities in Central and Eastern Europe* (2019).

[44] James Fowkes and Michaela Hailbronner, "Decolonizing Eastern Europe: A Global Perspective on 1989 and the World it Made", *International Journal of Constitutional Law*, XVII (2019), pp. 497-509.

their identities. Arguably, identity does not exist by itself. It needs some Other (and crucially various Others) to emerge.[45] Therefore, if one is interested in determining identity, Central and Eastern European legal identity in particular, one needs to compare and to do so in as many configurations as possible (not only West-East, but within the Eastern world). It is crucial to challenge the narratives that dissolve Central and Eastern European legal systems either within their Western counterparts (as samples of a more important representative) or within a common regional culture. Difference, or to use Jullien's vocabulary, distance needs to be asserted.

As a matter of fact, "distance" has already appeared in the comparatist's discourse: see, for instance, Frankenberg's call "for a rigorous experience of distance and difference".[46] Even less critical authors seem willing to value Jullien's vocabulary (for example, *écart*) as a warning against the possibility of full unification of laws.[47]

Now, the comparatist has to engage with other disciplines if she wants to be able to capture this distance (between cultures and, of equal importance, between various cultural resources existing within one given culture). Consider an example: there is a trend nowadays towards the constitutionalization of animal rights.[48] Despite such a strong level of protection, some polities decide to allow for cultural exceptions by virtue of which certain forms of violence towards animals are legally excused because they are

[45] Traditionally, the Other was the Western world. According to Krastev and Holmes, in time this constant comparison to the West generated a feeling of frustration among the Eastern imitators, which in turn facilitated the emergence of populism: Stephen Holmes and Ivan Krastev, *The Light That Failed* (2019). The thesis put forward by Holmes and Krastev constitutes only one plausible account of why countries from Central and Eastern Europe, such as Poland and Hungary, have experienced a serious rule of law and illiberalism crisis in recent years. For other complementary or alternative theories, see Martin Krygier, Adam Czarnota, and Wojciech Sadurski (eds.), *Anti-Constitutional Populism* (2022).

[46] Günter Frankenberg, *Comparative Law as Critique* (2016), p. 88.

[47] Jacques Ziller, "Comparison Within Multi-Level Polities and Governance Regimes", in Peter Cane, Herwig Hofmann, Eric C. Ip, and Peter Lindseth (eds), *The Oxford Handbook of Comparative Administrative Law* (2021), p. 392.

[48] See Jessica Eisen and Kristen Stilt, "Protection and Status of Animals", in Rainer Grote, Frauke Lachenmann, and Rüdiger Wolfrum (eds.), *Max Planck Encyclopedia of Comparative Constitutional Law* (2016); Anne Peters, "Introduction to Symposium on Global Animal Law (Part I): Animals Matter in International Law and International Law Matters for Animals", *AJIL Unbound*, CXI (2017), pp. 252-256.

considered to be an expression of culture.[49] We could therefore conclude that those jurisdictions offer less protection to animals, but it would be insufficiently critical to do so without unveiling the tensions that exist in that society with respect to animal welfare and how this specific issue connects to wider topics such as religion and communitarianism. "Animal welfare", "religion", "communitarianism" are all "cultural resources" that will compete with each other under a set of specific ideological circumstances, the battleground being always the expression of a historical trajectory which enables or disables the various "fighters" accordingly. We can legitimately expect that in a different society, the same cultural resources will end up acting along the lines of a very different dynamic.

At least three features of culture invite us to adopt an interdisciplinary approach in comparative legal research: transmissibility, transversality, and transformability.

Culture characterizes itself by transmissibility. It can be conceived as a heritage – a set of elements with normative value having been inscribed in the mind and behavior of a people over the long term and which is transmitted vertically, from one generation to the next. In this sense, it refers, *inter alia,* to the past of a given community and to the routes it has taken over time. That is why a historical analysis of the law is often essential to the comparatist who wishes to scrutinize the trajectory of institutions differently from local jurists who take them for granted and feel that they convey timeless truths. Indeed, "the traditionality of law is inescapable".[50] Thus, by empowering the comparatist to evoke the past of a law in order to answer the question of why this law has come to say what it says and why it does it in a certain way and not in another, interdisciplinarity (in this case, the study of law in its historical dimension) allows us to expose both the contingency of law's constructions and the cultural values of a people, thus

[49] See, for example, Carla M. Zoethout, "Ritual Slaughter and the Freedom of Religion: Some Reflections on a Stunning Matter", *Human Rights Quarterly,* XXXV (2013); Dushyant Thakur, "Resolving the Cultural Right-Animal Right Conflict in India: Analyzing Article 29(1) Through the Paradigm of Jallikattu", *Commonwealth Law Bulletin,* XLIV(3) (2018); Minjoo Oh and Jeffrey Jackson, "Animal Rights vs. Cultural Rights: Exploring the Dog Meat Debate in South Korea from a World Polity Perspective", *Journal of Intercultural Studies,* XXXII(1) (2011), pp. 31-56; Paul Waldau, "Religion and Animals", in Peter Singer (ed.), *In Defense of Animals* (2006), p. 69.

[50] Martin Krygier, "Law as Tradition", *Law and Philosophy,* V (1986), p. 237.

proving its "normality without reducing [its] particularity".[51] However, many historians today admit that a historical study cannot be limited to major political events or political figures, but that it is necessary to situate the past in the light of its cultural foundations and, consequently, to take into account a wider range of social fields (economy, arts, literature, religion, philosophy and others), particularly with a view to going beyond the supposed transparency of data and capture something of the complexity of meanings of symbols. In short, the comparatist will be led to do what historians dub "cultural history", thus embarking on a "multidisciplinary" as well as an interdisciplinary enterprise".[52] Therefore, the entry into history; it is also the entry into the territory of its neighboring disciplines: anthropology, geography, sociology, ethnology, bibliography, archeology, and even biology. The subject of historical studies has expanded so much that it is difficult to confine it to a given set of themes: today, "almost everything seems to have its own cultural history".[53]

Second, if culture (due to its "hereditary" character, so to speak) leads the comparatist to be interested in the historical dimension of law, the actuality of a law cannot be meticulously scrutinized without resorting to another one of culture's facets, namely transversality. Imagine a library shelf comprising several books side by side: one on economics, one on geography, one on art, one on politics, one on linguistics, and so on, and an arrow (culture) which would cross from one end to the other the bindings and pages of all books. This metaphor allows us to highlight at least three modalities of the transversal character of culture. First, it is reasonable to think that culture is transversal in the sense that it manifests itself everywhere.[54] It is ordinary.[55] In this sense, culture is not a separate book on the shelf existing in a relation of interdependence to other separate entities (the

[51] William Tabb, *The Postwar Japanese System [:] Cultural Economy and Economic Transformation* (1995), p. 23.

[52] Peter Burke, *What Is Cultural History?* (2008), p. 135.

[53] Ibid., p. 131.

[54] But see Duncan Kennedy, "Political Ideology and Comparative Law", in Mauro Bussani and Ugo Mattei (eds.), *The Cambridge Companion to Comparative Law* (2012), p. 54. Kennedy prefers to maintain ideology outside of culture.

[55] Raymond Williams, "Culture Is Ordinary", in Robin Gable (ed.), *Resources of Hope [:] Culture, Democracy, Socialism* (1989), p. 4.

other books: economics, philosophy, art, and so on) but a mode of being of these very entities, that is to say a "patterned conduct around a particular thematic identity".[56] Thus, it seems possible to conceive of culture as being consubstantial with the economic, the political, the historical, the demographic, religious or legal (the arrow being consubstantial with the books themselves). In other words, the relevance as a disciplinary field or specific sphere of activity is ensured by recurring references to a set of components conventionally considered as falling within that area. Therefore, instead of maintaining that there is culture in the economy, it would be more sensible to say that the economy is culture. Lawrence Rosen's words in relation to law suggest this direction: "carving [law] out as a separate domain and only then making note of its cultural connections distorts the nature of both culture and law".[57] Such a design of culture leads us to see it not as an historical artifact exclusively and to realize that culture also participates in the making of everyday life.

But culture can be said to be transversal in a second sense. That which makes a culture what it is – for example, what makes the Frenchness of the French culture – transcends all other identity traits of the participating members of that culture (sexual orientation, gender, social origin, religion, or other). Consequently, the part of the arrow that crosses the book "economics" is not the part of the arrow that goes through the "religion" book. In fact, transversality accounts for the fact that the set of values, symbols and behaviors that make a culture is shared horizontally by a sufficiently large number large number of people to denote a belonging to a community that stands out from any other community. The law, both as professional and national culture, differs from other professional cultures (those of economists, doctors, artists or others) and national ones. Therefore, the comparison with another professional community meant to shed some light on the professional world of law asks for an interdisciplinary approach. The time has come for the comparatist in law to accept that a cultural comparison presupposes the comparison of one national law to another, but also the comparison of law to another field of

[56] Mary Jane Collier, "Cultural and Intercultural Communication Competence: Current Approaches and Directions for Future Research", *International Journal of Intercultural Relations*, XIII (1989), p. 289.

[57] Lawrence Rosen, *Law as Culture* (2008), p. xii.

knowledge (is there any other discipline in charge of such cross-disciplinary musings?). What Henry Remak (1916-2009) claimed about comparative literature in 1971 is valid for the comparison of laws today: "Comparative literature is the study of literature beyond the confines of one particular country, and the study of the relationships between literature on the one hand and other areas of knowledge and belief, such as the arts [...], philosophy, history, the social sciences (e.g., politics, economics, sociology), the sciences, religion, etc., on the other. In brief, it is the comparison of one literature with another or others, and the comparison of literature with other spheres of human expression".[58]

Finally, culture's transformability opens the door to interdisciplinarity. At the same time as cultural theorists oppose it to the free will of the individual and insist on its collective character, they often add that culture is "always in the making", that it is "produced and renegotiated by individual agents through their actions and practices".[59] Although it is indisputable that culture comes to us from the past, its "present", so to say, is always in mutation, reworked depending on various ideals and, therefore, oriented towards the future. Any repetition of culture will make room for innovation (even if only so slightly from one decade to another).

To sum up, law's past, present, and future represents a matrix of cultural resources, some of which can be truly unique to that particular society whereas others are *prima facie* less unique, but the way they interact with each other inevitably speaks of their situatedness. These cultural resources are rarely visible at the surface of the law. Nor are there any guarantees that the insiders to that culture will know them fully or sensibly well. Interiority does not automatically constitute superior knowledge. Interiority and exteriority offer angles of vision, which are complementary and say nothing about the quality of knowledge one has arrived at. What matters is the degree to which the researcher, working from the perspective of his angle, will capture enough information to warrant our attention.

[58] Henry HH Remak, "Comparative Literature, Its Definition and Function", in Newton Stallknecht and Horst Frenz (eds.), *Comparative Literature, Method and Perspective* (1971), p. 3.

[59] Sjoerd Beugelsdijk and Robbert Maseland, *Culture in Economics* (2011), p. 10.

A positivist account of Belgian law by a Belgian scholar, let us say, is not superior to a positivist account of Belgian law by a Polish scholar simply by virtue of the first being the report of an insider. And vice-versa, whereas the encounter with foreign law lays the ground almost automatically for a novel, fresh, critical engagement with that law, all is a matter of distance. Legrand astutely observes that "[f]or a comparatist who is willing to offer an overture *to* the language of the foreign law-text, which is also an overture *of* the language of the law-text, there can be nothing that is quintessentially 'legal' or automatically outside the 'legal'".[60] Or in the same vein Samuel remarks: "theories rooted in disciplines outside law – disciplines such as sociology and economics – have provided and are continuing to provide information about law that eluded earlier jurists".[61] The question then becomes how far the researcher is ready to go in his or her analysis? Will they take into account this article or that decision? And how many of the cultural resources making a law what it is will the researcher be willing to explore? "What we aim to 'understand' is not total *culture* – an impossibility",[62] but something of significance from the vast underlying network of law's cultural resources.

NON-LEGAL UNITS OF COMPARISON FOR LEGAL MINDS

Now, the extent to which these cultural resources coming from other disciplines will themselves become units of comparisons will vary. Most of the time, the knowledge from other disciplines will be used with reference to one of the laws compared only. In this case, the foreign knowledge assumes at least two possible roles: an explicatory and a confrontational role.

Thus, one can use sociological data, for instance, to provide an account of at least one of the laws involved according to, let us say, a structural scheme of intelligibility whose purpose would be that

[60] Pierre Legrand, "Foreign Law, the Comparatist, and Culture: How It Is", in Cercel, Mercescu, and Sadowski (eds.), *Law, Culture and Identity in Central and Eastern Europe: A Comparative Engagement* (2023), p. 36 (emphasis in original).

[61] Geoffrey Samuel, "Interdisciplinarity and the Authority Paradigm: Should Law be Taken Seriously by Scientists and Social Scientists?", *Journal of Law and Society*, XXXVI (2009), p. 438.

[62] James Whitman, "The Neo-Romantic Turn", in Pierre Legrand and Roderick Munday (eds.), *Comparative Legal Studies: Traditions and Transitions* (2003), p. 337.

of exposing the interrelations between various social constructs having legal implications. Or, the researcher could use literature or history to provide an account of at least one of the laws involved according to, let us say, a hermeneutical scheme of intelligibility whose specific purpose would be that of understanding the deep meaning of certain legal institutions and why they took this form rather than another.[63] Disciplines do not commend the use of specific schemes of intelligibility, but it is manifest that the type of questions that disciplines asks determines for each field the suitability of some schemes rather than others. While philosophy will support well the dialectical scheme, sociology could easily lead to either a structural, causal, or auctorial scheme. In any case, the manner in which the researcher chooses to frame the object of analysis will orientate the researcher towards specific disciplines and therefore towards meaningful schemes of intelligibility. The result can be more than a mere explanation of law; it can amount to an actual confrontation of the law. For instance, in a contribution discussing comparatively the constitutional identity of Romania and Latvia, one co-author resorts to psychoanalysis (specifically to the concept of "agalma") in order to ascribe meaning to a legal concept, namely that of the "eternity clause". Psychoanalysis enables the author to propose a narrative that challenges the received opinion. The content of Article 152 of the Constitution of Romania regarding the limits of constitutional amendment is thus read "as a powerful symbolic device able to condense and conceal, in a nutshell, the specific traits that are foundational to the Romanian constitutional subject".[64] Only Romanian law, not the other law, here Latvian law, was filtered through the language of another discipline. Yet the passage of law through the mill of psychoanalysis offered a rich interpretative yield that facilitated the understanding of Romanian law for both insiders and outsiders.

[63] The notion of "schemes of intelligibility" was usefully borrowed from sociology and applied to (comparative) law by Geoffrey Samuel. See Samuel, "Taking Methods Seriously (Part One)", *Journal of Comparative Law*, II (2007); Samuel, "Taking Methods Seriously (Part Two)", *Journal of Comparative Law*, II (2007). In a nutshell, schemes of intelligibility refer to different modes of reading reality starting from questions which exhibit different purposes. See Jean-Michel Berthelot, *L'Intelligence du social* (1990).

[64] Cosmin Cercel and Jānis Pleps, "Eternity Clause as Agalma: Articulating Constitutional Identity in Romania and Latvia", in Cosmin Cercel, Alexandra Mercescu, and Mirosław Michał Sadowski, *Law, Culture and Identity in Central and Eastern Europe: A Comparative Engagement* (2023), pp. 167-190.

Under such scenarios as the ones cited above, there is no need for using the foreign discipline as a *comparator*. In other words, the knowledge received does not necessarily have to offer comparative insights. It can be mobilized in order to explain/confront one of the laws compared or both. One discipline, let us say, psychology could be used in explaining German law while a different discipline, let us say sociology, will be called upon to ascribe meaning to Croatian law (the comparison German law – Croatian law will then benefit from a *parallel interdisciplinarity* that, while not dialogical, makes the leap from a sterile, black-letter law, juxtaposition to a socially-informed and critical argument).

But while foreign disciplines need not act as comparators, they can do so. This is the case when one single discipline would provide us with ready-made comparative knowledge. In other words, comparative economics, comparative sociology, comparative history, comparative politics, comparative literature, comparative linguistics, or others would lend a hand, so to say, to the comparatist of laws wishing to move away from impoverished accounts of foreign law whose ambition does not go further than a purportedly objective restitution of "the law" and which therefore "find no need whatsoever to reach for discursive assistance so as to explain (comparative) legal analysis beyond what they regard as the proper sphere of legal discourse".[65] In this case, the units of comparison will be not only legal institutions, but constructs of a different disciplinary pedigree. Yet one can expect significant epistemic obstacles to rise in the way of such multi-layered comparisons. Leaving aside the fact that such disciplines display fragmented knowledge which can be confusing for a non-specialist, many of these disciplines seek to attain objectivization through quantitative data or various scientific protocols in which researchers put their faith as they hope that their work is nothing short of an accurate representation of the world. Therefore, it is not so easy to come across comparative knowledge compatible with a hermeneutical orientation typical of a culturalist apprehension of comparative law. As Legrand argues, comparative law is not the only discipline in need of an epistemic reshuffle. Ironically, comparatists who are ready to put their self at risk by "cross[ing] the door, the bridge, the border and going far away",[66] who in

[65] Legrand, note 30 above, p. 11.

[66] Nicole Lapierre, *Pensons ailleurs* (2006), p. 17.

other words have discarded the practice-oriented, law-centered, scientist (and more recently quantitativist) epistemic outlook long dominant in comparative legal thinking are likely to stumble upon knowledge that builds on epistemic assumptions similar to the orthodoxy:

> I observe that the epistemic considerations I raise are not specific to comparative law or indeed to law in general. Anthropologists, too, must face the quartet of issues I address. Such is the case also for sociologists, historians, or translators, who must likewise forsake representativeness, objectivity, or truth – and renounce the idea that the individual could labour hard enough so as agentially to generate any of these epistemic results.[67]

This being said, despite the many difficulties arising from interdisciplinary work, as will be illustrated two examples, it is not impossible to pursue such a double comparative endeavor where the units to be compared will not pertain to law only. The two examples constitute a failure and a success, respectively, in including comparative knowledge within the remit of comparative law. However, at a minimum, they both point to the existence of an undisciplined, aspiring to interdisciplinarity, epistemic trajectory.[68]

"Legal Origins" is well-known to comparatists as the theory that purports to have empirically identified the superiority of the common law tradition in terms of its economic performance.[69] Despite the authors' claims to the contrary, the literature is generally read as nonetheless instituting a ranking of legal systems with common law legal systems faring better.[70] Even if one is

[67] Legrand, note 30 above, p. 8.

[68] The difficulties of interdisciplinarity should not be underestimated. They are so important that we can legitimately ask if interdisciplinarity per se is achievable. For a cautionary approach pleading for indiscipline, rather than interdisciplinarity, see Legrand, *Negative Comparative Law* (2022), p. 200; Mercescu, note 1 above, pp. 267-311.

[69] Rafael La Porta, Florencio López-de-Silanes, Andrei Shleifer, and Robert W. Vishny, "Legal Determinants of External Finance", *Journal of Finance*, LII (1997), p. 1131; Edward Glaeser and Andrei Shleifer, "Legal Origins", *Quarterly Journal of Economics*, CXVII (2002), p. 1193; Rafael La Porta, Florencio López-de-Silanes, and Andrei Shleifer, "The Economic Consequences of Legal Origins", *Journal of Economic Literature*, XLVI (2008), p. 285.

[70] See, for instance, Poonam Puri, "Legal Origins, Investor Protection and

ready to accept that "Legal Origins" does not endorse hierarchies but merely states that legal systems differ in how they deal with various economic arrangements and that these differences can be traced back to their respective historical development, the theory remains problematic to that extent that it asserts the possibility to access the law (past and present, national and foreign) through objective measurements. Otherwise, epistemically speaking, "Legal Origins", a theory concocted through the mingling of (comparative) law, economics and history, represents a most fertile ground for reflecting on the (im)possibility of interdisciplinarity.[71]

When economics encountered law in the "Legal Origins" framework, economists were presented with several possibilities for discovering their discipline in a new light precisely due to another discipline's presence. Interdisciplinarity made visible its emancipatory potential. For instance, the measurements led the authors to conclude that different legal systems exhibit different "styles of social control of business".[72] This conclusion could have easily oriented Shleifer and colleagues towards the "varieties of capitalism" literature (see for instance, Peter A. Hall and David Soskice (eds.), *Varieties of Capitalism: The Institutional Foundations of Comparative Advantage* [2001]), a strand of economic thinking arguing, essentially, that different routes can be taken to reach similarly successful economic results. Therefore, institutions (including laws) are to be judged by reference to their own institutional (that is, political, economic, or social) context.[73] Indeed, liberal market economies, such as the United States or Australia, differ, in terms of how the firms interact with each other and with other actors, from coordinated market economies, such as Germany or Japan.[74] The former group of countries

Canada", *Brigham Young University Law Review* (2009), p. 1671; Bruno Deffains and Olivier Musy, "Droit et finance: quel bilan de la théorie des origines légales?", *Revue d'économie financière* (2018), p. 237.

[71] This is discussed in more detail in Simone Glanert, Alexandra Mercescu, and Geoffrey Samuel, *Rethinking Comparative Law* (2021), pp. 250-276.

[72] Rafael La Porta, Florencio López-de-Silanes, and Andrei Shleifer, "The Economic Consequences of Legal Origins", *Journal of Economic Literature*, XLVI (2008), p. 307.

[73] Peter A. Hall and David Soskice (eds.), *Varieties of Capitalism: The Institutional Foundations of Comparative Advantage* (2001).

[74] Hall and Soskice, "An Introduction to Varieties of Capitalism", in Hall and Soskice, note 73 above, pp. 1-68.

encourage firms to finance themselves through financial markets and therefore end up having a dispersed share ownership. In the latter, by contrast, firms resort less to financial markets and investors therefore need to obtain inside information about the firm's reputation and operation. Differences persist even within one category of economy. Thus, it appears that Northern European countries prefer to cooperate inside the same sector (industry-based coordination), whereas Japan or South Korea seem to promote a model in which coordination takes place between firms belonging to the same group, with competition remaining fierce between enterprises of the same industry (group-based coordination).[75] These various configurations are not failures in terms of economic outcomes, and law is not indifferent to these different models. As Pistor comments: "In contrast to LLS et al., we do not endorse a particular form of economic organizations – i.e. 'the market' – as optimal or superior, and instead suggest that different types of capitalist economies have proven remarkably successful in promoting economic growth and development".[76]

"Legal Origins" is an example of a theory in which a comparative discipline (here, comparative economics) could have been put to the use of comparative law. Instead, economics was seen as offering a universal yardstick against which the legal units had to be assessed. For James Whitman this was, at least partially, the fault of the comparative lawyers who rarely produce research that tries "to understand the role of law in the larger world of economic and political debate".[77] As a consequence, when economists entered the field of comparative law, they justifiably failed to grasp the significance of other possible classifications built on knowledge that is not strictly speaking legal and so resorted to a just distinction (common law-civil law) but one that had little interpretative potential in the particular context of their research:

> for example, when Andrei Shleifer and other leading economists decided to focus on the importance of the law for development, they seized, in a much-cited article, on the civil law-common law distinction. [...] Why did they think

[75] Ibid.

[76] Katharina Pistor, "Rethinking the 'Law and Finance' Paradigm", *Brigham Young University Law Review* (2009), p. 1663.

[77] James Whitman, "Consumerism versus Producerism: A Study in Comparative Law", *Yale Law Journal*, CXVII (2007), p. 340.

> the divide between the common law and civil law "families" was so important? The answer is that when they sat down to do their research, they found a comparative law literature that insisted that the common law-civil law divide was what mattered. They can hardly be blamed for believing what they read. Our comparative law literature, these economists failed to grasp, is mostly written for lawyers, not for social scientists. Unfortunately, the classifications comparativists have traditionally employed provide few answers to the kinds of policy questions posed by the core policy sciences - not only economics, but political science and sociology as well.[78]

Whitman's contribution is interesting for its content, being rich in historical, political, and sociological data, but merits attention for its methodological guidance as well. Indeed, the latter can be regarded as a warning and a call to comparatists for devising broad research questions that go beyond the mere technical concerns of the legal professionals.

In the case of the "Legal Origins" literature, if economics itself had been made the object of a comparative analysis, in other words, if the authors had included in their units of comparison economic knowledge about the various countries, a very different story would have been written in the name of the relation between law and economic performance. In any case, this example allows one to see the potential contribution of non-legal units of comparison.

A different example, where the author went all the way through and delineated his units of comparison with reference to knowledge coming from economics, history, and social philosophy is James Whitman's study on the two Western models of consumer protection.[79] Whitman convincingly drew a distinction between the *consumerist* legal culture of the United States and the *producerist* legal culture of European countries, such as France and Germany. The clash can be summarized as follows: for historical reasons, Americans tend to strongly protect consumers who, according to their beliefs, should have easy access to markets and benefit from lower prices; by contrast, European countries such as France and Germany, despite the growing emphasis on consumer protection,

[78] Ibid., p. 351.

[79] Ibid.

"remain far more oriented toward producer and distributor interests".[80] Thus, he relies on the dichotomy consumerism/producerism, a distinction on display in several disciplines from the beginning of the twentieth century. Whitman compares not only legal institutions, but whole mentalities reflected in distinct economic and political environments. Reaching beyond classical legal sources, Whitman is able to tell a complex story[81] and thus contradict some of the received knowledge.[82] And while the argument could go on and ultimately be contested (indeed, given the dynamics of European consumer law, we can legitimately ask whether Whitman's conclusions are still valid today, almost twenty years after the writing of his paper), this comparative study remains a methodologically inspiring piece of scholarship of the finest kind which successfully illustrates the merits of thinking with non-law about law.

ON SITUATION AND IDEOLOGY

Final cautionary remarks seem to be in order. One must not lose sight of the fact that the units of comparison herein addressed, be they strictly legal or non-legal, are non-natural categories because they are always someone's units and so is the link that brings them together (see, for instance, Legrand's statement on what happens, epistemically speaking, when he chooses to discuss French and Canadian law and refer them both to one particular notion, that of empowerment: "For I am indeed at work *inventing* an (unobjectivizable and untruthable) notion of empowerment through a 'thirding' of knowledge on account of which I can stage a forced negotiation between French and Canadian laws possibilitating my comparison".[83] There is indeed choice involved,

[80] Ibid., p. 340.

[81] Producerism is further deconstructed as it is shown that producer is a "broad, diffuse, and conflict-ridden category, and any given piece of legislation may favor one group of 'producers' over another. For example, sometime legislation favoring 'producer' interests may favor the interests of organized labor over the interests of investors, or of nonorganized labor": Ibid., p. 340.

[82] Whitman defends the analytic opposition between consumerism and producerism even though he is well aware of narratives that run counter to his claims. For instance, he quotes Victoria de Grazia's book, *Irresistible Empire* (2005), which documents how continental Europe has shifted towards an American consumerist model.

[83] Legrand, "The Guile and The Guise: Apropos of Comparative Law as We

in other words, *what* one compares, not unlike *how* one compares, is the outcome of more or less conscientious material and intellectual constraints (one can only ever know so much about law, foreign law, economics, history, etc. and in this 'knowing' one has purposes in mind, thus one never starts from ground zero). In any case, these units are not the expression of some truth (or else truth must be recognized as positioned thought). As Oliver Wendell Holmes, Jr. (1841-1935) put it, drawing on pragmatist philosophy:

> I assume that I am in the world not in me. Next when I say that a thing is true I only mean that I can't help believing it – but I have no grounds for assuming that my can't helps are cosmic can't helps and some reasons for thinking otherwise. I therefore define the truth as the system of my intellectual limitations.[84]

Or to quote Whitman again:

> It is not my aim to identify the 'correct' essential classification of any given system. [...] Good comparative law should never claim to offer any single correct classification. Classification in comparative law is not like Linnean classification in biology. It does not identify essential differences between legal systems comparable to the essential differences between animal species. Instead, classification in comparative law is necessarily ad hoc: it serves to explain how different legal orders can be classified in a variety of ways for the purpose of answering a variety of questions. Legal systems must always be viewed through a prism of multiple classifications. It is important to emphasize this methodological point, because it is a point that is so easy to miss[85].

This situatedness of comparative law is made obvious in a seminal contribution by Veronica Corcodel. She shows that acts of inclusion in respect of the object of comparative studies have almost always been corresponding acts of exclusion driven by

Know It", *Asian Journal of Comparative Law*, XVI (2021), p. 170.

84 *The Essential Holmes, Selections from Letters, Speeches, Judicial Opinions, and Other Writings of Oliver Wendell Holmes, Jr.*, ed. and intro. Richard Posner (1992), p. 107.

85 Whitman, note 76 above.

ideological/governance choices.[86] For instance, Roscoe Pound's was "a universal project for which he argued that only developed legal systems should be considered".[87] Other pre-war comparatists were open about their political stances.[88] By contrast, post-war masters of comparative law preferred to distance themselves from an evolutionary rhetoric and the vocabulary of political aims. Nonetheless, "they often reproduce[d] a disguised version of evolutionary thinking under a putatively universal vocabulary of scientific knowledge".[89] Corcodel remarks that "the distinction between (state) law and social/and or economic conditions continued [...] to be used in a way that produced exclusionary representations of the non-West".[90] A close inspection of the methodology of the most established post-war comparatists unveils their ideological background. René David was defending the superiority of the Western legal systems while Rudolf Schlesinger was interested too in finding the legal common core of civilized nations and consolidating international trade. For his part, Alan Watson, in postulating the autonomy of law vis-à-vis society, entertained a supposed agnosticism which itself was ideological as it refused to see the distributive effects of private law institutions.[91]

As should be clear from the above, rethinking the units of comparison so as to make room for non-legal questions and answers is also an invitation to reconsider comparative law's relation to ideology (a call to which comparatists have already been exposed in the 2003 seminal contribution by David Kennedy).[92] To

86 Corcodel, note 16 above.

87 Ibid., p. 139.

88 Ibid., p. 143. See also David Kennedy, "The Methods and the Politics", in Pierre Legrand and Roderick Munday (eds.), *Comparative Legal Studies: Traditions and Transitions* (2003), pp. 345-433. Writing from the position of self-awareness, Kennedy admits that "there is a politics to making known the politics of the profession – to translating our knowledge vocabularies into vocabularies of political contestation": Ibid., p. 432.

89 Corcodel, note 16 above, p. 144.

90 Ibid., p. 145.

91 Ibid., pp. 152-159.

92 Kennedy, note 88 above, pp. 345-433. At the end of his study, Kennedy offers the following advice: "Imagine each comparative-law project coming with an ideological and interest 'impact statement', articulating the effects that knowing this, rather than something else, might have on the distribution of ideas and things

the extent that the study of law (even comparatively) remains a matter of technicalities only, the initial transgressive potential of a research departing from the parochialism of national law is certain to be lost. Comparative law has the invaluable merit of suspending from the outset any idea of normativity as the main pillar of thinking about the law.[93] Comparisons force a reconnection of law to its material conditions, to life, and thus unveil how law relates to society, ultimately offering answers about law's "whereabouts". As a critical scholarly enterprise, comparison points to the fact that law does not own a transcendental condition from where it could speak "beyond any reasonable doubt". It also highlights that some general questions that we ask about law, oftentimes *ad nauseam*, cannot be answered at all, at least not in the abstract. With comparative law, suddenly, both the questions and the critique focusing on the "usual suspects" charged with infringing law's integrity and systematicity (for example, politics) are radically called into question. When dealing with two distinct legal orders, it no longer makes sense, from an intellectual point of view, to address the same typical normative questions raised within the confines of national scholarship.

As opposed to traditional dogmatic writings, whose utility has been defended for a long time and is taken for granted by most jurists, the act of putting together, in the same mental configuration, two or more legal systems represents an unnecessary (and not immediately useful) intervention. It is the researcher who generates this theoretical encounter and, therefore, it is they who bear a greater responsibility for why and how to compare. And so other disciplines might press the laws compared into more reflexive avenues of thought where ideological considerations are not shunned but critically engaged with. Relying on other sources than the legally binding, comparatists will be better situated to go a long way in formulating "critical ideas about the complex connections between a foreign law and the polylogical world that it inhabits, and that inhabits it", thus "enhanc[ing] comparative law's worldliness by accounting for foreignness's worldliness and for interpretive worldliness" and ultimately "ameliorat[ing] his

in the world". Ibid., p. 432.

93 Alexandra Mercescu, "What Kind of Critique for Central and Eastern European Legal Studies? Comparison As One of The Answers", *Folia Iuridica*, LXXXIX (2019).

reporting's integrity and attendant creditability".[94] The alternative, "a one-dimensional perspective reducing worldliness to empirical givenness" must be recognized "complicit with political and social domination (implausible decolonial gesticulation notwithstanding)".[95] In the context of pressing social issues like multiple wars, globalization, rule of law backsliding, democracy decay, artificial intelligence, it certainly does not seem the right time for comparative law to retreat into the aseptic, uninventive, fixist, disciplinarizing, non-reflexive, black and white world of positivism.

94 Legrand, note 60 above, p. 43.

95 Ibid., p. 43.

Chapter 21

Legal Images and Understandings of Law: Juristic Assumptions and Results, Student Evaluations and Choices

CSABA VARGA

We compare to get to know ourselves better. And we compare things that we know to have some common function. We therefore take their necessity and usefulness for granted, and by comparing them we are interested in why and in what ways the solutions adopted by individual legal cultures of various nations, which have been brought to our attention but are alien to us, prove to be more or less expedient than those we have developed and use ourselves. Our question is thus to clarify what kind of institutions and skills, procedures, and ways of reacting have been developed by man in his historical practice with the support of what kind of worldviews and background philosophies, and what kind of interplay between these has contributed to the adaptive use of the various known endowments in a given solution in a given culture to produce precisely this or that result in question.[1]

From this point of view, historical investigation is also a comparison, built up by comparing successive chronological sections of the past up to the present. For all the actors of all times are creators to the core, shapers of practice; in fact, they are not simply respondents to questions that can be logically deduced from abstract theories, but rather people who live with practical problem-solving, searching for and eventually choosing the most optimal answer to the challenges that arise in a given place and time, that is, the one that seems the most viable among the inevitable compromises. In successive times, the person responsible does no

[1] For example, Csaba Varga, "Comparative Law and Multicultural Legal Classes: Challenge or Opportunity?", in Csaba Varga (ed.), *Comparative Law and Multicultural Legal Classes: Challenge or Opportunity?* (2020), pp. 3-42.

more than either refine and improve these responses, or adapt them to the changed conditions, or try to found a completely new direction. In our human history, however spectacular, symbolic, and thus representative, that is, embodying human progress it may be, the result thus presented may be truly breathtaking indeed. Yet what is instructive from all this for its own environment and its afterlife, and thus requires analyzing it again and again, will be nothing other than the way of thinking – in short: problem-solving itself, which once led to the setting aside of any alternative that arose and to the reflection on and eventual acceptance of precisely this chosen one.[2]

THE HIDDEN PRESUPPOSITIONS OF JURISPRUDENCE

In every stray thought that arises and in our everyday thinking, as well as in the cultivation of our own scholarly field, behind our assertions and/or denials there is some intellectual background, or more precisely the whole sum of life-space images that lie presupposed behind the concrete object of thinking, which in fact provide the medium for the thought operations in question. They can be revealed and, with sufficient analytical interest, can be explored with an adequate approach. Not otherwise, of course, than as a purely logical presupposition and logically viewed. For it is logic that dictates that as soon as one speaks about anything, one has actually included their specimen in what one has to say – that is, either one has already accepted and been inspired by it, or one has also formed its wider (and, ultimately, even reaching the totality of our world, ultimately, ever expanding) underlying meaning as well. For by sheer logic it can indeed be shown that by positing any kind of *X*, a *Y*, as its precondition or organic accompaniment, is also, if implicitly, positively posited. As a logical necessity, all this means that we can count on some kind of their background presence when any thought appears in two ways: as a *presupposition*, so that we can speak of an object at all, and at the same time as a *consequence*, since by speaking of an object

[2] Regarding its theoretical foundations, see Varga, "A jog mint elméleti és történeti kutatások tárgya" [Law as an Object of Theoretical and Historical Research], in Barna Mezey (ed.), *Kölcsönhatások: Európa és Magyarország a jogtörténelem sodrásában* [Interactions: Europe and Hungary in the Maelstrom of Legal History] (2021), pp. 324-331.

we have implicitly betrayed something of this background object, and thus, symbolically speaking, we have re-enacted it as a refined and perhaps somewhat transformed variant.

We must therefore see it as a natural and self-evident interconnection that in the field of law, too, any intellectual expression of ours is also based on concepts and images of law itself. They are mostly not readable or visible, perhaps not even explicitly formulated, but only necessarily presupposed, since we can infer their presence. In general, they are not only not delineated, but also cannot be described or defined in retrospect, either exhaustively or even a little more precisely, if only by a small margin. They are simply the assumptions of our thinking. They are logically necessary, but unstated premises for a conclusion. They are like a set of undefined axioms described in a behavioral analysis, which, although without being stated in any way that can be markedly presupposed, nevertheless make one think and act in a definite way in everyday practice. And, as we have said, since they are present merely as the presupposition of a thought, rather than in any tangible form, nothing more can be known about them afterwards – only what can be assumed by means of intellectual reconstruction as the necessary presupposition of the assertion or negation posited as an original and stated conclusion of thought.

In contrast to which those law-pictures which are the so-called by-products, or even conscious constructions, of the jurisprudential thinking in question may now prove to be somewhat more concrete for the reconstruction – but of course only insofar as the thought process in question was itself the one which, by formulating any feature or property, that is, by explicitly asserting or denying it, definitively enriched this law-picture as its own result.

Such tacit, latent products, not even tangible in a symbolic sense, so to speak – at most, as we have seen, they can be inferred to some extent from abstractions of abstractions – have practically no epistemological value in themselves. As we have also seen, they do not really exist. It is only the reconstructive intellect, the constantly differentiating analysis, the freedom and omnipotence of conceptualisation that makes them communicable at all. Resisting any kind of reconstruction, we are confronted in their case with nothing more than a kind of hint, a sense of sensitivity, a *déjà vu* type of impression, even in the slightest hint of meaning, message or possible message. In epistemological terms, we might therefore consider them meaningless.

However, their practical importance is hardly affected. Such hints, suggestions, mental environments that in a certain direction give a positive or negative mood or even a feeling of homeliness, accompany our everyday life from moment to moment, full of new impressions. Their role in preserving and daily adapting the traditions that underpin our professional approach and condition our everyday self-positioning in the wider world is therefore of enormous importance. For it is a basic fact of everyday life that the majority of our interpretative stock relating to the outside world, the majority of our impressions of things, which are constantly being formed and perhaps not even consciously formulated, are not formed by what we have learned from the sciences, but by such and similar basic attitudes, conjectures, formless suggestions, which cannot even be strictly called information, and by the vague, unframed, blurred dream images that form the senseful background of our everyday lives. It is well known that we all have a single self, a single psyche. And it cannot be dismantled, cannot be divided into parts, cannot be distinguished from within as a set of functions. It is in such an environment and as a result of it that our sciences are also born, and that our social and personal assumptions that ensure our emotional, intellectual and positive or negative attitudes towards such or such phenomena and effects (that is, conditioning, which forms the medium of our scholarly thought and is mostly not even conscious), are also present as a smoldering background, both near and far.

The vast majority of jurisprudential work is obviously a doctrinal analysis or case-law review of the own law, based on the national legal system, that is appropriate to its authors. It is only a minority of the relevant research and literature that seeks to be a truly scholarly monograph, either on law in general or on a broader group, such as the European continental Civil Law, the Anglo–American Common Law, or the tribal or religious laws.

It can also be said that, in the average case, law appears in its ordinary everyday perception as a normative ordering force that ensures social order by issuing rules and by sanctioning, positively or negatively, the variations of behavior that conform or do not conform to them. Such a view of law is the typical background understanding for almost all public, private, and criminal law, as well as legal theory, and comparative jurisprudence. In fact, it is only certain distinct lines of enquiry that suggest or imply a different picture according to their specificity. For instance, sociology of law presents a model of the interaction between the normative spheres of social existence and the factors of social movement, whereas anthropology of law remains unchanged in its identification of customary law as invisible in reality but actualized on a case-by-case basis in a thousand faces, and yet ever-changing.[3] Even within legal theory itself, practically distinct from one school to another, natural law is the image of the respect for value, realism is the image of the judge's choice, Marxism is a kind of overall definition within prime economic functionality, and so on.

At this point, it should be noted that the three terms used in this context are not synonymous, but all express contents that characterize law, but from different perspectives. The original German *juristische Weltbild*[4] (in Russian правовая картина мира,[5] and in the present study, "legal world picture")[6] is used in the present writer's linguistic practice as "*law-picture*" [jogkép in Hungarian], meaning the implicit background images of law which can be inferred from a legal thought or a legal work as an indication of the law under discussion as background. In contrast, the original German *juristische Weltanschauung*[7] has a double meaning. It means, first and foremost and classically, what

[3] In fact, customary law as an object of legal anthropology is not a description of a momentary state that has just been stated and transcribed into a rule, but that thinking, and at the bottom of it, a mentality, which occasionally produces a decision on the basis of a question that arises. See Varga, "»Magyarok a nagyvilágban«: Nékám Sándor (1905–1982), a jogi személy, az afrikai szokásjog, a komparatisztika kutatója' [»Hungarians in the global world«: Alexander Nékám (1905–1982), researcher of the legal person, African customary law, and comparatistics], *Iustum Aequum Salutare*, XI (2015) 3, pp. 160-161.

[4] Varga, "Recht und Rechtsverwiklichung: Juristisches Weltbild, Subsumption und Manipulation", *Archiv für Rechts- und Sozialphilosophie*, LXX, no. 2 (1984), pp. 173-189.

[5] S. P. Khizhniak, «Соотношение наивных и научных правовых картин мира» [Correlation of Naive and Scientific Legal World Pictures], Известия высших учебных заведений – Поволжский регион (Гуманитарные науки: Филология) [News of Institutions of Higher Education – Volga Region (Humanitarian Sciences: Philology)] [Penza], no. 2 (2017), pp. 88-93.

[6] O. V. Kresin, "Comparative Law Days in Lausanne", *Journal of Comparative Law*, XVIII (2023), pp. 592-601.

[7] In its original classical sense, see Friedrich Engels – Karl Kautsky, "Juristen-Sozialismus", *Die Neue Zeit*, no. 2 (1887); monographically from Kilian Stein, *Die juristische Weltanschauung: Der Staat als Fetisch* (2010) and *Die juristische Weltanschauung: Das rechtstheoretische Potenzial der Marxschen »Kritik«* (2012). In the present sense, Varga, "Law, Understanding of Law, Application of Law", *Acta Juridica Hungarica*, LI, no. 2 (2010), pp. 20-32.

is known as the "juridical worldview"[8] or "juristic worldview"[9] [jogászi világnézet in Hungarian],[10] that is, the *lawyers' professional ideology,*[11] within the framework of which and in accordance with the expectations of which they operate the law professionally and which, therefore, irrespective of its content, is not a false ideology, as Marxism in its classical period saw it, but is part of the ontic of law in its different forms in different legal cultures. At the same time, irrespective of this foundation, it can also be understood as a "juristic world concept" [jogászi világkép in Hungarian], that is, the *lawyers' understanding of law* in a professional group or in an individual sense.

Truly interesting is how much asynchronicity can and does exist between the juridical worldview that is actually followed and the juristic world concept that is developed in and by the legal scholarship.

The *juridical worldview* is a kind of normative professional ideology, which is nothing other than the rule-based positivist approach traditionalized in the eighteenth and nineteenth centuries, according to which the legislator positively imposes norms and the law enforcer enforces their norm content by sanctioning the way of their implementation or application. This is the horizon of the legal function thus conceived; and this, its quasi-autotelic, self-sufficient sufficiency, has become the official ideology of the Continental legal order.[12] And even though times and expectations of law may have changed since, it is still what serves and satisfies the needs of law within the Civil Law of the European continent and is therefore no coincidence that its dogmatic doctrine is implicitly based on it, and that, consequently, our future jurists in our schools also acquire the subject of law under its approach and rule. These future jurists are thus coming out of a kind of scholarship

[8] See, for example, various online sources.

[9] See Varga, *The Place of Law in Lukács' World Concept* (3d ed.; 2012) resp. "The Contemporaneity of Lukács' Ideas with Modern Social Theoretical Thought: *The Ontology of Social Being* in Social Science Reconstruction with Regards to Constructs like Law", *Archiv für Rechts- und Sozialphilosophie,* XCIX, no. 1 (2013), pp. 42-54.

[10] Varga, *A jog helye Lukács György világképében* [The Place of Law in Lukács® World Concept] (1981), pp. 251-259.

[11] Ibid.

[12] See Varga, "Átalakulóban a jog?" [Is Law in Transformation?], *Állam- és Jogtudomány,* XXIII (1980), pp. 670-680.

and professional educational institutional view in which a historically theological formula prevails, a hierarchical structure almost mechanically broken down from God the Creator to the created, from this former "everything" to the latter's figurative "nothing", from the constitutional lord of the legal system down to the smallest human recipient, that is, from the legislator to the addressee. The basic theological image of the order of nature, that is, the *God* → *law* → *nature* sequence has thus become the pattern of the order of human conduct: *legislator* → *rule* → *enforcement by public authority*. Moreover, it is a formula with a quasi cause and effect interrelationship that can be clearly and uniquely traced and determined in any case, as required.[13]

While for more than a century kinds of *legal process reconstruction* have been developed by legal sciences, which, instead of unilateral effects, see law first and foremost in a medium of interactions, in the endless series of an infinite social interplay, which, contrary to the previous view, is not really about law, but about only one single fluid and diffuse factor, highlighted from the infinity of social movement arbitrarily or for analytical interest by us, jurists, and its constant and fluctuating interaction with other factors in its environment.

By way of illustration, one of these *juristic world concepts* was inspired by American *anthropological* research from the early twentieth century. It recognized that the social process itself is stochastic, full of randomness. Well, in practical terms, in everyday life we tend to act with a purely ordinary attention to detail, and although we sometimes perceive risks and sometimes consider dangers, we nevertheless choose and behave predominantly as prisoners of the moment's opportunities for self-interest. Accordingly, it is only in the casual need to reconsider or justify the choice made, among other things, that the law, the legal criterion, is ever considered.[14] So, breaking with the divine order suggested by the *theologicum*, which is clear, certain, predictable, and imposed with absolute precision, because it is backed by *providentia*, the divine fullness and self-sufficiency, everything is

[13] Werner Krawietz, "Die Lehre vom Stufenbau des Rechts – eine säkularisierte politische Theologie?", in Werner Krawietz and Helmut Schelsky (ed.), *Rechtssystem und gesellschaftliche Basis bei Hans Kelsen* (1984), pp. 255-271.

[14] Robert B. Edgerton, *Rules, Exceptions, and Social Order* (1985); Noel B. Reynolds, "Rule of Law in Legal and Economic Theory", in L. E. Kotsiris (ed.), *Law at the Turn of the 20th Century: International conference, Thessaloniki, 1993* (1994), pp. 357-376.

already in motion, changing from situation to situation here. As does the direction and emphasis of the approach. For it is precisely this world concept of law with an anthropological approach that reveals that "The essence of human life did not lie in following rules and in being rewarded by one's virtue but in making the best use of rules for one's own self-interest, depending on the situation".[15] Or, in other words, our life is somewhat decelebratedly practical, nestled in the practical incentives of everyday life.

A similar juristic world concept, albeit born out of an explanation of the development of European law, which eventually became the law *of the European Union*, was originally conceived as a description of the continental legal development in the early modern era. This is the analogy of the interdependence of the solar and planetary systems,[16] which, in their unity and in their dialectically distinct characteristics, show a continuous multipolar movement, a simultaneous centripetalism and centrifugalism, a continuum that is constantly in a state of flux and in practical evolutive solution, which happens to occur between the various responses of a normatively acting European Union center and the member States, that is, national legal systems, and the further moves generated by both of them, which are at the same time random, even if dominated by current policies. For this is what is produced by the bipolar fragmentation of the European Union›s legal reality, by the realization or non-realization of its central directives, interpreted in one way or another within the framework of nation-state sovereignty, then re-reacted by Brussels/Luxembourg/Strasbourg, and so on and so on.

It is an interesting coincidence, by not purely accidental, that the sociologism of the twentieth century began to form a functionalist vision of society from the notion of the self-propelling move of man-made reified structures, in which the vision of

[15] Edgerton, note 14 above, p. 13.

[16] As Kenneth Pennington, "Learned Law, Droit Savant, Gelehrtes Recht: The Tyranny of a Concept", *Rivista internazionale di diritto comune*, V (1994), pp. 197-209 as well as *Syracuse Journal of International Law and Commerce*, XX (1994), p. 215 concluded from Manlio Bellomo, *L'Europa del diritto comune* (6th ed.; 1993), pp. 205-206, there is "the imagery of the *Ius commune* as the sun and the *iura propria*, the legal norms of kingdoms, principalities, and city states as the planets to explain the relationship of the *Ius commune* and *iura propria*. [...] The *Ius commune* was not bookish law, was not the law of the greats, to be read, savored, and returned to the shelf, was not learned law in contrast to real law. It was the cauldron from which much of the precious metal of all European legal systems emerged".

the unidirectional mechanics of some kind of determination is replaced by the spontaneous movement of simultaneities built on and by a plural actor system and an uninterrupted series of social interactions. It was at the end of the nineteenth century that macro-physics' scientific vision of the world superseded the Newtonian vision of the world, which had promised the predictability of causality, to replace it with a vision of the outcomes of stochastic movements, which all that notwithstanding are certain in their mass and random statistical probabilities individually.

Instead of the mythical definition (inspired in its formulation by an unvarnished theological image of God) of a kind of primary act, or creative intervention or final determination, what has emerged is the functional interdependence of sub-complexes in interaction and the reality of interplay in this necessary, and thus practical, cooperation. And with the fact that it now focuses on an uninterrupted social practice, on the statistically averaged outcome of the motivational struggles of individuals, on interactions that actually take place, a change of perspective also takes place. For – surprise! – although in this latter context the *micro*-descriptions can only perceive chaos, a continuous interstice and floating in the constancy of attractions and repulsions, in its *macro*-descriptions it will nevertheless already infer the possibility and the fact of an *order resulting from chaos*, which ultimately emerges from its statistical generality. For in the mutuality of their multiplicity, even according to the formula of the solar and planetary system, the force which in all its movements tended to constantly and stubbornly seeking only the ways, principles, points of view and chances of ordering, proved to be finally decisive.[17]

It is no coincidence, therefore, that it is the same approach, the recognition of the *macro-order* that ultimately emerges *from micro-chaos*, that has laid the foundations of the modern economic vision, and the same vision has given rise to modern sociology as well. It has also a message for us to be more modest in our view of the universe: a kind of dynamism pervades our existence, always

[17] Varga, *Jogrendszerek, jogi gondolkodásmódok az európai egységesülés perspektívájában (Magyar körkép – európai uniós összefüggésben)* [Legal Systems, Judicial Ways of Thinking in the Perspective of European Unification (Hungarian Overview – in the Context of the European Union)] (2009), particularly at pp. 189-191, and "The Philosophy of European Law with 'Order Out of Chaos' Set-Up and Functioning", in *25th IVR World Congress: Law, Science and Technology*, Series B / No. 009/2012 (available online).

resulting in some kind of order, but always evolving. For here and there, too, order is stochastic: "Order is never complete and never can be".[18]

UNDERSTANDING OF LAW IN RESPONSES BY FUTURE PROFESSIONALS

It is not by chance, but as a legacy of the recognition of the explanatory power inherent in the exploration of the historicity of things, that legal education often starts with legal history as a foundational subject, and Roman law as a model in particular, followed by legal theory in order to introduce theoretical perspectives, and at some point – if at all, but here, with us, in any case – by a comparative legal discussion of the underlying legal cultures and their legal systems themselves, concentrating mainly on background mentalities and styles, and their basic concepts and some of their characteristic institutions. The Faculty of Law of the Pázmány Péter Catholic University (Budapest) has been familiar with this tripartite division from the beginning, so to speak, and as if the recognition of the systemic nature of this triad could be reflected in it, the optional final year discipline of "Comparative Legal Cultures and Judicial Thought" certainly builds on the basis of which the not insignificant body of legal knowledge accumulated by our students for the final examinations is combined with the aforementioned historical, theoretical, and comparative approach.[19]

What emerges from a comparative study of legal cultures is, first, that the world we know is not *the* world of law itself, but the image of one of the potentialities that can be, and in our case has been, realized here or there in world history; and it is not necessarily the best world, only the one we have best occupied by living within its ambits. Moreover, the very first property of all of those *other* worlds in this respect is nothing else than that they are

[18] Edgerton, note 14 above, p. 14.

[19] Varga, "The Philosophy of Teaching Legal Philosophy in Hungary", in Imer B. Flores and Gülriz Uygur (ed.), *Alternative Methods in the Education of Philosophy of Law and the Importance of Legal Philosophy in the Legal Education: Proceedings of the 23rd World Congress of the International Association for Philosophy of Law and Social Philosophy »Law and Legal Cultures in the 21st Century: Diversity and Unity« in Kraków, 2007* (2010), pp. 49-60; as well as *Iustum Aequum Salutare*, V, no. 2 (2009), pp. 165-184.

other. In what? In their basic principles; in respect of man and his community, and the transcendental roots of both; in the nature, the breadth, the need of support for the provision of order; and if they may differ so much on these ultimate issues, their varieties, in their modes of regulation, their institutions and their procedures, cover a field so vast, so wide and so diverse, that the representatives of another segment or variation of it sometimes do question whether a given species of it developed in another culture is law at all.[20]

In addition to their diversity, a fundamental feature of these cultures is the autochthonous character of their basic forms, that is, that they are the original products of times and places that are not mutually derived, that they are the product of their own living conditions and specific cultural milieu, that they function adequately in response to their own challenges, that is, that each of their varieties contains the genius *hic et nunc*, manifested in its own circle, which gives them their identity and ensures their functionality.[21]

Juridical worldviews and juristic world concepts? If we translate all these into abstractions and experiences derived from the knowledge of reality, and translate what we learn from a comparative study of legal cultures into a confrontation with our own culture, confronting it with others' different values, and in the process reflecting on the relative advantages and disadvantages that one side or the other can identify, we have a truly contrasted picture, in which we can see one in the mirror of the other. The present writer attempted to do this when his students were asked in the final year of the elective course on "Comparative Study of Legal Cultures and Judicial Thought" at the Faculty of Law of Pázmány Péter Catholic University, which has been offered

[20] According to my definition (see Varga, "Anthropological Jurisprudence? Leopold Pospíšil and the Comparative Study of Legal Cultures", in Institute of Comparative Law, Waseda University (ed.), *Law in East and West: On the Occasion of the 30th Anniversary of the Institute of Comparative Law, Waseda University* (1988), pp. 265-285) "(1) law is a global phenomenon integrating society as a whole [...] (2) law is a phenomenon settling conflicts of interests that emerge in social practice as fundamental [...] (3) law is a phenomenon possessing the supreme regulating and influencing power in a given society". By nature, see Varga, *The Paradigms of Legal Thinking* (2d ed,; 2012), ch. 6.1—law is process-like, multifactoral, and made up from acts.

[21] Varga, "Jog, jogi kultúra és jogi hagyomány" [Law, Legal Culture and Legal Tradition], *Iustum Aequum Salutare*, XVII, no. 1 (2021), pp. 191-219.

for several decades, about their impressions and preferences;[22] this process was repeated to specifically ask them about their preferences on the issue: "Which features of any legal cultures you have encountered do you find positive, progressive, more expedient, or even transposable, on the one hand, or even explicitly negative, detrimental, obstructive to the goals of the law as we know and believe it to be and therefore to be explicitly avoided, on the other, when confronted with our own legal culture, and why"?

Obviously, we should not look for mature perspectives or even a refined assessment in such and similar student answers as given in response, but rather impressions of the possibilities that can be formulated against the approaches and outlooks, institutional solutions that have historically been developed in Hungary, on the basis of the continental legal system – not necessarily in spite of them or to replace them, but at least to expand, supplement and/or enrich them. The students naturally reflect what they have already learned over five years, that is, their perception and understanding of the law as presented on the basis of their own juridical worldview, as well as the juristic world concepts of which they have acquired some knowledge and impressions. To a certain extent, the answers given are imbued with, and perhaps even benefit from, a certain idealism which is perhaps characteristic of this generation growing up. It is certain that this gives students the courage to seek ideals at all in a world that is now less receptive to the latter. All in all, their main benefit is to *gain perspective,* to gain both an internal and an external position which enables those students to understand more deeply the driving forces of their own system, and thus to be more successful in the long term than their peers who do not have it, in solving their future daily professional problems, and especially the bordering issues which will inevitably arise, and hopefully also to demonstrate creativity in building for the future.

From the foundation of Continental Civil Law on which our students are formed, the most striking attraction to them is obviously the recognition of the otherness of *Anglo-Saxon Common Law,* and so most of their comments have been about this. Accordingly,

[22] As a report, see Varga, "A magyar jog – tükörcserepekben" [Hungarian Law – in Mirror Tiles], *Magyar Jog* [Hungarian law], LXVIII (2021), pp. 227–235.

The very image of the human being in Anglo-Saxon legal culture is different, since it treats the individual as an adult, with confidence, as opposed to Continental law, which sees him as a mere subject of a system of orders from above. The judges in it, while they themselves make the law, approach cases with extreme humility: behind every case they see the unique, the unrepeatable, the »drama« that may have happened in the individual case, rather than a case to be »impersonally« forced into a set of facts previously defined by the law, that may make a case in law[23].

The precedent system creates opportunities to incorporate social perspectives, for example. A purely legal perspective can thus be enriched by external values. For it, therefore, law is not just a set of rules, but a constantly renewed attempt to solve the changing problems of a changing society. And this alone can meet the need for democracy more directly.

For them, judgment is always a choice between open options.

They reject conceptualisation and abstraction, and in problem-solving this can be much more useful than trying to fit a specific case into a formally predefined set of facts chosen from a reduced system of logical deduction. Induction is used instead of deduction, and although the law is necessarily abstract, it is also inductive in its interpretation.

In reaching his decision, the judge thinks in terms of the past and the present, and does not merely attempt to give a mechanical answer to the issue at hand.

The judge is also the guardian of the law and can therefore be more conservative.

The English judiciary tends to use simple ordinary language, while the tone of its decisions is personal and individual.

[23] This is der Tatbestand, that is, the sum of factual conditions that must be present for the legal consequence to be meted out. Or, as Max Weber's formal criterion of the law's rationality formulates it as a postulate: "every concrete legal decision is an 'application' of an abstract legal principle to a concrete 'fact'" ["jede konkrete Rechtsentscheidung »Anwendung«‹ eines abstrakten Rechtssatzes auf einen konkreten »Tatbestand« sei"].

Dictatorship in a common law system has not yet occurred.

This is mostly inspiring because, instead of thinking in deductive derivation that limits *ius* to *lex*, its judge can act much more flexibly and pragmatically when he can base his decision on examples that have already occurred instead of the simple and abstract order of the lawmaker. The judicial event will thus become the crystallisation of the law, in which and with which the court actually conveys the opinion of society.

Constitutional adjudication, which has led to the politicisation of law anywhere in the world, has not been adopted by the English to this day.

Anglo-Saxon legal system based on precedents is attractive because it assumes an analytical approach. This means that real life can shape the development of law. In addition, the jury system the English use also indicates that they take into account the opinion of the people, the lay people. As a result, civilians bear the fate of the legal order much more closely, since they have a say in its working. And last but not least, it is sympathetic that being a judge is not simply a profession, but the pinnacle of the legal profession as such, because only the most experienced make it to the final forum.

By allowing precedents to shape the law, they can follow social changes much more effectively. The judicial law-making, with its emphasis on judicial independence, allows the judge to take his own conscience into account during his decision-making. While there is no doubt that the development of precedent law is much more difficult for the average citizen to understand. Judging by jury, on the other hand, is forward-looking because it greatly helps the mapping of society, i.e. public opinion and public mood, in individual judicial decisions.

"If the law is more than some kind of a huge set of rules, then a kind of flexibility can also appear in it."

Jurors in the jury system are better suited to make an impartial decision on a given issue. Since both the defence and the prosecution are involved in their selection, their decision is more easily accepted by both parties. And while the precedent law system provides greater legitimacy to the judgment, thanks to its limitations, there will also be less chance of the court abusing its power.

The English judicial procedure and style is much more humane, direct and expressive than, for example, the more rigid, objective, academic approach similar to the French system and also known in our country. The atmosphere of a dialogical process, the judge's more direct approach to the case brings the law, justice, and comprehensibility closer to all actors. By describing all the circumstances of the case almost literally, the judge confirms that he understands all the circumstances of the case and that he deals with them in depth, because he wants to understand the positions of both parties. This makes the judgment more understandable, because it is more direct and acceptable to the losing party as well.

In the precedent system, they do not only focus on deciding cases at the moment, but on the one hand, they examine the past, the decisions made before, and on the other hand, they keep an eye on the future, to what extent their own decisions can shape the jurisprudence of the future.

It should be considered from the common law system that turning to the House of Lords as the highest appeal forum can be done with permission and in exceptional cases, and thus this highest level can deal with serious cases and problems that affect the legal system as a whole. At the same time, all this places a greater burden and responsibility on the lower-level courts.

In the Anglo-Saxon legal culture, the judge often uses open arguments, which makes it easier to adapt to social changes. Legal service is unique in each case. In general, its law is much more »flexible«, because the law itself, taken strictly, is outside the scope of the decision. Not only change, but also continuity is strongly present in it—as it is based on traditions and develops organically—and thus gives a sense of security at the same time.

The English judge does not interpret the law, the set of statutory instruments, but starts from the case, thinks about it, and then tries to find the best solution based on precedents as cases solved in the past. Such an approach

> can often be closer to the real legal truth, not just drawn from and eventually formulated in abstract terms.

> Everything is simply different in the Anglo-Saxon legal system. 'General norms' or 'application of law' mean completely different concepts to them. For them, the uniqueness of the case overrides the possibility of squeezing it into some kind of general situation, that is, the case is always specific and unrepeatable. Applying a pre-written formulation to this would mean that we are ignoring the specifics of the case in question.

As evidenced by the above, the Anglo-Saxon law-picture conveyed to our future lawyers is complex and suitable for contrast, since trust appears in its human-image premise, humility in its approach to cases, relative openness in addition to the sense of security of continuity and contingency in its system construction, and in its methodology a preference for the concreteness of the description to the domination of any kind of abstraction. Moreover, part of its view is the assumption of responsibility between the past and the future, and last but not least, more direct sociality and fuller legitimacy, in which the presence of dialogicity and the insight into the changeability of law also play a role.

The future lawyer mostly characterizes his own law, and thus *Continental Civil Law*, by what, how and why he sees as noticeable and especially sympathetic in a foreign legal concept. This may explain why our students have relatively few and modest direct things to say. As some of their observations show:

> Continental legal systems resemble a river moving in a pre-regulated channel. In other words, we have a huge body of law in front of us, and the rules contained in it determine our lives; we simply have to live by them.

> For me, continental law is the most transparent and easiest legal system to interpret.

> In our continental system, law is defined by definitions, which our legislators create and enact. These are quite general in nature. If the law were to appear in our country based on judicial decisions, the number of actions would increase in which the party involved would and perhaps rightly could claim that there is no special provision or rule for the given case, so the deed is free to be done.

> Our continental thinking starts from written law. The legal practitioner thinks in this system, so when solving a case, he conceptualises, i.e. reduces the real historical situation to predefined legal facts that may make a case in law. On the other hand, in Anglo-Saxon thinking rooted in the assumption of immemorial custom of the Realm, the applicable law is »everywhere«, so to speak, and therefore the judge not even conceptualise, since for him the totality of facts is interesting as a whole. As a result of his procedure, he can even create a new precedent, which, of course, according to its theoretical understanding, is not new, since the judge did not create it, but only recognized it, so to speak.

Striking on the one hand is the ease with which everything that our future lawyers learned for half a decade as the Hungarian implementation of the continental legal approach actually turns into an ideal-typical representation of the juridical worldview of this culture, and on the other hand, the inner conviction with which the whole of it, and especially its transparency, its simple and assumedly secure structure and operation are surrounded by natural sympathy. Basically, this is a service for one's own background culture, which, by providing or deciphering its interpretive key, not only creates an order that we can now thrive on, but also ensures the feeling of being at home, psychologically necessary for all living beings.[24]

Exemplification with the law-pictures of some historical or national establishments can also serve to provide a more precise overview and understanding of the characteristics of one's own law. Regarding the *law of ancient Greece,* for example, as an ancient root manifestation of law with the sign of early non-differentiation, it arises that

> The Greeks had a legal regime. They fought with arguments in front of the judicial body, but this was basically dominated by an oratorical and rhetorical character rather than a specifically legal one. For them, any argument could be relevant in law. Impartiality as crucial in modern Western

[24] Varga, "Law as Culture?", in Varga, *Comparative Legal Cultures: On Traditions Classified, their Rapprochement & Transfer, and the Anarchy of Hyper-rationalism* (2012), pp. 9-14 and, as a background, Dirk Baecker, *Wozu Kultur?* (2d ed.; 2001).

> legal cultures as a legacy from Roman law was alien to Greek culture.

This kind of thinking shows *classical Roman law* as something in-between, in a semi-state, in which philosophical reflection can play a role in its refinement and case resolution. But the semi-state of this intermediate openness is already indicated by the appearance of so-called professional commitment, which disciplines legal practitioner with his caste-like professional separation and at the same time mutual conventionalisation that may make the given community somewhat closed. Accordingly,

> Openness and closeness were present in the legal culture of the Romans, which of course changed from time to time. Arguments based on utility—now called public interest—multiplied in the late classical period. Arguments taken from philosophy (such as Stoicism) were considered acceptable if they appeared in a general guise such as references to *natura* or *aequum*. In this way, philosophy had an influence on the law, but only in a general way, and not one that could have directly guided the assessment of a problematic case in the direction of a specific solution.
>
> The law was vocationalised and professionalised by creating a necessarily small group of people who were socialised with the same ideals, with the same views on what types of arguments can be used in the assessment of given legal problems, and thereby made the legal discourse closed on the one hand, but on the other hand somewhat yet they left it open to the influence of the Romans' social life, morals, politics, and religion; as a product of all of this, their professionalism could then look at society through a half-open window.

As was visible from a previous casual opinion, the picture of Hungarian law is sometimes typified as French – first with or despite the recognition of the former's Latinic roots through the reception of Roman law, and then, for historical reasons, refined following German (Austrian-mediated) models. As a matter of fact, the former may be seen by students as a natural – because it is homely – model, but the *French law* regime itself is caricatured with some of its worst qualities. Because, so to speak:

> For the French, the case is identified by date and remembered by the name of the court, and the entire judgment is

condensed into one complex sentence. The judge cannot lay down general principles; he can only repeat legislation.

Therefore, it is not a coincidence either, but the experience of the naturalness and familiarity of one's own law, that the *Hungarian law* picture happens to be mentioned in such an evaluative context only as an object of criticism, as an object to be improved, merely as a *de lege lata* remark. For example, because

The Hungarian system would benefit from a plain and articulated language and stronger attention to individual cases.

The difference in the way of thinking of judges can be observed very well even within one legal system, since the judges' way of thinking is the result of the interplay of an extremely large number of moments. Broadly speaking, this way of thinking can be divided into two large groups: one is the legal positivist understanding of law-application, which strictly follows the letter of the law, and the other is the activist approach to the same process, also trying to interpret and enforce the original (at least assumed) will of the legislator. In Hungary, a cardinal legal principle laid down in Article 28 of the Basic Law[25] can provide a very good inspiration for this, according to which the courts interpret the statutory text primarily in accordance with its purpose and the Basic Law when applying the law. And when interpreting, it must be assumed that legislation cannot serve but goals within the ambit of common sense and common good, justifiable morally and economically as well.

The extremely heterogeneous nature of the judicial way of thinking and the consequent importance of the human factor, with the subjectivity of the entire law-application process involved, is well demonstrated by the fact that, even in the case of the same facts and the same legal

[25] "In the course of the application of law, courts shall interpret the text of laws primarily in accordance with their purpose and with the Fundamental Law. In the course of ascertaining the purpose of a law, consideration shall be given primarily to the preamble of that law and the justification of the proposal for, or for amending, the law. When interpreting the Fundamental Law or laws, it shall be presumed that they serve moral and economic purposes which are in accordance with common sense and the public good". *The Fundamental Law of Hungary* (2011) (available online).

> environment, two judicial forums often make completely different decisions from each other.
>
> It would be a positive message in Hungarian law if the limitations of judicial discretion could be somewhat expanded for the judge. In this way, the legislator would declare that he trusts the job exercised by and the expertise of the judge, that is, that he can adequately decide the case in question.

There are one or two scattered statements that convey a remarkable assessment of *Canadian law* and one of the characteristics of *Brazilian legal culture*, naturally from a domestic point of view. According to their testimony:

> Canadian law is exemplary in that it is codified without the system becoming rigid, because it pays special attention to the judicial process based on precedents. And it is very sympathetic that in legal education, Common Law is also taught in French and Civil Law in English. This makes it possible for different cultures to be interpreted in an inevitable interplay with each other, which can be a driving force, if, for example, a comprehensive private law codification will once take place in the European Union.

Respectively,

> The habit of *jeito*[26] in Brazilian law is problematic, as it means that the law is not necessarily the fastest and easiest way. For this type of thinking, the law serves only as a kind of supplement: the Brazilians use it if it serves the interests of both parties, and if it does not, they simply ignore it.

The so-called *religious rights* represent a new perspective; these are even closer to the ancient and common roots of the past and give the impression of the wisdom of a few millennia about the separation of law and other social organizing forces. They testify not only to the weight of the truly commonness of the former

[26] "'little way' is a Portuguese word to describe a method of finding a way to accomplish something by circumventing or bending the rules or transgressing social conventions". See the wikipedia entry; see also Keith S. Rosenn, "The Jeito: Brazil's Institutional Bypass of the Formal Legal System and Its Developmental Implications", *American Journal of Comparative Law*, XIX (1971), pp. 514-549; Rosenn, "*Brazil's Legal Culture: The Jeito Revisited*", *Florida International Law Journal*, I, no. 1 (1984), pp. 1-43.

communities and to the strength of their support, so to speak, unknown today, but also to a unity in community behaviour that, whether in the present comprehensive juristic worldviews or narrower law-pictures, is mostly only peripheral, assessed preferably in legal policies or legal sociological elaborations, sometimes separated from each other hopelessly distant, as they only appear as occasional issues of law and morality. It is still clear in them that:

> Unlike the English and continental systems, the law is not separated here: that what is desired by it is desired by every component of the normative superstructure of society, and what is accepted as fulfilment is not only the external conformity exhausted in avoiding breaking the rules, but the action that turns the spirit embodied in it into reality through internal initiative.
>
> If in Jewish and Islamic jurisprudence the parties can feel that their case is being judged on the basis of divinely revealed propositions, this greatly increases confidence in the court.

It may appear to be a specification of the above, a kind of reminder that in case of *classical Jewish law*:

> It is respectable that the rabbi's word decides everything. He is fully respected and seen as the most knowledgeable person whose word is unquestionable. His actual job is to know the entire Talmud and the Torah, and on the basis of this, be able to make a decision that pleases God in earthly legal disputes. And everyone must trust in this, since God could not be wrong in what He once revealed.

Going further to the historical uniqueness of divine revelation and at the same time to the requirements of living social practice, that is, to a certain unity of permanence and change, another notice, now relating to *Islamic law*, reminds us that

> All of Islamic law is based on revelation. Since it primarily formulates the rules of a religious community, the practice of religion—for example by regulating prayers and rites—is also part of it. It therefore regulates the legal status of family meticulously and rigidly, while also giving very detailed guidance on Islamic economic life. Since it is not man-made, not a kind of humans' law, it is a law that humans cannot change. Its rules with legal

> content are defined quite strictly and unchangeably in the Qur'an and the Sunnah, but they do not regulate all areas of life, so the use of analogy is widespread among their jurists.

From a theoretical legal point of view, it is worth noting that in connection with *canon law*, the student of law who happens to be preparing for his profession in a Catholic institution, does not mention its antiquity, the outstanding exemplary nature of some of its institutions, or its service that can and should be interpreted theologically, but the timeless merit of that it has ever been able to grasp all the assumable components of sociality. Or, one student opines that

> An extremely positive feature of canon law is the maintenance and development of those institutions that are most useful in terms of faith, social cohesion, and a worthwhile personal existence. This is what is perhaps most lacking in modern legal systems.

The characterization of the *legal establishments of the Far East* is not much different from the ones above either. It emphasizes in them the unchanged survival of ancient human wisdom and the sense of the one unity of totality with the completeness of connections. Which, by the fact that it serves to strengthen community and the integration that builds up society, prevents any kind of spontaneous or destructive social atomisation. Or, in other words, it makes the literary figure of Heinrich von Kleist (1777-1811), the Michael Kohlhaas phenomenon, that is, the obsessed community-deteriorating chase of justice,[27] unthinkable in society and excludes the socially destructive self-servicing that could still conquer in the European early modern age, the occurrence of "Fiat iustitia, et pereat mundus".[28] After all, attention is drawn here to the fact that:

[27] Heinrich Christian Caro, *Heinrich von Kleist und das Recht: Zum 100 jährigen Todestage Kleist's* (1911); Adolf Fink, "Michael Kohlhaas – ein noch anhängiger Prozeß: Geschichte und Kritik der bisher ergangenen Urteile", in Hans-Jürgen Becker, et al. (ed.), *Rechtsgeschichte als Kulturgeschichte: Festschrift für Adalbert Erler zum 70. Geburtstag* (1976), pp. 37-108; J. Hillis Miller, "Laying Down the Law in Literature: The Example of Kleist", *Cardozo Law Review*, XI (1989-1990), pp. 1491-1514; as well as Peter Ensberg (ed.), *Recht und Gerechtigkeit bein Heinrich von Kleist* (2002).

[28] Detlef Liebs, "Das Rechtssprichwort Fiat iustitia et pereat mundus", *JuristenZeitung*, LXX, no. 3 (6. Februar 2015), pp. 138-141; and also Ludwig von

While we examine and interpret a single selected slice of the world, that is to say while we treat it in pieces, the peoples of the Far East, with their unified worldview, perceive the whole in these ephemeral pieces.

Eastern "laws" seek unity and harmony, create consensus and aim for peaceful coexistence (similarly to primitive peoples); they don't focus on either the truth or the individual.

The mention of *ancient laws* here only reminds us of forced compliance with former constraints in old times, the lesson of which is primarily historical, that is, satisfying the need for direct derivation from current social conditions – even if its inner adaptability is often unrecognised. Because no more, the student appreciation only gets as far as

In the law of primitive societies, it seems at the same time barbaric and fair to apply the principle of »an eye for an eye, a tooth for a tooth«. To us, socialised in Western society, this seems cruel, while somehow everyone still feels its underlying truth.

While subsistence and survival may indeed make the consensus-based decision-making mechanism of tribal law inevitable, it obviously hinders any progress. In the end, such a decision-making procedure can easily turn into a »zero-sum game«, when the goal will be none other than the acceptance of a single idea.

As we have seen, these law-pictures are also cultural images. They are not justified by each other, but by the environment that created them and in which they fulfil their vocation.[29] Thus, their comparative historical study has double roots and lessons. In the fallibility of our world, it highlights how much what we see around us is a creation of our own history: a function of our environment,

Mises, *Human Action: A Treatise on Economics* (1998), p. 147.

[29] As asserted by Pierre Legrand, "Alterity: About Rules, For Example", in Peter Birks and Arianna Pretto (ed.), *Themes in Comparative Law: In Honour of Bernard Rudden* (2002), p. 21 as well, restating my arguments for the comparative study of legal cultures summarized in Varga, note 24 above, "Disciplinary Issues", pp. 9-102: "The main objectives of the comparatist […] must be to understand why a particular legal culture has been attracted to a particular genre of cultural product and to capture the trajectory of epistemological justification that has been followed by that culture".

the result of our interactions with all the factors of our external world at all times. No type or specimen is better or worse than its peers, just different,[30] because – even though in contact with others, borrowing from them, while exerting influence on them as well – it is nothing more than its own self, realized and continuously realizing in its particular world. For this very reason, their comparative and historical study can contribute to getting to know our own legal system, its inner philosophy, and the relative value of its solutions more deeply together with and in contrast to others.

30 Expressed by the words of a candid explorer of religions, this is the premise of suggesting that "their own culture as the 'latest' in time represented the heights of evolution". Alan W. Watts, *Myth and Ritual in Christianity* (1953), p. 9. Or, this is confirmed by recent theories of "progress". Jules Delvaille, *Essai sur l'histoire de l'idée de progrès jusquà la fin du XVIIIe siècle* (1910); Raymond Duncan Gastil, *Progress: Critical Thinking about Historical Change* (1993); Leo Marx and Bruce Mazlish (ed.), *Progress: Fact or Illusion?* (1996); Peter Wagner, *Progress: A Reconstruction* (2016) – which tend to associate every next step with the sign of "development", even though the various linguistic versions of *prōgressus* ("progress") originally neutrally meant only "displacement".

Chapter 22
Comparative Common Law Teaching: Why it is so Hard

CATHERINE VALCKE

In his seminal *Comparative Jurisprudence (I): What Was It Like to Try a Rat?*,[1] William Ewald called comparative law a "single-track enterprise".[2] By that he means that, regardless of the reason that one might have for wanting to do comparative law, there is, at bottom, only one way to go about it: "It makes no difference if your motive for the study is anthropological, or historical, or legal, or philosophical, or anything else: [...] you must go about your business in the same way. Differences of emphasis there will of course be, but not a fundamental difference of method".[3]

The object of the present article is to further explore the "single-trackedness" of comparative law and to unpack some of its implications for comparative legal education, in particular, for comparative legal education that involves common law systems. Reflecting on the current, widespread trend towards teaching law from a comparative perspective, caution is expressed against moving too quickly and too sweepingly to a comparative model, insofar as legal systems may not be equally amenable to it. In particular, the difficulties involved in teaching common law systems through direct comparison with civil law systems seem to have been largely overlooked.[4] Whereas the "single-track" of comparative law aligns well with all civil law systems – making these systems highly amenable to being taught trans-systemically, that is, through direct mutual comparison of their various

[1] W. Ewald, "Comparative Jurisprudence (I): What Was It Like to Try a Rat?", *University of Pennsylvania Law Review*, CXLIII (1994-1995), p. 1898.

[2] Ibid., p. 1951.

[3] Ibid., pp. 1946-1947.

[4] The present argument is confined to civil law and common law systems; its implications for other legal systems, whether aboriginal, religious, customary or any other, remain to be explored.

elements – it does not align well with common law systems, which operate on an altogether different "track". Comparative teaching of common law systems hence requires constant "track" switches, between that of the common law and that naturally supplied through comparative methodology, making it difficult to teach these systems trans-systemically with civil law systems. Although it is certainly possible to lay out side by side the various counterpart elements of a common law and a civil law system ("survey-style"), and although the civil law may perhaps be properly taught that way, such an exercise is ineffective for providing students with a deep understanding of the common law.

In what follows, a description of the "single track" of comparative law is followed by an outline of that track's alignment with the civil law and civilian legal education, and to its contrasting disalignment with the common law.[5] Concluding reflections consider the implications of this contrast for trans-systemic teaching of civil law and common law systems and suggest some other ways to enrich the teaching of these systems with a comparative dimension.

THE SCHOLARLY TRACK OF COMPARATIVE LAW

Whereas law can be studied (and taught) from the external perspective of the legal scholar or the internal perspective of the legal practitioner, *comparative* law is an exclusively scholarly endeavor. The comparative law scholar may, of course, aim to account for the various solutions and outcomes yielded by legal practice in the different systems studied – these systems' "law in action" rather than their mere "law in books".[6] But that is no different from the legal scholar attempting to make sense of the judicial output of their local system. The real difference is that comparative law is not "practiced" in the same way that law is. Whereas legal professionals divide in two groups – legal practitioners and legal scholars –, comparative law professionals (just as legal historians,

[5] For further details on that contrast, see C. Valcke, «From the Inside: French, German, and English Private Law», *Canadian Journal of Law and Jurisprudence*, XIX (2006), pp. 133-160.

[6] R. Pound, «Law in Books and Law in Action», *American Law Review*, XLIV (1910), p. 12

legal philosophers, economists of law, ...) at bottom are all scholars. In terms of epistemology, that is, comparative law can *only* be carried out from an observer standpoint – the external standpoint of the legal scientist – whereas law can be apprehended from an observer *or* a participant standpoint – the internal standpoint of the legal actors. There simply is no "practitioner" of comparative law (or legal history, or legal philosophy, or law and economics, ...) that could be identified as the counterpart to the legal practitioner.

That is not altogether surprising, seeing that any act of comparison requires viewing the compared entities from a distance, thus from an external standpoint. Comparison by definition entails viewing all the compared entities at once, which cannot be done from within any one of them: legal practitioners in any given legal system indeed see that system, and that system only – as foreign systems are normatively irrelevant to them, they treat these systems as sheer "noise".[7] It is, of course, possible for the observer of multiple legal systems to hop in and out of one, and then in and out of another, and so on in sequence: one could certainly seek to first adopt a legal practitioner standpoint in Japanese law, and then exit that standpoint so as to thereafter adopt the standpoint of an Argentinian legal practitioner, and so on for every legal system included in the study. But that is not a comparison so much as a series of successive (if internal) viewings.

Comparing two entities involves more than just viewing them successively. It involves bringing them together so as to *relate* them to one another in some direct fashion, as is done when saying "X is longer than Y". Successively viewing the length of X and the length of Y only allows for such statements as "X is this long" and "Y is that long", in absolute terms; it does not allow for such (properly comparative) judgments as "X is long*er than* Y", in relative terms.[8] Insofar as comparative law is about *relating* Japanese and Argentinian law to one another through the latter kind of statements, it operates on a plane that is necessarily removed from

[7] N. Luhmann, "L'unité du système juridique", *Archives de philosophie du droit*, XXXI (1989), p. 171.

[8] For an interesting discussion on point, see A. Ripstein, *Private Wrongs* (2016), p. 36. Ripstein, however, presses the argument one step further, suggesting that the two objects can be brought closer still, through such truly "relational" judgements as "above/below", which he contrasts with the "merely comparative" judgements of "taller/smaller than". No more than "mere comparativeness" is required for the above argument, however.

both these legal systems. Admittedly, the latter (comparative) statements may need to be *preceded* by the former: determining the respective lengths of X and Y in absolute terms may be a useful, perhaps necessary, first step to comparing them. So it may be that taking separate inside looks at Japanese and Argentine law is an essential preliminary to comparing these systems. The point only is that these remain two distinct operations, only the second one of which qualifies as comparative proper, which would confirm that comparative law itself necessarily operates on the outside, from an observer standpoint.

But Ewald says more than just that comparative law is single-tracked: he offers some thoughts about the nature of that track. Starting from a philosophical conception of law – law as "the applied moral philosophy [of a legal system]",[9] "an essentially cognitive enterprise [...] concerned with substantive values and with determining what ought to be done",[10] – he naturally views the first task of comparative law as being, correspondingly, "to interpret and make sense of the world's variety of such applied moral philosophies".[11] Hence is the single track of comparative law an essentially philosophical one: understanding foreign legal systems conceptualized as applied moral philosophies entails dealing in reasons and justifications, in particular, the reasons and justifications underlying the legal rules of the various systems under study. In sum, regardless of their particular motivation(s) for doing comparative law, comparative lawyers cannot but engage with it in the same way as do philosophical observers of law.[12]

THE SCHOLARLY TRACK OF CIVIL LAW TEACHING

Given their history and current structure and method, civil law systems operate very much on that same external, philosophical

[9] Ewald, note 1 above, p. 1951.

[10] Ibid.

[11] Ibid., p. 1949.

[12] Ewald however is careful to distinguish between the "object" and "execution" of comparative law. It is only with respect to the latter that comparative law borrows from legal philosophy; the "object" pursued by legal philosophy remains distinct from that of comparative law: "When I say that comparative law is an essentially philosophical enterprise, I do not wish to claim that its central concern should be to study questions of philosophy" (ibid., p. 1948.)

observer track.

It is well known that the civil law emerged as a scholarly tradition, from the writings of successive generations of thinkers reflecting on the Roman *Corpus Juris Civilis*, that Roman text being itself largely made up of reputable Roman jurists' "responses" to the legal issues of their time. The medieval merger of Canon with Roman law caused much theological writing to be added to that lot, the resulting body of materials eventually infiltrating all of continental Europe one way or another.[13] That European *Jus Commune*, as it came to be known, provided the groundwork for the various European civil codes that attended the advent of the nation state, through the eighteenth and nineteenth centuries.

These codes admittedly were more than just academic endeavours. Like all legal materials, they were meant to be put to use to resolve concrete human problems. Like all law, therefore, the civil law boasts a practical as well as a theoretical dimension, with the correspondingly bifurcated, scholarly and practitioner groups of professionals. Yet the distance between its theory and its practice remains slight, for the reasoning style of legal practitioners, and civilian legal practice more generally, are themselves heavily theoretical.

As the civil codes were meant to embody all the private law in their respective jurisdictions for centuries to come, their provisions naturally tended to be abstract, open-ended, and rationally ordered, allowing for their various practical ramifications to be gradually worked out, and adjusted over time, by the judges in the course of adjudication. Particularly noteworthy is the fact that, in doing so, the judges were to proceed largely as do scientists, that is, by way of a somewhat circular process combining deduction and induction: concrete rules would be logically derived from general principles, the soundness and accuracy of which would in turn be tested against custom and experience. Hence would the judges' subjectivities and personal inclinations be suppressed – as is purportedly done in science – in the service of objective truth and impartial judgment. Such qualifiers as "syllogistic" and "logically necessary" in fact have often been used to describe the

[13] Whereas the *Jus Commune* was formally "received" in Italy, Southern France and eventually Germany, for example, its reception was only informal in northern Europe. On the different forms and degrees of "reception" of law in new territories, see H. P. Glenn, "Persuasive Authority", *McGill Law Journal*, XXXII (1987), p. 261.

reasoning style and decisions of civil law judges,[14] which to this day remain highly impersonal and technical, as well as anonymous and dissent-free.[15]

Such strong cartesian undertones, already evident in Napoleon's 1804 *Code civil des français* (perhaps the most prominent of civil codes historically), came to underlie all aspects of contemporary civil law. In much the same way that philosophers' ideas galvanized the French revolutionaries, the ascendence of mind over matter informs civilian procedure (the inquisitorial process; de facto appeals; documentary evidence and court-appointed experts weighing more heavily than testimonial evidence and juries; ...),[16] sources and institutions (scholarly writings being treated as a quasi-source of law; the absence of a rule of precedent; reason-based arguments being preferred to history-based ones; ...),[17] even its substantive law (the moralistic flavor of delictual liability; the good faith doctrine; contract as actual party intention; ...).[18] Through and through, civil law institutions evince "the authority of Reason rather than the reason of authorities", as the famous saying goes.

Maximilian Emil Karl Weber (1864-1920) considered that legal systems express their view of law most loudly through their legal education programmes,[19] and the theoretical inclination of the civil

[14] "A rational judicial process involves always determination of issues in accordance with the requirements of formal logic. The judicial decision is a conclusion reached on the basis of syllogism: rules of law furnish the major premise, fact situations form the minor premise, and the conclusion follows with logical necessity". A. Yiannopoulos, *Louisiana Civil Law System* (1977), p. 89.

[15] For an interesting analysis of the diluted version of this in Quebec, see Rosalie Jukier, "Inside the Judicial Mind: Exploring Judicial Methodology in the Mixed Legal System of Quebec" (available online).

[16] A. D. Kessler, "Our Inquisitorial Tradition: Equity Procedure, Due Process, and the Search for an Alternative to the Adversarial", *Cornell Law Review* XC (2005), p. 1181; M. R. Damaška, *The Faces of Justice and State Authority: A Comparative Approach to the Legal Process* (1986).

[17] J. P. Dawson, *The Oracles of the Law* (1968); R. C. Van Caenegem, "The Common Law is Different: Ten Illustrations", in *Judges, Legislators and Professors* (1987).

[18] R. Sefton-Green, "A Vision of Social Justice in French Private Law: Paternalism and Solidarity", in H. Micklitz (ed.), *The Many Concepts of Social Justice in European Private Law* (2011), p. 237; C. Valcke, "Comparing Legal Styles", in P. Cserne (ed.), *The Many Faces of Style in Law and Legal Scholarship, International Journal of Law in Context, XV* (2019), pp. 274-296.

[19] Max Weber, *Economy and Society* (1978), Ch. 8 («Sociology of Law»), Part iii, p.

law is certainly palpable in civilian legal education. Mirroring the vertical structure of these systems' inquisitorial court procedure,[20] knowledge there tends to be dispensed top down, through the (higher, for already learned) masters enlightening their (lower, for still learning) pupils as to the conceptual necessity of legal rules that can be logically derived from a set of abstract first principles preliminarily posited as true. Hence is the "truth" of legal rules and principles thereby methodically uncovered before the pupils' eyes, as one would expect to see done in mathematics. The (didactic) teaching method is linear and vertical, just like the contents of the classes, which typically proceed from the general to the more concrete, the former being accorded far greater emphasis: the conceptual elegance of (pure) principles and ideas is underscored, while their (messy) application to the facts of concrete cases is comparatively neglected. As the pupils are expected to do no more than to (passively) ingest the information imparted to them, they rarely ask questions – how could anyone question the truth? – and classes can be very large, at any rate larger than at common law. Teaching styles admittedly vary across individual teachers, classes and schools in all legal systems, but the foregoing arguably captures a general tendency, or aspiration, peculiar to civil law systems, which serves to distinguish them from common law systems.

THE PRACTITIONER TRACK OF COMMON LAW TEACHING

All aspects of the common law in contrast bear the imprint of pragmatism, the view according to which reverence is first owed to facts, history, tradition, as their normative significance would far outweigh that of Reason, pure logic, free-floating ideas. Hence – insist the pragmatists, in flat opposition to the cartesians – what *is* ultimately should inform and determine what *ought* to be.

A focus on hard facts transpires from the history of the common law, and informs its characteristic institutional structures, method and substantive law. Historically, it emerged from the English writ system, a procedural maize initially so dense that it could only be navigated by the "counters", a group of uneducated individuals

776, and Part iv, pp. 784-794.

20 Damaška, note 16 above.

whose main, if strictly physical, talent was to perform, without slipping, the formulaic recitals associated with the various writs.[21] This talent earned them the right and duty to sit in court for days on end and come to develop therefrom an unmatched familiarity and expertise with the finicky details of court practice. Early English court practice indeed was not reducible to anything resembling a clear set of rational rules, with the result that no books could be written on it and it could only be learned through apprenticeship.[22] Although continental-style university law teaching did eventually catch up to England, the focus on hard facts and the view of legal training as best achieved "through doing" – through actually sitting in court – by then were already solidly entrenched: England's first professional lawyers, said "counters", were practically-minded individuals with little time for the high-flying ideas filling the classic Commentaries revered on the Continent.

That pragmatic, common sense view of law in many ways still molds the common law today, its procedure, sources, institutions and substantive law arguably standing as mirror opposites to those of the civil law. The legal process is centered on the trial – the actual re-enactment, before a jury of peers, of the facts sourcing the litigation, thus adversarial rather than inquisitorial, and horizontal rather than vertical in structure.[23] Whereas the civilians tend to associate objective adjudication and clear judgement with transcendence from the facts (as factual considerations would only serve to fog up principled reasoning with emotional bias), the common lawyers are prone to flying as close as possible to the ground (as justice removed from the hard facts of human life would amount to no justice at all).[24] Hence are real-life testimonials preferred to documentary evidence; appeals possible only upon permission; and expert witnesses appointed by the parties rather

[21] S. F. C. Milsom, *Historical Foundations of the Common Law* (1981), pp. 104ff.

[22] Weber describes as peculiarly English "the empirical training in the law as a craft; the apprentices learn from practitioners more or less in the course of actual legal practice". He then contrasts said "guildlike English method of having law taught by the lawyers" with continental-style law teaching, "in special schools, where the emphasis is placed on legal theory and 'science', that is, where legal phenomena are given rational and systematic treatment". Weber, note 19 above, Part iv, pp. 784-794.

[23] Damaška, note 16 above, uses the term «coordinate»/ «hierarchical» rather than «horizontal»/ «vertical».

[24] Valcke, note 5 above.

than the court.[25] Hence also are judicial decisions – first-hand reports from front-row observers in the factual re-enactment – valued more highly than any removed, scholarly commentary on it.[26] Hence also, finally, is argumentation anchored in (actual) human authorities more than remote (speculative) Reason.[27] In fact, as René David (1906-1991) famously explained,[28] the difference between common law and civil law systems reaches as far as into their respective conceptions of the "legal rule": what civilians regard as legal rules proper (for example, code provisions), common lawyers instead tend to view as just statements of principles, too broad and disembodied to be legally meaningful. To them, the "rule" proper would only really emerge from the principles' differentiated instantiations in various factual contexts – what the civilian downplay as mere "applications" of the rule.

That narrow, factual conception of the legal rule grounds what might be the common law's most important institutional feature, namely, the rule of precedent, and attendant distinction between the "holding" and *obiter dictum* of judicial decisions. In dictating that judges follow past cases when deciding new ones, the rule of precedent embodies no less than the rule of law imperative that "like cases be treated alike". Its operationalization, however, is no easy task, as it involves identifying, for any given past case, the part of it that must be followed – its specific "rule", or "holding"; the remainder constitutes mere (non-binding) "comment in passing", or *obiter dictum*. The "holding" of a case, one is told, is the part of it that "speaks directly" to the facts at hand, whereas its other parts, wherein the judge rises above the facts at hand to issue more abstract statements, also applicable in other situations, are mere *obiter dicta*.[29] However, which of the judge's statements speak to the facts directly *enough*, and which in contrast are to be considered *too* abstract, is a question that can never be clearly and definitively settled, as it remains a matter for debate, to be reopened whenever the factual context changes. To further complicate matters, in

[25] Kessler, note 16 above; Damaška, note 16 above.

[26] Dawson, note 17 above; Van Caenegem, note 17 above.

[27] See text accompanying note 17 above.

[28] R. David and C. Jauffret-Spinosi, *Les grands systèmes de droit contemporains* (11th ed.; 2002), §§69-71, 268, pp. 73-75, 265-266.

[29] S. Waddams, *Introduction to the Study of Law* (2004), p. 68.

each new factual context, the rule ends up being applied through a line-drawing exercise whose exact whereabouts remain highly elusive, as it partakes of "judgement" – which Aristotle described as involving human sensibilities other than logic – and thus defies any kind of pre-determined analytic process.[30]

In sum, the rampant cliché according to which the civil law and the common law would respectively proceed deductively and inductively[31] is as misleading with respect to the common law as it is with respect to the civil law. Civilian legal reasoning in fact tends to mimic scientific/philosophical reasoning in *combining* deduction and induction, its main defining feature accordingly being, not deduction so much as verticality. In contrast, the common law tends to proceed *neither* deductively *nor* inductively but rather horizontally, from case to case, or by analogical reasoning, which never rises above the facts.[32]

Such steadfast emphasis on the facts explains why legal education has, in common law systems, traditionally proceeded differently from civil law systems, namely, dialectically rather than didactically, by way of what is known as the "Socratic method". Rather than handing the students some ready-made, logical exposition of the law, the common law teacher aims to prompt them, through questions and answers, to form their own understanding of the reading materials. A class-wide movement of back and forth ensues, wherein the instructor effectively mediates the students' interaction, in a fashion highly reminiscent of the judicial role in the adversarial process. Teacher and students ultimately stand as equal contributors in the collective debate unfolding in the classroom, their rapport thus being more horizontal, less hierarchical, than it is in civilian legal education. The dialectical experience of the classroom moreover aims to mold students' intuitions as to what constitutes (relatively) "better" and "worse" arguments in different contexts, more than to get them to identify (absolutely) "right" or "wrong" answers, qualifying as

[30] G. J. Postema, «*A Similibus ad Similia:* Analogical Thinking in Law», in Douglas E. Edlin (ed.), *Common Law Theory* (2007), p. 120.

[31] See, for example, M. Bastarache, «Bijuralism and Harmonization: Genesis», Department of Justice Canada, Lunch and Learn Workshop on Bijuralism and the Judicial Function, 25 August 2022 (available online).

[32] Postema, note 30 above, pp. 124-126; Postema, «Classical Common Law Jurisprudence (Parts 1 and 2)» (available online).

such across contexts. Most significantly for present purposes, the students learn law "through doing" rather than "through being told about it", by actively participating in re-enacting the way that legal practitioners argue over the application of judicial holdings in new factual contexts. That is to say that, to common lawyers, law is somewhat analogous to swimming, in that regard: whereas one might usefully learn about swimming by reading what hydrodynamics treatises say about it, diving in the pool remains unavoidable for learning how to swim.

THE INCESSANT TRACK SWITCHES OF COMPARATIVE COMMON LAW TEACHING

The foregoing suggests that the highly theoretical nature of the civil law causes it to be aptly taught by reading treatises about it – that is, from a scholarly, external perspective – whereas the pragmatic nature of the common law calls for some sort of experiential learning, through apprenticeships, Socratic teaching or otherwise – that is, from the legal practitioner's internal perspective. It follows that trans-systemic teaching of several civil law systems is entirely possible, in fact likely desirable: in the same way that the parallel reading of aerodynamics and hydrodynamics treatises is an excellent way to learn about one or both of these sciences, German and French legal scholars have long drawn great benefit from laying side by side and comparing German and French legal rules. And French and German law instructors indeed commonly enrich their teaching by alerting the students to the French or German counterpart of the rule under study. The same, however, cannot be said where common law systems are concerned.

While it is certainly possible, indeed valuable, to lay side by side, from an external, observer standpoint, the civilian and common law counterparts of legal rules – which comparative lawyers have in fact usefully done for decades in the context of the various «common core» projects[33] – doing so reveals nothing about how rules are to be extracted from cases at common law, which remains the central and most difficult task to be performed by a common law practitioner. Teaching trans-systemically, in the

[33] R. B. Schlesinger and P. G. Bonassies (eds.), *Formation of Contracts: A Study of the Common Core of Legal Systems* (1968); A. Tunc (ed.), *International Encyclopedia of Comparative Law* (1983); M. Bussani and Ugo Mattei (eds)., *The Common Core of European Private Law* (2003).

context of a single course, the civil law and the common law rules pertaining to a given legal domain accordingly would require constant oscillation between the "observer track" (of the civil law) and the "practitioner track" (of the common law), lest the students emerge from that course with a poor, for external and superficial, understanding of the common law, one that fails to deliver the heart of common law reasoning. In other words, the instructor would need to constantly "switch tracks", from didactic to dialectic and back to didactic, teaching – to hop in and out of the pool so as to intersperse the swimming with bouts of hydrodynamics reading. *That* is why it is so hard to teach the common law comparatively.

Of course, that is not to say that common law students cannot benefit from comparative legal education. Year after year, upper-year students in my Civil Law course at the University of Toronto appreciate what it teaches them about ... the common law – that law they thought they understood from their first year of law school. That is, having already completed one full year of being thrown in the pool and figuring out how to swim, they are in a position to stand back and reflect on it on a meta level, which reflection at that point serves to deeply hone their understanding of what they were doing a year earlier. This does serve to confirm, however, that comparative law teaching involving common law systems is best achieved *sequentially* rather than *trans-systemically*: one first needs to gain an internal understanding of the common law, to thereafter come out of it and adopt the external perspective needed to usefully compare it to any other legal system.[34]

[34] This objection might apply to comparing common law systems among themselves: the various cases being authoritative only within their respective jurisdictions, it could be argued that little if any pedagogical value would be yielded through extending the analogies across cases of other jurisdictions.

Chapter 23

From the Center of the Margins: Reflections on Comparative Law Worldview from the Commonwealth Caribbean

ASYA OSTROUKH

Discussions on how to do comparative law, how to teach it, or what comparative law is have been ongoing for centuries. These topics are arguably among the most debatable within this area of legal knowledge. However, these discussions focus on larger countries and major legal systems. The implications of comparative law for the legal profession and society as well as its role in shaping the professional worldview of practicing lawyers and legal scholars in small, marginalized jurisdictions remain understudied but present a fruitful field for exploration. One such region traditionally overlooked in mainstream comparative law is the Caribbean.

Although not extensively studied in international legal scholarship, the broader Caribbean region has been a laboratory for comparative law, both on the practical-empirical and academic levels, from the onset of European colonization. A battleground for colonizing powers, situated at the crossroads of various legal traditions (both local and imported), the region has progressively crafted a map representing most legal traditions recognized by the science of comparative law.[1]

Not only does the Caribbean region provide diverse objects for macro-comparative legal studies – from local ramifications of the two major legal traditions (the Civil law and the Common law) to mixed jurisdictions (in Guyana, Saint Lucia, and Puerto Rico) and the almost extinct Socialist legal tradition (in Cuba) – but it also exemplifies a professional legal worldview that cannot

[1] For more about legal diversity of the Caribbean region and the legal traditions existing in this region, see A. Ostroukh, "Rewards and Challenges of Teaching Comparative Law in the Commonwealth Caribbean", *Louisiana Law Review*, LXXVI (2016), p. 1165.

be but comparative in order to produce any credible practical and theoretical conclusions and solutions. A law student, a practitioner, or a legal scholar in the Caribbean continuously engages (consciously or unconsciously) in comparative law, be it comparison of local law with the law of former colonizing powers, with law of neighboring States and territories, or with international law.

This chapter focuses on the significance of comparative law in the worldview of legal professionals in the Commonwealth Caribbean region. The author demonstrates that, taking into consideration the legal and cultural diversity of the region, comparative law holds a greater practical and academic significance for the Commonwealth Caribbean legal tradition and legal profession than in other parts of the world. By analyzing various salient features of the professional legal culture in the region, the author shows that the understanding of comparative law and its functions in the Commonwealth Caribbean differs significantly from mainstream jurisdictions, making this understudied region attractive for future comparative legal studies.

LEGAL COMPARISON AS INHERENT ELEMENT OF THE LEGAL PROFESSIONAL WORLDVIEW

In other jurisdictions, especially those that mainstream comparative law labels as major legal systems, legal comparison is merely one possible approach to discussing law. A method that is not necessarily used by many lawyers. In the Commonwealth Caribbean, however, legal comparison permeates all stages of interaction with legal matter: legislative drafting, adjudication, interpretation, application, practice, and study.

Lawyers in the Commonwealth Caribbean are comparativists by default, due to a great variety of legal systems in the region, their historical origins dating back to European colonization, the need to look at these legal systems through the lens of a unifying umbrella term "Commonwealth Caribbean law", and the necessity of adjusting laws of individual jurisdictions with international or CARICOM law.

Post-independence Commonwealth Caribbean legal professionals have always practiced a kind of intuitive comparative law. In shaping Commonwealth Caribbean jurisprudence, legislators and judges have looked at legal systems of Australia, Canada, United States, and New Zealand as potential donors of legal provisions and institutions for the region. For example, while reforming the rules of family law concerning divorce, Barbados legislators used Australian law and, while recognizing women's rights to financial support in a union other than marriage, Canadian law,[2] whereas condominium legislation in the Commonwealth Caribbean is based on the American Federal Housing Administration Model Act of 1961.[3]

Nowadays, legal comparison in the region is done for all known practical and educational functions of comparative law: applying and interpreting national law, reforming local legal systems, harmonization and unification projects, understanding local and foreign law better, improving international relations, and promoting critical thinking about law.[4]

Until recently, such comparison has often been intuitive and not guided by in-depth knowledge of comparative law principles and methodology. One might hope that with reintroduction of the course of comparative law and introduction of courses on foreign law (for example, Chinese Law and Institutions) at the Cave Hill Campus as well as with involvement of the Caribbean Association of Judicial Officers into a range of comparative-law projects and events, legal professionals in the Commonwealth Caribbean region will be better equipped to practice comparative law with a deeper understanding of its functions and methodology.

MIXITÉ AND HYBRIDISATION AS WAY OF PERCEIVING LAW

The worldview of the Commonwealth Caribbean comparativist is deeply rooted in *mixité* as a way of understanding the legal world. Even though most Commonwealth Caribbean countries and territories belong to the Common-law tradition, the simplistic single-component perception of legal systems and their straightforward

[2] D. Bradshaw, *Comparative Law: A Discipline for the Antillean Lawyer?* (1986), p. 22 (unpublished manuscript on file with author).

[3] G. Kodilinye, *Commonwealth Caribbean Property Law* (5th ed.; 2021).

[4] For more about functions of comparative law in a broader Caribbean, see Bradshaw, note 2 above.

categorization as Common law, Civil law, religious, customary, and so on is becoming less popular among regional comparativists. There are two reasons why *mixité* has become a common pattern in the thinking of Commonwealth Caribbean comparativists. The first reason is a general one – cultural and linguistic diversity in the Caribbean region as well as the history of its colonization with imposition of different religions, cultures, political powers, and legal systems over the same geographical space. The second reason is more specific to law, namely, the preservation of two mixed Civil-Common law jurisdictions in the Commonwealth Caribbean and one in non-Commonwealth Caribbean. The region is proud of showcasing three types of Civil–Common law mixture: English Common law and French, Quebec, and Louisiana Civil law in Saint Lucia (similar to Quebec and Louisiana); English Common law and Roman-Dutch law in Guyana (similar to South Africa and Sri Lanka); and American Common law and Spanish Civil law in Puerto Rico (similar to the Philippines).[5] However, mixed jurisdictions in the Caribbean, unlike Quebec, Louisiana, or South Africa, have demonstrated a substantially higher level of erosion (commonization) of the Civil law[6] – a factor which intensifies discussions on the purity and *mixité* of legal systems and encourages reflections on possible ways of withstanding commonization of local mixed jurisdictions.

Moreover, in recent years there has been a gradual transition from a narrow (classical) approach to *mixité* as a mixture of Civil-Common law traditions to a broader (pluralist) one recognizing multiple components of mixture (religious, customary, international, and non-state laws).[7] For instance, with respect to Guyana, its traditional binary understanding of mixed jurisdiction (as Civil-Common law mix) is gradually giving way to recognition of the third element of mixture: aboriginal rights of American Indians and their indigenous legal tradition.[8] Similarly, in light

[5] Ostroukh, note 1 above, p. 1221.

[6] Ibid.

[7] For the discussion of a narrow and a broad concept of *mixité* (also known as classical and pluralist respectively), see V. V. Palmer, "Mixed Legal Systems—The Origin of the Species", *Tulane European and Civil Law Forum*, XXVIII (2013), p. 103.

[8] For more about mixed legal system of Guyana, see C. Toppin-Allahar, "Guyana: 'Mosaic or Melting-Pot?", in S. Farran, E. Örücü and S. P. Donlan (eds.), *A Study of Mixed Legal Systems: Endangered, Entrenched or Blended?* (2014), pp. 37-58.

of consistent recognition by national and international authorities of indigenous claims to land advanced by the Maya in Belize, the legal system of this country can be considered as evolving into a mixed one. In other jurisdictions legal recognition of some religious traditions or non-formal customary law as well as legal transplants from other jurisdictions (United States, Canada, Australia, or European Union) has also encouraged the development of a perception of Commonwealth Caribbean legal systems as mixed.

Until recently, the major topic of discussion with respect to *mixité* in the region was erosion (commonization) of the Civil-law tradition[9] and possible ways of tackling this problem. However, since 2022, we also encounter instances of hybridization (civilization) of the Common-law tradition. One such example is the influence that the civilian principle of good faith in contracts, present in the Civil Code of Saint Lucia, has exercised on the development of employment and insurance law in Common-law jurisdictions by means of judgements of the Caribbean Court of Justice.[10] Some Caribbean judges consider looking at possible reception of civilian notions, principles, and ideas in the areas of civil procedure rules, procedural rules in family-law cases, and recognition of same-sex marriages.

Thus, it can be seen that Commonwealth Caribbean comparativists look at the world of law through the prism of *mixité,* understanding it from a pluralist approach. They are cognizant of both negative and positive effects of *mixité* and take deliberate decisions about mixing or not different elements of various legal traditions.

SUSTAINABLE USE OF COMPARATIVE LAW IN JUDICIAL DECISION-MAKING

Several scholars have criticized the excessive and uncritical reliance of Commonwealth Caribbean judges on British authorities and jurisprudence even after the acquisition of independence. Rose-Marie Belle Antoine reports that "[t]he countries of the Commonwealth Caribbean continue to exhibit perhaps excessive

[9] For more about the erosion of the Civil Law in Guyana and Saint Lucia, see R-M. B. Antoine, *Commonwealth Caribbean Law and Legal Systems* (2d ed.; 2008), pp. 61-71; Toppin-Allahar, note 8 above.

[10] For this point thanks are due to Peter Jamadar, Justice of the Caribbean Court of Justice.

tendencies of reliance on the form, structure, substance and content of the law as expressed in England".[11] Similarly, Howard N. Malcolm in his article "Towards the Emergence of Anglo-West Indian Jurisprudence" criticizes the lack of policy considerations and reflections on socio-economic context in Commonwealth Caribbean judgements as well as the uncritical reliance on British cases in judicial decision-making. He argues that "[...]despite political independence and the establishment of local legal education, the West Indian legal experience continues to be characterized by the uncritical and mechanical importation of English common law rules, practices and approaches to adjudication",[12] a condition that he describes as "post-colonial dependency syndrome".[13] This aligns with Winston Anderson's observation that "[t]he commonplace adherence of courts in the countries of the Commonwealth Caribbean to the decisions of the English courts is rooted in profound psychological and jurisprudential considerations of colonial domination".[14] To overcome this issue Malcolm suggests developing what he calls Anglo-West Indian jurisprudence to critically reassess English authorities and promote judicial activism in the Commonwealth Caribbean.[15] However, the very fact that Malcolm calls this new independent jurisprudence "Anglo-West Indian" is revealing as the choice of the words "Anglo" (instead of "Anglophone" or "English Speaking") and "West Indian" (instead of Commonwealth Caribbean) subtly reflects residues of colonial thinking.

Nevertheless, while acknowledging a pressing need for judicial emancipation from coloniality in legal thinking that still permeates the worldview of many judges in this region, it is crucial to recognize that many Commonwealth Caribbean judgements have significantly advanced the critical re-examination of British authorities and jurisprudence as well as their adaptation to needs and values of the Caribbean society through extensive use of

[11] Antoine, note 9 above, p. 39.

[12] H. N. Malcolm, "Towards the Emergence of an Anglo-West Indian Jurisprudence", *West Indian Law Journal*, XVIII (1993), p. 70.

[13] Ibid., p. 21.

[14] W. Anderson, "Double Renvoi and the Circulus Inextricabilis", in *Commonwealth Caribbean Legal Studies* (1992), p. 313.

[15] Malcolm, note 12 above, p. 70.

comparative law. Prominent judges like Aubry Fraser in cases such as *Lush v Duprey*,[16] *Luckie v Watson*,[17] and *Bernard v Jennings*[18] in the 1960s, as well as Roger Hamel-Smith in *Ramdass v Ramdass*[19] and *Rampersad v. Jattan*[20] in the 1980s, have adjusted a rather formalistic and rigid British case law on easements[21] of necessity to the local social context. In their decisions, the judges discuss important social policy considerations that are missing from British case law: the need for properly balancing the interests of the dominant and the servient owners and for fostering good neighborliness. The good neighborliness principle was also supported by sirs Vincent Frederick Floissac, Nicholas Joseph Orville Liverpool, and Charles Michael Dennis Byron for the mixed jurisdiction of Saint Lucia in *Michel and Another v Augier and Others*.[22] It must be emphasized that such adaption of British law to local context was done by the judges of the trial and appellate courts without a need to refer the issues to supreme judicial bodies, which confirms that judicial independence, activism, and comparative outlook are present at all levels of the Commonwealth Caribbean judiciary, albeit not widespread as yet.

Moreover, in *Michel and Another v Augier and Others* the three stellar judges Floissac, Byron, and Liverpool in the Court of Appeal of Eastern Caribbean States exhibited profound knowledge and application of comparative law. Considering the problem of the extent of a servitude, the judges made references to cases from Quebec, England, and Trinidad and Tobago, to the Civil Code of Louisiana as well as to a treatise on civil law from Quebec and eventually arrived at a very comparative decision by declaring that "[s]uch a demand has no legal foundation under the Quebec,

[16] (1966) 10 WIR (CA TT).

[17] Quoted by Alexis as 28 March 1962 (Fed SC) in F. Alexis, *H. Aubrey Fraser: Eminent Caribbean Jurist* (1985), p. 119.

[18] (1968) 13 WIR 222 (CA TT).

[19] TT 1989 HC 22.

[20] TT 1989 HC 138.

[21] Servitudes in the Civil-law tradition.

[22] (1994) 46 WIR 143.

Louisiana or St Lucia Civil Law. Nor is such a demand entertainable at common law". [23]

Another area of law where the Commonwealth Caribbean courts have used extensively comparative law is antigay criminal law provisions (also known as buggery or anti-sodomy laws) inherited from the colonial era. The courts struck down as unconstitutional and violating human rights the provisions criminalizing same-sex relations among the consenting adults in such countries as Trinidad and Tobago, Belize, Antigua and Barbuda, Saint Kitts and Nevis, Saint Vincent and the Grenadines, Barbados, and Dominica based on the extensive use of authorities from other jurisdictions. For example, in the most recent of such cases – *B.G. v Attorney General of the Commonwealth of Dominica*[24] – the judge makes extensive references to cases and other authorities from many jurisdictions, including Botswana, United Kingdom, United States, Nigeria, Kenya, India, Canada, and South Africa. It must be highlighted, however, that the victory over colonial antigay legislation was not achieved by the judiciary alone but was possible due to the efforts of other legal professionals and human rights activists, with the University of the West Indies Rights Advocacy Project (U-RAP) being at the forefront.

Additionally, in areas where English law is either non-existent or irrelevant, like indigenous land claims or condominium legislation, Commonwealth Caribbean courts have no choice but to forge their own legal paths, heavily relying on comparative law and referencing authorities from various jurisdictions.[25]

Thus, while excessive reliance on British authorities and legal formalism are still present in many Commonwealth Caribbean judgements and impede the development of an independent regional legal worldview, Commonwealth Caribbean courts have consistently shown a commitment to thoughtfully adapting British Common law to meet local needs and realities, and to engaging with legal principles from other jurisdictions. Further application

[23] (1994) 46 WIR 143 affirmed by the JCPC in *Michel v Augier and Others* (1995) 51 WIR 103.

[24] DOMHCV2019/0149.

[25] For use of authorities from other jurisdictions in cases concerning indigenous claims to land, see *Thomas and Arau Village Council v Attorney General of Guyana Geology and Mines Commission* GY 2009 HC 7 and in condominium cases *Seaport Construction Company Ltd v Residential Resort Developments Ltd and Others* BS 1988 SC 115.

of functionalist, sociological, historical, and cultural approaches to law is necessary to strengthen this trend. Such practices are increasingly present in the decisions of the Caribbean Court of Justice which is evolving into a multifunctional court instrumental for the development of regional legal worldview.

CARIBBEAN COURT OF JUSTICE AS A COMPARATIVE LAW COURT

One unique feature of the Caribbean legal landscape is the presence in the region of a judicial institution unmatched anywhere else in the world – the Caribbean Court of Justice (CCJ) – distinguished by its unparalleled dual jurisdiction. It operates both as a court of original jurisdiction for the interpretation and application of the Revised Treaty of Chaguaramas, which established the Caribbean Community (signed in 1973 and revised in 2001), and as the ultimate court of appeal for several Commonwealth Caribbean nations (Barbados, Belize, Guyana, Dominica, and Saint Lucia),[26] superseding in this role the Judicial Committee of the Privy Council (JCPC).

This dualist nature of the CCJ is pivotal in shaping local jurisprudence. Armand de Mestral insightfully observes that "[t]he different heads of jurisdiction, while formally separate, in fact come together when the Court draws upon fundamental principles such as the rule of law, fundamental principles of law, and various concepts drawn from common sources of international human rights law".[27]

However, this second jurisdiction of the CCJ has ignited robust jurisprudential and comparative-law debates, concentrating on two fundamental questions: whether the CCJ is a more appropriate appellate body for the Commonwealth Caribbean and what its role in the evolution of local legal traditions is.

The JCPC continues to serve the highest appellate court for the majority of the Commonwealth Caribbean independent countries.[28]

[26] Which makes almost one half of twelve independent Commonwealth Caribbean countries.

[27] A. de Mestral, "The Constitutional Functions of the Caribbean Court of Justice", *McGill Journal of Dispute Resolution*, I (2015), p. 74.

[28] A hilarious paradox is in that the seat of the CCJ is located in the Republic of Trinidad

Nonetheless, discussions regarding the appropriateness of this colonial-era court in addressing the needs of contemporary Caribbean society have been ongoing since these nations achieved independence. The JCPC, as an institution rooted in colonialism, remains an external entity in terms of geography, society, and culture. Attempts to integrate Caribbean representation on the JCPC, through appointments of justices such as Michael de la Bastide, Edward Zacca, Vincent Floissac, Hugh Wooding, and William Douglas, have largely been symbolic.[29] Given that some of them did not sit on any cases at all while others sat in very few cases, this measure can be considered as no more than political and legal tokenism that did not resolve the problem of appealing to a court that is geographically and culturally foreign to the Commonwealth Caribbean region.

Advocates for transitioning to the CCJ as the final regional court of appeal cite several reasons, including the prohibitive costs associated with appeals to the JCPC, which limit access to justice for many Caribbean residents.[30] A more compelling argument is that judges with regional training and extensive local experience cognizant of local socio-economic, political, and cultural realities are inherently better positioned to adapt laws to meet the societal needs of the region.[31] Moreover, the CCJ holds immense potential to disassociate regional law from its colonial past and to reconstruct it through the application of anticolonial legal methodology.

Since its establishment nearly two decades ago, the Caribbean Court of Justice has effectively functioned as a laboratory of comparative law or, to be more precise, as a comparative law court. This role is facilitated by several factors: both Commonwealth Caribbean mixed jurisdictions (Guyana and Saint Lucia) recognize the appellate jurisdiction of the CCJ; and two non-Commonwealth

and Tobago which still sends its appeals to the JCPC.

29 Interestingly, two of these judges – Wooding and de la Bastide – were strong proponents of transition from JCPC to a regional appellate court. H. Rawlins, *The Caribbean Court of Justice: The History and Analysis of the Debate* (2000), pp. 40 and 44.

30 For more about the history, functions, and prospects of the CCJ, see de Mestral, note 26 above; E. Rediker, "Courts of Appeal and Colonialism in the British Caribbean: A Case for the Caribbean Court of Justice", *Michigan Journal of International Law*, XXXV (2013), pp. 213-251; H. A. Young, *The Judicial Committee of the Privy Council and the Caribbean Court of Justice: Navigating Independence and Changing Political Environments* (2020).

31 The current generation of the justices of this court have received their education at Cave Hill Campus of the UWI.

Caribbean countries adhering to the Civil-law tradition—Haiti and Suriname—are CARICOM members recognizing the CCJ's original jurisdiction. Thus, having a potential to further interact with the pure Civil-law tradition, this court may exercise significant influence on the worldview of the legal community both in the Commonwealth and non-Commonwealth Caribbean.

The foundational mandate of the CCJ, as articulated in the preamble to the Agreement Establishing the CCJ (2001), is to "... play a determinative role in the further development of Caribbean jurisprudence through the judicial process". The CCJ itself in *Attorney General et al v Joseph and Boyce* extended this responsibility to other courts in the region highlighting that "[t]he main purpose in establishing this court is to promote the development of a Caribbean jurisprudence, *a goal which Caribbean courts are best equipped to pursue*" (emphasis added).[32]

While shaping regional jurisprudence, the CCJ in many cases gets involved in applying comparative law, and it does so deliberately. The CCJ's commitment to employing comparative law is evident in its efforts to preserve the Civil-law tradition within the region and to resist its potential erosion. In a notable Guyanese case *Ramdass v. Jairam*, the court, exercising its appellate jurisdiction, upheld the trial court's decision that equitable interests in immovable property are not recognised in Guyana.[33] CCJ also contributes to the recognition of the indigenous legal tradition, by using comparative law. In 2015, in the case *The Maya Leaders Alliance v the Attorney General of Belize*, the CCJ upheld the national Supreme Court's decision that the Maya indigenous communities of Southern Belize had rights to the lands they had customarily used and occupied. By referencing Australian and Canadian cases and international legal standards concerning indigenous claims to land, the court also affirmed that those traditional land rights constituted "*property equal in legitimacy to any other form of property under Belizean law*" (emphasis added),[34] thereby enriching the Belizean legal system with diverse constitutive elements. As a comparative law court, the CCJ not only fosters legal *mixité* and acknowledges indigenous legal traditions, but also plays

32 [2006] CCJ 3 AJ [18].

33 [2008] CCJ 6 (AJ).

34 *The Maya Leaders Alliance et al v the Attorney General of Belize* [2015] CCJ 15 (AJ).

an instrumental role in the decolonization and indigenization of Caribbean law. Serving as a court of original jurisdiction for all Commonwealth Caribbean countries and as an appellate court for five, the CCJ acts as a cohesive force, promoting the development of an autonomous Commonwealth Caribbean legal tradition.

Moreover, beyond its interpretative and appellate roles specified in the treaty establishing it, the CCJ is evolving into a versatile institution functioning as an international law court, a human rights court, and a constitutional court. It increasingly symbolizes legal independence for the Commonwealth Caribbean legal community, marking a jurisprudential departure from colonial legacies and transitioning towards a decolonized legal framework. It is no longer just a court (albeit a supreme one), but rather a symbol of legal independence, of jurisprudential break from colonial legacy, and of transition to decolonial law.

TEACHING LAW COMPARATIVELY AND TEACHING COMPARATIVE LAW[35]

Comparative law significantly influences the teaching of law in the Caribbean in its both traditional meanings, serving as a methodological approach and as a distinct academic discipline.

As a method, comparative law is woven into the fabric of almost all law courses at the University of the West Indies concerning both national and international law as well as courses relating to law and society (for example, jurisprudence). The region's legal diversity and the array of regional and global integration initiatives have made a comparative perspective fundamental to the law curriculum.[36] The teaching of law is not confined to Barbados, Jamaica, or Trinidad and Tobago where the three most important regional faculties of law are located but encompasses all Commonwealth Caribbean jurisdictions,[37] enhancing not only

[35] This title is inspired by the titles of two publications: Z. Péteri, "Teaching of Comparative Law and Comparative Law Teaching", *Acta Juridica Hungarica*, XLIII, nos. 3-4 (2002), pp. 243-261 and H. P. Glenn, "Teaching Comparative Law and Teaching Law Comparatively", in O. Leska and others (eds.), *Mélanges Maksymiliana Pazdana* (2005), pp. 951-960.

[36] Ostroukh, note 1 above, p. 1219.

[37] Most law courses devoted to the Commonwealth Caribbean law cover all or most of the following jurisdictions: Anguilla, Antigua and Barbuda, the Bahamas, Barbados, Belize,

comparative but multisystemic nature of legal education due to the inclusion of two mixed jurisdictions and relevant British law.[38]

The intrinsic recognition of the value of comparative law in the Commonwealth Caribbean distinguishes its teaching as a stand-alone course from other regions, where its importance often requires justification. Patrick Glenn's 2005 critique depicted comparative law as "a poorly attended elective subject", which was taught "non-comparatively" as "an exposition of foreign law with no reference or rapprochement with the law of the local jurisdiction".[39] However, his claims lacked empirical backing (for example, a report on how many law schools and in which jurisdictions he had studied). Of all that he is saying, for Cave Hill Campus only one thing is true: that comparative law is an elective course. Contrary to Glenn's observations, at Cave Hill Campus, comparative law is a well-attended course that robustly juxtaposes foreign legal principles with local law.

The need for teaching comparative law at UWI was reported as early as 1964, and the first class of the newly established faculty of law could take a comparative law course in 1972.[40] This course was taught by several international and local lecturers until 1997 and was reintroduced into the curriculum almost twenty years later in the academic year 2014–2015. Currently this is the only UWI campus that offers such a course. Comparative law at Cave Hill is a one-semester undergraduate course, unlike its typical graduate or postgraduate status elsewhere.

Not only is comparative law taught to undergraduate students at Cave Hill, but the Campus has recently initiated a two-semester professional development course of Comparative Civil law for the judges of the Caribbean region. This was done in response to the initiative of the Caribbean Association of Judicial Officers. In 2021 the Association held a webinar for judicial officers entitled "International Public and Private Law from the Civil Law

Bermuda (which is not strictly speaking a Caribbean territory, but very often covered by our law courses), British Virgin Islands, Cayman Islands, Dominica, Grenada, Guyana, Jamaica, Montserrat, St. Lucia, St. Kitts and Nevis, St. Vincent and the Grenadines, Trinidad and Tobago, and Turks and Caicos.

38 Ostroukh, note 1 above, p. 1219-1220.

39 Glenn, note 35 above, p. 954.

40 Bradshaw, note 2 above, p. 8.

Perspective: Relevance for Caribbean Judicial Practice". After the webinar, the organizers solicited feedback from the participants, which revealed that 100% of the participants would support future comparative-law initiatives. So, the association management expressed an interest in creating a training program in comparative Civil law for judicial officers in the Caribbean region and requested the Faculty of Law at Cave Hill to teach the course.[41] This initiative is particularly important to the region. First, because CARICOM, which originally consisted of exclusively Common-law countries, now includes two Civil-law jurisdictions — Haiti and Suriname. Second, because the Organization of Eastern Caribbean States includes two French overseas territories – Martinique and Guadeloupe – that have the status of associate members but are considered as full members for many of the Organization's activities.[42] Third, due to the already mentioned presence in the region of two mixed jurisdictions (Guyana and Saint Lucia). This initiative underscores the practical relevance of understanding the Civil-law tradition in a region characterized by legal pluralism and echoes with projects developed by some international law firms aimed at training their lawyers in the law of jurisdictions that are not familiar to them (Civil law for Common-law lawyers or vice versa).[43]

Specificity of teaching comparative law in the Commonwealth Caribbean, whether to undergraduate students or judges, is in that it is always taught to people who have already been exposed to, at the very least, intuitive comparative law, given that both the object and the method of teaching of all law courses in this region are comparative by default. This means that even undergraduate students come to the comparative-law classroom with an already formed general legal worldview and with some vision of comparative law (what to compare, how, and what for), and teaching of comparative law is only one of many factors that contribute to their professional culture.

[41] Letter from Peter Jamadar, Justice of the Caribbean Court of Justice, to Eddy Ventose, Dean and Professor of Law (2 September 2021) (on file with author).

[42] Organization of Eastern Caribbean States official website (available online).

[43] K. Clark, "Introduction", in B. S. Markesinis (ed.), The *Coming Together of the Common Law and the Civil Law* (2000), p. 8.

This already formed knowledge of what to compare, how and why manifests itself in the list of jurisdictions that students taking comparative law chose for their research and presentation.

The table depicts the list of jurisdictions chosen by students for group and individual presentations over six years of teaching comparative law as an undergraduate third-year elective course.

Europe	The Americas and the Caribbean	Africa	Asia/Middle East	Mixed Civil-Common law jurisdictions
Switzerland (2)	Cuba (3)	Somalia	China (3)	South Africa (3)
Germany (2)	USA (3)	Nigeria	Turkey (2)	Quebec (2)
France (2)	Haiti (2)		Saudi Arabia (2)	Israel (2)
Sweden	Brazil (3)		Maldives	Louisiana
Russia	Canada		North Korea	Scotland
Poland	Mexico		India	St Lucia
	Colombia			Malta
				Puerto Rico
				Sri Lanka

For their presentations, students could choose any jurisdiction, excepting the United Kingdom or Commonwealth Caribbean Common-law countries, because these jurisdictions are not considered to be foreign to them. They could choose, however, mixed jurisdictions of Saint Lucia and Guyana that provide a good opportunity for a comparative reflection. As follows from the table, the choice of jurisdictions in which Cave Hill students are interested demonstrates significant differences in comparative legal interests from mainstream jurisdictions. Out of thirty jurisdictions, some of which were chosen three or two times, the students have demonstrated the greatest interest in the law of the United States, China, Brazil, Cuba, and South Africa. A pattern that can be clearly seen from this list is a moderate interest in what is traditionally called major legal systems (the only exception being the United States) and legal systems from Europe, even though it is easier to research them given the abundance of translations and secondary sources. Rather, the students, for the most part, opted for postcolonial jurisdictions, many of which non-Western. Young comparativists also clearly demonstrate their fascination with the Socialist legal tradition, covering almost all the jurisdictions that, at least formally, claim their adherence to Socialist legal principles (China, North Corea, or Cuba) or that belonged to this tradition historically (Russia and Poland).[44] Interestingly, the list of students' preferences includes roughly most of Civil-Common law mixed jurisdictions known to the science of comparative law. Finally, students also choose legal systems of not just nation states, but also territories that are parts of larger states (Quebec, Louisiana, and Scotland). This distribution of students' preferences clearly demonstrates that, already prior to taking the comparative law course, they had their own legal worldview, and the course merely helped them to strengthen it.

Even more sophisticated is the teaching of comparative law to professional judges as people with an already formed professional worldview (both about the law in general and comparative law in particular) and as people who, in their turn, through their judgements, exercise substantial influence on forming the worldview of lawyers in this region. A good example of such already formed comparative-law worldview is the discussion that took place in the classroom in March 2024 about different names for units of macro-comparison. Some student judges admitted that it is more comfortable for them to call such units "legal systems" because this was the expression used in comparative law when they learned it. Exposing them to alternative approaches to classification of laws (legal traditions, legal cultures, jurisdictions, and others) was not without challenges, even though the students appreciated that all such alternatives did contribute to refining the discussion of classifications in comparative law.

Thus, formal teaching of comparative law as a stand-alone course is just one factor contributing to the development of the Commonwealth Caribbean lawyers' worldview. More influential in this respect is any type of previous exposure to comparative law (for example, through learning other law courses or practicing law) that affects one's professional legal culture.

Even though the question of the exact contribution of academic teaching of comparative law to the development of lawyers' worldview is debatable, it goes without saying that teaching comparative law has tremendous practical (applied) significance

[44] If we consider it a separate legal tradition. For criticism of the theory of the socialist legal tradition, see A. Ostroukh, "Russian Society and Its Civil Codes: A Long Way to Civilian Civil Law", *Journal of Civil Law Studies*, VI (2013), pp. 374-375.

for the region. For Commonwealth Caribbean lawyers the study of comparative law is not just a question of academic curiosity or a matter of acquiring good lawyer's manners to communicate with overseas clients or colleagues. Most constantly resort to comparative law while undertaking their routine professional activities. While drafting a new piece of national legislation. While applying law in mixed jurisdictions. While elaborating arguments for a judgement. While interpreting the law of CARICOM or international law. While writing a student essay for one of law courses.

The importance of this course for the legal profession has been emphasized by local practicing lawyers and legal scholars since the establishment of legal education in the region. Thus, in 1986 David Bradshaw, the then lecturer in comparative law and a barrister, wrote an extensive and convincing text "Comparative Law: A Discipline for the Antillean Lawyer?"[45] in which he meticulously explained the significance of this course not only for the Anglophone Caribbean, but also for Dutch overseas territories. In March 2024, the Chief Justice of Barbados, Sir Patterson Cheltenham, criticized the law program at Cave Hill Campus for alleged "intellectual attrition", lack of "academic rigor", and for being "populated with a lot of super soft options to get people over the bar".[46] Even though the course of comparative law was not subject to direct criticism from the Chief Justice, an unknown author found it appropriate to highlight the practical significance of this discipline for aspiring lawyers by stating that "[...]the third year Comparative Law course, with its wide analysis of legal systems, has practical use in analyzing and seeking to improve our own laws".[47]

Overall, Cave Hill Campus experience challenges Glenn's treatment of comparative law teaching and teaching comparative law as opposing educational strategies and his favoring the transition from teaching comparative law to integrating comparative-law method into teaching law in general.[48] Since

[45] Bradshaw, note 2 above.

[46] H-L. Evanson, "Chief Justice slams law at UWI", *The Nation*, (Bridgetown, 16 March 2024) (available online).

[47] "Room for more Law Options", *The Nation*, (Bridgetown, 20 March 2024),

[48] Glenn, note 35 above, p. 954.

the 1970s, the campus has embraced both, treating them as complementary approaches that together enhance the legal acumen and worldview of Caribbean legal professionals.

GRADUAL RECOGNITION AND APPLICATION OF DECOLONIAL COMPARATIVE LAW THEORY AND METHODOLOGY

The current stage in the evolution of comparative law in the Commonwealth Caribbean region is characterized by a gradual shift from a postcolonial to a decolonial approach.

The decolonial comparative law perspective acknowledges the role of comparative law in perpetuating colonialism and coloniality.[49] Modern (post Paris Congress) comparative law emerged at the time when major European countries were at the pinnacle of their colonial power, and, as in case of Great Britain, the development of comparative law was intrinsically linked to better organizing and controlling law and governance in its colonies.[50] Consequently, there has been a notable focus on studies of Caribbean societies and their laws from the perspective of outsiders, or colonizers. In the post-independence era, as interest from comparativists representing former colonizing countries in Caribbean legal systems waned and their approaches became outdated, the need for a native perspective in comparative studies became evident. What the Caribbean region needs now is comparative studies rooted in an insider's perspective aiming for the appropriation and indigenization (or rejection where necessary) of colonial laws to make them more suitable for modern local societies. Although colonialism as a governance system has long ended, coloniality as a worldview that permeates the legal system still persists. Comparative law can thus serve as a potent tool for national affirmation.

Acknowledging the academic and practical relevance of comparative law to the region and cognizant of its reflexive and

[49] For more about the decolonial approach to comparative law, see L. Salameh and R. Michaels, "Decolonial Comparative Law: A Conceptual Beginning", *Rabels Zeitschrift für ausländisches und internationales Privatrecht*, LXXXVI (2022), pp. 166-188.

[50] J. W. Cairns, "Development of Comparative Law in Great Britain", in M. Reimann and R. Zimmermann (eds.), *The Oxford Handbook of Comparative Law* (2006), pp. 138-141.

reformative potential, Commonwealth Caribbean comparativists remain skeptical of the established notions, classifications, and methods of mainstream comparative law. Thus, one major assumption of mainstream comparative law – assumed homogeneity[51] within a legal system – does not hold true in the Commonwealth Caribbean. The region's legal systems, just as local societies, comprise diverse and sometimes conflicting elements. For example, Guyana, known as the land of six people, has a legal system that blends British Common law, Roman-Dutch Civil law, and the indigenous legal traditions of American Indians. Even greater heterogeneity is encountered in the so-called notion of the "law of the Commonwealth Caribbean". Since the time of independence, it has been a common practice in the legal academia to teach and study different areas of law under a unifying title "Commonwealth Caribbean" (for example, Commonwealth Caribbean Constitutional Law, Commonwealth Caribbean Property Law, Commonwealth Caribbean Civil Procedure, Commonwealth Caribbean Law and Legal Systems). Although this genre of legal literature simplifies greatly the process of studying law, it comes at a significant cost. For many topics legal literature limits discussions to respective areas of law in major Commonwealth Caribbean jurisdictions like Jamaica, Barbados, and Trinidad and Tobago),[52] leaving other countries and territories at the periphery of the discussion and creating a false impression (especially in an outside reader) that statements and conclusions about the law of these major countries can be extended to other jurisdictions. This is particularly problematic when discussing mixed jurisdictions of Saint Lucia and Guyana where some areas of private law are still governed by civilian rules and notions (property and family law).

Another instance where the principle of assumed homogeneity falls short is in addressing indigenous land claims, which have distinct regional characteristics, as compared to other jurisdictions. Specifically, the presence in the Commonwealth Caribbean of the Jamaican Maroons, who consider themselves an indigenous nation, challenges conventional definitions of indigeneity.

[51] Salameh and Michaels, note 49 above, p. 172.

[52] For example, in the seminal textbook on property law, the discussion of the topic on discharge or modification of restrictive covenants is limited to Jamaica and Barbados, while the discussion of condominium legislation and case law is focused mostly on the Bahamas and Barbados (Kodilinye, note 3 above, pp. 135-145 and 104-114.

Originally, Maroons were runaway slaves who sometimes mixed with indigenous populations, such as the Taino in Jamaica. They formed their own communities during the late Spanish and early British colonization periods, surviving by planting and hunting.[53] Their identity is rooted in resistance to slavery and the official governments (both colonial and postcolonial) as well as communal land holding. However, they were not markedly different racially, linguistically, or culturally from Jamaica's broader Black population. Both terms – "indigenous" and "people"[54] – as applied to Jamaican Maroons, can be criticized under traditional approaches to indigeneity. Their history and identity might not align with the widespread definition of indigenous people as "the living descendants of pre-invasion inhabitants of lands now dominated by others".[55] However, a strong sense of identity and distinctiveness exhibited by Jamaican Maroons, does not allow us to dismiss their recognition as indigenous people, which necessitates a reconceptualization of traditional definitions of indigeneity that for a long time have reflected colonial vision of what it meant to be indigenous. This example of a failure to create a universal definition of indigeneity proves one of fundamental principles of decolonial theory, which "rejects coloniality's construction of national, racial, ethnic, religious, and gender classifications as universal categories".[56]

These examples illustrate how the Commonwealth Caribbean region can make significant original contribution to the growing field of decolonial comparative law. Through empirical evidence and grounded criticism provided by regional legal practitioners and academics, the region can articulate ways to overcome colonial mentality in legal thought, thus fostering truly independent comparative legal studies.

CONCLUSION

Comparative law research and education in the Commonwealth

[53] For the history of the Jamaican Maroons, see C. Mavis, *The Maroons of Jamaica, 1655-1796: A History of Resistance, Collaboration and Betrayal* (1988).

[54] "People" in the sense of an organized group of persons with common ethnic characteristics.

[55] S. J. Anaya, *Indigenous Peoples in International Law* (2d ed,; 2004), p. 3.

[56] Salaymeh and Michaels, note 49 above, p. 179.

Caribbean remain underdeveloped areas. However, the region, due to its geographical location, legal history, cultural diversity, and involvement in global and regional integration processes, is promising to comparativists from both inside and outside the Caribbean. There are still gaps in the legal map of the region that need filling, and certain parts of this map require redrawing to better reflect reality. The region also needs to develop its own distinctive version of comparative law, as simply following mainstream Western developments has proven impossible.

The diversity and specificity of the legal landscape in the region, as well as a strong tradition of regional lawyers to practice and study law comparatively, endow it with a great potential to develop its own independent comparative law worldview. Interestingly, unlike in many other regions, comparative law in the Commonwealth Caribbean has transcended academic interest and become integral to the legal practice. Thus, Commonwealth Caribbean courts, particularly the Caribbean Court of Justice, have played a pivotal role in using comparative law to develop local law. The regional judiciary has turned out to be the branch of the legal profession that is the most sensitive to law and society considerations; it has proven to be the most instrumental in rethinking and reshaping inherited colonial law in order to better suit the needs of the modern Caribbean society. While the CCJ has been at the forefront, other tiers of the regional judiciary (trial courts, national supreme courts, or the Supreme Court of the OECS) by means of their decisions, quite often based on comparative law, have actively participated in the process of decolonization and indigenization of regional law. Teaching comparative law to both undergraduate students and judges highlights significant regional specifics. Both groups of students come to their comparative law classes with an already formed intuitive view of comparative law while their practical and academic interests reflect regional vision of comparative law that often diverges from perspectives prevalent in more established legal systems.

Thus, the worldview of Commonwealth Caribbean comparativists is critical, pluriversal, and, at the very least, postcolonial, with a strong potential to evolve into a decolonial perspective. Regional comparativists are also optimistic about the reformative potential of comparative law and its significance for the legal profession.

INDEX OF NAMES

www.ingramcontent.com/pod-product-compliance
Lightning Source LLC
LaVergne TN
LVHW091521200926
848483LV00002B/269